Instructor's Manual
to accompany

BUSINESS MATHEMATICS
A Collegiate Approach

Eighth Edition

Nelda W. Roueche
Virginia H. Graves

Prentice
Hall

Upper Saddle River, New Jersey
Columbus, Ohio

10 9 8 7 6 5 4 3 2 1

ISBN 0-13-087338-1

CONTENTS

THE INSTRUCTOR'S MANUAL

in a Nutshell

The **Introduction** gives an overview of the course, providing suggestions for organizing and conducting it. Included are a day-by-day **course schedule** (for both a basic and a complete course) and an alternate outline for **nonconsecutive chapter order**. Testing procedure is discussed and **typical pop quiz questions** are given. **Six sample hour exams** and a **final exam** are included.

A discussion related to each individual chapter covers such aspects as **teaching suggestions** (points to emphasize in class), common **student difficulties** and mistakes to watch for, **examples to omit** for lower-ability classes, **additional background information** for the instructor's use (or to share with classes, if desired), **sources of additional information**, and **material to assist the instructor** in composing test problems.

Every problem in the text is worked out in complete detail, thus eliminating the time the instructor would have to spend in solving assignment problems.

60 Transparency Masters accompany the Instructor's Guide.

INTRODUCTION

There are probably as many variations in teaching procedure as there are instructors. An experienced instructor will have developed individualized procedures for conducting classes; and an instructor who has taught business math previously will need little guidance concerning the emphasis to give various topics or the scheduling of chapters over the term. Thus, the following recommendations are offered primarily for new instructors or for those with no previous experience in the two-year college or in teaching business math.

Teaching in a community college or junior college presents a unique challenge not found in other institutions. The students in a two-year college are unlike any of the students you may have known in another college or university. Most of them decided very late in their high school careers that they would go to college. Few have taken college-preparatory courses, and they probably did not do well in those they have had (math, in particular). Many are "late bloomers" -- students who only recently realized the importance of education and have just begun to make any serious effort in school. (Some still are not ready to make a serious effort and are enrolled only because "everyone else was going to college." These pose a special challenge.) Of course, some of your students have received degrees, have joined the workforce, and now have decided to come back to school for further education. For the most part, your students will want to learn and will work hard, but many of them will have poor study skills either because they did not learn them in high school or it has been several years since they have had to study. Never assume that any mathematical step is too simple to require explanation.

Classroom Procedure

The attitude of the instructor toward this course is the most important factor influencing the students' attitudes. If you are enthusiastic, lively, and make it apparent that you consider the course important, your students will also adopt this attitude. It is important to have the students like your course, because students usually work harder, learn more, and make better grades in courses they like. Even if (s)he does not like math in general, a student can still like your class in particular. So, be enthusiastic and cheerful; never let the session drag; and, above all, let the students know you are on their side.

Insofar as possible, always come to class on time. (If you are willing to make the supreme sacrifice, make a practice of arriving early, since this allows more time for student questions.) If your institution has attendance regulations, adhere to them religiously. Students cannot learn if they are not there. (Even normally excellent students often do not perform well on a test of information covered on a day when they were absent.)

First class session. At the first class meeting, introduce the class to the text. Give a general idea of the topics to be covered and of their business application. Announce your office number and office hours. Encourage the students to come see you immediately if they get lost -- not to wait several days until they are hopelessly behind. Stress that you are available and anxious to be of help. A syllabus containing all the information pertinent to the class should be handed to each student. Not only should you give them this written information, but also you should verbally inform the students of your course objectives, requirements, classroom procedures, testing procedures, and how you weigh the exams.

Questions on the previous assignment. At the beginning of each class, devote a few minutes to answering questions about the previous assignment. It will probably be necessary to work some problems on the board or overhead projector. Often, just setting up a problem will be sufficient. This period enables you to determine how well the class as a whole has mastered the assignment. If only a few students have questions, the topic has been sufficiently covered. If everyone seems to have questions, some reteaching is needed. (If no one has questions, it's probably Monday and they haven't done the assignment!)

Pop quizzes. At irregular intervals, give a short pop quiz on the previous assignment. This provides an added incentive for the students to study the assignment conscientiously. (The authors' ideas concerning pop quizzes are further explained under "Testing Procedures.")

Examples. Before explaining a new example, conduct a discussion of its business significance. Explain when this mathematical procedure is used, who performs it, and why. Describe its relationship to other topics. In other words, help the students understand the purpose in learning each procedure, and try to make sure they know when to use each. This is essential. It is a waste of time to teach business procedures if the students do not know when or how to apply what they have learned.

Students often "cannot see the forest for the trees." That is, they get so involved with the specific numbers of a problem that they fail to realize the basic procedure that is being used, the sequence of steps, or what must be found first in order to achieve the ultimate solution. Therefore, before using the specific numbers of an example, explain in general terms what the procedures will be. As the problem progresses, frequently recap through the current step; explain what has been found so far. In order to keep the students thinking about what is going on (rather than just copying it down), ask frequently what the next step should be -- even for arithmetic procedures or the solution to equations. (When incorrect suggestions are given, explain why that procedure would not work.)

Student participation. The authors strongly recommend that you encourage student participation in the class by asking frequent questions. Students tend to "tune out" an instructor who lectures the entire period, rather than thinking along. Thus, ask questions at every opportunity -- not questions usually directed to a specific individual, but thrown out to the class as a whole. When recent terminology comes into use, ask the class to define it. Ask the significance of various problems. Ask what formula or procedure should be used to solve certain kinds of problems. As solutions are obtained, ask what the results represent.

It is also vital that you encourage the students to ask questions. When examples are being given, we try to get our students to raise a question at any point if they get lost. It is better to explain right then how a step was accomplished, so that everyone can then follow the remainder of the explanation. Otherwise, the entire example will need to be re-explained. If a single person seems to be confused and is holding up the whole class, you might ask that student to stay after class or to come by during your office hours for help. As a general rule, however, when one student has a question, other students also have the same question.

Very few of your junior/community college students will ask anything but serious questions. (Only occasionally will you encounter a showoff or an antagonist.) Your problem will not be too many questions, but getting students to ask questions at all. Furthermore, because of their limited math background, some of the questions they do ask may seem trivial, unnecessary, or completely stupid. Keep in mind, however, that the role of a teacher is to help the student learn -- not to display your own profound knowledge or witty sarcasm. Never be sarcastic to a student, regardless of the question. To do so would quickly stifle all questions from all students, and an important means of teaching would be lost.

Assignment. The assignment should normally consist of two parts: problems on the topic that was introduced in this class period, and a reading assignment on the new material that will be covered in the next class. The authors have endeavored to make BUSINESS MATHEMATICS: A COLLEGIATE APPROACH readable and self-explanatory. Having the students study new mathematical procedures before you explain them in class will shorten the amount of class time required, thus allowing more class time for other things. Knowing that you give pop quizzes on the new descriptive material will motivate most students to study the assignment. (We would never quiz on the new problems before they are explained in class.)

Student boardwork. After the assignment has been made, the authors devote the remainder of the period to having the class try new problems at the board (and also at their desks). When new examples are worked under your supervision, you can correct mistakes or eliminate obstacles which might otherwise have made the assignment impossible for some students. Despite their halfhearted groans and complaints when it is their turn to go to the board, students readily admit that this is a valuable technique for learning new procedures.

When sending students to the board, send more than one at the same time. Those remaining at their desks work the problems on paper. Everyone works the same problem, which keeps anyone from being "put on the spot."

Obviously, to work problems from the previous assignment, give a pop quiz, introduce new material, and spend some time doing boardwork -- all in the same period -- will not be an easy feat to accomplish. Indeed, it will not always be possible. With the exception of the pop quiz (which is not always necessary), however, it will usually be possible to include all these procedures if you make a concentrated effort to keep the session moving. Do not move on to something new if it is obvious that you have left the class behind, but never spend more time than is necessary on any topic; certainly, never let the session drag.

Throughout the course, keep reinforcing that you are sympathetic toward the students and want to be of help. Encourage them to ask questions and to come by for extra help whenever needed. And, most important, be enthusiastic and make it obvious that you consider business math vital and want the students to learn as much as possible -- not just for the sake of grades but for their own sake as future business employees, employers, and consumers.

Course Content

In accordance with the business mathematics requirements of most two-year college programs, BUSINESS MATHEMATICS: A COLLEGIATE APPROACH was designed for use in either a one-term course or a two-term course. A survey of experienced business math instructors revealed no consensus regarding which topics are essential to the curriculum. Therefore, the individual instructor may well prefer to select those topics which (s)he considers most important, or those topics that best coordinate with other required courses in their college's business curriculum.

Some possible course schedules for basic or standard classes are listed later. As a general rule, the authors recommend that the instructor reduce the text material for basic classes by omitting the more difficult examples in most sections, rather than eliminating entire topics altogether. Considering their limited math background, most classes can probably complete only the basic course. The complete course may be studied when business math is used as an introductory course in a baccalaureate program or when the course covers two semesters.

In most instances, the chapters need not necessarily be studied in consecutive order and could well be rearranged at the instructor's discretion. There are a few exceptions, however. The review chapters should be studied first. It is recommended that the financial statements be studied prior to the chapter on markup, in order to provide a foundation for the markup topics. The chapters on simple interest and bank discount should be studied as a unit; they should precede the chapters related to compound interest, but need not necessarily be studied immediately beforehand. Since the chapters on markup, simple interest, and bank discount require the use of equations more than most other chapters, it might be advantageous to study these chapters as soon as possible following the review.

The sample course schedules on the following pages are based on 48 class meetings. The instructor may make appropriate adjustments for classes meeting fewer or more times. Teaching suggestions for the various chapters are offered with the problem solutions which conclude the manual. The problem solutions are worked out in detail, as the students' solutions should appear.

Sample Course Schedules

Basic Course				One-term Course			
Class Period	Lesson	Class Period	Lesson	Class Period	Lesson	Class Period	Lesson
1	Introduction; Appendices	25	Exam 3	1	Introduction; I-1,2; II-1,2	25	XII-2
2	I-1; II-1	26	XII-2	2	II-3; III-1,2	26	XIII-1
3	II-2,3	27	XIII-1	3	III-2,3	27	XIII-2
4	III-1,2	28	XIII-2,3	4	IV-1,2	28	XIII-3
5	III-3; I-2	29	XIV-2	5	IV-2,3	29	XIV-1
6	IV-1,4	30	Exam 4	6	IV-4,5	30	XIV-2
7	V-1	31	XV-1,2	7	V-1,2	31	XV-1,2,3
8	Exam 1	32	XV-3	8	Exam 1	32	Exam 4
9	V-2	33	XV-4	9	VI-1	33	XV-4
10	VI-1	34	XV-5	10	VI-2	34	XV-5
11	VI-3	35	XVI-1	11	VI-3	35	XVI-1
12	VII-1,2	36	XVI-2	12	VII-1,2	36	XVI-2
13	VIII-1,2,3	37	XVI-3	13	VIII-1,2,3	37	XVI-3
14	VIII-3,4	38	XVI-4	14	VIII-3,4	38	XVI-4
15	VIII-5	39	XVII-1,2	15	VIII-5,6	39	Exam 5
16	VIII-6	40	XVII-1,2	16	IX-1	40	XVII-1,2
17	IX-1	41	XVIII-1,2	17	Exam 2	41	XVII-3,4
18	Exam 2	42	XVIII-4	18	IX-2; X-1	42	XVIII-1,2
19	IX-2	43	XIX-1,2	19	X-1,2	43	XVIII-3,4
20	X-1,2	44	XX-1,2	20	X-1,2,3	44	XIX-1,2
21	X-1,2	45	XX-2,3	21	X-4	45	XX-1,2,3
22	XI-1	46	Exam 5	22	XI-1,2	46	Exam 6
23	XI-2	47	Review	23	XII-1	47	Review
24	XII-1	48	Final Exam	24	Exam 3	48	Final Exam

Two-Semester Course Schedule

First Semester				Second Semester			
Class Period	Lesson	Class Period	Lesson	Class Period	Lesson	Class Period	Lesson
1	Introduction; Appendices	25	VI-3	1	XI-1	25	XVI-3
		26	VII-1	2	XI-2	26	XVI-4
2	I-1	27	VII-2	3	XI-2	27	Exam(XV-XVI)
3	I-2	28	Review	4	XII-1		
4	II-1	29	Exam(V-VII)	5	XII-1	28	XVII-1
5	II-2	30	VIII-1,2	6	XII-2	29	XVII-2
6	II-3	31	VIII-3	7	XIII-1	30	XVII-3
7	II-3	32	VIII-4	8	XIII-2	31	XVII-3
8	III-1	33	VIII-5	9	XIII-2	32	XVII-4
9	III-2	34	VIII-5	10	XIII-3	33	XVII-4
10	III-3	35	VIII-6	11	XIV-1	34	XVIII-1
11	IV-1	36	VIII-6	12	XIV-1	35	XVIII-2
12	IV-2	37	IX-1	13	XIV-2	36	XVIII-3
13	IV-3	38	IX-1	14	XIV-2	37	XVIII-4
14	IV-4	39	IX-2	15	Review	38	XIX-1
15	IV-5	40	IX-3	16	Exam(XI-XIV)	39	XIX-1
16	Review	41	X-1	17	XV-1	40	XIX-2
17	Exam(Appendices-IV)	42	X-1,2	18	XV-2,3	41	XIX-2
		43	X-3	19	XV-4	42	XX-1
18	V-1	44	X-4	20	XV-4,5	43	XX-2
19	V-2	45	Review	21	XV-5	44	XX-2
20	VI-1	46	Exam(VIII-X)	22	XVI-1	45	XX-3
21	VI-1			23	XVI-2	46	Exam (XVII-XX)
22	VI-2	47	Review	24	XVI-2		
23	VI-2	48	Final Exam			47	Review
24	VI-3					48	Final Exam

Assignments

Problems are the most important part of any math book. Through good lectures, an instructor may overcome deficiencies in explanatory material. It is through working the problems, however, that the students obtain most knowledge of the mathematical procedures. Thus, the problems in BUSINESS MATHEMATICS: A COLLEGIATE APPROACH have been carefully prepared to cover all aspects of the various procedures without being more tedious than necessary.

Assigning no more than half the problems of each section should normally provide an adequate homework assignment. (The authors were careful to provide a surplus of problems so that the additional problems could be used for classwork, for review -- either assigned review or personal review by the student -- or for test questions.) However, if more than one topic is covered during a single class period, even half the related problems may prove too many. The instructor should always select the homework problems carefully to be certain that they adequately cover the material presented in class, that they cover only the examples explained in class, and that the assignment will require a reasonable amount of time to complete.

The authors believe that typical students will not give up on a difficult problem so easily, but will continue working until an answer is obtained, provided they will then know whether that answer is correct. Finding a solution to be incorrect, many students are then motivated to attack the problem again, trying to find the source of their mistakes. Therefore, we recommend that you assign problems for which the answers are given (or supplied by you). For those who do not share this philosophy, however, only the odd problem answers are printed at the back of the text.

Testing Procedures

The authors suggest giving unannounced pop quizzes periodically and announced hour exams every two to three weeks. We make a practice of allowing an extra class period between the last assignment and the final exam, so that questions about the final assignment can be answered before the students study for the exam.

Administrative policy may influence the giving of comprehensive mid-term and/or final examinations. We would not give a comprehensive mid-term unless required, preferring during the term to give only hour exams which cover all material studied since the last hour exam. School policy may also determine the influence of the final exam grade on the term grade. We would never count the exam grade more than 1/3 of the term grade. Many experienced instructors count the exam grade in proportion to the amount of time devoted to the exam. (For example, an exam lasting for two hours would be counted twice.) This policy usually results in the exam grade counting from 1/4 to 1/3 of the total grade.

Pop quizzes. Short, unannounced pop quizzes, given at irregular intervals, are an excellent device for motivating students to do assignments they might otherwise "put off until tomorrow." The authors prefer not to include problems which were assigned only the previous period, as this may penalize a student who made an honest effort but was unable to solve a problem. Rather, we suggest you ask terminology, formulas, or short explanations of when certain procedures should be used, their significance, or the distinctions between similar procedures -- things which must be learned before any practical application of the problems could be made. We do quiz on short procedures, very simple problems, or problems to which more than one class period has been devoted. We never ask a new problem which has not been explained in class.

The pop quizzes that we give usually consist of three to six questions which are worth one to two points each. We normally allow one minute of testing time per question. (When a problem which takes several minutes to solve is asked, it is counted as several points, allowing one minute of testing time for each point. Part credit is given for the formula, correct procedure, a value from a table, the answer, etc.) Each quiz is recorded according to the number of points that the student scored correctly. At the end of the term, all pop quiz grades are added together to count the equivalent to one hour exam.

Hour exams. A test should not be just a means of obtaining a grade for a student; but that, insofar as possible, the test should accurately reflect how much has been learned. An hour exam should ask only what has been covered in class (or assigned, in the case of descriptive material only), and the exam should give the same emphasis to various types of problems as was given in class. If students have mastered the problems assigned for homework, they should be well prepared for the problems on the exam. The instructor can encourage honesty by preparing separate exams for classes meeting several hours apart and by carefully proctoring the class during an exam.

This manual contains some sample pop quiz questions (page 12), as well as some sample exams and a final exam (page 17). These were prepared on the assumption that all chapters were studied and thus will not prove directly applicable when topics have been omitted. The exams are included primarily to illustrate the type of hour exams that the authors give. The hour exams should be

typed or word processed, allowing sufficient room for the solutions.
The test papers will be uniform and much easier to
grade.   (It is also more efficient to grade all the first pages,
then all the second pages, etc.)

Our exams usually contain a few objective questions.   These
questions usually count one point for each blank.   Questions on
terminology and business applications reveal the students'
understanding of the procedures.

The problems themselves are usually included in the same order
in which they were studied.   We assign points to the various
problems basically according to the amount of time and work which
each should take.   Rather than grading only the answer, we designate
on the key the number of points which each step of a problem will
count.   When grading the student papers, we allow partial credit for
all steps which were performed correctly, even if a previous step
has caused a numerical error.   (Points are subtracted for the point
where the error was made and for the final answer.)

The authors' objective in teaching business mathematics is to
teach mathematical procedures, rather than simply to provide
practice in arithmetic.   We feel that if students understand a
procedure and can carry it out using round numbers, they could also
perform it using more difficult numbers if necessary.   Thus, our
tests problems -- like the problems in BUSINESS MATHEMATICS: A
COLLEGIATE APPROACH -- contain primarily round numbers.   As a
result, students can often find the answer to a problem by trial and
error when they do not know the correct procedure.   Therefore, we
never allow credit for only the answer to a problem; the student
must always show an acceptable method for obtaining that answer.
(Perhaps it should be added here that, unless specific directions
have been given regarding what method to use, credit should always
be given for any mathematically correct method that accomplishes the
same purpose, even if it is not the same one presented in the text.)
Always be careful in constructing tests and exams that you give
specific directions, including the fact that all computations and
procedures should be shown on the test for partial and/or full
credit.

Since part credit has already been given on the individual
problems, we usually curve the final exam scores very little, if at
all.   Experience has shown that there is usually a wide gap
separating those students who have learned the material (and made
acceptable scores) and those who have not, thus making a curve
practically redundant.   A curve on the final exam grades, however,
may serve a more useful purpose, since there is not usually such a
distinct gap in exam scores. We prepare exams for separate classes
so that, insofar as possible, all will be of equal difficulty;

then, when a curve does seem necessary, we use the same curve for all classes, rather than curving each class separately.

Exam papers should be graded and returned promptly -- at the next class meeting if possible, so that the formulas and procedures will still be fresh and the students can readily understand their mistakes and benefit from your explanations. Many, if not most, students will correct their papers only if you require it and take the papers up afterwards (to be returned again).

The authors feel strongly that test papers are the students' property and should be returned to them to keep. Tests provide a valuable study aid when students prepare for the final examination. (Point out this fact to the class when you give back the first exam, and encourage all students to save their quizzes and exams papers for the entire term.) Of course, this practice requires that you prepare new exams each term, but this is a normal responsibility of the profession.

The question concerning make-up tests often comes up. Instead of having to act as a judge to determine if an excuse is legitimate or not, you might announce that no make-up exams will be given; rather, an optional comprehensive final exam will be given at the end of the term for those students who have missed exams and for those students who wish to take the final exam and drop their lowest exam grade. The authors have found this policy to be a positive motivator for students to take all exams on time and then to have the option of taking an extra exam (the final exam) in order to drop their lowest exam grade. If this policy is followed, then the final exam should count no more than other exams.

The final exam should ordinarily contain only those types of problems which have already been included on previous hour exams. The exam may contain very basic problems which were omitted earlier only because of time limitations; however, we would never ask a difficult variation of a basic problem unless it had been included on an earlier exam. (The only exception to this would be when no hour exam has been given on the material most recently studied. This is not a recommended procedure, however. The authors have found that students do not perform as well on recent material on the exam as they would have on an hour exam, because the topic never received concentrated, individual review.)

The testing procedures outlined above do involve more work for the instructor than might be considered adequate. However, it is our firm conviction that instructors should do all in their power to be fair to the students and to help them complete the course successfully.

Typical Pop Quiz Questions

1. Explain (or demonstrate) what it means when a number has an exponent of 3.

2. Write in words the value of this number: 0.022

3. Multiply: 4.813   (2 points)
                ×40.05

4. Round to the nearest tenth: 88.2463

5. Solve for x: 6x - x + 10 = 82 - 4x   (3 points)

6. What is the reciprocal of $\dfrac{5}{6}$

7. Compare 4 with 5, expressing the ratio three different ways. (3 points)

8. Percent means_____.

9. Express as a decimal: 75%;   12.5%;   0.4%   (3 points)

10. Express as a fraction: 2%;   35%; $11\dfrac{1}{9}$%   (3 points)

11. Express as a percent: $\dfrac{3}{8}$; .626;   3.6   (3 points)

12. Solve: 15% of _?_ = 57   (3 points)

13. What percent less than 20 is 7?   (2 points)

14. Another name for the mean is _____.

15. What does the term "MACRS" stand for?

16. What is the formula for finding straight-line depreciation?

17. A plant asset is to be depreciated by the declining-balance method for 10 years. What is the rate of depreciation each year? (4 points)

18. Which financial statement shows the firm's assets and liabilities?

19. Which financial statement shows the firm's net profit or loss?

20. What formula is used to determine the working capital (current) ratio?

21. A corporation has 20,000 shares of outstanding common stock and a declared dividend of $35,000. Determine the dividend per share. (3 points)

22. Partners G and H had a net profit of $68,000. If their partnership agreement does not specify how the profits are to be divided, each partner should receive_____.

23. Determine the 6% sales tax on an item marked $48.

24. What was the marked price of an item if the total price was $121.80 and the sales tax rate was 5%?

25. Express the tax rate 0.01446325+   (2 points)
    (a) as a percent with one decimal place
    (b) as an amount per $1,000, correct to cents

26. What kind of insurance covers each of the following:
    (a) smoke damage to a home   (4 points)
    (b) a tree limb falls on a car
    (c) a customer falls and breaks a leg
    (d) your car crashes into another vehicle

27. Explain "coinsurance clause." (2 points)

28. Fire insurance costs $0.75 per $100. Find the cost of insuring a $90,000 home. (2 points)

29. Determine the correct multiple for base automobile insurance for each of the following: (2 points)
    (a) a man, 44, drives 10 miles (each way) to work
    (b) a man, 18, has had driver training and uses the family car only for pleasure.

30. Compute the total base annual liability premium in Territory 3 for 100/200 bodily injury and $50,000 property damage insurance. (3 points)

31. Comprehensive-collision rates are determined by the Territory, the driver classification, and _____.

32. What is the main advantage and main disadvantage of term insurance? (2 points)

33. Compute the annual premium for a $50,000, 20-year pay policy issued at 25. (2 points)

34. Determine the weekly gross pay on an annual salary of $20,800. (2 points)

35. Janice is paid a commission rate of 8%. Determine her commission wages if she sold $5,400 worth of merchandise. (2 points)

36. What is the gross pay for an employee who worked 43 hours one week and is paid $10 an hour? Demonstrate the overtime excess method. (Assume overtime is paid.) (2 points)

37. (a) What is the Social Security deduction on a wage of $600?
    (b) How much does the employer pay?
        (2 points)

38. Determine the federal income tax deduction for a married woman claiming one allowance on a weekly salary of $410.(2 points)

39. The maximum Social Security taxable wages for each employee is_____.

40. What is the net cost rate factor for trade discounts of 20%, 15%, and 5%?

41. What is the single equivalent discount for the trade discounts given in the above problem?

42. If an invoice dated May 15 contained terms 2/10 EOM, what is the last date on which the cash discount may be taken?

43. What is the basic formula for determining selling price?

44. If a calculator costing $10.50 sells for $12.75 and a profit of $1.50 is made, how much were the expenses?

45. What formula would you use to find the percent of markup based on selling price?

46. If C = $60 and M = 20% of cost, find the selling price. (Do not compute markup separately.) (3 points)

47. A store has an overhead of 13% of sales and makes a net profit of 12% of sales. What is its percent of gross profit?

48. An item that regularly sells for $20 was sold for $15. What is the percent of markdown? (3 points)

49. What does "LIFO" mean?

50. Find the exact time between February 3, 2004 and June 3, 2004.

51. The face value of a simple interest note is called the_____.

52. If the interest on a 3-month loan of $1,000 is $17.50, what interest rate was charged? (3 points)

53. What formula would you use to find present value at simple interest?

54. What is the discount on a $1,600, 6-month note with a discount rate of 8%? (3 points)

55. The face value of a discounted note is the _____.

56. Under the U.S. rule, a partial payment is used to pay the _____ first, before the remaining part is deducted from the _____. (2 points)

57. Find the compound amount on $5,000 invested for 3 years at 6% compounded quarterly. (3 points)

58. If I want to find how much I would have to deposit today in order to have $2,000 in 4 years, what kind of problem is this?

59. What would I look for in a problem to determine whether it is a "compound amount" or an "amount of an annuity" problem?

60. What is the procedure (formula) used to find amount of an annuity?

61. How is a sinking fund used?

62. Find the semi-annual payment required to amortize a 10-year $10,000 loan, if money is worth 8% compounded semiannually.

Sample Hour Exams

The exam on the following pages are intended to be examples only; you may choose to test on different chapter groupings and to prepare your own exams, particularly for multiple classes and succeeding terms. These sample quizzes are typical of those which the authors would give if the complete text were covered. You may prepare additional problems to reflect the emphasis actually given to certain topics and may omit problems from topics not emphasized or not studied. The sample exams will probably prove a little long for basic classes; some problems should be eliminated or the exam could be split into two parts. From Chapter IV on, about 10-11 problems (not counting short-answer questions) usually constitute a sufficient hour exam for a basic class.

Each exam contains a total of 100 points; the final exam (which is suitable for a two-hour examination period) contains 250 points. Each blank of the introductory questions counts one point. The total points allotted to each of the remaining problems are in parentheses beside the problem. The answers are found after the Final Exam.

The chapter groupings covered by each sample exam are as follows:

       Exam 1. . . .Appendices - Chapter IV
       Exam 2. . . .Chapters V-VIII
       Exam 3. . . .Chapters IX-XI
       Exam 4. . . .Chapters XII-XIV
       Exam 5. . . .Chapters XV-XVI
       Exam 6. . . .Chapters XVII-XX

EXAM 1

Appendices - Chapter IV

Fill in the blanks.

_____1. What is the place value of 4 in the number 124,761?

_____2. The positive and negative whole numbers, along with zero, compose the set of _____.

_____3. Name the reciprocal of the fraction: $\frac{3}{8}$

_____4. $\frac{7}{2}$ is an example of a/an _____ fraction.

_____5. If a measurement is 4600' to the nearest hundred feet, there are _____ significant digits.

_____6. Express the ratio of "2 to 9" in two other forms.

_____7. Express a proportion using $\frac{X}{5}$ and $\frac{24}{60}$

_____8. Percent means_____.

_____9. The average that is the midpoint of a group of numbers is the _____.

_____10. Use the following graph to determine what percent of the numbers are 8 or smaller.

```
      6    7    8    9   10   11   12
     -+----+----+----+----+----+----+-
     -3σ  -2σ  -1σ   M   +1σ  +2σ  +3σ
```

_____11. Using the graph in Problem 10, what percent of items fall between ±1σ?

_____12. A price index of 247.4 means that an item which formerly cost $10 now costs _____.

13. Perform each indicated operation: (2 pts. ea.)

_____ (a) Round to the nearest hundredths: 231.4563

(b) $\dfrac{3}{4}$
$\dfrac{1}{3}$
$+\dfrac{5}{6}$
_____

(c) $15\dfrac{3}{8}$
$-11\dfrac{5}{6}$
_____

(d) $\begin{array}{r} 28.25 \\ \times \ \ 4.50 \\ \hline \end{array}$

(e) $\dfrac{224.4}{6.8}$

(f) $6\dfrac{1}{2} \times \dfrac{2}{3} \times 4\dfrac{1}{26}$

(g) $\dfrac{24}{\dfrac{3}{8}}$

14. Change to a decimal: (1 pt. ea.)

_____ (a) $\dfrac{5}{18}$

_____ (b) 5.62%

_____ (c) 10.82%

_____ (d) $\dfrac{1}{4}$%

15. Change to a fraction in lowest terms: (1 pt. ea.)

_____ (a) 0.9

_____ (b) 12.5%

_____ (c) $16\dfrac{2}{3}$%

16. Change to a percent: (1 pt ea.)

_____ (a) 0.7

_____ (b) 3.68

_____ (c) 0.012

17. Solve for T: (3 pts.)

$5\dfrac{T}{2} = 31$

18. Solve for p: (3 pts.)

$14(3p - 5) = 22p + 110$

19. What percent of 650 is 39? (3 pts.)

20. What percent less than 50 is 48? (3 pts.)

21. The sales price of a TV is $\frac{5}{8}$ of its regular price. If the sales price is $90, what is the regular price? (3 pts.)

22. The ratio of CDs to cassette tapes sold at Town Record was 5 to 6. Find the number of CDs sold if 30 tapes were sold. (3 pts.)

23. 25% of the purchase price of a home was payable at settlement. If the purchase price was $85,000, how much was due at settlement? (3 pts.)

24. During a holiday sale, the price of a pair of slacks dropped from $36 to $27. What percent reduction can the store advertise? (4 pts.)

25. Total sales at a department store were as follows: Dept. A, $6,500; Dept. B, $1,500; Dept. C, $4,800; Dept. D, $4,200. What was (a) the mean, (b) the median, and (c) the mode of these sales? (6 pts.)

26. Determine (a) Steve's average (mean) quality points per class and (b) his quality point average for the semester (his average per credit hour). He receives 4 quality points for each A, 3 points for each B, 2 points for each C, and 1 point for each D. His grades were as follows: (8 pts.)

Biology	4 hrs.	B	English	3 hrs.	C
Math	3 hrs.	B	Business	2 hrs.	A
History	3 hrs.	D	Phy. Ed.	1 hr.	A

27. Listed below are the years of experience at Fairlington Industries. Using intervals of 3 years, complete a frequency distribution, and compute (a) the mean, (b) the median, and (c) the most common interval (modal class) of experience. (9 pts.)

    8, 18, 3, 11, 10, 5, 9, 6, 14, 2, 4, 10, 6, 0, 19, 7, 13, 6, 22, 3, 4, 2, 8, 12.

28. Compute the standard deviation based on the following set of data: 6, 10, 18, 19, 22. (6 pts.)

29. Compute an index (price relative) for the price of a dozen large eggs, using 2001 as the base year: (5 pts.)

Year	Price
2001	$1.20
2002	1.08
2003	1.26

30. Construct a line graph showing the net sales, gross profit, and
    net profit for Abbott Publishing Co. during a 5-year period.
    (5 pts.)

	2002	2003	2004	2005	2006
Net Sales	$180,000	$210,000	$160,000	$220,000	$237,000
Gross Profit	110,000	112,000	100,000	105,000	108,000
Net Profit	25,000	28,000	10,000	18,000	20,000

EXAM 2

Chapters V - VIII

True or False:

_____1. Sales taxes are levied on both wholesale and retail sales.

_____2. A property tax is paid on the appraised value of real property.

_____3. The clause in many fire policies requiring coverage of a stipulated percent of value at the time of a fire in order to qualify for full reimbursement for damages is called a coinsurance clause.

_____4. The insurance contract that specifies in detail the provisions and limitations of the coverage is known as the indemnity.

Fill in the blanks:

_____5. The investment value available when any life insurance policy except term is terminated is called _____.

_____6. The portion of standard motor vehicle insurance which pays for damages caused by the policyholder to another vehicle or other property is called _____ insurance.

_____7. A check given in payment but not yet deducted from the drawee's bank account is called a/an_____ check.

_____8. The term that means net cash receipts exceeds the cash register total is cash_____.

_____9. Wages computed as a percent of the value of items sold or purchased is known as a/an _____.

_____10. The tax withheld from each employee's gross pay as determined by the person's gross earnings, martial status, and number of allowance is the_____.

11. Determine (a) the sales tax and (b) the marked price of a pair of sunglasses which has a total price of $19.95 if the sales tax rate is 5%. (3 pts.)

12. Determine the (a) the sales tax, (b) excise tax, and (c) total price of a fur coat that has a selling price of $18,000. The sales tax rate is 6% and the excise tax is 9%. (6 pts.)

13. Express the property tax rate 0.0124391+   (4 pts.)

    _____(a) as a percent correct to tenths

    _____(b) as an amount per C correct to cents

    _____(c) as an amount per M correct to cents

    _____(d) in whole mills

14. What is the assessed value of a building if the tax rate is $1.26 per C and the tax due is $1,890? (3 pts.)

15. Fire insurance on a building valued at $320,000 cost $0.64 per $100. (a) Compute the annual premium of this policy. (b) If the policy is canceled after 8 months by the policyholder, how much refund will be due on the canceled policy? (c) If the policy is canceled after 8 months by the insurance company, how much refund will be due on the canceled policy? (8 pts.)

16. Tempo Temporaries had a $100,000 fire. It was insured by Co. A for $200,000 and by Co. B for $300,000. All coinsurance clauses were met. How much of the damages will be paid by each? (5 pts.)

17. Tom Thompson is 30 years old, married and drives his car 10 miles each way to work. He lives in Territory 2. The car is a model K in age group 1. Thompson wants 100/200/50 liability coverage, $5,000 medical pay, full comprehensive, and $500-deductible collision insurance. Compute the total annual cost of his auto insurance. (8 pts.)

18. Bill Bland purchased a $60,000 whole life policy at age 25. (a) What is the annual premium of this policy? (b) How much could Bland borrow against the policy after 10 years? (c) If he stops paying premiums after 15 years, for how long would the same amount of coverage remain in force? (5 pts.)

19. Sonya White has become the beneficiary of a $50,000 life insurance policy at age 55. (a) If she selects the settlement option of a 10-year annuity, how much will she receive monthly? (b) Find the monthly amount for a life annuity with 10 years certain. (c) Which annuity pays more if she lives for 20 more years, and how much more? (9 pts.)

20. Reconcile the following bank statement: The checkbook balance showed a balance of $2,128.42, while the bank statement indicated a balance of $1,945.33. A service charge was $2.74, a returned check totaled $43.06. A deposit of $725.36 was not shown on the statement. Outstanding checks amounted to $296.80, $9.45, $77.96, $136.51, and $67.35.
(7 pts.)

21. A sales associate earned a salary of $75 plus a 5% commission on net sales in excess of $1,000. Last week, he sold $4,600 but $200 of sales were returned. Determine his gross wage. (6 pts.)

22. Determine the gross wages by both the standard overtime method and the overtime excess method for an employee who earned $9 per hour and worked 44 hours. Show computations for both methods. (6 pts.)

23. Andy works in the shipping department and makes a base rate of 75¢ per dozen pairs of socks packed. He receives a premium rate of 90¢ per dozen when he has packed more than 500 dozen per week. Determine his wages for a week in which he packed 605 dozen. (5 pts.)

24. Determine the (a) Social Security tax deduction, (b) Medicare tax deduction, (c) federal income tax deduction, and (d) net wages due for an employee who has a weekly gross wage of $1,230. She is married and claims 1 exemption. Her cumulative earnings prior to this week are $75,500. (6 pts.)

25. Complete lines 2 through 15 of Form 941 based on the following information: Total wages (all FICA taxable) of $30,000; another $2,000 taxable tips; Income tax of $5,600; Monthly deposits of: $4,400; $3,090; and $3,006. (9 pts.)

EXAM 3

CHAPTERS IX - XI

True-False.

_____1. Both current assets and plant asset can be recovered or depreciated over their useful life.

_____2. The book value of a plant asset is found by subtracting the accumulated depreciation from the asset's cost.

_____3. For income tax purposes, assets purchased after Dec. 31, 1986 must be depreciated by the declining-balance method.

_____4. If a business has assets of $80,000 and liabilities of $50,000, then the net worth is $130,000.

_____5. Net sales less cost of goods sold equals the operating expenses of a business.

Fill in the blanks.

_____6. Preferred stock which guarantees that dividends unpaid in any year(s) will accumulate until paid in full the next time(s) a dividend is paid is called

_____.

_____7. A business for which 2 or more individuals legally are jointly and separately liable, although responsibilities and profits may be divided in any way that is mutually agreeable is a _____.

_____8. Assigning the earliest costs to the cost of goods sold is the _____method of inventory valuation.

_____9. Assigning the latest costs to the cost of goods sold is the _____ method of inventory valuation.

_____10. The ratio of current assets to current liabilities is called the _____ratio.

11. An office machine was purchased in 2000 for $7,000. Determine its cost recovery each year, using the MACRS method for the 3-year class. Construct a cost recovery schedule. (6 pts.)

12. Refer to the previous problem (Problem #11). How much depreciation would be computed each year using the straight-line method, assuming the asset has a life of 4 years and will have a trade-in value of $1,000. (6 pts.)

13. Using the double declining-balance method, construct a depreciation schedule for equipment costing $3,000. It will be used for 5 years at which time it will be discarded as worthless. (7 pts.)

14. An asset costing $5,000 was purchased on May 1. The asset has a residual value of $200 after its useful life of 4 years. (a) How much depreciation can be claimed the first year if the straight-line method is used by the business? (b) How much depreciation can be claimed the second year? (6 pts.)

15. Overhead at a retail store is apportioned according to net sales for each department. Distribute their $50,000 overhead. (5 pts.)

Dept.	Net Sales
A	$40,000
B	23,000
C	27,000
D	10,000

16. Complete the following income statement: (10 pts.)

Vita, Inc. Income Statement For Year Ended December 31, 20X2				
Net sales		$180,000		$
Cost of Gds. Sold				
Beginning inventory	$40,500			
Net purchases	62,500			
Gds. available for sale			$	
Ending inventory	37,000			
Cost of gds. sold				$
Gross profit				$
Operating expenses		79,000		
Income before taxes				
Income tax		9,000		
Net income				$

17. Complete the following comparative balance sheet. Compute amounts and percents only for the blanks given. (15 pts.)

Vita, Inc. Comparative Balance Sheet, December 31, 20X2 and 20X1						
			Increase or (Decrease)		Percent of Total Assets	
	20X2	20X1	Amount	Percent	20X2	20X1
Assets						
Current assets						
Cash	$ 26,000	$ 30,000	$	$		%
Accounts receivable	48,000	40,000				
Mdse. inventory	143,000	140,000				
Total current assets	$	$				
Plant assets	$108,000	$ 90,000				%
Total assets	$	$				
Liabilities						
Current liabilities	$ 80,000	$ 70,000				
Long term liabilities	95,000	100,000	$	$		
Total liabilities	$	$				
Stockholders' Equity						
Common stock	$ 50,000	$ 50,000				
Retained earnings	100,000	80,000				
Total liabilities and stockholders' equity	$	$			%	

18. Based on problems 16 and 17, determine for 20X2 only (a) the working capital (or current) ratio; (b) the acid-test (or quick) ratio; and (c) the ratio of net income (after taxes) to average stockholders' equity. (7 pts.)

19. The average inventory at cost is $9,000 and $16,000 at retail. The net sales were $48,000 and the cost of goods sold was $36,000. (a) What is the turnover at cost? (b) What is the turnover at retail? (6 pts.)

20. Using (a) weighted average, (b) FIFO, and (c) LIFO, determine the cost of a 450-unit ending inventory from the following information: (8 pts.)

    Purchase #1   1,000 @ $1.80
    Purchase #2   1,600 @ 2.00
    Purchase #3   1,400 @ 2.20

21. The board of directors of the Office Systems, Inc. declared a cash dividend of $65,000. There are 4,000 shares of 9%, $100 par-value stock and 5,000 shares of common stock outstanding. What is the dividend per share to be paid to each class of stock? (6 pts.)

22. The partnership of M and S agreed to pay salaries of $25,000 to each; interest of 8% on investments of $6,000 and $5,000 respectively; and the remainder in the ratio of 3:1. How much of a $60,000 profit would each receive? (8 pts.)

EXAM 4

CHAPTERS XII - XIV

Fill in the blanks.

_____1. A reduction given for early payment of an invoice is a _____ discount.

_____2. A reduction from the list price of merchandise given to obtain the wholesale price, is a _____ discount.

_____3. The factor that multiples times list price to produce net cost (the product of the "percents paid" in a trade discount) is the _____.

_____4. The difference between the cost and the selling price of merchandise is called the _____.

_____5. A number or factor that multiples times cost to produce the selling price is called the _____.

_____6. The loss remaining when the sales price is less than cost is called the _____

_____7. A sales price that produces neither profit or loss and is the same as the total handling cost is a/an_____.

_____8. The net cost rate factor for trade discounts of 20/25/10 is _____.

_____9. The single equivalent discount for trade discounts of 20/25/10 is_____.

_____10. Which gives a business the higher markup, 25% on cost or 25% on selling price?

11. A box of computer paper has a list price of $15 less trade discounts of 20% and 10%. Find (a) the net cost rate factor, (b) the net price, and (c) the single equivalent discount. (6 pts.)

12. The list price of an office desk is $400, less 20% at Devine Furniture Co. The competitor's price for the same desk is $256. What additional discount must Devine offer to meet the competitor's price? (5 pts.)

13. Find the list price of an industrial sewing machine that has a net price of $280. The manufacturer offered trade discounts of 30% and 20%. (5 pts.)

14. The net cost of an item was $1,600. Additional freight charges of $16.20 and sales terms of 2/10 EOM were listed on the March 18 invoice. If the invoice was paid on April 10, how much was due? (5 pts.)

15. T shirts cost a department store $144 per dozen and sell for $18 each. (a) What percent markup on cost does this represent? (b) What is the percent markup on selling price? (8 pts.)

16. The cost of a picture frame is $8. The store's markup is 30% of cost. (a) What is the selling price? (b) What is the dollar amount of markup? (6 pts.)

17. A store has a cost of $30 and a selling price of $40. (a) What is its percent of markup based on cost? (b) What is its percent of markup based on selling price? (6 pts.)

18. The wholesale cost of a sweater is $15. The overhead runs 20% of cost and the retail store wants 15% for net profit. (a) What is the overhead? (b) What is the net profit? (c) What is the selling price? (8 pts.)

19. The latest income statement shows that operating expenses run 30% of sales and the net profit is 20% of sales. Based on these percents, for what price should they sell an item that cost $70 less 20%? (8 pts.)

20. A florist purchased 50 pots of tulips at $2 each. About 10% may die without selling. At what price should each pot be marked to obtain a gross profit of 35% on cost? (8 pts.)

21. A table lamp that cost $60 was marked to include a margin of 40% of the regular selling price. Later, the lamp was reduced by 30% of the marked price. (a) Find the regular price. (b) What was the sales price? (c) What percent markup on sales did the store obtain at the sales price? (9 pts.)

22. A travel bag at Allen Department Store was originally priced at $110. The price was later reduced to $77. What percent reduction can the store advertise? (6 pts.)

23. A television that regularly sells for $400 was reduced by 30%. The set had cost $300 and selling expenses are expected to be $20. Determine (a) the operating loss, (b) the absolute loss, and (c) the percent of absolute loss, based on wholesale cost. (10 pts.)

EXAM 5

CHAPTERS XV - XVI

True-False.

_____1. Simple interest is computed on the principal of the note while bank discount is computed on the proceeds.

_____2. The maturity value of a bank discount note is also called the face value.

_____3. The amount of money to be invested today that would yield a given amount of money in the future is called the present value.

Fill in the blanks.

_____4. The combination of time in which exact number of days is divided by 360 days is called the _____.

_____5. A person who signs a note promising to repay a loan is called the _____.

_____6. Assume a simple interest rate and a simple discount rate of 5% are charged on two notes. The borrower pays higher interest for the _____ note, based on the amount of money actually received from the bank.

_____7. The interest on a loan at 6% for a given time is $30. What would be the interest on that same loan for the same time at 4%?

_____8. Determine the exact number of days between January 15, 2002 and August 21, 2002.

9. Find the <u>interest</u> and <u>amount</u>: (4 pts. ea.)
   (a) $600 at 7% for 4 months:

   (b) $1,500 at 6% for 10 months:

10. How many months will it take for $400 to amount to $416 at 8% simple interest? (4 pts.)

11. Calculate the ordinary simple interest and exact simple interest on $1,460 at 9% for 90 days. (6 pts.)

12. A note for $2,500 is dated February 2 and matures in 5 months with interest at 6%. What amount will be due at maturity? (6 pts.)

13. An $800 note is drawn at 10% interest for 180 days. If money is worth 7%, find the present value of the note on the day it was drawn. (6 pts.)

14. A note for $6,000 is made at 8% interest for 180 days. Find the present value of the note 72 days before maturity if money is worth 10%. (8 pts.)

15. Find the bank discount and proceeds of a $1,500 note discounted at 8% for 60 days. (6 pts.)

16. A bank received proceeds of $19,840 on a 73 day note discounted from their Federal Reserve Bank. The face value of the note was $20,000. What exact discount rate was charged? (6 pts.)

17. The maturity values of two notes for 90 days are both $1,000. Compare the present value at 5% interest with the proceeds at 5% discount. (8 pts.)

18. On September 5, the proceeds of a note were $1,773. The maturity date is December 4. If the discount rate is 6%, what is the face value of the note? (7 pts.)

19. Deltaville Bank owned a $3,000 note discounted at 8% for 180 days. Thirty days before it was due, the bank rediscounted the note at 7%. (a) How much did Deltaville Bank loan originally? (b) How much did they receive when they sold the note? (c) How much money did Deltaville make? (10 pts.)

20. An invoice for $700 has sales terms 3/10, N/30. If a bank note is discounted at 9% in order to take advantage of the cash discount, (a) what will be the maturity value of the note? (b) How much will be saved by taking out the note? (8 pts.)

21. Fordyma Manufacturing Co. was the holder of a 5-month, $6,000 note dated April 20 with interest at 6%. Forty-five days before the note was due, Fordyma discounted the note at the bank at 8%. (a) How much did Fordyma receive for the note? (b) How much interest did it earn? (c) How much interest did the bank make? (9 pts.)

EXAM 6

CHAPTERS XVII - XX

True-False.

_____1. Under the U.S. rule, the partial payment is used first to pay the principal.

_____2. The total amount of extra money paid for credit buying is called the finance charge.

_____3. To find the number of periods for compounding interest, multiply number of years times number of periods per year.

_____4. To find the rate per period, multiply the yearly rate times the number of periods per year.

_____5. An annuity is a single deposit that remains invested for the entire time.

_____6. The beginning balance that an account must contain in order to receive an annuity from it until it is empty is the present value of an annuity.

_____7. If bonds are sold for a price that is more than face value, then they are sold at a discount.

_____8. To build up an account to a given amount by making regular payments is a sinking fund.

_____9. If one is asked to determine what regular payment must be made to discharge a debt, the amortization tables should be used.

10. Use the U.S. rule to determine the balance due on the maturity date of a $1,500 note at 6% for 150 days if a partial payment of $410 was made on the 40th day and another payment of $511 was made on the 100th day. (7 pts.)

11. A stereo is priced at $500. The time payment plan requires a 10% down payment and 24-monthly payments. For simplicity, the finance charge is computed at 6% nominal interest. Determine (a) the finance charge; (b) the monthly payment; and (c) the annual percentage rate that the dealer must disclose. (9 pts.)

12. Hilda Hess is buying furniture that cost $2,400 by making 12-monthly payments at 10% simple interest. (a) What is the total finance charge? (b) What is her monthly payment? (c) As she makes her 8th payment, she also wishes to pay her remaining balance. How much interest will she save by the rule of 78s? (d) Determine her remaining balance. (8 pts.)

13. If $3,000 is invested at 6% compounded quarterly, (a) what will be the compound amount after 10 years? (b) How much is interest? (7 pts.)

14. A 6%, $1,000 bond has a quoted price of 96. (a) How much does a buyer pay for the bond? (b) State the premium or discount. (c) What is the current yield on this bond? (6 pts.)

15. Find (a) the total amount of interest and (b) the balance after the quarter ended for Vernon Johnson's savings account. The bank pays 6% compounded daily. On July 1, his account contained $3,500. On August 7, he deposited $500 and he withdrew $300 on September 9. (8 pts.)

16. Tim Narvi opened a savings account on October 1, 2000 with a deposit of $900. The account paid 4% compounded quarterly. On January 1, 2001, he withdrew his balance and added enough money to purchase a $1,000 6-month CD with interest at 7% compounded monthly. (a) How much was his savings account balance on January 1 prior to the addition? (b) How much was his additional investment? (c) How much was his CD worth on July 1, 2001? (d) How much total interest had been earned? (12 pts.)

17. A business plans to replace some display fixtures in 3 years. They will need $40,000 for this project. What single deposit must be made now in a long-term investment that earns 8% compounded quarterly? (5 pts.)

18. Mark Leonardo deposits $50 each month for 2 years into an account earning 9% compounded monthly. (a) Determine the amount in the account in 2 years. (b) How much will Leonardo have deposited? (c) How much will be interest? (7 pts.)

19. At retirement, a teacher would like to receive an annuity of $600 quarterly for 10 years after she retires. If money is worth 10% compounded quarterly, (a) how much must she have when she retires so that she can finance this annuity? (b) How much will she actually receive from the annuity? (c) How much interest will this single deposit earn before the annuity ends? (8 pts.)

20. The Graystone Corp. issued $80,000 in 6-year bonds. A sinking fund at 8% compounded monthly was established in order to redeem the bonds. (a) What monthly payment must be deposited to the sinking fund? (b) How much of the maturity value will be deposits? (c) How much interest will the sinking fund earn? (7 pts.)

21. The Atwaters borrowed $36,000 to make home improvements. They signed a 9% mortgage with monthly payments for 7 years. (a) What was their monthly payment? (b) What was the total of their payments? (c) How much total interest will they pay? (7 pts.)

FINAL EXAM

Part I. Fill in the blanks.

_____1. Identify the place value of 7 in the number: 24,671,539

_____2. $\dfrac{19}{8}$ is a/an _____ fraction.

_____3. Express $\dfrac{3}{5}$ as a percent:

_____4. Express 12 1/2% as a fraction:

_____5. Find the median of these numbers: 54, 50, 47, 32

_____6. A price index of 182.4 means that an item which formerly cost $10 now costs_____.

_____7. A listing of numerical data in order of size is called a/an _____.

_____8. Express the tax rate 0.021435+ as a percent correct to tenths.

_____9. Round this number to the nearest hundredths: 65.3391

_____10. Henry's auto insurance policy includes 25/25/10 liability, $2,500 medical pay, comprehensive and $500-deductible collision. In a recent accident, he injured a husband and wife. The court awarded $18,000 and $15,000 to the couple. How much will the insurance company pay toward these costs?

_____11. The method of determining gross wages based on the number of units produced or finished is called _____.

_____12. The form that must be filed 4 times a year by the employer to report the employees' earnings, federal income tax and FICA tax liabilities is the _____.

_____13. The calculated value of a plant asset after depreciation or cost recovery has been deducted is known as _____.

_____14. Which gives a business the larger markup, 40% on cost or 40% on sales?

_____15. What is the net cost rate factor for the following chain discount: 20/20/30?

_____16. What is the single equivalent discount for the following chain discount: 25/30?

_____17. What is the selling price factor for a 33 1/3% markup on cost?

_____18. What is the selling price factor for a 33 1/3% markup on selling price?

_____19. The annual interest rate that must be disclosed to an installment buyer under the Truth in Lending Law is called the _____.

_____20. The process of repaying a loan (principal plus interest) by equal periodic payments is called _____.

_____21. Liabilities plus net worth equal _____ on the balance sheet.

_____22. Determine the inventory turnover at retail: average inventory at retail, $32,000; net sales, $200,000; cost of goods sold, $151,200.

Part II. Show all calculations on this test.

1. Find the value of this expression: $600\left(1\dfrac{8}{100} \times \dfrac{1}{3}\right)$ (4 pts)

2. During a sale, the Toy Shop's ratio of electronic sports games to electronic space games sold was 7:5.   Find the number of sports games, if 45 space games were sold. (4 pts.)

3. Find the selling price of a jacket if the gross profit was $11.50.   The gross profit was 25% of the selling price. (4 pts.)

4. The sale price for a set of golf clubs was $252, including a 5% sales tax.   (a) What was the sale price of the clubs before the tax was added?   (b) How much sales tax was included? (4 pts.)

5. What is the (a) cash value (nonforfeiture option) on a whole life insurance policy for $25,000 that has been in force for 10 years? (b) What is the amount of paid-up insurance? (6 pts.)

6. Insurance on Gabriel, Inc. is shared by two carriers as indicated below. There are 80% coinsurance clauses written into both policies. The fire inspector placed a $500,000 value on the building. Determine the compensation due from each on a $160,000 fire. (8 pts.)

   Co. A $200,000
   Co. B $150,000

7. The checkbook shows a balance of $896.62, while the bank statement indicates a balance of $962.61. A returned check totaled $19.34 and printing new checks cost $9.53. Interest of $5.25 was earned on the average balance. A deposit of $121.85 was not included on the statement. Outstanding checks are in the amount of $45.75, $32.11, $115.67, and $17.93. Reconcile the bank statement with the checkbook balance in good form. (7 pts.)

8. Molly earned $260 for the week. This included a $125 salary and a commission on net sales of $2,250. What is her commission rate? (4 pts.)

9. Determine by the overtime excess method the gross wages for an employee who earns $7.50 an hour for all regular hours and time-and-a-half for all hours over 40 in a week. He worked 45 hours last week. (5 pts.)

10. Determine the (a) federal income tax, (b) Social Security, (c) Medicare tax deductions for a single person with one allowance who made $632 last week. (d) What were the net wages? (4 pts.)

11. In 2002, Cora Kelly, Inc. purchased $9,000 in equipment of the 7-year class. Using MACRS, prepare a cost recovery schedule for this equipment for the first 4 years only. (5 pts.)

12. Using the declining-balance method of depreciation, construct a depreciation schedule for an asset costing $5,000 with an useful life of 5 years. The residual value is estimated to be $500. (8 pts.)

13. Determine (a) the annual depreciation by the straight-line method and (b) the book value at the end of the first year only for equipment that cost $3,600 with a scrap value of $200 and an estimated life of 5 years. (5 pts.)

14. The Daniel-Samuel partnership agreed to pay a $12,000 salary to
    Daniel; interest of 5% on their original investments of $40,000
    and $20,000 respectively; and any remaining profits in the ratio
    of 3:2. Distribute their profit of $48,000. (9 pts.)

15. Evaluate the following inventory by (a) weighted average, (b)
    FIFO, and (c) LIFO. (10 pts.)

Purchases	Ending Inventory
9 @ $ 8	12 items
10 @ 10	
6 @ 13	

16. The Owens Corp. declared a $420,000 cash dividend. Distribute
    the dividend to 10,000 shareholders of 6%, $100 par-value
    preferred and 50,000 shareholders of common. (6 pts.)

17. An invoice dated February 20 with sales terms of 3/15 EOM
    totaled $519.60 which included prepaid freight of $19.60. The
    merchandise is subject to trade discounts of 20% and 20%.
    Determine (a) the date by which the invoice must be paid in
    order to take advantage of the cash discount and (b) the amount
    that must be remitted if paid on or before that date. (7 pts.)

18. A coat cost a store $75. Its overhead is 20% of cost and its
    selling price is $100.   (a) How much markup does this sale
    include? (b) How much is the overhead? (c) Is a profit or loss
    made on the sale, and how much? (5 pts.)

19. Complete the following comparative balance sheet. (24 pts.)

	2002	2001	Increase or (Decrease) Amount	Percent	Percent of Total Assets 2002	2001
Assets						
Current assets						
Cash	$ 40,000	$ 32,000	$	$	%	%
Accounts receivable	60,000	48,000				
Mdse. inventory	180,000	200,000				
Current assets	$	$	$	$	%	%
Plant assets	$ 120,000	$ 100,000				
Total assets	$	$				
Liabilities						
Current liabilities	$ 80,000	$ 70,000				
Long term liabilities	140,000	170,000	$	$	%	%
Total liabilities	$	$				
Owner's equity						
Joe Phillips, capital	$ 180,000	$ 140,000				
Total liabilities & Owner's equity	$	$			%	%

20. A selling price of an item is $30. If the margin was 35% on retail selling price, (a) what was the cost and (b) what was the gross profit? (4 pts.)

21. A $100 power saw was closed out for $72. (a) What percent markdown did this represent? (b) The store had paid $80 less 20% and 12 1/2% for the saw, and selling expenses are 15% of the regular selling price. (c) How much operating profit or loss was made? (11 pts.)

22. A note is made on March 1 for $720 at 8% interest for 9 months. Determine (a) the interest and (b) the maturity value of the note. (5 pts.)

23. The principal of a 180-day note was $500. The interest rate charged was 8%. If money is worth 5%, what was the present value of the note 45 days before the maturity date? (8 pts.)

24. On January 31, the proceeds of a 5-month note were $931. If the bank discount had been computed at 6%, what was the face value of the note? (6 pts.)

25. First Federal Bank was the payee of a $4,000 note dated June 9 for 6 months discounted at 9%. First Federal rediscounted the note at 6% at another bank 60 days before it was due. (a) What amount had First Federal loaned the maker? (b) How much did First Federal receive when they sold the note? (c) How much interest did First Federal make? (d) How much interest did the second bank make? (10 pts.)

26. On March 3, Mary Clinton signed a note for $3,000 with interest at 8% for 270 days. She made payments of $680 on July 1 and $932 on August 30. How much will she owe on the due date? (16 pts.)

27. A camera cost $800 cash or it may be purchased for $50 down and 24 payments of $40 each. (a) What is the total cost of the camera on the installment plan? (b) How much extra does the buyer pay to finance this purchase? (c) What annual percentage rate is paid for the convenience of credit buying? (8 pts.)

28. If $5,000 is invested at 8% compounded semiannually, (a) what will the compound amount be in 3 years? (b) How much is interest? (8 pts.)

29. Conner wants to have $2,000 in 2 years for a down payment on a car. Passbook accounts earn 5% compounded monthly. (a) What single deposit now will mature to $2,000? (b) How much interest will the account earn? (8 pts.)

30. A father deposited $200 in his son's savings account on each birthday through his 21st birthday. (a) How much did the father deposit? (b) What amount was in the account after the 21st deposit, if the account earned 6% annual interest? (7 pts.)

31. A bakery borrowed $40,000 in order to purchase a new oven. Quarterly payments will be made for 8 years in order to amortize the 9% loan. (a) What is the amount of each payment? (b) How much total interest will be charged? (8 pts.)

ANSWERS TO EXAM PROBLEMS

Exam 1

1. 4 thousand

2. integers

3. $\dfrac{8}{3}$

4. improper

5. 2

6. $\dfrac{2}{9}$; 2:9

7. $\dfrac{X}{5} = \dfrac{24}{60}$

8. $\dfrac{1}{100}$ or

   hundredths

9. median

10. 16%

11. 68%

12. $24.74

13. (a) 231.46

    (b) $1\dfrac{11}{12}$

    (c) $3\dfrac{13}{24}$

    (d) 1,271.250

(e) 33

(f) 17½

(g) 64

14. (a) 0.277

    (b) 0.056

    (c) 0.1082

    (d) 0.0025

15. (a) $\dfrac{9}{10}$

    (b) $\dfrac{1}{8}$

    (c) $\dfrac{1}{6}$

16. (a) 70%

    (b) 368%

    (c) 1.2%

17. 72

18. 9

19. 6%

20. 4%

21. $144

22. 25

23. $21,250

24. 25%

25. (a) $4,250

    (b) $1,500

    (c) No mode

26. (a) 2.83

    (b) 2.625

27. (a) 7.5

    (b) 7.5

    (c) 6 - 8

28. 6

29. 90; 105

30. See attached

30.

	2002	2003	2004	2005	2006
Net Sales	$180,000	$210,000	$160,000	$220,000	$237,000
Gross Profit	110,000	112,000	100,000	105,000	108,000
Net Profit	25,000	28,000	10,000	18,000	20,000

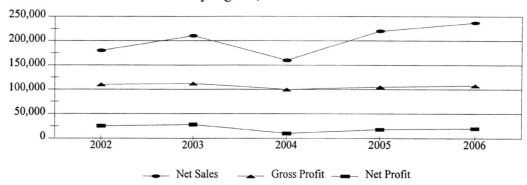

Abbott Publishing Co.

Key Figures, 2002-2006

Exam 2

1. false

2. true

3. true

4. false

5. nonforfeiture option

6. property damage

7. outstanding

8. over

9. commission

10. income tax

11. a. $19

    b. $0.95

12. a. $1,080

    b. $1,620

    c. $20,700

13. a. 1.3%

    b. $1.25 per C

    c. $12.44 per M

    d. 13 mills

14. $150,000

15. a. $2,048

    b. $409.60

    c. $682.67

16. A: $40,000

    B: $60,000

17. $635.60

18. a. $1,033.20

    b. $9,720.00

    c. 20 years, 300 days

19. a. $480

    b. $264

    c. 10-year certain pays $5,760 more

20. $2,082.62

21. $245

22. $414

23. $469.50

24. a. $43.40

    b. $17.84

    c. $194.00

    d. $974.76

25. line 2: $32,000
    line 3: $ 5,600
    line 5: $ 5,600
    line 6b: $3,720
    line 6d: $ 248
    line 7b: $ 928
    line 8: $4,896
    line 10: $4,896
    line 11: $10,496
    line 13: $10,496
    line 14: $10,495
    line 15: 0

Exam 3

1. false	6. cumulative
2. true	7. partnership
3. false	8. FIFO
4. false	9. LIFO
5. false	10. current or working capital

11.	Year	Book Value (End of Year)	Annual Depreciation	Accumulated Depreciation
	0	$7,000	—	—
	1	4,667	$2,333	$2,333
	2	1,556	3,111	5,444
	3	519	1,037	6,481
	4	0	519	7,000

12. $1,500

13.	Year	Book Value (End of Year)	Annual Depreciation	Accumulated Depreciation
	0	$3,000	—	----
	1	1,800	$1,200	$1,200
	2	1,080	720	1,920
	3	648	432	2,352
	4	389	259	2,611
	5	0	389	3,000

14. a. $800   b. $1,200

15. $20,000; $11,500; $13,500; $5,000

16.	Net sales		100.0%
	Goods available for sale	$103,000	57.2
	Cost of goods sold	66,000	36.7
	Gross profit	114,000	63.3
	Income before taxes	35,000	
	Net income	26,000	14.4

17.				Increase (Decrease)		Percent of Total Assets	
		20X2	20X1	Amount	Percent	20X2	20X1
	Cash			($4,000)	(13.3%)		
	Total current assets	$217,000	$210,000				
	Plant assets						30.0%
	Total assets	325,000	300,000				
	Lg.-term liabilities			(5,000)	(5.0)		
	Total liabilities	175,000	170,000				
	Retained earnings			20,000	25.0		
	Total liabilities & owners' equity	325,000	300,000			100.0%	

18. a. 2.71 to 1   b. 0.93 to 1   c. 18.6%

19. a. 4   b. 3

20. a. $909   b. $990   c. $810

21. $9 per share dividend preferred; $5.80 per share dividend common

22. M: $51,070
    S: $ 8,930

Exam 4

1. cash

2. trade

3. net cost rate factor

4. markup

5. selling price factor

6. absolute or gross loss

7. breakeven

8. 0.54

9. 46%

10. 25% of selling price

11. a. 0.72

    b. $10.80

    c. 28%

12. 20%

13. $500

14. $1,584.20

15. a. 50%

    b. 33⅓%

16. a. $10.40

    b. $2.40

17. a. 33⅓%

    b. 25%

18. a. $3

    b. $2.25

    c. $20.25

19. $112

20. $3

21. a. $100

    b. $70

    c. $14\frac{2}{7}$%

22. 30%

23. a. $40

    b. $20

    c. $6\frac{2}{3}$%

Exam 5

1. false

2. true

3. true

4. Bankers' Rule

5. Maker

6. discount

7. $20

8. 219 days

9. a. $14; $614

   b. $75; $1,575

10. 6 months

11. Ordinary: $32.85

    Exact: $32.40

12. $2,562.50

13. $811.59

14. $6,117.65

15. $20; $1,480

16. 4%

17. Present value: $987.65

    proceeds: $987.50

18. $1,800

19. a. $2,880.00

    b. $2,982.50

    c. $102.50

20. a. $682.41

    b. $17.59

21. a. $6,091.47

    b. $91.47

    c. $61.53

Exam 6

1. false	15. a. $56.35	
2. true	b. $3,756.35	
3. true	16. a. $927.27	
4. false	b. $72.73	
5. false	c. $1,035.51	
6. true	d. $62.78	
7. false	17. $31,539.73	
8. true	18. a. $1,309.42	
9. true	b. $1,200.00	
10. $401.32	c. $109.42	
11. a. $54	19. a. $15,061.67	
b. $21	b. $24,000.00	
c. 11.25%	c. $8,938.33	
12. a. $240	20. a. $869.33	
b. $220	b. $62,591.76	
c. $30.77	c. $17,408.24	
d. $849.23	21. a. $579.21	
13. a. $5,442.05	b. $48,653.64	
b. $2,442.05	c. $12,653.64	
14. a. $960		
b. Discount, $40		
c. 6.25%		

Final Exam

Part I.

1. 70 thousand

2. improper

3. 60%

4. $\dfrac{1}{8}$

5. 48.5

6. $18.24

7. array

8. 2.2%

9. 65.34

10. $25,000

11. production or piece meal

12. 941

13. book value

14. 40% on sales

15. 0.448

16. 0.475 or 47.5%

17. $\dfrac{4}{3}$

18. $\dfrac{3}{2}$

19. Annual percentage rate (APR)

20. amortization

21. total assets

22. 6.25 times

Part II.

1. 584

2. 63

3. $46

4. a. $240

   b. $12

5. a. $2,325

   b. $6,200

6. Co. A: $80,000

   Co. B: $60,000

7. $873

8. 6%

9. $356.25

10. a. $87.00

    b. $39.16

    c. $9.16

    d. $496.66

11. $1,286; $2,204; $1,574; $1,125

12. Annual Depreciation:

    $2,000

    $1,200

    $720

    $432

    $148

13. a. $680

    b. $2,920

14. Daniel: $33,800

    Samuel: $14,200

15. a. $120

    b. $138

    c. $102

16. $6 per share dividend preferred

    $7.20 per share dividend common

17. a. March 15

    b. $330

18. a. $25

    b. $15

    c. Profit, $10

19.				Increase (Decrease)		Percent of Total Assets	
		2002	2001	Amt.	Percent	2002	2001
	Cash			$ 8,000	25.0%	10.0%	8.4%
	Current assets	$280,000	$280,000	0	0	70.0	73.7
	Total assets	400,000	380,000	20,000	5.3	100.0	100.0
	Lg.-term liabilities			(30,000)	(17.6)	35.0	44.7
	Total liabilities	220,000	240,000				
	Total liab. & owners' equity	400,000	380,000			100.0	100.0

20. a. $19.50

    b. $10.50

21. a. 28%
    b. $56
    c. Operating profit, $1

22. a. $44

    b. $764

23. $516.77

24. $950

25. a. $3,817

    b. $3,960

    c. $143

    d. $40

26. $1,530

27. a. $1,010

    b. $210

    c. 25%

28. a. $6,326.60

    b. $1,326.60

29. a. $1,810.05

    b. $189.95

30. a. $4,200

    b. $7,998.97

31. a. $1,766.97

    b. $16,543.04

APPENDIX A

ARITHMETIC

Granted that many business math students are weak in arithmetic, the authors do not favor a lengthy review of arithmetic. There are several reasons for this. In the first place, most of these students know how the operations should be performed, having studied them repeatedly through their school days; they make mistakes because of haste and carelessness and because they are "bored to death" with another repetition of the same old things they have been studying since elementary school. Consequently, a thorough review of arithmetic seldom produces much improvement in students at this level. Furthermore, the widespread use of calculators in business today has greatly reduced the need for proficiency in the actual operations -- addition, subtraction, multiplication, and division. (The use of calculators, however, has in no way reduced the necessity for knowledge of mathematical procedures, of when each operation is required, and in what order they should be performed.) Also, a lengthy study of arithmetic is not a good motivating factor nor is it a realistic indication of forthcoming topics. Most important, a long study of arithmetic prohibits the inclusion of some important business procedures, which are the principal objective of the course.

With these facts in mind, the authors do not favor including the Appendix unless the arithmetic level of the students makes it essential. If it is included, we would not devote a great deal of class time to it. An alternative procedure might be to make the Appendix an out-of-class assignment entirely; the instructor could assign specific problems to be handed in at the end of the first week.

Most of the common procedures used in arithmetic are explained simply in terms of fundamental laws of algebra. This was done to let the student see there is a reason why these procedures are permissible. The intent was only to provide reassurance; we would not require the student to memorize these algebraic explanations. For the same reason, the basic number properties (commutative for addition and multiplication, associative for addition and multiplication, and the distributive property) are illustrated only with whole numbers. This simply serves as a reminder, since virtually all students have been introduced to the properties previously, and no student assignment problems for the number properties are included. If you feel some practice is necessary, however, you could easily select some values (including fractions and decimals) with which they could demonstrate the properties.

Appendix A - Arithmetic
Problem Solutions

Section 1, page 535

1. (a) millions   (d) hundred thousands
   (b) tens   (e) ones
   (c) billions

2. (a) ten millions   (d) hundred millions
   (b) ten thousands   (e) thousands
   (c) hundreds

3. (a) Six hundred thirty-three million, five hundred twenty
       thousand, four hundred eighty-one.
   (b) Twenty-five million, five hundred forty-three thousand,
       one hundred twenty-eight.
   (c) One hundred fifty million, two hundred eighty-six
       thousand, four hundred thirteen.
   (d) Six million, forty-six thousand, one hundred twenty-five.
   (e) Eight hundred twelve billion, three hundred forty-four
       million, six hundred one thousand, twenty-two.

4. (a) Eight hundred forty-two million, four hundred sixteen
       thousand, three hundred seventy-five.
   (b) Two billion, six hundred fifty-five million, one hundred
       twenty thousand, six hundred eighty-eight.
   (c) Forty-eight million, one hundred thirty-six thousand, four
       hundred seventy-two.
   (d) Eight million, one hundred eight thousand, twenty-seven.
   (e) Seven hundred sixty-two thousand, three hundred.

Section 2, page 546

1.		2.		3.		4.	
(a)	20	(a)	20	(a)	22	(a)	1,850
(b)	19	(b)	20	(b)	24	(b)	3,044
(c)	27	(c)	26	(c)	28	(c)	1,885
(d)	25	(d)	23	(d)	37	(d)	24,625
(e)	27	(e)	24	(e)	284	(e)	24,159
(f)	20	(f)	28	(f)	221	(f)	7,951
(g)	19	(g)	25	(g)	213	(g)	221,057
(h)	225	(h)	212	(h)	315	(h)	217,534
(i)	206	(i)	225	(i)	268	(i)	$ 8,788.45

5. (a)   206   6. (a)   217   7. (a)   8   8. (a)   26
    (b)   262   (b)   1,587   (b)   664   (b)   197
    (c) 1,412   (c)   10,914   (c)   1,921   (c)   1,094
                                           (d)   323   (d)   1,355

9. (a)   4,660   10. (a)   31,200
    (b)   6,400   (b)   88,000
    (c)   55,300   (c)   1,950
    (d)   11,200   (d)   157,500
    (e)   82,800   (e)   244,200
    (f) 2,075,000   (f)   118,800

11. (a)   1,824   12. (a)   1,645
     (b)   37,842   (b)   20,739
     (c)   381,351   (c) 2,833,330
     (d) 1,750,060   (d) 4,945,536

13. (a) 598   14. (a)   2,709
     (b) 746   (b) 12,744
     (c)   18   (c)   25
     (d)   26   (d)   293
     (e) 291   (e)   258

15. Daily Totals: Dept. Totals:
     Monday $ 2,457.47   Dept. #1 $ 2,404.35
     Tuesday   2,315.53   #2   3,002.09
     Wednesday   2,189.82   #3   2,651.89
     Thursday   2,361.51   #4   1,991.98
     Friday   2,732.17   #5   1,962.61
     Saturday   2,627.90   #6   2,671.48
                   $14,684.40 $14,684.40

16. Total Cost
$ 113.68
    126.60
    123.75
     44.25
     74.10
     53.70
      7.20
     25.30
  1,720.00
   124.75
    25.14
   285.90
 14,994.00
$17,718.37

Section 3, page 561

1. (a) $\dfrac{2}{3}$

  (b) $\dfrac{7}{3}$ or $2\dfrac{1}{3}$

  (c) $\dfrac{7}{9}$

  (d) $\dfrac{4}{7}$

  (e) $\dfrac{2}{3}$

  (f) $\dfrac{5}{3}$ or $1\dfrac{2}{3}$

  (g) $\dfrac{3}{4}$

  (h) $\dfrac{6}{5}$ or $1\dfrac{1}{5}$

  (i) $\dfrac{63}{107}$

  (j) $\dfrac{7}{12}$

2. (a) $\dfrac{4}{12}$; $\dfrac{9}{12}$

  (b) $\dfrac{7}{14}$; $\dfrac{8}{14}$

  (c) $\dfrac{4}{9}$; $\dfrac{6}{9}$

  (d) $\dfrac{6}{16}$; $\dfrac{1}{16}$

  (e) $\dfrac{15}{24}$; $\dfrac{4}{24}$

  (f) $\dfrac{12}{60}$; $\dfrac{15}{60}$; $\dfrac{40}{60}$

  (g) $\dfrac{12}{42}$; $\dfrac{7}{42}$; $\dfrac{21}{42}$

  (h) $\dfrac{21}{30}$; $\dfrac{12}{30}$; $\dfrac{10}{30}$

  (i) $\dfrac{8}{36}$; $\dfrac{27}{36}$; $\dfrac{30}{36}$

  (j) $\dfrac{24}{40}$; $\dfrac{10}{40}$; $\dfrac{25}{40}$

3. (a) By common denominator:

$$\dfrac{24}{56}, \ \dfrac{42}{56}, \ \dfrac{20}{56}, \ \dfrac{28}{56}, \ \dfrac{35}{56}, \ \dfrac{40}{56}$$

3. (a) (Continued)

By order of size:

$$\frac{5}{14}, \ \frac{3}{7}, \ \frac{1}{2}, \ \frac{5}{8}, \ \frac{5}{7}, \ \frac{3}{4}$$

(b) By common denominator:

$$\frac{42}{72}, \ \frac{60}{72}, \ \frac{54}{72}, \ \frac{56}{72}, \ \frac{45}{72}, \ \frac{39}{72}$$

By order of size:

$$\frac{13}{24}, \ \frac{7}{12}, \ \frac{5}{8}, \ \frac{3}{4}, \ \frac{7}{9}, \ \frac{5}{6}$$

4. (a) $\frac{13}{4}$ (e) $\frac{62}{5}$ (i) $\frac{113}{6}$

(b) $\frac{53}{8}$ (f) $\frac{61}{3}$ (j) $\frac{101}{11}$

(c) $\frac{58}{7}$ (g) $\frac{185}{7}$ (k) $\frac{107}{7}$

(d) $\frac{47}{9}$ (h) $\frac{65}{2}$ (l) $\frac{91}{12}$

5. (a) $2\frac{5}{6}$ (e) $16\frac{1}{3}$ (i) $5\frac{2}{3}$

(b) $9\frac{1}{5}$ (f) $3\frac{1}{12}$ (j) $11\frac{1}{5}$

(c) $8\frac{1}{2}$ (g) $15\frac{1}{3}$ (k) $11\frac{1}{3}$

(d) $3\frac{3}{7}$ (h) $13\frac{1}{2}$ (l) $9\frac{1}{2}$

6. (a) $\frac{13}{20}$ (c) $1\frac{11}{30}$ (e) $1\frac{4}{9}$ (g) $11\frac{9}{10}$ (i) $14\frac{31}{40}$

(b) $\frac{13}{24}$ (d) $1\frac{5}{24}$ (f) $2\frac{1}{9}$ (h) $9\frac{31}{36}$ (j) $37\frac{19}{30}$

7. (a) $\dfrac{1}{2}$ (c) $\dfrac{25}{56}$ (e) $\dfrac{1}{15}$ (g) $18\dfrac{5}{12}$ (i) $15\dfrac{2}{7}$

    (b) $\dfrac{11}{20}$ (d) $\dfrac{1}{12}$ (f) $11\dfrac{11}{12}$ (h) $20\dfrac{5}{6}$ (j) $20\dfrac{1}{2}$

8. (a) $\dfrac{5}{21}$ (c) $\dfrac{1}{2}$ (e) $\dfrac{1}{30}$ (g) $1\dfrac{1}{3}$ (i) 63

    (b) $\dfrac{7}{32}$ (d) $\dfrac{1}{8}$ (f) $2\dfrac{1}{7}$ (h) $2\dfrac{2}{5}$ (j) 12

9. (a) $\dfrac{1}{40}$ (b) $\dfrac{7}{32}$ (c) $24\dfrac{1}{2}$ (d) 28

10. (a) $\dfrac{1}{3}$ (c) $\dfrac{15}{16}$ (e) 1   (g) $1\dfrac{4}{5}$ (i) $\dfrac{3}{20}$

    (b) $\dfrac{5}{9}$ (d) 5   (f) $1\dfrac{1}{10}$ (h) 8   (j) $\dfrac{5}{27}$

Section 4, page 573

1. (a) thousandths   (d) hundreds   (g) ten thousandths

    (b) ones   (e) hundredths   (h) tenths

    (c) tens   (f) thousands   (i) hundred thousandths

2. (a) five tenths

    (b) six hundredths

    (c) eighteen thousandths

    (d) thirty-two hundredths

    (e) eight and six tenths

    (f) seventeen and forty-four hundredths

    (g) five hundred and one hundred three thousandths

    (h) nine and fifteen ten-thousandths

3. (a) 0.4

   (b) 0.25

   (c) 0.3

   (d) 0.7

   (e) 0.32

   (f) 0.075

   (g) $0.14\frac{2}{7}$ or 0.142857

   (h) $0.44\frac{4}{9}$ or $0.44\overline{4}$

   (i) $0.41\frac{2}{3}$ or $0.416\overline{6}$

   (j) $0.54\frac{6}{11}$ or $0.54\overline{54}$

   (k) $0.30\frac{10}{13}$ or 0.307692

   (l) $0.26\frac{12}{13}$ or 0.2692307

   (m) 6.0

   (n) $40\frac{3}{4}$ or 40.75

   (o) 5.4

   (p) $5.11\frac{1}{9}$ or $5.11\overline{1}$

   (q) $3.83\frac{1}{3}$ or $3.83\overline{3}$

   (r) 9.428

4. (a) $\frac{3}{50}$ (f) $\frac{1}{125}$

   (b) $\frac{2}{5}$ (g) $\frac{9}{250}$

   (c) $\frac{1}{4}$ (h) $\frac{91}{200}$

   (d) $\frac{13}{40}$ (i) $\frac{17}{400}$

   (e) $\frac{31}{200}$ (j) $\frac{23}{625}$

5. (a) 35.62   (e) 884.52   (i) 280   (m) 545,000
   (b) 26.45   (f) 1.6   (j) 0.003651   (n) 0.009945
   (c) 5.5663   (g) 265   (k) 52,500
   (d) 0.10488   (h) 881.2   (l) 0.00644

6. (a) 24.20   (e) 1743.891   (i) 866.256   (m) 596.369
    (b) 1.74   (f) 280.591   (j) 431.605
    (c) 1.3051   (g) 768.405   (k) 873.02
    (d) 196.244   (h) 899.553   (l) 422.96

7. (a) 46.95   (e) 7.811   (i) 29.0096   (m) 37.697
    (b) 3.725   (f) 3.845   (j) 142.344   (n) 48.2
    (c) 28.859   (g) 558.822   (k) 521.279   (o) 285.12
    (d) 240.316   (h) 12.929   (l) 455.045   (p) 68.894
                                                         (q) 4.5788

8. (a) 39.936   (e) 0.651   (i) 0.937464
    (b) 98.82   (f) 0.14617   (j) 0.013794
    (c) 2.9088   (g) 0.42148
    (d) 5.292   (h) 0.000145

9. (a) 78   (e) 136   (i) 0.344   (m) 440
    (b) 123   (f) 3,270   (j) 32.58   (n) 41
    (c) 46   (g) 1.27   (k) 0.78   (o) 321
    (d) 68   (h) 0.24   (l) 0.0645   (p) 0.28

APPENDIX B

METRIC AND CURRENCY CONVERSIONS

These two topics are independent of any other topic in the text; they may be studied at any point during the term.

1. Metric Conversion:

Students have some knowledge of the metric system having studied it in elementary and secondary schools. International students have, of course, used metrics to measure distance, weights, volume, and temperature. Though most people know about the metric system, there is still strong reluctance to convert completely in this country. Point out to students that international standards have become an important factor in international economic competition. Products in the global market place must be acceptable in terms of weights and measurements in all countries; they must comply with the international standard, the metric system.

Emphasize that the metric system is based on the number 10 (decimal system). In examples 1 and 2, students are shown how the movement of the decimal point to the right or left will increase or decrease the value of the measurement. Tables are used for metric to U.S. and U.S. to metric conversions. Students will multiply the actual number of given units by a table factor.

2. Currency Conversion:

The monetary conversion table in this section was taken from a newspaper. Be sure to explain that the values shown will fluctuate over time. Encourage students to check the newspaper daily during the study of this topic. Charting the changes of the U.S. dollar in another country's currency over a period of time would be interesting.

Appendix B - Metric & Currency Conversions
Problem Solutions

Section 1, page 584

1. (a) <u>10</u> meters

    (b) 1 <u>hectoliter</u>

    (c) 1 <u>milligram</u>

    (d) <u>0.1</u> liter

    (e) <u>100</u> centimeters

    (f) 1 <u>gram</u>

    (g) 1 <u>kilometer</u>

    (h) <u>0.001</u> liter

    (i) <u>1000</u> decigrams

    (j) 1 <u>milliliter</u>

    (k) <u>100</u> decameters

    (l) 1 <u>decagram</u>

2. (a) <u>1000</u> grams

    (b) 1 <u>decameter</u>

    (c) 1 <u>centiliter</u>

    (d) <u>0.001</u> meter

    (e) <u>0.001</u> kilometer

    (f) 1 <u>liter</u>

    (g) 1 <u>gram</u>

    (h) <u>100</u> centiliters

    (i) <u>10</u> decameters

    (j) 1 <u>decagram</u>

    (k) 1 <u>milliliter</u>

    (l) <u>0.1</u> kiloliter

3. (a) <u>360</u> liters

    (b) <u>4.5</u> meters

    (c) <u>2.150</u> grams

    (d) <u>800</u> meters

    (e) <u>425</u> centigrams

    (f) <u>1.88</u> hectoliters

    (g) <u>300</u> decimeters

    (h) <u>1.2</u> kilograms

    (i) <u>29</u> milligrams

    (j) <u>0.76</u> hectometers

4. (a) <u>150</u> meters

    (b) <u>1.25</u> meters

    (c) <u>360</u> grams

    (d) <u>2.137</u> liters

    (e) <u>1.475</u> kilograms

    (f) <u>1740</u> centigrams

4. (Continued)

   (g) <u>2.4</u> decaliters

   (h) <u>50000</u> millimeters

   (i) <u>7.5</u> kilometers

   (j) <u>0.362</u> kilograms

5. (a) 6 meters = <u>6.54</u> yards
       6(1.09 yds.) = 6.554

   (b) 50 kilograms = <u>110</u> pounds
       50(2.20 pounds) = 110

   (c) 10 liters = <u>10.6</u> quarts
       10(1.06 quarts) = 10.6

   (d) 80 kilometers = <u>49.68</u> miles
       80(0.621 miles) = 49.68

   (e) 20 centimeters = <u>7.88</u> inches
       20(0.394 inches) = 7.88

   (f) 0.5 liter = <u>16.9</u> ounces
       0.5(33.8 ounces) = 16.9

   (g) 5 meters = <u>16.4</u> feet
       5(3.28 feet) = 16.4

   (h) 400 grams = <u>14</u> ounces
       400(0.035 ounces) = 14

6. (a) 10 centimeters = <u>3.94</u> inches
       10(0.394 inches) = 3.94

   (b) 3 meters = <u>118.11</u> inches
       3(39.37 inches) = 118.11

   (c) 4 kilograms = <u>8.80</u> pounds
       4(2.20 pounds) = 8.80

   (d) 6 liters = <u>202.8</u> ounces
       6(33.8 ounces) = 202.8

   (e) 20 meters = <u>21.8</u> yards
       20(1.09 yards) = 21.8

   (f) 5 decimeters = <u>19.7</u> inches
       5(3.94 inches) = 19.7

6. (Continued)

    (g) 8 liters = <u>8.48</u> quarts
        8(1.06 quarts) = 8.48

    (h) 50 kilometers = <u>31.05</u> miles
        50 (0.621 miles) = 31.05

7. (a) 8 feet = <u>2.44</u> meters
        8(0.305 meters) = 2.44

    (b) 100 pounds = <u>45.4</u> kilograms
        100(0.454 kilograms) = 45.4

    (c) 4 quarts = <u>3.784</u> liters
        4(0.946 liters) = 3.784

    (d) 20 pints = <u>9.46</u> liters
        20(0.473 liters) = 9.46

    (e) 80 miles = <u>128.8</u> kilometers
        80(1.61 kilometers) = 128.8

    (f) 6 inches = <u>15.24</u> centimeters
        6(2.54 centimeters) = 15.24

    (g) 9 ounces = <u>255.6</u> grams
        9(28.4 grams) = 255.6

    (h) 5 gallons = <u>18.95</u> liters
        5(3.79 liters) = 18.95

8. (a) 8 inches = <u>20.32</u> centimeters
        8(2.54 centimeters) = 20.32

    (b) 10 miles = <u>16.1</u> kilometers
        10(1.61 kilometers) = 16.1

    (c) 8 ounces = <u>227.2</u> grams
        8(28.4 grams) = 227.2

    (d) 6 quarts = <u>5.676</u> liters
        6(0.946 liters) = 5.676

    (e) 3 pounds = <u>1362</u> grams
        3(454 grams) = 1362

8. (Continued)

   (f) 20 ounces = <u>0.6</u> liter
        20(0.030 liters) = 0.6

   (g) 6 feet = <u>1.83</u> meters
        6(0.305 meters) = 1.83

   (h) 50 gallons = <u>189.5</u> liters
        50(3.79 liters) = 189.5

9. (a) $C = \dfrac{5}{9}(F - 32)$

        $= \dfrac{5}{9}(77 - 32)$

        $= \dfrac{5}{9}(45)$

        $C = 25°$

   (b) $C = \dfrac{5}{9}(F - 32)$

        $= \dfrac{5}{9}(95 - 32)$

        $= \dfrac{5}{9}(63)$

        $C = 35°$

   (c) $C = \dfrac{5}{9}(F - 32)$

        $= \dfrac{5}{9}(59 - 32)$

        $= \dfrac{5}{9}(27)$

        $C = 15°$

   (d) $C = \dfrac{5}{9}(F - 32)$

        $= \dfrac{5}{9}(14 - 32)$

        $= \dfrac{5}{9}(-18)$

        $C = -10°$

   (e) $F = \dfrac{9}{5}C + 32$

        $= \dfrac{9}{5}(20) + 32$

        $= 36 + 32$

        $F = 68°$

   (f) $F = \dfrac{9}{5}C + 32$

        $= \dfrac{9}{5}(80) + 32$

        $= 144 + 32$

        $F = 176°$

9. (Continued)

(g) $F = \dfrac{9}{5}C + 32$

$= \dfrac{9}{5}(55) + 32$

$= 99 + 32$

$F = 131°$

(h) $F = \dfrac{9}{5}C + 32$

$= \dfrac{9}{5}(-5) + 32$

$= -9 + 32$

$F = 23°$

10. (a) $C = \dfrac{5}{9}(F - 32)$

$= \dfrac{5}{9}(104 - 32)$

$= \dfrac{5}{9}(72)$

$C = 40°$

(b) $C = \dfrac{5}{9}(F - 32)$

$= \dfrac{5}{9}(41 - 32)$

$= \dfrac{5}{9}(9)$

$C = 5°$

(c) $C = \dfrac{5}{9}(F - 32)$

$= \dfrac{5}{9}(68 - 32)$

$= \dfrac{5}{9}(36)$

$C = 20°$

(d) $C = \dfrac{5}{9}(F - 32)$

$= \dfrac{5}{9}(5 - 32)$

$= \dfrac{5}{9}(-27)$

$C = -15°$

(e) $F = \dfrac{9}{5}C + 32$

$= \dfrac{9}{5}(35) + 32$

$= 63 + 32$

$F = 95°$

(f) $F = \dfrac{9}{5}C + 32$

$= \dfrac{9}{5}(45) + 32$

$= 81 + 32$

$F = 113°$

10. (Continued)

(g) $F = \frac{9}{5}C + 32$

$= \frac{9}{5}(10) + 32$

$= 18 + 32$

$F = 50°$

(h) $F = \frac{9}{5}C + 32$

$= \frac{9}{5}(0) + 32$

$= 0 + 32$

$F = 32°$

11. (a) 120 inches = <u>304.8</u> centimeters
    120(2.54 centimeters) = 304.8

(b) 250 centimeters = <u>98.5</u> inches
    250(0.394 inches) = 98.5

(c) American car: 304.8 - 250 = 54.8 centimeters

12. (a) 100 yards = <u>91.4</u> meters
    100(0.914 meters) = 91.4

(b) 100 meters = <u>109</u> yards
    100(1.09 yards) = 109

(c) Swimming: 100 meters - 91.4 meters = 8.6 meters

13. (a) 5 feet 6 inches = 5 × 12 + 6 = 66 inches
    66 inches = <u>167.64</u> centimeters
    66(2.54 centimeters) = 167.64

(b) 120 pounds = <u>54.48</u> kilograms
    120(0.454 kilograms) = 54.48

14. (a) 5 feet 10 inches = 5 × 12 + 10 = 70 inches
    70 inches = <u>177.8</u> centimeters
    70(2.54 centimeters) = 177.8

(b) 170 pounds = <u>77.18</u> kilograms
    170(0.454 kilograms) = 77.18

15. 3000 miles = <u>4830</u> kilometers
    3000(1.61 kilometers) = 4830

15. (Continued)

    25000 miles = <u>40250</u> kilometers
    25000(1.61 kilometers) = 40250

16. (a) 40 ounces = <u>1136</u> grams
         40(28.4 grams) = 1136

    (b) 30 fluid ounces = <u>0.9</u> liters
         30(0.03 liters) = 0.9

17. (a) 20 grams = <u>0.7</u> ounces
         20(0.035 ounces) = 0.7

    (b) 1.75 kilograms = <u>3.85</u> pounds
         1.75(2.2 pounds) = 3.85

18. (a) 50 liters = <u>13.2</u> gallons
         50(0.264 gallons) = 13.2

    (b) 4 liters = <u>4.24</u> quarts
         4(1.06 quarts) = 4.24

19. (a) $95°F = \underline{35}°C$

$$C = \frac{5}{9}(F - 32)$$

$$= \frac{5}{9}(95 - 32)$$

$$= \frac{5}{9}(63)$$

$$C = 35°$$

(b) $30°C = \underline{86}°F$

$$F = \frac{9}{5}C + 32$$

$$= \frac{9}{5}(30) + 32$$

$$= 54 + 32$$

$$F = 86°$$

(c) New York: $35°C - 30°C = 5°C$

20. (a) $50°F = \underline{10°C}$

$$C = \frac{5}{9}(F - 32)$$

$$= \frac{5}{9}(50 - 32)$$

$$= \frac{5}{9}(18)$$

$$C = 10°$$

(b) $5°C = \underline{41°F}$

$$F = \frac{9}{5}C + 32$$

$$= \frac{9}{5}(5) + 32$$

$$= 9 + 32$$

$$F = 41°$$

(c) Madrid: $10°C - 5°C = 5°C$

Section 2, page 588

		U.S.($)	German(DM)	Japanese(¥)	Mexican($)
1.	(a)	$ 10	DM 18.19	¥ 1147	$ 94.82
	(b)	600	1091.10	68838	5689.20
	(c)	1,800	3273.30	206514	17067.60
2.	(a)	$ 20	DM 36.37	¥ 2295	$ 189.64
	(b)	500	909.25	57365	4741
	(c)	2,000	3637	229460	18964
3.	(a)	$1,546.32	DM2812	X	X
	(b)	466.74	X	¥ 53550	X
	(c)	357.52	X	X	$ 3390
4.	(a)	$1,932.90	DM3515	X	X
	(b)	108.91	X	¥ 12495	X
	(c)	143.01	X	X	$ 1356

1. (a) $10 × 1.8185 = 18.185 = DM18.19
$10 × 114.73 = 1147.3 = ¥1147
$10 × 9.482 = $94.82

(b) $600 × 1.8185 = DM1091.10
$600 × 114.73 = ¥68838
$600 × 9.482 = $5,689.20

1. (Continued)

    (c) $1,800 × 1.8185 = DM3273.30
        $1,800 × 114.73 = ¥206514
        $1,800 × 9.482 = $17,067.60

2. (a) $20 × 1.8185 = DM36.37
        $20 × 114.73 = ¥2294.6 = 2295
        $20 × 9.482 = $189.64

    (b) $500 × 1.8185 = DM909.25
        $500 × 114.73 = ¥57365
        $500 × 9.482 = $4,741

    (c) $2,000 × 1.8185 = DM3637
        $2,000 × 114.73 = ¥229460
        $2,000 × 9.482 = $18,964

3. (a) DM2812 × 0.5499   = 1546.318 = $546.32
    (b) ¥53550 × 0.008716 = $466.74
    (c) $3,390 × 0.105463 = 357.519 = $357.52

4. (a) DM3515 × 0.5499   = 1932.898 = $1,932.90
    (b) ¥12495 × 0.008716 = 108.906 = $108.91
    (c) $1,356 × 0.105463 = 143.007 = $143.01

5. $8,000 × 1.5039 = C$12031.20

6. $6,000 × 1.5039 = C$9023.40

7. $80 × ₣6.0976 = 487.808 = ₣487.81

8. $2,000 × ₣6.0976 = ₣12195.20

9. £50.144 × 1.6108 = 80.7719 = $80.77

10. £18.804 × 1.6108 = 30.29 × 2 = $60.58

11. DM158.18 × 0.5499 = $86.98

12. DM3.60 × 0.5499 = $1.98

13. (a) $3.99 × 1.8185 = DM7.26
     (b) $3.99 × 114.73 = 457.77 = ¥458
     (c) $3.99 × 1.5039 = C$6.00

14. (a) $4.29 × 0.6208 = £2.66
     (b) $4.29 × 9.482 = $40.68
     (c) $4.29 × 6.0976 = F26.16

CHAPTER I

REVIEW OF OPERATIONS

This chapter contains primarily items where students waste time unnecessarily or where mistakes are frequently made. Hence it should be included even if Appendix A has been studied. A few topics will overlap somewhat and so can be omitted. Emphasize the "Division" section, where denominators contain either fractions or decimals; errors of this type cause many mistakes in later problems. The operations with parentheses are also important because they cause problems in later studies of simple interest and discount; actually, this parentheses topic could be delayed until the simple interest chapter is studied.

In the section "Accuracy of Computation," the discussion regarding the number of tabular digits that must be used to ensure accuracy correct to the nearest cent might be delayed until the chapter on compound interest is covered.

Be sure to point out to the students the suggestions regarding "Problem Solving." Many students need a "plan of attack" in order to persist with problems that they don't immediately understand. Likewise, encourage students to read "How To Study Business Math" at the beginning of the text.

If your students will use calculators during this course, the section on "Using a Calculator" should prove helpful; many instructors find that their students require specific directions in order to operate calculators correctly. This topic is background for the series of "Calculator Techniques" that appear periodically throughout the text. If you do not permit the use of calculators during the Review chapters, it might be preferable to delay this topic until just before the students actually begin using their calculators.

CHAPTER 1 - REVIEW OF OPERATIONS
PROBLEM SOLUTIONS

Section 1, page 10

1. (a)   83   (b)   256   (c)   18 3
        ×   30   ×   50   ×   600
         2,490   12,800   109,800

    (d)   44   (e)   118   (f)   1641
        ×   1300   ×   3600   ×   302
         13 2   70 8   3 282
         44   354   492 3
         57,200   424,800   495,582

    (g)   1765   (h)   13202   (i)   423
        ×   405   ×   2009   ×   1070
         8 825   118 818   29 61
         706 0   26 404   423
         714,825   26,522,818   452,610

    (j)   34   (k)   5.2   (l)   0.48
        ×   6.4 1/2   ×   18 1/4   ×   28 1/3
         1 7   1 3   16
         13 6   41 6   2 24
         204   52   11 2
         219.3   94.9   13.60

    (m)   5.4   (n)   2.4
        ×   32 1/6   ×   3.5 3/4
         9   18
         10 8   1 20
         162   7 2
         173.7   8.58

    (o) 5^4 = 5 × 5 × 5 × 5 = 625

    (p) 4^8 = 4 × 4 × 4 × 4 × 4 × 4 × 4 × 4 = 65,536

    (q) 7^3 = 7 × 7 × 7 = 343

    (r) 2.01^2 = 2.01 × 2.01 = 4.0401

2. (a)   54
       ×   60
        3,240

(b)   362
    ×   80
     28,960

(c)   11 9
    ×   300
     35,700

(d)   57
    ×   1500
     28 500
     57
     85,500

(e)   353
    ×   2400
     141 200
     706
     847,200

(f)   3154
    ×   206
     18 924
     630 8
     649,724

(g)   6332
    ×   107
     44 324
     633 2
     677,524

(h)   20442
    ×   3002
     40 884
     61 326
     61,366,884

(i)   814
    ×   7060
     48 840
     5 698
     5,746,840

(j)   82
    ×   5.3 1/2
     4 1
     24 6
     410
     438.7

(k)   6.3
    ×   24 1/9
     7
     25 2
     126
     151.9

(l)   0.60
    ×   45 2/5
     24
     3 00
     24 0
     27.24

(m)   7.2
    ×   91 5/6
     6 0
     7 2
     648
     661.2

(n)   6.8
    ×   2.8 3/4
     51
     5 44
     13 6
     19.55

(o) $6^4 = 6 \times 6 \times 6 \times 6 = 1,296$

(p) $8^5 = 8 \times 8 \times 8 \times 8 \times 8 = 32,768$

(q) $10^3 = 10 \times 10 \times 10 = 1,000$

(r) $3.06^2 = 3.06 \times 3.06 = 9.3636$

3. (a) $\dfrac{48}{\frac{6}{7}} = \dfrac{48}{1} \div \dfrac{6}{7} = \dfrac{48}{1} \times \dfrac{7}{6} = 56$

(b) $\dfrac{72}{4\frac{1}{2}} = \dfrac{72}{1} \div \dfrac{9}{2} = \dfrac{72}{1} \times \dfrac{2}{9} = 16$

3. (Continued)

(c) $\dfrac{20}{0.5} = \dfrac{200}{5} = 40$ (d) $\dfrac{3.6}{0.12} = \dfrac{360}{12} = 30$

(e) $\dfrac{1.36}{0.8} = \dfrac{136}{80} = 1.7$ (f) Net sales: $ 66,708
                                 Cost of goods sold: −68,134
                                 Loss: <$ 1,426>

(g) Travel allowance: $ 300
      Travel expenses: −475
      Deficit: <$ 175>

(h) Net income: $ 82,500
      Partner's salaries: −100,000
      Deficit: <$ 17,500>

(i) Escrow for taxes: $ 2,575
      Taxes assessed: −3,100
      Balance: <$ 525>

4. (a) $\dfrac{111}{\dfrac{3}{5}} = 111 \div \dfrac{3}{5} = 111 \times \dfrac{5}{3} = 185$

(b) $\dfrac{85}{2\dfrac{1}{8}} = 85 \div \dfrac{17}{8} = 85 \times \dfrac{8}{17} = 40$

(c) $\dfrac{50}{0.4} = \dfrac{500}{4} = 125$ (d) $\dfrac{4.5}{0.15} = \dfrac{450}{15} = 30$

(e) $\dfrac{6.21}{0.3} = \dfrac{621}{30} = 20.7$ (f) Checkbook balance: $ 356.44
                                 Checks written: −372.60
                                 Deficit: <$ 16.16>

(g) Gross profit: $ 51,382
      Operating expenses: −56,309
      Loss: <$ 4,927>

(h) Advertising budget: $ 45,000
      Advertising expenditures: −49,810
      Deficit: <$ 4,810>

(i) Account balance: $ 1,620
      Payment: −1,682
      Deficit: <$ 62>

5. (a) $\left(1 + \dfrac{16}{100} \cdot \dfrac{1}{4}\right) = \left(1 + \dfrac{4}{100}\right) = \dfrac{104}{100} = \dfrac{26}{25}$ or $1\dfrac{1}{25}$

   (b) $\left(1 + \dfrac{7}{100} \cdot \dfrac{1}{3}\right) = \left(1 + \dfrac{7}{300}\right) = \dfrac{307}{300}$ or $1\dfrac{7}{300}$

   (c) $\left(1 - \dfrac{3}{100} \cdot \dfrac{1}{6}\right) = \left(1 - \dfrac{1}{200}\right) = \dfrac{199}{200}$

   (d) $\left(1 - \dfrac{4}{100} \cdot \dfrac{1}{2}\right) = \left(1 - \dfrac{2}{100}\right) = \dfrac{98}{100} = \dfrac{49}{50}$

   (e) $5,000\left(1 + \dfrac{18}{100} \cdot \dfrac{4}{9}\right) = 5,000\left(1 + \dfrac{2}{25}\right) = 5,000\left(\dfrac{27}{25}\right) = 5,400$

   (f) $1,500\left(1 + \dfrac{28}{100} \cdot \dfrac{2}{7}\right) = 1,500\left(1 + \dfrac{4}{50}\right) = 1,500\left(\dfrac{54}{50}\right) = 1,620$

   (g) $1,000\left(1 - \dfrac{6}{100} \cdot \dfrac{2}{5}\right) = 1,000\left(1 - \dfrac{6}{250}\right) = 1,000\left(\dfrac{244}{250}\right) = 976$

   (h) $500\left(1 - \dfrac{12}{100}g\right) = 500(1) - 500\left(\dfrac{12}{100}g\right) = 500 - 60g$

   (i) $300\left(1 + \dfrac{9}{100}b\right) = 300(1) + 300\left(\dfrac{9}{100}b\right) = 300 + 27b$

   (j) $j(kl + m) = j(kl) + j(m) = jkl + jm$

   (k) $w(1 - xy) = w(1) - w(xy) = w - wxy$

6. (a) $\left(1 + \dfrac{42}{100} \cdot \dfrac{1}{6}\right) = \left(1 + \dfrac{7}{100}\right) = \dfrac{107}{100}$ or $1\dfrac{7}{100}$

   (b) $\left(1 + \dfrac{3}{100} \cdot \dfrac{1}{5}\right) = \left(1 + \dfrac{3}{500}\right) = \dfrac{503}{500}$ or $1\dfrac{3}{500}$

   (c) $\left(1 - \dfrac{8}{100} \cdot \dfrac{1}{2}\right) = \left(1 - \dfrac{4}{100}\right) = \dfrac{96}{100} = \dfrac{24}{25}$

   (d) $\left(1 - \dfrac{21}{100} \cdot \dfrac{1}{3}\right) = \left(1 - \dfrac{7}{100}\right) = \dfrac{93}{100}$

6. (Continued)

(e) $900\left(1 + \dfrac{18}{100} \cdot \dfrac{2}{9}\right) = 900\left(1 + \dfrac{2}{50}\right) = 900\left(\dfrac{52}{50}\right) = 18(52) = 936$

(f) $720\left(1 + \dfrac{3}{100} \cdot \dfrac{5}{27}\right) = 720\left(1 + \dfrac{1}{180}\right) = 720\left(\dfrac{181}{180}\right) = 4(181) = 724$

(g) $1{,}000\left(1 - \dfrac{12}{100} \cdot \dfrac{10}{15}\right) = 1{,}000\left(1 - \dfrac{4}{10} \cdot \dfrac{1}{5}\right) = 1{,}000\left(1 - \dfrac{2}{5} \cdot \dfrac{1}{5}\right) =$

$1{,}000\left(1 - \dfrac{2}{25}\right) = 1{,}000\left(\dfrac{23}{25}\right) = 40(23) = 920$

(h) $600\left(1 - \dfrac{3}{100}b\right) = 600(1) - 600\left(\dfrac{3}{100}b\right) = 600 - 6(3b) = 600 - 18b$

(i) $400\left(1 + \dfrac{6}{100}x\right) = 400(1) + 400\left(\dfrac{6}{100}x\right) = 400 + 4(6x) = 400 + 24x$

(j) $a(bc + d) = a(bc) + a(d) = abc + ad$

(k) $e(1 - wh) = c(1) - e(wh) = e - ewh$

7. (a) $\begin{aligned}43.258 &= 43.3\\ 156.643 &= 156.6\\ 1{,}680.952 &= 1{,}681.0\end{aligned}$ (b) $\begin{aligned}8.9426 &= 8.94\\ 26.4453 &= 26.45\\ 60.0639 &= 160.06\end{aligned}$

(c) $\begin{aligned}18.92453 &= 18.925\\ 0.56641 &= 0.566\\ 337.00894 &= 337.009\end{aligned}$ (d) $\begin{aligned}5.08473 &= 5.1;\ 5.08;\ 5.085\\ 23.67521 &= 23.7;\ 23.68;\ 23.675\end{aligned}$

8. (a) $\begin{aligned}51.174 &= 51.2\\ 204.526 &= 204.5\\ 1{,}875.973 &= 1{,}876.0\end{aligned}$ (b) $\begin{aligned}9.3345 &= 9.33\\ 81.6666 &= 81.67\\ 104.1748 &= 104.17\end{aligned}$

(c) $\begin{aligned}15.04525 &= 15.045\\ 0.94368 &= 0.944\\ 257.00172 &= 257.002\end{aligned}$ (d) $\begin{aligned}8.06481 &= 8.1;\ 8.06;\ 8.065\\ 16.54546 &= 16.5;\ 16.55;\ 16.545\end{aligned}$

9. (a) $14.2 \times 12.35 = 175.4;\ 175$

(b) $4.56 \times 7.3 = 33.3;\ 33$

9. (Continued)

(c) 5.8 × 7.83 = 45.4; 45

(d) 1.111 × 3.85 = 4.28; 4.28

10. (a) 23.6 × 34.47 = 813.5; 813

(b) 8.11 × 4.7 = 38.1; 38

(c) 9.2 × 5.62 = 51.7; 52

(d) 7.634 × 8.25 = 62.98; 63.0

11. (a) $300 × 1.91301845
$300 × 2 = 600.00 (5 digits); 5 + 1 = 6 digits
$300 × 1.91302 = $573.91

(b) $500 × 1.52161826
$500 × 1.5 = 750.00 (5 digits); 5 + 1 = 6 digits
$500 × 1.52162 = $760.81

(c) $4,000 × 0.37440925
$4,000 × 0.4 = 1,600.00 (6 digits); 6 + 1 = 7 digits
$4,000 × 0.3744093 = $1,497.6372 = $1,497.64

(d) $20 × 19.08162643
$20 × 19 = 360.00 (5 digits); 5 + 1 = 6 digits
$20 × 19.0816 = $381.63

12. (a) $400 × 1.44354605
$400 × 1.4 = 560.00 (5 digits); 5 + 1 = 6 digits
$400 × 1.44355 = $577.42

(b) $600 × 1.81246018
$600 × 2 = 1,200.00 (6 digits); 6 + 1 = 7 digits
$600 × 1.812460 = $1,087.476 = $1,087.48

(c) $5,000 × 0.26423817
$5,000 × 0.3 = 1,500.00 (6 digits); 6 + 1 = 7 digits
$5,000 × 0.2642382 = $1,321.191 = $1,321.19

(d) $10 × 16.01964522
$10 × 16 = 160.00 (5 digits); 5 + 1 = 6 digits
$10 × 16.0196 = $160.196 = $160.20

Business Mathematics: A Collegiate Approach

1. (a) 3,120 - 48 + 188 - 251 = 3,009

    (b) 964 - 410 + 17 + 8 = 579

    (c) 76 × 9 ÷ 4 = 171   (d) 12 ÷ 8 × 46 = 69

    (e) $\frac{3}{8}$ × 400 = 150   (f) $\frac{4}{9}$(108) = 48

    (g) $\frac{2}{7}$(420) = 120   (h) $\frac{608}{8}$ × 12 = 912

2. (a) 4,261 - 36 + 216 - 378 = 4,063

    (b) 883 - 520 + 23 - 5 = 381

    (c) 66 × 6 ÷ 9 = 44   (d) 24 ÷ 6 × 5 = 20

    (e) $\frac{4}{5}$ × 55 = 44   (f) $\frac{3}{7}$(560) = 240

    (g) $\frac{5}{8}$(72) = 45   (h) $\frac{468}{9}$ × 18 = 936

3. (a) 136 × 22% = 29.92   (b) 582 × 30 × 5% = 873

    (c) 405 × 6.2% = 25.11   (d) 1,500 × 90% × 60% = 810

4. (a) 246 × 37% = 91.02   (b) 332 × 15 × 9% = 448.2

    (c) 308 × 4.8% = 14.784   (d) 2,700 × 40% × 80% = 864

5. (a) 0.1225 M+; 32 × MR = 3.92; 60 × MR = 7.35; 180 × MR = 22.05

    (b) 0.14 M+; 12 × MR = 1.68; 25 × MR = 3.5; 1,400 × MR = 196

    (c) $\frac{335 + 785}{1 - 0.80}$: 1 - 0.80 M+ → 0.2; 335 + 785 ÷ MR = 5,600

    (d) $\frac{874 - 56.42 - 21.26}{12.34 + 4.25}$: 12.34 + 4.25 M+ → 16.59;

         874 - 56.42 - 21.26 ÷ MR = 48

5. (Continued)

(e) $4,000(1 + 0.08 \times 24)$: 1 M+; 0.08×24 M+ $\rightarrow$ 1.92;
MR $\rightarrow$ 292 × 4,000 = 11,680

(f) $1,600\left(1 - \dfrac{3}{4} \times 9\%\right)$: 1 M+; $0.75 \times 9\%$ M- $\rightarrow$ 0.0675;
MR $\rightarrow$ 0.9325 × 1,600 = 1,492

(g) $720\left(1 + \dfrac{5}{8} \times 5\%\right)$: 1 M+; $0.625 \times 9\%$ M+ $\rightarrow$ 0.03125;
MR $\rightarrow$ 1.03125 × 720 = 742.50

(h) $\dfrac{126.9}{47 \times 15\%}$: $47 \times 15\%$ M+ $\rightarrow$ 7.05; 126.9 ÷ MR = 18

6. (a) 0.28 M+; 15 × MR = 4.2; 48 × MR = 13.44; 206 × MR = 57.68

(b) 0.65 M+; 18 × MR = 11.7; 34 × MR = 22.1; 2,740 × MR = 1,781

(c) $\dfrac{82 + 136}{1 - 0.75}$: $1 - 0.75 = 0.25$ M+ $\rightarrow$ 218 ÷ MR = 872

(d) $\dfrac{587 - 5.62 - 149.08}{24.9 + 3.92}$: $24.9 + 3.92 = \rightarrow 28.82$ M+;
$587 - 5.62 - 149.08 = \rightarrow 432.3$ ÷ MR = 15

(e) $3,200(1 + 0.09 \times 47)$: $0.09 \times 47 = \rightarrow 4.2 \times 3$ M+
$1 + $ MR $= 5.23 \times 3,200 = 16,736$

(f) $45\left(1 - \dfrac{2}{5} \times 8\%\right)$: $2 ÷ 5 = 0.4 \times 8\% \rightarrow 0.032$ M+ 1 - MR 1 =
$0.968 \times 45 = 43.56$

(g) $850\left(1 + \dfrac{1}{2} \times 12\%\right)$: $1 ÷ 2 = 0.5 \times 12\% \rightarrow 0.06$ M+ 1 + MR =
$1.06 \times 850 = 901$

(h) $\dfrac{1,029.6}{66 \times 20\%}$: $66 \times 20\% = 13.2$ M+ $1,029.6 ÷$ MR = 78

CHAPTER II

USING EQUATIONS

This chapter is not intended to be a complete review of equations, as it contains only those basic equation forms that will be required to solve other business math problems later in the text.

1. Basic Equations:

When solving examples for the class, keep emphasizing (1) that numbers or variables must be on the <u>same</u> side of the equation in order to be combined; and (2) in order to remove any number or variable from one side of the equation, one must perform the <u>opposite</u> operation from the one in which the term is now used. When illustrating examples, make a practice of asking what each next step should be, rather than just working straight through. Be sure the student realizes that $x = 1x$.

2. Written Problems:

Require the student to write the problem in English first and to show by drawing arrows how the mathematical equation is derived from it. Boardwork provides excellent practice for this; send the students to the board without their texts and dictate the problems, having them write down the essential words before expressing an equation. The assignment should also be done in this manner. Encourage the student to use a variable that is the first letter of the word the variable represents, rather than using x's and y's; this ensures that the student will know what the solution represents.

During the course of class discussion, the class might suggest a list of words which translate into an exact mathematical meaning:

Term	Meaning
of; as much as	"times" or "x" or "multiply"
is; was; gives; or any verb	"equals"; locates the equal marks of the equation
together; combined	"add"
increased by	"add"
decreased by	"subtract"
less	"subtract"

Term	Meaning
less than	"subtracted from"; the first number given <u>must</u> be subtracted from the second. Especially emphasize this, as students often put the terms down in reverse order.
more than	"added to"; as above, the first term should be written following the second, although this does not affect the solution as it did with subtraction.
per, out of	"divide" the first term by the second term.

Ratio should be covered well, since it is used in several later chapters. Many students have used proportion problems before, but they usually need review. Point out that cross products are most useful when the variable is in the denominator; other times, using cross products may create more work. The use of proportions will not be required in later chapters, however, so the topic may be omitted if the technique is unfamiliar to your students.

CHAPTER 2 - USING EQUATIONS
PROBLEM SOLUTIONS

Section 1, page 24

1. $x + 23 = 88$
$x + \cancel{23} - \cancel{23} = 88 - 23$
$x = 65$

2. $y + 15 = 68$
$y + \cancel{15} - \cancel{15} = 68 - 15$
$y = 53$

3. $x - 9 = 21$
$x - \cancel{9} + \cancel{9} = 21 + 9$
$x = 30$

4. $d - 8 = 52$
$d - \cancel{8} + \cancel{8} = 52 + 8$
$d = 60$

5. $4y = 112$
$\dfrac{\cancel{4}y}{\cancel{4}} = \dfrac{112}{4}$
$y = 28$

6. $7w = 434$
$\dfrac{\cancel{7}w}{\cancel{7}} = \dfrac{434}{7}$
$w = 62$

7. $12b = 108$
$\dfrac{\cancel{12}b}{\cancel{12}} = \dfrac{108}{12}$
$b = 9$

8. $6c = 246$
$\dfrac{\cancel{6}c}{\cancel{6}} = \dfrac{246}{6}$
$c = 41$

9. $8x - 6 = 18$
$8x - \cancel{6} + \cancel{6} = 18 + 6$
$8x = 24$
$\dfrac{\cancel{8}x}{\cancel{8}} = \dfrac{24}{8}$
$x = 3$

10. $18a - 4 = 86$
$18a - \cancel{4} + \cancel{4} = 86 + 4$
$18a = 90$
$\dfrac{\cancel{18}a}{\cancel{18}} = \dfrac{90}{18}$
$a = 5$

11.
$$7c + 48 = 125$$
$$7c + \cancel{48} - \cancel{48} = 125 - 48$$
$$7c = 77$$
$$\frac{\cancel{7}c}{\cancel{7}} - \frac{77}{7}$$
$$c = 11$$

12.
$$4t + 12 = 236$$
$$4t + \cancel{12} - \cancel{12} = 236 - 12$$
$$4t = 224$$
$$\frac{\cancel{4}t}{\cancel{4}} = \frac{224}{4}$$
$$t = 56$$

13.
$$26n + 3 = 601$$
$$26n + \cancel{3} - \cancel{3} = 601 - 3$$
$$26n = 598$$
$$\frac{\cancel{26}n}{\cancel{26}} = \frac{598}{26}$$
$$n = 23$$

14.
$$17d + 13 = 438$$
$$17d + \cancel{13} - \cancel{13} = 438 - 13$$
$$17d = 425$$
$$\frac{\cancel{17}d}{\cancel{17}} = \frac{425}{17}$$
$$d = 25$$

15.
$$8z - 8 = 2z + 52$$
$$8z - \cancel{8} + \cancel{8} = 2z + 52 + 8$$
$$8z = 2z + 60$$
$$8z - 2z = \cancel{2z} - \cancel{2z} + 60$$
$$6z = 60$$
$$\frac{\cancel{6}z}{\cancel{6}} = \frac{60}{6}$$
$$z = 10$$

16.
$$15q - 4 = 6q + 158$$
$$15q - \cancel{4} + \cancel{4} = 6q + 158 + 4$$
$$15q = 6q + 162$$
$$15q - 6q = \cancel{6q} - \cancel{6q} + 162$$
$$9q = 162$$
$$\frac{\cancel{9}q}{\cancel{9}} = \frac{162}{9}$$
$$q = 18$$

17.
$$7q = 5q + 16$$
$$7q - 5q = \cancel{5q} - \cancel{5q} + 16$$
$$2q = 16$$
$$\frac{\cancel{2}q}{\cancel{2}} = \frac{16}{2}$$
$$q = 8$$

18.
$$12v = 5v + 84$$
$$12v - 5v = \cancel{5v} - \cancel{5v} + 84$$
$$7v = 84$$
$$\frac{\cancel{7}v}{\cancel{7}} = \frac{84}{7}$$
$$v = 12$$

19.

$$6(y + 3) = y + 128$$
$$6y + 18 = y + 128$$
$$6y + \cancel{18} - \cancel{18} = y + 128 - 18$$
$$6y = y + 110$$
$$6y - y = \cancel{y} - \cancel{y} + 110$$
$$5y = 110$$
$$\frac{\cancel{5}y}{\cancel{5}} = \frac{110}{5}$$
$$y = 22$$

20.

$$8(x + 6) = x + 195$$
$$8x + 48 = x + 195$$
$$8x - x + 48 = \cancel{x} - \cancel{x} + 195$$
$$7x + 48 = 195$$
$$7x + \cancel{48} - \cancel{48} = 195 - 48$$
$$7x = 147$$
$$\frac{\cancel{7}x}{\cancel{7}} = \frac{147}{7}$$
$$x = 21$$

21.

$$8f + 22 = f + 57$$
$$8f + \cancel{22} - \cancel{22} = f + 57 - 22$$
$$8f = f + 35$$
$$8f - f = \cancel{f} - \cancel{f} + 35$$
$$7f = 35$$
$$\frac{\cancel{7}f}{\cancel{7}} = \frac{35}{7}$$
$$f = 5$$

22.

$$10r + 9 = r + 81$$
$$10r - r + 9 = \cancel{r} - \cancel{r} + 81$$
$$9r + 9 = 81$$
$$9r + \cancel{9} - \cancel{9} = 81 - 9$$
$$9r = 72$$
$$\frac{\cancel{9}r}{\cancel{9}} = \frac{72}{9}$$
$$r = 8$$

23.

$$15x - 6 = 7x + 10$$
$$15x - \cancel{6} + \cancel{6} = 7x + 10 + 6$$
$$15x = 7x + 16$$
$$15x - 7x = \cancel{7x} - \cancel{7x} + 16$$
$$8x = 16$$
$$\frac{\cancel{8}x}{\cancel{8}} = \frac{16}{8}$$
$$x = 2$$

24.

$$27k - 12 = 6k + 282$$
$$27k - 6k - 12 = \cancel{6k} - \cancel{6k} + 282$$
$$21k - 12 = 282$$
$$21k - \cancel{12} + \cancel{12} = 282 + 12$$
$$21k = 294$$
$$\frac{\cancel{21}k}{\cancel{21}} = \frac{294}{21}$$
$$k = 14$$

25.
$$2h - 10 = 32 - 4h$$
$$2h - \cancel{10} + \cancel{10} = 32 + 10 - 4h$$
$$2h = 42 - 4h$$
$$2h + 4h = 42 - \cancel{4h} + \cancel{4h}$$
$$6h = 42$$
$$\frac{\cancel{6}h}{\cancel{6}} = \frac{42}{6}$$
$$h = 7$$

26.
$$3t - 6 = 78 - 9t$$
$$3t + 9t - 6 = 78 - \cancel{9t} + \cancel{9t}$$
$$12t - 6 = 78$$
$$12t - \cancel{6} + \cancel{6} = 78 + 6$$
$$12t = 84$$
$$\frac{\cancel{12}t}{\cancel{12}} = \frac{84}{12}$$
$$t = 7$$

27.
$$6(x - 2) = 4x - 2$$
$$6x - 12 = 4x - 2$$
$$6x - \cancel{12} + \cancel{12} = 4x - 2 + 12$$
$$6x = 4x + 10$$
$$6x - 4x = \cancel{4x} - \cancel{4x} + 10$$
$$2x = 10$$
$$\frac{\cancel{2}x}{\cancel{2}} = \frac{10}{2}$$
$$x = 5$$

28.
$$8(m - 3) = 3m - 4$$
$$8m - 24 = 3m - 4$$
$$8m - 3m - 24 = \cancel{3m} - \cancel{3m} - 4$$
$$5m - 24 = -4$$
$$5m - \cancel{24} + \cancel{24} = -4 + 24$$
$$5m = 20$$
$$\frac{\cancel{5}m}{\cancel{5}} = \frac{20}{5}$$
$$m = 4$$

29.
$$\frac{3a}{8} = 48$$
$$\frac{\cancel{8}}{\cancel{3}} \cdot \frac{\cancel{3}a}{\cancel{8}} = 48 \cdot \frac{8}{3}$$
$$a = 16 \cdot 8$$
$$a = 128$$

30.
$$\frac{4e}{5} = 56$$
$$\frac{\cancel{5}}{\cancel{4}} \cdot \frac{\cancel{4}e}{\cancel{5}} = 56 \cdot \frac{5}{4}$$
$$e = 14 \cdot 5$$
$$e = 70$$

31.
$$\frac{r}{7} - 6 = 12$$
$$\frac{4}{7} - \cancel{6} + \cancel{6} = 12 + 6$$
$$\frac{r}{7} = 18$$
$$\frac{\cancel{7}}{1} \cdot \frac{r}{\cancel{7}} = 7 \cdot 18$$
$$r = 126$$

32.
$$\frac{x}{8} - 15 = 16$$
$$\frac{x}{8} - \cancel{15} + \cancel{15} = 16 + 15$$
$$\frac{x}{8} = 31$$
$$\cancel{8} \cdot \frac{x}{\cancel{8}} = 31 \cdot 8$$
$$x = 248$$

33.
$$\frac{3x}{5} + 8 = 98$$

$$\frac{3x}{5} + \cancel{8} - \cancel{8} = 98 - 8$$

$$\frac{3x}{5} = 90$$

$$\frac{\cancel{5}}{\cancel{3}} \cdot \frac{\cancel{3}x}{\cancel{5}} = \frac{5}{3} \cdot 90$$

$$x = 150$$

34.
$$\frac{6d}{7} + 9 = 81$$

$$\frac{6d}{7} + \cancel{9} - \cancel{9} = 81 - 9$$

$$\frac{6d}{7} = 72$$

$$\frac{\cancel{7}}{\cancel{6}} \cdot \frac{\cancel{6}d}{\cancel{7}} = 72 \cdot \frac{7}{6}$$

$$d = 12 \cdot 7$$

$$d = 84$$

35.
$$47 = \frac{3d}{4} - 22$$

$$47 + 22 = \frac{3d}{4} - \cancel{22} + \cancel{22}$$

$$69 = \frac{3d}{4}$$

$$\frac{4}{3} \cdot 69 = \frac{\cancel{3}d}{\cancel{4}} \cdot \frac{\cancel{4}}{\cancel{3}}$$

$$92 = d$$

36.
$$66 = \frac{2z}{5} - 8$$

$$66 + 8 = \frac{2z}{5} - \cancel{8} + \cancel{8}$$

$$74 = \frac{2z}{5}$$

$$\frac{5}{2} \cdot 74 = \frac{\cancel{2}z}{\cancel{5}} \cdot \frac{\cancel{5}}{\cancel{2}}$$

$$5 \cdot 37 = z$$

$$185 = z$$

Section 2, page 28

1. (a) $6x$ (b) $a + o$ (c) $n + 10$

(d) $n - 18$ (e) $\frac{2}{3}c$ (f) $\frac{1}{4}p + 5$

(g) $2(r + s)$ (h) $g = h - \$4$ (i) $d = 2(a + b)$

(j) $b = 8.5f$ (k) $m = \frac{1}{3}n - 9$ (l) $\$10b$

2. (a) $10y$ (b) $S + J$ (c) $n + 12$

(d) $n - 44$ (e) $\frac{1}{9}K$ (f) $\frac{1}{3}j + 17$

(g) $3(x + y)$ (h) $h = g - \$24$ (i) $c = 6(m + n)$

(j) $p = 5.5t$ (k) $l = \frac{2}{5}K - 1$ (l) $\$25t$

3. What number decreased by 26 yields 56?

$$n - 26 = 56$$
$$n - 26 + 26 = 56 + 26$$
$$n = 82$$

4. What number increased by 23 yields 84?

$$n + 23 = 84$$
$$n + 23 - 23 = 84 - 23$$
$$n = 61$$

5. Corner Market charges $1.50 less then Wilson's Mart.

$$\$12 = W - \$1.50$$
$$12 + 1.50 = W - 1.50 + 1.50$$
$$\$13.50 = W$$

6. July price was $4.99 less than April price.

$$J = A - \$4.99$$
$$J = \$10.99$$

$$\$10.99 = A - \$4.99$$
$$10.99 + 4.99 = A - 4.99 + 4.99$$
$$\$15.98 = A$$

7. Scott Shope charges $15 more than Garcia Co.

$$\$77 = G + \$15$$
$$77 - 15 = G + 15 - 15$$
$$\$62 = G$$

8. Quality Lumber charges $1.50 more than Handy Carpenter charges.

$$Q = H + \$1.50$$
$$Q = \$4.15$$

$$\$4.15 = H + \$1.50$$
$$4.15 - 1.50 = H + 1.50 - 1.50$$
$$\$2.65 = H$$

9. $\frac{3}{5}$ of sales were charge sales.

$$\frac{3}{5}s = c$$
$$\frac{3}{5}(\$3,000) = c$$
$$\$1,800 = c$$

10. $\frac{3}{5}$ of expenditures are payroll expenses.

$$\frac{3}{5}e = p$$
$$e = \$6,000$$

$$\frac{3}{5}(\$6,000) = p$$
$$3 \cdot \$1,200 = p$$
$$\$3,600 = p$$

11. $\frac{1}{4}$ of sales were repeat customers.

$$\frac{1}{4}s = r$$

$$\frac{1}{4}s = 800$$

$$\frac{\cancel{4}}{\cancel{1}} \cdot \frac{\cancel{1}}{\cancel{4}}s = 800 \cdot 4$$

$$s = 3,200$$

12. $\frac{2}{5}$ people held masters degrees.

$$\frac{2}{5}p = M$$

$$18 = M$$

$$\frac{2}{5}p = 18$$

$$\frac{\cancel{5}}{\cancel{2}} \cdot \frac{\cancel{2}}{\cancel{5}}p = 18 \cdot \frac{5}{2}$$

$$p = 9 \cdot 5$$

$$p = 45$$

13. 8 less than $\frac{2}{5}$ of employees took no sick leave.

$$\frac{2}{5}e - 8 = L$$

$$\frac{2}{5}e - 8 = 40$$

$$\frac{2}{5}e - \cancel{8} + \cancel{8} = 40 + 8$$

$$\frac{2}{5}e = 48$$

$$\frac{\cancel{5}}{\cancel{2}} \cdot \frac{\cancel{2}}{\cancel{5}}e = 48\left(\frac{5}{2}\right)$$

$$e = 120$$

14. $\frac{1}{2}$ of total sales less 15 were single-subject books.

$$\frac{1}{2}t - 15 = s$$

$$s = 50$$

$$\frac{1}{2}t - 15 = 50$$

$$\frac{1}{2}t - \cancel{15} + \cancel{15} = 50 + 15$$

$$\frac{1}{2}t = 65$$

$$\frac{\cancel{2}}{\cancel{1}} \cdot \frac{\cancel{1}}{\cancel{2}}t = 65 \cdot 2$$

$$t = 130$$

15. February utility expenses were 1.2 times March utility expenses.

$$F = 1.2M$$

$$\$192 = 1.2M$$

$$\frac{192}{1.2} = \frac{\cancel{1.2}}{\cancel{1.2}}M$$

$$\$160 = M$$

16. Before overhaul MPG were 0.75 MPG after overhaul.

$$b = 0.75a$$

$$b = 21$$

$$21 = 0.75a$$

$$\frac{21}{0.75} = \frac{\cancel{0.75}}{\cancel{0.75}}a$$

$$28 = a$$

17. 4,900 hours times rate per hour equals $1,176.

$$\$1,176 = 4,900\,x$$
$$\frac{1,176}{4,900} = \frac{\cancel{4,900}}{\cancel{4,900}}\,x$$
$$24\text{¢} = x$$

18. 40 hours times rate per hour equals $384.

$$40\,x = \$384$$
$$\frac{\cancel{40}\,x}{\cancel{40}} = \frac{342}{40}$$
$$x = \$9.60$$

19. Manager salaries are 1.8 times staff salaries. Total salaries are $280,000.

$$m = 1.8\,s$$

$$\$280,000 = 1.8\,s + s$$
$$280,000 = 2.8\,s$$
$$\frac{280,000}{2.8} = \frac{\cancel{2.8}}{\cancel{2.8}}\,s$$
$$\$100,000 = s$$

$$1.8(\$100,000) = m$$
$$\$180,000 = m$$

20. $2.90 is cost plus markup.

$$\$2.90 = C + M$$
$$M = 0.45\,C$$

$$\$2.90 = C + 0.45C$$
$$\$2.90 = 1.45C$$
$$\frac{2.90}{1.45} = \frac{\cancel{1.45}\,C}{\cancel{1.45}}$$
$$\$2 = C$$

$$M = \$2.90 - \$2.00$$
$$= \$0.90$$

21. Cellular phones and pagers equal 35 items. Cellular phones and pagers totaled $1,900.

$$c + p = 35$$
$$c = 35 - p$$

$$\$50(35 - p) + \$60p = \$1,900$$
$$1,750 - 50p + 60p = 1,900$$
$$\cancel{1,750} - \cancel{1,750} - 50p + 60p = 1,900 - 1,750$$
$$10p = 1,900 - 1,750$$
$$10p = 150$$
$$p = 15$$

$$c = 35 - p$$
$$c = 35 - 15$$
$$c = 20$$

-89-

22. Shorts plus jeans equaled 100 items.
     Shorts plus jeans totaled $1,955.

$$s + j = 100$$
$$s = 100 - j$$

$$\$15(100 - j) + \$28(j) = \$1,955$$
$$\$1,500 - 15j + 28j = 1,955$$
$$\cancel{1,500} - \cancel{1,500} - 15j + 28j = 1,955 - 1,500$$
$$13j = 455$$
$$\frac{\cancel{13}j}{\cancel{13}} = \frac{455}{13}$$
$$j = 35$$

$$s = 100 - j$$
$$s = 100 - 35$$
$$s = 65$$

23. Mortgage, taxes, and insurance equals $1,005.
     Mortgage is 9 times insurance. Taxes are $15
     more than insurance.

$$m + i + t = \$1,005$$
$$(9i) + (i) + (i + 15) = 1,005$$
$$11i + 15 = 1,005$$
$$11i = 1,005 - 15$$
$$\frac{\cancel{11}i}{\cancel{11}} = \frac{990}{11}$$
$$i = \$90$$

$$m = 9i$$
$$m = 9(\$90) = \$810$$

$$t = i + \$15$$
$$t = \$90 + \$15 = \$105$$

24. Carol plus Debbie plus Frieda practice 23 hours. Carol practices 2 times Frieda. Debbie practices 3 hours more than Frieda.

$$C + D + F = 23$$
$$(2F) + (F + 3) + F = 23$$
$$2F + F + 3 + F = 23$$
$$4F + 3 = 23$$
$$4F + \cancel{3} - \cancel{3} = 23 - 3$$
$$4F = 20$$
$$\frac{\cancel{4}F}{\cancel{4}} = \frac{20}{4}$$
$$F = 5$$

$$C = 2(5) = 10$$

$$D = 5 + 3 = 8$$

25. Brand A sold 3 times brands B and C together.

$$A = 3(B + C)$$
$$129 = 3(25 + C)$$
$$129 = 75 + 3C$$
$$129 - 75 = 3C$$
$$54 = 3C$$
$$\frac{54}{3} = \frac{\cancel{3}C}{\cancel{3}}$$
$$18 = C$$

26. Towel sales totaled 3 times umbrella and chair sales together.

$$t = 3(u + c)$$
$$54 = 3(12 + c)$$
$$54 = 36 + 3c$$
$$54 - 36 = \cancel{36} - \cancel{36} + 3c$$
$$18 = 3c$$
$$\frac{18}{3} = \frac{\cancel{3}c}{\cancel{3}}$$
$$6 = c$$

27. Jacket, slacks, and flannel shirt cost $137.
     Jacket cost 2.5 times slacks. Shirt cost $7
     less than slacks.

$$j + s + f = \$137$$
$$j = 2.5s$$
$$f = s - \$7$$

$$(2.5s) + (s) + (s - 7) = 137$$
$$4.5s - 7 = 137$$
$$4.5s = 137 + 7$$
$$4.5s = 144$$
$$\frac{\cancel{4.5}s}{\cancel{4.5}} = \frac{144}{4.5}$$
$$s = \$32$$

$$j = 2.5(\$32) = \$80$$
$$f = \$32 - \$7 = \$25$$

28. Woman's age plus mother's age plus sister's
     age equals 130 years.

$$w + m + s = 130$$
$$(w) + (1.5w) + (w - 10) = 130$$
$$w + 1.5w + w - 10 = 130$$
$$3.5w - \cancel{10} + \cancel{10} = 130 + 10$$
$$3.5w = 140$$
$$\frac{\cancel{3.5}w}{\cancel{3.5}} = \frac{140}{3.5}$$
$$w = 40$$

$$m = 1.5 \cdot 40 = 60$$
$$s = 40 - 10 = 30$$

29. Cotton leotards plus lycra leotards equal 54.
     Cotton plus lycra totaled $900.

$$c + l = 54$$
$$c = 54 - l$$

$$\$15(54 - l) + \$18l = \$900$$
$$810 - 15l + 18l = 900$$
$$\cancel{810} - \cancel{810} - 15l + 18l = 900 - 810$$
$$3l = 900 - 810$$
$$3l = 90$$
$$\frac{\cancel{3}l}{\cancel{3}} = \frac{90}{3}$$
$$l = 30$$

$$c = 54 - 30 = 24$$

30. Child's sleeping bag sales plus adult sleeping
     bag sales equal 60. Child's sleeping bag sales
     plus adult sleeping bag sales totaled $3,840.

$$c + a = 60$$
$$c = 60 - a$$

$$\$40(60 - a) + \$100a = \$3,840$$
$$2,400 - 40a + 100a = 3,840$$
$$\cancel{2,400} - \cancel{2,400} + 60a = 3,840 - 2,400$$
$$60a = 1,440$$
$$\frac{\cancel{60}a}{\cancel{60}} = \frac{1,440}{60}$$
$$a = 24$$

$$c = 60 - 24$$
$$c = 36$$

31. Canvas plus leather equaled 26 pairs.
     Canvas plus leather totaled $776.

$$C + L = 26$$
$$C = 26 - L$$

$$\$20(26 - L) + \$36L = \$776$$
$$520 - 20L + 36L = 776$$
$$520 + 16L = 776$$
$$16L = 776 - 520$$
$$16L = 256$$
$$\frac{\cancel{16}L}{\cancel{16}} = \frac{256}{16}$$
$$L = 16$$

$$C = 26 - 16 = 10$$

32. Hardback copies plus paperback copies equal 65.
     Hardback copies plus paperback copies totaled $1,356.

$$h + p = 65$$
$$p = 65 - h$$

$$\$28(h) + \$12(65 - h) = \$1,356$$
$$28h + 780 - 12h = 1,356$$
$$16h + \cancel{780} - \cancel{780} = 1,356 - 780$$
$$16h = 576$$
$$\frac{\cancel{16}h}{\cancel{16}} = \frac{576}{16}$$
$$h = 36$$

$$p = 65 - 36$$
$$p = 29$$

33. Friday plus Saturday equaled 275 tickets. Friday plus Saturday totaled $7,050.

$$f + s = 275$$
$$s = 275 - f$$

$$\$30(f) + \$22(275 - f) = \$7,050$$
$$30f + 6,050 - 22f = 7,050$$
$$8f + 6,050 = 7,050$$
$$8f = 7,050 - 6,050$$
$$8f = 1,000$$
$$\frac{\cancel{8}f}{\cancel{8}} = \frac{1,000}{8}$$
$$f = 125$$

$$s = 275 - 125 = 150$$

34. Microwave oven sales plus toaster oven sales equaled 25. Microwave sales plus toaster sales totaled $1,616.

$$m + t = 25$$
$$t = 25 - m$$

$$\$80(m) + \$32(25 - m) = \$1,616$$
$$80m + 800 - 32m = 1,616$$
$$48m + \cancel{800} - \cancel{800} = 1,616 - 800$$
$$48m = 816$$
$$\frac{\cancel{48}m}{\cancel{48}} = \frac{816}{48}$$
$$m = 17$$

$$t = 25 - 17$$
$$t = 8$$

35. Desk lamps and floor lamps equaled 200.
     Desk lamps and floor lamps totaled $5,165.

$$d + f = 200$$
$$d = 200 - f$$

$$\$19(200 - f) + \$40(f) = \$5,165$$
$$3,800 - 19f + 40f = 5,165$$
$$21f = 5,165 - 3,800$$
$$21f = 1,365$$
$$\frac{\cancel{21}f}{\cancel{21}} = \frac{1,365}{21}$$
$$f = 65$$

$$d = 200 - 65 = 135$$

36. National brand sales plus store brand sales
     equaled 50. National brand sales plus store
     brand sales totaled $36,170.

$$n + s = 50$$
$$s = 50 - n$$

$$\$990n + \$560(50 - n) = \$36,170$$
$$990n + 28,000 - 560n = 36,170$$
$$430n + \cancel{28,000} - \cancel{28,000} = 36,170 - 28,000$$
$$430n = 8,170$$
$$\frac{\cancel{430}n}{\cancel{430}} = \frac{8,170}{430}$$
$$n = 19$$

$$s = 50 - 19$$
$$s = 31$$

Section 3, page 33

1. (a) 8 to 21; 8:21; $\dfrac{8}{21}$ (b) 1 to 3; 1:3; $\dfrac{1}{3}$

  (c) 2 to 5; 2:5; $\dfrac{2}{5}$ (d) 5 to 8; 5:8; $\dfrac{5}{8}$

  (e) 9 to 4; 9:4; $\dfrac{9}{4}$ or

    2.25 to 1; 2.25:1; $\dfrac{2.25}{1}$

2. (a) 7 to 24; 7:24; $\dfrac{7}{24}$ (b) 1 to 9; 1:9; $\dfrac{1}{9}$

  (c) 3 to 5; 3:5; $\dfrac{3}{5}$ (d) 7 to 9; 7:9; $\dfrac{7}{9}$

  (e) 8 to 1; 8:1; $\dfrac{8}{1}$

3. (a)
$$\frac{c}{14} = \frac{2}{7}$$
$$\cancel{14}\left(\frac{c}{\cancel{14}}\right) = \left(\frac{2}{7}\right)14$$
$$c = 4$$

   (b)
$$\frac{3}{8} = \frac{r}{16}$$
$$16\left(\frac{3}{8}\right) = \cancel{16}\left(\frac{r}{\cancel{16}}\right)$$
$$6 = r$$

(c)
$$\frac{3}{g} = \frac{9}{24}$$
$$3(24) = 9(g)$$
$$72 = 9g$$
$$\frac{72}{9} = \frac{\cancel{9}g}{\cancel{9}}$$
$$8 = g$$

   (d)
$$\frac{15}{10} = \frac{9}{z}$$
$$15(z) = 9(10)$$
$$15z = 90$$
$$\frac{\cancel{15}z}{\cancel{15}} = \frac{90}{15}$$
$$z = 6$$

4. (a) $\dfrac{a}{18} = \dfrac{2}{9}$

      $9a = 2(18)$

      $9a = 36$

      $\dfrac{\cancel{9}a}{\cancel{9}} = \dfrac{36}{9}$

      $a = 4$

(b) $\dfrac{6}{21} = \dfrac{t}{14}$

      $21t = 6(14)$

      $21t = 84$

      $\dfrac{\cancel{21}t}{\cancel{21}} = \dfrac{84}{21}$

      $t = 4$

(c) $\dfrac{15}{k} = \dfrac{5}{8}$

      $5k = 8(15)$

      $5k = 120$

      $\dfrac{\cancel{5}k}{\cancel{5}} = \dfrac{120}{5}$

      $k = 24$

(d) $\dfrac{3}{2} = \dfrac{12}{d}$

      $3d = 2(12)$

      $3d = 24$

      $\dfrac{\cancel{3}d}{\cancel{3}} = \dfrac{24}{3}$

      $d = 8$

5. $\dfrac{\text{Carlita}}{\text{Susanne}} = \dfrac{8}{2} = \dfrac{4}{1}$

6. $\dfrac{\text{Karl}}{\text{Brian}} = \dfrac{6}{3} = \dfrac{2}{1}$

7. $\dfrac{\text{Experience}}{\text{Nonexperience}} = \dfrac{22}{4} = \dfrac{11}{2}$

8. $\dfrac{\text{Carter}}{\text{Doug}} = \dfrac{20}{25} = \dfrac{4}{5}$

9. $\dfrac{\text{Operating expenses}}{\text{Net sales}} = \dfrac{28}{100}$

$$\dfrac{28}{100} = \dfrac{x}{66,000}$$

$$66,000\left(\dfrac{28}{100}\right) = \left(\dfrac{x}{\cancel{66,000}}\right)\cancel{66,000}$$

$$\$18,480 = x$$

10. $\dfrac{\text{This year}}{\text{Last year}} = \dfrac{x}{105}$

$\dfrac{80}{100} = \dfrac{x}{105}$

$100x = 8,400$

$\dfrac{\cancel{100}\,x}{\cancel{100}} = \dfrac{8,400}{100}$

$x = 84$

11. $\dfrac{\text{Annuity}}{\text{Gross wages}} = \dfrac{15}{100}$

$\dfrac{15}{100} = \dfrac{\$33}{W}$

$15(W) = \$33(100)$

$15W = 3,300$

$\dfrac{\cancel{15}\,W}{\cancel{15}} = \dfrac{3,300}{15}$

$W = \$220$

12. $\dfrac{\text{Soup kitchen pledge}}{\text{Gross Wages}} = \dfrac{240}{x}$

$\dfrac{6}{100} = \dfrac{240}{x}$

$6x = 24,000$

$\dfrac{\cancel{6}\,x}{\cancel{6}} = \dfrac{24,000}{6}$

$x = \$4,000$

13. $\dfrac{\text{Men}}{\text{Women}} = \dfrac{3}{8}$

$\dfrac{3}{8} = \dfrac{6}{W}$

$3(W) = 8(6)$

$3W = 48$

$\dfrac{\cancel{3}\,W}{\cancel{3}} = \dfrac{48}{3}$

$W = 16$

14. $\dfrac{\text{Successful calls}}{\text{Unsuccessful calls}} = \dfrac{3}{7}$

$\dfrac{3}{7} = \dfrac{1,008}{x}$

$3x = 7,056$

$\dfrac{\cancel{3}\,x}{\cancel{3}} = \dfrac{7,056}{3}$

$x = 2,352$

15. $\dfrac{\text{Bus. Admin.}}{\text{Marketing}} = \dfrac{5}{2}$

$\dfrac{5}{2} = \dfrac{240}{M}$

$5(M) = 2(240)$

$5M = 480$

$\dfrac{\cancel{5}\,M}{\cancel{5}} = \dfrac{480}{5}$

$M = 96$

16. $\dfrac{\text{Omar}}{\text{Paul}} = \dfrac{2}{3}$

$\dfrac{2}{3} = \dfrac{76}{x}$

$2x = 228$

$\dfrac{\cancel{2}x}{\cancel{2}} = \dfrac{228}{2}$

$x = 114$

17. $\dfrac{\text{Team}}{\text{Individual}} = \dfrac{2}{7}$

$\dfrac{2}{7} = \dfrac{T}{1,260}$

$2(1,260) = 7(T)$

$2,520 = 7T$

$\dfrac{2,520}{7} = \dfrac{\cancel{7}T}{\cancel{7}}$

$360 = T$

18. $\dfrac{\text{Family}}{\text{Single}} = \dfrac{5}{2}$

$\dfrac{5}{2} = \dfrac{x}{26}$

$2x = 130$

$\dfrac{\cancel{2}x}{\cancel{2}} = \dfrac{130}{2}$

$x = 65$

19. $\dfrac{\text{Brand } X}{\text{Brand } Y} = \dfrac{3}{2}$

$\dfrac{3}{2} = \dfrac{54}{Y}$

$3(Y) = 2(54)$

$3Y = 108$

$\dfrac{\cancel{3}Y}{\cancel{3}} = \dfrac{108}{3}$

$Y = 36$

20. $\dfrac{\text{Current assets}}{\text{Current liabilities}} = \dfrac{2}{1}$

$\dfrac{2}{1} = \dfrac{88,500}{x}$

$2x = 88,500$

$\dfrac{\cancel{2}x}{\cancel{2}} = \dfrac{88,500}{2}$

$x = 44,250$

21. $$\frac{\text{Words}}{\text{Minutes}} = \frac{900}{30}$$

$$\frac{900}{30} = \frac{W}{210}$$

$$900(210) = 30(W)$$

$$189,000 = 30(W)$$

$$\frac{189,000}{30} = \frac{\cancel{30}W}{\cancel{30}}$$

$$6,300 = W$$

22. $$\frac{\text{Checks}}{\text{Minutes}} = \frac{1,500}{20}$$

$$\frac{1,500}{20} = \frac{x}{120}$$

$$20x = 180,000$$

$$\frac{\cancel{20}x}{\cancel{20}} = \frac{180,000}{20}$$

$$x = 9,000$$

23. $$\frac{\text{Boxes}}{\text{Minutes}} = \frac{10}{45}$$

$$\frac{10}{45} = \frac{8}{180}$$

$$10(180) = 45(B)$$

$$1,800 = 45B$$

$$\frac{1,800}{45} = \frac{\cancel{45}B}{\cancel{45}}$$

$$40 = B$$

24. $$\frac{\text{Dollars}}{\text{KWh}} = \frac{112}{1,400}$$

$$\frac{112}{1,400} = \frac{x}{1,850}$$

$$1,400x = 207,200$$

$$\frac{\cancel{1,400}x}{\cancel{1,400}} = \frac{207,200}{1,400}$$

$$x = \$148$$

25. $$\frac{\text{Pages}}{\text{Minutes}} = \frac{50}{5}$$

$$\frac{P}{60} = \frac{50}{5}$$

$$5(P) = 50(60)$$

$$5P = 3,000$$

$$P = 600$$

26. $$\frac{\text{Heartbeats}}{\text{Seconds}} = \frac{20}{15}$$

$$\frac{20}{15} = \frac{x}{60}$$

$$15x = 1,200$$

$$\frac{\cancel{15}x}{\cancel{15}} = \frac{1,200}{15}$$

$$x = 80$$

27. $\dfrac{\text{Hours}}{\text{Miles}} = \dfrac{6}{330}$

$\dfrac{6}{330} = \dfrac{x}{550}$

$330x = 3{,}300$

$\dfrac{\cancel{330}x}{\cancel{330}} = \dfrac{3{,}330}{330}$

$x = 10$

28. $\dfrac{\text{Hours}}{\text{Miles}} = \dfrac{3}{144}$

$\dfrac{3}{144} = \dfrac{x}{1{,}200}$

$144x = 3{,}600$

$\dfrac{\cancel{144}x}{\cancel{144}} = \dfrac{3{,}600}{144}$

$x = 25$

CHAPTER III

REVIEW OF PERCENT

Despite all the years when percent was studied in grade schools, most people still have trouble with it at least part of the time. Since percent is an integral part of so many phases of business, however, it is essential that students gain facility in working with percent. Percent probably has application to more areas of business than any other single topic; thus, if business math succeeds in teaching the correct use of percent, it will have been worthwhile.

1.   Basics:

Working with percents is difficult for the typical student because so many different procedures are required -- most of which seem rather similar on the surface. In teaching conversions among fractions, decimals, and percents, the authors do not talk about "moving the decimal point" back and forth; the student too often moves it the wrong way. We have found it helpful to define "percent" as "hundredths"; keep referring to this both now and in later sections. In <u>changing % to a decimal</u>, most students can handle the common percents (1% - 99%) fairly well; it is the less common percents which cause problems. Encourage the students, when they are confused or uncertain, to stop and analyze the percent by breaking it down and picking out the digit(s) representing an ordinary percent between 1% and 99%. (For instance, if uncertain how to represent 7.316% or 317.9% as a decimal, they decide where the 7% would go; then simply fit the other digits around the 7. This may not be a very mathematical approach, but at least it solves the problem.) Fractional percents always cause problems.
Point out that a fractional percent is less than 1% ($\frac{1}{4}$% means $\frac{1}{4}$ of 1%); thus, the first two decimal places must be zeros.

<u>Changing % to a fraction</u> usually causes no problems unless the percent itself contains a fraction. Students can usually master this procedure all right, but they often forget to multiply times the 100:

$$6 \frac{1}{4}\% = 6 \frac{1}{4} \times \frac{1}{100} = \frac{25}{4} \times \frac{1}{100} = \frac{25}{400} = \frac{1}{16}$$

Bring out this point or the student may often come up with $\frac{25}{100} = \frac{1}{4}$.

Changing a decimal to %. Emphasize "percent means hundredths" in reverse: hundredths = percent. Again, have the student pick out the ordinary percents between 1% and 99% (the first two decimal places) and fit the other digits around them.

Changing a fraction to %. Try to clarify for the student the distinction between a fraction and a fractional percent [i.e., ⅜ means ⅜ of the whole amount whereas ⅜% means ⅜ of (1% of the whole amount).]

2.   Percent Equation Forms:

After mastering conversion of percents, fractions, and decimals, your students will be ready to work with equation forms. We think your students will be successful with percent problems and "finding the missing part" by using an algebraic approach. The basic equation form for percent is ___% × ___ = ___. Once the student has learned this form, "finding the missing part" is simply a matter of filling in the given information and solving a simple equation. Make a practice of asking, "What is the basic percent form?" before working an example.

Make sure the students also master the problem of finding the % of increase or decrease (basic formula: ___% of original number = change?). This will be used both in the financial statements and in the retail sections.

The three types of percent applications are categorized for the student. Emphasize the terminology that identifies types 2 and 3 (the words "increase" or "decrease"); then, whether the problem is type 2 or 3 is determined by whether the question asks for a percent (type 2) or an amount (type 3).

The exercises for this section are divided into three parts -- corresponding to the three types of percent problems. Selected problems assigned from each set should enable the students to master each type, with individual concentration.

3.   Word Problems Containing Percents:

As in earlier word problems, the essential words of each problem should first be expressed in a sentence and the mathematical sentence (equation) translated directly from the English. Emphasize strongly that any percent in an equation must be a percent of something; otherwise, the student will write equations like "s - 15% = 56"; and then "the fun is on."

Again, the three types of percent applications are stipulated. Be sure to reiterate the distinguishing aspects of each.

The exercises for this section cover the three percent types in two parts. The first part covers all problem types in order as presented in the examples; the second part mixes the order, to give the student practice in determining the type of problem. The authors advise assigning selected problems from each part; even half of the problems in each part would be too many.

After the "review of percent" has been completed and students are comfortable with conversions, they will find the table on Percent Equivalents of Common Fractions to be very helpful in later chapters. You will probably refer students to this page throughout the study of business math.

Chapter 3 -- REVIEW OF PERCENT
PROBLEM SOLUTIONS

Section 1, page 44

(a)	(b)
1. 0.11	$\dfrac{11}{100}$
2. 0.23	$\dfrac{23}{100}$
3. 0.32	$\dfrac{8}{25}$
4. 0.18	$\dfrac{9}{50}$
5. 0.02	$\dfrac{1}{50}$
6. 0.06	$\dfrac{3}{50}$
7. 0.305	$\dfrac{61}{200}$

	(a)	(b)
8.	0.442	$\frac{221}{500}$
9.	0.0625	$\frac{1}{16}$
10.	0.0335	$\frac{67}{2,000}$
11.	1.74	$\frac{87}{50}$ or $1\frac{37}{50}$
12.	4.50	$\frac{9}{2}$ or $4\frac{1}{2}$
13.	1.284	$\frac{321}{250}$ or $1\frac{71}{250}$
14.	1.306	$\frac{653}{500}$ or $1\frac{153}{500}$
15.	0.008	$\frac{1}{125}$
16.	0.0048	$\frac{3}{625}$
17.	0.0175	$\frac{7}{400}$
18.	0.013	$\frac{13}{1,000}$
19.	1.05	$\frac{21}{20}$ or $1\frac{1}{20}$
20.	2.60	$\frac{13}{5}$ or $2\frac{3}{5}$
21.	0.0075	$\frac{3}{400}$
22.	0.00125	$\frac{1}{800}$
23.	0.004	$\frac{1}{250}$

	(a)	(b)
24.	0.0005	$\dfrac{1}{2,000}$
25.	0.00375	$\dfrac{3}{800}$
26.	0.008	$\dfrac{1}{125}$
27.	0.016	$\dfrac{2}{125}$
28.	0.875	$\dfrac{7}{8}$
29.	0.125	$\dfrac{1}{8}$
30.	0.082	$\dfrac{41}{500}$

31. 9%   32. 4%   33. 40%

34. 52%   35. 67.4%   36. 23.2%

37. 211%   38. 145%   39. 128%

40. 205%   41. 0.1%   42. 2.2%

43. 50%   44. 80%   45. 0.5%

46. 0.8%   47. 310%   48. 460%

49. 3%   50. 2%   51. 50%

52. 60%   53. 0.5%   54. 0.6%

55. $41.6\overline{6}\%$ or $41\dfrac{2}{3}\%$ 56. $44.4\overline{4}\%$ or $44\dfrac{4}{9}\%$ 57. 175%

58. 350%   59. 480%   60. 612.5%

Business Mathematics: A Collegiate Approach

Section 2, page 48

1.   8% of 700 = _?_

   (0.08)(700) = N

   56 = N

2.   15% of 460 = _?_

   (0.15)(460) = A

   69 = A

3.   20% of 640 = _?_

   (0.20)(640) = X

   128 = X

4.   40% of 520 = _?_

   (0.40)(520) = X

   208 = X

5.   25% of 78 = _?_

   (0.25)(78) = X

   19.5 = X

6.   42% of 90 = _?_

   (0.42)(90) = A

   37.8 = A

7.   _?_ = $\frac{3}{5}$% of 37,000

   X = (0.006)(37,000)

   X = 222

8.   _?_ = $\frac{3}{4}$% of 6,000

   X = (0.0075)(6,000)

   X = 45

9.   _?_ = $12\frac{1}{2}$% of 560

   X = (0.125)(560)

   X = 70

10. _?_ = 50.5% of 900

   X = (0.505)(900)

   X = 454.5

11. _?_ = $4\frac{1}{2}$% of 600

   N = (0.045)(600)

   N = 27

12. _?_ = 9.75% of 400

   X = (0.0975)(400)

   X = 39

13. 0.25% of 14,000 = _?_

$$(0.0025)(14,000) = A$$
$$35 = A$$

14. 0.20% of 12,000 = _?_

$$(0.002)(12,000) = X$$
$$24 = X$$

15. _?_% of 90 = 13

$$90X = 13$$
$$X = \frac{13}{90}$$
$$X = 14.4\overline{4}\%$$

16. _?_% of 100 = 12

$$100x = 12$$
$$x = \frac{12}{100}$$
$$x = 12\%$$

17. 28 = _?_% of 80

$$28 = 80x$$
$$\frac{28}{80} = x$$
$$\frac{7}{20} = x$$
$$x = 35\%$$

18. 450 = _?_% of 3,000

$$450 = 3,000X$$
$$\frac{450}{3,000} = X$$
$$15\% = X$$

19. 5.4 = _?_% of 180

$$5.4 = 180p$$
$$\frac{5.4}{180} = p$$
$$3\% = p$$

20. 45 = _?_% of 900

$$45 = 900p$$
$$\frac{45}{900} = p$$
$$5\% = p$$

21. _?_% of 18 = 4.5

$$18X = 4.5$$
$$X = \frac{4.5}{18}$$
$$X = 25\%$$

22. _?_% of 140 = 42

$$140X = 42$$
$$X = \frac{42}{140}$$
$$X = 30\%$$

23. 15% of ? = 48

$$0.15N = 48$$

$$N = \frac{48}{0.15}$$

$$N = 320$$

24. 120% of ? = 78

$$1.20A = 78$$

$$A = \frac{78}{1.2}$$

$$A = 65$$

25. 44% of ? = 33

$$0.44N = 33$$

$$N = \frac{33}{0.44}$$

$$N = 75$$

26. $11\frac{1}{2}$% of ? = 115

$$0.115N = 115$$

$$N = \frac{115}{0.115}$$

$$N = 1,000$$

27.   240 = 40% of ?

$$240 = 0.40A$$

$$\frac{240}{0.40} = A$$

$$600 = A$$

28.   196 = 28% of ?

$$196 = 0.28A$$

$$\frac{196}{0.28} = A$$

$$700 = A$$

29.

$$90 = 33\frac{1}{3}\% \text{ of } \underline{\ ?\ }$$

$$90 = \frac{1}{3}N$$

$$(3)(90) = N$$

$$270 = N$$

30.

$$50 = 33\frac{1}{3}\% \text{ of } \underline{\ ?\ }$$

$$50 = \frac{1}{3}A$$

$$(3)(50) = A$$

$$150 = A$$

31. 1.25% of ? = 100

$$0.0125A = 100$$

$$A = \frac{100}{0.0125}$$

$$A = 8,000$$

32. 4.5% of ? = 243

$$0.045A = 243$$

$$A = \frac{243}{0.045}$$

$$A = 5,400$$

33. 0.7% of $\underline{\ ?\ }$ = 3.5

$$0.007N = 3.5$$

$$N = \frac{3.5}{0.007}$$

$$N = 500$$

34. 0.9% of $\underline{\ ?\ }$ = 27

$$0.009N = 27$$

$$N = \frac{27}{0.90}$$

$$N = 3,000$$

35. 0.5% of $\underline{\ ?\ }$ = 48

$$0.005A = 48$$

$$A = \frac{48}{0.005}$$

$$A = 9,600$$

36. 0.75% of $\underline{\ ?\ }$ = 9

$$0.0075A = 9$$

$$A = \frac{9}{0.0075}$$

$$A = 1,200$$

37. Change = 7 - 5 = 2

___% of original = change

___% of 5 = 2

$$5X = 2$$

$$X = \frac{2}{5}$$

$$X = 40\%$$

38. Change = 180 - 150 = 30

___% of original = change

___% of 150 = 30

$$150X = 30$$

$$X = \frac{30}{150}$$

$$X = 20\%$$

39. Change = 55 - 44 = 11

___% of original = change

___% of 55 = 11

$$55X = 11$$

$$X = \frac{11}{55} = \frac{1}{5}$$

$$X = 20\%$$

40. Change = 150 - 105 = 45

___% of original = change

___% of 150 = 45

$$150X = 45$$

$$X = \frac{45}{150} = \frac{3}{10}$$

$$X = 30\%$$

41. Change = 325 - 130 = 195

$\underline{}$% of original = change

$\underline{}$% of 325 = 195

$325X = 195$

$X = \dfrac{195}{325} = \dfrac{3}{5}$

$X = 60\%$

42. Change = 260 - 26 = 234

$\underline{}$% of original = change

$\underline{}$% of 260 = 234

$260X = 234$

$X = \dfrac{234}{260}$

$X = 90\%$

43. Change = 135 - 108 = 27

$\underline{}$% of original = change

$\underline{}$% of 108 = 27

$108X = 27$

$X = \dfrac{27}{108} = \dfrac{1}{4}$

$X = 25\%$

44. Change = 300 - 200 = 100

$\underline{}$% of original = change

$\underline{}$% of 200 = 100

$200X = 100$

$X = \dfrac{100}{200} = \dfrac{1}{2}$

$X = 50\%$

45. Change = \$600 - \$597 = \$3

$\underline{}$% of original = change

$\underline{}$% of 600 = 3

$600X = 3$

$X = \dfrac{3}{600} = \dfrac{1}{200}$

$X = 0.5\%$

$\left(\text{or } \dfrac{1}{2}\%\right)$

46. Change = \$800 - \$794 = \$6

$\underline{}$% of original = change

$\underline{}$% of 800 = 6

$800X = 6$

$X = \dfrac{6}{800} = \dfrac{3}{400}$

$X = 0.75\%$

$\left(\text{or } \dfrac{3}{4}\%\right)$

47. $N + 25\%N = 90$

$1.25N = 90$

$N = \dfrac{90}{1.25}$

$N = 72$

48. $N + 40\%N = 77$

$1.40N = 77$

$N = \dfrac{77}{1.40}$

$N = 55$

49. $A - 25\%A = 36$

$A - 0.25A = 36$

$0.75A = 36$

$A = \dfrac{36}{0.75}$

$A = 48$

50. $A - 5\%A = 76$

$0.95A = 76$

$A = \dfrac{76}{0.95}$

$A = 80$

51. $N + 50\%N = 108$

$1.5N = 108$

$N = \dfrac{108}{1.5}$

$N = 72$

52. $N + 20\%N = 480$

$1.20N = 480$

$N = \dfrac{480}{1.20}$

$N = 400$

53. $A - 33\dfrac{1}{3}\%A = 150$

$\dfrac{2}{3}A = 150$

$A = (150)\dfrac{3}{2}$

$A - 225$

54. $A - 45\%A = 550$

$0.55A = 550$

$A = \dfrac{550}{0.55}$

$A = 1{,}000$

55. $A + 25\%A = 2{,}500$

$1.25A = 2{,}500$

$A = \dfrac{2{,}500}{1.25}$

$A = 2{,}000$

56. $A + 37.5\%A = 8{,}250$

$1.375A = 8{,}250$

$A = \dfrac{8{,}250}{1.375}$

$A = 6{,}000$

Section 3, page 51

1. Overhead is _?_% of sales?

   —— of $15,000 = $6,750

   $15,000X = 6,750$

   $X = \dfrac{6,750}{15,000}$

   $X = 45\%$

2. _?_% of sales was commission?

   ——% of $160,000 = $11,200

   $160,000X = 11,200$

   $X = \dfrac{11,200}{160,000}$

   $X = 7\%$

3. _?_% of budget was wages?

   ——% of $60,000 = $51,600

   $60,000X = 51,600$

   $X = \dfrac{51,600}{60,000}$

   $X = 86\%$

4. _?_% of total expenses were advertising costs?

   ——% of $280,000 = $33,600

   $280,000X = 33,600$

   $X = \dfrac{33,600}{280,000}$

   $X = 12\%$

5. 75% of revenue is advertisements.

   75% of $150,000 = A

   $0.75(150,000) = A$

   $\$112,500 = A$

6. 15% of investment was return.

   15% of $4,600 = R

   $(0.15)(4,600) = R$

   $\$690 = R$

7. 8% of cost paid in dividends.

   8% of $85 = D

   $0.08(85) = D$

   $\$6.80 = D$

8. 13% of enrollies are in managed care plans.

   13% of 40,000,000 = M

   $(0.13)(40,000,000) = M$

   $5,200,000 = M$

9. 20% of total income received from investments.

$$20\% \text{ of } T = \$10,200$$

$$0.20\,T = 10,200$$

$$T = \frac{10,200}{0.20}$$

$$T = \$51,000$$

10. 60% of votes won by candidate.

$$60\% \text{ of votes} = 492$$

$$0.60\,V = 492$$

$$V = \frac{492}{0.60}$$

$$V = 820$$

11. $60\frac{1}{4}\%$ of total assets represents inventory.

$$60\frac{1}{4}\% \text{ of } A = \$180,750$$

$$0.6025\,A = 180,750$$

$$A = \frac{180,750}{0.6025}$$

$$A = \$300,000$$

12. 48% of households watched Prime Events.

$$48\% \text{ of households} = 240$$

$$0.48\,H = 240$$

$$H = \frac{240}{0.48}$$

$$H = 500$$

13. $33\frac{1}{3}\%$ of collections are fees.

$$33\frac{1}{3}\% \text{ of } \$186,000 = F$$

$$\frac{1}{3}(186,000) = F$$

$$\$62,000 = F$$

14. Electricity charges equal $16\frac{2}{3}\%$ of monthly expenses.

$$16\frac{2}{3}\% \text{ of } \$8,700 = E$$

$$\frac{1}{6}\left(8,700\right) = E$$

$$\$1,450 = E$$

15. 25% of total production costs are raw materials.

$$25\% \text{ of total} = \$10$$

$$0.25\,T = 10$$

$$T = \frac{10}{0.25}$$

$$T = \$40$$

16. Gross profit was 8% of sales price.

$$\$18.80 = 8\% \text{ of sales}$$

$$18.80 = 0.08\,S$$

$$\frac{18.80}{0.08} = S$$

$$\$235 = S$$

17. Change = $37.98 - $36.00

= $1.98

___% of original = change

___% of 36 = $1.98

$36X = 1.98$

$X = \dfrac{1.98}{36}$

$X = 5.5\%$

18. Change = $1,015,200 - $940,000

= $75,200

___% of original = change

___% of $940,000 = $75,200

$940,000X = 75,200$

$X = \dfrac{75,200}{940,000}$

$X = 8\%$

19. Change = $52.80 - $50.00

= $2.80

___% of original = change

___% of $50 = $2.80

$50X = 2.80$

$X = \dfrac{2.80}{50}$

$X = 5.6\%$

20. Change = $263.22 - $246.00

= $17.22

___% of original = change

___% of $246 = $17.22

$246X = 17.22$

$X = \dfrac{17.22}{246}$

$X = 7\%$

21. Change = 12 - 8 = 4

___% of original = change

___% of 12 = 4

$12X = 4$

$X = \dfrac{4}{12} = \dfrac{1}{3}$

$X = 33\dfrac{1}{3}\%$

22. Change = $24 - $20 = $4

___% of original = change

___% of $24 = $4

$24X = 4$

$X = \dfrac{4}{24}$

$X = 16\dfrac{2}{3}\%$

23. Change = \$30.00 - \$28.20

$$= \$1.80$$

___% of original = change

___% of \$30 = \$1.80

$$30X = 1.80$$

$$X = \frac{1.80}{30}$$

$$X = 6\%$$

24. Change = \$8,800 - \$7,876

$$= \$924$$

___% of original = change

___% of \$8,800 = \$924

$$8,800X = 924$$

$$X = \frac{924}{8,800}$$

$$X = 10.5\%$$

25. Change = \$1,500.00 - \$1,312.50

$$= \$187.50$$

___% of original = change

___% of \$1,500 = \$187.50

$$1,500X = 187.50$$

$$X = \frac{187.50}{1,500}$$

$$X = 12\frac{1}{2}\%$$

26. Change = 18 - 15 = 3

___% of original = change

___% of 18 = 3

$$18X = 3$$

$$X = \frac{3}{18}$$

$$X = 16\frac{2}{3}\%$$

27. What number increased by 40% (of itself) yields 4,200?

$$N + 40\%N = 4,200$$

$$1.4N = 4,200$$

$$N = \frac{4,200}{1.4}$$

$$N = 3,000$$

28. What amount increased by 37.5% (of itself) equals 1,925?

$$N + 37.5\%N = 1,925$$

$$1.375N = 1,925$$

$$N = \frac{1,925}{1.375}$$

$$N = 1,400$$

29. What amount decreased by 20% (of itself) equals $36?

$$A - 20\%A = \$36$$

$$0.80A = 36$$

$$A = \frac{36}{0.80}$$

$$A = \$45$$

30. What amount decreased by 14% (of itself) equals 86?

$$A - 14\%A = 86$$

$$0.86A = 86$$

$$A = \frac{86}{0.86}$$

$$A = 100$$

31. $16\frac{2}{3}\%$ of customers were teenagers.

$$16\frac{2}{3}\% \text{ of } 930 = T$$

$$\frac{1}{6}\left(930\right) = T$$

$$155 = T$$

32. $1\frac{3}{4}\%$ of credit sales will be uncollectible.

$$1\frac{3}{4}\% \text{ of } \$6,500 = U$$

$$(0.0175)(6,500) = U$$

$$\$113.75 = U$$

33. Change = $206 - $200

$$= \$6$$

—% of original = change

—% of $200 = 6

$$200X = 6$$

$$X = \frac{6}{200}$$

$$X = \frac{3}{100}$$

$$X = 3\%$$

34. Change = $48 - $32 = $16

—% of original = change

—% of $32 = $16

$$32X = 16$$

$$X = \frac{16}{32}$$

$$X = 50\%$$

35. 17% of graduates secured jobs.

$$17\% \text{ of } G = 68$$

$$0.17G = 68$$

$$G = \frac{68}{0.17}$$

$$G = 400$$

36. 16% of total sales were returns.

$$16\%S = \$450$$

$$0.16S = 450$$

$$S = \frac{450}{0.16}$$

$$S = \$2,812.50$$

37. Change = \$23,000 - \$17,480

$$= \$5,520$$

—% of original = change

—% of \$23,000 = \$5,520

$$23,000X = 5,520$$

$$X = \frac{5,520}{23,000}$$

$$X = 24\%$$

38. Change = 1,820 - 1,729

$$= 91$$

—% of original = change

—% of 1,820 = 91

$$1,820X = 91$$

$$X = \frac{91}{1,820}$$

$$X = 5\%$$

39. —% of selling price was gross profit?

—% of \$480 - \$160

$$480X = 160$$

$$X = \frac{160}{480}$$

$$X = 33\frac{1}{3}\%$$

40. —% of sales representatives reached sales quota?

—% of 150 = 84

$$150X = 84$$

$$X = \frac{84}{150}$$

$$X = 56\%$$

41. Previous price increased by 18% yields latest price.

$$P + 18\%P = \$122.72$$

$$1.18P = 122.72$$

$$P = \frac{122.72}{1.18}$$

$$P = \$104$$

42. Cost increased by 20% yields new cost.

$$C + 20\%C = \$24$$

$$1.20C = 24$$

$$C = \frac{24}{1.20}$$

$$C = \$20$$

43. Price reduced by 30% (of itself) yields $2,100.

$$P - 30\%\,P = \$2,100$$

$$0.70\,P = 2,100$$

$$P = \frac{2,100}{0.70}$$

$$P = \$3,000$$

44. Net worth decreased by 10% yields current net worth.

$$W - 10\%\,W = \$225,000$$

$$0.90\,W = 225,000$$

$$W = \frac{225,000}{0.90}$$

$$W = \$250,000$$

45. Change = $63,000 - $60,000

$$= \$3,000$$

$$\underline{\quad}\% \text{ of original} = \text{change}$$

$$\underline{\quad}\% \text{ of } \$60,000 = \$3,000$$

$$60,000\,X = 3,000$$

$$X = \frac{3,000}{60,000}$$

$$X = 5\%$$

46. Change = 5,750 - 5,000

$$= 750$$

$$\underline{\quad}\% \text{ of original} = \text{change}$$

$$\underline{\quad}\% \text{ of } 5,000 = 750$$

$$5,000\,X = 750$$

$$X = \frac{750}{5,000}$$

$$X = 15\%$$

47. & 48. ANSWERS WILL VARY.

CHAPTER IV

BASIC STATISTICS AND GRAPHS

As a matter of convenience, the authors recommend that Chapter IV be included with the review material for testing. (Most of the review problems can be worked rather quickly, while many problems in succeeding chapters will take longer.)

1. Averages:

The ordinary arithmetic mean needs little attention and was included primarily for the sake of completeness. The weighted mean will be new to most students. They will be particularly interested in the calculation of grade point average, since most have no idea how it is obtained. Discuss the wording of problems to enable the student to distinguish when the ordinary mean is required and when the weighted mean is needed. Example 4 (average investment during the year) was included as preparation for the distribution of partnership profits and may be omitted if the instructor does not plan to teach that method.

2. Averages (Grouped Data):

Both this topic on the frequency distribution and the following topic on standard deviation can be understood by better students and may be included as introductory material for a group which will later be required to study statistics. However, the authors would probably omit these sections for most average (or below) classes.

For this first introduction to frequency distribution, a simplified method is used to represent class intervals and determine their midpoints. Given intervals 20-39, 40-59, etc., the midpoint is computed as the mean of the successive lower limits: $(20 + 40)/2 = 30$.

Many statistics texts present one of the following, more statistically correct procedures: (1) compute a midpoint that is the mean of the lower and upper limits of the class: $(20 + 39)/2 = 29.5$. More explicitly, (2) use the "real class limits" to find the mean of the upper and upper limits: $(19.5 + 39.45)/2 = 29.495$ or 29.5. Either of these methods makes only a slight difference in the computed arithmetic mean of the distribution and may cause more tedious calculations for students, since the text's intervals are specifically chosen to facilitate convenient midpoints.

Since all student problems will contain integer data, the text's intervals (and midpoints) are a satisfactory substitute for the more statistically continuous intervals 20.00 - 39.99, 40.00 - 59.99, etc. The midpoint for these intervals, by method (1) above, would be (20.00 + 39.99)/2 = 30.00, the same value computed using the text's method.

For better classes or to be more statistically correct, you may prefer assigning method (1) or (2). Alternatively, students may restate the given intervals (20-39) in continuous notation (20.00-39.99) and utilize method (1) to obtain the same midpoints as computed by the text's simplified method.

3.   Standard Deviation:

This topic may be included even if the section on grouped data has been omitted; brief reference is made to the preceding topic as an aid to visualizing the normal curve, but the frequency distribution is not used to compute standard deviation.

Students typically have difficulty in comprehending the normal curve as an ordinary graph, probably because it is often used without a vertical axis (specifying the number of times that each value occurred). It would thus be helpful to introduce the normal curve by graphing some actual data, such as the following:

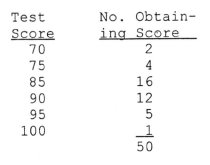

Test Score	No. Obtaining Score
70	2
75	4
85	16
90	12
95	5
100	1
	50

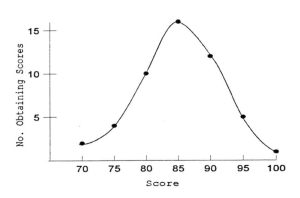

(The standard deviation for this example is approximately 6.5.) Emphasize that the normal curve distribution of scores would not apply in many specialized cases (such as the scores obtained by honor society members).

In discussing the percentage categories associated with the normal curve, begin with the intervals $\pm 1\sigma$, $\pm 2\sigma$, $\pm 3\sigma$. Emphasize that the standard deviation divides the range of values into six equal intervals along the horizontal axis. Thus, a simple horizontal-line graph can be used to illustrate standard deviation, as in Example 2.

The most important goal of this topic is for the students to gain an understanding of what "standard deviation" means, so that they will know what is being indicated when they hear the term used. Thus standard deviation is computed only by the simple formula used for ungrouped data:

(Example 2), $\sigma = \sqrt{\dfrac{\Sigma d^2}{n}}$

Although standard deviation is relatively simple for the student to compute, it is more difficult for the instructor to compose problems that have a whole-number solution. The following procedure will facilitate this composition somewhat:

	Procedure	Example

1. Decide what σ you want; square it and multiply by an arbitrary n which produces an even result. (This equals Σd^2.)

$\sigma = 3 \quad \sigma^2 = 9$
$n = 6 \qquad \underline{\times 6}$
$\qquad\qquad 54$

2. By trial and error, find n perfect squares whose sum equals the total above. Then find the square roots.

Sqs.	Roots
9	3
4	2
1	1
0	0
36	6
$\underline{4}$	$\underline{2}$
54	2)$\overline{14}$
	7

3
$7 \begin{cases} 2 \\ 1 \\ 0 \\ 6 \\ 2 \end{cases} 7$

3. Add the roots and divide by 2 to find the total for each set of + and - deviations. Assign + and - signs as desired. (See Deviations.)

4. Select any suitable mean; use your deviations to name the corresponding set of data. (See below.)

Deviations:
-3, -2, -2, 0, 1, 6;
or 3, 2, 2, 0, -1, -6

Let M = 50; then the data are:

47, 48, 48, 50, 51, 56; or 53, 52, 52, 50, 49, 44.

For the instructor's use in composing standard deviation problems, listed below are two sets of deviations which correspond to each indicated σ and n:

σ = 4 n = 5 d's:		σ = 6 n = 5 d's:		σ = 3 n = 6 d's:		σ = 5 n = 6 d's:		σ = 5 n = 6 d's:		σ = 6 n = 6 d's:	
-5	-6	-9	-7	-5	-4	-8	-8	-6	-8	-8	-7
-3	-3	-5	-4	-2	-2	-2	-4	-4	-5	-6	-7
-1	+1	+3	-3	-1	-2	-1	+1	-3	0	-3	-3
+3	+3	+4	+5	+2	+1	-1	+1	0	+3	+3	+3
+6	+5	+7	+9	+2	+2	+4	+2	+5	+4	+7	+6
				+4	+5	+8	+8	+8	+6	+7	+8

σ = 2 n = 8 d's:		σ = 4 n = 8 d's:		σ = 2 n = 10 d's:		σ = 3 n = 10 d's:		σ = 3 n = 10 d's:	
-4	-3	-8	-7	-5	-2	-7	-3	-5	-4
-1	-2	-2	-2	-1	-2	-2	-3	-3	-3
-1	-1	-1	-1	-1	-1	-1	-2	-2	-3
0	0	0	-1	0	-1	-1	-1	-1	-1
0	0	0	0	0	-1	0	-1	-1	-1
+1	+1	+1	0	0	0	0	-1	0	0
+2	+1	+3	+3	+1	0	+1	0	0	0
+3	+4	+7	+8	+2	0	+3	0	+3	+2
				+2	+2	+3	+4	+4	+5
				+2	+5	+4	+7	+5	+5

4.   Index Numbers:

Simple price relatives are easy for the student to compute and cause no problem. Because indexes are encountered so frequently in modern-day reports, the most important aspect of this topic is that the student learn to interpret indexes. Just reading an index (i.e., an index of 125.7 means an item which formerly cost $10 has increased to $12.57) can be learned easily. However, the key to correctly interpreting an index is understanding exactly what the base represents. Thus, price indexes such as Table 1 (example 2) only show how rapidly prices have increased or decreased; we can determine whether housing costs have increased faster in one locality than in another locality, or whether housing costs have increased faster than food costs in any given locality. However, separate indexes cannot be compared to determine which is more expensive unless they all refer to the same base amount (in dollars and cents); hence, Table 1 does not allow us to determine whether food is more expensive in Los Angeles or in New York, because a different base was used to compute the index for each locality (that is, the given food items which compose each base had cost a different amount in each locality). Neither does Table 1 allow us to know whether a family in Chicago spends more money for food or for housing). Understanding these restrictions in interpreting index numbers is not easy for the typical student. Emphasize that a comparison of the <u>actual</u> living costs in different cities is possible only with the <u>comparative</u> index in Table 2.

5. Graphs:

Every business person should be able to read and interpret graphs. A data disk containing templates for each problem has been prepared using the Excel® spreadsheet program. The disk accompanies the text. Students can complete, then convert, the spreadsheets to charts/graphs through the Chart Wizard. The problems can be worked manually also.

CHAPTER 4 – BASIC STATISTICS AND GRAPHS
PROBLEM SOLUTIONS

Section 1, page 63

1. (a) (1) The arithmetic mean:

$$\frac{10+22+29+22+45+30+43+18+39+28+59+41+42+40+12}{15}$$

$$= \frac{480}{15} = 32$$

(2) The median:

10, 12, 18, 22, 22, 28, 29, <u>30</u>, 39, 40, 41, 42, 43, 45, 59

$$\frac{15}{2} = 7+; \text{ so } 8^{\text{th}} \text{ number } = 30$$

(3) The mode: 22 (occurs twice)

1. (Continued)

    (b) (1) The arithmetic mean:

$$\frac{170 + 154 + 120 + 133 + 142 + 161 + 115 + 121 + 130 + 154}{10}$$

$$= \frac{1,400}{10} = 140$$

       (2) The median:

115, 120, 121, 130, 133, 142, 154, 154, 161, 170

$\frac{10}{2} = 5$; so median is the arithmetic mean of 5th and 6th numbers: $\frac{133 + 142}{2} = 137.5$

       (3) The mode: 154 (occurs twice)

2. (a) (1) The arithmetic mean:

$$\frac{20 + 18 + 20 + 16 + 22 + 19 + 21 + 23 + 17 + 20 + 24}{11}$$

$$= \frac{220}{11} = 20$$

       (2) The median:

16, 17, 18, 19, 20, 20, 20, 21, 22, 23, 24

$\frac{11}{2} = 5+$; so 6th number = 20

       (3) The mode: 20 (occurs 3 times)

    (b) (1) The arithmetic mean:

$$\frac{342 + 332 + 351 + 343 + 347 + 348 + 340 + 352 + 344 + 351 + 349 + 341}{12}$$

$$= \frac{4,140}{12} = 345$$

2. (b) (Continued)

   (2) The median:

   332, 340, 341, 342, 343, 344, 347, 348, 349, 351, 351, 352

   $\frac{12}{2}$ = 6; so median is the arithmetic mean of the 6th
   and 7th numbers: $\frac{344 + 347}{2}$ = 345.5

   (3) The mode: 351 (occurs twice)

3.

Final Grade	Quality Points		Credit Hours		
D	1	×	3	=	3
C	2	×	3	=	6
A	4	×	4	=	16
B	3	×	5	=	15
	10		15		40

(a) Average quality points per class: $\frac{10}{4}$ = 2.50

(b) Average per credit hour: $\frac{40}{15}$ = 2.6$\overline{6}$

4.

Final Grade	Quality Points		Credit Hours		
A	4	×	3	=	12
B	3	×	3	=	9
A	4	×	3	=	12
C	2	×	2	=	4
C	2	×	1	=	2
	15		12		39

(a) Average quality points per class: $\frac{15}{5}$ = 3.0

(b) Average per credit hour: $\frac{39}{12}$ = 3.25

5.

Job	# in Job		Weekly Wages		
Manager	1	×	$1,000	=	$ 1,000
Sales representative	4	×	450	=	1,800
Technician	10	×	550	=	5,500
Office support	5	×	400	=	2,000
	20		$2,400		$10,300

5. (Continued)

(a) Mean wage per job: $\dfrac{\$2,400}{4} = \$600$

(b) Mean wage per employee: $\dfrac{\$10,300}{20} = \$515$

6.

Job	# in Job		Weekly Wages		
Manager	1	×	$1,200	=	$1,200
Stylist	6	×	600	=	3,600
Receptionist	2	×	450	=	900
Custodian	1	×	350	=	350
	10		$2,600		$6,050

(a) Mean wage per job: $\dfrac{\$2,600}{4} = \$650$

(b) Mean wage per employee: $\dfrac{\$6,050}{10} = \$605$

7.

Store	Price		# Sold		
A	$ 85	×	12	=	$1,020
B	135	×	8	=	1,080
C	96	×	22	=	2,112
D	89	×	20	=	1,780
E	112	×	9	=	1,008
F	107	×	9	=	963
	$624		80		$7,963

(a) Mean price per store: $\dfrac{\$624}{6} = \$104$

(b) Mean price per vacuum sold: $\dfrac{\$7,963}{80} = 99.5375$

　　　　　　　　　　　　　　　　or $99.54

8.

Store	Price		# Sold		
Compuland	$ 70	×	50	=	$ 3,500
ComputerWorld	85	×	42	=	3,570
Computer Connection	103	×	30	=	3,090
	$285		122		$10,160

(a) Mean price per store: $\dfrac{\$258}{3} = \$86$

8. (Continued)

(b) Mean price per cartridge: $\dfrac{\$10,160}{122} = \$83.28$

9.

Date		Change	Amount of Investment		Months Invested		
January	1	---	$5,000	×	2	=	$10,000
March	1	-$200	4,800	×	5	=	24,000
August	1	+ 400	5,200	×	1	=	5,200
September	1	- 600	4,600	×	4	=	18,400
					12		$57,600

$\dfrac{\$57,600}{12} = \$4,800$ average investment per month

10.

Date		Change	Amount of Investment		Months Invested		
January	1	---	$20,000	×	4	=	$ 80,000
May	1	+$15,000	35,000	×	3	=	105,000
August	1	- 2,000	33,000	×	3	=	99,000
November	1	+ 5,000	38,000	×	2	=	76,000
					12		$360,000

$\dfrac{\$360,000}{12} = \$30,000$ average investment per month

11. $108,000, $110,000, $130,000, $133,000, $138,000, $140,000, $151,000. $\dfrac{7}{2} = 3+$; so median is 4th number = $133,000

12. $155, $180, $194, $265, $290, $300, $350, $375, $400

$\dfrac{9}{2} = 4.5$; so median is 5th number: $290

13. $79, $79, $82, $82, $82, $86, $86, $94, $124, $130, $158

The mode: $82 (occurs 3 times)

14. $18, $18, $18, $18, $25, $25, $33, $33, $42, $58, $58, $61, $99. The mode: $18 (occurs 4 times)

15. (a) The mean:

$$48 + 50 + 54 + 60 + 48 + 54 + 56 + 60 +$$

$$\frac{59 + 68 + 52 + 60 + 51 + 60 + 45 + 47}{16}$$

$$= \frac{872}{16} = 54.5 \text{ hours}$$

(b) The median:

$$45, 47, 48, 48, 50, 51, 52, \underline{54, 54}, 56, 59, 60, 60, 60, 60, 68$$

$\frac{16}{2} = 8$; so median is the arithmetic mean of 8th and 9th

numbers: $\frac{54 + 54}{2} = 54$ hours

(c) The mode: 60 hours (occurs 4 times)

16. (a) The mean:

$$\frac{3 + 5 + 1 + 2 + 8 + 6 + 3 + 7 + 9 + 12}{10} = \frac{56}{10} = 5.6 \text{ years}$$

(b) The median:

$$1, 2, 3, 3, 5, 6, 7, 8, 9, 12$$

$\frac{10}{2} = 5$; so median is the arithmetic mean of 5th and 6th

numbers: $\frac{5 + 6}{2} = \frac{11}{2} = 5.5$ years

(c) Modal class: 3 years (occurs twice)

17. (a) The mean:

$$\frac{1600 + 1630 + 1640 + 1630 + 1620 + 1640 + 1560 + 1640 + 1620}{9}$$

$$= \frac{14,580}{9} = 1,620$$

17. (Continued)

(b) The median:

1560, 1600, 1620, 1620, <u>1630</u>, 1630, 1640, 1640, 1640

$\frac{9}{2}$ = 4+; so 5th number = 1,630

(c) The mode: 1,640 (occurs 3 times)

18. (a) The mean:

$$\frac{26 + 15 + 9 + 12 + 22 + 20 + 15}{7} = \frac{119}{7} = 17 \text{ cars}$$

(b) The median:

9, 12, 15, <u>15</u>, 20, 22, 26

$\frac{7}{2}$ = 3.5; so 4th number = 15 cars

(c) Modal number: 15 cars (occurs twice)

Section 2, page 69

1.

Class Interval	Tally	f	Midpoint	f × Midpoint
80 - 99	//	2	90	180
60 - 79	⅃⅂⁊	5	70	350
40 - 59	⅃⅂⁊	5	50	250
20 - 39	⅃⅂⁊ ////	9	30	270
0 - 19	////	4	10	40
		25		1,090

(a) Mean: $\frac{1,090}{25}$ = 43.6

(b) Median: (1) $\frac{25}{2}$ = 12.5

(2) 4 + 8.5 = 12.5

(3) $\frac{8.5}{9}$ × 20 = 18.88888̄ = 18.89

(4) 20 + 18.89 = 38.89

1. (Continued)

(c) Modal class: 20 - 39

2.

Class Interval	Tally	f	Midpoint	f × Midpoint
60 - 69	////	4	65	260
50 - 59	///	3	55	165
40 - 49	//	2	45	90
30 - 39	L/H/	5	35	175
20 - 29	L/H/ //	7	25	175
10 - 19	L/H/ /	6	15	90
0 - 9	///	3	5	15
		30		970

(a) Mean: $\dfrac{970}{30}$ = 32.3$\overline{3}$

(b) Median: (1) $\dfrac{30}{2}$ = 15

(2)   3 + 6 + 6 = 15

(3) $\dfrac{6}{7}$ × 10 = 8.57

(4)   20 + 8.57 = 28.57

(c) Modal class: 20 - 29

3.

Class Interval	Tally	f	Midpoint	f × Midpoint
$1,000 - 1,099	////	4	$1,050	$ 4,200
900 - 999	L/H/	5	950	4,750
800 - 899	L/H/ ///	8	850	6,800
700 - 799	L/H/ /	6	750	4,500
600 - 699	////	4	650	2,600
500 - 599	///	3	550	1,650
		30		$24,500

(a) Mean: $\dfrac{\$24,500}{30}$ = 816.6\overline{6}$

(b) Median: (1) $\dfrac{30}{2}$ = 15

(2)   3 + 4 + 6 + 2 = 15

(3) $\dfrac{2}{8}$ × 100 = $25

(4) $800 + $25 = $825

3. (Continued)

(c) Modal class: $800 - $899

4.

Class Interval	Tally	f	Midpoint	f × Midpoint
$500 - 549	////	4	$525	$2,100
450 - 499	//	2	475	950
400 - 449	LH7 /	6	425	2,550
350 - 399	/	1	375	375
300 - 349	//	2	325	650
250 - 299	//	2	275	550
200 - 249	///	3	225	675
		20		$7,850

(a) Mean: $\dfrac{\$7,850}{20} = \$392.50$

(b) Median: (1) $\dfrac{20}{2} = 10$

(2) $3 + 2 + 2 + 1 + 2 = 10$

(3) $\dfrac{2}{6} \times 50 = 16.6\overline{6}$

(4) $400 + $16.67 = $416.67

(c) Modal class: 400 - 449

5.

Class Interval	Tally	f	Midpoint	f × Midpoint
$350 - 449	//	2	$400	$ 800
250 - 349	////	4	300	1,200
150 - 249	LH7 ///	8	200	1,600
50 - 149	LH7 /	6	100	600
		20		$4,200

(a) Mean: $\dfrac{\$4,200}{20} = \$210$

(b) Median: (1) $\dfrac{20}{2} = 10$

(2) $6 + 4 = 10$

(3) $\dfrac{4}{8} \times \$100 = \$50$

(4) $150 + $50 = $200

(c) Modal class: $150 - $249

6.

Class Interval	Tally	f	Midpoint	f × Midpoint
1,000 - 1,099	//	2	1,050	2,100
900 - 999	////	4	950	3,800
800 - 899	////	4	850	3,400
700 - 799	//// /	6	750	4,500
600 - 699	////	5	650	3,250
500 - 599	////	4	550	2,200
400 - 499	/	1	450	450
		26		19,700

(a) Mean: $\dfrac{19,700}{26}$ = 757.69 or 758

(b) Median: (1) $\dfrac{26}{2}$ = 13

   (2)   1 + 4 + 5 + 3 = 13

   (3) $\dfrac{3}{6}$ × 100 = 50

   (4)   700 + 50 = 750

(c) Modal class: 700 - 799

7.

Class Interval	Tally	f	Midpoint	f × Midpoint
21 - 23	/	1	22.5	22.5
18 - 20	//	2	19.5	39.0
15 - 17	//	2	16.5	33.0
12 - 14	////	4	13.5	54.0
9 - 11	/	1	10.5	10.5
6 - 8	//// ////	9	7.5	67.5
3 - 5	////	5	4.5	22.5
0 - 2	//	2	1.5	3.0
		26		252.0

(a) Mean: $\dfrac{252}{26}$ = 9.69

(b) Median: (1) $\dfrac{26}{2}$ = 13

   (2)   2 + 5 + 6 = 13

   (3) $\dfrac{6}{9}$ × 3 = 2

   (4)   6 + 2 = 8

(c) Modal class: 6 - 8

8.

Class Interval	Tally	f	Midpoint	f × Midpoint
$10,000 - 11,999	///	3	$11,000	$33,000
8,000 - 9,999	⅃⅂⅂⅂ ///	8	9,000	72,000
6,000 - 7,999	///	3	7,000	21,000
4,000 - 5,999	⅃⅂⅂⅂	5	5,000	25,000
2,000 - 3,999	⅃⅂⅂⅂	5	3,000	15,000
		24		$166,000

(a) Mean: $\dfrac{\$166,000}{24} = \$6,916.67$

(b) Median: (1) $\dfrac{24}{2} = 12$

(2) $5 + 5 + 2 = 12$

(3) $\dfrac{2}{3} \times \$2,000 = \$1,333.33$

(4) $\$6,000 + \$1,333.33 = \$7,333.33$

(c) Modal class: $8,000 - $9,999

Section 3, page 74

1. (a) 50%
   (b) 2.5%
   (c) 34% + 13.5% = 47.5%
   (d) 13.5% + 34% + 34% +
       13.5% + 2.5% = 97.5%
   (e) 16% × 50 = 8
   (f) 84% × 50 = 42

2. (a) 50%
   (b) 2.5%
   (c) 34%
   (d) 2.5% + 13.5% = 16.0%
   (e) 0.68(100) = 68
   (f) 0.50(100) = 50

3.

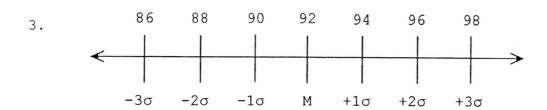

(a) 13.5% + 34% + 13.5% + 2.5% = 97.5%
(b) 34% + 13.5% + 2.5% = 50%
(c) 34% + 34% = 68%
(d) 13.5% + 2.5% = 16%
(e) 16% of 31 = 4.96 or 5 days
(f) 50% of 31 = 15.5 or 16 days
(g) 68% of 31 = 21.08 or 21 days

4.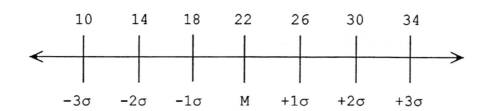

(a) 68% + 13.5% = 81.5%
(b) 2.5%
(c) 16%
(d) 84%
(e) 0.50(6,000) = 3,000
(f) 0.68(6,000) = 4,080
(g) 0.025(6,000) =   150

5. (a)

Mean	d	d^2	Standard Deviation
8	−5	25	$\sigma = \sqrt{\dfrac{\Sigma d^2}{n}}$
10	−3	9	
12	−1	1	$= \sqrt{\dfrac{80}{5}}$
16	+3	9	
			$= \sqrt{16}$
$5\overline{)65} = 13$	$\dfrac{+6}{0}$	$\Sigma d^2 = \dfrac{36}{80}$	$\sigma = \pm 4$

(b)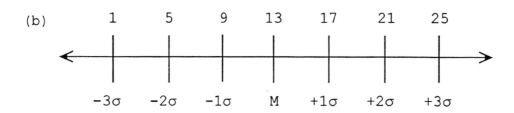

(c) ±1σ: 68% of 5 numbers = 3.4; we have 3: 10, 12, 16.

±2σ: 95% of 5 numbers = 4.75 or 5; all numbers are between 5 and 21.

6. (a)

Mean	d	d^2	Standard Deviation
41	-9	81	$\sigma = \sqrt{\dfrac{\Sigma d^2}{n}}$
45	-5	25	$= \sqrt{\dfrac{180}{5}}$
53	+3	9	
54	+4	16	$= \sqrt{36}$
$\dfrac{57}{5\overline{)250}} = 13$	$\dfrac{+7}{0}$	$\Sigma d^2 = \dfrac{49}{180}$	$\sigma = \pm6$

(b)

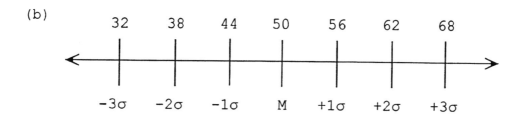

(c) $\pm1\sigma$: 68% of 5 numbers = 3.4; we have 3: 45, 53, 54.

$\pm2\sigma$: 95% of 5 numbers = 4.75; we have all numbers.

7. (a)

Mean	d	d^2	Standard Deviation
28	-8	64	$\sigma = \sqrt{\dfrac{\Sigma d^2}{n}}$
34	-2	4	
35	-1	1	$= \sqrt{\dfrac{150}{6}}$
35	-1	1	$= \sqrt{25}$
40	+4	16	$\sigma = \pm 5$
44	+8	64	
$6\overline{)216} = 36$	0	$\Sigma d^2 = 150$	

(b)

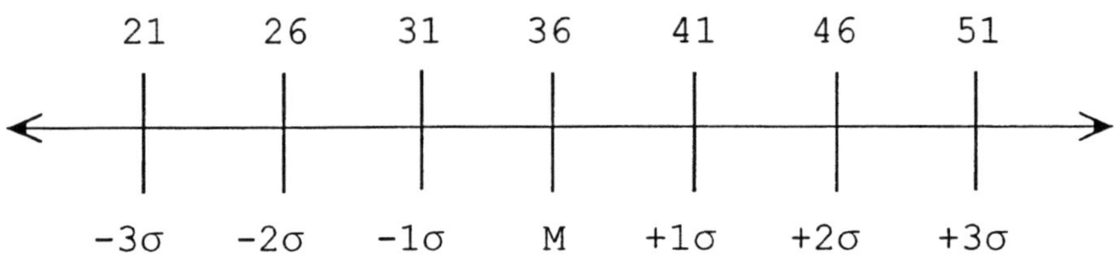
21
26
31
36
41
46
51
-3σ
-2σ
-1σ
M
+1σ
+2σ
+3σ

(c) $\pm 1\sigma$: 68% of 6 numbers = 4.08; we have 4: 34, 35, 35, 40.

$\pm 2\sigma$: 95% of 6 numbers = 5.7 or 6; we have all 6 numbers between 26 and 46.

8. (a)

Mean	d	d^2	Standard Deviation
26	-4	16	$\sigma = \sqrt{\dfrac{\Sigma d^2}{n}}$
29	-1	1	
29	-1	1	$= \sqrt{\dfrac{32}{8}}$
30	0	0	
30	0	0	$= \sqrt{4}$
31	+1	1	$\sigma = \pm 2$
32	+2	4	
$\dfrac{33}{8\overline{)240}} = 30$	$\dfrac{+3}{0}$	$\Sigma d^2 = \dfrac{9}{32}$	

(b)

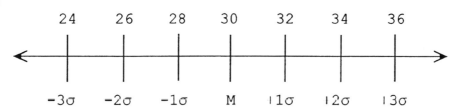

(c) ±1σ: 68% of 8 numbers = 5.44; we have 6: 29, 29, 30, 30, 31, 32.

±2σ: 95% of 8 numbers = 7.6; we have all 8 numbers.

*See note at the end of this section.

9. (a)

Mean	d	d^2	Standard Deviation
31	-9	81	$\sigma = \sqrt{\dfrac{\Sigma d^2}{n}}$
32	-8	64	
35	-5	25	$= \sqrt{\dfrac{288}{8}}$
41	1	1	
44	4	16	$= \sqrt{36}$
44	4	16	
46	6	36	$\sigma = \pm 6$
47	7	49	

$8\overline{)320} = 40 \qquad \overline{0} \qquad \Sigma d^2 = \overline{288}$

(b)

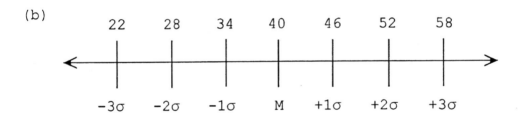

```
      22    28    34    40    46    52    58
      |     |     |     |     |     |     |
<-----+-----+-----+-----+-----+-----+-----+----->

     -3σ   -2σ   -1σ    M    +1σ   +2σ   +3σ
```

(c) ±1σ: 68% of 8 numbers = 5.44; we have 5: 35, 41, 44, 44, 46.

±2σ: 95% of 8 numbers = 7.6 or 8; we have all 8 numbers between 28 and 52.

10. (a)

Mean	d	d^2	Standard Deviation
55	-5	25	$\sigma = \sqrt{\dfrac{\Sigma d^2}{n}}$
57	-3	9	
58	-2	4	$= \sqrt{\dfrac{90}{10}}$
59	-1	1	
59	-1	1	$= \sqrt{9}$
60	0	0	$\sigma = \pm 3$
60	0	0	
63	+3	9	
64	+4	16	
65	+5	25	
$10\overline{)600} = 60$	0	$\Sigma d^2 = 90$	

(b)

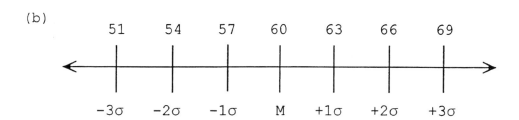

(c) $\pm 1\sigma$: 68% of 10 numbers = 6.8; we have 7: 57, 58, 59, 59, 60, 60, 63.

$\pm 2\sigma$: 95% of 10 numbers = 9.5; we have all 10.

11. (a)

Mean	d	d^2	Standard Deviation
23	-7	49	$\sigma = \sqrt{\dfrac{\Sigma d^2}{n}}$
24	-6	36	
25	-5	25	$= \sqrt{\dfrac{200}{8}}$
31	1	1	
31	1	1	$= \sqrt{25}$
34	4	16	$\sigma = \pm 5$
36	6	36	
36	6	36	

$8\overline{)240} = 30$ $\dfrac{}{0}$ $\Sigma d^2 = 200$

(b)

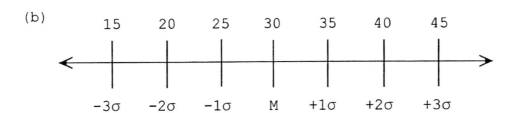

(c) ±1σ: 68% of 8 numbers = 5.44; we have 4: 25, 31, 31, 34.

±2σ: 95% of 8 numbers = 7.6 or 8; we have all 8 numbers between 20 and 40.

*See note at the end of this section.

12. (a)

Mean	d	d^2	Standard Deviation
68	−5	25	$\sigma = \sqrt{\dfrac{\Sigma d^2}{n}}$
72	−1	1	
72	−1	1	$= \sqrt{\dfrac{40}{10}}$
73	0	0	
73	0	0	$= \sqrt{4}$
73	0	0	$\sigma = \pm 2$
74	+1	1	
75	+2	4	
75	+2	4	
$\underline{75}$	$\underline{+2}$	$\underline{4}$	

$10\overline{)730} = 73 \qquad 0 \qquad \Sigma d^2 = 40$

(b)

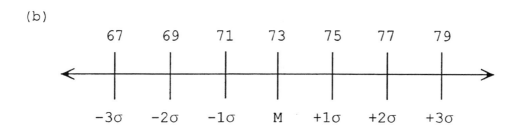

(c) $\pm 1\sigma$: 68% of 10 numbers = 6.8; we have 9: 72, 72, 73, 73, 73, 74, 75, 75, 75.

$\pm 2\sigma$: 95% of 10 numbers = 9.5; we have all 9.

*See note at the end of this section.

13. (a)

Mean	d	d^2	Standard Deviation
14	-6	36	$\sigma = \sqrt{\dfrac{\Sigma d^2}{n}}$
15	-5	25	
16	-4	16	$= \sqrt{\dfrac{160}{10}}$
18	-2	4	
20	0	0	$= \sqrt{16}$
20	0	0	$\sigma = \pm 4$
23	3	9	
23	3	9	
25	5	25	
26	6	36	

$10\overline{)200} = 20 \qquad \overline{0} \qquad \Sigma d^2 = \overline{160}$

(b)

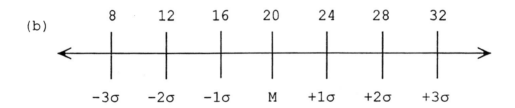

(c) ±1σ: 68% of 10 numbers = 6.8 or 7; we have 6: 16, 18, 20, 20, 23, 23.

±2σ: 95% of 10 numbers = 9.5 or 10; we have all 10 numbers between 12 and 28.

*See note at the end of this section.

14. (a)

Mean	d	d^2	Standard Deviation
74	-7	49	$\sigma = \sqrt{\dfrac{\Sigma d^2}{n}}$
79	-2	4	
80	-1	1	$= \sqrt{\dfrac{90}{10}}$
80	-1	1	
81	0	0	$= \sqrt{9}$
81	0	0	$\sigma = \pm 3$
82	+1	1	
84	+3	9	
84	+3	9	

$\dfrac{85}{10 \overline{)810}} = 81 \qquad \dfrac{+4}{0} \qquad \dfrac{16}{\Sigma d^2 = 90}$

(b)

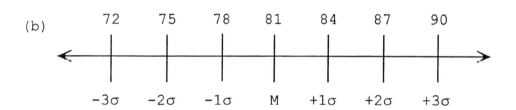

(c) ±1σ: 68% of 10 numbers = 6.8; we have 8: 79, 80, 80, 81, 81, 82, 84, 84.

±2σ: 95% of 10 numbers = 9.5; we have all 10.

*See note at the end of this section.

Note: When the expected number of given values does not fall within each interval ($\pm 1\sigma$, $\pm 2\sigma$, $\pm 3\sigma$), it means that the given data is not normally distributed, or, as is the case with the problems used in this text, the sample size is too small to even apply normal curve attributes.

Section 4, page 79

1. (a) $1,619.00
   (b) $164.40
   (c) $14.05
   (d) New York (176.6)
   (e) Los Angeles (145.2)
   (f) Dallas (142.3)
   (g) New York (255.3)
   (h) New York (143.9)
   (i) Atlanta (125.8)

2. (a) $1,537.00
   (b) $23.34
   (c) $128.40
   (d) New York (114.3)
   (e) Dallas (95.3)
   (f) New York (460.5)
   (g) Atlanta (101.9)
   (h) Dallas (233.4)
   (i) Seattle (232.8)

3.

Year	Price	Index (1998 = 100)
1998	$1.50	Base year $= 100$
1999	1.47	$\dfrac{1.47}{1.50} \times 100 = 0.98 \times 100 = 98$
2000	1.65	$\dfrac{1.65}{1.50} \times 100 = 1.10 \times 100 = 110$
2001	1.80	$\dfrac{1.80}{1.50} \times 100 = 1.20 \times 100 = 120$
2002	1.95	$\dfrac{1.95}{1.50} \times 100 = 1.30 \times 100 = 130$

4.

Year	Price	Index (1997 = 100)
1997	$0.50	Base year = 100
1998	0.45	$\dfrac{0.45}{0.50} \times 100 = 0.90 \times 100 = 90$
1999	0.55	$\dfrac{0.55}{0.50} \times 100 = 1.10 \times 100 = 110$
2000	0.60	$\dfrac{0.60}{0.50} \times 100 = 1.20 \times 100 = 120$
2001	0.70	$\dfrac{0.70}{0.50} \times 100 = 1.40 \times 100 = 140$

5.

Year	Price	Index (1990 = 100)
1990	$0.60	Base year = 100
1995	0.42	$\dfrac{0.42}{0.60} \times 100 = 0.70 \times 100 = 70$
1999	0.75	$\dfrac{0.75}{0.60} \times 100 = 1.25 \times 100 = 125$
2001	0.84	$\dfrac{0.84}{0.60} \times 100 = 1.40 \times 100 = 140$

6.

Year	Price	Index (1996 = 100)
1996	$0.80	Base year = 100
1998	0.84	$\dfrac{0.84}{0.80} \times 100 = 1.05 \times 100 = 105$
2000	0.72	$\dfrac{0.72}{0.80} \times 100 = 0.90 \times 100 = 90$
2002	0.76	$\dfrac{0.76}{0.80} \times 100 = 0.95 \times 100 = 95$

Section 5, page 85

1.

Mean Salaries for Office Managers

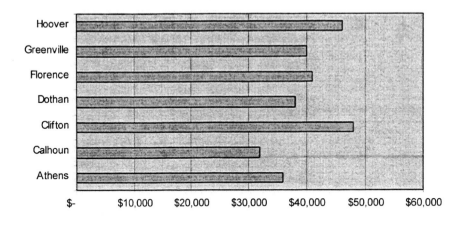

2.

Charles County Seniors, College Acceptance, 200X

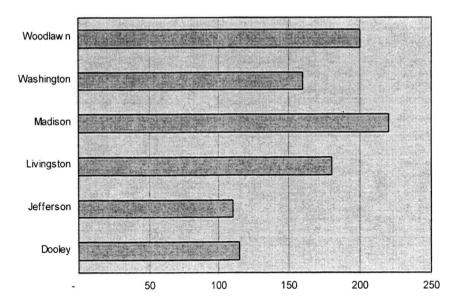

3.

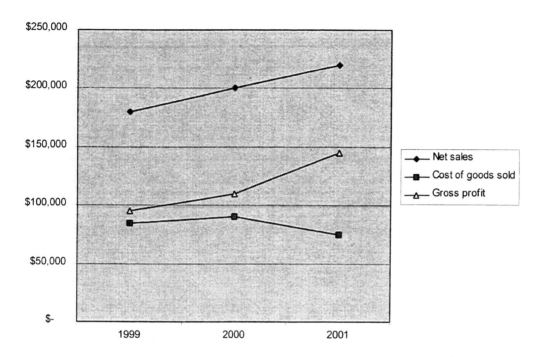

Coleman Interiors, Inc.

4.

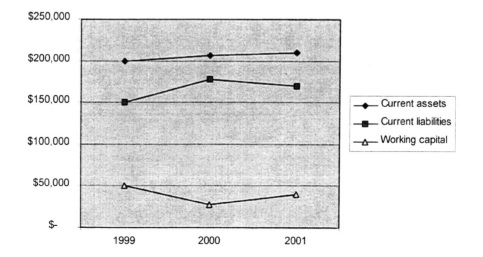

Solomon Repair Services

5.

American Insurance Co.

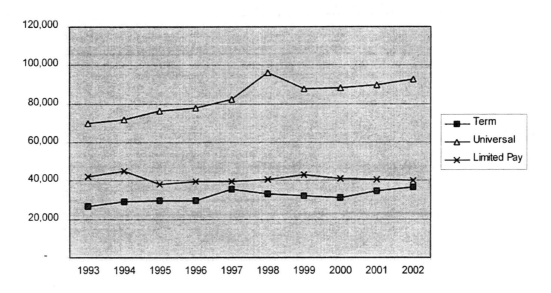

6.

Brown Company, July Expenses, 20X1

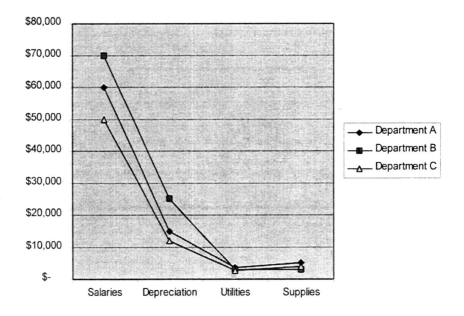

7.   Federal Budget Income Sources

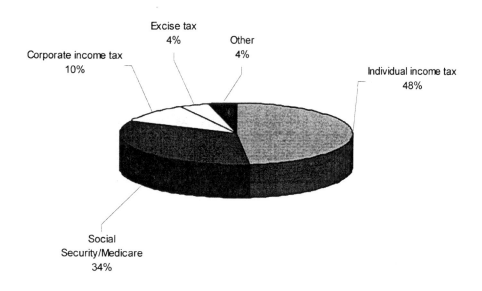

8.   Federal Budget Expenditures

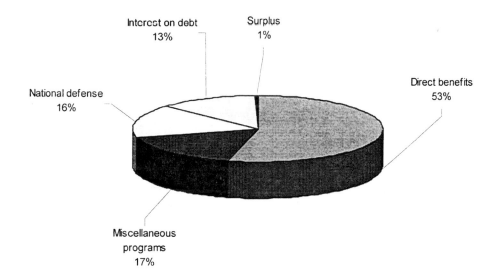

9.

Wadge Industries

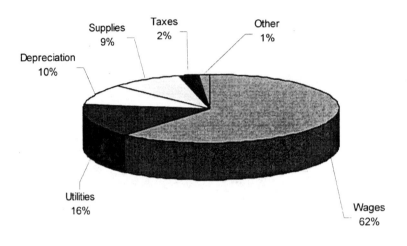

10.

Bostick Technologies

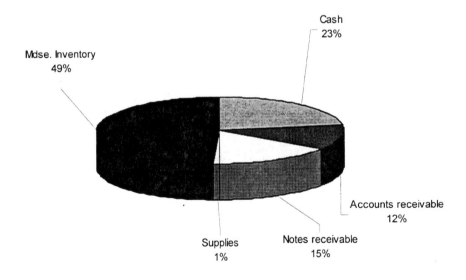

CHAPTER V

TAXES

Taxes in this chapter are limited to sales tax and property tax. (Payroll deductions for income tax and FICA taxes are included in Chapter VIII, Wages and Payrolls. However, the study of income tax for individuals or corporations was not included, as it was thought that neither could be covered sufficiently as a single unit of a business math course to be of any practical use.)

1.   Sales Taxes:

The computation of sales tax to be charged on a purchase is simple and will require little attention. The main objective for this topic is to teach the student to find the marked selling price when the sales tax and the tax rate are known (example 2); and to find the marked price when the total price (tax included) and the tax rate are known (example 3). Invariable, some students will try to solve example 3 by finding 6% of the total price and then subtracting to obtain the marked price. Explain that this is impossible, since the tax is 6% of $130 (the marked price), not 6% of $137.80 (the total price); and 6% of different numbers can never produce the same result (except with very small amounts about $2 or less). Be sure the student can work this problem by proper mathematical methods and do not accept only the answer. (If you use round numbers for your problems, the student may use the above "subtraction method" and then simply give as the answer the round number closest to what was obtained. Other students will select potential marked prices at random until they find the one which results in the correct total price.) This is one topic where the authors often make exception to the customary practice of using round numbers; here we frequently use marked prices containing cents -- but cents which result in a sales tax that comes out to the exact cent.

In discussing excise taxes (illustrated in example 4), you may wish to mention the following justifications for excise taxes: (1) the tax on luxury commodities primarily taxes those in upper-income brackets; (2) they discourage use of socially harmful commodities (alcohol and tobacco); (3) primary users help finance the expenditures they benefit from (gas and auto taxes to support highway construction); (4) excise taxes help curtail purchase of scarce products or imported products (as a protection for American industries). Excise taxes account for only about 4% of Federal budget receipts as compared with 48% for receipts of individual income taxes and 10% for corporate income taxes.

Most students are unaware of the use tax. However, all states that impose a sales tax also impose a use tax. The use tax is confined to the initial use of goods purchased from outside the state and brought into the state for use within the state. This tax is collected either (1) by the out-of-state vendor and sent to the state or (2) from the purchaser after bringing the item into the state. In some states, the use tax form is included with the state income tax form, and is payable during income tax time. Students would be interested to learn of their state's policy on payment of the use tax. Many states experience difficulty in collecting these taxes. Some state legislatures are considering legislation to tax all retail sales within the state regardless of the purchase's residency.

2.   **Property Tax**:

In discussing property taxes, stress the importance of assessed value (as opposed to market value) in calculating the tax. Your students would be interest to know the general policy followed in your locality for determining assessed value, as well as what the tax rate in you area is. Many localities are now using assessments that are supposedly 100% of market value, but this is still usually somewhat less than the selling prices actually being paid when real estate changes owners.

CHAPTER 5 - TAXES
PROBLEM SOLUTIONS

Section 1, page 98

1.

	Marked Price	Sales Tax Rate	Sales Tax	Total Price
(a)	$15.75	4%	$0.63	$16.38
(b)	66.00	8	5.28	71.28
(c)	32.50	6	1.95	34.45
(d)	41.00	5	2.05	43.05
(e)	58.00	6	3.48	61.48
(f)	24.00	7	1.68	25.68
(g)	36.00	8	2.88	38.88
(h)	87.00	5	4.35	91.35

1. (Continued)

(a)   4% · Price = Tax

    $0.04(\$15.75) =$

        $\$0.63 = T$

  $\$15.75 + \$0.63 =$ Total price

       $\$16.38 = TP$

(b) 8% · Price = Tax

    $0.08(\$66) =$

      $\$5.28 = T$

  $\$66.00 + \$5.28 =$ Total price

      $\$71.28 = TP$

(c) 6% · Price = Tax

    $0.06P = \$1.95$

       $P = \$32.50$

  $\$32.50 + \$1.95 =$ Total price

      $\$34.45 = TP$

(d) 5% · Price = Tax

    $0.05P = \$2.05$

       $P = \$41$

  $\$41.00 + \$2.05 =$ Total price

      $\$43.05 = TP$

(e) 6% · Price = Tax

    $0.06P = \$3.48$

       $P = \$58$

  $\$58.00 + \$3.48 =$ Total price

      $\$61.48 = TP$

(f) $P + 7\%P =$ Total price

    $1.07P = \$25.68$

       $P = \$24$

  $\$25.68 - \$24.00 =$ Tax

       $\$1.68 = T$

(g) $P + 8\%P =$ Total price

    $1.08P = \$38.88$

       $P = \$36$

  $\$38.88 - \$36.00 =$ Tax

      $\$2.88 = T$

(h) $P + 5\%P =$ Total price

    $1.05P = \$91.35$

       $P = \$87$

  $\$91.35 - \$87.00 =$ Tax

      $\$4.35 = T$

2.

	Marked Price	Sales Tax Rate	Sales Tax	Total Price
(a)	$83.00	5 %	$4.15	$87.15
(b)	12.00	4½	0.54	12.54
(c)	65.00	6	3.90	68.90
(d)	26.00	7	1.82	27.82
(e)	34.00	5½	1.87	35.87
(f)	43.00	8	3.44	46.44
(g)	94.00	6	5.64	99.64
(h)	47.00	9	4.23	51.23

2. (Continued)

(a) $5\% \cdot$ Price = Tax

   $0.05(\$83) =$

    $\$4.15 = T$

   $\$83.00 + \$4.15 =$ Total price

     $\$87.15 = TP$

(b) $4\tfrac{1}{2}\% \cdot$ Price = Tax

   $0.045(\$12) =$

    $\$0.54 = T$

   $\$12.00 + \$0.54 =$ Total price

     $\$12.54 = TP$

(c) $6\% \cdot$ Price = Tax

   $0.06P = \$3.90$

    $P = \$65$

   $\$65.00 + \$3.90 =$ Total price

     $\$68.90 = TP$

(d) $7\% \cdot$ Price = Tax

   $0.07P = \$1.82$

    $P = \$26$

   $\$26.00 + \$1.82 =$ Total price

     $\$27.82 = TP$

(e) $5.5\% \cdot$ Price = Tax

   $0.055P = \$1.87$

    $P = \$34$

   $\$34.00 + \$1.87 =$ Total price

     $\$35.87 = TP$

(f) $P + 8\%P =$ Total price

   $1.08P = \$46.44$

    $P = \$43$

   $\$46.44 - \$43.00 =$ Tax

     $\$3.44 = T$

(g) $P + 6\%P =$ Total price

   $1.06P = \$99.64$

    $P = \$94$

   $\$99.64 - \$94.00 =$ Tax

     $\$5.64 = T$

(h) $P + 9\%P =$ Total price

   $1.09P = \$51.23$

    $P = \$47$

   $\$51.23 - \$47.00 =$ Tax

     $\$4.23 = T$

3. $6\% \cdot$ Price = Tax

  $0.06(\$29) =$

   $\$1.74 = T$

  $\$29.00 + \$1.74 =$ Total price

    $\$30.74 = TP$

4. $5\% \cdot$ Price = Tax

  $0.05(\$98) =$

   $\$4.90 = T$

  $\$98.00 + \$4.90 =$ Total price

    $\$102.90 = TP$

5. 9% · Price = Tax
    0.09($310) =
    $27.90 = T

    $310.00 + $27.90 = Total price
    $337.90 = TP

6. 7% · Price = Tax
    0.07($220) =
    $15.40 = T

    $220.00 + $15.40 = Total price
    $235.40 = TP

7. (a) 6% · Price = Tax
         $0.06P = \$5.34$
         $P = \$89$

    (b) $89.00 + $5.34 = Total price
         $94.34 = TP

8. (a) 7% · Price = Tax
         $0.07P = \$5.53$
         $P = \$79$

    (b) $79.00 + $5.53 = Total price
         $84.53 = TP

9. (a) 15% · Price = Tax
         $0.15P = \$7.50$
         $P = \$50$

    (b) $50.00 + $7.50 = Total price
         $57.50 = TP

10. (a) 12% · Price = Tax
         $0.12P = \$30$
         $P = \$250$

    (b) $250 + $30 = Total price
         $280 = TP

11. (a) Price + 4.5% Price = Total price
         $1.045P = \$198.55$
         $P = \$190$

    (b) $198.55 - $190.00 - Tax
         $8.55 = T

12. (a) Price + 7% Price = Total price
         $1.07P = \$178.69$
         $P = \$167$

    (b) $178.69 - $167.00 = Tax
         $11.69 = T

13. (a) Price + 5% Price = Total price
         $1.05P = \$93.45$
         $P = \$89$

    (b) $93.45 - $89.00 = Tax
         $4.45 = T

14. (a) Price + 6.5% Price = Total price

$$1.065P = \$172.53$$

$$P = \$162$$

(b) $172.53 - $162.00 = Tax

$$\$10.53 = T$$

15. (a) Price + 6.5% Price = Total price

$$1.065P = \$66.03$$

$$P = \$62$$

(b) $66.03 - $62.00 = Tax

$$\$4.03 = T$$

16. (a) Price + 8% Price = Total price

$$1.08P = \$156.60$$

$$P = \$145$$

(b) $156.60 - $145.00 = Tax

$$\$11.60 = T$$

17. (a) Price + 8% Price = Total price

$$1.08P = \$93.96$$

$$P = \$87$$

(b) $93.96 - $87.00 = Tax

$$\$6.96 = T$$

18. (a) Price + 6% Price = Total price

$$1.06P = \$284.08$$

$$P = \$268$$

(b) $284.08 - $268.00 = Tax

$$\$16.08 = T$$

19. (a) Price + 5% Price + 15% Price = Total price

$$1.20P = \$15.60$$

$$P = \$13$$

(b) 5% · Price = Sales tax

$$0.05(\$13) =$$

$$\$0.65 = ST$$

(c) 15% · Price = Excise tax

$$0.15(\$13) =$$

$$\$1.95 = ET$$

20. (a) Price + 6% Price + 10% Price = Total price

$$1.16P = \$58$$

$$P = \$50$$

20. (Continued)

    (b) 6% · Price = Sales tax

$$0.06(\$50) =$$
$$\$3 = ST$$

    (c) 10% · Price = Excise tax

$$0.01(\$50) =$$
$$\$5 = ET$$

21. (a) Price + 7% Price + 13% Price = Total price

$$1.20 P = \$84$$
$$P = \$70$$

    (b) 7% · Price = Sales tax

$$0.07(\$70) =$$
$$\$4.90 = ST$$

    (c) 13% · Price = Import tax

$$0.13(\$70) =$$
$$\$9.10 = IT$$

22. (a) Price + 6% Price + 12% Price = Total price

$$1.18 P = \$495.60$$
$$P = \$420$$

    (b) 6% · Price = Sales tax

$$0.06(\$420) =$$
$$\$25.20 = ST$$

    (c) 12% · Price = Excise tax

$$0.12(\$420) =$$
$$\$50.40 = ET$$

23. (a) Price + 6% Price + 12% Price = Total price

$$1.18(\$25,000) =$$
$$\$29,500 = TP$$

    (b) 6% · Price = Sales tax

$$0.06(\$25,000) =$$
$$\$1,500 = ST$$

    (c) 12% · Price = Import tax

$$0.12(\$25,000) =$$
$$\$3,000 = IT$$

24. (a) Price + 7% Price + 10% Price = Total price

$$1.17(\$37,000) =$$
$$\$43,290 = TP$$

    (b) 7% · Price = Sales tax

$$0.07(\$37,000) =$$
$$\$2,590 = ST$$

    (c) 10% · Price = Import tax

$$0.10(\$37,000) =$$
$$\$3,700 = IT$$

Section 2, page 104

1. (a) 1.85%
    (b) $1.85 per C
    (c) $18.45 per M
    (d) 19 mills

2. (a) 2.25%
    (b) $2.25 per C
    (c) $22.47 per M
    (d) 23 mills

3. (a) 1.93%
    (b) $1.93 per C
    (c) $19.24 per M
    (d) 20 mills

4. (a) 1.41%
    (b) $1.41 per C
    (c) $14.07 per M
    (d) 15 mills

5. Rate $= \dfrac{\$24,000,000}{\$980,000,000} = 0.0244897+$

    (a) 2.5%   (b) $2.45 per C   (c) $24.49 per M   (d) 25 mills

6. Rate $= \dfrac{\$23,000,000}{\$660,000,000} = 0.034848+$

    (a) 3.5%   (b) $3.49 per C   (c) $34.85 per M   (d) 35 mills

7.

	Rate	Assessed Value	Tax
(a)	2.8%	$94,000	$2,632
(b)	$1.25 per C	59,200	740
(c)	$12.40 per M	75,000	930
(d)	2.1%	50,000	1,050
(e)	$2.60 per C	68,000	1,768
(f)	$18.80 per M	65,000	1,222
(g)	1.4%	82,000	1,148
(h)	$3.20 per C	74,500	2,384
(i)	$9.60 per M	95,000	912

(a) R = 2.8%   R × V = T
     V = $94,000   2.8% × $94,000 =
     T = ? $2,632 = T

(b) R = $1.25 per C   R × V = T
     V = $59,200 $1.25 × $59,200 =
       = 592 hundred $740 = T
     T = ?

7. (Continued)

(c) R = $12.40 per M   R × V = T
     V = $75,000 $12.40 × $75 =
       = 75 thousand $930 = T
     T = ?

(d) R = 2.1%   R × V = T
     V = ?   2.1%V = $1,050
     T = $1,050   V = $50,000

(e) R = $2.60 per C   R × V = T
     V = ? $2.60V = $1,768
     T = $1,768   V = 680 hundred
                                 V = $68,000

(f) R = $18.80 per M   R × V = T
     V = ? $18.80V = $1,222
     T = $1,222   V = 65 thousand
                                 V = $65,000

(g) R = ?%   R × V = T
     V = $82,000   R × $82,000 = $1,148
     T = $1,148   R = 0.014 = 1.4%

(h) R = ? per M   R × V = T
     V = $74,500   R × $745 = $2,384
       = 745 hundred   R = $3.20 per C
     T = $2,384

(i) R = ? per M   R × V = T
     V = $95,000   R × $95 = $912
       = 95 thousand   R = $9.60 per M
     T = $912

8.

	Rate	Assessed Value	Tax
(a)	1.8%	$ 75,000	$ 1,350
(b)	$2.10 per C	88,000	1,848
(c)	$11.20 per M	65,000	728
(d)	2.4%	94,000	2,256
(e)	$1.15 per C	120,000	1,380
(f)	$15.30 per M	200,000	3,060
(g)	1.75%	600,000	10,500
(h)	$1.50 per C	45,000	675
(i)	$13 per M	540,000	7,020

8. (Continued)

    (a) R = 1.8%   R × V = T
        V = $75,000   0.018 × $75,000 =
        T = ? $1,350 = T

    (b) R = $2.10 per C   R × V = T
        V = $88,000 $2.10 × $88,000 =
          = 880 hundred $1,848 = T
        T = ?

    (c) R = $11.20 per M   R × V = T
        V = $65,000 $11.20 × $65 =
          = 65 thousand $728 = T
        T = ?

    (d) R = 2.4%   R × V = T
        V = ?   0.024V = $2,256
        T = $2,256   V = $94,000

    (e) R = $1.15 per C   R × V = T
        V = ? $1.15V = $1,380
        T = $1,380   V = 1200 hundred
                                  V = $120,000

    (f) R = $15.30 per M   R × V = T
        V = ? $15.30V = $3,060
        T = $3,060   V = 200 thousand
                                    V = $200,000

    (g) R = ?%   R × V = T
        V = $600,000   R × $600,000 = $10,500
        T = $10,500   R = 0.0175 = 1.75%

    (h) R = ? per C   R × V = T
        V = $45,000   R × $450 = $675
          = 450 hundred   R = $1.50 per C
        T = $675

    (i) R = ? per M   R × V = T
        V = $540,000   R × $540 = $7,020
          = 540 thousand   R = $13 per M
        T = $7,020

9. R = 1.8%   R × V = T
    V = $35,000   0.018 × $35,000 =
    T = ? $630 = T

10. R = 2.8%
    V = $85,000
    T = ?

    R × V = T
    0.028 × $85,000 =
    $2,380 = T

11. R = $2.05 per C
    V = $90,000
      = 900 hundred
    T = ?

    R × V = T
    $2.05 × $900 =
    $1,845 = T

12. R = $1.12 per C
    V = $130,000
    T = 1300 hundred
    T = ?

    R × V = T
    $1.12 × $1,300 =
    $1,456 = T

13. R = $1.95 per C
    V = ?
    T = $429

    R × V = T
    $1.95V = $429
        V = 220 hundred
        V = $22,000

14. R = $1.85 per C
    V = ?
    T = $1,702

    R × V = T
    $1.85V = $1,702
        V = 920 hundred
        V = $92,000

15. R = $12.75 per M
    V = ?
    T = $918

    R × V = T
    $12.75V = $918
        V = 72 thousand
        V = $72,000

16. R = $9.45 per M
    V = ?
    T = $4,725

    R × V = T
    9.45V = $4,725
        V = 500 thousand
        V = $500,000

17. R = ?%
    V = $84,000
    T = $2,016

    R × V = T
    R × $84,000 = $2,016
        R = 0.024 = 2.4%

18. R = ?%
    V = $267,000
    T = $4,806

    R × V = T
    R × $267,000 = $4,806
        R = 0.018
        R = 1.8%

19. R = ? mills   R × V = T
     V = $35,000   R × $35 = $525
       = 35 thousand   R = 15 mills
     T = $525

20. R = ? mills   R × V = T
     V = $600,000   R × $600,000 = $10,800
     T = $10,800   R = 0.018
                                                   R = 18 mills

21. R = ? per C   R × V = T
     V = $180,000   R × $1,800 = $3,960
       = 1800 hundred   R = $2.20 per C
     T = $3,960

22. R = ? per C   R × V = T
     V = $98,000   R × $980 = $1,666
       = 980 hundred   R = $1.70 per C
     T = $1,666

23. First Year
     R = ? per C   R × V = T
     V = $95,000   R × $950 = $1,349
       = 950 hundred   R = $1.42 per C
     T = $1,349

     Second Year
     R = $1.50 per C ($1.42 + $0.08)   R × V = T
     V = ? $1.50V = $1,434
     T = $1,434   V = 956 hundred
                                                V = $95,600

     Increase in value = $95,600 - $95,000 = $600

24. First Year
     R = ? per C   R × V = T
     V = $800,000   R × $8,000 = $10,560
       = 8000 hundred   R = $1.32 per C
     T = $10,560

     Second Year
     R = $1.42 per C ($1.32 + $0.10)   R × V = T
     V = ? $1.42V = $11,644
     T = $11,644   V = 8200 hundred
                                                V = $820,000

24. (Continued)

    Increase in value = $820,000 - $800,000 = $20,000

25. <u>First Year</u>
    R = 1.3%   R × V = T
    V = ?   1.3%V = $390
    T = $390   V = $30,000

    Second year value = $30,000 + $4,000 = $34,000

    <u>Second Year</u>
    R = ?%   R × V = T
    V = $34,000   R × $34,000 = $544
    T = $544   R = 0.016 = 1.6%

26. <u>First Year</u>
    R = 1.6%   R × V = T
    V = ?   0.016V = $5,440
    T = $5,440   V = $340,000

    <u>Second Year</u>
    R = ?%   R × V = T
    V = $341,000 ($340,000 + $1,000)   R × $341,000 = $5,797
    T = $5,797   R = 0.017
                                                  R = 1.7%

CHAPTER VI

INSURANCE

Insurance rates vary greatly from locality to locality and from company to company, according to the special features of various policies. However, it was thought that business students should gain some knowledge of how premiums are computed for the major types of insurance.

1.   Business Insurance:

The authors did not feel that the computation of premiums for various types of business insurance differed greatly enough to justify separate study. Therefore, the other major forms of business insurance are merely discussed, and principal attention is given to fire insurance.

Example 4 illustrates the distribution of loss between the carrier and the insured when the coinsurance clause is not met. Actually, some insurance agents will not even write a fire policy unless the required level of coverage is purchased.

Multiple carriers, both when coinsurance requirements are met (example 5) and not met (example 6) could be omitted from a basic course.

2.   Motor Vehicle Insurance

This topic would be of particular interest to those students who own cars. However, the instructor may wish to omit automobile insurance from basic courses because it involves so many variables -- the age of the driver and the amount of driving done (as well as sex and marital status, for younger drivers), the territory in which the driver lives, and the make and age of the automobile, as well as the amount of insurance that is purchased. An alternative would be to assign this topic as a reading assignment only (without problems), in order that the student might gain at least some idea of the factors influencing automobile insurance.

Table 6-3 (Driver Classifications) contains multiples only for drivers with satisfactory driving records. Drivers who have been involved in accidents or received citations for moving violations would be classified in other tables containing higher multiples. (Many companies and insurance boards issue tables of actual rates, rather than using driver multiples. These multiples produce similar rates, however, and emphasize to the student the wide differences in rates associated with various driver classifications.) Due to rising claims, some companies are no longer accepting new policyholders, even with good driving records; however, regulations in some states may require all companies to share responsibility for insuring a pool of drivers who are poor risks.

Inform your students how much minimum liability insurance is required in your state. This information may be obtained from the state board of insurance or from a local insurance agent. Be certain the student realizes that liability insurance protects only the other driver when a person is at fault; if a driver is at fault in an accident, his/her own car is insured only if collision insurance is carried.

3. Life Insurance

Life insurance is considered a necessity by the large majority of Americans. Thus, this topic serves, not to convince students of its necessity, but to familiarize them with the principal kinds of coverage available and their relative costs. The American Council of Life Insurance (1001 Pennsylvania Ave., NW, Washington, DC 20004-2599) publishes a number of interesting and informative booklets about life insurance, most of which are available free in single copies to educators. You may write for their catalog of publications and audio-visual aids. Of particular interest may be the annual Fact Book of Life Insurance (along with its alternating Fact Book Update), which gives the latest nationwide figures concerning all types of life insurance. You may wish to visit or have your students visit the Internet site: www.insure.com. Various consumer terms and issues are defined and discussed here.

The annual premiums shown in Table 6-7 are not those of any particular company, but attempt to approximate average rates. It is difficult to compare premium rates of different companies, because their policies may include different special features, as well as differences in nonforfeiture values. Be sure your students realize that premium cost alone is not the only thing they should consider when purchasing life insurance.

The section on settlement options is less important, since most policy benefits are taken in lump-sum payments. Therefore, the instructor may wish to omit this section from basic courses.

CHAPTER 6 - INSURANCE
PROBLEM SOLUTIONS

Section 1, page 118

		Structure Value	Contents Value	Class	Territory	Premium
1.	(a)	$350,000	$64,000	B	1	$2,466
	(b)	580,000	78,000	A	2	3,894
2.	(a)	$575,000	$82,000	C	1	$4,443
	(b)	840,000	55,000	D	3	8,428

1. (a) $0.56 \times \$3,500 = \$1,960.00$ Structure
$0.79 \times \$\ \ \ 640 = \underline{\ \ \ \ \ 505.60}$ Contents
$\$2,465.60$
or $2,466 Total

(b) $0.58 \times \$5,800 = \$3,364.00$ Structure
$0.68 \times \$\ \ \ 780 = \underline{\ \ \ \ \ 530.40}$ Contents
$\$3,894.40$
or $3,894 Total

2. (a) $0.66 \times \$5,750 = \$3,795.00$ Structure
$0.79 \times \$\ \ \ 820 = \underline{\ \ \ \ \ 647.80}$ Contents
$\$4,442.80$
or $4,443 Total

(b) $0.93 \times \$8,400 = \$7,812.00$ Structure
$1.12 \times \$\ \ \ 550 = \underline{\ \ \ \ \ 616.00}$ Contents
$\$8,428.00$ Total

		Amount of Insurance	Term	Canceled By	Premium	Refund Due
3.	(a)	$ 290,000	1 year	X	$2,262	X
	(b)	770,000	6 months	X	4,204	X
	(c)	830,000	9 months	Insured	5,503	$ 971
	(d)	1,500,000	4 months	Carrier	3,900	7,800

(a) $0.78 \times \$2,900 = \$2,262$ Annual premium

(b) $0.78 \times \$7,700 = \$6,006$ Annual premium
For a 6 month policy: $70\% \times \$6,006 = \$4,204$

3. (Continued)

(c) 0.78 × $8,300 = $6,474 Annual premium
Canceled by insured 9 months:
85% × $6,474 = $5,502.90 or $5,503 Premium

Refund = $6,474 - $5,503 = $971

(d) 0.78 × $15,000 = $11,700 Annual premium
Canceled by carrier after 4 months:

$$\frac{4}{12} \times \$11,700 = \$3,900 \text{ Premium}$$

Refund = $11,700 - $3,900 = $7,800

		Amount of Insurance	Term	Canceled By	Premium	Refund Due
4.	(a)	$ 260,000	1 year	X	$ 2,028	X
	(b)	590,000	3 months	X	1,841	X
	(c)	720,000	7 months	Insured	4,212	$1,404
	(d)	2,800,000	10 months	Carrier	18,200	3,640

(a) 0.78 × $2,600 = $2,028 Annual premium

(b) 0.78 × $5,900 = $4,602 Annual premium
For a 3-month policy: 40% × $4,602 = $1,840.80 or $1,841

(c) 0.78 × $7,200 = $5,616 Annual premium
Canceled by insured after 7 months:
75% × $5,616 = $4,212 Premium

Refund = $5,616 - $4,212 = $1,404

(d) 0.78 × $28,000 = $21,840 Annual premium
Canceled by carrier after 10 months:

$$\frac{5}{6} \times \$21,840 = \$18,200 \text{ Premium}$$

Refund = $21,840 - $18,200 = $3,640

5.

	Property Value	Coins. Clause	Insurance Required	Insurance Carried	Amount of Loss	Indemnity
(a)	$ 500,000	80%	$400,000	$200,000	$250,000	$125,000
(b)	440,000	80	352,000	352,000	90,000	90,000
(c)	600,000	90	540,000	450,000	420,000	350,000
(d)	900,000	80	720,000	600,000	780,000	600,000
(e)	1,000,000	80	800,000	700,000	950,000	700,000

(a) Insurance required = 80% × $500,000 = $400,000

$$\frac{\text{Insurance carried}}{\text{Insurance required}} = \frac{\$200,000}{\$400,000} = \frac{1}{2}$$

$\frac{1}{2}$ × $250,000 = $125,000 Indemnity

(b) Insurance required = 80% × $440,000 = $352,000
Since insurance carried equals insurance required, $90,000 is fully covered.

(c) Insurance required = 90% × $600,000 = $540,000

$$\frac{\text{Insurance carried}}{\text{Insurance required}} = \frac{\$450,000}{\$540,000} = \frac{5}{6}$$

$\frac{5}{6}$ × $420,000 = $350,000 Indemnity

(d) Insurance required = 80% × $900,000 = $720,000

$$\frac{\text{Insurance carried}}{\text{Insurance required}} = \frac{\$600,000}{\$720,000} = \frac{5}{6}$$

$\frac{5}{6}$ × $780,000 = $650,000, which exceeds the amount of

insurance carried ($600,000) so compensation will be limited to $600,000.

(e) Insurance required = 80% × $1,000,000 = $800,000

$$\frac{\text{Insurance carried}}{\text{Insurance required}} = \frac{\$700,000}{\$800,000} = \frac{7}{8}$$

$\frac{7}{8}$ × $950,000 = $831,250, which exceeds the amount of

insurance carried ($700,000) so compensation will be limited to $700,000.

6.

	Property Value	Coins. Clause	Insurance Required	Insurance Carried	Amount of Loss	Indemnity
(a)	$ 300,000	80%	$ 240,000	$200,000	$ 180,000	$150,000
(b)	750,000	90	675,000	500,000	135,000	100,000
(c)	600,000	90	540,000	360,000	450,000	300,000
(d)	400,000	80	320,000	300,000	380,000	300,000
(e)	1,500,000	80	1,200,000	900,000	1,500,000	900,000

(a) Insurance required = 80% × $300,000 = $240,000

$$\frac{\text{Insurance carried}}{\text{Insurance required}} = \frac{\$200,000}{\$240,000} = \frac{5}{6}$$

$\frac{5}{6}$ × $180,000 = $150,000 Indemnity

(b) Insurance required = 90% × $750,000 = $675,000

$$\frac{\text{Insurance carried}}{\text{Insurance required}} = \frac{\$500,000}{\$675,000} = \frac{20}{27}$$

$\frac{20}{27}$ × $135,000 = $100,000 Indemnity

(c) Insurance required = 90% × $600,000 = $540,000

$$\frac{\text{Insurance carried}}{\text{Insurance required}} = \frac{\$360,000}{\$540,000} = \frac{2}{3}$$

$\frac{2}{3}$ × $450,000 = $300,000 Indemnity

(d) Insurance required = 80% × $400,000 = $320,000

$$\frac{\text{Insurance carried}}{\text{Insurance required}} = \frac{\$300,000}{\$320,000} = \frac{15}{16}$$

$\frac{15}{16}$ × $380,000 = $356,250, which exceeds the amount of

insurance carried ($300,000) so indemnity will be $300,000.

(e) Insurance required = 80% × $1,500,000 = $1,200,000

$$\frac{\text{Insurance carried}}{\text{Insurance required}} = \frac{\$900,000}{\$1,200,000} = \frac{3}{4}$$

6. (e) (Continued)

$\frac{3}{4}$ × \$1,500,000 = \$1,125,000, which exceeds the amount of insurance carried (\$900,000) so indemnity will be \$900,000.

	Company	Amount of Policy	Ratio of Coverage	Amount of Loss	Compensation
7. (a)	N	\$440,000	22/53	\$477,000	\$198,000
	O	620,000	31/53		279,000
(b)	I	\$750,000	15/28	\$840,000	\$450,000
	N	400,000	2/7		240,000
	S	250,000	5/28		150,000

(a) Total coverage = \$440,000 + \$620,000 = \$1,060,000

N pays $\frac{\$440,000}{\$1,060,000} = \frac{22}{53}$; $\frac{22}{53}$ × \$477,000 = \$198,000

O pays $\frac{\$620,000}{\$1,060,000} = \frac{31}{53}$; $\frac{31}{53}$ × \$477,000 = $\underline{\$279,000}$
$\qquad\qquad\qquad\qquad\qquad\qquad\qquad$ \$477,000

(b) Total coverage = \$750,000 + \$400,000 + \$250,000
$\qquad\qquad\qquad$ = \$1,400,000

I pays $\frac{\$750,000}{\$1,400,000} = \frac{15}{28}$; $\frac{15}{28}$ × \$840,000 = \$450,000

N pays $\frac{\$400,000}{\$1,400,000} = \frac{2}{7}$; $\frac{2}{7}$ × \$840,000 = \$240,000

S pays $\frac{\$250,000}{\$1,400,000} = \frac{5}{28}$; $\frac{5}{28}$ × \$840,000 = $\underline{\$150,000}$
$\qquad\qquad\qquad\qquad\qquad\qquad\qquad$ \$840,000

	Company	Amount of Policy	Ratio of Coverage	Amount of Loss	Compensation
8. (a)	A	\$200,000	2/7	\$140,000	\$ 40,000
	T	500,000	5/7		100,000
(b)	R	\$ 90,000	9/24	\$120,000	\$ 45,000
	I	62,000	31/120		31,000
	S	50,000	5/24		25,000
	K	38,000	19/20		19,000

8. (Continued)

(a) Total coverage = $200,000 + $500,000 = $700,000

A pays $\dfrac{\$200,000}{\$700,000} = \dfrac{2}{7}$; $\dfrac{2}{7} \times \$140,000 = \$ 40,000$

T pays $\dfrac{\$500,000}{\$700,000} = \dfrac{5}{7}$; $\dfrac{5}{7} \times \$140,000 = \dfrac{\$100,000}{\$140,000}$

(b) Total coverage = $90,000 + $62,000 + $50,000 + $38,000
        = $240,000

R pays $\dfrac{\$90,000}{\$240,000} = \dfrac{3}{8}$; $\dfrac{3}{8} \times \$120,000 = \$ 45,000$

I pays $\dfrac{\$62,000}{\$240,000} = \dfrac{31}{120}$; $\dfrac{31}{120} \times \$120,000 = \$ 31,000$

S pays $\dfrac{\$50,000}{\$240,000} = \dfrac{5}{24}$; $\dfrac{5}{24} \times \$120,000 = \$ 25,000$

K pays $\dfrac{\$38,000}{\$240,000} = \dfrac{19}{120}$; $\dfrac{19}{120} \times \$120,000 = \dfrac{\$ 19,000}{\$120,000}$

	Property Value	Coins. Clause	Ins. Req.	Ins. Carried	Fire Loss
9. (a)	$600,000	80%	$480,000	$320,000	$450,000
(b)	800,000	70	560,000	480,000	770,000

(continued)

	Total Indemnity	Policy Co. Value	Co's Ratio	Co's Payment
(a)	$300,000	I $200,000	5/8	$187,500
		J 120,000	3/8	112,500
(b)	660,000	K 280,000	7/12	385,000
		L 200,000	5/12	275,000

(a) Insurance required = 80% × $600,000 = $480,000
    Insurance carried = $200,000 + $120,000 = $320,000

$\dfrac{\text{Insurance carried}}{\text{Insurance required}} = \dfrac{\$320,000}{\$480,000} = \dfrac{2}{3}$

9. (a) (Continued)

$$\frac{2}{3} \times \$450,000 = \$300,000 \text{ Total indemnity}$$

I pays $\dfrac{\$200,000}{\$320,000} = \dfrac{5}{8}$; $\dfrac{5}{8} \times \$300,000 = \$187,500$

J pays $\dfrac{\$120,000}{\$320,000} = \dfrac{3}{8}$; $\dfrac{3}{8} \times \$300,000 = \underline{\$112,500}$
$\$300,000$

(b) Insurance required = 70% × $800,000 = $560,000
Insurance carried = $280,000 + $200,000 = $480,000

$$\frac{\text{Insurance carried}}{\text{Insurance required}} = \frac{\$480,000}{\$560,000} = \frac{6}{7}$$

$$\frac{6}{7} \times \$770,000 = \$660,000 \text{ Total indemnity}$$

K pays $\dfrac{\$280,000}{\$480,000} = \dfrac{7}{12}$; $\dfrac{7}{12} \times \$660,000 = \$385,000$

L pays $\dfrac{\$200,000}{\$480,000} = \dfrac{5}{12}$; $\dfrac{5}{12} \times \$660,000 = \underline{\$275,000}$
$\$660,000$

		Property Value	Coins. Clause	Ins. Req.	Ins. Carried	Fire Loss
10.	(a)	$900,000	80%	$720,000	$640,000	$450,000
	(b)	350,000	90	315,000	250,000	189,000

(continued)

		Total Indemnity	Policy Co. Value		Co's Ratio	Co's Payment
	(a)	$400,000	M	$240,000	3/8	$150,000
			N	400,000	5/8	250,000
	(b)	150,000	O	150,000	3/5	90,000
			P	100,000	2/5	60,000

(a) Insurance required = 80% × $900,000 = $720,000
Insurance carried = $240,000 + $400,000 = $640,000

10. (a) (Continued)

$$\frac{\text{Insurance carried}}{\text{Insurance required}} = \frac{\$640,000}{\$720,000} = \frac{8}{9};$$

$$\frac{8}{9} \times \$450,000 = \$400,000 \text{ Total indemnity}$$

M pays $\dfrac{\$240,000}{\$640,000} = \dfrac{3}{8}; \dfrac{3}{8} \times \$400,000 = \$150,000$

N pays $\dfrac{\$400,000}{\$640,000} = \dfrac{5}{8}; \dfrac{5}{8} \times \$400,000 = \$250,000$

(b) Insurance required = 90% × $350,000 = $315,000
Insurance carried = $150,000 + $100,000 = $250,000

$$\frac{\text{Insurance carried}}{\text{Insurance required}} = \frac{\$250,000}{\$315,000} = \frac{50}{63};$$

$$\frac{50}{63} \times \$189,000 = \$150,000 \text{ Total indemnity}$$

O pays $\dfrac{\$150,000}{\$250,000} = \dfrac{3}{5}; \dfrac{3}{5} \times \$150,000 = \$ 90,000$

P pays $\dfrac{\$100,000}{\$250,000} = \dfrac{2}{5}; \dfrac{2}{5} \times \$150,000 = \$ 60,000$

11. R = $0.60 per $100   P = R · V
    V = $180,000   = $0.60 × $1,800
      = $1,800 hundreds   P = $1,080
    P = ? (3 months)
                                  40% × $1,080 = $432 (3 months)

12. R = $0.82 per $100   P = R · V
    V = $370,000   = $0.82 × $3,700
      = $3,700 hundreds   P = $3,034
    P = ? (6 months)
                                  70% × $3,034 = $2,123.8 so
                                              = $2,124 (6 months)

13. R = $0.90 per $100   P = R · V
    V = $630,000   = $0.90 × $6,300
      = $6,300 hundreds   P = $5,670
    P = ?

13. (Continued)

   (a) Canceled by the insured:
       60% × $5,670 = $3,402 Premium
       $5,670 - $3,402 = $2,268 Refund

   (b) Canceled by the insured:

       $\frac{5}{12}$ × $5,670 = $2,363 Premium

       $5,670 - $2,363 = $3,307 Refund

14. R = $1.05 per $100   P = R · V
    V = $1,800,000   = $1.05 × $18,000
      = $18,000 hundreds   P = $18,900
    P = ? (8 months)

   (a) Canceled by the insurer:
       80% × $18,900 = $15,120 Premium
       $18,900 - $15,120 = $3,780 Refund

   (b) Canceled by the carrier:

       $\frac{8}{12}$ = $\frac{2}{3}$ × $18,900 = $12,600 Premium

       $18,900 - $12,600 = $6,300 Refund

15. Insurance required = 80% × $680,000 = $544,000
    Insurance carried = $600,000 (which exceeds insurance
    required)

   (a) $80,000
   (b) $500,000
   (c) $600,000

16. Insurance required = 90% × $2,000,000 = $1,800,000
    Insurance carried = $1,900,000 (which exceeds insurance
    required)

   (a) $50,000
   (b) $800,000
   (c) $1,900,000

17. Insurance required = 90% × $5,000,000 = $4,500,000

$$\frac{\text{Insurance carried}}{\text{Insurance required}} = \frac{\$3,500,000}{\$4,500,000} = \frac{7}{9}$$

(a) Indemnity = $\frac{7}{9}$ × $36,000 = $28,000

(b) Indemnity = $\frac{7}{9}$ × $2,700,000 = $2,100,000

(c) Indemnity = $3,500,000 (Maximum = face value)

18. Insurance required = 80% × $1,000,000 = $800,000

$$\frac{\text{Insurance carried}}{\text{Insurance required}} = \frac{\$700,000}{\$800,000} = \frac{7}{8}$$

(a) Indemnity = $\frac{7}{8}$ × $180,000 = $157,500

(b) Indemnity = $\frac{7}{8}$ × $600,000 = $525,000

(c) Indemnity = $700,000 (Maximum = face value)

19. Insurance required = 90% × $300,000 = $270,000

$$\frac{\text{Insurance carried}}{\text{Insurance required}} = \frac{\$240,000}{\$270,000} = \frac{8}{9}$$

(a) Indemnity = $\frac{8}{9}$ × $81,000 = $72,000

(b) Indemnity = $\frac{8}{9}$ × $189,000 = $168,000

(c) Indemnity = $240,000 (Maximum = face value)

20. Insurance required = 90% × $620,000 = $558,000

$$\frac{\text{Insurance carried}}{\text{Insurance required}} = \frac{\$500,000}{\$558,000} = \frac{250}{279}$$

(a) Indemnity = $\frac{500}{558}$ × $11,160 = $10,000

20. (Continued)

    (b) Indemnity $= \dfrac{250}{279} \times \$223,200 = \$200,000$

    (c) Indemnity $= \dfrac{250}{279} \times \$600,000 = \$537,634$ (which exceeds

       insurance carried; so maximum is $500,000.)

21. Total insurance = \$240,000 + \$340,000 + \$420,000 = \$1,000,000

    A pays $\dfrac{\$240,000}{\$1,000,000} = \dfrac{6}{25}$ or 24%

    B pays $\dfrac{\$340,000}{\$1,000,000} = \dfrac{17}{50}$ or 34%

    C pays $\dfrac{\$420,000}{\$1,000,000} = \dfrac{21}{50}$ or 42%

    (a) A = 24% × \$50,000 = \$12,000
        B = 34% × \$50,000 = \$17,000
        C = 42% × \$50,000 = <u>\$21,000</u>
                                 \$50,000

    (b) A = 24% × \$900,000 = \$216,000
        B = 34% × \$900,000 = \$306,000
        C = 42% × \$900,000 = <u>\$378,000</u>
                                 \$900,000

    (c) A = 24% × \$1,000,000 = \$ 240,000
        B = 34% × \$1,000,000 = \$ 340,000
        C = 42% × \$1,000,000 = <u>\$ 420,000</u>
                                 \$1,000,000

22. Total insurance = \$550,000 + \$410,000 + \$640,000 = \$1,600,000

    Dee pays $= \dfrac{\$550,000}{\$1,600,000} = \dfrac{11}{32}$ or 34.375%

    Fee pays $= \dfrac{\$410,000}{\$1,600,000} = \dfrac{41}{160}$ or 25.625%

    Gee pays $= \dfrac{\$640,000}{\$1,600,000} = \dfrac{2}{5}$ or 40%

22. (Continued)

    (a) Dee = 34.375% × \$256,000 = \$ 88,000

        Fee = 25.625% × \$256,000 = \$ 65,600

        Gee = 40%   × \$256,000 = <u>\$102,400</u>
                                          \$256,000

    (b) Dee = 34.375% × \$384,000 = \$132,000

        Fee = 25.625% × \$384,000 = \$ 98,400

        Gee = 40%   × \$384,000 = <u>\$153,600</u>
                                          \$384,000

    (c) Dee = 34.375% × \$1,600,000 = \$ 550,000

        Fee = 25.625% × \$1,600,000 = \$ 410,000

        Gee = 40%   × \$1,600,000 = <u>\$ 640,000</u>
                                         \$1,600,000

23. Insurance carried = \$300,000 + \$350,000 + \$250,000 + \$100,000
                               = \$1,000,000

AA pays $\dfrac{\$300,000}{\$1,000,000} = \dfrac{3}{10}$ or 30%

BB pays $\dfrac{\$350,000}{\$1,000,000} = \dfrac{35}{100}$ or 35%

CC pays $\dfrac{\$250,000}{\$1,000,000} = \dfrac{25}{100}$ or 25%

DD pays $\dfrac{\$100,000}{\$1,000,000} = \dfrac{1}{10}$ or 10%

    (a) AA = 30% × \$72,000 = \$21,600
        BB = 35% × \$72,000 = \$25,200
        CC = 25% × \$72,000 = \$18,000
        DD = 10% × \$72,000 = <u>\$ 7,200</u>
                              \$72,000

    (b) AA = 30% × \$600,000 = \$180,000
        BB = 35% × \$600,000 = \$210,000
        CC = 25% × \$600,000 = \$150,000
        DD = 10% × \$600,000 = <u>\$ 60,000</u>
                              \$600,000

23. (Continued)

   (c) AA = 30% × $1,000,000 = $ 300,000
         BB = 35% × $1,000,000 = $ 350,000
         CC = 25% × $1,000,000 = $ 250,000
         DD = 10% × $1,000,000 = $ 100,000
                                       $1,000,000

24. Insurance carried = $200,000 + $280,000 + $320,000 + $350,000
                         = $1,150,000

U pays $\dfrac{\$200,000}{\$1,150,000} = \dfrac{4}{23}$

V pays $\dfrac{\$280,000}{\$1,150,000} = \dfrac{28}{115}$

W pays $\dfrac{\$320,000}{\$1,150,000} = \dfrac{32}{115}$

X pays $\dfrac{\$350,000}{\$1,150,000} = \dfrac{7}{23}$

 (a) U pays $= \dfrac{4}{23} \times \$920,000 = \$16,000$

       V pays $= \dfrac{28}{115} \times \$920,000 = \$22,400$

       W pays $= \dfrac{32}{115} \times \$920,000 = \$25,600$

       X pays $= \dfrac{7}{23} \times \$920,000 = \underline{\$28,000}$
                                      $92,000

 (b) U pays $= \dfrac{4}{23} \times \$207,000 = \$\ 36,000$

       V pays $= \dfrac{28}{115} \times \$207,000 = \$\ 50,400$

       W pays $= \dfrac{32}{115} \times \$207,000 = \$\ 57,600$

       X pays $= \dfrac{7}{23} \times \$207,000 = \underline{\$\ 63,000}$
                                      $207,000

24. (Continued)

(c) U pays = $\dfrac{4}{23}$ × \$1,150,000 = \$ 200,000

V pays = $\dfrac{28}{115}$ × \$1,150,000 = \$ 280,000

W pays = $\dfrac{32}{115}$ × \$1,150,000 = \$ 320,000

X pays = $\dfrac{7}{23}$ × \$1,150,000 = $\underline{\underline{\text{\$ 350,000}}}$
$\qquad\qquad\qquad\qquad\qquad\qquad\qquad\quad$ \$1,150,000

25. (a) Insurance required = 80% × \$2,500,000 = \$2,000,000
Insurance carried = \$700,000 + \$800,000 = \$1,500,000

$\dfrac{\text{Insurance carried}}{\text{Insurance required}} = \dfrac{\$1,500,000}{\$2,000,000} = \dfrac{3}{4}$

$\dfrac{3}{4}$ × \$2,200,000 = \$1,650,000 (Exceeds total face value so

\$1,500,000 is total indemnity paid.)

(b) American = $\dfrac{\$700,000}{\$1,500,000} = \dfrac{7}{15}$ × \$1,500,000 = \$700,000

Liberty = $\dfrac{\$800,000}{\$1,500,000} = \dfrac{8}{15}$ × \$1,500,000 = \$800,000

26. (a) Insurance required = 90% × \$3,000,000 = \$2,700,000
Insurance carried = \$1,000,000 + \$1,100,000 = \$2,100,000

$\dfrac{\text{Insurance carried}}{\text{Insurance required}} = \dfrac{\$2,100,000}{\$2,700,000} = \dfrac{7}{9}$

$\dfrac{7}{9}$ × \$2,880,000 = \$2,240,000 (Exceeds total face value so

\$2,100,000 is total indemnity paid.)

(b) Co X pays = $\dfrac{\$1,000,000}{\$2,100,000} = \dfrac{10}{21}$ × \$2,100,000 = \$1,000,000

Co Y pays = $\dfrac{\$1,100,000}{\$2,100,000} = \dfrac{11}{21}$ × \$2,100,000 = \$1,100,000

27. Insurance required = 80% × $6,000,000 = $4,800,000
    Insurance carried = $1,200,000 + $1,800,000 + $1,000,000
                       = $4,000,000

$$\frac{\text{Insurance carried}}{\text{Insurance required}} = \frac{\$4,000,000}{\$4,800,000} = \frac{5}{6}$$

(a) $\frac{5}{6}$ × $4,500,000 = $3,750,000

(b) Dickson pays = $\frac{\$1,200,000}{\$4,000,000}$ = $\frac{3}{10}$ × $3,750,000 = $1,125,000

    Eagle pays   = $\frac{\$1,800,000}{\$4,000,000}$ = $\frac{9}{20}$ × $3,750,000 = $1,687,500

    Franklin pays = $\frac{\$1,000,000}{\$4,000,000}$ = $\frac{1}{4}$ × $3,750,000 = $ 937,500

28. Insurance required = 80% × $5,000,000 = $4,000,000
    Insurance carried = $2,000,000 + $1,000,000 + $800,000
                       = $3,800,000

$$\frac{\text{Insurance carried}}{\text{Insurance required}} = \frac{\$3,800,000}{\$4,000,000} = \frac{19}{20}$$

(a) $\frac{19}{20}$ × $3,500,000 = $3,325,000

(b) Prentice pays = $\frac{\$2,000,000}{\$3,800,000}$ = $\frac{10}{19}$ × $3,325,000 = $1,750,000

    Randell pays = $\frac{\$1,000,000}{\$3,800,000}$ = $\frac{5}{19}$ × $3,325,000 = $ 875,000

    Quincy pays   = $\frac{\$800,000}{\$3,800,000}$ = $\frac{4}{19}$ × $3,325,000 = $ 700,000

Section 2, page 130

1. (a)
	Territory 2
$ 91.00	15/30 Bodily injury
97.00	$10,000 Property damage
63.00	$1,000 Medical pay
$251.00	Base premium
× 1.20	Driver classification
$301.20	Annual premium

(b)
	Territory 1
$ 88.00	50/50 Bodily injury
86.00	$25,000 Property damage
67.00	$5,000 Medical pay
$241.00	Base premium
× 1.30	Driver classification
$313.30	Annual premium

(c)
	Territory 3
$136.00	100/200 Bodily injury
107.00	$50,000 Property damage
74.00	$10,000 Medical pay
$317.00	Base premium
× 1.65	Driver classification
$523.05	Annual premium

2. (a)
	Territory 1
$ 83.00	25/25 Bodily injury
85.00	$10,000 Property damage
62.00	$1,000 Medical pay
$230.00	Base premium
× 1.10	Driver classification
$253.00	Annual premium

(b)
	Territory 2
$103.00	50/100 Bodily injury
101.00	$50,000 Property damage
66.00	$2,500 Medical pay
$270.00	Base premium
× 1.55	Driver classification
$418.50	Annual premium

2. (Continued)

(c)   Territory 3
    $144.00   300/300 Bodily injury
     108.00 $100,000 Property damage
      74.00 $10,000 Medical pay
    $326.00   Base premium
    × 1.50   Driver classification
    $489.00   Annual premium

3. (a) $ 52.00   Comprehensive (Model A, Age 3, Territory 1)
        77.00 $250-deductible collision
      $129.00   Base premium
      × 1.40   Driver classification
      $180.60   Annual premium

   (b) $ 69.00   Comprehensive (Model J, Age 1, Territory 2)
       108.00 $500-deductible collision
      $177.00   Base premium
      × 1.90   Driver classification
      $336.30   Annual premium

   (c) $ 70.00   Comprehensive (Model L, Age 2, Territory 2)
       112.00 $500-deductible collision
      $182.00   Base premium
      × 1.40   Driver classification
      $254.80   Annual premium

4. (a) $ 70.00   Comprehensive (Model N, Age 2, Territory 1)
       130.00 $250-deductible collision
      $200.00   Base premium
      × 1.00   Driver classification
      $200.00   Annual premium

   (b) $ 69.00   Comprehensive (Model J, Age 1, Territory 2)
       108.00 $500-deductible collision
      $177.00   Base premium
      × 1.10   Driver classification
      $194.70   Annual premium

   (c) $ 58.00   Comprehensive (Model A, Age 3, Territory 3)
        85.00 $500-deductible collision
      $143.00   Base premium
      × 1.45   Driver classification
      $207.35   Annual premium

5.
	<u>Territory 2</u>
$ 97.00	25/50 Bodily injury
97.00	$10,000 Property damage
<u>63.00</u>	$1,000 Medical pay
$257.00	Base premium
<u>× 1.70</u>	Driver classification (Male, 20, not principal operator, D.T., 6 miles)
$436.90	Annual premium

6.
	<u>Territory 1</u>
$ 86.00	25/50 Bodily injury
86.00	$25,000 Property damage
<u>65.00</u>	$2,500 Medical pay
$237.00	Base premium
<u>× 1.00</u>	Driver classification (Female, 32, 5 miles to work)
$237.00	Annual premium

7.
$ 77.00	Comprehensive (Model N, Age 1, Territory 1)
<u>140.00</u>	$250-deductible collision
$217.00	Base premium
<u>× 1.50</u>	Driver classification (Female, 27, uses in business)
$325.50	Annual premium

8.
$ 54.00	Comprehensive (Model C, Age 4, Territory 3)
<u>78.00</u>	$500-deductible collision
$132.00	Base premium
<u>× 2.60</u>	Driver classification (Unmarried male, 21, owner, 6 miles to work)
$343.20	Annual premium

9.
	<u>Territory 3</u>
$131.00	100/100 Bodily injury
107.00	$50,000 Property damage
74.00	$10,000 Medical pay
58.00	Comprehensive (Model B, Age 2)
<u>85.00</u>	$500-deductible collision
$455.00	Base premium
<u>× 1.00</u>	Driver classification (No young operator, 2½ miles)
$455.00	Annual premium

10.   Territory 2
     $ 97.00   25/50 Bodily injury
       95.00 $5,000 Property damage
       63.00 $1,000 Medical pay
       86.00   Comprehensive (Model N, Age 1)
      164.00 $250-deductible collision
     $505.00   Base premium
     × 1.00   Driver classification (Female, 66, pleasure)
     $505.00   Annual premium

11.   Territory 2
     $101.00   50/50 Bodily injury
       97.00 $10,000 Property damage
       66.00 $2,500 Medical pay
       57.00   Comprehensive (Model K, Age 4)
       91.00 $500-deductible collision
     $412.00   Base premium
     × 1.40   Driver classification (No young operator, 11 miles)
     $576.80   Annual premium

12.   Territory 1
     $ 91.00   100/100 Bodily injury
       87.00 $50,000 Property damage
       70.00 $10,000 Medical pay
       55.00   Comprehensive (Model A, Age 1)
       76.00 $500-deductible collision
     $379.00   Base premium
     × 1.20   Driver classification (Young, married male, 24, 4
                miles to work)
     $454.80   Annual premium

13.

	Damages/ Court Award	Insurance Company Pays	Insured Pays
Person A	$ 30,000	$30,000	$ 0
Person B	65,000	50,000	15,000
Car	25,000	10,000	15,000
	$120,000	(a) $90,000	(b) $30,000

14.

	Damages/ Court Award	Insurance Company Pays	Insured Pays
Person A	$20,000	$15,000	$ 5,000
Person B	40,000	15,000	25,000
Car	15,000	10,000	5,000
	$75,000	(a) $40,000	(b) $35,000

15. (a) All $20,000 should be covered by Bruce's comprehensive insurance (unless the policy had a deductible for comprehensive coverage).

(b) None.

16. (a) All $1,800 damage should be covered by his insurance company (unless he has a deductible on the comprehensive coverage).

(b) None

17.

	Damages/ Court Award	Insurance Company Pays	Insured Pays
Driver	$ 48,000	$15,000	$33,000
Passenger	60,000	15,000	45,000
Car	12,000	5,000	7,000
Van	7,000	6,500	500
	$127,000	(a) $41,500	(b) $85,500

18.

	Damages/ Court Award	Insurance Company Pays	Insured Pays
Driver	$ 10,000	$10,000	$ 0
Passenger	75,000	25,000	50,000
Car	13,000	10,000	3,000
Truck	26,000	25,750	250
	$124,000	(a) $70,750	(b) $53,250

19.

	Damages/ Court Award	Insurance Company Pays	Insured Pays
Widow	$400,000	$100,000	$300,000
Gemini	110,000	100,000	10,000
Edmund's doctor bills	3,000	1,000	2,000
Car	15,000	15,000	0
Truck	2,000	1,750	250
	$530,000	(a) $217,750	(b) $312,250

20.

	Damages/ Court Award	Insurance Company Pays	Insured Pays
Widower	$500,000	$200,000	$300,000
Passenger	50,000	50,000	0
Jerde car	17,000	16,500	500
Jennings Car	20,000	20,000	0
Jerde medical	25,000	10,000	15,000
	$612,000	(a) $296,500	(b) $315,500

Section 3, page 145

1.

	Applicant and Age	Type of Policy	Face Value	Annual Premium
(a)	Male, 20	10-year term	$ 15,000	$ 103.20
(b)	Male, 45	Whole life	50,000	1,689.50
(c)	Female, 25	20-pmt. life	20,000	511.80
(d)	Female, 30	Variable universal	100,000	2,217.00

(a) $ 6.88	(b) $ 33.79	(c) $ 25.59	(d) $ 22.17
× 15	× 50	× 20	× 100
$103.20	$1,689.50	$511.80	$2,217.00

2.

	Applicant and Age	Type of Policy	Face Value	Annual Premium
(a)	Male, 18	10-year term	$10,000	$ 68.10
(b)	Male, 35	Variable universal	75,000	2,315.25
(c)	Female, 40	Lmt-pmt. life	35,000	1,253.00
(d)	Female, 35	Whole life	50,000	986.50

2. (Continued)

(a) $ 6.81   (b) $ 30.87   (c) $35.80   (d) $ 19.73
   ×   10   ×   75   ×   35   ×   50
   $68.10 $2,315.25 $1,253 $986.50

3.

	Yrs. in Force	Type of Policy	Face Value	Nonforfeiture Option	Nonforfeiture Value
(a)	20	Whole life	$100,000	Cash value	$25,100
(b)	5	20-pay. life	50,000	Paid-up ins.	$10,900
(c)	10	Whole life	125,000	Extend. term	18 yrs. 91 days
(d)	3	Var. universal	150,000	Cash value	$6,600

(a) $ 251   (b) $ 218   (c) 18 years and 91 days
   ×   100   ×   50
   $25,100 $10,900

(d) $ 44
   ×   150
   $6,600

4.

	Yrs. in Force	Type of Policy	Face Value	Nonforfeiture Option	Nonforfeiture Value
(a)	5	20-pmt. life	$ 60,000	Cash value	$ 4,440
(b)	15	Whole life	80,000	Paid-up ins.	$30,960
(c)	20	Whole life	25,000	Extend. term	22 yrs. 37 days
(d)	40	Var. universal	140,000	Cash value	$417,060

(a) $ 74   (b) $ 387   (c) 22 years and 137 days
   ×   60   ×   80   in extended term
   $4,440 $30,960   insurance

(d) $ 2,979
   ×   140
   $417,060

5.

	Beneficiary				Settlement	Monthly Annuity	
	Sex	Age	Face Value	Option Chosen	Years	Amount
(a)	M	60	$ 55,000	Fixed no. of years	16	$353.65
(b)	F	50	75,000	Fixed amt. per mo.	20	425.00
(c)	F	65	100,000	Life annuity	--	656.00
(d)	F	45	150,000	Guaranteed annuity	20	666.00

5. (Continued)

(a) $ 6.43
    ×   55
    $353.65

(b) $\frac{425}{75} = 5.66\overline{6}$ so 20 years

(c) $ 6.56
    ×   100
    $656.00

(d) $ 4.44
    ×   150
    $666.00

6.

	Beneficiary			Settlement	Monthly Annuity	
	Sex	Age	Face Value	Option Chosen	Years	Amount
(a)	M	56	$100,000	Fixed no. of years	15	$689
(b)	M	50	45,000	Fixed amt. per mo.	16	290
(c)	F	55	80,000	Life annuity	--	424
(d)	F	60	125,000	Guaranteed annuity	10	750

(a) $ 6.89
    ×   100
    $689.00

(b) $\frac{\$290}{45} = 6.44$ so 16 years

(c) $ 5.30
    ×   80
    $424.00

(d) $ 6.00
    ×   125
    $750.00

7. (a) 20-payment life:
       $ 28.06 (age 25)
       ×   85
       $2,385.10 Annual premium

   (b) Whole life:
       $ 17.22 (age 25)
       ×   85
       $1,463.70 Annual premium

   (c) $2,385.10 Annual premium
       ×   20 years (paid up)
       $ 47,702 Total premium

   (d) $1,463.70 Annual premium
       ×   30 years
       $ 43,911 Total premium

8. (a) 20-payment life:
       $ 29.84 (age 28)
       ×   55
       $1,641.20 Annual premium

   (b) Whole life:
       $ 18.64 (age 28)
       ×   55
       $1,025.20 Annual premium

   (c) $ 1,641.20 Annual premium
       ×   20 years (paid up)
       $32,824.00 Total premium

   (d) $ 1,025.20 Annual premium
       ×   40 years
       $41,008.00 Total premium

9. (a) <u>10-year term</u>: (b) $ 355 Annual premium
        $ 7.10 (set back to 25)   ×   10 years
        ×   50 $3,550 Total premium
        $355.00 Annual premium

    (c) <u>Whole life</u>: (d) $8,610 Whole life
        $ 17.22 (set back to 25)   -3,550 10-year term
        ×   50 $5,060 Savings
        $ 861.00 Annual premium
        ×   10 years
        $8,610.00 Total premium

    (e) Term = 0; Whole life = $50,000

10. (a) <u>10-year term</u>: (b) $ 173.60 Annual premium
        $ 8.68 (set back to 35)   ×   10 years
        ×   20 $1,736.00 Total premium
        $173.60 Annual premium

    (c) <u>Whole life</u>: (d) $4,798 Whole life
        $ 23.99 (set back to 35)   -1,736 10-year term
        ×   20 $3,062 Savings
        $ 479.80 Annual premium

        $ 479.80 Annual premium
        ×   10 years
        $4,798.00 Total premium

    (e) Term = 0; Whole life = $20,000

11. (a) <u>At age 30</u>:   <u>At age 20</u>:
        $ 19.73 Whole life $ 15.46 Whole life
        ×   75   ×   75
        $1,479.75 Annual premium $1,159.50 Annual premium

        $1,479.75 Annual premium at age 30
        -1,159.50 Annual premium at age 20
        $ 320.25 Annual savings

    (b) $ 1,479.75 Annual premium
        ×   35 years
        $51,791.25 Total premiums at age 30

    (c) $ 1,159.50 Annual premium
        ×   45 years
        $52,177.50 Total premiums at age 20

11. (Continued)

    (d) If he takes out the policy at age 20, he gets 10 more years of insurance protection, and the policy builds cash value during those extra 10 years.

12. (a) <u>At age 40</u>:

        $35.55 Variable universal
        ×   100
        $3,555 Annual premium

       <u>At age 30</u>:

        $ 26.05 Variable universal
        ×   100
        $2,605.00 Annual premium

        $3,555 Annual premium at age 40
       <u>-2,605</u> Annual premium at age 30
        $ 950 Annual savings

    (b) $ 3,555 Annual premium
        ×   20 years
        $71,100 Total premium
              to age 60

    (c) $ 2,605 Annual premium
        ×   30 years
        $78,150 Total premiums
              to age 60

    (d) Purchased at age 30, he would have 10 more years to build cash value to age 60 plus insurance coverage for ages 30 to 60.

13. (a) <u>Annual premium</u>:
        $28.06
        ×   100
        $2,806

    (b) <u>Cash value</u>:
        $ 187
        ×   100
        $18,700

    (c) <u>Paid-up</u>:
        $ 507
        ×   100
        $50,700

    (d) 28 years and 186 days for extended term

14. (a) <u>Annual premium</u>:
        $17.22 (at age 25)
        × 200
        $3,444

    (b) <u>Cash value</u>:
        $ 93 (10 years in
        ×   200 force)
        $18,600

    (c) <u>Paid-up insurance</u>:
        $ 248 (10 years in force)
        ×   200
        $49,600

    (d) <u>Extended term</u>:
        18 years 91 days

15. $ 319
     ×   40
     $12,760 Cash value

16. $ 251
    ×   65
    $16,315 Cash value

17. (a) <u>Variable universal</u>:
$ 1,030
× 150
$154,500 Cash value

   (b) <u>Whole life</u>:
$ 251
× 150
$37,650 Cash value

18. (a) <u>Variable universal</u>:
$ 321
× 100
$32,100 Cash value

   (b) <u>20-payment life</u>:
$ 187
× 100
$18,700 Cash value

19. (a) <u>Fixed # of years = 14</u>:
$ 7.71
× 80
$616.80 per month

   (b) <u>Fixed amount</u>:

$$\frac{\$770}{80} = 9.625$$

Closest table value = $9.60; so $770 per month payments would last approximately 10 years

20. (a) <u>Fixed # of years = 20</u>:
$ 5.66
× 75
$424.50 per month

   (b) <u>Fixed amount</u>:

$$\frac{480}{75} = 6.40$$

Closest table value = $6.43; so $480 per month payments would last approximately 16 years.

21. (a) <u>Life annuity</u>:

$ 4.60
× 125
$575.00/month for life

   (b) <u>Life annuity guaranteed for 20 years</u>:
$ 4.44
× 125
$555.00 per month

22. (a) <u>Life annuity</u>:

$ 6.13
× 50
$306.50/month for life

   (b) <u>Life annuity guaranteed for 10 years</u>:
$ 6.00
× 50
$ 300.00/month per life

23. (a) <u>Fixed # of years = 10</u>:

$ 9.60
× __50__
$ 480 per month
× __120__ months
$57,600 Total annuity

(b) <u>Life annuity with 10-years certain</u>:

$ 5.28
× __50__
$ 264
× __156__ months
$41,184

(c) She gained $16,416 (and gained $7,600 over face value).

24. (a) <u>Fixed # of years = 20</u>:

$ 5.66
× __45__
$254.70 per month
× __240__ months
$61,128 Total annuity

(b) <u>Life annuity guaranteed for 20 years</u>:

$ 5.00
× __45__
$225.00 per month
× __360__ months
$81,000 Total annuity

(c) He lost $19,872 ($81,000 - $61,128) but still gained $16,128 over the cash value.

25. (a) <u>Life annuity</u>:
$ 5.16
× __90__
$464.40 per month

(b) $ 464.00
× __204__ months
$94,737.60 Total received

(c) <u>Life annuity guaranteed 20 years</u>:
$ 4.80
× __90__
$432.00 per month

$ 432
× __204__ months
$88,128 Total received

(d) Jennifer gained $6,609.60 ($94,737.60 - $88,128), but secondary beneficiary lost $15,552 ($432 × 36 months).

26. (a) <u>Life annuity</u>:
$ 6.13
× __70__
$429.10 per month

(b) $ 429.10
× __192__ months
$82,387.20 Total annuity

(c) <u>Life annuity guaranteed 20 years</u>:
$ 5.46
× __70__
$382.20 per month

$ 382.20
× __192__ months
$73,382.40 Total annuity

(d) She gained $9,004.80 ($82,387.20 - $73,382.40), but secondary beneficiary lost $18,345.60 ($382.20 × 48 months).

CHAPTER VII

CHECKBOOK AND CASH RECORDS

This is an example of easy topics inserted between more difficult ones, thus allowing the student a short "breather." Checkbook records introduces the student to the various forms customarily used in connection with a bank checking account -- several types of checks, the check register, the deposit slip, and the bank statement. Three types of endorsements are also explained. From a mathematical standpoint, the purpose of this topic is to teach the student how to reconcile a bank statement. The format taught lists under the "checkbook balance" side all of the entries that must be made by the bookkeeper to the business's records. NOW accounts are included to present checking accounts that earn interest. Reiterate that such accounts usually require the owner to maintain a substantial minimum balance in order to earn interest.

As a part of the class discussion of cash records, mention that, although it is almost impossible to handle quantities of money constantly without making an error, employers expect the cashier to be as careful as possible in making change. Some businesses even make the cashier personally responsible for shortages; this is particularly true if the cashier has taken a check without getting it approved and the check later "bounces."

Business Mathematics: A Collegiate Approach

CHAPTER 7 - CHECKBOOK AND CASH RECORDS
PROBLEM SOLUTIONS

Section 1, page 160

1.

```
#360    Balance
        Brought
        Forward  $3,645.26
Nov. 2 20 xx
To  Gold Supply
    Co.
For Office supplies,
    $176, plus sales
    tax, $7.92
        Amount
        Check     $  183.92
        Deposit    --------
        Balance    $3,461.34
```

```
#361    Balance
        Brought
        Forward  $3,461.34
Nov. 3 20 xx
To  Baltimeier
    Computer Co.
For Computer,
    $940, plus
    sales tax, $42.30
        Amount
        Check     $  982.30
        Deposit    --------
        Balance    $2,479.04
```

```
#362    Balance
        Brought
        Forward  $2,479.04
Nov. 3 20 xx
To: Garman, Inc.

For: Merchandise


        Amount
        Check     $1,250.00
        Deposit   $  374.46
        Balance   $1,603.50
```

```
#363    Balance
        Brought
        Forward  $1,603.50
Nov. 4 20 xx
To: U.S. Postal
    Service
For: Postage
    stamps

        Amount
        Check     $   64.00
        Deposit    --------
        Balance   $1,539.50
```

2.

```
#5622   Balance
        Brought
        Forward  $5,246.48
June 3 20 xx
To  Hodge
    Manufacturing Co.
For Merchandise


        Amount
        Check     $3,100.00
        Deposit    -----
        Balance   $2,146.48
```

```
#5623   Balance
        Brought
        Forward  $2,146.48
June 3 20 xx
To  Scully Ins.
    Agency
For Qtr. liability
    insurance
    premium
        Amount
        Check     $  550.00
        Deposit    1,687.32
        Balance   $3,283.80
```

2. (Continued)

```
┌─────────────────────────────────┐   ┌─────────────────────────────────┐
│ #5624   Balance                 │   │ #5625   Balance                 │
│         Brought                 │   │         Brought                 │
│         Forward  $3,283.80      │   │         Forward $3,157.80       │
│ June 4 20 xx                    │   │ June 5 20 xx                    │
│ To   Connelly                   │   │ To   Charlie's                  │
│    Office Products              │   │    Computer Services            │
│ For  Off. supplies $120         │   │ For  Computer repair            │
│    + sales tax $6               │   │                                 │
│                                 │   │                                 │
│         Amount                  │   │         Amount                  │
│         Check     $  126.00     │   │         Check     $   75.42     │
│         Deposit    --------      │   │         Deposit    --------      │
│         Balance   $3,157.80     │   │         Balance   $3,082.38     │
└─────────────────────────────────┘   └─────────────────────────────────┘
```

3.

Bank Reconciliation			
Bank Balance	$605.75	Checkbook Balance	$142.12
Less: Outstanding checks			
$ 86.20			
122.48			
250.39		Less:	
12.56	-471.63	Service charge	- 8.00
Adjusted Balance	$134.12	Adjusted Balance	$134.12

4.

Bank Reconciliation			
Bank Balance	$1,472.66	Checkbook Balance	$1,539.90
Add: Outstanding deposit	+ 600.00		
	$2,072.66		
Less: Outstanding checks			
$264.25			
188.60			
54.56		Less:	
37.35	- 544.76	Service charge	- 12.00
Adjusted Balance	$1,527.90	Adjusted Balance	$1,527.90

5.

Bank Reconciliation			
Bank Balance	$1,814.41	Checkbook Balance	$1,077.97
Add: Outstand. deposit	+ 334.82	Add: Interest	+ 5.15
	$2,149.23		$1,083.12
Less: Outstand. checks		Less:	
$176.00		Service charge $10.45	
440.60		Check printing 9.20	
519.16	-1,135.76	Returned check 50.00	- 69.65
Adjusted Balance	$1,013.47	Adjusted Balance	$1,013.47

6.

Bank Reconciliation			
Bank Balance	$3,424.53	Checkbook Balance	$3,371.15
Add: Outstanding deposit	+ 477.25		
	$3,901.78		
Less: Outstanding checks		Less:	
$144.51		Returned check $68.00	
76.00		Debit memo 15.00	
400.62	- 621.13	Service charge 7.50	- 90.50
Adjusted Balance	$3,280.65	Adjusted Balance	$3,280.65

7.

Bank Reconciliation			
Bank Balance	$ 845.32	Checkbook Balance	$1,348.29
Add: Outstand. deposit	+ 800.00	Add: Interest	+ 8.48
	$1,645.32		$1,356.77
		Less:	
		Correction to	
		deposit charge $ 2.00	
		Service charge 6.55	
		Returned check 165.65	
Less: Outstand. checks	- 477.75	Printing charge 15.00	- 189.20
Adjusted Balance	$1,167.57	Adjusted Balance	$1,167.57

8.

Bank Reconciliation			
Bank Balance	$2,260.91	Checkbook Balance	$1,313.55
Add: Outstand. deposit	+ 646.48	Add:	
	$2,907.39	Electronic	
		Deposit	$921.50	
		Interest	10.22	+ 931.72
			$2,245.27
		Less:	
		ATM withdrawal	$364.00
		ATM fee	4.50
Less: Outstand. checks	-1,050.62	Debit Memo	20.00	- 388.50
Adjusted Balance	$1,856.77	Adjusted Balance	$1,856.77

9.

Bank Reconciliation			
Bank Balance	$2,675.71	Checkbook Balance	$1,352.18
Add: Outstand. deposit	+ 836.24		
	$3,511.95		
Less: Outstand. checks			
#224 $ 376.28			
#229 54.62		Less:	
#232 282.44		Returned check $400.00	
#233 1,856.43	-2,569.77	Service charge 10.00	- 410.00
Adjusted Balance	$ 942.18	Adjusted Balance	$ 942.18

10.

Bank Reconciliation			
Bank Balance	$4,928.28	Checkbook Balance	$3,803.59
Add: Outstanding deposit	+1,667.50		
	$6,595.78		
Less: Outstanding checks			
$ 540.00			
34.86			
46.38			
600.60		Less:	
190.23		Ret. check $250.00	
1,642.12	-3,054.19	Service chg. 12.00	- 262.00
Adjusted Balance	$3,541.59	Adjusted Balance	$3,541.59

11.

Bank Reconciliation			
Bank Balance	$1,525.34	Checkbook Balance	$1,079.27
Add: Outstand. deposit	+ 234.03		
	$1,759.37		
Less: Outstand. checks			
#231 $ 78.33			
#237 262.13		Less:	
#239 4.34		Bank charges $18.45	
#242 361.15	- 705.95	7.40	- 25.85
Adjusted Balance	$1,053.42	Adjusted Balance	$1,053.42

12.

Bank Reconciliation			
Bank Balance	$1,412.23	Checkbook Balance	$2,780.52
Add: Outstanding deposit	+2,556.89		
	$3,969.12		
Less: Outstanding checks			
$1,001.61			
87.42		Less:	
90.64		Returned check $55.27	
74.20	+1,253.87	Service charge 10.00	- 65.27
Adjusted Balance	$2,715.25	Adjusted Balance	$2,715.25

Section 2, page 169

1.

```
┌─────────────────────────────────────────────────────┐
│                   Kitchens, Inc.                    │
│                 Daily Cash Report                   │
├─────────────────────────────────────────────────────┤
│ Date:                                               │
│ Register:    No. 9                                  │
│ Clerk:       Tom Bruno                              │
├─────────────────────────────────────────────────────┤
│ Pennies                          52  $    0.52      │
│ Nickels                          68       3.40      │
│ Dimes                            30       3.00      │
│ Quarters                         74      18.50      │
│ Halves                            2       1.00      │
│ Ones                             34      34.00      │
│ Fives                            12      60.00      │
│ Tens                             15     150.00      │
│ Twenties                         10     200.00      │
│ Other currency ($100)             1     100.00      │
│ Checks (listed separately):                         │
│                         $50.25                      │
│                          36.36                      │
│                          15.98                      │
│                          48.00                      │
│                          67.57        +218.16       │
│ Total cash                            $788.58       │
│    Less:  change fund                 -100.00       │
│    Net cash receipts                  $688.58       │
│    Cash over (subtract)               ----          │
│    Cash short (add)                   +  0.90       │
│    Cash register total                $689.48       │
└─────────────────────────────────────────────────────┘
```

$0.90 short

2.

Prime Cut Meat Shop Daily Cash Report		
Date: Register: No. 4 Clerk: Kate Calloway		
Pennies	52	$ 0.52
Nickels	65	3.25
Dimes	46	4.60
Quarters	50	12.50
Halves	3	1.50
Ones	71	71.00
Fives	18	90.00
Tens	6	60.00
Twenties	5	100.00
Other currency ($50)	1	50.00
Checks (listed separately):		
$ 68.45		
81.80		
35.14		
108.00		
74.44		
56.85		
92.75		
52.63		
Total cash		+570.06
Less: change fund		$963.43
Net cash receipts		-200.00
Cash over (subtract)		$763.43
Cash short (add)		----
Cash register total		+ 0.64
		$764.07

Cash short $0.64

3.

```
┌─────────────────────────────────────────────────┐
│                  Hair, Inc.                     │
│              Daily Cash Report                  │
├─────────────────────────────────────────────────┤
│ Date:                                           │
│ Register:                                       │
│ Clerk:                                          │
├─────────────────────────────────────────────────┤
│ Pennies                        22   $   0.22    │
│ Nickels                        74       3.70    │
│ Dimes                          53       5.30    │
│ Quarters                       15       3.75    │
│ Halves                          1       0.50    │
│ Ones                           36      36.00    │
│ Fives                          18      90.00    │
│ Tens                           12     120.00    │
│ Twenties                        5     100.00    │
│ Other currency ($50)            1      50.00    │
│ Checks (listed separately):                     │
│                          $25                    │
│                           30                    │
│                           42                    │
│                           30                    │
│                           35          +162.00   │
│ Total Cash                           $571.47    │
│    Less:  change fund                 - 75.00   │
│    Net cash receipts                 $496.47    │
│    Cash over (subtract)               -  0.25   │
│    Cash short (add)                   ----      │
│    Cash register total               $496.22    │
└─────────────────────────────────────────────────┘
```

Cash over $0.25

4.

L & M Emporium		
Daily Cash Report		
Date:		
Register:		
Clerk: Janet Yates		
Pennies	60	$ 0.60
Nickels	24	1.20
Dimes	48	4.80
Quarters	62	15.50
Halves	2	1.00
Ones	27	27.00
Fives	10	50.00
Tens	14	140.00
Twenties	15	300.00
Other currency		
Checks (listed separately):		
	$56.12	
	89.95	
	97.75	
	66.18	
		+310.00
Total Cash		$850.10
Less: change fund		- 75.00
Net cash receipts		$775.10
Cash over (subtract)		- 0.62
Cash short (add)		----
Cash register total		$774.48

Cash over $0.62

5.

USA Chips Co. Over and Short Summary				
Date	Total Sales	Net Cash Receipts	Cash Over	Cash Short
June 3	$1,045.68	$1,045.70	$0.02	--
June 4	1,172.49	1,172.49	--	--
June 5	1,099.46	1,100.00	0.54	--
June 6	1,153.33	1,153.25	--	$0.08
June 7	1,155.21	1,155.16	--	0.05
Totals	$5,626.17	$5,626.60	$0.56	$0.13

Total cash receipts	$5,626.60
Total cash short (add)	+ 0.13
Total cash over (subtract)	− 0.56
Total cash register readings	$5,626.17

Cash over	$0.56
Cash short	−0.13
Cash over	$0.43 for the week

6.

Auto Parts, Inc. Over and Short Summary				
Date	Total Sales	Net Cash Receipts	Cash Over	Cash Short
May 15	$1,252.99	$1,253.44	$0.45	$ --
May 16	1,342.01	1,342.21	0.20	--
May 17	1,304.68	1,303.68	--	1.00
May 18	1,313.12	1,313.12	--	--
May 19	1,359.75	1,359.88	0.13	--
Totals	$6,572.55	$6,572.33	$0.78	$1.00

Total cash receipts	$6,572.33
Total cash short (add)	+ 1.00
Total cash over (subtract)	− .78
Total cash register readings	$6,572.55

Cash over	−$0.78
Cash short	+1.00
Cash over	$ 0.22 for the week

CHAPTER VIII

WAGES AND PAYROLLS

This is one of the most important chapters in the book and should be taught thoroughly. Because every business must prepare a payroll, more of your students will have occasion to apply this information than probably any other single topic. Calculators will facilitate completion of the payroll problems in this chapter, and the authors encourage their use.

1.   Salary:

Although an annual salary is often quoted to an employee, the salary is actually paid weekly, biweekly, monthly, or semimonthly. Example 1 shows the student how an annual salary is divided into one of the four payment methods.

2.   Commission:

Basic commission problems are easy as most students have probably studied them at some time previously. Variations including sliding-scale commissions, drawing accounts, salary, and quota can be learned without difficulty. The topic on "commission agents," although not difficult, might be omitted from basic courses.

3.   Hourly Rate Basis:

This is the most important method of wage determination, since a large portion of the U.S. working force is paid by the hour. Conduct a discussion of standard wage practices, including the current minimum wage, hours per work week, overtime rates, and so on. Example 3, which involves overtime paid on a daily basis as well as weekly, may be omitted from basic courses. Similarly, example 4 (overtime computation for salaried workers) is also optional for basic classes. Overtime excess should be included for all classes, as the method is becoming widely used in some areas.

4.   Production Basis:

The production basis for determining wages has been losing popularity in recent years; thus, if time is short, the instructor may wish to omit Examples 3 and 4, which are related to incentives and charge-backs.

5. Net Weekly Payrolls:

This section is the heart of the chapter and should be covered in detail. Emphasize that Social Security is deducted only on a base amount ($76,200 in 2000) while Medicare is deducted on the total gross wages for each employee. Stress that these two deductions are matched by the employer. Describe how the base amounts have increased through the years, and today Medicare no longer has a maximum taxable base. The tax rates have increased also. These changes in FICA have been necessary to keep the programs solvent.

Point out the difference in income tax that would be deducted for married persons and for single persons having the same gross wages. The students would be interested in seeing schedules showing the various annual income brackets and the income tax which must be paid within each. (This may be obtained from the instructions to your own 1040 return, from an office of Internal Revenue, or from the following web site: www.irs.gov.)

If at all possible, have your students deduct Social Security and Federal income tax at the current rates, rather than using the tables in the text after they have become out of date. These tables may be obtained from the Internal Revenue Service. You can call the form/publication division at 1-800-829-3676 or download them from www.irs.gov/forms_pubs/index.html. If your state requires that state income tax be deducted, obtain withholding tables from your state department of revenue and have the students include this deduction in their problems.

Remind the students that time can be saved by listing all the FICA deductions for the entire payroll, then all the federal tax deductions, and so forth. Be sure they are aware of the built-in checks among the various totals and subtotals on the payroll.

6. Quarterly Earnings Records and Returns:

Despite improvements in the quarterly report (#941), many students have difficulty with the form. It must be emphasized that line 2 lists all wages earned during that quarter only that were subject to income tax, while lines 6a and 6c list taxable Social Security wages and tips which may differ from the wages on line 2. Since Medicare has no base amount, line 7 may differ from lines 6a and 6c.

Although most workers now pay Social Security on all wages, enough employers and executives exceed the current base amount to make it essential that the student understand the concepts in examples 2 and 3. The examples must be taught slowly and with a great deal of explanation. Sometimes a fellow student helps a confused student "see the light." By all means have the class try these problems at the board before attempting the assignment.

The authors strongly suggest that you obtain actual #941 forms from IRS for your students. Using the actual forms and being able to read the complete directions has greatly enhanced student understanding in many cases.

Example 4 again presents the concept of determining taxable wages, this time for unemployment taxes. This example could easily be omitted if time is short.

CHAPTER 8 - WAGES AND PAYROLLS
PROBLEM SOLUTIONS

Sections 1 and 2, page 181

		ANNUAL SALARY	MONTHLY	SEMIMONTHLY	WEEKLY	BIWEEKLY
1.	(a)	$ 48,000	$ 4,000	$2,000	$ 923.08	$1,846.15
	(b)	72,000	6,000	3,000	1,384.62	2,769.23
	(c)	24,000	2,000	1,000	461.54	923.08
2.	(a)	$150,000	$12,500	$6,250	$2,884.62	$5,769.23
	(b)	33,600	2,800	1,400	646.15	1,292.31
	(c)	96,000	8,000	4,000	1,846.15	3,692.31

1. (a) $\dfrac{\$48,000}{12} = \$4,000/\text{monthly}$

$\dfrac{\$48,000}{24} = \$2,000/\text{semimonthly}$

$\dfrac{\$48,000}{52} = \$923.08/\text{weekly}$

$\dfrac{\$48,000}{26} = \$1,846.15/\text{biweekly}$

1. (Continued)

(b) $6,000 × 12 = $72,000/annual

$$\frac{\$72,000}{24} = \$3,000/semiannual$$

$$\frac{\$72,000}{52} = \$1,384.62/weekly$$

$$\frac{\$72,000}{26} = \$2,769.23/biweekly$$

(c) $1,000 × 24 = $24,000/annual

$$\frac{\$24,000}{12} = \$2,000/monthly$$

$$\frac{\$24,000}{52} = \$461.54/weekly$$

$$\frac{\$24,000}{26} = \$923.08/biweekly$$

2. (a) $$\frac{\$150,000}{12} = \$12,500/monthly$$

$$\frac{\$150,000}{24} = \$6,250/semimonthly$$

$$\frac{\$150,000}{52} = \$2,884.62/weekly$$

$$\frac{\$150,000}{26} = \$5,769.23/biweekly$$

(b) $2,800 × 12 = $33,600/annual

$$\frac{\$33,600}{24} = \$1,400/semimonthly$$

$$\frac{\$33,600}{52} = \$646.15/weekly$$

$$\frac{\$33,600}{26} = \$1,292.31/biweekly$$

2. (Continued)

(c) $4,000 × 24 = $96,000/annual

$$\frac{\$96,000}{12} = \$8,000/\text{monthly}$$

$$\frac{\$96,000}{52} = \$1,846.15/\text{weekly}$$

$$\frac{\$96,000}{26} = \$3,692.31/\text{biweekly}$$

		SALARY	QUOTA	RATE	NET SALES	COMMISSION	GROSS WAGE
3.	(a)	X	X	6 %	$ 9,500	$ 570	X
	(b)	X	X	5½	7,200	396	X
	(c)	X	X	4	6,100	244	X
	(d)	$ 200	X	5	4,400	220	$ 420
	(e)	110	X	7	6,000	420	530
	(f)	X	$ 500	4½	9,900	423	X
	(g)	175	200	8	5,700	440	615
	(h)	80	1,000	6	6,400	324	404
	(i)	200	1,400	5	13,800	620	820
4.	(a)	X	X	8 %	$13,000	$1,040	X
	(b)	X	X	7	80,000	5,600	X
	(c)	X	X	7.5	25,000	1,875	X
	(d)	$ 300	X	6	20,000	1,200	$1,500
	(e)	400	X	9	17,000	1,530	1,930
	(f)	X	$ 500	10	18,000	1,750	X
	(g)	500	1,000	8	40,000	3,120	3,620
	(h)	1,200	2,000	5½	32,000	1,650	2,850
	(i)	200	600	9	37,000	3,276	3,476

3. (a)   % × S = C   (b)   % × S = C
  6% × $9,500 =   5.5% × S = $396
     $570 = C   S = $7,200

 (c)   % × S = C
  X($6,100) = $244
      X = 4%

 (d)   % × S = C   Salary + Commission = Gross
  5% × $4,400 =   Wage
     $220 = C $200 + $220 = GW
                  $420 = GW

 (e) Salary + Commission = Gross wage
     $110 + C = $530
        C = $420

   % × S = C
  7% × S = $420
     S = $6,000

 (f) Net sales - Quota = Net sales subject to commission
   $9,900 - $500 = $9,400

      % × S = C
  4.5% × $9,400 =
     $423 = C

 (g) Net sales - Quota = Net sales subject to commission
   $5,700 - $200 = $5,500

     % × S = C   Salary + Commission = Gross
  8% × $5,500 =   Wage
     $440 = C $175 + $440 = GW
                  $615 = GW

 (h) Salary + Commission = Gross wage
     $80 + C = $404
       C = $324

   % × S = C
  6% × S = $324
     S = $5,400

  $5,400 Net sales subjected to commission
  +1,000 Quota
  $6,400 Net sales

3. (Continued)

(i) $13,800 Net sales
     - 1,400 Quota
     $12,400 Net sales subject to Commission

             % × S = C $820 Gross wage
       5% × $12,400 =   -620 Commission
               $620 = C $200 Salary

4. (a)   % × S = C   (b) % × S = C
        8% × $13,000 =   7% × S = $5,600
               $1,040 = C   S = $80,000

    (c)   % × S = C
          % × $25,000 = $1,875
                    X = 7.5%

    (d)   % × S = C   Salary + Commission = Gross
          6% × $20,000 =   Wage
                 $1,200 = C $300 + $1,200 = GW
                                              $1,500 = GW

    (e) Salary + Commission = Gross wage
               $400 + C = $1,930
                      C = $1,530

          % × S = C
        9% × S = $1,530
             S = $17,000

    (f) $18,000 Net sales   % × S = C
         -    500 Quota   10% × $17,500 =
         $17,500 Net sales subject $1,750 = C
                 to commission

    (g) $40,000 Net sales   % × S = C
         - 1,000 Quota   8% × $39,000 =
         $39,000 Net sales subject $3,120 = C
                 to commission

         $ 500 Salary
         +3,120 Commission
         $3,620 Gross wage

    (h) $2,850 Gross wage   % × S = C
         -1,200 Salary   5.5% × S = $1,650
         $1,650 Commission   S = $30,000

4. (h) (Continued)

$30,000 Net sales subject to commission
+ 2,000 Quota
$32,000 Net sales

(i) $37,000 Net sales
    -    600 Quota
    $36,400 Net sakes subject
           to commission

$%$ × S = C
9% × $36,400 =
    $3,276 = C

$3,476 Gross wage
-3,276 Commission
$ 200 Salary

5. $7,500 Sales
   - 350 Sales returns
   $7,150 Net sales

$%$ × S = C
6% × $7,150 =
    $429 = C

6. $10,900 Sales
   -   500 Sales returns
   $10,400 Net sales

$%$ × S = C
7% × $10,400 =
    $728 = C

7. $%$ × S = C
   7% × S = $10,500
        S = $150,000

8. $%$ × S = C
   8% × S = $10,800
        S = $135,000

9. (a) $13,600 Net sales
       - 2,000 × 3.5% = $ 70
       $11,600
       - 4,000 × 5% =   200
       $ 7,600 × 6% =   456
                       $726

   (b) $726 Commission
       -350 Drawing account
       $376 Amount due

10. (a) $16,000 Net sales
        - 6,000 × 4%   = $240
        $10,000
        - 5,000 × 4.5% = 225
        $ 5,000 × 5%   = 250
                        $715

    (b) $715 Commission
        -250 Drawing account
        $465 Amount due

11. $300 Gross wage
    -120 Salary
    $180 Commission

    % × S = C
5% × S = $180
      S = $3,600

12. $810 Gross wage
    - 90 Salary
    $720 Commission

    % × S = C
6% × S = $720
      S = $12,000

13. $3,000 Sales
    -    50 Sales returns
    $2,950 Net sales

$2,950 Net sales
-   200 Quota
$2,750 Net sales subject
      to commission

     % × S = C
4% × $2,750 =
    $110 = C

$175 Salary
+110 Commission
$285 Gross wage

14. $8,000 Sales
    -   100 Sales returns
    $7,900 Net sales

$7,900 Net sales
-   300 Quota
$7,600 Net sales subject
      to commission

     % × S = C
6% × $7,600 =
    $456 = C

$150 Salary
+456 Commission
$606 Gross wage

15. Marshall's net sales
    Quota
    Net sales subject to commission $1,700

$2,200
-   500
$1,700

     % × S = C
6% × $1,700 =
    $102 = C

Department sales
Sales returns
Net sales subject to override $10,050

$10,100
-    50
$10,050

      % × S = C
1.5% × $10,050 =
    $150.75 = C

Salary $160
Commission +102
Override +150.75
       $412.75

16.
Hamm's net sales	$5,000
Quota	− 500
Net sales subject to commission	$4,500

% × S = C
7% × $4,500 =
$315 = C

% × S = C
1% × $35,000 =
$350 = C

Department sales	$35,400
Sales returns	− 400
Net sales subject to commission	$35,000

Salary	$150
Commission	+315
Override	+350
Gross wage	$815

17.

OZARK OFFICE SUPPLY
Payroll for Week Ending June 11, 20XX

NAME	NET SALES							COMM. RATE	GROSS COMM.
	M	T	W	TH	F	S	TOTAL		
Dempsey, J.	$396	$375	$280	$195	$304	$400	$1,950	8%	$156.00
Gold, K.	266	483	501	442	455	423	2,570	10	257.00
Keller, E.	322	388	404	425	421	500	2,460	9	221.40
Miller, M.	329	284	292	275	360	410	1,950	8	156.00
Wright, C.	340	465	488	492	502	613	2,900	7	203.00
								Total	$993.40

18.

WASHINGTON SPORTING GOODS, INC.
Payroll for Week Ending May 15, 20XX

NAME	NET SALES							COMM. RATE	GROSS COMM.
	M	T	W	TH	F	S	TOTAL		
Dodd, D.	$ 925	$ 742	$ 957	$ 896	$ 850	$ 750	$5,120	10%	$ 512
Hayes, B.	1,256	1,345	1,384	1,390	1,400	1,450	8,225	8	658
Jenkins, P.	660	782	778	840	860	780	4,700	7	329
Moody, A.	1,306	984	1,000	1,105	800	905	6,100	8	488
Owens, K.	864	700	1,010	1,496	580	800	5,400	9	486
								Total	$2,473

19.

ROZELLA COMPUTER CO.
Payroll for Week Ending October 4, 20XX

| NAME | SALES | | | QUOTA | COMM. SALES | COMM. RATE | GROSS COMM. | SALARY | GROSS WAGES |
	GROSS	R&A	NET						
Bellis, E.	$6,340	$40	$6,300	--	$6,300	8%	$ 504	$ 80	$ 584
Chambers, D.	5,820	70	5,750	$ 800	4,950	6	297	--	297
Duggan, C.	4,690	50	4,640	--	4,640	5	232	100	332
Meyer, C.	6,500	--	6,500	1,000	5,500	6	330	120	450
Quader, E.	6,332	82	6,250	500	5,750	8	460	--	460
						Total	$1,823	$300	$2,123

20.

COPPER ENTERPRISE, INC.
Payroll for Week Ending November 4, 20xx

| NAME | SALES | | | QUOTA | COMM. SALES | COMM. RATE | GROSS COMM. | SALARY | GROSS WAGES |
	GROSS	R&A	NET						
Barnes, D.	$ 7,500	$100	$ 7,400	--	$ 7,400	8%	$ 592	$110	$ 702
Cordel, Y.	10,680	80	10,600	$1,000	9,600	7	672	--	672
Leiter, L.	9,844	64	9,780	--	9,780	5	489	200	689
Murphy, D.	12,000	--	12,000	1,200	10,800	9	972	150	1,122
Ward, J.	8,956	26	8,920	630	8,300	8	664	--	664
						Total	$3,389	$460	$3,849

21.   220 lbs. × $0.65 = $ 143
          175 lbs. × 0.52 =   91
          460 lbs. × 0.48 =   220.80
          200 lbs. × 6.30 = 1,260
          Gross proceeds $1,714.80
    Freight $ 98.40
    Insurance   100.00
    Commission 102.89
                      - 301.29
        Net proceeds $1,413.51

22.   600 × $0.68 = $ 408
          500 × 0.40 =   200
          150 × 4.80 =   720
          175 × 6.40 = 1,120
          Gross proceeds $2,448.00
    Freight $ 72.00
    Insurance   56.00
    Commission 122.40
                      - 250.40
        Net proceeds $2,197.60

23.   5 × $70 = $ 350
          10 × 36 =   360
           3 × 61 =   183
           2 × 57 =   114
           4 × 45 =   180
          Prime cost $1,187.00
    Shipping $96
    Insurance   55
    Commission   59.35
                      + 210.35
        Gross cost $1,397.35

24.   25 × $ 76 = $1,900
          16 ×   52 =   832
          10 ×   48 =   480
           6 × 195 = 1,170
          Prime cost $4,382.00
    Shipping $ 98.00
    Insurance   87.00
    Commission 175.28
                      + 360.28
        Gross cost $4,742.28

Section 3, page 191

1.							CRISTO CLEANING SERVICE Payroll for Week Ending May 5, 20XX		
Name	M	T	W	TH	F	S	Total Hours	Rate Per Hour	Gross Wages
Becker, P.	8	8	7	7	6	0	36	$6.50	$ 234.00
Doyle, D.	8	7	8	9	8	0	40	6.75	270.00
Margo, D.	5	8	7	8	8	3	39	5.80	226.20
Murray, A.	8	7	7	7	7	2	38	6.25	237.50
Richards, B.	6	6	6	6	6	6	36	6.00	216.00
Stark, R.	8	9	9	8	6	0	40	7.10	284.00
Wu, Y.	9	8	8	7	5	0	37	7.00	259.00
								Total	$1,726.70

2.							THE HEARN CO. Payroll for Week Ending June 2, 20XX		
Name	M	T	W	TH	F	S	Total Hours	Rate Per Hour	Gross Wages
Burke, A.	8	7	5	8	8	0	36	$ 9.50	$ 342.00
Carter, F.	6	8	8	8	8	2	40	11.25	450.00
Keeney, K.	9	6	8	7	8	0	38	10.70	406.60
Poole, R.	8	8	7	7	7	3	40	10.45	418.00
Quinn, B.	5	7	6	9	9	3	39	12.00	468.00
Schick, B.	9	8	7	8	8	0	40	9.40	376.00
Weiman, T.	8	8	9	9	3	0	37	9.75	360.75
								TOTAL	$2,821.35

3.

SAUNDERS, INC.
Payroll for Week Ending December 6, 20XX

Name	M	T	W	TH	F	S	Total Hours	Reg. Hours	Hourly Rate	Over-time Hours	Over-time Rate	Reg. Wages	Over-time Wages	Total Gross Wages
Agnew	8	8	8	8	8	0	40	40	$17.50	—	$26.25	$ 700	— —	$ 700.00
Barski	8	7	9	8	7	3	42	40	16.50	2	24.75	660	$ 49.50	709.50
Clancy	6	8	7	8	8	0	37	37	16.00	—	24.00	592	— —	592.00
Ibar	7	8	8	9	8	5	45	40	17.20	5	25.80	688	129.00	817.00
Nozek	8	8	6	9	8	4	43	40	17.00	3	25.50	680	76.50	756.50
Totals												$3,320	$255.00	$3,575.00

4.

MAHONEY ELECTRONICS, INC.
Payroll for Week Ending June 14, 20XX

Name	M	T	W	TH	F	S	Total Hours	Reg. Hours	Hourly Rate	Over-time Hours	Over-time Rate	Reg. Wages	Over-time Wages	Total Gross Wages
Austin	9	8	8	7	8	0	40	40	$10.50	—	$15.75	$ 420	— —	$ 420.00
Coté	8	9	9	8	8	0	42	40	11.50	2	17.25	460	$ 34.50	494.50
Jarvis	6	7	8	8	6	4	39	39	10.00	—	15.00	390	— —	390.00
Osuna	9	9	8	9	6	5	46	40	9.90	6	14.85	396	89.10	485.10
Way	8	8	8	9	7	4	44	40	13.00	4	19.50	520	78.00	598.00
Totals												$2,186	$201.60	$2,387.60

5.

Name		M	T	W	TH	F	S	S	Total Hours	Rate Per Hour	Base Wages	Total Gross Wages
Coffey	RT	6	8	7	8	7	0	0	36	$ 8.00	$228.00	
	1½	0	0	0	1	0	0	0	1	12.00	12.00	
	DT	0	0	0	0	0	0	4	4	16.00	64.00	$ 364.00
Hanson	RT	7	8	8	8	7	2	0	40	8.50	340.00	
	1½	0	0	2	0	0	6	0	8	12.75	102.00	
	DT	0	0	0	0	0	0	0	0	17.00	--	442.00
Yoder	RT	8	5	8	8	8	3	0	40	8.60	344.00	
	1½	1	0	0	1	0	1	0	3	12.90	38.70	
	DT	0	0	0	0	0	0	3	3	17.20	51.60	434.30
											Total	$1,240.30

6.

Name		M	T	W	TH	F	S	S	Total Hours	Rate Per Hour	Base Wages	Total Gross Wages
Amsbry	RT	0	8	8	7	8	0	0	31	$10.00	$310.00	
	1½	0	0	1	0	0	0	0	1	15.00	15.00	
	DT	6	0	0	0	0	0	0	6	20.00	120.00	$ 445.00
Emory	RT	0	8	8	8	8	8	0	40	9.00	360.00	
	1½	0	0	2	0	1	0	0	3	13.50	40.50	
	DT	8	0	0	0	0	0	0	8	18.00	144.00	544.50
Williams	RT	0	8	8	8	8	5	0	37	15.00	555.00	
	1½	0	2	0	0	0	0	0	2	22.50	45.00	
	DT	0	0	0	0	0	0	5	5	30.00	150.00	750.00
											Total	$1,739.50

		POSITION	REGULAR HOURS PER WEEK	REGULAR SALARY	HOURS WORKED	GROSS WAGES
7.	(a)	Sales manager	40	$336	45	$399.00
	(b)	Office manager	38	304	44	368.00
	(c)	Plant manager	(varies)	437	46	465.50
8.	(a)	Administrative Assistant	40	$540	43	$600.75
	(b)	Executive Secretary	36	522	46	710.50
	(c)	Supervisor	(varies)	506	44	529.00

7. (a) $\dfrac{\$336}{40}$ = $8.40 regular hourly rate

$$
\begin{array}{rcl}
40 \times \$\ 8.40 &=& \$336 \\
5 \times\ \ 12.60 &=& \underline{\ \ 63} \\
& & \$399
\end{array}
$$

(b) $\dfrac{\$304}{38}$ = $8.00 regular hourly rate

$$
\begin{array}{rcl}
40 \times \$\ 8.00 &=& \$320 \\
4 \times\ \ 12.00 &=& \underline{\ \ 48} \\
& & \$368
\end{array}
$$

(c) $\dfrac{\$437}{46}$ = $9.50 regular hourly rate

$$
\begin{array}{rcl}
40 \times \$\ 9.50 &=& \$380 \\
6 \times\ \ 14.25 &=& \underline{\ \ 85.50} \\
& & \$465.50
\end{array}
$$

8. (a) $\dfrac{\$540}{40}$ = $13.50 regular hourly rate

$$
\begin{array}{rcl}
40 \times \$13.50 &=& \$540 \\
3 \times\ \ 20.25 &=& \underline{\ \ 60.75} \\
& & \$600.75
\end{array}
$$

(b) $\dfrac{\$522}{36}$ = $14.50 regular hourly rate

$$
\begin{array}{rcl}
40 \times \$14.50 &=& \$580 \\
6 \times\ \ 21.75 &=& \underline{\ \ 130.50} \\
& & \$710.50
\end{array}
$$

8. (Continued)

(c) $\dfrac{\$506}{44}$ = $11.50 regular hourly rate

$$40 \times \$11.50 = \$460$$
$$4 \times 17.25 = \underline{69}$$
$$\$529$$

	EMPLOYEE	HOURS	RATE PER HOUR	GROSS EARNINGS
9. (a)	G	43	$ 5.60	$249.20
(b)	H	45	7.70	365.75
(c)	I	47	8.50	429.25
10. (a)	J	42	$10.00	$430.00
(b)	K	46	15.40	754.60
(c)	L	48	13.50	702.00

9. (a) (1) $40 \times \$5.60 = \$224.00$
 $ 3 \times 8.40 = \underline{25.20}$
 $\$249.20$
 (2) $43 \times \$5.60 = \$240.80$
 $ 3 \times 2.80 = \underline{8.40}$
 $\$249.20$

(b) (1) $40 \times \$ 7.70 = \$308.00$
 $ 5 \times 11.55 = \underline{57.75}$
 $\$365.75$
 (2) $45 \times \$7.70 = \$346.50$
 $ 5 \times 3.85 = \underline{19.25}$
 $\$365.75$

(c) (1) $40 \times \$ 8.50 = \$340.00$
 $ 7 \times 12.75 = \underline{89.25}$
 $\$429.25$
 (2) $47 \times \$8.50 = \$399.50$
 $ 7 \times 4.25 = \underline{29.75}$
 $\$429.25$

10. (a) (1) $40 \times \$10 = \$400$
 $ 2 \times 15 = \underline{30}$
 $\$430$
 (2) $42 \times \$10 = \$420$
 $ 2 \times 5 = \underline{10}$
 $\$430$

(b) (1) $40 \times \$15.40 = \$616.00$
 $ 6 \times 23.10 = \underline{138.60}$
 $\$754.60$
 (2) $46 \times \$15.40 = \$708.40$
 $ 6 \times 7.70 = \underline{46.20}$
 $\$754.60$

(c) (1) $40 \times \$13.50 = \$540$
 $ 8 \times 20.25 = \underline{162}$
 $\$702$
 (2) $48 \times \$13.50 = \$648$
 $ 8 \times 6.75 = \underline{54}$
 $\$702$

11.

KING APPLIANCES, INC.
Payroll for Week Ending February 15, 20XX

Name	M	T	W	TH	F	S	Total Hours	Rate Per Hour	Over-time Hours	Over-time Excess Rate	Regular Rate Wages	Over-time Excess Wages	Total Gross Wages
Dinh	8	8	10	8	9	5	48	$5.50	8	$2.75	$ 264.00	$ 22.00	$ 286.00
Horn	8	9	8	9	9	6	49	6.40	9	3.20	313.60	28.80	342.40
Rook	7	8	10	10	8	4	47	7.30	7	3.65	343.10	25.55	368.65
Soka	9	9	8	8	8	0	42	7.90	2	3.95	331.80	7.90	339.70
Vern	8	9	9	6	10	8	50	7.60	10	3.80	380.00	38.00	418.00
										Totals	$1,632.50	$122.25	$1,754.75

12.

LEARY VIDEO SALES AND SERVICE
Payroll for Week Ending December 3, 20XX

Name	M	T	W	TH	F	S	Total Hours	Rate Per Hour	Over-time Hours	Over-time Excess Rate	Regular Rate Wages	Over-time Excess Wages	Total Gross Wages
Chung	8	8	9	9	8	0	42	$10.20	2	$5.10	$ 428.40	$ 10.20	$ 438.60
Hampton	7	8	8	8	8	6	45	12.50	5	6.25	562.50	31.25	593.75
Kramer	8	8	8	8	8	4	44	11.40	4	5.70	501.60	22.80	524.40
Rhoades	9	8	7	8	8	8	48	10.50	8	5.25	504.00	42.00	546.00
Sherman	8	8	5	8	6	11	46	12.00	6	6.00	552.00	36.00	588.00
										Totals	$2,548.50	$142.25	$2,690.75

Section 4, page 199

1.

	M	T	W	TH	F	Total
Stone, Tom	128	140	155	158	167	748

```
Base production     500 × $0.52 = $260.00
Premium production  248 × $0.70 =  173.60
Gross wage                       $433.60
```

2.

	M	T	W	TH	F	Total
Taylor, Melissa	85 doz.	92 doz.	100 doz.	98 doz.	105 doz.	480 doz.

```
Base production     300 × $0.95 = $285
Premium production  180 × $1.10 =  198
Gross wage                       $483
```

3.

	M	T	W	TH	F	Total
Gross production	325	344	346	350	342	1,707
Less: Spoilage	5	6	2·	0	1	14
Net production	320	338	344	350	341	1,693

```
Net production       1,693
Base production     -1,000 × $0.15 = $150.00
Premium production     693 ×  0.24 =  166.32
                                     $316.32
Docking               14 × $0.08 = -   1.12
Gross wages                          $315.20
```

4.

	M	T	W	TH	F	Total
Gross production	26	34	28	34	29	151
Less: Spoilage	2	0	0	3	1	6
Net production	24	34	28	31	28	145

4. (Continued)

```
Net production        145
Base production      -100 × $2.00 = $200
Premium production     45 ×  2.60 =   117
                                    $317
Docking               6 × $0.50 = -   3
Gross wages                         $314
```

5.

PACIFIC TOOL CO.
Payroll for Week Ending April 5, 20XX

Name	\multicolumn{5}{c}{NET PIECES PRODUCED}	Total Net Pieces	Rate Per Piece	Gross Wages Earned
	M	T	W	TH	F			
Abbott, A.	64	78	76	84	90	392	$1.00	$ 392.00
Breck, J.	71	77	78	79	86	391	1.03	402.73
Dunn, M.	56	58	62	65	67	308	1.01	311.08
Jones, B.	80	89	88	85	97	439	1.04	456.56
Simon, C.	75	75	82	86	89	407	1.02	415.14
Woods, V.	84	85	89	86	91	435	1.05	456.75
Yoe, T.	88	85	88	90	92	443	1.06	469.58
							Total	$2,903.84

6.

RICHMOND FABRICS
Payroll for Week Ending April 16, 20XX

Name	\multicolumn{5}{c}{NET PIECES PRODUCED}	Total Net Pieces	Rate Per Piece	Gross Wages Earned
	M	T	W	TH	F			
Adams, K.	90	88	100	101	102	481	$0.75	$ 360.75
Green, N.	95	100	105	108	108	516	0.80	412.80
Hart, M.	115	112	114	114	104	559	0.90	503.10
Lester, A.	109	110	120	125	121	585	0.92	538.20
Potter, D.	112	126	120	121	120	599	0.80	479.20
Randolph, T.	116	122	106	110	110	564	0.96	541.44
Wilkins, E.	109	101	104	105	106	525	0.87	456.75
							Total	$3,292.24

7.

STROZIER MANUFACTURING CO.
Payroll for Week Ending January 18, 20XX

Name	NET PIECES PRODUCED						Reg. Time Prod.	Rate Per Piece	Over-time Prod.	Over-time Rate	Reg. Wages	Over-time Wages	Total Gross Wages
	M	T	W	TH	F	S							
Chang	56	58	60	62	66	50	302	$0.60	50	$0.90	$ 181.20	$ 45.00	$ 226.20
Evans	60	61	64	67	70	45	322	0.68	45	1.02	218.96	45.90	264.86
Hall	72	75	75	79	78	70	379	0.70	70	1.05	265.30	73.50	338.80
Long	65	70	76	71	75	63	357	0.74	63	1.11	264.18	69.93	334.11
Thomas	61	71	73	76	74	68	355	0.68	68	1.02	241.40	69.36	310.76
Totals											$1,171.04	$303.69	$1,474.73

8.

JAMESTOWN CABLE CO.
Payroll for Week Ending July 27, 20XX

Name	NET PIECES PRODUCED						Reg. Time Prod.	Rate Per Piece	Over-time Prod.	Over-time Rate	Reg. Wages	Over-time Wages	Total Gross Wages
	M	T	W	TH	F	S							
Baylor	80	82	81	88	85	46	416	$0.68	46	$1.02	$ 282.88	$ 46.92	$ 329.80
Downes	92	101	102	99	104	66	498	0.72	66	1.08	358.56	71.28	429.84
Kelly	89	91	73	84	89	45	426	0.94	45	1.41	400.44	63.45	463.89
Harvey	80	94	95	90	81	36	440	0.88	36	1.32	387.20	47.52	434.72
Scully	77	68	78	80	84	61	387	0.92	61	1.38	356.04	84.18	440.22
Totals											$1,785.12	$313.35	$2,098.47

9.

SCHNELL ATHLETIC EQUIPMENT
Payroll for Week Ending August 12, 20XX

Name		DAILY PRODUCTION					Total Prod.	Net Quota	Production	Rate	Base Wages	Total Gross Wages
		M	T	W	TH	F						
Allen	GP	39	48	50	51	46		200	Base:	$0.88	$176.00	$ 198.10
	S	1	2	0	1	2			Premium:	0.95	26.60	
	NP	38	46	50	50	44	228		Chargeback:	0.75	(4.50)	
Dill	GP	36	41	49	54	50		150	Base:	0.92	138.00	210.84
	S	0	2	2	0	0			Premium:	0.99	75.24	
	NP	36	39	47	54	50	226		Chargeback:	0.60	(2.40)	
Edwards	GP	54	58	64	60	63		250	Base:	0.70	175.00	207.70
	S	3	1	1	0	0			Premium:	0.80	35.20	
	NP	51	57	63	60	63	294		Chargeback:	0.50	(2.50)	
Jenks	GP	48	49	53	59	66		300	Base:	0.85	230.35	228.75
	S	1	0	2	1	0			Premium:	0.93	---	
	NP	47	49	51	58	66	271		Chargeback:	0.40	(1.60)	
Strong	GP	65	68	73	75	79		275	Base:	0.86	236.50	306.82
	S	3	1	1	2	1			Premium:	0.96	73.92	
	NP	62	67	72	73	78	352		Chargeback:	0.45	(3.60)	
										Total		$1,152.21

10.

SIMON TEXTILES, INC.
Payroll for Week Ending May 6, 20XX

Name		DAILY PRODUCTION					Total Prod.	Net Quota	Production	Rate	Base Wages	Total Gross Wages
		M	T	W	TH	F						
Ballard	GP	100	94	95	90	86		300	Base:	$0.88	$264.00	
	S	1	0	2	2	2	458		Premium:	0.94	148.52	$ 410.42
	NP	99	94	93	88	84			Chargeback:	0.30	(2.10)	
Galano	GP	65	72	85	92	90		250	Base:	0.95	237.50	
	S	0	1	2	1	1	399		Premium:	0.98	146.02	382.52
	NP	65	71	83	91	89			Chargeback:	0.20	(1.00)	
Maddox	GP	101	106	110	112	100		350	Base:	0.92	322.00	
	S	0	0	2	4	4	519		Premium:	0.96	162.24	480.24
	NP	101	106	108	108	96			Chargeback:	0.40	(4.00)	
Pierson	GP	75	70	63	68	76		350	Base:	0.98	339.08	
	S	1	0	3	2	0	346		Premium:	1.00	---	336.44
	NP	74	70	60	66	76			Chargeback:	0.44	(2.64)	
Stewart	GP	99	97	100	101	99		300	Base:	0.89	267.00	
	S	0	1	2	1	1	491		Premium:	0.95	181.45	446.95
	NP	99	96	98	100	98			Chargeback:	0.30	(1.50)	
											Total	$2,056.57

1.

LESSIN PRINTING CO.
Payroll for Week Ending February 3, 20XX

Employee (Addl. Deps.)	Allow- ances	Gross Wages	DEDUCTIONS					Net Wages Due
			Social Security	Medi- care	Fed. Inc. Tax	Other (Ins.)	Total Deductions	
Beasley (0)	M-2	$ 545	$ 33.79	$ 7.90	$ 47	$10	$ 98.69	$ 446.31
Kirtley (1)	M-2	860	53.32	12.47	95	14	174.79	685.21
Mason (0)	S-1	772	47.86	11.19	126	10	195.05	576.95
Musser (2)	M-3	751	46.56	10.89	71	18	146.45	604.55
Smith (3)	M-4	687	42.59	9.96	52	22	126.55	560.45
Totals		$3,615	$224.12	$52.41	$391	$74	$741.53	$2,873.47

2.

ATKINS GARDEN SHOP
Payroll for Week Ending April 26, 20XX

Employee (Addl. Deps.)	Allow- ances	Gross Wages	DEDUCTIONS					Net Wages Due
			Social Security	Medi- care	Fed. Inc. Tax	Other (Ins.)	Total Deductions	
Donley (0)	M-2	$ 735	$ 45.57	$10.66	$ 76	$ 8	$140.23	$ 594.77
Moran (2)	M-3	766	47.49	11.11	72	16	146.60	619.40
Pepper (0)	S-1	643	39.87	9.32	90	8	147.19	495.81
Robb (1)	S-2	695	43.09	10.08	89	12	154.17	540.83
Ticer (3)	M-4	728	45.14	10.56	58	20	133.70	594.30
Totals		$3,567	$221.16	$51.73	$385	$64	$721.89	$2,845.11

3.

GRAYSTONE HARDWARE CO.
Payroll for Week Ending June 14, 20XX

Empl. No.	Allow-ances	Total Hours	Rate Per Hour	Gross Wages	DEDUCTIONS					Net Wages Due
					Social Security	Medicare	Fed. Income Tax	Other (Union Dues)	Total Deds.	
44	S-1	40	$13.50	$ 540.00	$ 33.48	$ 7.83	$ 66	$ 8.00	$115.31	$ 424.69
45	M-1	39	14.50	565.50	35.06	8.20	58	8.50	109.76	455.74
46	M-2	40	14.00	560.00	34.72	8.12	50	8.50	101.34	458.66
47	S-2	40	15.75	630.00	39.06	9.14	72	9.00	129.20	500.80
48	S-1	38	15.00	570.00	35.34	8.27	71	9.00	123.61	446.39
			Totals	$2,865.50	$177.66	$41.56	$317	$43.00	$579.22	$2,286.28

4.

RAMERIZ COMPUTER SERVICES
Payroll for Week Ending March 22, 20XX

Empl. No.	Allow-ances	Total Hours	Rate Per Hour	Gross Wages	DEDUCTIONS					Net Wages Due
					Social Security	Medicare	Fed. Income Tax	Other (Union Dues)	Total Deductions	
205	M-1	40	$14.50	$ 580	$ 35.96	$ 8.41	$ 61	$ 8.50	$113.87	$ 466.13
206	M-2	40	12.80	512	31.74	7.42	43	7.50	89.66	422.34
207	S-1	35	15.00	525	32.55	7.61	63	9.00	112.16	412.84
208	S-2	40	14.75	590	36.58	8.56	66	8.50	119.64	470.36
209	M-3	39	14.00	546	33.85	7.92	39	8.50	89.27	456.73
			Totals	$2,753	$170.68	$39.92	$272	$42.00	$524.60	$2,228.40

5.

SWARTS SALES CORP.
Payroll for Week Ending February 17, 20XX

Empl. No.	Allowances	Net Sales	Comm. Rate	Gross Wages	DEDUCTIONS					Net Wages Due
					Social Security	Medi-care	Fed. Income Tax	Other (United Way)	Total Deductions	
G-4	S-0	$7,600	8.5%	$ 646	$ 40.05	$ 9.37	$105	$ 64.60	$219.02	$ 426.98
G-5	M-2	7,500	7	525	32.55	7.61	44	52.50	136.66	388.34
G-6	M-1	7,800	8	624	38.69	9.05	67	62.40	177.14	446.86
G-7	M-3	8,000	8.5	680	42.16	9.86	60	68.00	180.02	499.98
G-8	S-1	7,400	7.5	555	34.41	8.05	68	55.50	165.96	389.04
Totals				$3,030	$187.86	$43.94	$344	$303.00	$878.80	$2,151.20

6.

ERRY MUSIC CO.
Payroll for Week Ending April 5, 20XX

Empl. No.	Allowances	Net Sales	Comm. Rate	Gross Wages	DEDUCTIONS					Net Wages Due
					Social Security	Medicare	Fed. Income Tax	Other (Charity Fund)	Total Deductions	
A-10	S-0	$5,600	12 %	$ 672	$ 41.66	$ 9.74	$113	$ 33.60	$198.00	$ 474.00
A-11	M-1	6,000	11	660	40.92	9.57	73	33.00	156.49	503.51
A-12	M-2	5,600	10.5	588	36.46	8.53	53	29.40	127.39	460.61
A-13	S-1	6,200	10	620	38.44	8.99	84	31.00	162.43	457.57
A-14	M-3	5,400	11.5	621	38.50	9.00	51	31.05	129.55	491.45
Totals				$3,161	$195.98	$45.83	$374	$128.05	$773.86	$2,387.14

7.

KING ASSOCIATES, INC.
Payroll for Week Ending June 11, 20XX

Employee No.	Allow-ances	Net Prod.	Rate Per Piece	Gross Wages	DEDUCTIONS					Net Wages Due
					Social Security	Medicare	Fed. Income Tax	Other (Ins.)	Total Deductions	
54 (2)	S-2	6,200	$0.10	$ 620	$ 38.44	$ 8.99	$ 70	$20	$137.43	$ 482.57
55 (1)	M-2	5,800	0.12	696	43.15	10.09	70	15	138.24	557.76
56 (2)	M-3	4,400	0.15	660	40.92	9.57	57	20	127.49	532.51
57 (0)	S-1	5,000	0.13	650	40.30	9.43	93	10	152.73	497.27
58 (1)	S-1	4,000	0.16	640	39.68	9.28	90	15	153.96	486.04
	Totals			$3,266	$202.49	$47.36	$380	$80	$709.85	$2,556.15

8.

PALGUTA SALES AND SERVICES, INC.
Payroll for Week Ending September 21, 20XX

Employee No.	Allow-ances	Net Prod.	Rate Per Piece	Gross Wages	DEDUCTIONS					Net Wages Due
					Social Security	Medicare	Fed. Inc. Tax	Other (Ins.)	Total Deductions	
22 (2)	S-2	6,500	$0.11	$ 715	$ 44.33	$10.37	$ 95	$ 26	$175.70	$ 539.30
23 (3)	M-2	5,400	0.13	702	43.52	10.18	71	33	157.70	544.30
24 (2)	M-3	3,800	0.15	570	35.34	8.27	44	26	113.61	456.39
25 (0)	S-0	5,000	0.12	600	37.20	8.70	94	12	151.90	448.10
26 (1)	S-1	4,500	0.14	630	39.06	9.14	87	19	154.20	475.80
	Totals			$3,217	$199.45	$46.66	$388	$116	$753.11	$2,463.89

9.

MCVEIGH INDUSTRIES
Payroll for Week Ending October 8, 20XX

Empl.	Allow-ances	Hours Worked	Reg. Wages	Over-time Wages	Total Gross Wages	DEDUCTIONS					Net Wages Due
						Social Security	Medi-care	Fed. Income Tax	Other (Ins.)	Total Deductions	
E	M-3	41	$ 700	$ 26.25	$ 726.25	$ 45.03	$ 0.53	$ 66	$10	$131.56	$ 594.69
F	M-2	45	600	112.50	712.50	44.18	10.33	73	10	137.51	574.99
G	S-0	48	580	174.00	754.00	46.75	10.93	136	10	203.68	550.32
H	S-1	43	660	74.25	734.25	45.52	10.65	115	10	181.17	553.08
	Totals		$2,540	$387.00	$2,927.00	$181.48	$42.44	$390	$40	$653.92	$2,273.08

10.

L. D. PAPE TUTORIAL SERVICES
Payroll for Week Ending February 22, 20XX

Empl.	Allow-ances	Hours Worked	Reg. Wages	Over-time Wages	Total Gross Wages	DEDUCTIONS					Net Wages Due
						Social Security	Medi-care	Fed. Income Tax	Other (Ins.)	Total Deductions	
A	S-2	42	$ 580	$ 93.50	$ 623.50	$ 38.66	$ 9.04	$ 70	$10	$127.70	$ 495.80
B	M-2	44	640	96.00	736.00	45.63	10.67	76	10	142.30	593.70
C	S-0	41	600	22.50	622.50	38.60	9.03	99	10	156.63	465.87
D	M-3	43	540	60.75	600.75	37.25	8.71	48	10	103.96	496.79
	TOTALS		$2,360	$222.75	$2,582.75	$160.14	$37.45	$293	$40	$530.59	$2,052.16

11.

DAWES EQUIPMENT, INC.
Payroll for Week Ending January 5, 20XX

Empl.	Allow-ances	Net Reg. Produc-tion	Over-time Produc-tion	Reg. Piece Rate	Reg. Wages	Over-time Wages	Total Gross Wages	DEDUCTIONS					Net Wages Due
								Social Security	Medi-care	Fed. Inc. Tax	Other (Ins.)	Total Deduc-tions	
#20	M-2	890	75	$0.60	$ 534	$ 67.50	$ 601.50	$ 37.29	$ 8.72	$ 56	$ 30.08	$132.09	$ 469.41
21	M-0	850	50	0.64	544	48.00	592.00	36.70	8.58	71	29.60	145.88	446.12
22	S-2	825	35	0.72	594	37.80	631.80	39.17	9.16	72	31.59	151.92	479.88
23	M-1	800	45	0.88	704	59.40	763.40	47.33	11.07	88	38.17	184.57	578.83
Totals					$2,376	$212.70	$2,588.70	$160.49	$37.53	$287	$129.44	$614.46	$1,974.24

12.

J. V. GRAY ACCOUNTING SOFTWARE
Payroll for Week Ending November 15, 20XX

Empl. No.	Allow-ances	Net Reg. Produc-tion	Over-time Produc-tion	Reg. Piece Rate	Reg. Wages	Over-time Wages	Total Gross Wages	DEDUCTIONS					Net Wages Due
								Social Security	Medi-care	Fed. Income Tax	Other	Total Deduc-tions	
#1	S-2	1,000	100	$0.50	$ 500	$ 75.00	$ 575.00	$ 35.65	$ 8.34	$ 63	$ 23.00	$129.99	$ 445.01
2	M-0	1,100	70	0.56	616	58.80	674.80	41.84	9.78	83	26.99	161.61	513.19
3	M-2	850	30	0.60	510	27.00	537.00	33.29	7.79	46	21.48	108.56	428.44
4	M-3	900	40	0.70	630	42.00	672.00	41.66	9.74	59	26.88	137.28	534.72
Totals					$2,256	$202.80	$2,458.80	$152.44	$35.65	$251	$98.35	$537.44	$1,921.36

Section 6, page 223

Problem 1

2	Total wages and tips, plus other compensation					2	15,000	
3	Total income tax withheld from wages, tips, and sick pay					3	2,250	
4	Adjustment of withheld income tax for preceding quarters of calendar year					4	—	
5	Adjusted total of income tax withheld (line 3 as adjusted by line 4 — see instructions) . .					5	2,250	
6	Taxable social security wages	6a	15,000	× 12.4% (.124) =		6b	1,860	
	Taxable social security tips	6c	—	× 12.4% (.124) =		6d		
7	Taxable Medicare wages and tips	7a	15,000	× 2.9% (.029) =		7b	435	

8 Total social security and Medicare taxes (add lines 6b, 6d, and 7b). Check here if wages
   are not subject to social security and/or Medicare tax . . . . ▶ ☐ | 8 | 2,295 |

9 Adjustment of social security and Medicare taxes (see Instructions for required explanation)
   Sick Pay $_____ ± Fractions of Cents $_____ ± Other $_____ = | 9 | — |

10 Adjusted total of social security and Medicare taxes (line 8 as adjusted by line 9 — see
   instructions) . . . . | 10 | 2,295 |

11 **Total taxes** (add lines 5 and 10) . . . . | 11 | 4,545 |

12 Advance earned income credit (EIC) payments made to employees . . . . | 12 | — |

13 Net taxes (subtract line 12 from line 11). **If $1,000 or more, this must equal line 17,
   column (d) below (or line D of Schedule B (Form 941)** . . . . | 13 | 4,545 |

14 Total deposits for quarter, including overpayment applied from a prior quarter . . . . | 14 | 4,545 |

15 **Balance due** (subtract line 14 from line 13). See instructions . . . . | 15 | — |

Problem 2

2	Total wages and tips, plus other compensation					2	40,000	
3	Total Income tax withheld from wages, tips, and sick pay					3	5,900	
4	Adjustment of withheld income tax for preceding quarters of calendar year					4	—	
5	Adjusted total of income tax withheld (line 3 as adjusted by line 4 — see instructions) . .					5	5,900	
6	Taxable social security wages	6a	4,000	× 12.4% (.124) =		6b	4,960	
	Taxable social security tips	6c	—	× 12.4% (.124) =		6d	—	
7	Taxable Medicare wages and tips	7a	4,000	× 2.9% (.029) =		7b	1,160	

8 Total social security and Medicare taxes (add lines 6b, 6d, and 7b). Check here if wages
   are not subject to social security and/or Medicare tax . . . . ▶ ☐ | 8 | 6,120 |

9 Adjustment of social security and Medicare taxes (see Instructions for required explanation)
   Sick Pay $_____ ± Fractions of Cents $_____ ± Other $_____ = | 9 | — |

10 Adjusted total of social security and Medicare taxes (line 8 as adjusted by line 9 — see
   instructions) . . . . | 10 | 6,120 |

11 **Total taxes** (add lines 5 and 10) . . . . | 11 | 12,020 |

12 Advance earned income credit (EIC) payments made to employees . . . . | 12 | — |

13 Net taxes (subtract line 12 from line 11). **If $1,000 or more, this must equal line 17,
   column (d) below (or line D of Schedule B (Form 941)** . . . . | 13 | 12,020 |

14 Total deposits for quarter, including overpayment applied from a prior quarter . . . . | 14 | 12,020 |

15 **Balance due** (subtract line 14 from line 13). See instructions . . . . | 15 | — |

Problem 3

2	Total wages and tips, plus other compensation	**2**	50,000		
3	Total income tax withheld from wages, tips, and sick pay	**3**	7,500		
4	Adjustment of withheld income tax for preceding quarters of calendar year	**4**	—		
5	Adjusted total of income tax withheld (line 3 as adjusted by line 4 — see instructions) . .	**5**	7,500		
6	Taxable social security wages . . . . **6a** 44,000 × 12.4% (.124) =	**6b**	5,456		
	Taxable social security tips . . . . **6c** 6,000 × 12.4% (.124) =	**6d**	744		
7	Taxable Medicare wages and tips . . . . **7a** 50,000 × 2.9% (.029) =	**7b**	1,450		
8	Total social security and Medicare taxes (add lines 6b, 6d, and 7b). Check here if wages are not subject to social security and/or Medicare tax . . . . ▶ ☐	**8**	7,650		
9	Adjustment of social security and Medicare taxes (see Instructions for required explanation) Sick Pay $_____ ± Fractions of Cents $_____ ± Other $_____ =	**9**	—		
10	Adjusted total of social security and Medicare taxes (line 8 as adjusted by line 9 — see instructions)	**10**	7,650		
11	**Total taxes** (add lines 5 and 10)	**11**	15,150		
12	Advance earned income credit (EIC) payments made to employees	**12**	—		
13	Net taxes (subtract line 12 from line 11). **If $1,000 or more, this must equal line 17, column (d) below (or line D of Schedule B (Form 941)**	**13**	15,150		
14	Total deposits for quarter, including overpayment applied from a prior quarter	**14**	15,150		
15	**Balance due** (subtract line 14 from line 13). See instructions	**15**	—		

Problem 4

2	Total wages and tips, plus other compensation	**2**	41,000		
3	Total income tax withheld from wages, tips, and sick pay	**3**	5,400		
4	Adjustment of withheld income tax for preceding quarters of calendar year	**4**	—		
5	Adjusted total of income tax withheld (line 3 as adjusted by line 4 — see instructions) . .	**5**	5,400		
6	Taxable social security wages . . . . **6a** 38,000 × 12.4% (.124) =	**6b**	4,712		
	Taxable social security tips . . . . **6c** 3,000 × 12.4% (.124) =	**6d**	372		
7	Taxable Medicare wages and tips . . . . **7a** 41,000 × 2.9% (.029) =	**7b**	1,189		
8	Total social security and Medicare taxes (add lines 6b, 6d, and 7b). Check here if wages are not subject to social security and/or Medicare tax . . . . ▶ ☐	**8**	6,273		
9	Adjustment of social security and Medicare taxes (see Instructions for required explanation) Sick Pay $_____ ± Fractions of Cents $_____ ± Other $_____ =	**9**	—		
10	Adjusted total of social security and Medicare taxes (line 8 as adjusted by line 9 — see instructions)	**10**	6,273		
11	**Total taxes** (add lines 5 and 10)	**11**	11,673		
12	Advance earned income credit (EIC) payments made to employees	**12**	—		
13	Net taxes (subtract line 12 from line 11). **If $1,000 or more, this must equal line 17, column (d) below (or line D of Schedule B (Form 941)**	**13**	11,673		
14	Total deposits for quarter, including overpayment applied from a prior quarter	**14**	11,673		
15	**Balance due** (subtract line 14 from line 13). See instructions	**15**	—		

Problem 5

2	Total wages and tips, plus other compensation					2	29,500
3	Total income tax withheld from wages, tips, and sick pay					3	4,200
4	Adjustment of withheld income tax for preceding quarters of calendar year					4	—
5	Adjusted total of income tax withheld (line 3 as adjusted by line 4 — see instructions) ..					5	4,200
6	Taxable social security wages	6a	26,000	× 12.4% (.124) =		6b	3,224
	Taxable social security tips	6c	1,500	× 12.4% (.124) =		6d	186
7	Taxable Medicare wages and tips	7a	29,500	× 2.9% (.029) =		7b	856
8	Total social security and Medicare taxes (add lines 6b, 6d, and 7b). Check here if wages are not subject to social security and/or Medicare tax .... ▶ ☐					8	4,266
9	Adjustment of social security and Medicare taxes (see Instructions for required explanation) Sick Pay $_____ ± Fractions of Cents $_____ ± Other $_____ =					9	—
10	Adjusted total of social security and Medicare taxes (line 8 as adjusted by line 9 — see instructions)					10	4,266
11	**Total taxes** (add lines 5 and 10)					11	8,466
12	Advance earned income credit (EIC) payments made to employees					12	—
13	Net taxes (subtract line 12 from line 11). **If $1,000 or more, this must equal line 17, column (d) below (or line D of Schedule B (Form 941)**					13	8,466
14	Total deposits for quarter, including overpayment applied from a prior quarter					14	8,466
15	**Balance due** (subtract line 14 from line 13). See instructions					15	—

Problem 6

2	Total wages and tips, plus other compensation					2	57,000
3	Total income tax withheld from wages, tips, and sick pay					3	9,000
4	Adjustment of withheld income tax for preceding quarters of calendar year					4	—
5	Adjusted total of income tax withheld (line 3 as adjusted by line 4 — see instructions) ..					5	9,000
6	Taxable social security wages	6a	50,000	× 12.4% (.124) =		6b	6,200
	Taxable social security tips	6c	5,000	× 12.4% (.124) =		6d	620
7	Taxable Medicare wages and tips	7a	57,000	× 2.9% (.029) =		7b	1,653
8	Total social security and Medicare taxes (add lines 6b, 6d, and 7b). Check here if wages are not subject to social security and/or Medicare tax .... ▶ ☐					8	8,473
9	Adjustment of social security and Medicare taxes (see Instructions for required explanation) Sick Pay $_____ ± Fractions of Cents $_____ ± Other $_____ =					9	—
10	Adjusted total of social security and Medicare taxes (line 8 as adjusted by line 9 — see instructions)					10	8,473
11	**Total taxes** (add lines 5 and 10)					11	17,473
12	Advance earned income credit (EIC) payments made to employees					12	—
13	Net taxes (subtract line 12 from line 11). **If $1,000 or more, this must equal line 17, column (d) below (or line D of Schedule B (Form 941)**					13	17,473
14	Total deposits for quarter, including overpayment applied from a prior quarter					14	17,473
15	**Balance due** (subtract line 14 from line 13). See instructions					15	—

Business Mathematics: A Collegiate Approach

		1st Qtr.	2nd Qtr.	3rd Qtr.	4th Qtr.
7.	G	$19,500	$19,000	$19,000	$18,200
	H	21,000	25,000	29,000	1,200
	I	26,000	26,000	24,200	0
8.	J	$ 7,000	$15,500	$16,000	$16,000
	K	18,900	18,400	19,600	19,300
	L	31,000	30,000	15,200	0

	Employee	Cumulative Earnings	4th Qtr. Earnings	Social Security Earnings	Medicare Earnings
9.	1	$ 66,000	$18,000	$10,200	$18,000
	2	55,000	29,000	21,200	29,000
	3	80,000	28,000	0	28,000
10.	4	$ 68,000	$20,000	$ 8,200	$20,000
	5	64,000	15,500	12,200	15,500
	6	100,000	25,000	0	25,000

11.

Empl	1st Quarter Gross Wages	Inc. Tax	Soc. Sec. Wages	2nd Quarter Gross Wages	Inc. Tax	Soc. Sec. Wages	3rd Quarter Gross Wages	Inc. Tax	Soc. Sec. Wages	4th Quarter Gross Wages	Inc. Tax	Soc. Sec. Wages
A	$ 6,800	$ 980	$ 6,800	$ 7,400	$1,036	$ 7,400	$ 7,500	$ 1,050	$ 7,500	$ 7,900	$ 1,106	$ 7,900
B	17,600	1,960	17,600	20,800	2,072	20,800	18,000	2,100	18,000	19,300	2,242	19,300
C	18,800	2,492	18,800	18,600	2,604	18,600	20,700	2,818	20,700	20,500	2,775	18,100
D	29,000	4,060	29,000	29,500	3,990	29,500	28,900	4,046	17,700	28,800	4,032	0
Total	72,200	9,492	72,200	76,300	9,702	76,300	75,100	10,014	63,900	76,500	10,155	45,300

12.

Empl	1st Quarter Gross Wages	Inc. Tax	Soc. Sec. Wages	2nd Quarter Gross Wages	Inc. Tax	Soc. Sec. Wages	3rd Quarter Gross Wages	Inc. Tax	Soc. Sec. Wages	4th Quarter Gross Wages	Inc. Tax	Soc. Sec. Wages
E	$ 6,200	$ 940	$ 6,200	$12,800	$1,470	$12,800	$12,800	$1,470	$12,800	$13,000	$1,506	$13,000
F	15,500	1,900	15,500	16,400	2,200	16,400	16,800	2,350	16,800	16,900	2,358	16,900
G	20,000	2,520	20,000	20,000	2,520	20,000	20,000	2,520	20,000	20,000	2,520	16,200
H	30,000	3,030	30,000	35,000	3,200	35,000	35,000	3,200	11,200	36,000	3,240	0
Total	71,700	8,390	71,700	84,200	9,390	84,200	84,600	9,540	60,800	85,900	9,624	46,100

Problem 13

2	Total wages and tips, plus other compensation				2	75,100
3	Total income tax withheld from wages, tips, and sick pay				3	10,014
4	Adjustment of withheld income tax for preceding quarters of calendar year				4	–
5	Adjusted total of income tax withheld (line 3 as adjusted by line 4 – see instructions)				5	10,014
6	Taxable social security wages	6a	63,900	× 12.4% (.124) =	6b	7,924
	Taxable social security tips	6c	–	× 12.4% (.124) =	6d	–
7	Taxable Medicare wages and tips	7a	75,100	× 2.9% (.029) =	7b	2,178
8	Total social security and Medicare taxes (add lines 6b, 6d, and 7b). Check here if wages are not subject to social security and/or Medicare tax ▶ ☐				8	10,102
9	Adjustment of social security and Medicare taxes (see Instructions for required explanation) Sick Pay $_____ ± Fractions of Cents $_____ ± Other $_____ =				9	–
10	Adjusted total of social security and Medicare taxes (line 8 as adjusted by line 9 – see instructions)				10	10,102
11	**Total taxes** (add lines 5 and 10)				11	20,116
12	Advance earned income credit (EIC) payments made to employees				12	–
13	Net taxes (subtract line 12 from line 11). **If $1,000 or more, this must equal line 17, column (d) below (or line D of Schedule B (Form 941)**				13	20,116
14	Total deposits for quarter, including overpayment applied from a prior quarter				14	20,116
15	**Balance due** (subtract line 14 from line 13). See instructions				15	–

Problem 14

2	Total wages and tips, plus other compensation				2	84,600
3	Total income tax withheld from wages, tips, and sick pay				3	9,540
4	Adjustment of withheld income tax for preceding quarters of calendar year				4	–
5	Adjusted total of income tax withheld (line 3 as adjusted by line 4 – see instructions)				5	9,540
6	Taxable social security wages	6a	60,800	× 12.4% (.124) =	6b	7,539
	Taxable social security tips	6c	–	× 12.4% (.124) =	6d	–
7	Taxable Medicare wages and tips	7a	84,600	× 2.9% (.029) =	7b	2,453
8	Total social security and Medicare taxes (add lines 6b, 6d, and 7b). Check here if wages are not subject to social security and/or Medicare tax ▶ ☐				8	9,992
9	Adjustment of social security and Medicare taxes (see Instructions for required explanation) Sick Pay $_____ ± Fractions of Cents $_____ ± Other $_____ =				9	–
10	Adjusted total of social security and Medicare taxes (line 8 as adjusted by line 9 – see instructions)				10	9,992
11	**Total taxes** (add lines 5 and 10)				11	19,532
12	Advance earned income credit (EIC) payments made to employees				12	–
13	Net taxes (subtract line 12 from line 11). **If $1,000 or more, this must equal line 17, column (d) below (or line D of Schedule B (Form 941)**				13	19,532
14	Total deposits for quarter, including overpayment applied from a prior quarter				14	19,532
15	**Balance due** (subtract line 14 from line 13). See instructions				15	–

Problem 15

2	Total wages and tips, plus other compensation				**2**	76,500	
3	Total income tax withheld from wages, tips, and sick pay				**3**	10,155	
4	Adjustment of withheld income tax for preceding quarters of calendar year				**4**	—	
5	Adjusted total of income tax withheld (line 3 as adjusted by line 4 — see instructions) . .				**5**	10,155	
6	Taxable social security wages	**6a**	45,300	× 12.4% (.124) =	**6b**	5,617	
	Taxable social security tips	**6c**	—	× 12.4% (.124) =	**6d**	—	
7	Taxable Medicare wages and tips	**7a**	76,500	× 2.9% (.029) =	**7b**	2,219	
8	Total social security and Medicare taxes (add lines 6b, 6d, and 7b). Check here if wages are not subject to social security and/or Medicare tax . . . . ▶ ☐				**8**	7,836	
9	Adjustment of social security and Medicare taxes (see Instructions for required explanation) Sick Pay \$_____ ± Fractions of Cents \$_____ ± Other \$_____ =				**9**	—	
10	Adjusted total of social security and Medicare taxes (line 8 as adjusted by line 9 — see instructions)				**10**	7,836	
11	**Total taxes** (add lines 5 and 10)				**11**	17,991	
12	Advance earned income credit (EIC) payments made to employees				**12**	—	
13	Net taxes (subtract line 12 from line 11). **If \$1,000 or more, this must equal line 17, column (d) below (or line D of Schedule B (Form 941)**				**13**	17,991	
14	Total deposits for quarter, including overpayment applied from a prior quarter				**14**	17,991	
15	**Balance due** (subtract line 14 from line 13). See instructions				**15**	—	

Problem 16

2	Total wages and tips, plus other compensation				**2**	85,900	
3	Total income tax withheld from wages, tips, and sick pay				**3**	9,624	
4	Adjustment of withheld income tax for preceding quarters of calendar year				**4**	—	
5	Adjusted total of income tax withheld (line 3 as adjusted by line 4 — see instructions) . .				**5**	9,624	
6	Taxable social security wages	**6a**	46,100	× 12.4% (.124) =	**6b**	5,716	
	Taxable social security tips	**6c**	—	× 12.4% (.124) =	**6d**	—	
7	Taxable Medicare wages and tips	**7a**	85,900	× 2.9% (.029) =	**7b**	2,491	
8	Total social security and Medicare taxes (add lines 6b, 6d, and 7b). Check here if wages are not subject to social security and/or Medicare tax . . . . ▶ ☐				**8**	8,207	
9	Adjustment of social security and Medicare taxes (see Instructions for required explanation) Sick Pay \$_____ ± Fractions of Cents \$_____ ± Other \$_____ =				**9**	—	
10	Adjusted total of social security and Medicare taxes (line 8 as adjusted by line 9 — see instructions)				**10**	8,207	
11	**Total taxes** (add lines 5 and 10)				**11**	17,831	
12	Advance earned income credit (EIC) payments made to employees				**12**	—	
13	Net taxes (subtract line 12 from line 11). **If \$1,000 or more, this must equal line 17, column (d) below (or line D of Schedule B (Form 941)**				**13**	17,831	
14	Total deposits for quarter, including overpayment applied from a prior quarter				**14**	17,831	
15	**Balance due** (subtract line 14 from line 13). See instructions				**15**	—	

		1st Qtr.	2nd Qtr.	3rd Qtr.	4th Qtr.
17. (a)	G	$ 7,000	0	0	0
	H	7,000	0	0	0
	I	7,000	0	0	0
(b)	Total	$21,000	0	0	0

(c) 1st Qtr. only
State   = .036 × $21,000 = $756
Federal = .008 × $21,000 = $168

		1st Qtr.	2nd Qtr.	3rd Qtr.	4th Qtr.
18. (a)	J	$ 7,000	0	0	0
	K	7,000	0	0	0
	L	7,000	0	0	0
(b)	Total	$21,000	0	0	0

(c) 1st Qtr. only
State   = .036 × $21,000 = $756
Federal = .008 × $21,000 = $168

		1st Qtr.	2nd Qtr.	3rd Qtr.	4th Qtr.
19. (a)	A	$ 6,800	200	0	0
	B	7,000	0	0	0
	C	7,000	0	0	0
	D	7,000	0	0	0
(b)	Total	$21,800	200	0	0

(c) 1st Qtr.
State   = .036 × $27,800 = $1,001
Federal = .008 × $27,800 = $ 222

2nd Qtr.
State   = .036 × $200 = $7.20
Federal = .008 × $200 = $1.60

		1st Qtr.	2nd Qtr.	3rd Qtr.	4th Qtr.
20. (a)	E	$ 6,200	800	0	0
	F	7,000	0	0	0
	G	7,000	0	0	0
	H	7,000	0	0	0
(b)	Total	$27,200	800	0	0

20. (Continued)

   (c) 1st Qtr.
        State   = .029 × $27,200 = $789
        Federal = .008 × $27,200 = $218

        2nd Qtr.
        State   = .029 × $800 = $23.20
        Federal = .008 × $800 = $ 6.40

21. (a) Maximum Social Security taxable earnings:
        $ 76,200 × .062 = $4,724
    (b) $500,000 × .0145 = $7,250
    (c) $ 7,000 × .008 = $ 56
    (d) $ 7,000 × .054 = $ 378

22. (a) Maximum Social Security taxable earnings:
        $ 76,200 × .062 = $ 4,724
    (b) $1,000,000 × .0145 = $14,500
    (c) $ 7,000 × .008 = $ 56
    (d) $ 7,000 × .054 = $ 378

CHAPTER IX

DEPRECIATION AND OVERHEAD

These topics are grouped together since both involve the distribution of business expenses.

1.   Depreciation:

Depreciation and cost recovery are basically the same. Both refer to the allocation of a plant asset's cost over its estimated useful life. Since a plant asset is used by a business for several years, it would be improper to write off (or expense) the total cost in one year. Depreciation and cost recovery are systematic methods of allocating the cost over the useful life of the plant asset.

Prior to 1981, a business generally could use any of the traditional depreciation methods for income tax purposes. With the Economic Recovery Tax Act of 1981 and the Tax Reform Act of 1986 the rules were changed. For assets placed in service after December 31, 1986, a business must use the Modified Accelerated Cost Recovery System (MACRS) or a variation of straight-line depreciation for tax purposes.

Depreciation methods are still used in financial accounting since the AICPA and FASB (Financial Accounting Standards Board) do not recognize the MACRS method for use in financial accounting records and reports, because the method allocates depreciation over a shorter period of time than the estimated useful life.

One difference between depreciation and cost recovery that should be pointed out to students is that a plant asset is depreciated down to its residual value, which may or may not be zero. With MACRS, a plant asset's cost is fully recovered (brought down to zero).

Another major difference is in the first year of depreciation and cost recovery. Using depreciation, the first-year's write-off could be apportioned according to the length of use, whereas MACRS simply assume that all newly acquired plant assets (except real property) taken together will average a half-year of use. This half-year is built into the tables.

The 1986 Tax Reform Act uses a combination of the 200% (or double) declining-balance method and later the straight-line method -- both long-established procedures. Having grown accustomed to the convenience of tabular factors for their calculations (or in their computer programs), however, many accounting firms prefer to continue that approach under the 1986 Act. Thus, the text also presents the MACRS method using multiplicative factors.

In addition to the MACRS method, the text introduces all traditional depreciation methods, with emphasis on straight line and double declining balance. Discussion and examples are also included for the units-of-production method. Emphasize, however, that the units-of-production method, while it has been used historically, is not recommended by accountants.

Point out the differences between the straight-line method and the declining-balance method: the straight-line method involves the *depreciable base* distributed over a period of years. The declining-balance method distributes the *cost* over the years ending with the residual value as the book value in the final year. Both the straight-line method and the units-of-production method use the depreciable base.

After each depreciation method is introduced and examples given, a "quick practice" is provided. This is to give the students some feedback before going on to the next depreciation method and before doing the assignment. These problems would be good exercises to do in class and then checked before continuing into the next method.

2.   Partial Years:

Students should have a good understanding of different depreciation methods before attempting partial years and proration. Students understand the concept of proration when an asset is purchased at some time other than the beginning of a year. Straight line proration for a partial year is usually not difficult for them. Difficulty does arrive with proration for a partial year for the accelerated methods. It may be helpful to explain that a business wants to take the full allowable amount of depreciation each year and to do so, the unused portion of depreciation from the previous year must be included. This section may be omitted for basic courses.

3.   Overhead:

This is a rather simple topic and serves to renew the confidence of a student who has been experiencing difficulty with previous topics. It is also a good application of ratio. Be sure the student checks each problem to verify that the individual allocations total the full amount of overhead.

CHAPTER 9 - DEPRECIATION AND OVERHEAD
PROBLEM SOLUTIONS

Quick Practice - Straight line, page 232

1. (a) Annual depr. $= \dfrac{\$7,500 - \$300}{6 \text{ years}} = \$1,200/\text{yr.}$

   (b) Annual depr. $= \dfrac{\$5,800 - \$400}{9 \text{ years}} = \$600/\text{yr.}$

   (c) Annual depr. $= \dfrac{\$2,900 - \$700}{4 \text{ years}} = \$550/\text{yr.}$

Depreciation Schedule

Year	Book Value (End of Year)	Annual Depreciation	Accumulated Depreciation
0	$2,900	--	--
1	2,350	$550	$ 550
2	1,800	550	1,100
3	1,250	550	1,650
4	700	550	2,200

2. (a) Annual depr. $= \dfrac{\$20,000 - \$2,000}{10 \text{ years}} = \$1,800/\text{yr.}$

   (b) Annual depr. $= \dfrac{\$12,000 - \$800}{8 \text{ years}} = \$1,400/\text{yr.}$

   (c) Annual depr. $= \dfrac{\$6,000 - \$400}{7 \text{ years}} = \$800/\text{yr.}$

Depreciation Schedule

Year	Book Value (End of Year)	Annual Depreciation	Accumulated Depreciation
0	$6,000	--	--
1	5,200	$800	$ 800
2	4,400	800	1,600
3	3,600	800	2,400
4	2,800	800	3,200
5	2,000	800	4,000
6	1,200	800	4,800
7	400	800	5,600

Quick Practice - Declining Balance, page 235

1. (a) Rate = $2 \times \dfrac{1}{5} = \dfrac{2}{5}$ or 40%

   First year depr.   = 40% × $1,900 = $760
   Book value   = $1,900 - $760 = $1,140

   Second year depr. = 40% × $1,140 = $456
   Book value   = $1,140 - $456 = $684

   Third year depr. = 40% × $684 = $274
   Book value   = $684 - $274 = $410

   Fourth year depr. = 40% × $410 = $164
   Book value   = $410 - $164 = $246

   Fifth year depr. = book value end of fourth year = $246
   Book value   = 0

   (b) Rate = $2 \times \dfrac{1}{4} = \dfrac{2}{4} = \dfrac{1}{2}$ or 50%

   First year depr. = 50% × $800 = $400
   Book value   = $800 - $400 = $400

   Second year depr. = 50% × $400 = $200
   Book value   = $400 - $200 = $200

   Third year depr. = 50% × $200 = $100
   Book value   = $200 - $100 = $100

   Fourth year depr. = book value end of third year = $100
   Book value   = 0

   (c) Rate = $2 \times \dfrac{1}{6} = \dfrac{2}{6} = \dfrac{1}{3}$

   First year depr.   = $\dfrac{1}{3}$ × $1,800 = $600

   Book value   = $1,800 - $600 = $1,200

   Second year depr. = $\dfrac{1}{3}$ × $1,200 = $400

   Book value   = $1,200 - $400 = $800

1. (c) (Continued)

Third year depr. $= \frac{1}{3} \times \$800 = \$267$

Book value $= \$800 - \$267 = \$533$

Fourth year depr. $= \frac{1}{3} \times \$533 = \$178$

Book value $= \$533 - \$178 = \$355$

Fifth year depr. $= \frac{1}{3} \times \$355 = \$118$

Book value $= \$355 - \$118 = \$237$

Sixth year depr. $= \frac{1}{3} \times \$237 = \$79$ but this amount

would bring book value above residual value of $150.

Sixth year depr. = $237 - $150 = $87.

Depreciation Schedule

Year	Book Value (End of Year)	Annual Depreciation	Accumulated Depreciation
0	$1,800	--	--
1	1,200	$600	$ 600
2	800	400	1,000
3	533	267	1,267
4	355	178	1,445
5	237	118	1,563
6	150	87	1,650

2. (a) Rate $= 2 \times \frac{1}{5} = \frac{2}{5}$ or 40%

First year depr. $= 40\% \times \$4,200 = \$1,680$
Book value $= \$4,200 - \$1,680 = \$2,520$

Second year depr. $= 40\% \times \$2,520 = \$1,008$
Book value $= \$2,520 - \$1,008 = \$1,512$

Third year depr. $= 40\% \times \$1,512 = \$605$
Book value $= \$1,512 - \$605 = \$907$

Fourth year depr. $= 40\% \times \$907 = \$363$
Book value $= \$907 - \$363 = \$544$

2. (a) (Continued)

Fifth year depr.   = book value end of fourth year = $544
Book value   = 0

(b) Rate = $2 \times \dfrac{1}{8} = \dfrac{1}{4}$ = or 25%

First year depr.   = 25% × $5,000 = $1,250
Book value   = $5,000 - $1,250 = $3,750

Second year depr. = 25% × $3,750 = $938
Book value   = $3,750 - $938 = $2,812

Third year depr.   = 25% × $2,812 = $703
Book value   = $2,812 - $703 = $2,109

Fourth year depr. = 25% × $2,109 = $527
Book value   = $2,109 - $527 = $1,582

Fifth year depr.   = 25% × $1,582 = $396
Book value   = $1,582 - $396 = $1,186

Sixth year depr.   = 25% × $1,186 = $297
Book value   = $1,186 - $297 = $889

Seventh year depr. = 25% × $889 = $222
Book value   = $889 - $222 = $667

Eight year depr.   = book value end of seventh year = $667
Book value   = 0

(c) Rate = $2 \times \dfrac{1}{3} = \dfrac{2}{3}$

First year depr.   = $\dfrac{2}{3}$ × $1,500 = $1,000

Book value   = $1,500 - $1,000 = $500

Second year depr. = $\dfrac{2}{3}$ × $500 = $333

Book value   = $500 - $333 = $167

Third year depr.   = $167 - $50 = $117

2. (c) (Continued)

Depreciation Schedule

Year	Book Value (End of Year)	Annual Depreciation	Accumulated Depreciation
0	$1,500	--	--
1	500	$1,000	$1,000
2	167	333	1,333
3	50	117	1,450

Quick Practice - Units of Production, page 237

1. (a) Rate $= \dfrac{\$7,500 - \$300}{90,000 \text{ units}} = \$0.08$ per unit

Year	Units Produced	×	Unit Rate	=	Annual Depreciation
1	18,000	×	$0.08	=	$1,440
2	20,000	×	0.08	=	1,600
3	25,000	×	0.08	=	2,000
4	19,000	×	0.08	=	1,520
5	8,000	×	0.08	=	640

(b) Rate $= \dfrac{\$8,100 - \$600}{30,000 \text{ units}} = \$0.25$ per unit

Year	Units Produced	×	Unit Rate	=	Annual Depreciation
1	10,000	×	$0.25	=	$2,500
2	8,000	×	0.25	=	2,000
3	7,000	×	0.25	=	1,750
4	5,000	×	0.25	=	1,250

(c) Rate $= \dfrac{\$2,600 - \$200}{200,000 \text{ units}} = \$0.012$ per unit

Year	Units Produced	×	Unit Rate	=	Annual Depreciation
1	35,000	×	$0.012	=	$420
2	44,000	×	0.012	=	528
3	40,000	×	0.012	=	480
4	33,000	×	0.012	=	396
5	28,000	×	0.012	=	336
6	20,000	×	0.012	=	240

2. (a) Rate = $\dfrac{\$17,000 - \$1,000}{400,000 \text{ units}}$ = $0.04 per unit

Year	Units Produced	×	Unit Rate	=	Annual Depreciation
1	62,000	×	$0.04	=	$2,480
2	80,000	×	0.04	=	3,200
3	78,000	×	0.04	=	3,120
4	75,000	×	0.04	=	3,000
5	64,000	×	0.04	=	2,560
6	41,000	×	0.04	=	1,640

(b) Rate = $\dfrac{\$32,000 - \$2,000}{500,000 \text{ units}}$ = $0.06 per unit

Year	Units Produced	×	Unit Rate	=	Annual Depreciation
1	100,000	×	$0.06	=	$6,000
2	125,000	×	0.06	=	7,500
3	105,000	×	0.06	=	6,300
4	90,000	×	0.06	=	5,400
5	80,000	×	0.06	=	4,800

(c) Rate = $\dfrac{\$3,000 - \$1,200}{60,000 \text{ units}}$ = $0.03 per unit

Year	Units Produced	×	Unit Rate	=	Annual Depreciation
1	10,000	×	$0.03	=	$300
2	25,000	×	0.03	=	750
3	16,000	×	0.03	=	480
4	9,000	×	0.03	=	270

Quick Practice - MACRS, page 242

1. (a)

Year	Annual Cost Recovery
1	$1,000
2	1,333
3	444
4	223*

*Rounded up to fully recover cost

1. (Continued)

(b)

Year	Annual Cost Recovery
1	$ 829
2	1,420
3	1,015
4	725
5	518
6	518
7	518
8	257*

*Rounded down to equal cost

Cost Recovery Schedule

(c)

Year	Book Value (End of Year)	Annual Recovery	Accumulated Cost Recovery
0	$4,500	--	--
1	3,600	$ 900	$ 900
2	2,160	1,440	2,340
3	1,296	864	3,204
4	778	518	3,722
5	260	518	4,240
6	0	260*	4,500

*Rounded up to equal book value, fifth year

2. (a)

Year	Annual Cost Recovery
1	$1,286
2	2,204
3	1,574
4	1,125
5	803
6	803
7	803
8	402

(b)

Year	Annual Cost Recovery
1	$1,440
2	2,304
3	1,382
4	829
5	829
6	416*

*Rounded up to fully recover cost

2. (Continued)

Cost Recovery Schedule

(c) Year	Book Value (End of Year)	Annual Recovery	Accumulated Cost Recovery
0	$2,800	--	--
1	1,867	$ 933	$ 933
2	623	1,244	2,177
3	208	415	2,592
4	0	208*	2,800

*Rounded to equal third year book value

Section 1, page 247

1. (a)

Cost	$6,000
Scrap Value	- 400
Depreciable base	$5,600

$$\text{Annual depr.} = \frac{\$5,600}{8} = \$700$$

Year	Book Value (End of Year)	Annual Depreciation	Accumulated Depreciation
0	$6,000	--	--
1	5,300	$700	$ 700
2	4,600	700	1,400
3	3,900	700	2,100
4	3,200	700	2,800
5	2,500	700	3,500
6	1,800	700	4,200
7	1,100	700	4,900
8	400	700	5,600

(b) Depreciation rate $= 2 \times \dfrac{1}{5} = \dfrac{2}{5}$ or 40%

First year depr. $= 40\% \times \$4,000 = \$1,600$
Book value $= \$4,000 - \$1,600 = \$2,400$

Second year depr. $= 40\% \times \$2,400 = \$960$
Book value $= \$2,400 - \$960 = \$1,440$

Third year depr. $= 40\% \times \$1,440 = \$576$
Book value $= \$1,440 - \$576 = \$864$

Fourth year depr. $= 40\% \times \$864 = \$346$
Book value $= \$864 - \$346 = \$518$

Business Mathematics: A Collegiate Approach

1. (b) (Continued)

Fifth year depr. = $518 - $200 = $318

Year	Book Value (End of Year)	Annual Depreciation	Accumulated Depreciation
0	$4,000	--	--
1	2,400	$1,600	$1,600
2	1,440	960	2,560
3	864	576	3,136
4	518	346	3,482
5	200	318*	3,800

*Adjusted to equal fifth year book value

(c) MACRS Cost Recovery Schedule - 3 yr. class

Year	Book Value (End of Year)	Annual Cost Recovery	Accumulated Cost Recovery
0	$1,400	--	--
1	933	$467	$ 467
2	311	622	1,089
3	104	207	1,296
4	0	104	1,400

(d) MACRS Cost Recovery Schedule - 7 yr. class

Year	Book Value (End of Year)	Annual Cost Recovery	Accumulated Cost Recovery
0	$3,600	--	--
1	3,086	$514	$ 514
2	2,204	882	1,396
3	1,574	630	2,026
4	1,124	450	2,476
5	803	321	2,797
6	482	321	3,118
7	161	321	3,439
8	0	161	3,600

2. (a)

Cost	$17,000
Residual value	- 500
Depreciable base	$16,500

Annual depr. $= \dfrac{\$16,500}{10} = \$1,650$

-254-

2. (a) (Continued)

Year	Book Value (End of Year)	Annual Depreciation	Accumulated Depreciation
0	$17,000	--	--
1	15,350	$1,650	$ 1,650
2	13,700	1,650	3,300
3	12,050	1,650	4,950
4	10,400	1,650	6,600
5	8,750	1,650	8,250
6	7,100	1,650	9,900
7	5,450	1,650	11,550
8	3,800	1,650	13,200
9	2,150	1,650	14,850
10	500	1,650	16,500

(b) Depreciation rate = $2 \times \dfrac{1}{6} = \dfrac{1}{3}$

First year depr. = $\dfrac{1}{3} \times \$8,000 = \$2,667$

Book value = $\$8,000 - \$2,667 = \$5,333$

Second year depr. = $\dfrac{1}{3} \times \$5,333 = \$1,778$

Book value = $\$5,333 - \$1,778 = \$3,555$

Third year depr. = $\dfrac{1}{3} \times \$3,555 = \$1,185$

Book value = $\$3,555 - \$1,185 = \$2,370$

Fourth year depr. = $\dfrac{1}{3} \times \$2,370 = \$790$

Book value = $\$2,370 - \$790 = \$1,580$

Fifth year depr. = $\dfrac{1}{3} \times \$1,580 = \$527$

Book value = $\$1,580 - \$527 = \$1,053$

Sixth year depr. = $\$1,053 - \$600 = \$453$

2. (b) (Continued)

Year	Book Value (End of Year)	Annual Depreciation	Accumulated Depreciation
0	$8,000	--	--
1	5,333	$2,667	$2,667
2	3,555	1,778	4,445
3	2,370	1,185	5,630
4	1,580	790	6,420
5	1,053	527	6,947
6	600	453*	7,400

*Adjusted so book value equals $600

(c) MACRS Cost Recovery Schedule - 3 yr. class

Year	Book Value (End of Year)	Annual Cost Recovery	Accumulated Cost Recovery
0	$5,500	--	--
1	3,667	$1,833	$1,833
2	1,223	2,444	4,277
3	408	815	4,292
4	0	408*	4,700

*Adjusted

(d) MACRS Cost Recovery Schedule - 5 yr. class

Year	Book Value (End of Year)	Annual Cost Recovery	Accumulated Cost Recovery
0	$7,400	--	--
1	5,920	$1,480	$1,480
2	3,552	2,368	3,848
3	2,131	1,421	5,269
4	1,279	852	6,121
5	427	852	6,973
6	0	427*	7,400

*Adjusted

3. Cost $6,800

Residual value - 500

Depreciable base $6,300

Annual depr. $= \dfrac{\$6,300}{7 \text{ yrs.}} = \$900$

3. (Continued)

Depreciation Schedule

Year	Book Value (End of Year)	Annual Depreciation	Accumulated Depreciation
0	$6,800	--	--
1	5,900	$900	$ 900
2	5,000	900	1,800
3	4,100	900	2,700
4	3,200	900	3,600
5	2,300	900	4,500
6	1,400	900	5,400
7	500	900	6,300

4. Cost $4,450   Annual depr. $= \dfrac{\$4,050}{5} = \$810$
   Residual value − 400
   Depreciable base $4,050

Depreciation Schedule

Year	Book Value (End of Year)	Annual Depreciation	Accumulated Depreciation
0	$4,450	--	--
1	3,640	$810	$ 810
2	2,830	810	1,620
3	2,020	810	2,430
4	1,210	810	3,240
5	400	810	4,050

5. Cost $1,200   Annual depr. $= \dfrac{\$900}{6} = \$150$
   Salvage value − 300
   Depreciable base $ 900

6. Cost $18,000   Annual depr. $= \dfrac{\$17,800}{8} = \$2,225$
   Residual value − 200
   Depreciable base $17,800

7. Cost $38,000   Annual depr. $= \dfrac{\$32,000}{8} = \$4,000$
   Residual value − 6,000
   Depreciable base $32,000

8. Cost $43,000   Annual depr. $= \dfrac{\$42,000}{12} = \$3,500$
   Residual value − 1,000
   Depreciable base $42,000

9. Depreciation rate $= 2 \times \dfrac{1}{6} = \dfrac{2}{6} = \dfrac{1}{3}$

First year depr. $= \dfrac{1}{3} \times \$12,000 = \$4,000$

Book value $= \$12,000 - \$4,000 = \$8,000$

Second year depr. $= \dfrac{1}{3} \times \$8,000 = \$2,667$

Book value $= \$8,000 - \$2,667 = \$5,333$

Third year depr. $= \dfrac{1}{3} \times \$5,333 = \$1,778$

Book value $= \$5,333 - \$1,778 = \$3,555$

Fourth year depr. $= \dfrac{1}{3} \times \$3,555 = \$1,185$

Book value $= \$3,555 - \$1,185 = \$2,370$

Fifth year depr. $= \dfrac{1}{3} \times \$2,370 = \$790$

Book value $= \$2,370 - \$790 = \$1,580$

Sixth year depr. $= \$1,580 - \$800 = \$780$

Depreciation Schedule

Year	Book Value (End of Year)	Annual Depreciation	Accumulated Depreciation
0	$12,000	--	--
1	8,000	$4,000	$ 4,000
2	5,333	2,667	6,667
3	3,555	1,778	8,445
4	2,370	1,185	9,630
5	1,580	790	10,420
6	800	780*	11,200

*Adjusted so book value equals $800 (residual value)

10. Depreciation rate $= 2 \times \dfrac{1}{10} = \dfrac{1}{5}$ or 20%

10. (Continued)

Depreciation Schedule

Year	Book Value (End of Year)	Annual Depreciation	Accumulated Depreciation
0	$15,000	--	--
1	12,000	$3,000	$ 3,000
2	9,600	2,400	5,400
3	7,680	1,920	7,320
4	6,144	1,536	8,856
5	4,915	1,229	10,085
6	3,932	983	11,068
7	3,146	786	11,854
8	2,517	629	12,483
9	2,014	503	12,986
10	2,000	14*	13,000

*Adjusted so book value equals $2,000

11. Depreciation rate $= 2 \times \dfrac{1}{4} = \dfrac{2}{4} = \dfrac{1}{2}$ or 50%

Depreciation Schedule

Year	Book Value (End of Year)	Annual Depreciation	Accumulated Depreciation
0	$6,000	--	--
1	3,000	$3,000	$3,000
2	1,500	1,500	4,500
3	750	750	5,250
4	0	750*	6,000

*Adjusted so book value equals $0 (scrap value)

12. Depreciation rate $= 2 \times \dfrac{1}{5} = \dfrac{2}{5}$ or 40%

Depreciation Schedule

Year	Book Value (End of Year)	Annual Depreciation	Accumulated Depreciation
0	$700	--	--
1	420	$280	$280
2	252	168	448
3	151	101	549
4	91	60	609
5	0	91*	700

*Adjusted so book value equals $0

13. Depreciation rate $= 2 \times \dfrac{1}{8} = \dfrac{2}{8} = \dfrac{1}{4}$ or 25%

Depreciation Schedule

Year	Book Value (End of Year)	Annual Depreciation	Accumulated Depreciation
0	$800	--	--
1	600	$200	$200
2	450	150	350
3	337	113	463
4	253	84	547
5	190	63	610
6	142	48	658
7	106	36	694
8	100	6*	700

*Adjusted so book value equals $100 (residual value)

14. Depreciation rate $= 2 \times \dfrac{1}{7} = \dfrac{2}{7}$

Depreciation Schedule

Year	Book Value (End of Year)	Annual Depreciation	Accumulated Depreciation
0	$6,300	--	--
1	4,500	$1,800	$1,800
2	3,214	1,286	3,086
3	2,296	918	4,004
4	1,640	656	4,660
5	1,171	469	5,129
6	836	335	5,464
7	500	336*	5,800

*Adjusted so book value equals $500

15.

Cost Recovery Schedule - 5 yr. class

Year	Book Value (End of Year)	Annual Cost Recovery	Accumulated Cost Recovery
0	$6,200	--	--
1	4,960	$1,240	$1,240
2	2,976	1,984	3,224
3	1,786	1,190	4,414
4	1,072	714	5,128
5	358	714	5,842
6	0	358*	6,200

*Adjustment necessary due to rounding to whole dollars

16.

Cost Recovery Schedule - 7 yr. class

Year	Book Value (End of Year)	Annual Cost Recovery	Accumulated Cost Recovery
0	$10,000	--	--
1	8,571	$1,429	$ 1,429
2	6,122	2,449	3,878
3	4,373	1,749	5,627
4	3,124	1,249	6,876
5	2,232	892	7,768
6	1,340	892	8,660
7	448	892	9,552
8	0	448*	10,000

*Adjustment so book value equals $0

17.

Year	Cost	×	Cost Recovery Factor	=	Cost Recovery (Rounded)
1	$800,000	×	0.030423	=	$24,338
2	800,000	×	0.031746	=	25,397
3	800,000	×	0.031746	=	25,397

18.

Year	Cost	×	Cost Recovery Factor	=	Cost Recovery (Rounded)
1	$2,500,000	×	0.034848	=	$87,120
2	2,500,000	×	0.036364	=	90,910
3	2,500,000	×	0.036364	=	90,910

19.

Year	27.5-Year $600,000	5-Year $25,000	Total Cost Recovery
1	$20,909	$ 5,000	$25,909
2	21,818	8,000	29,818
3	21,818	4,800	26,618
	$64,545	$17,800	$82,345

20.

Year	39-Year $2,000,000	5-Year $4,500	Total Cost Recovery
2000	$ 49,146	$ 900	$ 50,046
2001	51,282	1,440	52,722
2002	51,282	864	52,146
	$151,710	$3,204	$154,914

21. (a)

	Cost	$3,000
	Salvage value	- 300
	Depreciable base	$2,700

Rate = $\dfrac{\$2,700}{300,000 \text{ units}}$

= $0.009 per unit

Year	Annual Units	×	Unit Rate	=	Annual Depreciation
1	75,000	×	$0.009	=	$ 675
2	82,000	×	0.009	=	738
3	76,000	×	0.009	=	684
4	67,000	×	0.009	=	603
	300,000				$2,700

(b)

	Cost	$5,700
	Salvage value	- 300
	Depreciable base	$5,400

Rate = $\dfrac{\$5,400}{300,000 \text{ units}}$

= $0.018 per unit

Year	Annual Units	×	Unit Rate	=	Annual Depreciation
1	70,000	×	$0.018	=	$1,260
2	80,000	×	0.018	=	1,440
3	88,000	×	0.018	=	1,584
4	62,000	×	0.018	=	1,116
	300,000				$5,400

(c)

	Cost	$6,800
	Salvage value	- 500
	Depreciable base	$6,300

Rate = $\dfrac{\$6,300}{300,000 \text{ units}}$

= $0.021 per unit

Year	Annual Units	×	Unit Rate	=	Annual Depreciation
1	56,000	×	$0.021	=	$1,176
2	58,000	×	0.021	=	1,218
3	60,000	×	0.021	=	1,260
4	55,000	×	0.021	=	1,155
5	40,000	×	0.021	=	840
6	31,000	×	0.021	=	651
	300,000				$6,300

22. (a)

	Cost	$8,100
	Residual value	- 600
	Depreciable base	$7,500

Rate = $\dfrac{\$7,500}{300,000 \text{ units}}$

= $0.025 per unit

22. (a) (Continued)

Year	Annual Units	×	Unit Rate	=	Annual Depreciation
1	62,000	×	$0.025	=	$1,550
2	79,000	×	0.025	=	1,975
3	85,000	×	0.025	=	2,125
4	74,000	×	0.025	=	1,850
	300,000				$7,500

(b)

Cost	$9,700	Rate =	$9,600
Residual value	− 100		300,000 units
Depreciable base	$9,600		= $0.032 per unit

Year	Annual Units	×	Unit Rate	=	Annual Depreciation
1	55,000	×	$0.032	=	$1,760
2	76,000	×	0.032	=	2,432
3	84,000	×	0.032	=	2,688
4	78,000	×	0.032	=	2,496
5	7,000	×	0.032	=	224
	300,000				$9,600

(c)

Cost	$15,000	Rate =	$12,000
Residual value	− 3,000		300,000 units
Depreciable base	$12,000		= $0.04 per unit

Year	Annual Units	×	Unit Rate	=	Annual Depreciation
1	50,000	×	$0.04	=	$ 2,000
2	53,000	×	0.04	=	2,120
3	56,000	×	0.04	=	2,240
4	52,000	×	0.04	=	2,080
5	44,000	×	0.04	=	1,760
6	45,000	×	0.04	=	1,800
	300,000				$12,000

23. Straight-line method:

Cost	$4,200	Annual Depr. = $\dfrac{\$4,000}{5}$ = $800
Residual value	− 200	
Depreciable base	$4,000	

23. (Continued)

Declining-balance method:

Rate = $2 \times \dfrac{1}{5} = \dfrac{2}{5}$ or 40%

First year depr.   = 40% × $4,200 = $1,680
Book value   = $4,200 - $1,680 = $2,520

Second year depr. = 40% × $2,520 = $1,008
Book value   = $2,520 - $1,008 = $1,512

Third year depr. = 40% × $1,512 = $605
Book value   = $1,512 - $605 = $907

MACRS method:

First year cost recovery = 0.2   × $4,200 = $ 840
Second year cost recovery = 0.32 × $4,200 = $1,344
Third year cost recovery = 0.192 × $4,200 = $ 806

Year	Straight Line	Declining Balance	MACRS
1	$800	$1,680	$ 840
2	800	1,008	1,344
3	800	605	806

24. Straight-line method:

Cost $19,000   Annual Depr. = $\dfrac{\$16,000}{5 \text{ yrs.}}$ = $3,200
Residual value   - 3,000
Depreciable base $16,000

Declining-balance method:

Rate = $2 \times \dfrac{1}{5} = \dfrac{2}{5}$ or 40%

First year depr.   = 40% × $19,000 = $7,600
Book value   = $19,000 - $7,600 = $11,400

Second year depr. = 40% × $11,400 = $4,560
Book value   = $11,400 - $4,560 = $6,840

24. (Continued)

Third year depr.   = 40% × $6,840 = $2,736
Book value   = $6,840 - $2,736 = $4,104

MACRS Method:

First year cost recovery = 0.2   × $19,000 = $3,800
Second year cost recovery = 0.32 × $19,000 = $6,080
Third year cost recovery = 0.192 × $19,000 = $3,648

Year	Straight Line	Declining Balance	MACRS
1	$3,200	$7,600	$3,800
2	3,200	4,560	6,080
3	3,200	2,736	3,648

Section 2, page 250

1. (a) MACRS Cost Recovery Schedule - 5 yr. class

Year	Book Value (End of Year)	Annual Cost Recovery	Accumulated Cost Recovery
0	$9,000	--	--
1	7,200	$1,800	$1,800
2	4,320	2,880	4,680
3	2,592	1,728	6,408
4	1,555	1,037	7,445
5	518	1,037	8,482
6	0	518	9,000

(b) Cost $4,900   Straight-line method:
    Residual value - 400
    Depreciable base $4,500 $\frac{\$4,500}{5}$ = $900 per full year

First year = $\frac{1}{3}$ of a year; $\frac{1}{3}$ × $900 = $300

Sixth year = $\frac{2}{3}$ of a year; $\frac{2}{3}$ × $900 = $600

1. (b) (Continued)

Depreciation Schedule

Year	Book Value (End of Year)	Annual Depreciation	Accumulated Depreciation
0	$4,900	--	--
1	4,600	$300	$ 300
2	3,700	900	1,200
3	2,800	900	2,100
4	1,900	900	3,000
5	1,000	900	3,900
6	400	600	4,500

(c) Depreciable base = $2,600

Depreciation rate = $2 \times \dfrac{1}{4} = \dfrac{2}{4} = \dfrac{1}{2}$ or 50%

First year = $\dfrac{3}{4}$ of a year; $\dfrac{3}{4} \times 50\% \times \$2,600 = \$975$

Depreciation Schedule

Year	Book Value (End of Year)	Annual Depreciation	Accumulated Depreciation
0	$2,600	--	--
1	1,625	$975	$ 975
2	812	813	1,788
3	406	406	2,194
4	203	203	2,397
5	0	203*	2,600

*Adjusted to bring book value to $0

2. (a) MACRS Cost Recovery Schedule - 5 yr. class

Year	Book Value (End of Year)	Annual Cost Recovery	Accumulated Cost Recovery
0	$100,000	--	--
1	80,000	$20,000	$ 20,000
2	48,000	32,000	52,000
3	28,800	19,200	71,200
4	17,280	11,520	82,720
5	5,760	11,520	94,240
6	0	5,760	100,000

2. (Continued)

(b) Cost $6,000   Annual depr. = $\dfrac{\$5,400}{4}$ = $1,350

     Residual value $-$ 600

     Depreciable base $5,400

First year   = $\dfrac{1}{3}$ of a year; $\dfrac{1}{3}$ × $1,350 = $450

Fourth year = $\dfrac{2}{3}$ of a year; $\dfrac{2}{3}$ × $1,350 = $900

Depreciation Schedule

Year	Book Value (End of Year)	Annual Depreciation	Accumulated Depreciation
0	$6,000	--	--
1	5,550	$ 450	$ 450
2	4,200	1,350	1,800
3	2,850	1,350	3,150
4	1,500	1,350	4,500
5	600	900	5,400

(c) Rate = $2 \times \dfrac{1}{3} = \dfrac{2}{3}$

First year = $\dfrac{5}{6}$ of a year; $\dfrac{5}{6}$ × $\dfrac{2}{3}$ × $1,800 = $1,000

Depreciation Schedule

Year	Book Value (End of Year)	Annual Depreciation	Accumulated Depreciation
0	$1,800	--	--
1	800	$1,000	$1,000
2	267	533	1,533
3	89	178	1,711
4	0	89	1,800

3. Cost $4,600   Straight-line method:

    Trade-in value $-$ 400

    Depreciable base $4,200 $\dfrac{\$4,200}{7}$ = $600 per full year

First year   = $\dfrac{2}{12}$ of a year; $\dfrac{2}{12}$ × $600 = $100

Eighth year = $\dfrac{10}{12}$ of a year; $\dfrac{10}{12}$ × $600 = $500

3. (Continued)

Depreciation Schedule

Year	Book Value (End of Year)	Annual Depreciation	Accumulated Depreciation
0	$4,600	--	--
1	4,500	$100	$ 100
2	3,900	600	700
3	3,300	600	1,300
4	2,700	600	1,900
5	2,100	600	2,500
6	1,500	600	3,100
7	900	600	3,700
8	400	500	4,200

4. Cost $1,860   Annual depr. $= \dfrac{\$1,800}{5} = \$360$
    Residual value $-\ \ \ 60$
    Depreciable base $1,800

First year $= \dfrac{7}{12}$ of a year; $\dfrac{7}{12} \times \$360 = \$210$

Sixth year $= \dfrac{5}{12}$ of a year; $\dfrac{5}{12} \times \$360 = \$150$

Depreciation Schedule

Year	Book Value (End of Year)	Annual Depreciation	Accumulated Depreciation
0	$1,860	--	--
1	1,650	$210	$ 210
2	1,290	360	570
3	930	360	930
4	570	360	1,290
5	210	360	1,650
6	60	150	1,800

5. Declining-balance rate: $2 \times \dfrac{1}{3} = \dfrac{2}{3}$

First year $= \dfrac{5}{12}$ of a year; $\dfrac{5}{12} \times \dfrac{2}{3} \times \$900 = \$250$

5. (Continued)

Depreciation Schedule

Year	Book Value (End of Year)	Annual Depreciation	Accumulated Depreciation
0	$900	--	--
1	650	$250	$250
2	217	433	683
3	72	145	828
4	50	22*	850

*Adjusted

6. Rate $= 2 \times \dfrac{1}{6} = \dfrac{1}{3}$

First year $= \dfrac{7}{12}$ of a year; $\dfrac{7}{12} \times \dfrac{1}{3} \times \$27,000 = \$5,250$

Depreciation Schedule

Year	Book Value (End of Year)	Annual Depreciation	Accumulated Depreciation
0	$27,000	--	--
1	21,750	$5,250	$ 5,250
2	14,500	7,250	12,500
3	9,667	4,833	17,333
4	6,445	3,222	20,555
5	4,297	2,148	22,703
6	2,865	1,432	24,135
7	2,000	865*	25,000

*Adjusted so book value equals $2,000

Section 3, page 253

1. (a)

Dept.	Ratio of floor space	Overhead charge
#1	$\dfrac{800}{4,500} = \dfrac{8}{45}$	$\$13,500 \times \dfrac{8}{45} = \$\ 2,400$
2	$\dfrac{1,000}{4,500} = \dfrac{2}{9}$	$\$13,500 \times \dfrac{2}{9} = \ \ \ 3,000$
3	$\dfrac{1,200}{4,500} = \dfrac{12}{45}$	$\$13,500 \times \dfrac{12}{45} = \ \ \ 3,600$
4	$\dfrac{1,500}{4,500} = \dfrac{3}{9}$	$\$13,500 \times \dfrac{3}{9} = \ \ \underline{4,500}$

Total overhead = $13,500

(b)

Dept.	Ratio of floor space	Overhead charge
#16	$\dfrac{500}{2,000} = \dfrac{1}{4}$	$\$32,000 \times \dfrac{1}{4} = \$\ 8,000$
17	$\dfrac{300}{2,000} = \dfrac{3}{20}$	$\$32,000 \times \dfrac{3}{20} = \ \ \ 4,800$
18	$\dfrac{400}{2,000} = \dfrac{1}{5}$	$\$32,000 \times \dfrac{1}{5} = \ \ \ 6,400$
19	$\dfrac{800}{2,000} = \dfrac{2}{5}$	$\$32,000 \times \dfrac{2}{5} = \ \underline{12,800}$

Total overhead = $32,000

2. (a)

Dept.	Ratio of floor space	Overhead charge
M	$\dfrac{2,000}{6,000} = \dfrac{1}{3}$	$\$48,000 \times \dfrac{1}{3} = \$16,000$
N	$\dfrac{1,000}{6,000} = \dfrac{1}{6}$	$\$48,000 \times \dfrac{1}{6} = \ \ 8,000$
O	$\dfrac{1,600}{6,000} = \dfrac{4}{15}$	$\$48,000 \times \dfrac{4}{15} = \ 12,800$
P	$\dfrac{1,400}{6,000} = \dfrac{7}{30}$	$\$48,000 \times \dfrac{7}{30} = \ \underline{11,200}$

Total overhead = $48,000

2. (Continued)

(b)

Dept.	Ratio of floor space	Overhead charge
Q	$\dfrac{900}{2,500} = \dfrac{9}{25}$	$15,000 \times \dfrac{9}{25} = \$ 5,400$
R	$\dfrac{800}{2,500} = \dfrac{8}{25}$	$15,000 \times \dfrac{8}{25} = 4,800$
S	$\dfrac{300}{2,500} = \dfrac{3}{25}$	$15,000 \times \dfrac{3}{25} = 1,800$
T	$\dfrac{500}{2,500} = \dfrac{1}{5}$	$15,000 \times \dfrac{1}{5} = \underline{3,000}$

Total overhead = $15,000

3. (a)

Dept.	Ratio of net sales	Overhead charge
W	$\dfrac{30,000}{70,000} = \dfrac{3}{7}$	$56,000 \times \dfrac{3}{7} = \$24,000$
X	$\dfrac{15,000}{70,000} = \dfrac{3}{14}$	$56,000 \times \dfrac{3}{14} = 12,000$
Y	$\dfrac{14,000}{70,000} = \dfrac{1}{5}$	$56,000 \times \dfrac{1}{5} = 11,200$
Z	$\dfrac{11,000}{70,000} = \dfrac{11}{70}$	$56,000 \times \dfrac{11}{70} = \underline{8,800}$

Total overhead = $56,000

(b)

Dept.	Ratio of net sales	Overhead charge
AA	$\dfrac{20,000}{72,000} = \dfrac{5}{18}$	$36,000 \times \dfrac{5}{18} = \$10,000$
BB	$\dfrac{22,000}{72,000} = \dfrac{11}{36}$	$36,000 \times \dfrac{11}{36} = 11,000$
CC	$\dfrac{14,000}{72,000} = \dfrac{7}{36}$	$36,000 \times \dfrac{7}{36} = 7,000$
DD	$\dfrac{16,000}{72,000} = \dfrac{2}{9}$	$36,000 \times \dfrac{2}{9} = \underline{8,000}$

Total overhead = $36,000

4. (a)

Dept.	Ratio of net sales	Overhead charge
O	$\dfrac{45,000}{120,000} = \dfrac{3}{8}$	$\$84,000 \times \dfrac{3}{8} = \$31,500$
V	$\dfrac{24,000}{120,000} = \dfrac{1}{5}$	$\$84,000 \times \dfrac{1}{5} = 16,800$
E	$\dfrac{36,000}{120,000} = \dfrac{3}{10}$	$\$84,000 \times \dfrac{3}{10} = 25,200$
R	$\dfrac{15,000}{120,000} = \dfrac{1}{8}$	$\$84,000 \times \dfrac{1}{8} = \underline{10,500}$

Total overhead = $84,000

(b)

Dept.	Ratio of net sales	Overhead charge
H	$\dfrac{62,000}{240,000} = \dfrac{31}{120}$	$\$96,000 \times \dfrac{31}{120} = \$24,800$
E	$\dfrac{68,000}{240,000} = \dfrac{17}{60}$	$\$96,000 \times \dfrac{17}{60} = 27,200$
A	$\dfrac{64,000}{240,000} = \dfrac{4}{15}$	$\$96,000 \times \dfrac{4}{15} = 25,600$
D	$\dfrac{46,000}{240,000} = \dfrac{23}{120}$	$\$96,000 \times \dfrac{23}{120} = \underline{18,400}$

Total overhead = $96,000

5. (a)

Dept.	Ratio of # employees	Overhead charge
#22	$\dfrac{40}{100} = \dfrac{2}{5}$	$\$18,000 \times \dfrac{2}{5} = \$\ 7,200$
33	$\dfrac{10}{100} = \dfrac{1}{10}$	$\$18,000 \times \dfrac{1}{10} = 1,800$
44	$\dfrac{30}{100} = \dfrac{3}{10}$	$\$18,000 \times \dfrac{3}{10} = 5,400$
55	$\dfrac{20}{100} = \dfrac{1}{5}$	$\$18,000 \times \dfrac{1}{5} = \underline{3,600}$

Total overhead = $18,000

5. (Continued)

(b)

Dept.	Ratio of # employees	Overhead charge
#10	$\frac{2}{15}$	$\$30,000 \times \frac{2}{15} = \$ \ 4,000$
11	$\frac{4}{15}$	$\$30,000 \times \frac{4}{15} = \ \ \ 8,000$
12	$\frac{3}{15} = \frac{1}{5}$	$\$30,000 \times \frac{1}{5} = \ \ \ 6,000$
13	$\frac{6}{15} = \frac{2}{5}$	$\$30,000 \times \frac{2}{5} = \ \ \underline{12,000}$

Total overhead = $30,000

6. (a)

Dept.	Ratio of # employees	Overhead charge
#66	$\frac{12}{60} = \frac{1}{5}$	$\$54,000 \times \frac{1}{5} = \$10,800$
77	$\frac{15}{60} = \frac{1}{4}$	$\$54,000 \times \frac{1}{4} = \ 13,500$
88	$\frac{13}{60}$	$\$54,000 \times \frac{13}{60} = \ 11,700$
99	$\frac{20}{60} = \frac{1}{3}$	$\$54,000 \times \frac{1}{3} = \ \underline{18,000}$

Total overhead = $54,000

(b)

Dept.	Ratio of # employees	Overhead charge
#14	$\frac{8}{20} = \frac{2}{5}$	$\$19,000 \times \frac{2}{5} = \$ \ 7,600$
15	$\frac{4}{20} = \frac{1}{5}$	$\$19,000 \times \frac{1}{5} = \ \ \ 3,800$
16	$\frac{5}{20} = \frac{1}{4}$	$\$19,000 \times \frac{1}{4} = \ \ \ 4,750$
17	$\frac{3}{20}$	$\$19,000 \times \frac{3}{20} = \ \ \underline{2,850}$

Total overhead = $19,000

7.

Dept.	Ratio of Floor space	Overhead charge
Accounting	$\dfrac{200}{1,500} = \dfrac{2}{15}$	$60,000 \times \dfrac{2}{15} = \$\ 8,000$
General office	$\dfrac{300}{1,500} = \dfrac{1}{5}$	$60,000 \times \dfrac{1}{5} = 12,000$
Marketing	$\dfrac{400}{1,500} = \dfrac{4}{15}$	$60,000 \times \dfrac{4}{15} = 16,000$
Service/repairs	$\dfrac{600}{1,500} = \dfrac{2}{5}$	$60,000 \times \dfrac{2}{5} = \underline{\ 24,000}$

Total overhead = $60,000

8.

Dept.	Ratio of Floor space	Overhead charge
Pharmacy	$\dfrac{4}{24} = \dfrac{1}{6}$	$14,400 \times \dfrac{1}{6} = \$\ 2,400$
Home Health Equip.	$\dfrac{10}{24} = \dfrac{5}{12}$	$14,400 \times \dfrac{5}{12} = 6,000$
Cosmetics	$\dfrac{8}{24} = \dfrac{1}{3}$	$14,400 \times \dfrac{1}{3} = 4,800$
Greeting cards	$\dfrac{2}{24} = \dfrac{1}{12}$	$14,400 \times \dfrac{1}{12} = \underline{\ 1,200}$

Total overhead = $14,400

9.

Dept.	Ratio of net sales	Overhead charge
Biographies	$\dfrac{60,000}{200,000} = \dfrac{3}{10}$	$40,000 \times \dfrac{3}{10} = \$12,000$
Adv./Mysteries	$\dfrac{44,000}{200,000} = \dfrac{11}{50}$	$40,000 \times \dfrac{11}{50} = 8,800$
Computer/Software	$\dfrac{42,000}{200,000} = \dfrac{21}{100}$	$40,000 \times \dfrac{21}{100} = 8,400$
Romance	$\dfrac{38,000}{200,000} = \dfrac{19}{100}$	$40,000 \times \dfrac{19}{100} = 7,600$
Sports	$\dfrac{16,000}{200,000} = \dfrac{2}{25}$	$40,000 \times \dfrac{2}{25} = \underline{\ 3,200}$

Total overhead = $40,000

10.

Dept.	Ratio of net sales	Overhead charge
Men's clothing	$\frac{10}{50} = \frac{1}{5}$	$20,000 \times \frac{1}{5} = \$ 4,000$
Women's clothing	$\frac{12}{50} = \frac{6}{25}$	$20,000 \times \frac{6}{25} = 4,800$
Shoes	$\frac{8}{50} = \frac{4}{25}$	$20,000 \times \frac{4}{25} = 3,200$
Small appliances	$\frac{20}{50} = \frac{2}{5}$	$20,000 \times \frac{2}{5} = \underline{\quad 8,000}$

Total overhead = $20,000

11.

Dept.	Ratio of # employees	Overhead charge
Lawn/Garden	$\frac{7}{30}$	$90,000 \times \frac{7}{30} = \$21,000$
Appliances	$\frac{8}{30} = \frac{4}{15}$	$90,000 \times \frac{4}{15} = 24,000$
Automotive	$\frac{5}{30} = \frac{1}{6}$	$90,000 \times \frac{1}{6} = 15,000$
Bldg. supplies	$\frac{6}{30} = \frac{1}{5}$	$90,000 \times \frac{1}{5} = 18,000$
Paint	$\frac{4}{30} = \frac{2}{15}$	$90,000 \times \frac{2}{15} = \underline{\quad 12,000}$

Total overhead = $90,000

12.

Dept.	Ratio of # employees	Overhead charge
Branch A	$\frac{5}{40} = \frac{1}{8}$	$50,000 \times \frac{1}{8} = \$ 6,250$
Branch B	$\frac{9}{40}$	$50,000 \times \frac{9}{40} = 11,250$
Branch C	$\frac{8}{40} = \frac{1}{5}$	$50,000 \times \frac{1}{5} = 10,000$
Branch D	$\frac{6}{40} = \frac{3}{20}$	$50,000 \times \frac{3}{20} = 7,500$
Branch E	$\frac{12}{40} = \frac{3}{10}$	$50,000 \times \frac{3}{10} = \underline{\quad 15,000}$

Total overhead = $50,000

CHAPTER X

FINANCIAL STATEMENTS AND RATIOS

The income statement and the balance sheet are studied in order to acquaint the student with the most common financial statements. They also provide excellent practice in working with percents.

Both of these financial statements will be new to most students; thus, they provide an introduction to the methods used to determine the financial condition of a business. The authors would not require at this point that the student be able to personally construct either statement in detail, but would leave that requirement to a later accounting course. A sufficient business math objective would be that the student be able to complete the calculations on a given statement, along with the required percents.

1.   The Income Statement:

The income statement can provide an excellent foundation for the chapter on markup (which is typically very difficult for many students to comprehend). This section contains introductory material for the basic markup formula, C + M = S. We would require the student to learn the basic calculations contained on the income statement, as this is essential to an understanding of markup:

         Net Sales
        -Cost of Goods Sold
         Gross Profit
        -Operating Expenses
         Net Profit (or Net Loss)

Thus, the student should be able to construct a simple statement such as example 1.

Be sure the student realizes that all percents on the income statement are based on net sales. This also provides an introduction to markup as a percent of selling price.

Comparative statements offer a good example of finding percents of increase or decrease. A weak student may experience difficulty in completing the basic calculations for the separate years, however. Thus, the instructor may wish to omit horizontal analysis for basic classes.

2.   The Balance Sheet:

Again, students should know the basic facts presented by the balance sheet: Assets = Liabilities + New Worth. They should know that the percents on the balance sheet are based on the total assets.

Business ratios may not be very meaningful to students who have never studied bookkeeping or accounting. Therefore, the instructor may wish to include only two or three of the more common ratios or to omit them altogether.

Note: Because of the errors incurred when individual entries were rounded off, some of the percent columns (in both examples and student problems) do not add to the exact total, correct to the nearest tenth percent. Where rounding errors have occurred, an asterisk marks the percents with a footnote giving an explanation.

3.   Inventory Turnover:

Inventory turnover is presented both at cost and at retail, based on average inventories computed by the student. Historical percentages from the income statement are used to convert inventory at sales value to its comparable cost value, prior to calculating the inventory turnover at cost. This topic may be omitted if time is short, and the following topic on inventory valuation methods could still be included.

4.   Inventory Valuation:

Inventory values were used without question in the preceding turnover section as well as in the financial statements. The weighted-average; the first-in, first-out; and the last-in, first-out methods of inventory valuation (at cost) are briefly introduced here to demonstrate the wide variations in values which can be obtained. Emphasize strongly the effect that these different valuations produce on the gross profit (both amount and percent). Most students will blindly accept the figures on any financial statement, believing that dollars-and-cents figures cannot be misrepresented. An important aspect of this topic is to help them realize that, in the hands of a knowledgeable business person, the same set of facts can often be made to look different ways, to serve the best interests of the business at the time.

CHAPTER 10 - FINANCIAL STATEMENTS AND RATIOS
PROBLEM SOLUTIONS

Sections 1 & 2, page 280

1.

Davie & Associates Income Statement For Year Ending Dec. 31, 20X2				
Income from sales:				
Sales	$ 520,000		104.0%	
Sales discount	20,000		4.0%	
Net sales		$ 500,000		100.0%
Cost of goods sold:				
Inventory, Jan. 1	$ 82,000			
Net purchases	150,000			
Goods avail. for sale	232,000			
Inventory, Dec. 31	83,000			
Cost of goods sold		149,000		29.8%
Gross profit		$ 351,000		70.2%
Operating Expenses				
Salaries	$ 200,000		40.0%	
Depreciation	32,000		6.4%	
Utilities	18,000		3.6%	
Maintenance	16,500		3.3%	
Advertising	10,000		2.0%	
Insurance	8,500		1.7%	
Office supplies	8,000		1.6%	
Miscellaneous	7,000		1.4%	
Total expenses		$ 300,000		60.0%
Net income from operations		51,000		10.2%
Income taxes		14,000		2.8%
Net income after taxes		$ 37,000		7.4%

2.

Prentice Sporting Goods
Income Statement
For Year Ending Dec. 31, 20X2

Income from sales:				
Sales	$ 760,000		105.6%	
Sales discounts	40,000		5.6%	
Net sales		$ 720,000		100.0%
Cost of goods sold:				
Inventory, Jan.1	$ 55,000			
Net purchases	300,000			
Goods avail. for sale	355,000			
Inventory, Dec. 31	48,000			
Cost of goods sold		307,000		42.6%
Gross profit		$ 413,000		57.4%
Operating expenses:				
Salaries	$ 196,000		27.2%	
Rent	80,000		11.1%	
Depreciation	18,000		2.5%	
Insurance	12,000		1.7%	
Utilities	10,000		1.4%	
Office supplies	6,000		0.8%	
Advertising	2,500		0.3%	
Miscellaneous	1,500		0.2%	
Total expenses		$ 326,000		45.3%
Net income from operations		87,000		12.1%
Income taxes		26,000		3.6%
Net income after taxes		$ 61,000		8.5%

3.

Madison & Co. Balance Sheet, December 20X1					
				%	%
Assets					
Current Assets:					
Cash		$ 27,000		4.7%	
Accounts receivable		32,000		5.6%	
Notes receivable		20,000		3.5%	
Inventory		45,000		7.8%	
Total current assets			$ 124,000		21.6%
Plant assets:					
Building	$ 300,000				
Less: Accum. Depreciation	30,000				
Net building		$ 270,000		47.0%	
Truck	38,000				
Less: Accum. Depreciation	18,000				
Net truck		20,000		3.5%	
Land		160,000			
Total plant assets			$ 450,000		78.4%
Total assets			$ 574,000		100.0%
Liabilities and Owner's Equity					
Current liabilities:					
Accounts payable		$ 34,000		5.9%	
Notes payable		46,000		8.0%	
Total current liabilities			$ 80,000		13.9%
Long-term liabilities:					
Mortgage			229,000		39.9%
Total liabilities			$ 309,000		53.8%
Owner's equity			265,000		46.2%
Total liabilities and owner's equity			$ 574,000		100.0%

4.

Tucker, Connor, and Riva Co. Balance Sheet December 31, 20X1					
				%	%
Assets					
Current assets:					
Cash		$ 36,000		4.5%	
Accounts receivable		45,000		5.6%	
Notes receivable		10,000		1.3%	
Inventory		83,000		10.4%	
Total current assets			$ 174,000		21.8%
Plant assets:					
Building	$ 450,000				
Less: Accum. Depreciation	25,000				
Net building		425,000		53.2%	
Land		200,000		25.0%	
Total plant assets			$ 625,000		78.2%
Total assets			$ 799,000		100.0%
Liabilities and owners' equity					
Current liabilities:					
Accounts payable		62,000		7.8%	
Notes payable		20,000		2.5%	
Total current liabilities			$ 82,000		10.3%
Long-term liabilities					
Mortgage			350,000		43.8%
Total liabilities			$ 432,000		54.1%
Owners' equity			367,000		45.9%
Total liabilities and owner's equity			$ 799,000		100.0%

5.

Noor Floor Co. Comparative Income Statement For Years Ending Dec. 31, 20X2 and 20X1						
			Increase or (Decrease)		Percent of Net Sales	
	20X2	20X1	Amount	Percent	20X2	20X1
Income:						
Net sales	$ 325,000	$ 300,000	$ 25,000	8.3%	100.0%	100.0%
Cost of goods sold:						
Inventory, Jan. 1	$ 90,000	$ 82,000	8,000	9.8%	27.7%	27.3%
Purchases	135,000	150,000	(15,000)	-10.0%	41.5%	50.0%
Goods avail. for sale	225,000	232,000	(7,000)	-3.0%	69.2%	77.3%
Inventory, Dec. 31	81,000	90,000	(9,000)	-10.0%	24.9%	30.0%
Cost of goods sold	144,000	142,000	2,000	1.4%	44.3%	47.3%
Gross profit	181,000	158,000	23,000	14.6%	55.7%	52.7%
Expenses:						
Salaries	$ 90,000	$ 60,000	30,000	50.0%	27.7%	20.0%
Rent	44,000	42,500	1,500	3.5%	13.5%	14.2%
Advertising	6,000	6,000	-	0.0%		
Depreciation	5,000	5,500	(500)	-9.1%	1.5%	1.8%
Utilities	3,000	2,800	200	7.1%	0.9%	0.9%
Miscellaneous	5,000	2,200	2,800	127.3%	1.5%	0.7%
Total expenses	153,000	119,000	34,000	28.6%	47.1%	39.7%
Net income	$ 28,000	$ 39,000	(11,000)	-28.2%	8.6%	13.0%

6.

Ellett Heating and Air Conditioning Co. Comparative Income Statement For Years Ending Dec. 31, 20X2 and 20X1						
			Increase or (Decrease)		Perent of Net Sales	
	20X2	20X1	Amount	Percent	20X2	20X1
Income:						
Net sales	$ 512,000	$ 500,000	12,000	2.4%	100.0%	100.0%
Cost of goods sold:						
Inventory, Jan. 1	$ 100,000	$ 95,000	5,000	5.3%	19.5%	19.0%
Purchases	200,000	225,000	(25,000)	-11.1%	39.1%	45.0%
Goods avail. for sale	300,000	320,000	(20,000)	-6.3%	58.6%	64.0%
Inventory, Dec. 31	96,000	100,000	(4,000)	-4.0%	18.8%	20.0%
Cost of goods sold	204,000	220,000	(16,000)	-7.3%	39.8%	44.0%
Gross profit	308,000	280,000	28,000	10.0%	60.2%	56.0%
Expenses:						
Salaries	170,000	149,000	21,000	14.1%	33.2%	29.8%
Office supplies	25,000	22,000	3,000	13.6%	4.9%	4.4%
Shop supplies	15,000	17,500	(2,500)	-14.3%	2.9%	3.5%
Depreciation	10,000	11,500	(1,500)	-13.0%	2.0%	2.3%
Utilities	8,000	6,300	1,700	27.0%	1.6%	1.3%
Advertising	2,000	1,000	1,000	100.0%	0.4%	0.2%
Miscellaneous	1,000	800	200	25.0%	0.2%	0.2%
Total expenses	231,000	208,100	22,900	11.0%	45.1%	41.6%
Net income	$ 77,000	$ 71,900	5,100	7.1%	15.0%	14.4%

7.

			Increase or (Decrease)		Percent of Total Assets	
Davie & Associates **Comparative Balance Sheet** **December 31, 20X2 and 20X1**						
	20X2	20X1	Amount	Percent	20X2	20X1
Assets						
Current assets:						
Cash	$ 27,000	$ 33,000	$ (6,000)	-18.2%	5.8%	6.8%
Accounts receivable	52,000	48,000	4,000	8.3%	11.3%	9.9%
Inventory	83,000	82,000	1,000	1.2%	18.0%	16.9%
Total current assets	162,000	163,000	(1,000)	-0.6%	35.1%	33.6%
Toal plant assets	300,000	322,000	(22,000)	-6.8%	64.9%	66.4%
Total assets	462,000	485,000	(23,000)	-4.7%	100.0%	100.0%
liabilities and Equity						
Current liabilities	79,000	85,000	(6,000)	-7.1%	17.1%	17.5%
Long-term liabilities	150,000	172,000	(22,000)	-12.8%	32.5%	35.5%
Total liabilities	229,000	257,000	(28,000)	-10.9%	49.6%	53.0%
Stockholders's equity:						
Preferred stock	45,000	45,000	-	0.0%	9.7%	9.3%
Common stock	80,000	78,000	2,000	2.6%	17.3%	16.1%
Retained earnings	108,000	105,000	3,000	2.9%	23.4%	21.6%
Total equity	233,000	228,000	5,000	2.2%	50.4%	47.0%
Total liabilities and equity	$ 462,000	$ 485,000	(23,000)	-4.7%	100.0%	100.0%

8.

Prentice Sporting Goods Comparative Balance Sheet December 31, 20X2 and 20X1						
			Increase or (Decrease)		Percent of Total Assets	
	20X2	20X1	Amount	Percent	20X2	20X1
Assets						
Current assets:						
Cash	$ 15,000	$ 12,000	3,000	25.0%	6.7%	5.8%
Accounts receivable	62,000	50,000	12,000	24.0%	100.0%	24.2%
Inventory	48,000	55,000	(7,000)	-12.7%	21.5%	26.6%
Total current assets	125,000	117,000	8,000	6.8%	56.1%	56.5%
Total plant assets	98,000	90,000	8,000	8.9%	43.9%	43.5%
Total assets	223,000	207,000	16,000	7.7%	100.0%	100.0%
Liabilities and Owners' equity						
Current liabilities	57,000	50,000	7,000	14.0%	25.6%	24.2%
Long-term liabilities	10,000	8,000	2,000	25.0%	4.5%	3.9%
Total liabilities	67,000	58,000	9,000	15.5%	30.0%	28.0%
Stockholders' equity:						
Preferred stock	25,000	25,000	-	0.0%	11.2%	12.1%
Common stock	70,000	68,000	2,000	2.9%	31.4%	32.9%
Retained earnings	61,000	56,000	5,000	8.9%	27.4%	27.1%
Total equity	156,000	149,000	7,000	4.7%	70.0%	72.0%
Total liabilities and equity	$ 223,000	$ 207,000	16,000	7.7%	100.0%	100.0%

9. (a) Working capital ratio:

$$\frac{\text{Current assets}}{\text{Current liabilities}} = \frac{\$124,000}{\$80,000} = 1.6 \text{ to } 1$$

(b) Acid-test ratio:

$$\frac{\text{Quick assets}}{\text{Current liabilities}} = \frac{\$79,000}{\$80,000} = 1.0 \text{ to } 1$$

(c) Ratio of net sales to net working capital:

$$\frac{\text{Net sales}}{\text{Current assets} - \text{Current liabilities}} = \frac{\$300,000}{\$124,000 - \$80,000}$$

$$= 6.8 \text{ to } 1$$

9. (Continued)

(d) Book value of stock:

$$\frac{\text{Owners' equity}}{\text{Number of shares of stock}} = \frac{\$265,000}{5,000} = \$53$$

10. (a) Working capital ratio:

$$\frac{\text{Current assets}}{\text{Current liabilities}} = \frac{\$174,000}{\$82,000} = 2.1 \text{ to } 1$$

(b) Acid-test ratio:

$$\frac{\text{Quick assets}}{\text{Current liabilities}} = \frac{\$91,000}{\$82,000} = 1.1 \text{ to } 1$$

(c) Ratio of net sales to net working capital:

$$\frac{\text{Net sales}}{\text{Current assets} - \text{Current liabilities}} = \frac{\$425,000}{\$174,000 - \$82,000}$$

$$= 4.6\%$$

(d) Book value of stock:

$$\frac{\text{Owners' equity}}{\text{Number of shares of stock}} = \frac{\$367,000}{8,000} = \$45.88$$

11. (a) Working capital ratio:

$$\frac{\text{Current assets}}{\text{Current liabilities}} = \frac{\$162,000}{\$79,000} = 2.1 \text{ to } 1$$

(b) Acid-test ratio:

$$\frac{\text{Quick assets}}{\text{Current liabilities}} = \frac{\$79,000}{\$79,000} = 1 \text{ to } 1$$

(c) Percent of net income (after taxes) to average net worth:

$$\text{Average net worth} = \frac{\$233,000 + \$228,000}{2} = \$230,500$$

11. (c) (Continued)

$$\frac{\text{Net income after taxes}}{\text{Average net worth}} = \frac{\$37,000}{\$230,500} = 16.1\%$$

(d) Ratio of net sales to average total assets:

$$\text{Average total assets} = \frac{\$462,000 + \$485,000}{2} = \$473,500$$

$$\frac{\text{Net sales}}{\text{Average total assets}} = \frac{\$500,000}{\$473,500} = 1.1 \text{ to } 1$$

(e) Accounts receivable turnover:

Average accounts receivable =

$$\frac{\$52,000 + \$48,000}{2} = \$50,000$$

$$\frac{\text{Net sales}}{\text{Average accounts receivable}} = \frac{\$500,000}{\$50,000} = 10 \text{ times}$$

(f) Average age of accounts receivable:

$$\frac{365}{\text{Average accounts receivable}} = \frac{365}{10} = 36.5 \text{ day}$$

12. (a) Working capital ratio:

$$\frac{\text{Current assets}}{\text{Current liabilities}} = \frac{\$125,000}{\$57,000} = 2.2 \text{ to } 1$$

(b) Acid-test ratio:

$$\frac{\text{Quick assets}}{\text{Current liabilities}} = \frac{\$77,000}{\$57,000} = 1.4 \text{ to } 1$$

(c) Percent of net income (after taxes) to average net worth:

$$\text{Average net worth} = \frac{\$156,000 + \$149,000}{2} = \$152,500$$

$$\frac{\text{Net income after taxes}}{\text{Average net worth}} = \frac{\$61,000}{\$152,500} = 40\%$$

12. (Continued)

(d) Ratio of net sales to average total assets:

$$\text{Average total assets} = \frac{\$223,000 + \$207,000}{2} = \$215,000$$

$$\frac{\text{Net sales}}{\text{Average total assets}} = \frac{\$720,000}{\$215,000} = 3.3 \text{ to } 1$$

(e) Accounts receivable turnover:

$$\text{Average accounts receivable} = \frac{\$62,000 + \$50,000}{2} = \$56,000$$

$$\frac{\text{Net sales}}{\text{Average accounts receivable}} = \frac{\$720,000}{\$56,000} = 12.9 \text{ times}$$

(f) Average age of accounts receivable:

$$\frac{365}{\text{Average accounts receivable}} = \frac{365}{12.9} = 28.3 \text{ day}$$

Section 3, page 290

1. Inventory
   at retail:
   $ 75,000
     63,000
     72,000
     84,000
   $294,000

$$\text{Average inventory} \atop \text{(at retail)} = \frac{\$294,000}{4} = \$73,500$$

2. Inventory
   at retail:
   $120,000
    104,000
    116,000
    124,000
   $464,000

$$\text{Average inventory} \atop \text{(at retail)} = \frac{\$464,000}{4} = \$116,000$$

3. (a) Cost $ 74,000   (b) Inventory
   +40% cost   + 29,600   at retail:
   Retail $103,600 $103,600
                                     100,000
                                     104,000
                                     102,000
                                    $409,600

                                 Average inventory = $409,600
                                 (at retail)   ─────────
                                                         4
                                                   = $102,400

4. (a) Cost $180,000   (b) Inventory
   +30% cost   + 54,000   at retail:
   Retail $234,000 $234,000
                                     236,000
                                     245,000
                                     200,000
                                    $915,000

                                 Average inventory = $915,000
                                 (at retail)   ─────────
                                                         4
                                                   = $228,750

5. Inventory turnover = $\dfrac{\text{Net sales}}{\text{Average inventory at retail}}$

                      = $\dfrac{\$279,300}{\$73,500}$

                      = 3.8 times

6. Inventory turnover = $\dfrac{\text{Net sales}}{\text{Average inventory at retail}}$

                      = $\dfrac{\$430,000}{\$116,000}$

                      = 3.7 times

7. From problems 1 and 5:
   Average inventory at retail = $73,500;
   Cost of goods sold = $176,400

7. (Continued)

    (a) Cost = 60% of retail
             = 0.60($73,500)
       C = $44,100

    (b) $\text{Turnover} = \dfrac{\text{Cost of goods sold}}{\text{Average inventory at cost}}$

$$= \dfrac{\$176,400}{\$44,100}$$

$$= 4 \text{ times}$$

8. From problems 2 and 6:
   Average inventory at retail = $116,000;
   Cost of goods sold = $340,000

    (a) Cost = 75% of retail
             = 0.75($116,000)
       C = $87,000

    (b) $\text{Turnover} = \dfrac{\text{Cost of goods sold}}{\text{Average inventory at cost}}$

$$= \dfrac{\$340,000}{\$87,000}$$

$$= 3.9 \text{ times}$$

9. Inventory
   at retail:
   $116,000
    124,000
    125,000
    126,000
   $491,000

$$\text{Average inventory (at retail)} = \dfrac{\$491,000}{4} = \$122,750$$

$$\text{Turnover} = \dfrac{\text{Net sales}}{\text{Average inventory at retail}} = \dfrac{\$392,800}{\$122,750} = 3.2 \text{ times}$$

10. Inventory
    at retail:
    $ 68,000
     72,000
     70,000
     64,000
    $274,000

$$\text{Average inventory (at retail)} = \dfrac{\$274,000}{4} = \$68,500$$

10. (Continued)

$$\text{Turnover} = \frac{\text{Net sales}}{\text{Average inventory at retail}} = \frac{\$239,750}{\$68,500} = 3.5 \text{ times}$$

11. From problem 9:
    Average inventory at retail = $122,750;
    Cost of goods sold = $250,410

    (a) Cost = 60% of retail
           = 0.60($122,750)
        C = $73,650

       Average inventory at
       cost = $73,650

    (b) $\frac{\text{Cost of goods sold}}{\text{Average inventory at cost}}$

       $= \frac{\$250,410}{\$73,650} = 3.4 \text{ times}$

12. From problem 10:
    Average inventory at retail = $68,500;
    Cost of goods sold = $145,000

    (a) Cost = 70% of retail
           = 0.70($68,500)
        C = $47,950

    (b) $\frac{\text{Cost of goods sold}}{\text{Average inventory at cost}}$

       $= \frac{\$145,000}{\$47,950} = 3.0 \text{ times}$

Section 4, page 294

1. (a) 10 @ $5.10 = $ 51
        30 @ 5.20 = 156
        20 @ 5.25 = 105
        60 units $312

    (1) Weighted average:

        $\frac{\$312}{60}$ = $5.20 average cost

        15 @ $5.20 = $78 inventory value

    (2) FIFO:
        15 @ $5.25 = $78.75 inventory value

    (3) LIFO:
        10 @ $5.10 = $51
         5 @ 5.20 = 26
        15 units $77 inventory value

1. (Continued)

    (b) 25 @ $7.40 = $185.00
          45 @ 7.50 = 337.50
          <u>30</u> @ 7.65 = <u>229.50</u>
        100 units $752.00

      (1) <u>Weighted average</u>:

$$\frac{\$752}{100} = \$7.52 \text{ average cost}$$

          40 @ $7.52 = $300.80 inventory value

      (2) <u>FIFO</u>:
          30 @ $7.65 = $229.50
          <u>10</u> @ 7.50 = <u>75.00</u>
          40 units $304.50 inventory value

      (3) <u>LIFO</u>:
          25 @ $7.40 = $185.00
          <u>15</u> @ 7.50 = <u>112.50</u>
          40 units $297.50 inventory value

2. (a) 50 @ $8.60 = $ 430
        40 @ 8.65 =   346
        <u>30</u> @ 9.00 =   <u>270</u>
      120 units $1,046

      (1) <u>Weighted average</u>:

$$\frac{\$1,046}{120} = \$8.72 \text{ average cost}$$

          35 @ $8.72 = $305.20 inventory value

      (2) <u>FIFO</u>:
          30 @ $9.00 = $270.00
          <u> 5</u> @ 8.65 = <u>43.25</u>
          35 units $313.25 inventory value

      (3) <u>LIFO</u>:
          35 @ $8.60 = $301.00 inventory value

    (b) 18 @ $25.00 = $ 450.00
        22 @ 25.10 =   552.20
        <u>26</u> @ 25.05 = <u>651.30</u>
      66 units $1,653.50

2. (b) (Continued)

   (1) Weighted average:

   $$\frac{\$1,653.50}{66} = \$25.05 \text{ average cost}$$

   28 @ $25.05 = $701.40 inventory value

   (2) FIFO:
   26 @ $25.05 = $651.30
   <u>2</u> @ 25.10 = <u> 50.20</u>
   28 units $701.50 inventory value

   (3) LIFO:
   18 @ $25.00 = $450.00
   <u>10</u> @ 25.10 = <u> 251.00</u>
   28 units $701.00 inventory value

3.   31 @ $116 = $ 3,596
     32 @ 118 =   3,776
     40 @ 120 =   4,800
     44 @ 121 =   5,324
     28 @ 125 =   3,500
   <u> 25</u> @ 126 = <u> 3,150</u>
    200 units $24,146

   (a) Weighted average:

   $$\frac{\$24,146}{200} = \$120.73 \text{ average cost}$$

   10 @ $120.73 = $1,207.30 inventory value

   (b) FIFO:
   10 @ $126 = $1,260 inventory value

   (c) LIFO:
   10 @ $116 = $1,160 inventory value

4. 17 @ $17.30 = $ 294.10
   16 @ 17.40 =   278.40
   15 @ 18.45 =   276.75
  <u> 24</u> @ 18.50 = <u> 444.00</u>
   72 units $1,293.25

4. (Continued)

   (a) Weighted average:

$$\frac{\$1,293.25}{72} = \$17.96 \text{ average cost}$$

      20 @ $17.96 = $359.20 inventory value

   (b) FIFO:
      20 @ $18.50 = $370 inventory value

   (c) LIFO:
      17 @ $17.30 = $294.10
       3 @ 17.40 =   52.20
      20 units $346.30 inventory value

5.   40 @ $35 = $1,400
    80 @ 34 = 2,720
    60 @ 32 = 1,920
    70 @ 30 = 2,100
  250 units $8,140

   (a) Weighted average:

$$\frac{\$8,140}{250} = \$32.56 \text{ average cost}$$

      60 @ $32.56 = $1,953.60 inventory cost

   (b) FIFO:
      60 @ $30 = $1,800 inventory cost

   (c) LIFO:
      40 @ $35 = $1,400
      20 @ 34 =   680
      60 units $2,080 inventory cost

6. 25 @ $52.00 = $1,300.00
   22 @ 52.20 = 1,148.40
   13 @ 52.30 =   679.90
   60 units $3,128.30

   (a) Weighted average:

$$\frac{\$3,128.30}{60} = \$52.14 \text{ average cost}$$

      26 @ $52.14 = $1,355.64 inventory value

6. (Continued)

    (b) <u>FIFO</u>:
        13 @ $52.30 = $ 679.90
        <u>13</u> @ 52.20 = <u>   678.60</u>
        26 units $1,358.50 inventory value

    (c) <u>LIFO</u>:
        25 @ $52.00 = $1,300.00
        <u> 1</u> @ $52.20 = <u>   52.20</u>
        26 units $1,352.20 inventory value

7.

	Wt. Avg.		FIFO		LIFO	
Net sales		$40,000.00		$40,000		$40,000
Cost of goods sold:						
Beg. inventory	$ 0		$ 0		$ 0	
Purchases	<u>24,146.00</u>		<u>24,146</u>		<u>24,146</u>	
Goods available	$24,146.00		$24,146		$24,146	
Endg. inventory	<u>1,207.30</u>		<u>1,260</u>		<u>1,160</u>	
Cost of goods		<u>22,938.70</u>		<u>22,886</u>		<u>22,986</u>
Gross profit		$17,061.30		$17,114		$17,014
% gross profit		42.7%		42.8%		42.5%

8.

	Wt. Avg.		FIFO		LIFO	
Net sales		$5,000.00		$5,000.00		$5,000.00
Cost of goods sold:						
Beg. inventory	$ 0		$ 0		$ 0	
Purchases	<u>1,293.25</u>		<u>1,293.25</u>		<u>1,293.25</u>	
Goods available	$1,293.25		$1,293.25		$1,293.25	
Endg. inventory	<u>359.20</u>		<u>370.00</u>		<u>346.30</u>	
Cost of goods		<u>934.05</u>		<u>923.25</u>		<u>946.95</u>
Gross profit		$4,065.95		$4,076.75		$4,053.05
% gross profit		81.3%		81.5%		81.1%

CHAPTER XI

DISTRIBUTION OF PROFITS AND LOSS

This chapter contains a brief description of the three basic forms of business -- proprietorship, partnership, and corporation -- as an introduction to the distribution of profits among owners.

1. Distribution of Profits in a Corporation:

The specific characteristics of the various classes of stock may be somewhat confusing to most students. Therefore, we would require the student to know only those aspects essential to the mathematics of computing dividends per share.

Note: Uninformed investors often do not realize that there may be no relation between the par value and the market value of a stock. This has caused a trend toward nonparvalue stock; thus, no par values are given for common stock in the text problems.

Point out that stock dividends are often given in lieu of cash dividends. Because of the time restrictions of a business math course, the purchasing of stock was not included. You may wish to bring current newspaper stock exchange listings to class and conduct a discussion of stock purchasing.

The cash dividend per share and earnings per share are usually different. The cash dividend per share is the amount of cash that investors receive for each share of stock owned. The earnings per share measures the amount of net income earned by common shareholders during the year. Since the board of directors often does not declare a cash dividend or it will declare a cash dividend for less than the total net income, the two numbers are rarely the same. Another complication arises when the number of outstanding shares changes during the year. A weighted average calculation is necessary to determine the average number of outstanding common stock shares before determining the earnings per share.

No problems require weighted average calculation. Our purpose was to introduce the topic since the earnings per share is important to business; it is included in financial reports.

2. Distribution of Profits in a Partnership:

Distribution of partnership profits is studied after cash dividends because of the numerous ways in which partnership profits may be distributed. Students usually experience no difficulty in learning the separate methods which may be used; however, mistakes are often made when several methods are combined. Emphasize that salary and/or interest must be deducted from the total profits before the ratio is applied. The student should always check to be certain that the amounts assigned to the various partners equal the exact total profit of the partnership.

No examples or problems were included on distribution of net loss since the authors felt this topic was beyond the scope of the business math course. Students may question "what if" there is a net loss. Questions of this nature often arise when discussing example 6 (b) where there is a shortage of net income to cover the interest and salary. It is important for students to understand that with a net loss, the interest and salary would be allocated to the partners (as stipulated by their agreement) which would <u>add</u> to the net loss [not subtract from the net income as in example 6 (b)] to determine each partner's share.

The instructor may wish to conserve time by omitting one or more of the methods shown for distributing profits in a partnership.

CHAPTER 11
DISTRIBUTION OF PROFITS AND LOSS
PROBLEM SOLUTIONS

Section 1, page 307

1. (a) $\dfrac{\$63,000}{45,000 \text{ shares}}$ = $1.40 dividend per share common

(b) 6% × $100 par value = $6 dividend per share preferred

$6 × 10,000 shares = $60,000

$100,000 Total dividend
- 60,000 Total preferred dividend
$ 40,000 Total common dividend

$\dfrac{\$40,000}{50,000 \text{ shares}}$ = $0.80 dividend per share common

(c) 5% × $50 par value × 2 years = $5 dividend per share
                                    preferred

1. (c) (Continued)

$5 × 40,000 shares = $200,000

$220,000 Total dividend
-200,000 Total preferred dividend
$ 20,000 Total common dividend

$$\frac{\$20,000}{20,000 \text{ shares}} = \$1 \text{ dividend per share common}$$

2. (a) $\frac{\$91,000}{65,000 \text{ shares}} = \$1.40$ dividend per share common

(b) 5% × $100 par value = $5 dividend per share preferred

$5 × 30,000 shares = $150,000

$174,000 Total dividend
-150,000 Total preferred dividend
$ 24,000 Total common dividend

$$\frac{\$24,000}{40,000 \text{ shares}} = \$0.60 \text{ dividend per share common}$$

(c) 6% × $50 par value × 2 years = $6 dividend per share
preferred

$6 × 20,000 shares = $120,000

$150,000 Total dividend
-120,000 Total preferred dividend
$ 30,000 Total common dividend

$$\frac{\$30,000}{60,000 \text{ shares}} = \$0.50 \text{ dividend per share common}$$

3. (a) Dividend per share:
7% × $100 par value = $7 dividend per share preferred

$7 × 60,000 shares = $420,000

$450,000 Total dividend
-420,000 Total preferred dividend
$ 30,000 Total common dividend

3. (a) (Continued)

$$\frac{\$30,000}{30,000 \text{ shares}} = \$1 \text{ dividend per share common}$$

Earnings per share:

$$\frac{\$900,000 - \$420,000}{30,000 \text{ shares}} = \$16 \text{ earnings per share}$$

(b) Dividend per share:
8% × $50 par value = $4 dividend per share preferred

$4 × 20,000 shares = $80,000

$150,000 Total dividend
- 80,000 Total preferred dividend
$ 70,000 Total common dividend

$$\frac{\$70,000}{10,000 \text{ shares}} = \$7 \text{ dividend per share common}$$

Earnings per share:

$$\frac{\$200,000 - \$80,000}{10,000 \text{ shares}} = \$12 \text{ earnings per share}$$

4. (a) Dividend per share:
5% × $100 par value = $5 dividend per share preferred

$5 × 70,000 shares = $350,000

$450,000 Total dividend
-350,000 Total preferred dividend
$100,000 Total common dividend

$$\frac{\$100,000}{50,000 \text{ shares}} = \$2 \text{ dividend per share common}$$

Earnings per share:

$$\frac{\$600,000 - \$350,000}{50,000 \text{ shares}} = \$5 \text{ earnings per share}$$

4. (Continued)

    (b) <u>Dividend per share</u>:
       7% × $50 par value = $3.50 dividend per share preferred

       $3.50 × 90,000 shares = $315,000

       $400,000 Total dividend
       <u>-315,000</u> Total preferred dividend
       $ 85,000 Total common dividend

$$\frac{\$85,000}{25,000 \text{ shares}} = \$3.40 \text{ dividend per share common}$$

       <u>Earnings per share</u>:

$$\frac{\$800,000 - \$315,000}{25,000 \text{ shares}} = \$19.40 \text{ earnings per share}$$

5. $\dfrac{\text{Total dividend}}{\text{Total shares}} = \dfrac{\$136,000}{80,000} = \$1.70$ dividend per share common

6. $\dfrac{\text{Total dividend}}{\text{Total shares}} = \dfrac{\$137,500}{50,000} = \$2.75$ dividend per share common

7. 7% × $100 par value = $7 dividend per share preferred

    $7 × 20,000 shares = $140,000

    $175,000 Total dividend
    <u>-140,000</u> Total preferred dividend
    $ 35,000 Total common dividend

$$\frac{\$35,000}{10,000 \text{ shares}} = \$3.50 \text{ dividend per share common}$$

8. 8% × $100 par value = $8 dividend per share preferred

    $8 × 15,000 shares = $120,000

    $135,000 Total dividend
    <u>-120,000</u> Total preferred dividend
    $ 15,000 Total common dividend

8. (Continued)

$$\frac{\$15,000}{5,000 \text{ shares}} = \$3 \text{ dividend per share common}$$

9. 8% × $50 par value = $4 dividend per share preferred

$4 × 1,500 shares = $6,000

$10,000 Total dividend
$\underline{- \ 6,000}$ Total preferred dividend
$ 4,000 Total common dividend

$$\frac{\$4,000}{500 \text{ shares}} = \$8 \text{ dividend per share common}$$

10. 7% × $50 par value = $3.50 dividend per share preferred

$3.50 × 3,000 shares = $10,500

$12,000 Total dividend
$\underline{-10,500}$ Total preferred dividend
$ 1,500 Total common dividend

$$\frac{\$1,500}{1,000 \text{ shares}} = \$1.50 \text{ dividend per share common}$$

11. 6% × $100 par value = $6

$6 × 65,000 shares = $390,000 but only $325,000 total dividend

$$\frac{\$325,000}{65,000 \text{ shares}} = \$5 \text{ dividend per share preferred}$$

0 dividend per share common

12. 6% × $100 par value = $6

$6 × 30,000 shares = $180,000 but only $150,000 total dividend

$$\frac{\$150,000}{30,000 \text{ shares}} = \$5 \text{ dividend per share preferred}$$

0 dividend per share common

13. 7% × $50 par value × 2 years = $7 dividend per share
                                                preferred

    $7 × 4,000 shares = $28,000

    $77,000 Total dividend
    -28,000 Total preferred dividend
    $49,000 Total common dividend

    $\dfrac{\$49,000}{5,000 \text{ shares}}$ = $9.80 dividend per share common

14. 8% × $100 par value = $8 × 2 years = $16 dividend per share
                                                preferred

    $16 × 25,000 shares = $400,000

    $425,000 Total dividend
    -400,000 Total preferred dividend
    $ 25,000 Total common dividend

    $\dfrac{\$25,000}{10,000 \text{ shares}}$ = $2.50 dividend per share common

15. 8% × $50 × 3 years = $12 dividend per share preferred

    $12 × 3,000 shares = $36,000

    $40,000 Total dividend
    -36,000 Total preferred dividend
    $ 4,000 Total common dividend

    $\dfrac{\$4,000}{8,000 \text{ shares}}$ = $0.50 dividend per share common

16. 7% × $100 par value = $7 × 3 years = $21 dividend per share
                                                preferred

    $21 × 6,000 shares = $126,000

    $140,000 Total dividend
    -126,000 Total preferred dividend
    $ 14,000 Total common dividend

16. (Continued)

$$\frac{\$14,000}{5,000 \text{ shares}} = \$2.80 \text{ dividend per share common}$$

17. $5\% \times \$100$ par value $\times$ 2 years = $10 dividend per share
                                                    preferred

    $10 × 10,000 shares = $100,000

    $130,000 Total dividend
    <u>-100,000</u> Total preferred dividend
    $ 30,000 Total common dividend

$$\frac{\$30,000}{6,000 \text{ shares}} = \$5 \text{ dividend per share common}$$

18. $5\% \times \$50$ par value = $2.50 $\times$ 2 years = $5 dividend per share
                                                          preferred

    $5 × 4,000 shares = $20,000

    $50,000 Total dividend
    <u>-20,000</u> Total preferred dividend
    $30,000 Total common dividend

$$\frac{\$30,000}{15,000 \text{ shares}} = \$2 \text{ dividend per share common}$$

19. $6\% \times \$50$ par value = $3 dividend per share preferred (stock
                                           is non-cumulative)

    $3 × 10,000 shares = $30,000

    $45,000 Total dividend
    <u>-30,000</u> Total preferred dividend
    $15,000 Total common dividend

$$\frac{\$15,000}{6,000 \text{ shares}} = \$2.50 \text{ dividend per share common}$$

20. 8% × $50 par value = $4 dividend per share preferred

    $4 × 16,000 shares = $64,000

    $65,000 Total dividend
    -64,000 Total preferred dividend
    $ 1,000 Total common dividend

    $$\frac{\$1,000}{4,000 \text{ shares}} = \$0.25 \text{ dividend per share common}$$

21. (a) 5% × $50 par value = $2.50 dividend per share preferred

    $2.50 × 15,000 shares = $37,500

    $90,000 Total dividend
    -37,500 Total preferred dividend
    $52,500 Total common dividend

    $$\frac{\$52,500}{10,000 \text{ shares}} = \$5.25 \text{ dividend per share common}$$

    (b) $$\frac{\$150,000 - \$37,500}{10,000 \text{ shares}} = \$11.25 \text{ earnings per share}$$

22. (a) 9% × $50 par value = $4.50 dividend per share preferred

    $4.50 × 8,000 shares = $36,000

    $64,000 Total dividend
    -36,000 Total preferred dividend
    $28,000 Total common dividend

    $$\frac{\$28,000}{7,000 \text{ shares}} = \$4 \text{ dividend per share common}$$

    (b) $$\frac{\$78,000 - \$36,000}{7,000 \text{ shares}} = \$6 \text{ earnings per share}$$

Section 2, page 314

1. (a) 1 + 3 = 4 shares

$$K = \frac{1}{4} \times \$60,000 = \$15,000$$

$$L = \frac{3}{4} \times \$60,000 = \underline{\$45,000}$$
$$\$60,000$$

(b) $A = \dfrac{\$5,000}{\$18,000} = \dfrac{5}{18};\quad \dfrac{5}{18} \times \$21,600 = \$\ 6,000$

$B = \dfrac{\$6,000}{\$18,000} = \dfrac{1}{3};\quad \dfrac{1}{3} \times \$21,600 = \$\ 7,200$

$C = \dfrac{\$7,000}{\$18,000} = \dfrac{7}{18};\quad \dfrac{7}{18} \times \$21,600 = \underline{\$\ 8,400}$
$$\$21,600$$

(c)

	S	T	U
Investment	$30,000	$35,000	$15,000
Interest rate	× 6%	× 6%	× 6%
Interest	$ 1,800	$ 2,100	$ 900

Total interest = $1,800 + $2,100 + $900 = $4,800

$16,000 Total profit
– 4,800 Interest
$11,200 To be shared in a ratio of 2:2:1

2 + 2 + 1 = 5 shares

$$S = \frac{2}{5} \times \$11,200 = \$4,480$$

$$T = \frac{2}{5} \times \$11,200 = \$4,480$$

$$U = \frac{1}{5} \times \$11,200 = \$2,240$$

SUMMARY

	S	T	U	Check
Interest	$1,800	$2,100	$ 900	$ 6,280
Ratio	4,480	4,480	2,240	6,580
Total	$6,280	$6,580	$3,140	3,140
				$16,000

1. (Continued)

(d)

	V	W	X
Investment	$30,000	$28,000	$24,000
Interest rate	× 5%	× 5%	× 5%
Interest	$ 1,500	$ 1,400	$ 1,200

Total interest = $1,500 + $1,400 + $1,200 = $4,100

$43,700 Total profit
- 4,100 Interest
-15,000 Salary to V
$24,600 To be shared in ratio of investments

$$V = \frac{\$30,000}{\$82,000} = \frac{15}{41}; \quad \frac{15}{41} \times \$24,600 = \$9,000$$

$$W = \frac{\$28,000}{\$82,000} = \frac{14}{41}; \quad \frac{14}{41} \times \$24,600 = \$8,400$$

$$X = \frac{\$24,000}{\$82,000} = \frac{12}{41}; \quad \frac{12}{41} \times \$24,600 = \$7,200$$

SUMMARY

	V	W	X	Check
Interest	$ 1,500	$1,400	$1,200	$25,500
Salary	15,000	--	--	9,800
Ratio	9,000	8,400	7,200	8,400
Total	$25,500	$9,800	$8,400	$43,700

2. (a) 2 + 1 = 3 shares

$$G = \frac{2}{3} \times \$90,000 = \$60,000$$

$$H = \frac{1}{3} \times \$90,000 = \frac{\$30,000}{\$90,000}$$

(b) $$I = \frac{\$18,000}{\$48,000} = \frac{3}{8}; \quad \frac{3}{8} \times \$72,000 = \$27,000$$

$$J = \frac{\$16,000}{\$48,000} = \frac{1}{3}; \quad \frac{1}{3} \times \$72,000 = \$24,000$$

$$K = \frac{\$14,000}{\$48,000} = \frac{7}{24}; \quad \frac{7}{24} \times \$72,000 = \frac{\$21,000}{\$72,000}$$

2. (Continued)

(c)

	L	M	N
Investment	$40,000	$30,000	$10,000
Interest rate	× 7%	× 7%	× 7%
Interest	$ 2,800	$ 2,100	$ 700

Total interest = $2,800 + $2,100 + $700 = $5,600

$20,000 Total net profit
<u>- 5,600</u> Interest
$14,400 To be shared in a ratio of 3:2:1

3 + 2 + 1 = 6 shares

$L = \frac{3}{6}; \frac{1}{2} \times \$14,400 = \$7,200$

$M = \frac{2}{6}; \frac{1}{3} \times \$14,400 = \$4,800$

$N = \frac{1}{6}; \frac{1}{6} \times \$14,400 = \$2,400$

SUMMARY

	L	M	N	Check
Interest	$ 2,800	$2,100	$ 700	$10,000
Ratio	7,200	4,800	2,400	6,900
Total	$10,000	$6,900	$3,100	3,100
				$20,000

(d)

	P	Q	R
Investment	$10,000	$15,000	$17,000
Interest rate	× 6%	× 6%	× 6%
Interest	$ 600	$ 900	$ 1,020

Total interest = $600 + $900 + $1,020 = $2,520

$29,000 Total net profit
- 2,520 Interest
<u>- 8,000</u> Salary to R
$18,480 To be divided in a ratio of their investments

$P = \frac{\$10,000}{\$42,000} = \frac{5}{21}; \frac{5}{21} \times \$18,480 = \$4,400$

$Q = \frac{\$15,000}{\$42,000} = \frac{5}{14}; \frac{5}{14} \times \$18,480 = \$6,600$

2. (d) (Continued)

$$R = \frac{\$17,000}{\$42,000} = \frac{17}{42}; \quad \frac{17}{42} \times \$18,480 = \$7,480$$

SUMMARY

	P	Q	R	Check
Interest	$ 600	$ 900	$ 1,020	$ 5,000
Salary	--	--	8,000	7,500
Ratio	4,400	6,600	7,480	16,500
Total	$5,000	$7,500	$16,500	$29,000

3. Each should receive $\frac{1}{2}$ of the $50,000 = $25,000 each

4. Each should receive $\frac{1}{2}$ of the $18,000 = $9,000 each

5. 2 + 3 + 1 = 6 shares

(a) $Q = \frac{2}{6}; \quad \frac{1}{3} \times \$42,000 = \$14,000$

$R = \frac{3}{6}; \quad \frac{1}{2} \times \$42,000 = \$21,000$

$S = \frac{1}{6}; \quad \frac{1}{6} \times \$42,000 = \underline{\$\ 7,000}$

$$\$42,000$$

(b) $Q = \frac{1}{3} \times (\$18,000) = (\$\ 6,000)$

$R = \frac{1}{2} \times (\$18,000) = (\$\ 9,000)$

$S = \frac{1}{6} \times (\$18,000) = \underline{(\$\ 3,000)}$

$$(\$18,000)$$

6. 3 + 2 + 2 = 7 shares

(a) $L = \frac{3}{7}; \quad \frac{3}{7} \times \$35,000 = \$15,000$

$M = \frac{2}{7}; \quad \frac{2}{7} \times \$35,000 = \$10,000$

6. (a) (Continued)

$$N = \frac{2}{7}; \quad \frac{2}{7} \times \$35,000 = \underline{\$10,000}$$
$$\$35,000$$

(b) $L = \frac{3}{7} \times (\$5,600) = (\$2,400)$

$M = \frac{2}{7} \times (\$5,600) = (\$1,600)$

$N = \frac{2}{7} \times (\$5,600) = \underline{(\$1,600)}$
$$(\$5,600)$$

7. Total salaries = $10,000 × 3 partners = $30,000
   $50,000 profit − $30,000 salaries = $20,000 to be divided
   25%/30%/45%

Bob   = 25% × $20,000 = $5,000

Chris = 30% × $20,000 = $6,000

Doug = 45% × $20,000 = $9,000

	SUMMARY			
	Bob	Chris	Doug	Check
Salary	$10,000	$10,000	$10,000	$15,000
% Distrib.	5,000	6,000	9,000	16,000
Total	$15,000	$16,000	$19,000	19,000
				$50,000

8. Total salaries = $12,000 × 3 partners = $36,000
   $40,000 profit − $36,000 salaries = $4,000 to be divided
   25%/35%/40%

Lynn   = 25% × $4,000 = $1,000

Monica = 35% × $4,000 = $1,400

Nancy = 40% × $4,000 = $1,600

8. (Continued)

SUMMARY

	Lynn	Monica	Nancy	Check
Salary	$12,000	$12,000	$12,000	$13,000
% Distrib.	1,000	1,400	1,600	13,400
Total	$13,000	$13,400	$13,600	13,600
				$40,000

9. Total of their *initial* investments = $16,000 + $24,000
$$= \$40,000$$

$$\text{Julie} = \frac{\$16,000}{\$40,000} = \frac{2}{5}; \quad \frac{2}{5} \times \$75,000 = \$30,000$$

$$\text{Greta} = \frac{\$24,000}{\$40,000} = \frac{3}{5}; \quad \frac{3}{5} \times \$75,000 = \underline{\$45,000}$$
$$\$75,000$$

10. Total of their *initial* investments = $20,000 + $25,000
$$= \$45,000$$

$$\text{Matt} = \frac{\$20,000}{\$45,000} = \frac{4}{9}; \quad \frac{4}{9} \times \$27,000 = \$12,000$$

$$\text{Bob} = \frac{\$25,000}{\$45,000} = \frac{5}{9}; \quad \frac{5}{9} \times \$27,000 = \underline{\$15,000}$$
$$\$27,000$$

11. Total salaries = $6,000 × 2 partners = $12,000
$64,800 profit - $12,000 salaries = $52,800 to be divided
in the ratio of second-year investments.

$$\text{Julie} = \frac{\$20,000}{\$44,000} = \frac{5}{11}; \quad \frac{5}{11} \times \$52,800 = \$24,000$$

$$\text{Greta} = \frac{\$24,000}{\$44,000} = \frac{6}{11}; \quad \frac{6}{11} \times \$52,800 = \$28,800$$

SUMMARY

	Julie	Greta	Check
Salary	$ 6,000	$ 6,000	$30,000
Ratio	24,000	28,800	34,800
Total	$30,000	$34,800	$64,800

12. Total salaries = $19,000 + $22,000 = $41,000
    $74,000 profit - $41,000 salaries = $33,000 to be divided
    in the ratio of current year investments.

Matt $= \dfrac{\$30,000}{\$55,000} = \dfrac{6}{11}$; $\dfrac{6}{11} \times \$33,000 = \$18,000$

Bob $= \dfrac{\$25,000}{\$55,000} = \dfrac{5}{11}$; $\dfrac{5}{11} \times \$33,000 = \$15,000$

SUMMARY

	Matt	Bob	Check
Salary	$19,000	$22,000	$37,000
Ratio	18,000	15,000	37,000
Total	$37,000	$37,000	$74,000

13. (a) Tom's average investment:

Date	Change	Amount of Investment		Mos. Invested		
January 1		$20,000	×	5	=	$100,000
June 1	-$4,000	16,000	×	3	=	48,000
Sept. 1	+ 1,000	17,000	×	4	=	68,000
				12		$216,000

$\dfrac{\$216,000}{12 \text{ mos.}} = \$18,000$ Tom's average investment

(b) $26,000 Steve's average investment
     +18,000 Tom's average investment
     $44,000 Total average investment

Steve $= \dfrac{\$26,000}{\$44,000} = \dfrac{13}{22}$; $\dfrac{13}{22} \times \$77,000 = \$45,500$

Tom $= \dfrac{\$18,000}{\$44,000} = \dfrac{9}{22}$; $\dfrac{9}{22} \times \$77,000 = \underline{\$31,500}$
$\$77,000$

14. (a) James' average investment:

Date	Change	Amount of Investment		Mos. Invested		
January 1		$40,000	×	4	=	$160,000
May 1	-$ 5,000	35,000	×	6	=	210,000
Nov. 1	+ 20,000	55,000	×	2	=	110,000
				12		$480,000

$$\frac{\$480,000}{12 \text{ mos.}} = \$40,000 \text{ James' average investment}$$

(b) $40,000 James' average investment
+50,000 George's average investment
$90,000 Total average investment

$$\text{James} = \frac{\$40,000}{\$90,000} = \frac{4}{9}; \quad \frac{4}{9} \times \$270,000 = \$120,000$$

$$\text{George} = \frac{\$50,000}{\$90,000} = \frac{5}{9}; \quad \frac{5}{9} \times \$270,000 = \underline{\$150,000}$$
$$\$270,000$$

15. (a) Pete's average investment:

Date	Change	Amount of Investment		Mos. Invested		
January 1		$25,000	×	2	=	$ 50,000
March 1	-$3,000	22,000	×	4	=	88,000
July 1	+ 6,000	28,000	×	6	=	168,000
				12		$306,000

$$\frac{\$306,000}{12 \text{ mos.}} = \$25,500 \text{ Pete's average investment}$$

(b) Interest: Mark = 6% × $22,000 = $1,320
             Pete = 6% × $25,500 = $1,530

$30,000 Total profit
- 2,850 Total interest
$27,150 To be shared equally

$$\frac{\$27,150}{2} = \$13,575 \text{ each}$$

15. (b) (Continued)

SUMMARY

	Mark	Pete	Check
Interest	$ 1,320	$ 1,530	$14,895
Ratio	13,575	13,575	15,105
Total	$14,895	$15,105	$30,000

16. (a) Kalid's average investment:

Date	Change	Amount of Investment		Mos. Invested		
January 1		$18,000	×	5	=	$ 90,000
June 1	+$3,000	21,000	×	4	=	84,000
Oct. 1	− 1,000	20,000	×	3	=	60,000
				12		$234,000

$$\frac{\$234,000}{12 \text{ mos.}} = \$19,500 \text{ Kalid's average investment}$$

(b) Interest: Amin = 8% × $26,000 = $2,080
             Kalid = 8% × $19,500 = $1,560

$40,000 Total profit
− 3,640 Total interest
$36,360 To be shared equally

$$\frac{\$36,360}{2} = \$18,180 \text{ each}$$

SUMMARY

	Amin	Kalid	Check
Interest	$ 2,080	$ 1,560	$20,260
Ratio	18,180	18,180	19,740
Total	$20,260	$19,740	$40,000

17. (a) Interest: Margaret = 6% × $16,000 = $ 960
             Katherine = 6% × $30,000 = $1,800

$14,000 Total profit
− 2,760 Total interest
− 5,000 Salary to Margaret
$ 6,250 To be divided equally

$$\frac{\$6,250}{2} = \$3,120 \text{ each}$$

17. (a) (Continued)

SUMMARY

	Margaret	Katherine	Check
Interest	$ 960	$1,800	$ 9,080
Salary	5,000	--	4,920
Ratio	3,120	3,120	$14,000
Total	$9,080	$4,920	

(b) $7,000 Total profit
    -2,760 Total interest
    -5,000 Salary to Margaret
 ($ 760) To be divided equally

$$\frac{(\$760)}{2} = (\$380)$$

SUMMARY

	Margaret	Katherine	Check
Interest	$ 960	$1,800	$5,580
Salary	5,000	--	1,420
Ratio	(380)	(380)	$7,000
Total	$5,580	$1,420	

18. (a) Interest: Nelly = 7% × $15,000 = $1,050
                    Jane = 7% × $18,000 = $1,260

$24,000 Total profit
- 2,310 Total interest
-10,000 Salary to Jane
$11,690 To be shared equally

$$\frac{\$11,690}{2} = \$5,845 \text{ each}$$

SUMMARY

	Nelly	Jane	Check
Interest	$1,050	$ 1,260	$ 6,895
Salary	--	10,000	17,105
Ratio	5,845	5,845	$24,000
Total	$6,895	$17,105	

(b) $12,000 Total net profit
    - 2,310 Total interest
    -10,000 Salary to Jane
 ($ 310) To be divided equally

18. (b) (Continued)

$$\frac{(\$310)}{2} = (\$155) \text{ each}$$

SUMMARY

	Nelly	Jane	Check
Interest	$1,050	$ 1,260	$ 895
Salary	--	10,000	11,105
Ratio	(155)	(155)	$12,000
Total	$ 895	$11,105	

19. (a) Interest: Tim = 7% × $10,000 = $700
    Chrisy = 7% × $ 9,000 = $630
    Barbara = 7% × $ 8,000 = $560

    $27,390 Total profit
    - 1,890 Total interest
    -12,000 Total salaries
    $13,500 To be divided in the ratio of investments

    Tim = $\frac{10}{27}$ × $13,500 = $5,000

    Chrisy = $\frac{9}{27}$ × $13,500 = $4,500

    Barbara = $\frac{8}{27}$ × $13,500 = $4,000

SUMMARY

	Tim	Chrisy	Barbara	Check
Interest	$ 700	$ 630	$ 560	$ 9,700
Salary	4,000	4,000	4,000	9,130
Ratio	5,000	4,500	4,000	8,560
Total	$9,700	$9,130	$8,560	$27,390

(b) $13,350 Total profit
    - 1,890 Total interest
    -12,000 Total salaries
    ($ 540) To be divided in the ratio of investments

    Tim = $\frac{10}{27}$ × ($540) = ($200)

    Chrisy = $\frac{9}{27}$ × ($540) = ($180)

19. (b) (Continued)

Barbara $= \dfrac{8}{27} \times (\$540) = (\$160)$

SUMMARY

	Tim	Chrisy	Barbara	Check
Interest	$ 700	$ 630	$ 560	$ 4,500
Salary	4,000	4,000	4,000	4,450
Ratio	(200)	(180)	(160)	4,400
Total	$4,500	$ 4,450	$4,400	$13,350

20. (a) Interest: Hal $= 6\% \times \$50,000 = \$3,000$
Jeff $= 6\% \times \$40,000 = \$2,400$
Steve $= 6\% \times \$30,000 = \$1,800$

$48,000 Total net profit
- 7,200 Total interest
-36,000 Total salaries
$ 4,800 To be divided in the ratio of their investments

Hal $= \dfrac{\$50,000}{\$120,000} = \dfrac{5}{12}; \quad \dfrac{5}{12} \times \$4,800 = \$2,000$

Jeff $= \dfrac{\$40,000}{\$120,000} = \dfrac{1}{3}; \quad \dfrac{1}{3} \times \$4,800 = \$1,600$

Steve $= \dfrac{\$30,000}{\$120,000} = \dfrac{1}{4}; \quad \dfrac{1}{4} \times \$4,800 = \$1,200$

SUMMARY

	Hal	Jeff	Steve	Check
Interest	$ 3,000	$ 2,400	$ 1,800	$17,000
Salary	12,000	12,000	12,000	16,000
Ratio	2,000	1,600	1,200	15,000
Total	$17,000	$16,000	$15,000	$48,000

(b) $39,000 Total net profit
- 7,200 Total interest
-36,000 Total salaries
($ 4,200) To be divided in the ratio of their investments

Hal $= \dfrac{5}{12} \times (\$4,200) = (\$1,750)$

Jeff $= \dfrac{1}{3} \times (\$4,200) = (\$1,400)$

20. (b) (Continued)

Steve = $\frac{1}{4}$ × ($4,200) = ($1,050)

SUMMARY

	Hal	Jeff	Steve	Check
Interest	$ 3,000	$ 2,400	$ 1,800	$13,250
Salary	12,000	12,000	12,000	13,000
Ratio	(1,750)	(1,400)	(1,050)	12,750
Total	$13,250	$13,000	$12,750	$39,000

21. (a) Interest: Richard = 5% × $20,000 = $1,000
Sarah = 5% × $40,000 = $2,000
Ted = 5% × $30,000 = $1,500

$16,000 Total profit
- 4,500 Total interest
-10,000 Total salaries
$ 1,500 To be divided in a 1:3:2 ratio

1 + 3 + 2 = 6 shares

Richard = $\frac{1}{6}$ × $1,500 = $250

Sarah = $\frac{1}{2}$ × $1,500 = $750

Ted = $\frac{1}{3}$ × $1,500 = $500

SUMMARY

	Richard	Sarah	Ted	Check
Interest	$1,000	$2,000	$1,500	$ 1,250
Salary	--	5,000	5,000	7,750
Ratio	250	750	500	7,000
Total	$1,250	$7,750	$7,000	$16,000

(b) $13,300 Total profit
- 4,500 Total interest
-10,000 Total salaries
($ 1,200) To be divided in a 1:3:2 ratio

1 + 3 + 2 = 6 shares

21. (b) (Continued)

$$\text{Richard} = \frac{1}{6} \times (\$1,200) = (\$200)$$

$$\text{Sarah} = \frac{1}{2} \times (\$1,200) = (\$600)$$

$$\text{Ted} = \frac{1}{3} \times (\$1,200) = (\$400)$$

SUMMARY

	Richard	Sarah	Ted	Check
Interest	$1,000	$2,000	$1,500	$ 800
Salary	--	5,000	5,000	6,400
Ratio	(200)	(600)	(400)	6,100
Total	$ 800	$6,400	$6,100	$13,350

22. (a) Interest: Connor = 6% × $22,000 = $1,320
            Dave   = 6% × $28,000 = $1,680
            Edwin = 6% × $30,000 = $1,800

```
 $45,000 Total net profit
-  4,800 Total interest
- 30,000 Total salaries
 $10,200 To be divided in a 1:1:2 ratio
```

$$\text{Connor} = \frac{1}{4} \times \$10,200 = \$2,550$$

$$\text{Dave} = \frac{1}{4} \times \$10,200 = \$2,550$$

$$\text{Edwin} = \frac{1}{2} \times \$10,200 = \$5,100$$

SUMMARY

	Connor	Dave	Edwin	Check
Interest	$ 1,320	$ 1,680	$ 1,800	$13,870
Salary	10,000	10,000	10,000	14,230
Ratio	2,550	2,550	5,100	16,900
Total	$13,870	$14,230	$16,900	$45,000

(b)
```
  $32,000  Total net profit
-   4,800  Total interest
-  30,000  Total salaries
($ 2,800)  To be divided in a 1:1:2 ratio
```

22. (b) (Continued)

$$\text{Connor} = \frac{1}{4} \times (\$2,800) = (\$\ 700)$$

$$\text{Dave} = \frac{1}{4} \times (\$2,800) = (\$\ 700)$$

$$\text{Edwin} = \frac{1}{2} \times (\$2,800) = (\$1,400)$$

SUMMARY

	Connor	Dave	Edwin	Check
Interest	$ 1,320	$ 1,680	$ 1,800	$10,620
Salary	10,000	10,000	10,000	10,980
Ratio	(700)	(700)	(1,400)	10,400
Total	$10,620	$10,980	$10,400	$32,000

CHAPTER XII

COMMERCIAL DISCOUNTS

Discounts are an important application of percent in business. This chapter looks at two of the most common discounts -- trade discounts and cash discounts.

1. Trade Discounts:

Most students could already find a net cost by computing the discount and subtracting. However, efficient computation of trade discounts makes use of the formula, % Paid × List = Net, and the student should be encouraged (if not required) to use it. Students can really appreciate this formula when chain discounts are introduced. Also, they can easily learn to apply the formula; finding the complement of the discount (the percent paid) poses no problem for most students.

When first teaching how to find the single equivalent discount rate, use only discounts (with no list price mentioned), to demonstrate that list has no influence on the equivalent discount percent. Emphasize that the equivalent discount rate is not equal to the sum of the series discounts.

By applying simple equation-solving techniques, students generally have no trouble finding other variations of the discount problem. When the discount rate is found using % Paid × L = N, point out that the equation solution represents the % paid, and must be converted to the equivalent discount percent.

The following table of net cost rate factors is included for your convenience in composing trade discount problems:

Trade Discount	Net Cost Rate Factor	Trade Discount	Net Cost Rate Factor
10/5	.855	20/20/10	.576
10/10	.81	25/20/5	.57
10/15	.765	40/5	.57
20/5	.76	30/20	.56
20/10	.72	20/20/12.5	.56
20/12.5	.7	25/20/10	.54
20/10/5	.684	40/10	.54
20/15	.68	30/25	.525
25/10	.675	25/20/15	.51
30/5	.665	40/15	.51
20/20	.64	30/30	.49
30/10	.63	30/20/12.5	.49
20/10/12.5	.63	25/20/20	.48
20/20/5	.608	25/25/20	.45
25/20	.6	30/25/20	.42

2.   Cash Discounts:

Discuss the meaning of sales terms -- by what date an invoice must be paid to take the discount, how much discount may be taken, and the last date when the full net amount must be paid. As simple as this seems, some students have trouble getting it straight. The word "net" is particularly misleading, since it refers to the full amount here, whereas "net" in the trade discounts section referred to the amount remaining after a discount.

Stress the importance to a business of taking advantage of these cash discounts. Emphasize that it is even profitable to borrow money in order to take advantage of cash discounts, since bank rates are less than cash discount rates (when both are considered on an annual basis). The following formula is used to determine the cost of discounts not taken:

$$\frac{\text{Discount \%}}{100\% - \text{Discount \%}} \times \frac{360}{\text{Credit period} - \text{Discount period}}$$

Even though an invoice is paid in 10 days, it is the amount of time by which payment is early that determines the corresponding bank rate. For example, on an invoice with credit terms of 2/10, n/30, a 2% savings over a 20-day period is equivalent to simple interest at 36.7%.

$$\frac{2\%}{100\% - 2\%} \times \frac{360}{30 - 10} = 36.7$$

Money would thus be saved on a cash discount by borrowing at any note lower then 36.7%.

Examples 4 and 5, dealing with partial payments on an invoice, may be omitted from basic course.

CHAPTER 12 - COMMERCIAL DISCOUNTS
PROBLEM SOLUTIONS

Section 1, page 327

1.

	Trade Discounts	% Paid (or Net Cost Rate Factor)	List	Net Cost	Single Equivalent Discount %
(a)	20%	80%	$ 72	$ 57.60	x
(b)	25%	75%	240	180.00	x
(c)	40%	60%	170	102.00	x
(d)	$33\frac{1}{3}$%	$66\frac{2}{3}$%	108	72.00	x
(e)	20%, 25%	60%	290	174.00	40%
(f)	$22\frac{2}{9}$%,10%	$\frac{7}{10}$ or 70%	150	105.00	30%
(g)	$37\frac{1}{2}$%,30%	$\frac{7}{16}$ or $43\frac{3}{4}$%	160	70.00	$56\frac{1}{4}$%
(h)	20/40/30	33.6%	500	168.00	66.4%

(a) Net cost rate factor = 0.80
$\quad$ % Pd × L = N
$\quad$ 0.80 × $72 =
$\qquad$ $57.60 = N

(b) Net cost rate factor = 0.75 or $\frac{3}{4}$
$\quad$ % Pd × L = N
$\quad$ 0.75 × $240 =
$\qquad$ $180 = N

(c) Net cost rate factor = 0.60
$\quad$ % Pd × L = N
$\quad$ 0.60 × L = $102

$$L = \frac{102}{0.60}$$

$$L = \$170$$

1. (Continued)

(d) Net cost rate factor = $66\frac{2}{3}\%$ = $\frac{2}{3}$

Trade discount = $33\frac{1}{3}\%$ or $\frac{1}{3}$

% Pd × L = N

$$\frac{2}{3}L = \$72$$

$$L = 72\left(\frac{3}{2}\right)$$

$$L = \$108$$

(e) Net cost rate factor = (0.80)(0.75) = 0.60
   % Pd × L = N
   0.60 × \$290 =
        \$174 = N

Single equivalent discount:
        100%
        −60
        40%

(f) Net cost rate factor = $\left(\frac{7}{9}\right)\left(\frac{9}{10}\right)$ = $\frac{7}{10}$ or 0.70

% Pd × L = N

$$\frac{7}{10} \times \$150 =$$

$$\$105 = N$$

Single equivalent discount:
        100%
        −70
        30%

(g) Net cost rate factor = $\left(\frac{5}{8}\right)\left(\frac{7}{10}\right)$ = $\frac{7}{16}$ or 0.4375

1. (g) (Continued)

$$\% \text{ Pd} \times L = N$$

$$\frac{7}{16} L = \$70$$

$$L = 70 \left(\frac{16}{7} \right)$$

$$L = \$160$$

Single equivalent discount:
$$
\begin{array}{r}
100.00\% \\
-43.75 \\
\hline
56.25\%
\end{array}
$$

(h) Net cost rate factor = $(0.80)(0.60)(0.70) = 0.336$

$$\% \text{ Pd} \times L = N$$
$$0.336 L = \$168$$
$$L = \$500$$

Single equivalent discount:
$$
\begin{array}{r}
100.0\% \\
-33.6 \\
\hline
66.4\%
\end{array}
$$

2.

	Trade Discounts	% Paid (or Net Cost Rate Factor)	List	Net Cost	Single Equivalent Discount %
(a)	15%	85%	$240	$204.00	x
(b)	45%	55%	30	16.50	x
(c)	12.5%	87.5%	8	7.00	x
(d)	10%	90%	40	36.00	x
(e)	20%,15%	68%	50	34.00	32%
(f)	25%,10%	67.5%	280	189.00	32.5%
(g)	$33\frac{1}{3}\%$,40%	40%	360	144.00	60%
(h)	20/25/10	54%	600	324.00	46%

2. (Continued)

(a) Net cost rate factor = 0.85
   % Pd × L = N
   0.85 × $240 =
        $204 = N

(b) Net cost rate factor = 0.55
   % Pd × L = N
   0.55 × $30 =
        $16.50 = N

(c) Net cost rate factor = 0.875
   % Pd × L = N
   0.875 × L = $7
         L = $8

(d) Net cost rate factor = 0.90
   Trade discount = 10%

   % Pd × L = N
      0.90L = $36
          L = $40

(e) Net cost rate factor = (0.80)(0.85) = 0.68
   % Pd × L = N
   0.68 × $50 =
        $34 = N

   Single equivalent discount:
           100%
           -68
            32%

(f) Net cost rate factor = (0.75)(0.9) = 0.675
   % Pd × L = N
   0.675 × $280 =
        $189 = N

   Single equivalent discount:
           100.0%
           -67.5
            32.5%

(g) Net cost rate factor = $\left(\dfrac{2}{3}\right)\left(\dfrac{3}{5}\right) = \dfrac{2}{5}$ or 0.40

   % Pd × L = N
      0.40L = $144
          L = $360

2. (g) (Continued)

Single equivalent discount:
```
      100%
      -40
      60%
```

(h) Net cost rate factor = $(0.8)(0.75)(0.9) = 0.54$

% Pd × L = N

$0.54L = \$324$

$L = \$600$

Single equivalent discount:
```
      100%
      -54
      46%
```

3. (a) % Pd × L = N
   $0.55 \times \$109 =$
   $\$59.95 = N$

(b) % Pd × L = N
   $0.65 \times \$500 =$
   $\$325 = N$

(c) % Pd × L = N

$\dfrac{5}{8} \times \$40 =$

$\$25 = N$

(d) % Pd × L = N

$\dfrac{8}{9} \times \$18 =$

$\$16 = N$

4. (a) % Pd × L = N
   $0.8 \times \$190 =$
   $\$152 = N$

(b) % Pd × L = N
   $0.90 \times \$750 =$
   $\$675 = N$

(c) % Pd × L = N
   $0.7 \times \$110 =$
   $\$77 = N$

(d) % Pd × L = N
   $0.85 \times \$80 =$
   $\$68 = N$

5.
```
       20 × $7    = $140.00
       36 × $3    =  108.00
        5 × $6    =   30.00
     10.5 × $8    =   84.00
       12 × $2    =   24.00
   Total list       $386.00
   Less:  25%      -  96.50
   Net              $289.50
   Plus:  Freight  + 27.00
   Total due        $316.50
```

6. 5 × $20   = $ 100.00
    2 × 12 × $70 =   1,680.00
    6 × $150   =   900.00
   10 × $29   =   290.00
    8 × $45   =   360.00
   Total list $3,330.00
   Less: 30%   - 999.00
   Net $2,331.00
   Plus: Freight +   12.50
   Total due $2,343.50

7. (a) 1. Net cost rate factor = (0.8)(0.8) = 0.64

        2.   % Pd × L = N
           0.64 × $45 =
                $28.80 = N

        3. Single equivalent discount = 100% - 64% = 36%

    (b) 1. Net cost rate factor = (0.85)(0.75) = 0.6375

        2.   % Pd × L = N
           0.6375 × $20 =
                 $12.75 = N

        3. Single equivalent discount = 100% - 63.75% = 36.25%

    (c) 1. Net cost rate factor = $(0.9)(0.745)\left(\dfrac{2}{3}\right)$ = 0.447

        2.   % Pd × L = N
           0.447 × $40 =
                $17.88 = N

        3. Single equivalent discount = 100% - 44.7% = 55.3%

    (d) 1. Net cost rate factor = (0.75)(0.80)(0.85) = 0.51

        2.   % Pd × L = N
           0.51 × $200 =
                 $102 = N

        3. Single equivalent discount = 100% - 51% = 49%

8. (a) 1. Net cost rate factor = (0.9)(0.85) = 0.765

8. (a) (Continued)

   2.   % Pd × L = N
      0.765 × $20 =
         $15.30 = N

   3. Single equivalent discount:
         100.0%
       - 76.5
         23.5%

(b) 1. Net cost rate factor = (0.8)(0.875) = 0.7

   2.   % Pd × L = N
      0.7 × $26 =
         $18.20 = N

   3. Single equivalent discount:
         100%
       - 70
         30%

(c) 1. Net cost rate factor = (0.8)(0.7)(0.95) = 0.532

   2.   % Pd × L = N
      0.532 × $35 =
         $18.62 = N

   3. Single equivalent discount:
         100.0%
       - 53.2
         46.8%

(d) 1. Net cost rate factor = $(0.75)\left(\dfrac{2}{3}\right)(0.9) = 0.45$

   2.   % Pd × L = N
      0.45 × $30 =
         $13.50 = N

   3. Single equivalent discount:
         100%
       - 45
         55%

9. Cotrone Co.:
   Net cost rate factor = (0.75)(0.80)(0.90) = 0.54
   Single equivalent discount = 100% - 54% = 46%

9. (Continued)

Hodgkins:
Net cost rate factor = (0.85)(0.60) = 0.45
Single equivalent discount = 100% - 45% = 55%

Thus, Hodgkins Distributors offers a better discount.

10. Home Decor:
Net cost rate factor = (0.65)(0.9) = 0.585
Single equivalent discount = 100% - 58.5% = 41.5%

Carpet City:
Net cost rate factor = (0.8)(0.8)(0.95) = 0.608
Single equivalent discount = 100% - 60.8% = 39.2%

Thus, Home Decor offers a better discount.

11. $\% \text{ Pd} \times L = N$

$(0.8)(0.85)L = \$2.04$

$0.68L = 2.04$

$L = \dfrac{2.04}{0.68}$

$L = \$3$

12. $\% \text{ Pd} \times L = N$

$(0.75)(0.9)L = \$5.40$

$0.675L = 5.40$

$L = \$8$

13. $\% \text{ Pd} \times L = N$

$(0.65)(0.9)L = \$29.25$

$0.585L = 29.25$

$L = \dfrac{29.25}{0.585}$

$L = \$50$

14. $\% \text{ Pd} \times L = N$

$\left(\dfrac{2}{3}\right)\left(\dfrac{9}{10}\right)L = \$6.30$

$\dfrac{3}{5}L = 6.30$

$L = \$10.50$

15. $\% \text{ Pd} \times L = N$

$X(\$10) = \$6$

$X = \dfrac{6}{10}$

$X = 60\%$

Thus, 100% - 60% = 40%

16. $\% \text{ Pd} \times L = N$

$X(\$330) = \$297$

$X = \dfrac{297}{330}$

$X = 90\%$

Thus, 100% - 90% = 10%

17. (a)   % Pd × L = N
     (0.8)(X)($60) = $42
              48X = 42
                X = $\dfrac{42}{48}$

                X = 87.5%

     Thus, additional discount
     needed = 100% − 87.5%
            = 12.5%

   (b) Net cost rate factor =
       (0.8)(0.875) = 0.70

       Single equivalent
       discount = 100% − 70%
                = 30%

18. (a)   % Pd × L = N
       (0.75)(X)($180) = $108
                  135X = 108
                     X = 80%

     Thus, additional discount
     needed = 100% − 80% = 20%

   (b) Net cost rate factor =
       (0.75)(0.80) = 0.60

       Single equivalent
       discount = 100% − 60%
                = 40%

19. (a) Crabtree Pet Supplies:
        % Pd × L = N

        $\dfrac{5}{6}$ × $30 =

           $25 = N

        Hannah's Pet Mart:
         % Pd × L = N
        0.65 × $35 =
            $22.75 = N

   (b)   % Pd × L = N

        $\left(\dfrac{5}{6}\right)$ (X) ($30) = $22.75

                   25X = 22.75

                    X = 91%

       So, additional discount
       needed by Crabtree =
       100% − 91% = 9%

20. (a) Jerde's Kitchen Bazar:
        % Pd × L = N
        (0.6)($70) =
            $42 = N

        Melrose Inc:
         % Pd × L = N
        (0.8)($60) =
            $48 = N

   (b)   % Pd × L = N
       (0.80)(X)($60) = $42
                  48X = 42
                    X = 87.5%

       Thus, additional discount
       needed by Melrose =
       100.0% − 87.5% = $12\dfrac{1}{2}$%

21. (a) Shenandoah Furniture:
    % Pd × L = N

$$\frac{2}{3} \times \$480 =$$

    $320 = N

Dickens Co.:
    % Pd × L = N
0.75 × $400 =
    $300 = N

(b)   % Pd × L = N

$$\left(\frac{2}{3}\right)(X)(\$480) = \$300$$

    320X = 300

    X = 93.75%

So, additional discount
needed by Shenandoah =
100% - 93.75% = 6.25%

22. (a) Plymouth Distributors:
    % Pd × L = N
(0.80)($150) =
    $120 = N

Thomas Wholesalers:
    % Pd × L = N
(0.60)($180) =
    $108 = N

(b)   % Pd × L = N
(0.80)(X)($150) = $108
    120X = 108
    X = 90%

So, additional discount
needed by Plymouth =
100% - 90% = 10%

23. (a) Thelma's:
    % Pd × L = N
0.875 × $200 =
    $175 = N

Johnson:
    % Pd × L = N
0.50 × $280 =
    $140 = N

(b)   % Pd × L = N
(0.875)(X)($200) = $140
    175X = 140
    X = 80%

So, additional discount
needed by Thelma's
Accessories = 100% - 80%
    = 20%

24. (a) Martin Co.:
    % Pd × L = N
(0.8)(0.875)($180) =
    $126 = N

Jergan's Outlet:
    % Pd × L = N
(0.625)($240) =
    $150 = N

(b)   % Pd × L = N
(0.625)(X)($240) = $126
    150X = 126
    X = 84%

So, additional discount
needed by Jergan's =
100% - 84% = 16%

Section 2, page 334

1. (a) No discount
   (b) 3%
   (c) 1%
   (d) 2%
   (e) 3%
   (f) 2%

2. (a) No discount
   (b) 1%
   (c) 2%
   (d) 1%
   (e) 3%
   (f) 2%

3. (a) No discount
   Amount due = $824

   (b) % Pd × L = N
   (0.98)$600 =
   $588 = N

   (c) % Pd × L = N
   (0.98)$325 =
   $318.50 = N

   (d) No discount
   Amount due = $780

   (e) % Pd × L = N
   (0.98)$450 =
   $441 = N

   (f) % Pd × L = N
   (0.97)$860 =
   $834.20 = N

   (g) % Pd × L = N
   (0.96)$550 =
   $528 = N

4. (a) No discount
   Amount due = $1,200

   (b) % Pd × L = N
   (0.98)$4,700 =
   $4,606 = N

   (c) % Pd × L = N
   (0.97)$800 =
   $776 = N

   (d) No discount
   Amount due = $940

   (e) % Pd × L = N
   (0.98)$5,500 =
   $5,390 = N

   (f) % Pd × L = N
   (0.97)$6,300 =
   $6,111 = N

   (g) % Pd × L = N
   (0.98)$2,600 =
   $2,548 = N

5.

	Amount of Invoice	Sales Terms	Credit Toward Account	Net Payment Made	Amount Still Due
(a)	$2,000	2/10, n/30	$500	$490.00	$1,500
(b)	860	1/10, n/30	300	297.00	560
(c)	670	2/10, n/60	450	441.00	220
(d)	790	3/15, n/30	400	388.00	390
(e)	560	4/10, n/60	360	345.60	200

(a) % Pd × Cr = N
(0.98)$500 =
$490 = N
Amount due = $2,000 - $500
= $1,500

(b) % Pd × Cr = N
(0.99)$300 =
$297 = N
Amount due = $860 - $300
= $560

(c) % Pd × Cr = N
(0.98)Cr = $441
Cr = $450
Amount due = $670 - $450
= $220

(d) % Pd × Cr = N
(0.97)Cr = $388
Cr = $400
Amount due = $790 - $400
= $390

(e) Credit to account = $560 - $200 = $360
% Pd × L = N
(0.96)$360 =
$345.60 = N

6.

	Amount of Invoice	Sales Terms	Credit Toward Account	Net Payment Made	Amount Still Due
(a)	$3,500	2/10, n/30	$1,750	$1,715	$1,750
(b)	4,800	1/10, n/30	2,000	1,980	2,800
(c)	880	3/10, n/30	500	485	380
(d)	5,600	4/10, n/30	1,000	960	4,600
(e)	2,200	2/10, n/30	1,200	1,176	1,000

(a) % Pd × Cr = N
(0.98)$1,750 =
$1,715 = N

Amount due = $3,500
-1,750
$1,750

(b) % Pd × Cr = N
(0.99)$2,000 =
$1,980 = N

Amount due = $4,800
-2,000
$2,800

(c) % Pd × Cr = N
(0.97)Cr = $485
Cr = $500

(d) % Pd × Cr = N
(0.96)Cr = $960
Cr = $1,000

6. (c) (Continued)   (d) (Continued)

          Amount due = $880   Amount due = $5,600
                      -500   -1,000
                      $380 $4,600

      (e) Credit to account = $2,200 - $1,000 = $1,200
              % Pd × Cr = N
          (0.98)$1,200 =
                $1,176 = N

7. Total cost $383.20   % Pd × L = N
   Less: Freight   - 33.20   (0.8)(0.8)(0.97)$350 =
   Merchandise cost $350.00 $217.28 = N

   Cost after discount $217.28
   Add back freight   + 33.20
   Total amount due $250.48

8. Total cost $2,546.45   % Pd × L = N
   Less: Freight   - 46.45   (0.7)(0.9)(0.97)$2,500 =
   Merchandise cost $2,500.00 $1,527.75 = N

   Cost after discount $1,527.75
   Add back freight   + 46.45
   Total amount due $1,574.20

9.   8 × $ 8.00 = $ 64   % Pd × L = N
     10 ×   18.00 =   180   (0.7)(0.75)(0.98)$334 =
     30 ×   1.20 =   36 $171.84 = N
     36 ×   1.50 =   54
                     $334

   Cost after discounts $171.84
   Add: freight   + 12.95
   Total amount due $184.79

10.   3 × $216 = $ 648   % Pd × L = N
      2 × 141 =   282   (0.8)(0.7)(0.98)$1,980 =
    0.5 × 180 =   90 $1,086.62 = N
      4 × 240 =   960
                  $1,980

10. (Continued)

Cost after discount $1,086.62
Add back freight   +   50.00
Total amount due $1,136.61

11.   <u>Discount</u>   <u>Net Amount Due</u>
    March 3 $ 850   No discount $ 850.00
    March 10   1,000   1% × $1,000   990.00
    March 15   620   2% × $ 620   607.60
                        Total due $2,447.60

12.   <u>Discount</u>   <u>Net Amount Due</u>
    July 6 $ 500   No discount $ 500
    July 11   1,350   2% × $1,350   1,323
    July 16   1,800   3% × $1,800   1,746
                        Total due $3,569

13. (a) $\frac{1}{4}$ of $1,200 = $300 credit desired

         % Pd × Cr = N
    (0.98)$300 =
          $294 = N

    (b) Balance due = $1,200 - $300 = $900

         % Pd × L = N
    (0.99)$900 =
          $891 = N

    (c) Total paid = $294 + $891 = $1,185

14. (a) $\frac{1}{2}$ of $5,000 = $2,500 credit desired

           % Pd × Cr = N
    (0.97)($2,500) =
           $2,425 = N

    (b) Balance due = $5,000 - $2,500 = $2,500

           % Pd × L = N
    (0.99)($2,500) =
           $2,475 = N

14. (Continued)

   (c) Total paid = $2,425 + $2,475 = $4,900

15. (a)   % Pd × Cr = N   (b) Balance due:
            (0.97)Cr = $421.95 $870
                  Cr = $435   −435
                                                $435

16. (a)   % Pd × Cr = N   (b) Balance due:
            (0.98)Cr = $490 $1,500
                  Cr = $500   − 500
                                                $1,000

CHAPTER XIII

MARKUP

Markup is one of the most important topics in business mathematics. Unfortunately, it is also one of the most difficult for students to comprehend and apply, and the authors have not found all the answers for teaching it. Hopefully, a good foundation has been laid through study of the income statement --cost, overhead, and net profit expressed in terms of dollars and cents. This chapter will require slow and careful explanations, as well as a great deal of practice and boardwork.

The terminology should be familiar from the income statement but may need to be reviewed if it has been some time since the income statement was studied. The fundamental selling price formula, C + M = S, may also need review. As part of the introductory discussion, point out that selling price is not always a matter of personal choice; competition or the manufacturer's recommended selling price (often printed on the merchandise) may force merchants to sell at a lower price than they would otherwise use.

1.   Markup Based on Cost:

Discuss example 2 thoroughly in order to drive home the importance of a carefully calculated markup. Note, however, that it is common practice to mark an item $24.98 or $24.99 instead of $25.00, because of the psychological effect on the customer.

Most students have studied simple markup based on cost as an application of percent in the primary and secondary schools, and they can already find this selling price by adding cost plus markup. However, markup based on selling price (the one most often used in business) is impossible to compute using addition; therefore, the instructor should immediately start requiring the student to substitute the decimal (or fractional) equivalent for markup, thus obtaining the selling price by multiplication (example 3b). Emphasize that the students cannot substitute just "20%" for the markup; they may substitute "20% of C" (1/5 C or 0.2C). Failure to include the "C" is a common mistake when markup problems are first introduced. Have the students form the habit of combining the C's before they substitute the actual dollar cost; this is important, for it eliminates many mistakes.

Students often have difficulty with problems which ask them to "find the percent of markup based on cost" or to "find the percent

of markup based on selling price" (example 5). These problems are
solved using the formulas "__?% of C = M" and "__?% of S = M";
however, many students often jumble the variables. You could simply
insist that they memorize the formulas. However, the students will
have more success with these problems if the situation has meaning
to them, rather than just attempting to apply abstract formulas.
(Bringing "meaning" to markup procedures is the real teaching
challenge of this chapter.)   The instructor could also help the
students by rephrasing the question as "What percent of cost is the
margin?" thus enabling them to write the formulas directly from the
English.   However, that is a leading question and not necessarily
recommended. The best approach seems to be to help the student
really understand what is to be found; when this has been
accomplished, the formulas will be logical and students will not be
so likely to misplace the variables.

After the solution to example 5a has been found, relate it back
to the pricing procedure: show that the 25% markup will produce the
same margin and thus result in the correct selling price. Treat
example 5b in a similar manner: check your answer to prove that the
$15 markup used is actually 20% of the selling price. The diagrams
will help the students visualize (and internalize) the
relationships.

The selling price factor is discussed in order to point out
that, if a number of items are to be priced using the same markup,
it is not necessary to start with the original equation each time.
Many students would fail to apply this fact if it were not
specifically mentioned.

2.   Markup Based on Selling Price:

Having studied the income statement earlier, students will
realize that, since expenses and net profit are stated as a percent
of net sales on the income statement, it is desirable to price
merchandise by using a markup based on selling price. However, the
idea of finding a markup that is a certain percent of a selling
price which is also unknown "boggles the mind" of many students.

Before discussing example 1, it will help to prepare the class
for the equation-solving techniques that will be required,
particularly if some time has elapsed since the review chapters were
studied. Use an equation such as $15 + 2x = 5x$ to introduce the idea
of having to subtract on both sides of the equation. This brief
refresher will enable the students to learn much more quickly the
procedure for markup based on selling price. The diagram for
example 1 breaks down the selling price and will help the students
understand that the markup condition is .met.

When solving C + M = S using the markup based on selling price, reemphasize that the students may substitute "1/5 S" for a "20% markup on sales." As before, insist that the S's be combined before the dollar amount is substituted for cost. This type of problem is sometimes easier and quicker for students to apply when the markup percent can be conveniently expressed as a fraction. With this in mind, almost all of the problems in this chapter contain percents that are the equivalents of frequently-used common fractions. (Be sure that students have learned the percent equivalents listed after Section 3 of Chapter III.)

For your own convenience, you may wish to know the relationship that exists between markup percent based on cost and markup percent based on sales. When the percent of markup based on cost is known, the corresponding percent markup based on sales may be found as follows: (1) express the markup percent on cost as a fraction, $\frac{n}{d}$, (2) now write a fraction with the same numerator and with a denominator that is the sum of the original numerator plus denominator, $\frac{n}{n + d}$; (3) convert this fraction to a percent and you have the equivalent percent of markup based on sales. Some examples follow:

Percent of markup based on cost	Corresponding percent of markup based on sale
$66\frac{2}{3}\% = \frac{2}{3}$	$\frac{2}{2 + 3} = \frac{2}{5} = 40\%$
$60\% = \frac{3}{5}$	$\frac{3}{3 + 5} = \frac{3}{8} = 37\frac{1}{2}\%$
$50\% = \frac{1}{2}$	$\frac{1}{1 + 2} = \frac{1}{3} = 33\frac{1}{3}\%$
$33\frac{1}{3}\% = \frac{1}{3}$	$\frac{1}{1 + 3} = \frac{1}{4} = 25\%$
$28\frac{4}{7}\% = \frac{2}{7}$	$\frac{2}{2 + 7} = \frac{2}{9} = 22\frac{2}{9}\%$
$25\% = \frac{1}{4}$	$\frac{1}{1 + 4} = \frac{1}{5} = 20\%$
$16\frac{2}{3}\% = \frac{1}{6}$	$\frac{1}{1 + 6} = \frac{1}{7} = 14\frac{2}{7}\%$
$14\frac{2}{7}\% = \frac{1}{7}$	$\frac{1}{1 + 7} = \frac{1}{8} = 12\frac{1}{2}\%$
$12\frac{1}{2}\% = \frac{1}{8}$	$\frac{1}{1 + 8} = \frac{1}{9} = 11\frac{1}{9}\%$
$11\frac{1}{9}\% = \frac{1}{9}$	$\frac{1}{1 + 9} = \frac{1}{10} = 10\%$

Likewise, the percent markup on selling price can be converted to its equivalent percent markup on cost by using this shortcut formula: $\dfrac{n}{d - n}$.

3.   **Marking Perishables**:

This section outlines the general procedure to follow in pricing perishables: Find (a) the cost; (b) the total value of sales; (c) the quantity of goods expected to sell; and (d) the marked price per unit. The only aspect needing special attention is step (d), finding the marked price per unit; the student may try to use the original amount purchased, rather than using the amount expected to sell. (This also happens in example 2.)

Point out that it is common practice in retail businesses to round up any fraction, regardless of how small, to the next cent. Thus, if handsoap is priced "4 bars for $1.89," then separate bars would cost 48¢ each, even though the exact price was only 47-1/4¢ each.

CHAPTER 13 - MARKUP
PROBLEM SOLUTIONS

Section 1, page 348

1. (a) 1.   C + M = S
$80 + M = $95
M = $15

2. OH = 15% × C
= (0.15)$80
OH = $12

3.   M = OH + P
$15 = $12 + P
$3 = P

(b) 1.   C + M = S
$55 + M = $73
M = $18

2. OH = 40% × C
= (0.4)$55
OH = $22

3.   M = OH + P
$18 = $22 + P
-$4 = P (loss)

(c) 1.   C + M = S
$75 + M = $89
M = $14

2. OH = 20% × C
= (0.2)$75
OH = $15

1. (c) (Continued)

    3.   M = OH + P
        $14 = $15 + P
       -$1 = P (loss)

 (d) 1.   C + M = S   2. OH = 25% × S
       $33 + M = $40   = (0.25)$40
            M = $7   OH = $10

    3.   M = OH + P
       $7 = $10 + P
     -$3 = P (loss)

 (e) 1.   C + M = S   2. OH = 15% × S
       $72 + M = $96   = (0.15)$96
            M = $24   OH = $14.40

    3.   M = OH + P
        $24 = $14.40 + P
    $9.60 = P

2. (a) 1.   C + M = S   2. OH = 20% × C
       $16 + M = $20   = (0.20)$16
            M = $4   OH = $3.20

    3.   M = OH + P
        $4 = $3.20 + P
    $0.80 = P

 (b) 1.   C + M = S   2. OH = 25% × C
       $50 + M = $66   = (0.25)$50
            M = $16   OH = $12.50

    3.   M = OH + P
       $16 = $12.50 + P
    $3.50 = P

 (c) 1.   C + M = S   2. OH = 30% × C
       $30 + M = $35   = (0.30)$30
            M = $5   OH = $9

    3.   M = OH + P
       $5 = $9 + P
     -$4 = P (loss)

2. (Continued)

(d) 1.   C + M = S
         $85 + M = $100
              M = $15

   2. OH = 12.5% × S
         = (0.125)$100
      OH = $12.50

   3.   M = OH + P
      $15 = $12.50 + P
     $2.50 = P

(e) 1.   C + M = S
         $56 + M = $64
              M = $8

   2. OH = 15% × S
         = (0.15)$64
      OH = $9.60

   3.   M = OH + P
       $8 = $9.60 + P
    -$1.60 = P (loss)

3.

	% Markup on Cost	Spf	Cost	Selling Price	Markup	% Markup on Selling Price
(a)	40 %	1.4	$90	$126	$36	$28\frac{4}{7}$ %
(b)	20	1.2	60	72	12	$16\frac{2}{3}$
(c)	$12\frac{1}{2}$	$\frac{9}{8}$ or 1.125	32	36	4	$11\frac{1}{9}$
(d)	25	1.25	12	15	3	20
(e)	60	1.6	40	64	24	$37\frac{1}{2}$
(f)	$22\frac{2}{9}$	$\frac{11}{9}$ or $1.22\frac{2}{9}$	54	66	12	18.18
(g)	$33\frac{1}{3}$	$\frac{4}{3}$ or $1.33\frac{1}{3}$	27	36	9	25

(a) Spf = 1 + .40 = 1.4

   1.4 × C = S
   1.4($90) =
       $126 = S

   M = S - C
     = $126 - $90
   M = $36

   ___% of S = M
   ___%($126) = $36
      126x = 36
         x = $28\frac{4}{7}$%

3. (Continued)

(b) Spf = 1 + .20 = 1.20

Spf × C = S	M = S − C	___% of S = M
1.2($60) =	= $72 − $60	___%($72) = $12
$72 = S	M = $12	72x = 12

$$x = \frac{1}{6} \text{ or}$$

$$16\frac{2}{3}\%$$

(c) Spf = 1 + $\frac{1}{8}$ = $\frac{9}{8}$

Spf × C = S	M = S − C	___% of S = M
	= $36 − $32	___%($36) = $4
$\frac{9}{8}$($32) =	M = $4	36x = 4
$36 = S		

$$x = \frac{1}{9} \text{ or}$$

$$11\frac{1}{9}\%$$

(d) Spf = 1 + .25 = 1.25

Spf × C = S	M = S − C	___% of S = M
1.25C = $15	= $15 − $12	___%($15) = $3
C = $12	M = $3	15x = 3

$$x = \frac{1}{5} \text{ or}$$

$$20\%$$

(e) Spf = 1 + .60 = 1.60

Spf × C = S	M = S − C	___% of S = M
1.6C = $64	= $64 − $40	___%($64) = $24
C = $40	M = $24	64x = 24
		x = 37.5%

(f)

M = S − C	___% of C = M	___% of S = M
M = $66 − $54	___%($54) = $12	___%($66) = $12
M = $12	54x = 12	66x = 12
		x = 18.18%

$$x = \frac{2}{9} \text{ or}$$

$$22\frac{2}{9}\%$$

3. (f) (Continued)

$$Spf = 1 + \frac{2}{9} = \frac{11}{9} \quad or \quad 1.22\frac{2}{9}$$

(g)
C = S − M	___% of C = M	___% of S = M
= \$36 − \$9	___%(\$27) = \$9	___%(\$36) = \$9
C = \$27	27x = 9	36x = 9

$$x = \frac{1}{3} \quad or \quad\quad\quad x = \frac{1}{4} \quad or$$

$$33\frac{1}{3}\% \quad\quad\quad\quad 25\%$$

$$Spf = 1 + \frac{1}{3} = \frac{4}{3} \quad or \quad 1.33\overline{3}$$

4.

	% Markup on Cost	Spf	Cost	Selling Price	Markup	% Markup on Selling Price
(a)	25 %	1.25	\$40	\$50	\$10	20 %
(b)	33\frac{1}{3}	1.3\overline{3} or \frac{4}{3}	60	80	20	25
(c)	20	1.2	20	24	4	16\frac{2}{3}
(d)	50	1.5	64	96	32	33\frac{1}{3}
(e)	10	1.1	50	55	5	9.\overline{09}
(f)	16\frac{2}{3}	1.16\frac{2}{3} or \frac{7}{6}	36	42	6	14\frac{2}{7}
(g)	60	1.6	30	48	18	37.5

(a) $Spf = 1 + .25 = 1.25$

1.25 × C = S	M = S − C	___% of S = M
1.25(\$40) =	= \$50 − \$40	___%(\$50) = \$10
\$50 = S	M = \$10	50x = 10
		x = 20%

(b) $Spf = 1 + \frac{1}{3} = \frac{4}{3}$

Spf × C = S	M = S − C	___% of S = M
	= \$80 − \$60	___%(\$80) = \$20
$\frac{4}{3}$(\$60) =	M = \$20	80x = 20
		x = 25%
\$80 = S		

4. (Continued)

(c) Spf = 1 + .20 = 1.20

Spf × C = S	M = S − C	___% of S = M
1.2($20) =	= $24 − $20	___%($24) = $4
$24 = S	M = $4	24x = 4

$$x = 16\frac{2}{3}\%$$

(d) Spf = 1 + .50 = 1.50

Spf × C = S	M = S − C	___% of S = M
1.5C = $96	= $96 − $64	___%($96) = $32
C = $64	M = $32	96x = 32

$$x = 33\frac{1}{3}\%$$

(e) Spf = 1 + .10 = 1.10

Spf × C = S	M = S − C	___% of S = M
1.1C = $55	= $55 − $50	___%($55) = $5
C = $50	M = $5	55x = 5

$$x = 9.\overline{09}\%$$

(f)
M = S − C	___% of C = M	___% of S = M
= $42 − $36	___%($36) = $6	___%($42) = $6
M = $6	36x = 6	42x = 6

$$x = 16\frac{2}{3}\% \qquad x = 14\frac{2}{7}\%$$

$$Spf = 1 + \frac{1}{6} = \frac{7}{6}$$

(g)
C = S − M	___% of C = M	___% of S = M
= $48 − $18	___%($30) = $18	___%($48) = $18
C = $30	30x = 18	48x = 18
	x = 60%	x = 37.5%

$$Spf = 1 + .60 = 1.60$$

5. (a) Spf = 1.42

(b)
Spf × C = S
1.42($13) =
$18.46 = S

(c) M = S − C
= $18.46 − $13
M = $5.46

6. (a) Spf = 1.2

(b)
Spf × C = S
1.2($15) =
$18 = S

(c) M = S − C
= $18 − $15
M = $3

7. Cost per pair: $\dfrac{\$48}{12} = \$4$

$$M = S - C$$
$$= \$5 - \$4$$
$$M = \$1$$

(a) ___% of C = M
$$\_\_\%(\$4) = \$1$$
$$4x = 1$$
$$x = \frac{1}{4}$$
$$x = 25\%$$

(b) ___% of S = M
$$\_\_\%(\$5) = \$1$$
$$5x = 1$$
$$x = \frac{1}{5}$$
$$x = 20\%$$

8. Cost per pen: $\dfrac{\$18}{12} = \$1.50$

$$M = S - C$$
$$= \$2.00 - \$1.50$$
$$M = \$0.50$$

(a) ___% of C = M
$$\_\_\%(\$1.50) = \$0.50$$
$$1.50x = 0.50$$
$$x = 33\frac{1}{3}\%$$

(b) ___% of S = M
$$\_\_\%(\$2) = \$0.50$$
$$2x = 0.50$$
$$x = 25\%$$

9. (a) Spf $= 1 + .37\frac{1}{2} = 1.375$

(or $\frac{11}{8}$)

(b)
$$\text{Spf} \times C = S$$
$$\frac{11}{8}(\$8) = \$11$$
$$\frac{11}{8}(\$4.80) = \$6.60$$
$$\frac{11}{8}(\$6.40) = \$8.80$$
$$\frac{11}{8}(\$16.40) = \$22.55$$

(c) C + M = S
$$\$8 + M = \$11$$
$$M = \$3$$

___% of S = M
$$\_\_\%(\$11) = \$3$$
$$11x = 3$$
$$x = 27\frac{3}{11}\%$$

10. (a) Spf = 1.4

(b)
$$\text{Spf} \times C = S$$
$$1.4(\$14) = \$19.60$$
$$1.4(\$9) = \$12.60$$
$$1.4(\$25) = \$35.00$$
$$1.4(\$30) = \$42.00$$

10. (Continued)

(c) $M = S - C$
     $\quad = \$19.60 - \$14.00$
     $M = \$5.60$

$\underline{\quad}\% \text{ of } S = M$
$\underline{\quad}\%(\$19.60) = \$5.60$
$\qquad 19.60x = 5.60$
$\qquad\quad x = 28\dfrac{4}{7}\%$

11. (a) $\quad C + M = S$
     $\quad C + 30\%C =$
     $\qquad 1.3C = \$78$
     $\qquad\quad C = \$60$

     $M = S - C$
     $\quad = \$85 - \$68$
     $M = \$17$

(b) $\quad C + M = S$
     $\quad C + 25\%C =$
     $\qquad 1.25C = \$85$
     $\qquad\quad C = \$68$

$\underline{\quad}\% \text{ of } S = M$
$\underline{\quad}\%(\$85) = \$17$
$\qquad 85x = 17$
$\qquad\quad x = 20\%$

12. (a) $\quad C + M = S$
     $\quad C + 50\%C =$
     $\qquad 1.5C = \$135$
     $\qquad\quad C = \$90$

     $M = S - C$
     $\quad = \$80 - \$50$
     $M = \$30$

(b) $\quad C + M = S$
     $\quad C + 60\%C =$
     $\qquad 1.6C = \$80$
     $\qquad\quad C = \$50$

$\underline{\quad}\% \text{ of } S = M$
$\underline{\quad}\%(\$80) = \$30$
$\qquad 80x = 30$
$\qquad\quad x = 37.5\%$

13. (a) $\% \text{ Pd} \times L = \text{Net cost}$
     $0.50(\$70) = N$
     $\qquad \$35 = N$

     $\% \text{ Pd} \times L = \text{Net selling price}$
     $0.75(\$70) = N$
     $\qquad \$52.50 = N$

(b) $\quad C + M = S$
     $\$35 + M = \$52.50$
     $\qquad\quad M = \$17.50$

$\underline{\quad}\% \text{ of } C = M$
$\underline{\quad}\%(\$35) = \$17.50$
$\qquad 35x = 17.50$
$\qquad\quad x = 50\%$

(c) $\underline{\quad}\% \text{ of } S = M$
$\underline{\quad}\%(\$52.50) = \$17.50$
$\qquad 52.50x = 17.50$
$\qquad\quad x = 33\dfrac{1}{3}\%$

14. (a)   % Pd × L = Net cost   % Pd × L = Net selling price
            0.60($55) = N   0.90($55) = N
                 $33 = N $49.50 = N

    (b) M = S - C   ___% of C = M
          = $49.50 - $33.00   ___%($33) = $16.50
        M = $16.50   33x = 16.50
                                            x = 50%

    (c)   ___% of S = M
        ___%($49.50) = $16.50
              49.50x = 16.50
                   x = $33\frac{1}{3}$%

15. Total cost = $115 + $20 = $135

    Cost per detector = $\frac{\$135}{15}$ = $9

    (a)   C + M = S   (b) M = S - C   ___% of S = M
          C + 25%C =   = $11.25 - $9   ___%($11.25) = $2.25
          1.25($9) =   M = $2.25   11.25x = 2.25
             $11.25 = S   x = 20%

16. Total cost = $1,850 + $100 = $1,950

    Cost per racket = $\frac{\$1,950}{10}$ = $195

    (a)   C + M = S   (b) M = S - C   ___% of S = M
                                = $260 - $195   ___%($260) = $65
          C + $\frac{1}{3}$C =   M = $65   260x = 65
                                                        x = 25%
          $\frac{4}{3}$($195) =

             $260 = S

17. Total cost = $120 + $24 = $144

    Cost per bottle = $\frac{\$144}{6}$ = $24

17. (Continued)

(a)   C + M = S   (b) M = S - C   ___% of S = M
         C + 60%C =   = \$38.40 - \$24 ___%(\$38.40) = \$14.40
        1.6(\$24) =   M = \$14.40   38.40x = 14.40
          \$38.40 = S

$$x = 37\frac{1}{2}\%$$

18. Total cost = \$1,870 + \$50 = \$1,920

$$\text{Cost per golf club} = \frac{\$1,920}{12} = \$160$$

(a)   C + M = S   (b) M = S - C   ___% of S = M
         C + 25%C =   = \$200 - \$160 ___%(\$200) = \$40
      1.25(\$160) =   M = \$40   200x = 40
          \$200 = S   x = 20%

Section 2, page 353

1.

	% Markup on Selling Price	Spf	Cost	Selling Price	Markup	% Markup on Cost
(a)	25 %	$\frac{4}{3}$	\$30	$\underline{\$40}$	$\underline{\$10}$	$33\frac{1}{3}\%$
(b)	$37\frac{1}{2}$	$\frac{8}{5}$ or 1.6	35	$\underline{56}$	$\underline{21}$	$\underline{60}$
(c)	$33\frac{1}{3}$	$\frac{3}{2}$ or 1.5	$\underline{28}$	42	$\underline{14}$	$\underline{50}$
(d)	50	$\frac{1}{.5}$ or 2	$\underline{6}$	12	$\underline{6}$	$\underline{100}$
(e)	$\underline{10}$	$\frac{10}{9}$	18	$\underline{20}$	2	$11\frac{1}{9}$

(a) Spf = $\frac{4}{3}$ C + M = S   ___% of C = M
                  \$30 + M = \$40   ___%(\$30) = \$10
                      M = \$10   30x = 10

Spf × C = S

$\frac{4}{3}$(\$30) =

      \$40 = S

$$x = 33\frac{1}{3}\%$$

1. (Continued)

(b) Spf = $\dfrac{8}{5}$ or 1.6

$$C + M = S$$
$$\$35 + M = \$56$$
$$M = \$21$$

___% of C = M
___%($35) = $21
$$35x = 21$$
$$x = 60\%$$

Spf × C = S

$$\dfrac{8}{5}(\$35) =$$

$$\$56 = S$$

(c) Spf = $\dfrac{3}{2}$ or 1.5

$$C + M = S$$
$$\$28 + M = \$42$$
$$M = \$14$$

___% of C = M
___%($28) = $14
$$28x = 14$$
$$x = 50\%$$

Spf × C = S

$$\dfrac{3}{2}C = \$42$$

$$C = \$28$$

(d) Spf = $\dfrac{1}{.5}$ or 2

$$C + M = S$$
$$\$6 + M = \$12$$
$$M = \$6$$

___% of C = M
___%($6) = $6
$$6x = 6$$
$$x = 100\%$$

Spf × C = S

$$\dfrac{1}{.5}C = \$12$$

$$C = \$6$$

(e)
$$C + M = S$$
$$\$18 + \$2 =$$
$$\$20 = S$$

___% of S = M
___%($20) = $2
$$20x = 2$$
$$x = 10\%$$

___% of C = M
___%($18) = $2
$$18x = 2$$
$$x = 11\dfrac{1}{9}\%$$

Spf = $\dfrac{10}{9}$

2.

	% Markup on Selling Price	Spf	Cost	Selling Price	Markup	% Markup on Cost
(a)	40%	$1.66\overline{6}$ or $\frac{5}{3}$	$ 15	$ 25	$10	$66\frac{2}{3}$ %
(b)	60	2.5 or $\frac{5}{2}$	22	55	33	150
(c)	20	1.25 or $\frac{5}{4}$	72	90	18	25
(d)	15	1.1765 or $\frac{20}{17}$	102	120	18	17.65
(e)	25	1.25 or $\frac{5}{4}$	24	30	6	20

(a) Spf = $1.66\overline{6}$ or $\frac{5}{3}$

$$C + M = S$$
$$\$15 + M = \$25$$
$$M = \$10$$

$$\underline{\quad}\% \text{ of } C = M$$
$$\underline{\quad}\%(\$15) = \$10$$
$$15x = 10$$
$$x = 66\frac{2}{3}\%$$

Spf × C = S
$$\frac{5}{3}(\$15) =$$
$$\$25 = S$$

(b) Spf = 2.5 or $\frac{5}{2}$

$$C + M = S$$
$$\$22 + M = \$55$$
$$M = \$33$$

$$\underline{\quad}\% \text{ of } C = M$$
$$\underline{\quad}\%(\$22) = \$33$$
$$22x = 33$$
$$x = 150\%$$

Spf × C = S
2.5($22) =
$55 = S

(c) Spf = 1.25 or $\frac{5}{4}$

M = S − C
= $90 − $72
M = $18

$$\underline{\quad}\% \text{ of } C = M$$
$$\underline{\quad}\%(\$72) = \$18$$
$$72x = 18$$
$$x = 25\%$$

Spf × C = S
1.25(C) = $90
C = $72

(d) Spf = 1.1765 or

$\frac{20}{17}$

M = S − C
= $120 − $102
M = $18

$$\underline{\quad}\% \text{ of } C = M$$
$$\underline{\quad}\%(\$102) = \$18$$
$$102x = 18$$
$$x = 17.65\%$$

2. (d) (Continued)

$$\text{Spf} \times C = S$$

$$\frac{20}{17}C = \$120$$

$$C = \$102$$

(e)

	C + M = S	___% of C = M	___% of S = M
	\$24 + \$6 =	___%(\$24) = \$6	___%(\$30) = \$6
	\$30 = S	24x = 6	30x = 6
		x = 25%	x = 20%

$$\text{Spf} = \frac{5}{4} \text{ or } 1.25$$

3. (a) Spf = 1.42857 or $\frac{10}{7}$

(b) $\text{Spf} \times C = S$

$$\frac{10}{7}(\$14) =$$

$$\$20 = S$$

(c) M = S − C
   = \$20 − \$14
   M = \$6

4. (a) Spf = 1.538 or $\frac{20}{13}$

(b) $\text{Spf} \times C = S$

$$\frac{20}{13}(\$5.20) =$$

$$\$8.00 = S$$

(c) M = S − C
   = \$8.00 − \$5.20
   M = \$2.80

5. (a) ___% of S = M

$$37\frac{1}{2}\%S = \$15$$

$$0.375S = 15$$

$$S = \$40$$

(b) C + M = S
   C + \$15 = \$40
       C = \$25

6. (a) ___% of S = M
   0.60S = \$5.40
       S = \$9.00

(b)   C + M = S
   C + \$5.40 = \$9.00
        C = \$3.60

7. (a) Spf = 2.5 or $\frac{5}{2}$

(b)

$$Spf \times C = S$$
$$2.5(\$5) = \$12.50$$
$$2.5(\$6.40) = \$16.00$$
$$2.5(\$7.20) = \$18.00$$
$$2.5(\$8.50) = \$21.25$$

(c)

$$M = S - C$$
$$= \$12.50 - \$5.00$$
$$M = \$7.50$$

___% of C = M
$$\_\_\_\%(\$5) = \$7.50$$
$$5x = 7.50$$
$$x = 150\%$$

8. (a) Spf = 1.33$\overline{3}$ or $\frac{4}{3}$

(b)

$$Spf \times C = S$$

$$\frac{4}{3}(\$\ 6) = \$\ 8.00$$

$$\frac{4}{3}(\$\ 9.90) = \$13.20$$

$$\frac{4}{3}(\$18) = \$24.00$$

$$\frac{4}{3}(\$14.40) = \$19.20$$

(c)

$$M = S - C$$
$$= \$8.00 - \$6.00$$
$$M = \$2$$

___% of C = M
$$\_\_\_\%(\$6) = \$2$$
$$6x = 2$$
$$x = 33\frac{1}{3}\%$$

9. (a) Total sales revenue:
$$20\ @\ \$60 = \$1,200$$
$$16\ @\ \$54 = 864$$
$$9\ @\ \$46 = 414$$
$$5\ @\ \$36 = \underline{\ \ \ \ 180}$$
Total $2,658

Total sales $2,658
Total cost   −2,215
Total margin $ 443

(b)

___% of C = M
$$\_\_\_\%(\$2,215) = \$443$$
$$2,215x = 443$$
$$x = 20\%$$

(c)

___% of S = M
$$\_\_\_\%(\$2,658) = \$443$$
$$2,658x = 443$$
$$x = 16\frac{2}{3}\%$$

10. (a) Total sales revenue:
       45 @ $18 = $ 810
       10 @ $15 =   150
       15 @ $12 =   180
       Total $1,140

       Total sales $1,140
       Total cost   - 912
       Total margin $ 228

    (b) ___% of C = M
         ___%($912) = $228
              912x = 228
                 x = 25%

    (c) ___% of S = M
         ___%($1,140) = $228
            1,140x = 228
                 x = 20%

11. (a) 50% on cost:

       Spf = 1 + .50 = 1.50

       50% on selling price:

       Spf = $\dfrac{1}{.5}$ = 2.0

       Larger Spf belongs to 50% on selling price, so it will yield the larger gross profit.

    (b) 20% on cost:

       Spf = 1 + .20 = 1.20

       28% on selling price:

       Spf = $\dfrac{1}{.72}$ = 1.3$\overline{8}$

       28% on selling price yields a larger Spf, thus a larger gross profit.

12. (a) 30% on cost:

       Spf = 1.3

       30% of selling price:

       Spf = 1.42857

       Larger Spf belongs to 30% on selling price, so it will yield the larger gross profit.

    (b) 40% on cost:

       Spf = 1.4

       31% on selling price:

       Spf = 1.449275

       Larger Spf belongs to 31% on selling price, so it will yield the larger gross profit.

13. (a) M = $37\dfrac{1}{2}$%S = $\dfrac{3}{8}$S

       Spf = $\dfrac{8}{5}$ or 1.6

    (b) Spf × C = S
        1.6C = $192
           C = $120

13. (Continued)

(c) $\quad$ C + M = S
$\qquad$ \$120 + M = \$192
$\qquad\qquad$ M = \$72

___% of C = M
___%(\$120) = \$72
$\qquad$ 120x = 72
$\qquad\qquad$ x = 60%

14. (a) $\quad$ M = $33\frac{1}{3}$%S = $\frac{1}{3}$S

$\qquad$ Spf = $\frac{3}{2}$ or 1.5

(b) Spf × C = S

$\qquad$ $\frac{3}{2}$C = \$33

$\qquad\qquad$ C = \$22

(c) $\quad$ C + M = S
$\qquad$ \$22 + M = \$33
$\qquad\qquad$ M = \$11

___% of C = M
___%(\$22) = \$11
$\qquad$ 22x = 11
$\qquad\qquad$ x = 50%

15. (a) $\quad$ C + M = S
$\qquad$ C + 35%S = S
$\qquad\qquad$ C = 0.65(\$340)
$\qquad\qquad$ C = \$221

(b) Spf = $\frac{1}{.65}$ or $\frac{20}{13}$ or 1.538

16. (a) $\quad$ C + M = S
$\qquad$ C + 30%S = S
$\qquad\qquad$ C = 0.70(\$100)
$\qquad\qquad$ C = \$70

(b) Spf = $\frac{1}{.7}$ or $\frac{10}{7}$ or 1.42857

17. % Pd × L = Net cost

$\qquad$ $\frac{5}{6}$(\$42) = N

$\qquad\qquad$ \$35 = N

M = OH + P
M = 25%S + 5%S
M = 30%S

$\quad$ C + $\quad$ M = S
C + 30%S = S
$\qquad\qquad$ C = 70%S
$\qquad\qquad$ \$35 = 0.7S
$\qquad\qquad$ \$50 = S

18. % Pd × L = Net cost
$\quad$ 0.80(\$40) = N
$\qquad\quad$ \$32 = N

M = OH + P
M = 25%S + 50%S
M = 75%S

$\quad$ C + M = S
C + 75%S = S
$\qquad\qquad$ \$32 = 0.25S
$\qquad\qquad$ \$128 = S

Section 3, page 357

1.

	Quantity Bought	Cost per Unit	Total Cost	Markup on Cost	Total Sales	Pct. to Spoil	Amt. to Sell	Selling Price
(a)	70 lbs.	$0.60	$ 42	20 %	$ 50.40	10%	63 lbs.	$0.80 lb.
(b)	20 dz.	1.40	28	25	35.00	5	19 dz.	1.85 dz.
(c)	50	4.00	200	$12\frac{1}{2}$	225.00	4	48	4.69

(a) Total cost = 70 × $0.60 = $42
    Amount to spoil = 10% × 70 lbs. = 7 lbs.
    Amount to sell = 70 lbs. - 7 lbs. = 63 lbs.

$$\begin{array}{ll} C + M = S & \text{No. to sell} \times \text{price} = \text{Total sales} \\ C + 20\%C = & 63p = \$50.40 \\ 1.2(\$42) = & p = \$\ 0.80 \\ \$50.40 = S & \end{array}$$

(b) Total cost = 20 dz. × $1.40 = $28
    Amount to spoil = 5% × 20 dz. = 1 dz.
    Amount to sell = 20 dz. - 1 dz. = 19 dz.

$$\begin{array}{ll} C + M = S & \text{No. to sell} \times \text{price} = \text{Total sales} \\ C + 25\%C = & 19p = \$35 \\ 1.25(\$28) = & p = \$1.85 \\ \$35 = S & \end{array}$$

(c) Total cost = 50 × $4 = $200
    Amount to spoil = 4% × 50 = 2
    Amount to sell = 50 - 2 = 48

$$\begin{array}{ll} C + M = S & \text{No. to sell} \times \text{price} = \text{Total sales} \\ C + \frac{1}{8}C = & 48p = \$225 \\ \frac{9}{8}(\$200) = & p = \$4.69 \\ \$225 = S & \end{array}$$

2.

	Quantity Bought	Cost per Unit	Total Cost	Markup on Cost	Total Sales	Pct. to Spoil	Amt. to Sell	Selling Price
(a)	100 lbs.	$0.36	$ 36	50%	$ 54	7%	93 lbs.	$0.59 lb.
(b)	125 lbs.	6.00	750	40	1,050	4	120 lbs.	8.75 lb.
(c)	100 doz.	1.80	198	30	257.40	10	99 doz.	2.60 doz.

(a) Total cost = 100 × $0.36 = $36
Amount to spoil = 7% × 100 lbs. = 7 lbs.
Amount to sell = 100 lbs. - 7 lbs. = 93 lbs.

$$C + M = S \qquad \text{No. to sell} \times \text{price} = \text{Total sales}$$
$$C + 50\%C = \qquad\qquad 93p = \$54$$
$$1.5(\$0.36) = \qquad\qquad p = \$ 0.59/\text{lb.}$$
$$\$54 = S$$

(b) Total cost = 125 × $6 = $750
Amount to spoil = 4% × 125 lbs. = 5 lbs.
Amount to sell = 125 lbs. - 5 lbs. = 120 lbs.

$$C + M = S \qquad \text{No. to sell} \times \text{price} = \text{Total sales}$$
$$C + 40\%C = \qquad\qquad 120p = \$1,050$$
$$1.4(\$750) = \qquad\qquad p = \$8.75/\text{lb.}$$
$$\$1,050 = S$$

(c) Total cost = 110 × $1.80 = $198
Amount to spoil = 10% × 110 = 11 doz.
Amount to sell = 110 doz. - 11 doz. = 99 doz.

$$C + M = S \qquad \text{No. to sell} \times \text{price} = \text{Total sales}$$
$$C + 30\%C = \qquad\qquad 99p = \$257.40$$
$$1.3(\$198) = \qquad\qquad p = \$2.60/\text{doz.}$$
$$\$257.40 = S$$

3.

	Quantity Bought	Cost per Unit	Total Cost	Markup on Cost	Total Sales	(Cont. below)
(a)	80 lbs.	$0.40	$32	20%	$ 38.40	
(b)	25	3.00	75	40	105.00	

	Amount at Reg. Price	% at Reduced Price	Amount at Reduced Price	Reduced Price	Reg. S.P.
(a)	76 lbs.	5%	4 lbs.	$0.35	$0.49/lb.
(b)	23	8	2	2.50	4.35

3. (Continued)

(a) Total cost = 80 × $0.40 = $32
     5% × 80 lbs. = 4 lbs. sold at reduced price
     80 lbs. - 4 lbs. = 76 lbs. to sell at regular price

         C + M = S   Regular + Reduced = Total sales
     C + 20%C =   76p + 4($0.35) = $38.40
     1.2($32) =   76p + 1.40 = 38.40
         $38.40 = S   76p = 37
                                                 p = $0.49

(b) Total cost = 25 × $3 = $75
     8% × 25 = 2 to sell at reduced price
     25 - 2 = 23 to sell at regular price

         C + M = S   Regular + Reduced = Total sales
     C + 40%C =   23p + 2($2.50) = $105
     1.4($75) =   23p + 5 = 105
         $105 = S   23p = 100
                                              p = $4.35

4.

	Quantity Bought	Cost per Unit	Total Cost	Markup on Cost	Total Sales (Cont. below)
(a)	160 lbs.	$0.90	$ 144	50%	$ 216
(b)	250	4.00	1,000	36	1,360

	Amount at Reg. Price	% at Reduced Price	Amount at Reduced Price	Reduced Price	Reg. S.P.
(a)	144 lbs.	10%	16 lbs.	$1.00	$1.39
(b)	240	4	10	3.00	5.55

(a) Total cost = 160 × $0.90 = $144
     10% × 160 lbs. = 16 lbs. sold at reduced price
     160 lbs. - 16 lbs. = 144 lbs. to sell at regular price

         C + M = S   Regular + Reduced = Total sales
     C + 50%C =   144p + 16($1) = $216
     1.5($144) =   144p + 16 = 216
         $216 = S   144p = 200
                                              p = $1.39/lb.

4. (Continued)

(b) Total cost = 250 × \$4 = \$1,000
4% × 250 lbs. = 10 lbs. sold at reduced price
250 lbs. - 10 lbs. = 240 lbs. to sell at regular price

$$C + M = S \qquad \text{Regular} + \text{Reduced} = \text{Total sales}$$
$$C + 36\%C = \qquad 240p + 10(\$3) = \$1,360$$
$$1.36(\$1,000) = \qquad 240p + 30 = 1,360$$
$$\$1,360 = S \qquad 240p = 1,330$$
$$p = \$5.55/\text{lb.}$$

5. Referring to Problem 1(a):
Total sales = 70 lbs. × \$0.80 = \$56

(a) $\quad C + M = S$
$\quad\quad \$42 + M = \$56$
$\quad\quad\quad\quad M = \$14$

(b) ___% of C = M
$\quad$ ___%(\$42) = \$14
$\quad\quad\quad 42x = 14$
$$x = 33\frac{1}{3}\%$$

(c) ___% of S = M
$\quad$ ___%(\$56) = \$14
$\quad\quad\quad 56x = 14$
$\quad\quad\quad\quad x = 25\%$

6. Referring to Example 2:
Total sales = 30 cakes × \$0.46 + 10 cakes × \$0.30
$\quad\quad\quad\quad S = \$16.80$

(a) $\quad C + M = S$
$\quad\quad \$12 + M = \$16.80$
$\quad\quad\quad\quad M = \$4.80$

(b) ___% of C = M
$\quad$ ___%(\$12) = \$4.80
$\quad\quad\quad 12x = 4.80$
$\quad\quad\quad\quad x = 40\%$

(c) $\quad$ ___% of S = M
$\quad$ ___%(\$16.80) = \$4.80
$\quad\quad 16.80x = 4.80$
$\quad\quad\quad\quad x = 28.57\%$
$$\text{or } 28\frac{4}{7}\%$$

7. Total cost = 200 lbs. × \$0.60 = \$120
Amount expected to spoil = 10% × 200 lbs. = 20 lbs.
Amount expected to sell = 200 lbs. - 20 lbs. = 180 lbs.

7. (Continued)

$$
\begin{array}{rl}
C + M &= S \\
C + 15\%C &= \\
1.15(\$120) &= \\
\$138 &= S
\end{array}
\qquad
\begin{array}{l}
\text{Amount to sell} \times \text{price} = \text{Total sales} \\
\qquad\qquad 180p = \$138 \\
\qquad\qquad\quad p = \$0.77/\text{lb.}
\end{array}
$$

8. Total cost = 500 × $2 = $1,000
   Amount expected to spoil = 10% × 500 = 50
   Amount expected to sell = 500 - 50 = 450

$$
\begin{array}{rl}
C + M &= S \\
C + 55\%C &= \\
1.55(\$1,000) &= \\
\$1,550 &= S
\end{array}
\qquad
\begin{array}{l}
\text{Amount to sell} \times \text{price} = \text{Total sales} \\
\qquad\qquad 450p = \$1,550 \\
\qquad\qquad\quad p = \$3.45/\text{ea.}
\end{array}
$$

9. Total cost = 300 lbs. × $0.72 = $216
   Amount expected to spoil = 7% × 300 lbs. = 21 lbs.
   Amount expected to sell = 300 lbs. - 21 lbs. = 279 lbs.

$$
\begin{array}{rl}
C + M &= S \\
C + 25\%C &= \\
1.25(\$216) &= \\
\$270 &= S
\end{array}
\qquad
\begin{array}{l}
\text{Amount to sell} \times \text{price} = \text{Total sales} \\
\qquad\qquad 279p = \$270 \\
\qquad\qquad\quad p = \$0.97/\text{lb.}
\end{array}
$$

10. Total cost = 40 × $2.50 = $100
    Amount expected to spoil = 15% × 40 = 6
    Amount expected to sell = 34

$$
\begin{array}{rl}
C + M &= S \\
C + 80\%C &= \\
1.8(\$100) &= \\
\$180 &= S
\end{array}
\qquad
\begin{array}{l}
\text{Amount to sell} \times \text{price} = \text{Total sales} \\
\qquad\qquad 34p = \$180 \\
\qquad\qquad\; p = \$5.30/\text{ea.}
\end{array}
$$

11. Total cost = 20 doz. × $6 = $120
    Amount expected to spoil = 5% × 20 dz. = 1 doz.
    Amount expected to sell = 20 doz. - 1 doz. = 19 doz.

$$
\begin{array}{rl}
C + M &= S \\
C + 45\%C &= \\
1.45(\$120) &= \\
\$174 &= S
\end{array}
\qquad
\begin{array}{l}
\text{No. to sell} \times \text{price} = \text{Total sales} \\
\qquad\qquad 19p = \$174 \\
\qquad\qquad\; p = \$9.16/\text{doz.}
\end{array}
$$

12. Total cost = 400 doz. × $0.60 = $240
    Amount expected to spoil = 20% × 400 doz. = 80 doz.
    Amount expected to sell = 400 doz. - 80 doz. = 320 doz.

           C + M = S   No. to sell × price = Total sales
         C + 40%C =   320p = $336
        1.4($240) =   p = $1.05/doz.
            $336 = S

13. Total cost = 50 loaves × $0.55 = $27.50
    10% × 50 loaves = 5 loaves will be sold at $0.40/ea.
    50 - 5 = 45 loaves to sell at regular price

            C + M = S   Regular + Reduced = Total sales
          C + 60%C =   45p + 5($0.40) = $44
        1.6($27.50) =   45p + 2 =   44
              $44 = S   45p =   42
                                              p = $0.94/ea.

14. Total cost = 120 lbs. × $0.46 = $55.20
    20% × 120 cupcakes = 24 cupcakes will be sold at
                         reduced price
    100 - 24 = 96 cupcakes to sell at regular price

            C + M = S   Regular + Reduced = Total sales
          C + 50%C =   96p + 24($0.48) = $82.80
        1.5($55.20) =   96p + 11.52 =   82.80
            $82.80 = S   96p =   71.28
                                              p = $0.75/ea.

15. Total cost = 75 × $120 = $9,000
    12% × 75 = 9 jackets will be sold at $118 each
    75 - 9 = 66 jackets left to sell at regular price

            C + M = S   Regular + Reduced = Total sales
          C + 35%C =   66p + 9($118) = $12,150
        1.35($9,000) =   66p + 1,062 = 12,150
            $12,150 = S   66p =   11,088
                                              p = $168

16. Total cost = 20 × $150 = $3,000
    25% × 20 bags = 5 bags will be sold at reduced price
    20 - 5 = 15 bags to sell at regular price

16. (Continued)

$$
\begin{aligned}
C + M &= S \\
C + 40\%C &= \\
1.4(\$3,000) &= \\
\$4,200 &= S
\end{aligned}
$$

$$
\begin{aligned}
\text{Regular} + \text{Reduced} &= \text{Total sales} \\
15p + 5(\$180) &= \$4,200 \\
15p + 900 &= 4,200 \\
15p &= 3,300 \\
p &= \$220/ea.
\end{aligned}
$$

CHAPTER XIV

MARKDOWN

This chapter is a continuation of retailing problems. For basic courses, the instructor may wish to omit some of the examples.

1.   Actual Selling Price:

Markup based on selling price can seldom be mastered in one assignment. This topic attempts to solidify what has been taught previously, as well as to introduce markup as related to sale or discount prices. Again, emphasize the diagrams to help solidify the concepts being presented.

Students get confused using $C + M = S$ to find both the regular list and the actual selling price. For that reason, the authors have used subscripts in the formulas to differentiate between markup at the regular selling price and markup at the actual selling price. Emphasize the difference between S_1 and S_2 and M_1 and M_2. Ask students to identify the information given in each problem. Have them label all information before attempting to solve the problem.

Since these problems require several steps, the instructor may wish to omit one or more (example 3 is the most difficult). Example 4 re-emphasizes the trade discounts studied earlier.

The students' success with these problems depends on their abilities to read, and the instructor can help them learn what to look for. Emphasize the following strongly: (a) If a problem gives "x% markup," that information is to be used in the fundamental selling price formula, $C + M = S$. (b) When the problem gives "y% discount," that information is applied to the discount formula, % Pd × L = N. ("Net price" can represent either net cost or net selling price, depending on whether a company is buying at a trade discount or is offering to sell its own merchandise at a trade discount.)

Example 2 gives the percent markup at the regular selling price and asks the student to find the percent markup at the sales price. Example 3 gives the percent markup at the sales price and asks for the percent markup at the regular selling price. In both cases, however, the general plan of attack is almost identical and traces the merchandise chronologically from the time it enters the store: (a) determine the cost; (b) determine the regular selling (list) price; (c) use this information to compute the margin (either at the regular price or at the sale price); and (d) then find the percent

markup requested, using _?%_ S = M.   (The questions in the problems
will help the students perform the steps in correct order.)

Example 4 involves trade discounts but is also worked in a
similar order: (a) compute the cost; (b) determine what the actual
selling price will be; and (c) determine what list price, less the
given discounts, will leave the desired net (selling) price obtained
in (b). When the same problem contains both markup percents and
discount percents, students often do "the right thing at the wrong
time." Remind them to subtract only _discount_ percents from 100% to
obtain % paid; _markup_ percents are converted to their equivalent
fraction for substitution in the selling price formula, C + M = S.

Unlike most problems, problems like example 4 are more
difficult for the instructor to make out than for the student to
work -- at least if they are to contain only whole amounts. In
order to ensure a round number at the final solution, it is
generally necessary to start near the end and work backwards. When
making up problems of this type, the authors follow the following
procedure: (1) Experiment with a round-number marked price and
various combinations of chain discounts until you obtain a selling
price that is divisible by several different numbers. (Or, choose
a selling price that is divisible by several different numbers and
experiment with various discounts off the marked price until you
find a combination which will produce a round-number marked price.)
(2) Select a markup percent and determine the corresponding cost.
(3) Experiment with various combinations of list price discounts
until you find a combination that will divide into your cost and
produce a whole list price.

For your convenience, several additional combinations
applicable to example 4 are given here. L = wholesale list price
and MP = retailer's marked price. As before, C = cost, S = selling
price, and M = margin.

L = $425 less 20/10
C = $306
M = 25% S
S = $408
MP = $600 less 20/15

L = $600 less 20/20
C = $384
M = 20% S
S = $480
MP = $800 less 25/20

L = $500 less 25/30
C = $300
M = 25% S
S = $375
MP = $600 less 25/16 $\frac{2}{3}$

L = $320 less 25/20
C = $192
M = 33 1/3% S
S = $288
MP = $450 less 20/20

```
L  = $500 less 25/30          L  = $400 less 25/20
C  = $300                     C  = $240
M  = 37 1/2% S                M  = 25% S
S  = $480                     S  = $320
MP = $750 less 20/20          MP = $500 less 20/20

L  = $400 less 30/10 or
     $350 less 20/10
C  = $252
M  = 33 1/3% S
S  = $378
MP = $600 less 30/10 or
     $630 less 25/20 or
     $525 less 20/10
```

This section is probably the only instance where the tabular problems at the beginning of the assignment are harder than the written problems. The reason is that the written problems guide the students' work by asking questions in the same order as their work should proceed. Thus, the instructor may wish to either omit the tabular problems in this instance or tell the students to work them by fitting the percents into the appropriate places of the written problems. [(a) and (b) correspond to 3 and 4; (c) and (d) correspond to 5 and 6; (e) and (f) correspond to 7 and 8; and (g) and (h) correspond to 9 and 10.]

2. Markdown vs. Loss:

The point to emphasize is that wholesale cost does not represent the entire amount which a company has invested in merchandise. Be sure the students understand the difference between operating loss and absolute loss. The diagrams will help clarify this. Example 2 computes operating loss, and example 3 includes absolute loss. The percent of absolute loss is also computed, based on wholesale cost, and diagrammed in detail. The major objective of example 4 is to find the largest percent reduction that can be offered without suffering an operating loss. Example 5 determines the overall profit or loss on multiple items sold at different prices.

CHAPTER 14 - MARKDOWNS
PROBLEM SOLUTIONS

Section 1, page 368

1.

	Cost	% Regular Markup (M_1)	Reg. Price (S_1)	% Discount	Sale Price (S_2)	% Sale Markup (M_2)
(a)	$ 50	40%C	$ 70	x	$ 62.50	20%S
(b)	48	$33\frac{1}{3}$%C	64	x	57.60	$16\frac{2}{3}$S%
(c)	28	30%S	40	20 %	32.00	$12\frac{1}{2}$%S
(d)	30	25%S	40	10	36.00	$16\frac{2}{3}$%S
(e)	27	46%S	50	10	45.00	40%S
(f)	148.75	40.5%S	250	30	175.00	15%S
(g)	240	60%S	600	$33\frac{1}{3}$/20	320.00	25%S
(h)	128	60%S	320	$37\frac{1}{2}$/20	160.00	20%S

(a) $C + M_1 = S_1$ $C + M_2 = S_2$
    $C + 40\%C = S_1$ $C + 20\%S_2 = S_2$
          $1.4C = \$70$ $C = 80\%S_2$
             $C = \$50$ $\$50 = 0.80S_2$
                                    $\$62.50 = S_2$

(b) $C + M_1 = S_1$ $C + M_2 = S_2$

    $C + \frac{1}{3}C = S_1$ $C + \frac{1}{6}S_2 = S_2$

       $\frac{4}{3}C = \$64$ $C = \frac{5}{6}S_2$

          $C = \$48$ $\$48 = \frac{5}{6}S_2$

                                  $\frac{6}{5}(48) = S_2$

                                  $\$57.60 = S_2$

1. (Continued)

(c)

$$C + M_1 = S_1$$
$$C + 30\%S_1 = S_1$$
$$C = 70\%S_1$$
$$\frac{1}{.7}(\$28) = S_1$$
$$\$40 = S_1$$

$$\% \text{ Pd} \times L = N$$
$$80\%(\$40) = S_2$$
$$\$32 = S_2$$

$$C + M_2 = S_2$$
$$\$28 + M_2 = \$32$$
$$M_2 = \$4$$

$$\underline{\quad}\% \text{ of } S_2 = M_2$$
$$\underline{\quad}\%(\$32) = \$4$$
$$32x = 4$$
$$x = 12\frac{1}{2}\%$$

(d)

$$C + M_1 = S_1$$
$$C + 25\%S_1 = S_1$$
$$C = 75\%S_1$$
$$\$30 = 0.75S_1$$
$$\$40 = S_1$$

$$\% \text{ Pd} \times L = N$$
$$90\%(\$40) = S_2$$
$$\$36 = S_2$$

$$C + M_2 = S_2$$
$$\$30 + M_2 = \$36$$
$$M_2 = \$6$$

$$\underline{\quad}\% \text{ of } S_2 = M_2$$
$$\underline{\quad}\%(\$36) = \$6$$
$$36x = 6$$
$$x = 16\frac{2}{3}\%$$

(e)

$$C + M_2 = S_2$$
$$C + 40\%S_2 = S_2$$
$$C = 60\%(\$45)$$
$$C = \$27$$

$$\% \text{ Pd} \times L = N$$
$$90\%S_1 = S_2$$
$$90\%S_1 = \$45$$
$$S_1 = \$50$$

$$C + M_1 = S_1$$
$$\$27 + M_1 = \$50$$
$$M_1 = \$23$$

$$\underline{\quad}\% \text{ of } S_1 = M_1$$
$$\underline{\quad}\%(\$50) = \$23$$
$$50x = 23$$
$$x = 46\%$$

1. (Continued)

(f) $C + M_2 = S_2$ $\% \text{ Pd} \times L = N$

$C + 15\%S_2 = S_2$ $70\%S_1 = S_2$

$C = 85\%(\$175)$ $70\%S_1 = \$175$

$C = \$148.75$ $S_1 = \$250$

$C + M_1 = S_1$ $\underline{\quad}\% \text{ of } S_1 = M_1$

$\$148.75 + M_1 = \$250.00$ $\underline{\quad}\%(\$250) = \$101.25$

$M_1 = \$101.25$ $250x = 101.25$

$x = 40.5\%$

(g) $\% \text{ Pd} \times L = \text{Net Cost}$ $C + M_2 = S_2$

$60\%(\$400) = C$ $C + 25\%S_2 = S_2$

$\$240 = C$ $C = 75\%S_2$

$\dfrac{1}{.75}(\$240) = S_2$

$\$320 = S_2$

$\% \text{ Pd} \times L = N$ $C + M_1 = S_1$

$\left(\dfrac{2}{3}\right)\left(\dfrac{4}{5}\right)S_1 = S_2$ $\$240 + M_1 = \$600$

$M_1 = \$360$

$\dfrac{8}{15}S_1 = \$320$

$S_1 = \$600$

$\underline{\quad}\% \text{ of } S_1 = M_1$

$\underline{\quad}\%(\$600) = \$360$

$600x = 360$

$x = 60\%$

(h) $\% \text{ Pd} \times L = \text{Net Cost}$ $C + M_2 = S_2$

$(80\%)(80\%)\$200 = C$ $C + 20\%S_2 = S_2$

$0.64(200) = C$ $C = 80\%S_2$

$\$128 = C$ $\dfrac{1}{.8}(\$128) = S_2$

$\$160 = S_2$

1. (h) (Continued)

$$\% \ Pd \ \times \ L \ = \ N$$

$$\left(\frac{5}{8}\right)\left(\frac{4}{5}\right)S_1 \ = \ S_2$$

$$\frac{1}{2}S_1 \ = \ \$160$$

$$S_1 \ = \ \$320$$

$$\underline{\hspace{1cm}}\% \ of \ S_1 \ = \ M_1$$

$$\underline{\hspace{1cm}}\%(\$320) \ = \ \$192$$

$$320x \ = \ 192$$

$$x \ = \ 60\%$$

$$C \ + \ M_1 \ = \ S_1$$

$$\$128 \ + \ M_1 \ = \ \$320$$

$$M_1 \ = \ \$192$$

2.

	Cost	% Regular Markup(M_1)	Reg. Price(S_1)	% Discount	Sale Price(S_2)	% Sale Markup(M_2)
(a)	$ 40	30%C	$ 52	x	$ 50	20%S
(b)	600	50%C	900	x	800	25%S
(c)	36	40%S	60	25 %	45	20%S
(d)	52	35%S	80	20	64	18.75%S
(e)	27	43.75%S	48	37.5	30	10%S
(f)	105	58%S	250	40	150	30%S
(g)	28	72%S	100	30/10	56	50%S
(h)	360	42.4%S	625	20/20	400	10%S

(a)
$$C \ + \ M_1 \ = \ S_1$$
$$C \ + \ 30\%C \ = \ S_1$$
$$130\%C \ = \ \$52$$
$$C \ = \ \$40$$

$$C \ + \ M_2 \ = \ S_2$$
$$C \ + \ 20\%S_2 \ = \ S_2$$
$$C \ = \ 80\%S_2$$
$$\$40 \ = \ 0.80S_2$$
$$\$50 \ = \ S_2$$

(b)
$$C \ + \ M_1 \ = \ S_1$$
$$C \ + \ 50\%C \ = \ S_1$$
$$150\%C \ = \ \$900$$
$$C \ = \ \$600$$

$$C \ + \ M_2 \ = \ S_2$$
$$C \ + \ 25\%S_2 \ = \ S_2$$
$$C \ = \ 75\%S_2$$
$$\$600 \ = \ 0.75S_2$$
$$\$800 \ = \ S_2$$

2. (Continued)

(c) $C + M_1 = S_1$ % Pd × L = N

    $C + 40\%S_1 = S_1$ $75\%(\$60) = S_2$

          $C = 60\%S_1$ $\$45 = S_2$

       $\$36 = 0.60S_1$

       $\$60 = S_1$

     $C + M_2 = S_2$ ___% of $S_2 = M_2$

  $\$36 + M_2 = \$45$ ___%$(\$45) = \$9$

       $M_2 = \$9$ $45x = 9$

                           $x = 20\%$

(d) $C + M_1 = S_1$ % Pd × L = N

    $C + 35\%S_1 = S_1$ $80\%(\$80) = S_2$

          $C = 65\%S_1$ $\$64 = S_2$

       $\$52 = 0.65S_1$

       $\$80 = S_1$

     $C + M_2 = S_2$ ___% of $S_2 = M_2$

  $\$52 + M_2 = \$64$ ___%$(\$64) = \$12$

       $M_2 = \$12$ $64x = 12$

                         $x = 18.75\%$

(e) $C + M_2 = S_2$ % Pd × L = N

    $C + 10\%S_2 = S_2$ $62.5\%S_1 = S_2$

          $C = 90\%S_2$ $0.625S_1 = \$30$

          $C = 0.90(\$30)$ $S_1 = \$48$

          $C = \$27$

     $C + M_1 = S_1$ ___% of $S_1 = M_1$

  $\$27 + M_1 = \$48$ ___%$(\$48) = \$21$

       $M_1 = \$21$ $48x = 21$

                         $x = 43.75\%$

2. (Continued)

(f) $C + M_2 = S_2$ % Pd × L = N

$C + 30\%S_2 = S_2$ $60\%S_1 = S_2$

$C = 70\%S_2$ $0.60S_1 = \$150$

$C = 0.70(\$150)$ $S_1 = \$250$

$C = \$105$

$C + M_1 = S_1$ ___% of $S_1 = M_1$

$\$105 + M_1 = \$250$ ___%$(\$250) = \$145$

$M_1 = \$145$ $250x = 145$

$x = 58\%$

(g) % Pd × L = Net Cost $C + M_2 = S_2$

$70\%(\$40) = C$ $C + 50\%S_2 = S_2$

$\$28 = C$ $C = 50\%S_2$

$\$28 = 0.50S_2$

$\$56 = S_2$

% Pd × L = N $C + M_1 = S_1$

$(70\%)(80\%)S_1 = S_2$ $\$28 + M_1 = \$100$

$0.56S_1 = \$56$ $M_1 = \$72$

$S_1 = \$100$

___% of $S_1 = M_1$

___%$(\$100) = \$72$

$100x = 72$

$x = 72\%$

(h)   % Pd × L = Net Cost $C + M_2 = S_2$

$(75\%)(80\%)\$600 = C$ $C + 10\%S_2 = S_2$

$0.60(600) = C$ $C = 90\%S_2$

$\$360 = C$ $\$360 = 0.90S_2$

$\$400 = S_2$

2. (h) (Continued)

$$\% \text{ Pd} \times \text{L} = \text{Net Cost}$$
$$(80\%)(80\%)S_1 = S_2$$
$$0.64S_1 = \$400$$
$$S_1 = \$625$$

$$C + M_1 = S_1$$
$$\$360 + M_1 = \$625$$
$$M_1 = \$265$$

$$\underline{\quad}\% \text{ of } S_1 = M_1$$
$$\underline{\quad}\%(\$625) = \$265$$
$$625x = 265$$
$$x = 42.4\%$$

3. (a)
$$C + M_1 = S_1$$
$$C + 45\%C = \$87$$
$$1.45C = 87$$
$$C = \$60$$

(b)
$$C + M_2 = S_2$$
$$C + 25\%S_2 = S_2$$
$$C = 75\%S_2$$
$$\frac{1}{.75}(\$60) = S_2$$
$$\$80 = S_2$$

4. (a)
$$C + M_1 = S_1$$
$$C + 25\%C = S_1$$
$$1.25C = \$90$$
$$C = \$72$$

(b)
$$C + M_2 = S_2$$
$$C + 10\%S_2 = S_2$$
$$C = 90\%S_2$$
$$\$72 = 0.90S_2$$
$$\$80 = S_2$$

5. (a)
$$C + M_1 = S_1$$
$$C + 37.5\%S_1 = S_1$$
$$C = 62.5\%S_1$$
$$\$800 = 0.625S_1$$
$$\$1,280 = S_1$$

(b)
$$\% \text{ Pd} \times \text{L} = \text{N}$$
$$75\%(\$1,280) = S_2$$
$$\$960 = S_2$$

(c)
$$C + M_2 = S_2$$
$$\$800 + M_2 = \$960$$
$$M_2 = \$160$$

$$\underline{\quad}\% \text{ of } S_2 = M_2$$
$$\underline{\quad}\%(\$960) = \$160$$
$$960x = 160$$
$$x = 16\frac{2}{3}\%$$

6. (a)
$$C + M_1 = S_1$$
$$C + \frac{1}{3}\%S_1 = S_1$$
$$C = \frac{2}{3}S_1$$
$$\$424 = \frac{2}{3}S_1$$
$$\frac{3}{2}(424) = S_1$$
$$\$636 = S_1$$

(b)
$$\% \text{ Pd} \times L = N$$
$$80\%(\$636) = S_2$$
$$0.80(636) = S_2$$
$$\$508.80 = S_2$$

(c)
$$C + M_2 = S_2$$
$$\$424 + M_2 = \$508.80$$
$$M_2 = \$84.80$$

$$\underline{}\% \text{ of } S_2 = M_2$$
$$\underline{}\%(\$508.80) = \$84.80$$
$$508.80x = 84.80$$
$$x = 16\frac{2}{3}\%$$

7. (a)
$$C + M_1 = S_1$$
$$C + 55\%S_1 = S_1$$
$$C = 45\%S_1$$
$$\$18 = 0.45S_1$$
$$\$40 = S_1$$

(b)
$$\% \text{ Pd} \times L = N$$
$$75\%S_1 = S_2$$
$$0.75(\$40) = S_2$$
$$\$30 = S_2$$

(c)
$$C + M_2 = S_2$$
$$\$18 + M_2 = \$30$$
$$M_2 = \$12$$

$$\underline{}\% \text{ of } S_2 = M_2$$
$$\underline{}\%(\$30) = \$12$$
$$30x = 12$$
$$x = 40\%$$

8. (a)
$$C + M_1 = S_1$$
$$C + 30\%S_1 = S_1$$
$$C = 70\%S_1$$
$$\$126 = 0.70S_1$$
$$\$180 = S_1$$

(b)
$$\% \text{ Pd} \times L = N$$
$$90\%S_1 = S_2$$
$$0.90(\$180) = S_2$$
$$\$162 = S_2$$

(c)
$$C + M_2 = S_2$$
$$\$126 + M_2 = \$162$$
$$M_2 = \$36$$

$$\underline{}\% \text{ of } S_2 = M_2$$
$$\underline{}\%(\$162) = \$36$$
$$162x = 36$$
$$x = 22.2\overline{2}\%$$

9. (a) % Pd × L = N
$$75\%S_1 = S_2$$
$$0.75S_1 = \$90$$
$$S_1 = \$120$$

(b)
$$C + M_2 = S_2$$
$$C + 40\%S_2 = S_2$$
$$C = 60\%S_2$$
$$C = 0.60(\$90)$$
$$C = \$54$$

(c)
$$C + M_1 = S_1$$
$$\$54 + M_1 = \$120$$
$$M_1 = \$66$$

___% of $S_1 = M_1$
___%($120) = $66
$$120x = 66$$
$$x = 55\%$$

10. (a) % Pd × L = N
$$85\%S_1 = S_2$$
$$0.85S_1 = \$51$$
$$S_1 = \$60$$

(b)
$$C + M_2 = S_2$$
$$C + 20\%S_2 = S_2$$
$$C = 80\%S_2$$
$$C = 0.80(\$51)$$
$$C = \$40.80$$

(c)
$$C + M_1 = S_1$$
$$\$40.80 + M_1 = \$60$$
$$M_1 = \$19.20$$

___% of $S_1 = M_1$
___%($60) = $19.20
$$60x = 19.20$$
$$x = 32\%$$

11. (a) % Pd × L = N
$$87.5\%S_1 = S_2$$
$$0.875S_1 = \$63$$
$$S_1 = \$72$$

(b)
$$C + M_2 = S_2$$
$$C + 20\%S_2 = S_2$$
$$C = 80\%S_2$$
$$C = 0.80(\$63)$$
$$C = \$50.40$$

(c)
$$C + M_1 = S_1$$
$$\$50.40 + M_1 = \$72$$
$$M_1 = \$21.60$$

___% of $S_1 = M_1$
___%($72) = $21.60
$$72x = 21.60$$
$$x = 30\%$$

12. (a) % Pd × L = N
$$60\%S_1 = S_2$$
$$0.60S_1 = \$45$$
$$S_1 = \$75$$

(b)
$$C + M_2 = S_2$$
$$C + 30\%S_2 = S_2$$
$$C = 70\%S_2$$
$$C = 0.70(\$45)$$
$$C = \$31.50$$

12. (Continued)

(c)
$$C + M_1 = S_1$$
$$\$31.50 + M_1 = \$75$$
$$M_1 = \$43.50$$

$$\underline{}\% \text{ of } S_1 = M_1$$
$$\underline{}\%(\$75) = \$43.50$$
$$75x = 43.50$$
$$x = 58\%$$

13. (a)
$$\% \text{ Pd} \times L = \text{Net Cost}$$
$$(70\%)(75\%)\$140 = C$$
$$0.525(140) = C$$
$$\$73.50 = C$$

(b)
$$C + M_2 = S_2$$
$$C + \frac{1}{3}S_2 = S_2$$
$$C = \frac{2}{3}S_2$$
$$\frac{3}{2}(\$73.50) = S_2$$
$$\$110.25 = S_2$$

(c)
$$\% \text{ Pd} \times L = N$$
$$60\% S_1 = S_2$$
$$0.60 S_1 = \$110.25$$
$$S_1 = \$183.75$$

14. (a)
$$\% \text{ Pd} \times L = \text{Net Cost}$$
$$(60\%)(90\%)\$200 = C$$
$$(0.54)\$200 = C$$
$$\$108 = C$$

(b)
$$C + M_2 = S_2$$
$$C + 25\% S_2 = S_2$$
$$C = 75\% S_2$$
$$\$108 = 0.75 S_2$$
$$\$144 = S_2$$

(c)
$$\% \text{ Pd} \times L = N$$
$$80\% S_1 = S_2$$
$$0.80 S_1 = \$144$$
$$S_1 = \$180$$

15. (a)
$$\% \text{ Pd} \times L = N$$
$$70\%(\$50) = N$$
$$\$35 = N$$

(b)
$$C + M_2 = S_2$$
$$C + 60\% S_2 = S_2$$
$$C = 40\% S_2$$
$$\$35 = 0.40 S_2$$
$$\$87.50 = S_2$$

15. (Continued)

   (c) % Pd × L = N

   $87.5\%S_1 = S_2$

   $0.875S_1 = \$87.50$

   $S_1 = \$100$

16. (a) % Pd × L = N

   $50\%(\$15) = N$

   $\$7.50 = N$

   (b) $C + M_2 = S_2$

   $C + 40\%S_2 = S_2$

   $C = 60\%S_2$

   $\$7.50 = 0.60S_2$

   $\$12.50 = S_2$

   (c) % Pd × L = N

   $\dfrac{2}{3}S_1 = S_2$

   $\dfrac{2}{3}S_1 = \$12.50$

   $S_1 = \$18.75$

Section 2, page 376

1.

	Regular Selling Price(S_1)	Markdown %	Markdown Amt.	Sale Price(S_2)	Whole-sale cost	Over-head	Total Handling Cost	Operating Profit or (Loss)
(a)	$50	40 %	$20	$30	$22	$4	$26	$ 4
(b)	30	30	9	21	19	3	22	(1)
(c)	45	$22\frac{2}{9}$	10	35	23	8	31	4
(d)	18	$11\frac{1}{9}$	2	16	12	7	19	(3)
(e)	60	10	6	54	50	9	59	(5)
(f)	40	20	8	32	18	8	26	6

(a) Markdown amount = $50 × 40% = $20
   Sale price = $50 - $20 = $30
   THC = $22 + $4 = $26
   Profit = $30 - $26 = $4

1. (Continued)

(b) Markdown percent = (on right)
    Sale price = $30 - $9 = $21
    THC = $19 + $3 = $22
    Loss = $22 - $21 = -$1

  ___% of original = change
   ___%($30) = $9
    30x = 9
     x = 30%

(c) Markdown amt. = $45 - $35 = $10
    Markdown percent = (on right)
    THC = $35 - $4 = $31
    Wholesale cost = $31 - $8 = $23

  ___% of original = change
   ___%($45) = $10
    45x = 10
     $x = 22\frac{2}{9}\%$

(d) Wholesale cost = $19 - $7 = $12
    Sale price = $19 - $3 = $16
    Markdown amount = $18 - $16 = $2
    Markdown percent = (on right)

  ___% of original = change
   ___%($18) = $2
    18x = 2
     $x = 11\frac{1}{9}\%$

(e) Overhead = $59 - $50 = $9
    Sale price = $59 - $5 = $54
    Regular price = $54 + $6 = $60
    Markdown percent = (on right)

  ___% of original = change
   ___%($60) = $6
    60x = 6
     x = 10%

(f) Regular price = (on right)
    Markdown amt. = $40 - $32 = $8
    THC = $32 - $6 = $26
    Wholesale cost = $26 - $8 = $18

  % Pd × L = N
   $80\%S_1$ = $32
    S_1 = $40

2.

	Regular Selling Price(S_1)	Markdown %	Markdown Amt.	Sale Price(S_2)	Whole-sale cost	Over-head	Total Handling Cost	Operating Profit or (Loss)
(a)	$20	10 %	$ 2	$18	$14	$ 3	$17	$ 1
(b)	15	20	3	12	9	5	14	(2)
(c)	60	40	24	36	24	7	31	5
(d)	80	12.5	10	70	66	10	76	(6)
(e)	48	31.25	15	33	28	14	42	(9)
(f)	24	50	12	12	6	4	10	2

2. (Continued)

(a) Markdown amount = $20 × 10% = $2
    Sale price = $20 - $2 = $18
    THC = $14 + $3 = $17
    Profit = $18 - $17 = $1

(b) Markdown percent = (on right)   ___% of original = change
    Sale price = $15 - $3 = $12   ___%($15) = $3
    THC = $9 + $5 = $14   15x = 3
    Loss = $12 - $14 = -$2   x = 20%

(c) Markdown amt. = $60 - $36 = $24   ___% of original = change
    Markdown percent = (on right)   ___%($60) = $24
    THC = $36 - $5 = $31   60x = 24
    Wholesale cost = $31 - $7 = $24   = 40%

(d) Wholesale cost = $76 - $10 = $66   ___% of original = change
    Sale price = $76 - $6 = $70   ___%($80) = $10
    Markdown amount = $80 - $70 = $10   80x = 10
    Markdown percent = (on right)   x = 12.5%

(e) Overhead = $42 - $28 = $14   ___% of original = change
    Sale price = $42 - $9 = $33   ___%($48) = $15
    Regular price = $33 + $15 = $48   48x = 15
    Markdown percent = (on right)   x = 31.25%

(f) Regular price = (on right)   ___% Pd × L = N
    Markdown amt. = $24 - $12 = $12   50%$S_1$ = $12
    THC = $12 - $2 = $10 S_1 = $24
    Wholesale cost = $10 - $4 = $6

3.

	Regular Selling Price(S_1)	Markdown %	Markdown Amt.	Sale Price(S_2)	Whole-sale Cost	Over-head	Total Handling Cost	Operating Loss	Gross Loss	Loss %
(a)	$36	$16\frac{2}{3}$%	$ 6	$30	$32	$3	$35	$ 5	$2	6.25%
(b)	60	40	24	36	40	6	46	10	4	10
(c)	40	25	8	32	35	8	43	11	3	8.57
(d)	90	30	27	63	70	4	74	11	7	10

3. (Continued)

(a) $S_1 - MD = S_2$

$\$36 - \$6 = S_2$

$\$30 = S_2$

___% of original = change

___%($\$36$) = $\$6$

$36x = 6$

$x = 16\frac{2}{3}\%$

THC = C + OH

THC = $\$32 + \$3$

THC = $\$35$

$THC - S_2 = OL$

$\$35 - \$30 = OL$

$\$5 = OL$

GL = C − OH

GL = $\$32 - \$30$

GL = $\$2$

___% of C = GL

___%($\$32$) = $\$2$

$32x = 2$

$x = 6.25\%$

(b) ___% of original = change

40%($\$60$) = MD

$\$24 = MD$

$S_1 - MD = S_2$

$\$60 - \$24 = S_2$

$\$36 = S_2$

OL = $THC - S_2$

$\$10 = THC - \$36$

$\$46 = THC$

THC = C + OH

$\$46 = \$40 + OH$

$\$6 = OH$

GL = $C - S_2$

GL = $\$40 - \$36$

GL = $\$4$

___% of C = GL

___%($\$40$) = $\$4$

$40x = 4$

$x = 10\%$

(c) % Pd × L = N

$80\%S_1 = \$32$

$S_1 = \$40$

$S_1 - MD = S_2$

$\$40 - MD = \$32$

MD = $\$8$

THC = C + OH

$\$43 = C + \$8$

$\$35 = C$

OL = $THC - S_2$

OL = $\$43 - \$32$

OL = $\$11$

3. (c) (Continued)

$$GL = C - S_2 \qquad \underline{\quad}\% \text{ of } C = GL$$
$$GL = \$35 - \$32 \qquad \underline{\quad}\%(\$35) = \$3$$
$$GL = \$3 \qquad\qquad 35x = 3$$
$$\qquad\qquad\qquad\qquad\qquad x = 8.57\%$$

(d) $\% \text{ Pd} \times L = N \qquad MD = S_1 - S_2$
$\qquad 70\% S_1 = \$63 \qquad MD = \$90 - \$63$
$\qquad\qquad S_1 = \$90 \qquad MD = \$27$

$$GL = C - S_2 \qquad THC = C + OH$$
$$\$7 = C - \$63 \qquad THC = \$70 + \$4$$
$$\$70 = C \qquad\qquad THC = \$74$$

$$\underline{\quad}\% \text{ of } C = GL \qquad OL = THC - S_2$$
$$\underline{\quad}\%(\$70) = \$7 \qquad OL = \$74 - \$63$$
$$70x = 7 \qquad\qquad OL = \$11$$
$$x = 10\%$$

4.

	Regular Selling Price (S_1)	Markdown %	Amt.	Sale Price (S_2)	Whole-sale Cost	Over-head	Total Handling Cost	Operating Loss	Gross Loss	Loss %
(a)	$40	25 %	$10	$30	$35	$2	$37	$ 7	$ 5	$14\frac{2}{7}\%$
(b)	48	$33\frac{1}{3}$	16	32	40	4	44	12	8	20
(c)	56	25	14	42	45	6	51	9	3	$6\frac{2}{3}$
(d)	90	20	18	72	80	8	88	16	8	10

(a) $\quad S_1 - MD = S_2 \qquad \underline{\quad}\% \text{ of original} = \text{change}$
$\qquad \$40 - \$10 = S_2 \qquad\qquad \underline{\quad}\%(\$40) = MD$
$\qquad\qquad \$30 = S_2 \qquad\qquad\qquad 40x = 10$
$\qquad\qquad\qquad\qquad\qquad\qquad\qquad x = 25\%$

$$THC = C + OH \qquad OL = THC - S_1$$
$$THC = \$35 + \$2 \qquad OL = \$37 - \$30$$
$$THC = \$37 \qquad\qquad OL = \$7$$

4. (a) (Continued)

$GL = C - S_2$　　　　　　　　___% of C = GL

$GL = \$35 - \$30$　　　　　___%(35) = 5

$GL = \$5$　　　　　　　　　　$35x = 5$

　　　　　　　　　　　　　　　　$x = 14.29\%$ or $14\frac{2}{7}\%$

(b)　% Pd × L = N　　　　　$MD = S_1 - S_2$

　　$\frac{2}{3}$(48) = S_2　　　　$MD = \$48 - \$32$

　　　　　　　　　　　　　　$MD = \$16$

　　　　$\$32 = S_2$

　　　OL = THC - S_2　　　THC = C + OH

　$\$12 = THC - \$32$　　　$\$44 = \$40 + OH$

　$\$44 = THC$　　　　　　　$\$4 = OH$

　　GL = C - S_2　　　　　　___% of C = GL

　　GL = $\$40 - \$32$　　　___%(40) = 8

　　GL = $\$8$　　　　　　　　$40x = 8$

　　　　　　　　　　　　　　　　$x = 20\%$

(c)　% Pd × L = N　　　　　$MD = S_1 - S_2$

　　　$75\%S_1 = \$42$　　　$MD = \$56 - \$42$

　　　　　$S_1 = \$56$　　　$MD = \$14$

　　THC = C + OH　　　　　OL = THC - S_2

　$\$51 = C + \$6$　　　　　OL = $\$51 - \$42$

　$\$45 = C$　　　　　　　　OL = $\$9$

　　GL = C - S_2　　　　　　___% of C = GL

　　GL = $\$45 - \$42$　　　___%(45) = 3

　　GL = $\$3$　　　　　　　　$45x = 3$

　　　　　　　　　　　　　　　　$x = 6\frac{2}{3}\%$

(d)　% Pd × L = N　　　　　$MD = S_1 - S_2$

　　　$80\%S_1 = \$72$　　　$MD = \$90 - \$72$

　　　　　$S_1 = \$90$　　　$MD = \$18$

4. (d) (Continued)

$$GL = C - S_2$$
$$\$8 = C - \$72$$
$$\$80 = C$$

$$THC = C + OH$$
$$THC = \$80 + \$8$$
$$THC = \$88$$

$$OL = THC - S_2$$
$$OL = \$88 - \$72$$
$$OL = \$16$$

$$\underline{\quad}\% \text{ of } C = GL$$
$$\underline{\quad}\%(\$80) = \$8$$
$$80x = 8$$
$$x = 10\%$$

5. $\% \text{ Pd} \times L = N$
$$70\%S_1 = S_2$$
$$70\%(\$210) = S_2$$
$$\$147 = S_2$$

$$THC = C + 25\%C$$
$$THC = 125\%(\$130)$$
$$THC = \$162.50$$

$$OL = THC - S_2$$
$$OL = \$162.50 - \$147$$
$$OL = \$15.50$$

6. $\% \text{ Pd} \times L = N$
$$70\%S_1 = S_2$$
$$70\%(\$35) = S_2$$
$$\$24.50 = S_2$$

$$THC = C + 15\%C$$
$$THC = 115\%(\$23)$$
$$THC = \$26.45$$

$$OL = THC - S_2$$
$$OL = \$26.45 - \$24.50$$
$$OL = \$1.95$$

7. $\% \text{ Pd} \times L = N$
$$75\%S_1 = S_2$$
$$75\%(\$40) = S_2$$
$$\$30 = S_2$$

$$THC = C + 20\%C$$
$$THC = 120\%(\$26)$$
$$THC = \$31.20$$

$$OL = THC - S_2$$
$$OL = \$31.20 - \$30$$
$$OL = \$1.20$$

8. $\% \text{ Pd} \times L = N$
$$60\%S_1 = S_2$$
$$60\%(\$45) = S_2$$
$$\$27 = S_2$$

$$THC = C + 20\%C$$
$$THC = 120\%(\$25)$$
$$THC = \$30$$

$$OL = THC - S_2$$
$$OL = \$30 - \$27$$
$$OL = \$3$$

9. (a) Markdown amount $= \$54 - \$45 = \$9$

$$\underline{\quad}\% \text{ of original} = \text{change}$$
$$\underline{\quad}\%(\$54) = \$9$$
$$54x = 9$$
$$x = 16\frac{2}{3}\%$$

9. (Continued)

(b)   % Pd × L = Net Cost
     (80%)(85%)$50 = C
             $34 = C

THC = C + OH   OP = S_2 - THC
THC = $34.00 + $5.40   OP = $45.00 - $39.50
THC = $39.40   OP = $5.60

10. (a) Markdown amount = $120 - $84 = $36

____% of original = change
____%($120) = $36
      120x =   36
         x = 30%

(b)   % Pd × L = Net Cost
     (90%)(80%)$80 = C
         $57.60 = C

THC = C + OH   OP = S_2 - THC
THC = $57.60 + $10.40   OP = $84 - $68
THC = $68.00   OP = $16

11. (a)   C + OH + P = S_1
     C + 20%S + 10%S = S_1
                    C = 70%S_1

     $\dfrac{1}{.7}$($140) = S_1

              $200 = S_1

(b) % Pd × L = N   OH = 20%S_1
        50%S_1 = S_2 OH = 0.20($200)
     50%($200) = S_2 OH = $40
        $100 = S_2

11. (b) (Continued)

$$THC = C + OH$$
$$THC = \$140 + \$40$$
$$THC = \$180$$

$$OL = THC - S_2$$
$$OL = \$180 - \$100$$
$$OL = \$80$$

(c)
$$GL = C - S_2$$
$$GL = \$140 - \$100$$
$$GL = \$40$$

$$\underline{\quad}\% \text{ of } C = GL$$
$$\underline{\quad}\%(\$140) = \$40$$
$$140x = 40$$
$$x = 28\frac{4}{7}\%$$

12. (a)
$$C + OH + P = S_1$$
$$C + 10\%S + 40\%S = S_1$$
$$C = 50\%S_1$$
$$\frac{1}{.5}(\$90) = S_1$$
$$\$180 = S_1$$

(b)
$$\% \text{ Pd} \times L = N$$
$$40\%S_1 = S_2$$
$$40\%(\$180) = S_2$$
$$\$72 = S_2$$

$$OH = 10\%S_1$$
$$OH = 10\%(\$180)$$
$$OH = \$18$$

$$THC = C + OH$$
$$THC = \$90 + \$18$$
$$THC = \$108$$

$$OL = THC - S_2$$
$$OL = \$108 - \$72$$
$$OL = \$36$$

(c)
$$GL = C - S_2$$
$$GL = \$90 - \$72$$
$$GL = \$18$$

$$\underline{\quad}\% \text{ of } C = GL$$
$$\underline{\quad}\%(\$90) = \$18$$
$$90x = 18$$
$$x = 20\%$$

13. (a)
$$\% \text{ Pd} \times L = \text{Net Cost}$$
$$(80\%)(80\%)\$7.50 = C$$
$$(0.64)7.50 = C$$
$$\$4.80 = C$$

$$\frac{\$4.80}{12} = \$0.40/\text{each}$$

13. (a) (Continued)

$$C + 30\%C + 20\%C = S_1$$
$$1.5(\$0.40) = S_1$$
$$\$0.60 = S_1$$

(b) $THC = C + OH$
$$THC = C + 30\%C$$
$$THC = 1.3(\$0.40)$$
$$THC = \$0.52$$

$$S_1 - THC = \text{Max. MD}$$
$$\$0.60 - \$0.52 = MD$$
$$\$0.08 = MD$$

(c) $\_\_\%$ of original = change
$$\_\_\%(\$0.60) = \$0.08$$
$$0.60x = 0.08$$
$$x = 13\frac{1}{3}\%$$

14. (a) $\% \text{ Pd} \times L = \text{Net Cost}$ $\qquad \dfrac{\$4.20}{12} = \$0.35/\text{each}$
$$\left(\frac{2}{3}\right)(90\%)\$7 = C$$
$$\$4.20 = C$$

$$C + M_1 = S_1$$
$$C + 60\%C = S_1$$
$$160\%(0.35) = S_1$$
$$\$0.56 = S_1$$

(b) $THC = 140\%C$
$$THC = 140\%(0.35)$$
$$THC = \$0.49$$

(c) $\qquad S_1 - THC = \text{Max. MD}$ $\qquad \_\_\%$ of original = change
$$\$0.56 - \$0.49 = MD \qquad \qquad \_\_\%(\$0.56) = \$0.07$$
$$\$0.07 = MD \qquad \qquad 0.56x = 0.07$$
$$x = 12.5\%$$

15. (a) $\% \text{ Pd} \times L = \text{Net Cost}$ $\qquad \dfrac{\$43.20}{12} = \$3.60/\text{each}$
$$(60\%)(80\%)\$90 = C$$
$$\$43.20 = C$$

$$C + M_1 = S_1$$
$$C + 25\%C + 50\%C = S_1$$
$$175\%(\$3.60) = S_1$$
$$\$6.30 = S_1$$

(b) $THC = 125\%C$
$$THC = 125\%(\$3.60)$$
$$THC = \$4.50$$

15. (b) (Continued)

$$S_1 - THC = \text{Max. MD}$$
$$\$6.30 - \$4.50 = MD$$
$$\$1.80 = MD$$

(c) ___% of original = change
$$\underline{\quad}\%(\$6.30) = \$1.80$$
$$6.30x = 1.80$$
$$x = 28.57\%$$

16. (a)
$$\% \text{ Pd} \times L = \text{Net Cost}$$
$$(80\%)(80\%)\$30 = C$$
$$\$19.20 = C$$

$$\frac{\$19.20}{12} = \$1.60/\text{each}$$

$$C + M_1 = S_1$$
$$C + 25\%C + 10\%C = S_1$$
$$135\%(\$1.60) = S_1$$
$$\$2.16 = S_1$$

(b) THC = 125%C
THC = 125%($1.60)
THC = $2.00

$$S_1 - THC = \text{Max. MD}$$
$$\$2.16 - \$2.00 = MD$$
$$\$0.16 = MD$$

(c) ___% of original = change
$$\underline{\quad}\%(\$2.16) = \$0.16$$
$$2.16x = 0.16$$
$$x = 7.4\%$$

17. (a) Total cost = 200 × $2.80 = $560
OH = 15% × $560 = $84
Total handling cost = $560 + $84 = $644
Total sales = $670 (below)

180 × $3.50 = $630
 20 × $2.00 = + 40
                $670

(b) Total sales ($670) exceeds total handling cost ($644) = operating profit

(c) OP = S - THC
OP = $670 - $644
OP = $26

___% of C = OP
___%($560) = $26
560x = 26
x = 4.6%

18. (a) Total cost = 50 × $40 = $2,000
       OH = 20% of $2,000 = $400
       Total handling cost = $2,000 + $400 = $2,400
       Total sales = $2,550 (below)

           40 × $55 = $2,200
           10 × $35 = +   350
                      $2,550

    (b) Total sales ($2,550) exceeds total handling cost ($2,400)
        = operating profit

    (c) OP = S - THC   ___% of C = OP
        OP = $2,550 - $2,400   ___%($2,400) = $150
        OP = $150   2,400x =   150
                                           x = 7.5%

19. (a) Total cost = 25 × $4 = $100
       Total handling cost = 130% × $100 = $130
       Total sales = $143 (below)

           18 × $6 = $108
            7 × $5 = + 35
                     $143

    (b) Total sales ($143) exceeds total handling cost ($130) =
        operating profit

    (c) OP = S - THC   ___% of C = OP
        OP = $143 - $130   ___%($100) = $13
        OP = $13   100x =   13
                                         x = 13%

20. (a) Total cost = 50 × $1.50 = $75
       Total handling cost = 125% × $75 = $93.75
       Total sales = $91.40 (below)

           38 × $1.90 = $72.20
           12 × $1.60 = +19.20
                        $91.40

    (b) Total handling cost ($93.75) exceeds total sales ($91.40)
        = operating loss

    (c) OL = THC - S   ___% of C = OL
        OL = $93.75 - $91.40   ___%($75) = $2.35
        OL = $2.35   75x =   2.35
                                        x = 3.1%

Comprehensive Problems
Chapters 12, 13, 14

Section 3, page 379

1. (a) Total cost before trade discount:
       80 × $20 = $1,600

       Total cost after trade discount:
       ___% Pd × L = N
       70%($1,600) = N
             $1,120 = N

   (b) $\frac{\$1,120}{2}$ = $560 = credit for half the balance

       10 days from invoice date = 2% discount

       ___% Pd × Credit = Net payment
             98%($560) = N
              $548.80 = N

   (c) 20 days from invoice date = 1% discount

       ___% Pd × Balance = N
             99%($560) = N
              $554.40 = N

   (d) Total cost = $548.80 + $554.40 = $1,103.20

       Individual cost = $\frac{\$1,103.20}{80}$ = $13.79 each

   (e)   C + M = S
       C + 20%C + 20%C = S
               140%C = S
         140%($13.79) = S
              $19.31 = S

   (f) ___% Pd × S_1 = S_2
        60%($19.31) = $11.59

   (g) Total revenue:
       50 × $19.31 = $ 965.50
       30 × $11.59 = + __347.70__
                      $1,313.20

1. (Continued)

   (h) Total handling cost = 120%($1,103.20) = $1,323.84

   Operating loss = Total handling cost ($1,323.84) - Total sales ($1,313.20) = $10.64

   (i)   ___% of C = OL
       ___%($1,103.20) = $10.64
            1,103.20x =   10.64
                   x = 0.964% or 1.0%

2. (a) Total cost before trade discount:
       60 × $105 = $6,300

   Total cost after trade discount:
   ___% Pd × L = N
   75%($6,300) = N
        $4,725 = N

   (b) $\frac{1}{3}$ × $4,725 = $1,575 = credit for $\frac{1}{3}$ the balance

   10 days from invoice date = 2% discount

   ___% Pd × Credit = Net payment
       98%($1,575) = N
         $1,543.50 = N

   (c) Balance due = $4,725 - $1,575 = $3,150

   20 days from invoice date = 1% discount

   ___% Pd × Balance = N
       99%($3,150) = N
         $3,118.50 = N

   (d) Total cost = $1,543.50 + $3,118.50 = $4,662

   Individual cost = $\frac{$4,662}{60}$ = $77.70 each

   (e)   C + M = S
       C + 10%C + 20%C = S
                130%C = S
         130%($77.70) = S
              $101.01 = S

2. (Continued)

   (f) $\underline{}$% Pd × S_1 = S_2
       90%($101.01) = S_2
              $90.91 = S_2

   (g) Total revenue:
       45 × $101.01 = $4,545.45
       15 × $ 90.91 = $\underline{+1,363.65}$
                      $5,909.10

   (h) Total handling cost = 110%($4,662) = $5,128.20

       Operating profit = Total sales ($5,909.10) - Total
       handling cost ($5,128.20) = $780.90

   (i) $\underline{}$% of C = OP
       $\underline{}$%($4,662) = $780.90
              4,662x =   780.90
                   x = 16.8%

3. (a) Total cost before trade discount:
       100 × $125 = $12,500

       Total cost after trade discount:
           $\underline{}$% Pd × L = N
       (85%)(80%)$12,500 = N
                  $8,500 = N

       Net cost after cash discount:
       $\underline{}$% Pd × L = N
       97%($8,500) = N
             $8,245 = N

       Net merchandise cost   = $8,245
       Freight charge   = $\underline{+35}$
       Amount of Sept. 12 payment = $8,280

   (b) Total cost $8,280 and individual cost = $\dfrac{\$8,280}{100}$ = $82.80

   (c)   C + M = S
       C + 25%C + 15%C = S
               140%C = S
           140($82.80) = S
               $115.92 = S

3. (Continued)

    (d) Reduced selling price:

$$\underline{\quad}\% \ Pd \times S_1 = S_2$$
$$50\%(\$115.92) = S_2$$
$$\$57.96 = S_2$$

    (e) Total revenue:

$$75 \times \$115.92 = \$ \ 8,694$$
$$25 \times \$ \ 57.96 = \underline{+ \ 1,449}$$
$$\$10,143$$

    (f) Total handling cost = 125%($8,280) = $10,350

        Operating loss = Total handling cost ($10,350) - Total selling price ($10,143) = $207

    (g)

$$\underline{\quad}\% \ of \ C = OL$$
$$\underline{\quad}\%(\$8,280) = \$207$$
$$8,280x = 207$$
$$x = 2.5\%$$

4. (a) Total cost before trade discount:

$$1,500 \times \$3 = \$4,500$$

       Total cost after trade discount:

$$\underline{\quad}\% \ Pd \times L = N$$
$$80\%(\$4,500) = N$$
$$\$3,600 = N$$

       Net cost after cash discount:

$$\underline{\quad}\% \ Pd \times L = N$$
$$98\%(\$3,600) = N$$
$$\$3,528 = N$$

       Net merchandise cost = $3,528
       Freight charge   = $\underline{+ \quad 20}$
                        $3,548

    (b) Total cost = $3,548 and individual cost = $\dfrac{\$3,548}{1,500} = \$2.37$

    (c)

$$C + M = S$$
$$C + 20\%C + 15\%C = S$$
$$135\%C = S$$
$$135\%(\$2.37) = S$$
$$\$3.20 = S$$

4. (Continued)

(d) Reduced selling price:
$$\underline{\quad}\% \ P_d \times S_1 = S_2$$
$$40\%(\$3.20) = S_2$$
$$\$1.28 = S_2$$

(e) Total revenue:
$$1{,}000 \times \$3.20 = \$3{,}200$$
$$500 \times \$1.28 = \underline{+\quad 640}$$
$$\$3{,}840$$

(f) Total handling cost = $120\%(\$3{,}548) = \$4{,}257.60$

Operating loss = Total handling cost ($4,257.60) - Total selling price ($3,840) = $417.60

(g)
$$\underline{\quad}\% \ of \ C = OL$$
$$\underline{\quad}\%(\$3{,}548) = \$417.60$$
$$3{,}548x = 417.60$$
$$x = 11.8\%$$

CHAPTER XV

SIMPLE INTEREST

Students often experience difficulty with simple interest and simple discount problems. This happens because the formulas and procedures for the two types of notes are so similar that the students confuses them. As each formula is introduced, insist that students memorize it. Also, emphasize the term "face value." Refer to the principal of a simple interest note as the face value. Later in Chapter XVI, refer to the maturity value of a simple discount note as the face value. The authors have found that this repetitive practice has helped students see the similarities and differences between both types of notes. The instructor may also point out that the <u>face value</u> multiplied times <u>rate</u> and <u>time</u> equals the <u>rent</u> (or interest or discount) on both notes.

1. Basic Simple Interest:

This topic introduces the terminology related to simple interest, as well as the basic simple interest formulas: $I = Prt$; $M = P + I$; and $M = P(1 + rt)$. The "time" in this first section is always expressed in even months, thus allowing the students to become familiar with the formulas and their use while keeping the computation very simple. When one of the variables other than interest itself is to be found, the students should use the formula $I = Prt$, if possible; stress that P, r, or t can be found using $I = Prt$ provided the interest, I, is given or can be determined. Be sure students use a capital P in the interest formulas, so as not to confuse it later with the proceeds, p.

When demonstrating the formula $M = P(1 + rt)$, emphasize the correct procedure with the parentheses: the "rt" is multiplied together before adding the "1". Only then can the parentheses be multiplied times the principal, P.

2. Ordinary Time and Exact Time:

In the remaining problems of this chapter and the next, exact time will be used if the problem contains sufficient information with which to determine the exact time (that is, if the problem mentions an exact calendar date). Both ordinary and exact time are calculated in this topic for purposes of comparison. Exact time is sometimes found by adding the exact days of each month between the dates in question, but this is inefficient and unnecessary; exact time should be found from the outset using the table, "The Number of Each Day of the Year."

3.   Ordinary Interest and Exact Interest:

Ordinary and exact time is easy for students to understand; but why ordinary and exact "interest" should refer to the number of days per year is impossible to explain. Consequently, students often become confused when a problem refers to both. (Just tell them to remember that "time" refers to the length of the loan, so "interest" must refer to the other.)

Interest is calculated using the three combinations of time and interest that are used in business, in order to demonstrate the popularity of the Bankers' Rule: $\dfrac{\text{exact days}}{360}$. Succeeding problems should be worked using the Bankers' Rule (Type I) unless otherwise directed or unless the given information is insufficient to find exact time. Type II $\left(\dfrac{\text{exact days}}{365}\right)$ is also emphasized, to a lesser extent, since its usage has increased somewhat in recent years.

Problems 5 through 12 are designed to teach the students that, besides principal, changes in both rate and time produce a similar change in interest. (That is, interest varies directly as principal, rate, and time; or, interest is directly proportional to principal, rate and time.) Problems 13 through 16 again utilize the Type II calculations.

The instructor might like to show the students the 6%, 60-day method which is a shortcut. Although it is not taught in the text, the method might be introduced by the instructor at this point. The method works this way: When the time is 60 days and the rate is 6%, the interest charged will always be $\dfrac{1}{100}$ or 1% of the principal: $I = P \times \dfrac{6}{100} \times \dfrac{1}{6} = P \times \dfrac{1}{100}$

Instruct the students to mentally move the decimal point of the principal two places to the left.

The 6%, 60-day method can be applied to other problems also. For example, $1,000 at 6%, for 30-days is $\dfrac{30}{60}$ or $\dfrac{1}{2}$ the interest charged at 6%, 60 days: I_{6-60} = $10

$$I_{6-30} = \frac{1}{2} \times \$10 = \$5$$

4.   Simple Interest Notes:

When discussing the use and terminology of the simple interest note, especially emphasize that the face value of this note is the principal of the loan -- the amount the borrower will have to spend. Remind the students that interest is computed using the Bankers' Rule (unless directions are given for exact interest). The suggestions offered for topic 1 also apply to the problems in this section.

5.   Present Value:

The idea of present value as simply another definition of principal is not difficult for students to accept; however, when two interest rates are involved, it usually takes a while for "present value" to develop any meaning for the students. Keep repeating frequently the basic definition: "Present value is the amount that would have to be invested at the rate money is worth in order to have the same maturity value as the actual investment will have." It also helps to identify "present value" as the amount that would have to be deposited "at the present time"; it is not difficult for students to later alter this idea, when "present value" is used to refer to the relative value on any day prior to the maturity date. It may help fix the concept in the students' minds if, during class discussion, you have several students express the meaning of "present value" in their own words.

It might be well worth the time to take a few minutes to have the entire class write on paper what the term "present value" conveys to them. (This would also be a good pop quiz question at the following class meeting.)

The authors have found it is better not to have students memorize the present value formula $P = \dfrac{M}{1 + rt}$, as a separate formula. Rather, have them first write the maturity value formula, $M = P(1 + rt)$, which they already know, and then obtain the present value formula by dividing by the parentheses. Weaker math students will be much more successful using this approach, since they tend to misplace the variables when they try to memorize these as separate formulas. Eventually, most students will be able to write the present value formula directly, by merely thinking about the required division with the parentheses; (you can "see the wheels turning" as they start to write the formula).

When working examples for the class, emphasize that the "$1 + rt$" must be combined first, as they were previously. Also remind the students that "a fraction is an indicated division; since the denominator now contains a fraction, we are dividing by a fraction -- which means we must invert and multiply to obtain the solution."

Requiring the students to make a diagram for each problem helps students form a mental picture of the situation. It helps them understand the problem -- what is given, which facts go together, what must be found, and in which order. (Later on, the diagram will help students determine which type of problem this is and what formula is called for.)

The instructor may use examples such as the following to help the students visualize, before working a problem, whether the present value (on the day the investment is made) will be more or less than the face value. You might show several examples, some where the actual rate is greater than the rate money is worth, and vice versa. The demonstration might proceed somewhat as follows:

Instructor: Suppose I make an investment at 8%. I will draw an arrow to indicate the maturity value of the investment.

Now suppose money is usually worth 12%. If my principal were invested at 12%, would the maturity value be more or less? (Wait for class to answer.) Since the maturity value would be larger at the rate money is worth, I will draw an arrow which extends beyond the first arrow.

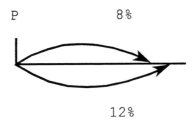

In order to determine the size of the present value, we must be considering investments which have the same maturity value. So, I will adjust the arrow representing the investment at the rate money is worth until its maturity value coincides with the actual maturity value.

P   8%

P.V.   12%

Now we see that the origin of the arrow representing the investment at the rate money is worth is at a point smaller than the actual investment. This point also represents the present value, so we see that the present value is less than the actual principal. To put it another way: a smaller investment, invested at 12%, would earn more interest and would thus amount to the same maturity value. Hence, our actual 8% investment is not worth as much as its face value, because anyone else could take <u>less</u> money, invest it at the rate money is worth, and end up with the same amount we will have. This same conclusion is stated in the text. However, the demonstration above will help students understand <u>why</u> this must be so.

When finding present value on a day other than the original date, stress computing the time correctly. (Some students try to use the time until the date in question, rather than the time from that date until maturity.)

CHAPTER 15 - SIMPLE INTEREST
PROBLEM SOLUTIONS

Section 1, page 388

1. (a) P = $600   I = Prt   M = P + I
       r = 10%   = $600 × 0.10 × 1   = $600 + $60
       t = 1 year   I = $60   M = $660

   (b) P = $600   I = Prt   M = P + I
       r = 10%   = $600 × 0.10 × 0.5   = $600 + $30
       t = $\frac{6}{12}$ = 0.5   I = $30   M = $630

   (c) P = $1,200   I = Prt   M = P + I
       r = 8%   = $1,200 + $32
       t = $\frac{4}{12}$ = $\frac{1}{3}$ = $1,200 × 0.08 × $\frac{1}{3}$ M = $1,232

                     I = $32

1. (Continued)

(d) $P = \$800$
     $r = 8.5\%$
     $t = \dfrac{3}{12} = 0.25$

$I = Prt$
  $= \$800 \times 0.085 \times 0.25$
$I = \$17$

$M = P + I$
  $= \$800 + \$17$
$M = \$817$

(e) $P = \$2,400$
     $r = 9\%$
     $t = \dfrac{9}{12} = 0.75$

$I = Prt$
  $= \$2,400 \times 0.09 \times 0.75$
$I = \$162$

$M = P + I$
  $= \$2,400 + \$162$
$M = \$2,562$

2. (a) $P = \$700$
        $r = 9\%$
        $t = 1$ year

$I = Prt$
  $= \$700 \times 0.09 \times 1$
$I = \$63$

$M = P + I$
  $= \$700 + \$63$
$M = \$763$

(b) $P = \$700$
     $r = 9\%$
     $t = \dfrac{6}{12} = 0.5$

$I = Prt$
  $= \$700 \times 0.09 \times 0.5$
$I = \$31.50$

$M = P + I$
  $= \$700 + \$31.50$
$M = \$731.50$

(c) $P = \$1,400$
     $r = 8\%$
     $t = \dfrac{3}{12} = 0.25$

$I = Prt$
  $= \$1,400 \times 0.08 \times 0.25$
$I = \$28$

$M = P + I$
  $= \$1,400 + \$28$
$M = \$1,428$

(d) $P = \$2,400$
     $r = 6.5\%$
     $t = \dfrac{9}{12} = 0.75$

$I = Prt$
  $= \$2,400 \times 0.065 \times 0.75$
$I = \$117$

$M = P + I$
  $= \$2,400 + \$117$
$M = \$2,517$

(e) $P = \$840$
     $r = 7\%$
     $t = \dfrac{8}{12} = \dfrac{2}{3}$

$I = Prt$
  $= \$840 \times 0.07 \times \dfrac{2}{3}$
$I = \$39.20$

$M = P + I$
  $= \$840 + \$39.20$
$M = \$879.20$

3. (a) $M = P(1 + rt)$

  $= \$600(1 + 0.10 \cdot 1)$

  $= 600(1 + 0.10)$

  $= 600(1.10)$

  $M = \$660$

$I = M - P$
  $= \$660 - \$600$
$I = \$60$

3. (Continued)

(c) $M = P(1 + rt)$

$\qquad = \$1,200\left(1 + \dfrac{8}{100} \cdot \dfrac{1}{3}\right)$

$\qquad = \ 1,200\left(1 + \dfrac{8}{300}\right)$

$\qquad = \ 1,200\left(\dfrac{308}{300}\right)$

$M = \$1,232$

$I = M - P$
$\qquad = \$1,232 - \$1,200$
$I = \$32$

(e) $M = P(1 + rt)$

$\qquad = \$2,400(1 + 0.09 \cdot 0.75)$

$\qquad = \ 2,400(1 + 0.0675)$

$\qquad = \ 2,400(1.0675)$

$M = \$2,562$

$I = M - P$
$\qquad = \$2,562 - \$2,400$
$I = \$162$

4. (a) $M = P(1 + rt)$

$\qquad = \$700(1 + 0.09 \cdot 1)$

$\qquad = \ 700(1.09)$

$M = \$763$

$I = M - P$
$\qquad = \$763 - \$700$
$I = \$63$

(c) $M = P(1 + rt)$

$\qquad = \$1,400(1 + 0.08 \cdot 0.25)$

$\qquad = \ 1,400(1.02)$

$M = \$1,428$

$I = M - P$
$\qquad = \$1,428 - \$1,400$
$I = \$28$

(e) $M = P(1 + rt)$

$\qquad = \$840(1 + 0.07 \cdot \dfrac{2}{3})$

$\qquad = \ 840(1.04667)$

$M = \$879.20$

$I = M - P$
$\qquad = \$879.20 - \$840$
$I = \$39.20$

5. P = \$3,000

    r = ?

    $t = \dfrac{9}{12} = 0.75$

    I = \$180

    I = Prt

    \$180 = \$3,000 × r × 0.75

    180 =   2,250r

    8% = r

6. P = \$2,000

    r = ?

    $t = \dfrac{6}{12} = 0.5$

    I = \$90

    I = Prt

    \$90 = \$2,000 × r × 0.5

    90 = 1,000r

    9% = r

7. P = \$1,500
    r = 7%
    t = ?
    I = \$1,587.50 - \$1,500 = \$87.50

    I = Prt
    \$87.50 = \$1,500 × 0.07 × t
    87.50 = 105t
    0.833$\overline{3}$ = t
    t = 0.8333 × 12 mos.
    = 10 mos.

8. P = \$880
    r = 7.5%
    t = ?
    I = \$896.50 - \$880.00 = \$16.50

    I = Prt
    \$16.50 = \$880 × 0.075 × t
    16.50 = 66t
    0.25 = t
    t = 0.25 × 12 months
    = 3 months

9. P = \$6,000

    r = ?

    $t = \dfrac{6}{12} = 0.5$

    I = \$6,300 - \$6,000 = \$300

    I = Prt

    \$300 = \$6,000 × r × 0.5

    300 = 3,000r

    10% = r

10. P = \$1,600

    r = ?

    $t = \dfrac{3}{12} = 0.25$

    I = \$1,636 - \$1,600 = \$36

    I = Prt

    \$36 = \$1,600 × r × 0.25

    36 = 400r

    9% = r

11. P = ?

    r = 14%

    $t = \dfrac{18}{12} = 1.5$

    M = $9,680

$$M = P(1 + rt)$$
$$\$9,680 = P(1 + 0.14 \cdot 1.5)$$
$$9,680 = P(1 + 0.21)$$
$$9,680 = P(1.21)$$
$$\$8,000 = P$$

12. P = ?

    r = 8%

    $t = \dfrac{36}{12} = 3$

    M = $14,880

$$M = P(1 + rt)$$
$$\$14,880 = P(1 + 0.08 \cdot 3)$$
$$14,880 = P(1.24)$$
$$\$12,000 = P$$

13. Play the "What If" game. What if P = $1,000. Since the investment is to double at 16%, the interest must be $1,000.

    P = $1,000

    r = 16%

    t = ?

    I = $1,000

$$I = Prt$$
$$\$1,000 = \$1,000 \times 0.16 \times t$$
$$1,000 = 160t$$
$$6.25 = t \text{ or } 6\tfrac{1}{4} \text{ years}$$

14. Have the student pick any principal amount. Example:
    Choose P = $1,000
            r = ?
            t = 20
            I = $1,000

$$I = Prt$$
$$\$1,000 = \$1,000 \times r \times 20$$
$$1,000 = 20,000r$$
$$5\% = t$$

Section 2, page 390

1. (a) May   31 =   151 day   (b) Sept. 15 =   258 day
      March 6 = <u>- 65 day</u>   June   5 = <u>-156 day</u>
                 86 days   102 days

1. (Continued)

(c) Dec. 10 = 344 day
    July 10 = <u>-191 day</u>
                153 days

(d) Nov. 28 = 332 day
    Jan. 14 = <u>- 14 day</u>
                318 days

(e) May 31, 2000 = 152 day
    Feb. 12, 2000 = <u>- 43 day</u>
    (leap year)   109 days

(f) Dec. 31, 2001 = 365 day
    Sept. 23, 2001 = <u>-266 day</u>
                       99 days
    April 1, 2002 = <u>+ 91 day</u>
                      190 days

(g) Dec. 31, 2003 = 365 day
    July 4, 2003 = <u>-185 day</u>
                     180 days
    March 4, 2004 = <u>+ 63 day</u>
    (leap year)   243 days

(h) Dec. 31, 1999 = 365 day
    Nov. 15, 1999 = <u>-319 day</u>
                      46 days
    June 6, 2000 = <u>+158 day</u>
    (leap year)   204 days

2. (a) December 6 = 340 day
        November 9 = <u>-313 day</u>
                       27 days

    (b) October 18 = 291 day
        April   12 = <u>-102 day</u>
                      189 days

    (c) December 25 = 359 day
        May   27 = <u>-147 day</u>
                        212 days

    (d) November 23 = 327 day
        February 7 = <u>- 38 day</u>
                       289 days

    (e) April 3, 2000 = 94 day
        Jan. 16, 2000 = <u>-16 day</u>
                          78 days

    (f) Dec. 31, 2001 = 365 day
        Aug.   5, 2001 = <u>-217 day</u>
                          148 days
        March 12, 2002 = <u>+ 71 day</u>
                          219 days

    (g) Dec. 31, 2003 = 365 day
        June 25, 2003 = <u>-176 day</u>
                         189 days
        April 3, 2004 = <u>+ 94 day</u>
        (leap year)   283 days

    (h) Dec. 31, 2007 = 365 day
        Dec. 15, 2007 = <u>-349 day</u>
                          16 days
        May   1, 2000 = <u>+122 day</u>
        (leap year)   138 days

3. (a) 233 day = Aug. 21
         <u>+ 30 days</u>
         263 day = Sept. 20

    (b) 287 day = Oct. 14
         <u>+ 60 days</u>
         347 day = Dec. 13

    (c) 169 day = June 18
         <u>+120 days</u>
         289 day = Oct. 16

    (d)   60 day = Mar.   1
         <u>+200 days</u>
         260 day = Sept. 17

3. (Continued)

(e) 198 day = July 17
    +150 days
     348 day = Dec. 14

(f) 327 day = Nov. 23
    +180 days
     507 day
    -365 days
     142 day = May 22

4. (a) 246 day = Sept. 3
       + 60 days
        306 day = Nov. 2

   (b)   39 day = Feb. 8
        +270 days
         309 day = Nov. 5

   (c) 163 day = June 12
       + 90 days
        253 day = Sept. 10

   (d)   3 day = Jan. 3
        +300 days
         303 day = Oct. 30

   (e) 121 day = May 1
       +180 days
        301 day = Oct. 28

   (f) 292 day = Oct. 19
       +150 days
        442 day
       -365 day   = Dec. 31
         77 day   = March 18

5. (a) Due date = February 18 + 6 months = August 18

       August   18 = 230 day
       February 18 = - 49 day
                       181 days

   (b) Due date = May 24 + 3 months = August 24

       August 24 = 236 day
       May   24 = -144 day
                     92 days

   (c) Due date = January 26, 2002 + 9 months = October 26, 2002

       October 26 = 299 day
       January 26 = - 26 day
                      273 days

   (d) Due date = March 30, 2006 + 4 months = July 30, 2006

       July 30 = 211 day
       March 30 = - 89 day
                    122 days

5. (Continued)

   (e) Due date = January 13, 2004 + 5 months = June 13, 2004

   ```
   June      13 =   165 day
   January 13 = - 13 day
   (leap year)    152 days
   ```

6. (a) Due date = August 7 + 4 months = December 7

   ```
   December 7 =   341 day
   August    7 = -219 day
                  122 days
   ```

   (b) Due date = May 26 + 2 months = July 26

   ```
   July 26 =   207 day
   May   26 = -146 day
               61 days
   ```

   (c) Due date = January 5, 2000 + 8 months = September 5, 2000

   ```
   September 5 =   249 day
   January    5 = -   5 day
   (leap year)    244 days
   ```

   (d) Due date = July 18, 2003 + 4 months = November 18, 2003

   ```
   November 18 =   322 day
   July        18 = -199 day
                    123 days
   ```

   (e) Due date = February 3, 2008 + 3 months = May 3, 2008

   ```
   May        3 =   124 day
   February 3 = - 34 day
   (leap year)     90 days
   ```

Section 3, page 394

1. (a) <u>Ordinary interest</u>
   $P = \$2,190$ $I = Prt$

   $r = 8\%$ $= \$2,190 \times 0.08 \times 0.125$

   $t = \dfrac{45}{360} = 0.125$ $I = \$21.90$

1. (a) (Continued)

Exact interest

$P = \$2,190$

$r = 8\%$

$t = \dfrac{45}{365}$

$I = Prt$

$= \$2,190 \times 0.08 \times \dfrac{45}{365}$

$I = \$21.60$

(b) Ordinary interest

$P = \$2,920$

$r = 9\%$

$t = \dfrac{60}{360} = \dfrac{1}{6}$

$I = Prt$

$= \$2,920 \times 0.09 \times \dfrac{1}{6}$

$I = \$43.80$

Exact interest

$P = \$2,920$

$r = 9\%$

$t = \dfrac{60}{365}$

$I = Prt$

$= \$2,920 \times 0.09 \times \dfrac{60}{365}$

$I = \$43.20$

2. (a) Ordinary interest

$P = \$6,500$

$r = 7\%$

$t = \dfrac{90}{360} = 0.25$

$I = Prt$

$= \$6,500 \times 0.07 \times 0.25$

$I = \$113.75$

Exact interest

$P = \$6,500$

$r = 7\%$

$t = \dfrac{90}{365} = \dfrac{18}{73}$

$I = Prt$

$= \$6,500 \times 0.07 \times \dfrac{18}{73}$

$I = \$112.19$

(b) Ordinary interest

$P = \$5,200$

$r = 6.5\%$

$t = \dfrac{120}{360} = \dfrac{1}{3}$

$I = Prt$

$= \$5,200 \times 0.065 \times \dfrac{1}{3}$

$I = \$112.67$

2. (b) (Continued)

Exact interest

$P = \$5,200$

$r = 6.5\%$

$t = \dfrac{120}{365} = \dfrac{24}{73}$

$I = Prt$

$= \$5,200 \times 0.065 \times \dfrac{24}{73}$

$I = \$111.12$

3. Due date = June 6 + 4 months = October 6

$P = \$8,000$

$r = 14\%$

Type I: $t = \dfrac{\text{Exact time}}{\text{Ordinary interest}} = \dfrac{122}{360}$

$I = Prt$

$= \$8,000 \times 0.14 \times \dfrac{122}{360}$

$I = \$379.56$

Type II: $t = \dfrac{\text{Exact time}}{\text{Exact interest}} = \dfrac{122}{365}$

$I = Prt$

$= \$8,000 \times 0.14 \times \dfrac{122}{365}$

$I = \$374.36$

Type III: $t = \dfrac{\text{Ordinary time}}{\text{Ordinary interest}} = \dfrac{4}{12} = \dfrac{1}{3}$

$I = Prt$

$= \$8,000 \times 0.14 \times \dfrac{1}{3}$

$I = \$373.33$

4. Due date = September 5 + 2 months = November 5 = 61 days

$P = \$10,000$

$r = 9\%$

Type I: $t = \dfrac{\text{Exact time}}{\text{Ordinary interest}} = \dfrac{61}{360}$

4. (Continued)

$$I = Prt$$
$$= \$10,000 \times 0.09 \times \frac{61}{360}$$
$$I = \$152.50$$

Type II: $\quad t = \dfrac{\text{Exact time}}{\text{Exact interest}} = \dfrac{61}{365}$

$$I = Prt$$
$$= \$10,000 \times 0.09 \times \frac{61}{365}$$
$$I = \$150.41$$

Type III: $\quad t = \dfrac{\text{Ordinary time}}{\text{Ordinary interest}} = \dfrac{2}{12} = \dfrac{1}{6}$

$$I = Prt$$
$$= \$10,000 \times 0.09 \times \frac{1}{6}$$
$$I = \$150.00$$

5. $P = \$3,000$, $t = \dfrac{90}{360} = 0.25$ year

(a) $r = 5\%$

$$I = Prt$$
$$= \$3,000 \times 0.05 \times 0.25$$
$$I = \$37.50$$

(b) $r = 10\%$

$$I = Prt$$
$$= \$3,000 \times 0.10 \times 0.25$$
$$I = \$75$$

(c) $r = 15\%$

$$I = Prt$$
$$= \$3,000 \times 0.15 \times 0.25$$
$$I = \$112.50$$

(d) $r = 7.5\%$

$$I = Prt$$
$$= \$3,000 \times 0.075 \times 0.25$$
$$I = \$56.25$$

6. $P = \$6,000$, $t = \dfrac{60}{360} = \dfrac{1}{6}$

6. (Continued)

(a) r = 8%

   I = Prt

   $\quad = \$6,000 \times 0.08 \times \dfrac{1}{6}$

   I = $80

(b) r = 4%

   I = Prt

   $\quad = \$6,000 \times 0.04 \times \dfrac{1}{6}$

   I = $40

(c) r = 12%

   I = Prt

   $\quad = \$6,000 \times 0.12 \times \dfrac{1}{6}$

   I = $120

(d) r = 6%

   I = Prt

   $\quad = \$6,000 \times 0.06 \times \dfrac{1}{6}$

   I = $60

7. P = $4,000, r = 12%

(a) $t = \dfrac{90}{360} = 0.25$

   I = Prt

   $\quad = \$4,000 \times 0.12 \times 0.25$

   I = $120

(b) $t = \dfrac{30}{360} = \dfrac{1}{12}$

   I = Prt

   $\quad = \$4,000 \times 0.12 \times \dfrac{1}{12}$

   I = $40

(c) $t = \dfrac{120}{360} = \dfrac{1}{3}$

   I = Prt

   $\quad = \$4,000 \times 0.12 \times \dfrac{1}{3}$

   I = $160

(d) $t = \dfrac{270}{360} = 0.75$

   I = Prt

   $\quad = \$4,000 \times 0.12 \times 0.75$

   I = $360

8. P = $2,400, r = 7%

(a) $t = \dfrac{30}{360} = \dfrac{1}{12}$

   I = Prt

   $\quad = \$2,400 \times 0.07 \times \dfrac{1}{12}$

   I = $14

(b) $t = \dfrac{90}{360} = 0.25$

   I = Prt

   $\quad = \$2,400 \times 0.07 \times 0.25$

   I = $42

8. (Continued)

(c) $t = \dfrac{45}{360} = 0.125$

(d) $t = \dfrac{180}{360} = 0.5$

$I = Prt$
$\quad = \$2,400 \times 0.07 \times 0.125$
$I = \$21$

$I = Prt$
$\quad = \$2,400 \times 0.07 \times 0.5$
$I = \$84$

9. At $r = 8\%$, $I = \$36$

(a) $\dfrac{16\%}{8\%} = 2;$ $I = \$36 \times 2 = \$72$

(b) $\dfrac{10\%}{8\%} = \dfrac{5}{4};$ $I = \$36 \times \dfrac{5}{4} = \$45$

(c) $\dfrac{12\%}{8\%} = \dfrac{3}{2};$ $I = \$36 \times \dfrac{3}{2} = \$54$

10. At $r = 9\%$, $I = \$50$

(a) $\dfrac{18\%}{9\%} = 2;$ $I = \$50 \times 2 = \$100$

(b) $\dfrac{4.5\%}{9\%} = 0.5;$ $I = \$50 \times 0.5 = \$25$

(c) $\dfrac{13.5\%}{9\%} = 1.5;$ $I = \$50 \times 1.5 = \$75$

11. At $t = 120$ days, $I = \$40$

(a) $t = \dfrac{60}{120} = 0.5;$ $I = \$40 \times 0.5 = \$20$

(b) $t = \dfrac{300}{60} = 5;$ $I = \$20 \times 5 = \$100$

$\left(\text{or } t = \dfrac{300}{120} = 2.5; \ I = 40 \times 2.5 = \$100 \right)$

(c) $t = \dfrac{240}{120} = 2;$ $I = \$40 \times 2 = \$80$

12. At t = 30 days, I = $80

    (a) $\dfrac{120}{30} - 4;$ I = $80 × 4 = $320

    (b) $\dfrac{60}{30} = 2;$ I = $80 × 2 = $160

    (c) $\dfrac{90}{30} = 3;$ I = $80 × 3 = $240

13. (a) P = $2,190   June 5 = 156 day
         r = 10%   April 5 = - 95 day
         $t = \dfrac{61}{365}$ 61 days

      I = Prt

        = $2,190 × 0.10 × $\dfrac{61}{365}$

      I = $36.60

   (b) At 5%, $\dfrac{5}{10} = 0.5;$ I = $36.60 × 0.5 = $18.30

   (c) At 15%, $\dfrac{15}{10} = 1.5;$ I = $36.60 × 1.5 = $54.90

14. (a) P = $1,095   October 10 = 283 day
         r = 12%   July   10 = -191 day
         $t = \dfrac{92}{365}$ 92 days

      I = Prt

        = $1,095 × 0.12 × $\dfrac{92}{365}$

      I = $33.12

   (b) At 6%, $\dfrac{6}{12} = 0.5;$ I = $33.12 × 0.5 = $16.56

   (c) At 15%, $\dfrac{15}{12} = 1.25;$ I = $33.12 × 1.25 = $41.40

15. (a) P = $1,460   I = Prt

    r = 9.5% $= \$1,460 \times 0.095 \times \dfrac{150}{365}$

    $t = \dfrac{150}{365}$ I = $57

    (b) At t = 180 days, $\dfrac{180}{150} = \dfrac{5}{6}$; $I = \$57 \times \dfrac{5}{6} = \$68.40$

    (c) At t = 270 days, $\dfrac{270}{150} = \dfrac{9}{5}$; $I = \$57 \times \dfrac{9}{5} = \$102.60$

16. (a) P = $2,555   I = Prt

    r = 8% $= \$2,555 \times 0.08 \times \dfrac{1}{6}$

    $t = \dfrac{60}{360} = \dfrac{1}{6}$ I = $33.60

    (b) At 90 days, $\dfrac{90}{60} = 1.5$; $I = \$33.60 \times 1.5 = \$50.40$

    (c) At 360 days, $\dfrac{360}{60} = 6$; $I = \$33.60 \times 6 = \$201.60$

Section 4, page 400

1. & 2. (a) $5,000.00   (f) $5,000.00
         (b) William J. McDaniel   (g) 9%
         (c) Cardinal Bank   (h) 30 days
         (d) May 1, 20xx   (i) $37.50
         (e) May 31, 20xx   (j) $5,037.50

3.

	Principal	Rate	Date	Due Date	Time	Interest	Maturity Value
(a)	$4,800	9%	2/12	11/9	270 days	$324.00	$5,124.00
(b)	900	11	4/22	6/21	60 days	16.50	916.50
(c)	4,500	12	8/21	11/21	3 mos.	138.00	4,638.00
(d)	800	10	4/4	7/13	100 days	20.00	820.00

    (a) November 9 = 313 day
        February 12 = - 43 day
                      270 days

3. (a) (Continued)

$I = Prt$
$= \$4,800 \times 0.09 \times 0.75$
$I = \$324$

$M = P + I$
$= \$4,800 + \$324$
$M = \$5,124$

(b) April 22 = 112 day
$\underline{+\ 60\ days}$
Due date = 172 day = June 21

$I = Prt$

$= \$900 \times 0.11 \times \dfrac{1}{6}$

$I = \$16.50$

$M = P + I$
$= \$900.00 + \$16.50$
$M = \$916.50$

(c) Due date = August 21 + 3 months = November 21

November 21 = 325 day
August   21 = $\underline{-233\ day}$
92 days

$I = Prt$

$= \$4,500 \times 0.12 \times \dfrac{92}{360}$

$I = \$138$

$M = P + I$
$= \$4,500 + \$138$
$M = \$4,638$

(d) July 13 = 194 day
$\underline{-100\ days}$
Due date =   94 day = April 4

$I = Prt$

$\$20 = P \times 0.09 \times \dfrac{5}{18}$

$20 = 0.025P$

$\$800 = P$

$M = P + I$
$= \$800 + \$20$
$M = \$820$

4.

	Principal	Rate	Date	Due Date	Time	Interest	Maturity Value
(a)	$9,000	8%	5/15	6/4	20 days	$40	$9,040
(b)	1,800	9	7/12	11/9	120 days	54	1,854
(c)	3,600	10	6/20	9/20	3 mos.	92	3,692
(d)	5,400	6	1/20	3/21	60 days	54	5,454

4. (Continued)

(a) June 4 = 155 day
    May 15 = <u>-135 day</u>
                20 days

$I = Prt$ $M = P + I$
                                   $= \$9{,}000 + \$40$
    $= \$9{,}000 \times 0.08 \times \dfrac{1}{18}$ $M = \$9{,}040$

$I = \$40$

(b) July 12 = 193 day
                <u>+120 days</u>
    Due date = 313 day = November 9

$I = Prt$ $M = P + I$
                                   $= \$1{,}800 + \$54$
    $= \$1{,}800 \times 0.09 \times \dfrac{1}{3}$ $M = \$1{,}854$

$I = \$54$

(c) June 20 + 3 months = September 20

    September 20 = 263 day
    June   20 = <u>-171 day</u>
                    92 days

$I = Prt$ $M = P + I$
                                   $= \$3{,}600 + \$92$
    $= \$3{,}600 \times 0.10 \times \dfrac{92}{360}$ $M = \$3{,}692$

$I = \$92$

(d) March 21 = 80 day
                <u>-60 days</u>
    Due date = 20 day = January 20

    $I = Prt$ $M = P + I$
                                    $= \$5{,}400 + \$54$
    $\$54 = P \times 0.06 \times \dfrac{1}{6}$ $M = \$5{,}454$

    $54 = 0.01P$

$\$5{,}400 = P$

5. May   24, 2003 = 144 day
   January 24, 2003 = - 24 day
                      120 days

   $P = \$6,000$
   $r = 9\%$
   $t = \dfrac{120}{365}$

   $I = Prt$

   $= \$6,000 \times 0.09 \times \dfrac{120}{365}$

   $I = \$177.53$

   $M = P + I$
   $= \$6,000.00 + \$177.53$
   $M = \$6,177.53$

6. April   5 = 95 day
   January 5 = - 5 day
               90 days

   $P = \$2,920$
   $r = 8\%$
   $t = \dfrac{90}{365} = \dfrac{18}{73}$

   $I = Prt$

   $= \$2,920 \times 0.08 \times \dfrac{18}{73}$

   $I = \$57.60$

   $M = P + I$
   $= \$2,920.00 + \$57.60$
   $M = \$2,977.60$

7. Due date = December 5, 2000 = 340 day (leap year)
              October   5, 2000 = -279 day
                                   61 days

   $t = \dfrac{61}{360}$

   $I = Prt$

   $= \$400 \times 0.105 \times \dfrac{61}{360}$

   $I = \$7.12$

   $M = P + I$
   $= \$400.00 + \$7.12$
   $M = \$407.12$

8. Due date = March   18, 2001 = 77 day
              February 18, 2001 = -49 day
                                   28 days

   $t = \dfrac{28}{360} = \dfrac{7}{90}$

8. (Continued)

$I = Prt$

$= \$6,000 \times 0.12 \times \dfrac{7}{90}$

$I = \$56$

$M = P + I$
$= \$6,000 + \$56$
$M = \$6,056$

9. $t = \dfrac{10}{12} = \dfrac{5}{6}$

$I = Prt$

$= \$2,000 \times 0.09 \times \dfrac{5}{6}$

$I = \$150$

$M = P + I$
$= \$2,000 + \$150$
$M = \$2,150$

10. $t = \dfrac{6}{12} = 0.5$

$I = Prt$
$= \$9,000 \times 0.08 \times 0.5$
$I = \$360$

$M = P + I$
$= \$9,000 + \$360$
$M = \$9,360$

11. August   14 =   226 day
February 14 = $\underline{- \text{ 45 day}}$
          181 days

$I = \$2,298.60 - \$2,190.00$
$= \$108.60$

$t = \dfrac{181}{365}$

$I = Prt$

$\$108.60 = \$2,190 \times r \times \dfrac{181}{365}$

$108.60 = 1,086r$

$10\% = r$

12. November 10 =   314 day
June   10 = $\underline{-161 \text{ day}}$
          153 days

$I = \$5,727.45 - \$5,475.00$
$= \$252.45$

$t = \dfrac{153}{365}$

12. (Continued)

$$I - Prt$$

$$\$252.45 = \$5,475 \times r \times \frac{153}{365}$$

$$252.45 = 2,295r$$

$$11\% = r$$

13. $I = Prt$ $\qquad t = \frac{18}{73} \times 365 \text{ days} = 90 \text{ days}$

$$\$18 = \$730 \times 0.10 \times t$$

$$18 = 73t$$

$$\frac{18}{73} = t$$

14. $I = Prt$

$$\$162 = \$3,650 \times 0.09 \times t$$

$$162 = 328.5t$$

$$0.493151 = t$$

$$0.493151 \times 365 \text{ days} = 180 \text{ days}$$

15. $I = Prt$ $\qquad t = \frac{36}{48} = 0.75; \ 0.75 \times 12 \text{ mos.} = 9 \text{ mos.}$

$$\$36 = \$400 \times 0.12 \times t \qquad \text{or } 0.75 \times 360 \text{ days} = 270 \text{ days}$$

$$36 = 48t$$

$$\frac{36}{48} = t$$

16. $I = Prt$

$$\$30 = \$2,000 \times 0.06 \times t$$

$$30 = 120t$$

$$0.25 = t$$

$$0.25 \times 12 \text{ months} = 3 \text{ months or}$$
$$0.25 \times 360 \text{ days} \ = 90 \text{ days}$$

17. P = ?

   r = 14%

   $t = \dfrac{180}{360} = 0.5$

   I = \$105

          I = Prt
\$105 = P × 0.14 × 0.5
  105 = 0.07P
\$1,500 = P

18. P = ?

   r = 9%

   $t = \dfrac{120}{360} = \dfrac{1}{3}$

   I = \$48

          I = Prt
\$48 = $P × 0.09 × \dfrac{1}{3}$
 48 = 0.03P
\$1,600 = P

19. December 6 = 340 day
September 7 = <u>-250 day</u>
             90 days

   P = ?

   r = 10%

   $t = \dfrac{90}{360} = 0.25$

   M = \$3,075

          $M = P(1 + rt)$
\$3,075 = P(1 + 0.10 · 0.25)
 3,075 = P(1.025)
\$3,000 = P

20. July 14 = 195 day
April 15 = <u>-105 day</u>
             90 days

   P = ?

   r = 10%

   $t = \dfrac{90}{360} = 0.25$

   M = \$7,380

          $M = P(1 + rt)$
\$7,380 = P(1 + 0.10 · 0.25)
 7,380 = P(1.025)
\$7,200 = P

Section 5, page 405

1.

	Maturity Value	Rate	Time	Present Value
(a)	$ 735	12%	150 days	$ 700
(b)	2,484	14	90 days	2,400

(a) $M = P(1 + rt)$

$$\$735 = P\left(1 + 0.12 \cdot \frac{5}{12}\right)$$

$$735 = P(1 + 0.05)$$

$$735 = P(1.05)$$

$$\$700 = P$$

(b) $M = P(1 + rt)$

$$\$2,484 = P(1 + 0.14 \cdot 0.25)$$

$$2,484 = P(1 + 0.035)$$

$$2,484 = P(1.035)$$

$$\$2,400 = P$$

2.

	Maturity Value	Rate	Time	Present Value
(a)	$6,450	10%	270 days	$6,000
(b)	2,020	8	45 days	2,000

(a) $M = P(1 + rt)$

$$\$6,450 = P(1 + 0.10 \cdot 0.75)$$

$$6,450 = P(1 + 0.075)$$

$$6,450 = P(1.075)$$

$$\$6,000 = P$$

(b) $M = P(1 + rt)$

$$\$2,020 = P(1 + 0.08 \cdot 0.125)$$

$$2,020 = P(1 + 0.01)$$

$$2,020 = P(1.01)$$

$$\$2,000 = P$$

3.

	Principal	Rate	Time	Maturity Value	Rate Money is Worth	Present Value
(a)	$6,000	10%	90 days	$6,150	9%	$6,014.67
(b)	8,000	12	120 days	8,320	15	7,923.81

(a) $I = Prt$
   $= \$6,000 \times 0.10 \times 0.25$
   $I = \$150$

$M = P + I$
   $= \$6,000 + \$150$
$M = \$6,150$

$$M = P(1 + rt)$$

$$\$6,150 = P(1 + 0.09 \cdot 0.25)$$

$$6,150 = P(1 + 0.0225)$$

$$6,150 = P(1.0225)$$

$$\$6,014.67 = P$$

3. (Continued)

(b) I = Prt

$$= \$8{,}000 \times 0.12 \times \frac{1}{3}$$

I = \$320

M = P + I
= \$8,000 + \$320
M = \$8,320

$$M = P(1 + rt)$$

$$\$8{,}320 = P\left(1 + 0.15 \cdot \frac{1}{3}\right)$$

$$8{,}320 = P(1 + 0.05)$$

$$8{,}320 = P(1.05)$$

$$\$7{,}923.81 = P$$

4.

	Principal	Rate	Time	Maturity Value	Rate Money is Worth	Present Value
(a)	$5,400	7%	180 days	$5,589	8%	$5,374.04
(b)	9,000	9	120 days	9,270	6	9,088.24

(a) I = Prt
= \$5,400 × 0.07 × 0.5
I = \$189

M = P + I
= \$5,400 + \$189
M = \$5,589

$$M = P(1 + rt)$$

$$\$5{,}589 = P(1 + 0.08 \cdot 0.5)$$

$$5{,}589 = P(1 + 0.04)$$

$$5{,}589 = P(1.04)$$

$$\$5{,}374.04 = P$$

(b) I = Prt

$$= \$9{,}000 \times 0.09 \times \frac{1}{3}$$

I = \$270

M = P + I
= \$9,000 + \$270
M = \$9,270

4. (b) (Continued)

$$M = P(1 + rt)$$

$$\$9,270 = P\left(1 + 0.06 \cdot \frac{1}{3}\right)$$

$$9,270 = P(1 + 0.02)$$

$$9,270 = P(1.02)$$

$$\$9,088.24 = P$$

5.

	Principal	Rate	Time	Maturity Value	Rate Money is Worth	Days Before Maturity Date	Present Value
(a)	$9,000	12%	300 days	$9,900	10%	180 days	$9,428.57
(b)	7,500	15	120 days	7,875	12	60 days	7,720.59

(a) I = Prt

$$= \$9,000 \times 0.12 \times \frac{5}{6}$$

I = $900

M = P + I
= $9,000 + $900
M = $9,900

$$M = P(1 + rt)$$

$$\$9,900 = P(1 + 0.10 \cdot 0.5)$$

$$9,900 = P(1 + 0.05)$$

$$9,900 = P(1.05)$$

$$\$9,428.57 = P$$

(b) I = Prt

$$= \$7,500 \times 0.15 \times \frac{1}{3}$$

I = $375

M = P + I
= $7,500 + $375
M = $7,875

$$M = P(1 + rt)$$

$$\$7,875 = P\left(1 + 0.12 \cdot \frac{1}{6}\right)$$

$$7,875 = P(1 + 0.02)$$

$$7,875 = P(1.02)$$

$$\$7,720.59 = P$$

6.

	Principal	Rate	Time	Maturity Value	Rate Money is Worth	Days Before Maturity Date	Present Value
(a)	$30,000	10%	120 days	$31,000	9%	60 days	$30,541.87
(b)	50,000	8	270 days	53,000	11	180 days	50,236.97

(a) I = Prt

$$= \$30,000 \times 0.10 \times \frac{1}{3}$$

I = $1,000

M = P + I
= $30,000 + $1,000
M = $31,000

$$M = P(1 + rt)$$

$$\$31,000 = P\left(1 + 0.09 \cdot \frac{1}{6}\right)$$

$$31,000 = P(1 + 0.015)$$

$$31,000 = P(1.015)$$

$$\$30,541.87 = P$$

(b) I = Prt
= $50,000 × 0.08 × 0.75
I = $3,000

M = P + I
= $50,000 + $3,000
M = $53,000

$$M = P(1 + rt)$$

$$\$53,000 = P(1 + 0.11 \cdot 0.5)$$

$$53,000 = P(1 + 0.055)$$

$$53,000 = P(1.055)$$

$$\$50,236.97 = P$$

7. September 15 = 258 day
July   15 = -196 day
                  62 days

P = ?

r = 9%

$$t = \frac{62}{360}$$

M = $4,062

$$M = P(1 + rt)$$

$$\$4,062 = P\left(1 + 0.09 \cdot \frac{62}{360}\right)$$

$$4,062 = P(1 + 0.0155)$$

$$4,062 = P(1.0155)$$

$$\$4,000 = P$$

8. April   19 =   109 day
   January 19 = $\underline{-\ 19\ \text{day}}$
                    90 days

   P = ?

   r = 8.5%

   t = $\dfrac{90}{360}$ = 0.25

   M = $20,425

$M = P(1 + rt)$

$20,425 = P(1 + 0.085 \cdot 0.25)$

$20,425 = P(1 + 0.02125)$

$20,425 = P(1.02125)$

$20,000 = P$

9. April   15 =   105 day
   January 15 = $\underline{-\ 15\ \text{day}}$
                    90 days

   P = ?

   r = 11%

   t = $\dfrac{90}{360}$ = 0.25

   M = $6,165

$M = P(1 + rt)$

$6,165 = P(1 + 0.11 \cdot 0.25)$

$6,165 = P(1 + 0.0275)$

$6,165 = P(1.0275)$

$6,000 = P$

10. October 6 =   279 day
    April   9 = $\underline{-\ 99\ \text{day}}$
                   180 days

    P = ?

    r = 10%

    t = $\dfrac{180}{360}$ = 0.5

    M = $2,520

$M = P(1 + rt)$

$2,520 = P(1 + 0.10 \cdot 0.5)$

$2,520 = P(1 + 0.05)$

$2,520 = P(1.05)$

$2,400 = P$

11. June   8 =   159 day
    February 8 = $\underline{-\ 39\ \text{day}}$
                   120 days

11. (Continued)

$P = \$3,500$ $I = Prt$ $M = P + I$

$r = 15\%$ $= \$3,500 \times 0.15 \times \dfrac{1}{3}$ $= \$3,500 + \$175$

$t = \dfrac{120}{360} = \dfrac{1}{3}$ $I = \$175$ $M = \$3,675$

$M = ?$

$P = ?$ (present value) $M = P(1 + rt)$

$r = 18\%$ $\$3,675 = P\left(1 + 0.12 \cdot \dfrac{1}{3}\right)$

$t = \dfrac{1}{3}$ $3,675 = P(1 + 0.04)$

$M = \$3,675$ $3,675 = P(1.04)$

$\$3,533.65 = PV$

12. September 3 = 246 day
    July   3 = $\underline{-184\ day}$
                  62 days

$P = \$4,500$ $I = Prt$ $M = P + I$

$r = 8\%$ $= \$4,500 \times 0.08 \times \dfrac{62}{360}$ $= \$4,500 + \$62$

$t = \dfrac{62}{360}$ $I = \$62$ $M = \$4,562$

$M = ?$

$P = ?$ (present value) $M = P(1 + rt)$

$r = 9\%$ $\$4,562 = P\left(1 + 0.09 \cdot \dfrac{62}{360}\right)$

$t = \dfrac{62}{360}$ $4,562 = P(1 + 0.0155)$

$M = \$4,562$ $4,562 = P(1.0155)$

$\$4,492.37 = PV$

13. June   12 =   163 day
    February 12 = − 43 day
                   120 days

$P = \$6,000$ $I = Prt$ $M = P + I$
                                                          $= \$6,000 + \$220$
$r = 11\%$ $= \$6,000 \times 0.11 \times \dfrac{1}{3}$ $M = \$6,220$

$t = \dfrac{120}{360} = \dfrac{1}{3}$ $I = \$220$

$M = ?$

$P = ?$ (present value) $M = P(1 + rt)$

$r = 12\%$ $\$6,220 = P\left(1 + 0.12 \cdot \dfrac{1}{3}\right)$

$t = \dfrac{1}{3}$ $6,220 = P(1 + 0.04)$

$M = \$6,220$ $6,220 = P(1.04)$

                          $\$5,980.77 = PV$

14. July   18 =   199 day
    February 18 = − 49 day
                   150 days

$P = \$48,000$ $I = Prt$ $M = P + I$
                                                          $= \$48,000 + \$1,600$
$r = 8\%$ $= \$48,000 \times 0.08 \times \dfrac{5}{12}$ $M = \$49,600$

$t = \dfrac{150}{360} = \dfrac{5}{12}$ $I = \$1,600$

$M = ?$

$P = ?$ (present value) $M = P(1 + rt)$

$r = 9\%$ $\$49,600 = P\left(1 + 0.09 \cdot \dfrac{5}{12}\right)$

$t = \dfrac{5}{12}$ $49,600 = P(1 + 0.0375)$

$M = \$49,600$ $49,600 = P(1.0375)$

                          $\$47,807.23 = PV$

15. August 16 = 228 day
    May   16 = -136 day
                  92 days

P = $12,000   I = Prt   M = P + I
                                                 = $12,000 + $460
r = 15%   = $12,000 × 0.15 × $\frac{92}{360}$ M = $12,460

t = $\frac{92}{360}$ I = $460

M = ?

August 16 = 228 day
July   17 = -198 day
              30 days

P = ? (present value) $M = P(1 + rt)$

r = 12% $12,460 = P\left(1 + 0.12 \cdot \frac{1}{12}\right)$

t = $\frac{30}{360} = \frac{1}{12}$ $12,460 = P(1 + 0.01)$

M = $12,460 $12,460 = P(1.01)$

                           $12,336.63 = PV$

16. November 20 = 324 day
    April   20 = -110 day
                  214 days

P = $18,000   I = Prt   M = P + I
                                                 = $18,000 + $1,070
r = 10%   = $18,000 × 0.10 × $\frac{214}{360}$ M = $19,070

t = $\frac{214}{360}$ I = $1,070

M = ?

November 20 = 324 day
September 21 = -264 day
               60 days

16. (Continued)

P = ? (present value)

r = 9%

$t = \dfrac{60}{360} = \dfrac{1}{6}$

M = $19,070

$M = P(1 + rt)$

$\$19,070 = P\left(1 + 0.09 \cdot \dfrac{1}{6}\right)$

$19,070 = P(1 + 0.015)$

$19,070 = P(1.015)$

$\$18,788.18 = PV$

17. May   17 = 137 day
    January 17 = $\underline{- \ 17 \ \text{day}}$
                 120 days

P = $2,500

r = 9%

$t = \dfrac{120}{360} = \dfrac{1}{3}$

M = ?

I = Prt

$= \$2,500 \times 0.09 \times \dfrac{1}{3}$

I = $75

M = P + I
  = $2,500 + $75
M = $2,575

May   17 = 137 day
April 17 = $\underline{-107 \ \text{day}}$
            30 days

P = ? (present value)

r = 7.5%

$t = \dfrac{30}{360} = \dfrac{1}{12}$

M = $2,575

$M = P(1 + rt)$

$\$2,575 = P\left(1 + 0.075 \cdot \dfrac{1}{12}\right)$

$2,575 = P(1 + 0.00625)$

$2,575 = P(1.00625)$

$\$2,559.01 = PV$

18. June   25 = 176 day
    January 25 = $\underline{- \ 25 \ \text{day}}$
                 151 days

18. (Continued)

$P = \$6,000$ $I = Prt$ $M = P + I$
$= \$6,000 + \$151$
$r = 6\%$ $= \$6,000 \times 0.06 \times \dfrac{151}{360}$ $M = \$6,151$

$t = \dfrac{151}{360}$ $I = \$151$

$M = ?$

$$\begin{array}{l} \text{June } 25 = 176 \text{ day} \\ \text{May } 26 = \underline{-146 \text{ day}} \\ \phantom{\text{May } 26 = } 30 \text{ days} \end{array}$$

$P = ?$ (present value) $M = P(1 + rt)$

$r = 7\%$ $\$6,151 = P\left(1 + 0.07 \cdot \dfrac{1}{12}\right)$

$t = \dfrac{30}{360} = \dfrac{1}{12}$ $6,151 = P(1 + 0.005833)$

$6,151 = P(1.005833)$

$M = \$6,151$ $\$6,115.33 = PV$

19. $30,000 cash now: $30,700 in $31,500 in
                           3 months: 6 months:

$PV = \$30,000$

$PV = \dfrac{M}{(1 + rt)}$ $PV = \dfrac{M}{(1 + rt)}$

$= \dfrac{\$30,700}{(1 + 0.12 \cdot 0.25)}$ $= \dfrac{\$31,500}{(1 + 0.12 \cdot 0.5)}$

$= \dfrac{30,700}{(1 + 0.03)}$ $= \dfrac{31,500}{(1 + 0.06)}$

$= \dfrac{30,700}{(1.03)}$ $= \dfrac{31,500}{(1.06)}$

$PV = \$29,805.83$ $PV = \$29,716.98$

$30,000 cash now is the best offer because it has the highest present value.

20. $155,000 cash now: $163,000 in $165,000 in
                                4 months: 9 months:

PV = $155,000

$$PV = \frac{M}{(1 + rt)}$$

$$= \frac{\$163,000}{\left(1 + 0.09 \cdot \dfrac{1}{3}\right)}$$

$$= \frac{163,000}{(1 + 0.03)}$$

$$= \frac{163,000}{(1.03)}$$

$$PV = \$158,252.42$$

$$PV = \frac{M}{(1 + rt)}$$

$$= \frac{\$165,000}{(1 + 0.09 \cdot 0.75)}$$

$$= \frac{165,000}{(1 + 0.0675)}$$

$$= \frac{165,000}{(1.0675)}$$

$$PV = \$154,566.74$$

$163,000 in 4 months is the best offer because it has the
highest present value.

CHAPTER XVI

BANK DISCOUNT

Since banks in some regions issue primarily simple discount notes, this topic can be of equal importance with simple interest. However, if the banks in your area do not use bank discount and if time is short, you might omit this chapter.

1.　Simple Discount Notes:

Bank discount will be a new topic to most students. When introduced to bank discount, many students have an uneasy feeling that the borrower pays the interest twice; the fact that bank discount is computed and deducted in advance gives students the idea that the interest has already been paid. Explain that, if a borrower signs a note and the bank gives him a check for $990, then he has only borrowed $990; he has not paid the bank anything extra. When the time of the note has expired and he pays back $1,000, only then does he pay any interest. The distinction is that he pays interest computed on the $1,000 which he paid back, rather than on the $990 which he received.

Like the simple interest note, the simple discount note has interest computed on its face value. However, the face value of the discount note is its <u>maturity value</u>; thus, interest is paid on the amount which will be paid back rather than on the amount which was received. This cannot be overemphasized. The amount which the borrower will be able to spend on the discount note is the proceeds. The other parts of the discount note are the same as for the interest note.

Advise the students to learn the new formulas carefully, so as not to confuse them with the interest formulas. Point out that proceeds should be represented with a lowercase p. Because of the similarity of $M = P(1 + rt)$ and $p = M(1 - dt)$, several mistakes are common. From force of habit, the student may (a) add $1 + dt$ instead of subtracting and (b) invert the fraction obtained from combining the terms in parentheses.

Examples 1 and 3 are included to make comparisons between simple interest and simple discount. Example 4 shows the calculation of an exact discount by a Federal Reserve bank, which typifies the use of a 365-day year.

2.   Maturity Value (and Rediscounting Notes):

This topic deals with finding what maturity value would result in the given proceeds. Here again, the authors would not ask students to memorize the maturity value formula, $M = \dfrac{p}{1 - dt}$, as a separate formula. As before, we would have them write the basic discount formula, $p = M(1 - dt)$, and obtain the maturity value formula by dividing by the parentheses.

Also included in this topic are examples of rediscounting a discounted note (Example 2) and discounting an interest note (Example 3). Either or both of these examples could be eliminated from a basic course. The two examples are somewhat similar: When the note is sold, (a) proceeds are first computed on the maturity value of the note in question. (Maturity value must first be calculated for the simple interest note, Example 3.) Then, (b) the amount which the original payee made on the note is the difference between the proceeds which the note sold for and the amount which was originally lent. (The proceeds which were lent must be computed for the discount note, Example 2.) Diagrams are very helpful in explaining these problems.

Notice that diagrams for the discount problems are drawn using broken lines, to distinguish them from the simple interest problems.

3.   Discounting Notes to Take Advantage of Cash Discounts:

This section provides an opportunity to correlate several business math topics. Cash discount is reviewed, while giving a practical application of the preceding topic -- finding the maturity value required to have a specific proceeds remaining.

When cash discount was originally studied prior to interest, it was stated that these discounts represented a substantial savings to businesses. Only after having studied interest, however, can students now fully appreciate this fact. The text points out that a 13.5% annual bank rate on a pro rata basis is equivalent to interest of 3/4% of the face value; thus, 1-1/4% is saved when the sales terms are 2/10, n/30. It is even more impressive to consider the annual bank discount rate that the 2% cash discount rate corresponds to. To illustrate, work the following example:

Invoice: $360	if M = $360	D = Mdt
Terms: 2/10, n/30	D = $7.20	$7.20 = $360 × d × $\dfrac{20}{360}$
Cash discount: $7.20	t = 20 days	36% = d
	d = ?	

This is quite astonishing to most students. You might prepare some similar problems to include with the assignment. (Notice that t corresponds to the number of days by which payment is early. See also the commentary on cash discounts in Chapter XII of this Manual.)

Of course, some savings would be made on notes taken out for various periods of time. For the sake of uniformity in problems, however, we are assuming that the firm would have sufficient funds to pay the net amount of the invoice on the last day of the quoted terms. Thus, the note is to be taken out simply to save money, rather than because money would not be available on the date the invoice is due. The bank note, therefore is signed on the last day of the discount period and is due on the day when the invoice would have been paid anyway (the last day when the net amount is due, as specified in the sales terms).

Example 1 illustrates the procedures for these problems: (a) determine the amount required to pay the invoice, taking advantage of the cash discount; (b) determine the maturity value of a note with exactly the proceeds computed in part (a); and (c) compute the savings -- the difference between the net amount of the invoice and the maturity value of the note (both due on the last day specified by the sales terms). After part (a) has been computed, the instructor can make part (b) obvious by asking something similar to the following: "We need $670.50 to pay the invoice. Thus, we need to sign a note for which we will have $670.50 to spend. What do we call the amount available to spend on a discounted note? (Class answers, 'Proceeds.') Since we know the proceeds, then, we must find the maturity value of that note."

4. Summary of Simple Interest and Simple Discount:

As a general rule, the authors do not advocate separate review sections, since students tend to think the review contains all materials for which they would be responsible. Simple interest and bank discount has proved to be an exception, however, for many students have a difficult time distinguishing between the various simple interest and bank discount problems unless they are neatly categorized under a topic heading. Thus, this summary contains a list of the distinguishing characteristics of the two notes and terminology associated with each, as well as an assortment of both types of problems.

CHAPTER 16 - BANK DISCOUNT
PROBLEM SOLUTIONS

Section 1, page 417

1. (a) $2,400   (b) A. Sample Borrower
   (c) North Star Savings Assoc.   (d) January 30, 19xx
   (e) March 31, 19xx   (f) 10%
   (g) 60 days   (h) $40
   (i) $2,360   (j) $2,400

2. (a) $1,500   (b) Mason R. & Joan D.
                                       Weatherford
   (c) North Carolina National Bank (d) July 15, 19x1
   (e) October 13, 19x1   (f) 12%
   (g) 90 days   (h) $45
   (i) $1,455   (j) $1,500

3.

	Maturity Value	Discount Rate	Date	Due Date	Time	Bank Discount	Proceeds
(a)	$9,000	8%	10/5	11/4	30 days	$ 60	$8,940
(b)	7,600	15	2/25	11/22	270 days	855	6,745
(c)	5,000	10	5/14	8/12	90 days	125	4,875
(d)	3,000	9	7/5	9/3	60 days	45	2,955

(a) October 5   =   278 day
                   + 30 days
    Due date   =   308 day = November 4

   M = $9,000   D = Mdt   p = M - D
                                            = $9,000 - $60
   d = 8%   = $9,000 × 0.08 × $\frac{1}{1}$ p = $8,940

   t = $\frac{30}{360}$ = $\frac{1}{12}$ D = $60

   D = ?

   p = ?

(b) February 25 =   56 day
                   +270 days
    Due date   =   326 day = November 22

3. (b) (Continued)

$M = \$7,600$ $D = Mdt$ $p = M - D$

$d = 15\%$ $= \$7,600 \times 0.15 \times \dfrac{3}{4}$ $= \$7,600 - \$855$

$t = \dfrac{270}{360} = \dfrac{3}{4}$ $D = \$855$ $p = \$6,745$

$D = ?$

$p = ?$

(c) August 12 = 224 day
   May   14 = -134 day
                90 days

$M = \$5,000$ $D = Mdt$ $p = M - D$

$d = 10\%$ $= \$5,000 \times 0.10 \times \dfrac{1}{4}$ $= \$5,000 - \$125$

$t = \dfrac{90}{360} = \dfrac{1}{4}$ $D = \$125$ $p = \$4,875$

$D = ?$

$p = ?$

(d) September 3 = 246 day
               - 60 days
   Date   = 186 day = July 5

$M = \$3,000$ $D = Mdt$ $p = M - D$

$d = 9\%$ $= \$3,000 \times 0.09 \times \dfrac{1}{6}$ $= \$3,000 - \$45$

$t = \dfrac{60}{360} = \dfrac{1}{6}$ $D = \$45$ $p = \$2,955$

$D = ?$

$p = ?$

4.

	Maturity Value	Discount Rate	Date	Due Date	Time	Bank Discount	Proceeds
(a)	$ 4,500	8%	5/15	8/13	90 days	$ 90	$4,410
(b)	6,200	9	4/10	8/8	120 days	186	6,014
(c)	9,000	10	9/20	10/20	30 days	75	8,925
(d)	10,000	11	5/18	11/14	180 days	550	9,450

4. (Continued)

(a) May 15   =   135 day
                 + 90 days
    Due date =   225 day = August 13

    M = $4,500   D = Mdt   p = M - D
                                          = $4,500 - $90
    d = 8%   = $4,500 × 0.08 × 0.2   p = $4,410

    $t = \frac{90}{360} = \frac{1}{4}$ D = $90

       or 0.25

    D = ?

    p = ?

(b) April 10 =   100 day
                 +120 days
    Due date =   220 day = August 8

    M = $6,200   D = Mdt   p = M - D
                                          = $6,200 - $186
    d = 9%   = $6,200 × 0.09 × $\frac{1}{3}$ p = $6,014

    $t = \frac{120}{360} = \frac{1}{3}$ D = $186

    D = ?

    p = ?

(c) October   20 =   293 day
    September 20 =   -263 day
                      30 days

    M = $9,000   D = Mdt   p = M - D
                                          = $9,000 - $75
    d = 10%   = $9,000 × 0.10 × $\frac{1}{12}$ p = $8,925

    $t = \frac{30}{360} = \frac{1}{12}$ D = $75

    D = ?

    p = ?

4. (Continued)

(d) November 14 = 318 day
$$\underline{-180 \text{ days}}$$
Date = 138 day = May 18

M = \$10,000   D = Mdt   p = M − D
                   = \$10,000 × 0.11 × 0.5   = \$10,000 − \$550
d = 11%   D = \$550   p = \$9,450

$t = \dfrac{180}{360} = 0.5$

D = ?

p = ?

5. (a) M = \$3,650   D = Mdt   p = M − D
                                           = \$3,650 − \$27
   d = 9% $= \$3,650 \times 0.09 \times \dfrac{30}{365}$ p = \$3,623

   $t = \dfrac{30}{365}$ D = \$27

   D = ?

   p = ?

(b) M = \$7,300   D = Mdt   p = M − D
                                        = \$7,300 − \$264
    d = 11% $= \$7,300 \times 0.11 \times \dfrac{120}{365}$ p = \$7,036

    $t = \dfrac{120}{365}$ D = \$264

    D = ?

    p = ?

(c) M = \$1,095   D = Mdt   p = M − D
                                        = \$1,095 − \$40.50
    d = 15% $= \$1,095 \times 0.15 \times \dfrac{90}{365}$ p = \$1,054.50

    $t = \dfrac{90}{365}$ D = \$40.50

    D = ?

    p = ?

6. (a) M = $2,920   D = Mdt   p = M - D
                                                    = $2,920 - $48
       d = 10%   = $2,920 × 0.10 × $\frac{60}{365}$ p = $2,872

       t = $\frac{60}{365}$ D = $48

       D = ?

       p = ?

   (b) M = $4,380   D = Mdt   p = M - D
                                                    = $4,380 - $388.80
       d = 12%   = $4,380 × 0.12 × $\frac{54}{73}$ p = $3,991.20

       t = $\frac{270}{365}$ D = $388.80

         = $\frac{54}{73}$

       D = ?

       p = ?

   (c) M = $14,600   D = Mdt   p = M - D
                                                    = $14,600 - $324
       d = 9%   = $14,600 × 0.09 × $\frac{18}{73}$ p = $14,276

       t = $\frac{90}{365}$ D = $324

         = $\frac{18}{73}$

       D = ?

       p = ?

7.

	Maturity Value	Disc. Rate	Time	Discount	Proceeds	Equiv. Simple Int. Rate
(a)	$4,000	12%	90 days	$120	$3,880	12.5 %
(b)	8,000	15	150	500	7,500	16.0
(c)	7,200	13	120	312	6,888	13.5
(d)	5,400	10	60	90	5,310	10.25

   (a) D = Mdt   p = M - D
                                        = $4,000 - $120
         = $4,000 × 0.12 × $\frac{1}{4}$ p = $3,880

       D = $120

7. (a) (Continued)

$$I = Prt$$

$$\$120 = \$3,880 \cdot r \cdot \frac{1}{4}$$

$$120 = 970r$$

$$0.1237113 = r$$

$$12.5\% = r \text{ (nearest 1/4\%)}$$

(b) $D = Mdt$

$$= \$8,000 \times 0.15 \times \frac{5}{12}$$

$$D = \$500$$

$p = M - D$
$= \$8,000 - \$500$
$p = \$7,500$

$$I = Prt$$

$$\$500 = \$7,500 \cdot r \cdot \frac{5}{12}$$

$$500 = 3,125r$$

$$0.16 = r$$

$$16\% = r$$

(c) $D = Mdt$

$$= \$7,200 \times 0.13 \times \frac{1}{3}$$

$$D = \$312$$

$p = M - D$
$= \$7,200 - \$312$
$p = \$6,888$

$$I = Prt$$

$$\$312 = \$6,888 \cdot r \cdot \frac{1}{3}$$

$$312 = 2,296r$$

$$0.1358885 = r$$

$$13.5\% = r \text{ (nearest 1/4\%)}$$

7. (Continued)

(d) D = Mdt

$$= \$5,400 \times 0.10 \times \frac{1}{6}$$

D = \$90

                p = M − D
                  = \$5,400 − \$90
                p = \$5,310

I = Prt

$$\$90 = \$5,310 \cdot r \cdot \frac{1}{6}$$

90 = 885r

0.1016949 = r

10.25% = r (nearest 1/4%)

8.

	Maturity Value	Disc. Rate	Time	Discount	Proceeds	Equiv. Simple Int. Rate
(a)	$ 6,600	8%	120 days	$176	$ 6,424	8.25%
(b)	12,000	10	270	900	11,100	10.75
(c)	10,000	9	90	225	9,775	9.25
(d)	5,400	7	300	315	5,085	7.50

(a) D = Mdt

$$= \$6,600 \times 0.08 \times \frac{1}{3}$$

D = \$176

                p = M − D
                  = \$6,600 − \$176
                p = \$6,424

I = Prt

$$\$176 = \$6,424 \cdot r \cdot \frac{1}{3}$$

8.219 = r

8.25% = r (nearest 1/4%)

(b) D = Mdt
     = \$12,000 × 0.10 × 0.75
   D = \$900

                p = M − D
                  = \$12,000 − \$900
                p = \$11,100

8. (b) (Continued)

$$I = Prt$$
$$\$900 = \$11,100 \cdot r \cdot 0.75$$
$$0.108108 = r$$
$$10.75\% = r \text{ (nearest 1/4\%)}$$

(c)
$$D = Mdt$$
$$= \$10,000 \times 0.09 \times 0.25$$
$$D = \$225$$

$$p = M - D$$
$$= \$10,000 - \$225$$
$$p = \$9,775$$

$$I = Prt$$
$$\$225 = \$9,775 \cdot r \cdot 0.25$$
$$0.092072 = r$$
$$9.25\% = r \text{ (nearest 1/4\%)}$$

(d)
$$D = Mdt$$
$$= \$5,400 \times 0.07 \times \frac{5}{6}$$
$$D = \$315$$

$$p = M - D$$
$$= \$5,400 - \$315$$
$$p = \$5,085$$

$$I = Prt$$
$$\$315 = \$5,085 \cdot r \cdot \frac{5}{6}$$
$$0.074345 = r$$
$$7.50\% = r \text{ (nearest 1/4\%)}$$

9.

	Maturity Value	Discount Rate	Date	Due Date	Time	Proceeds
(a)	$4,320	14%	1/9	6/9	5 mos.	$4,066.32
(b)	6,000	9	10/3	12/3	2 mos.	5,908.50
(c)	6,500	12	3/17	6/15	90 days	6,305.00
(d)	9,000	10	5/20	11/16	180 days	8,550.00

(a)
$$D = Mdt$$
$$= \$4,320 \times 0.14 \times \frac{151}{360}$$
$$D = \$253.68$$

$$p = M - D$$
$$= \$4,320.00 - \$253.68$$
$$p = \$4,066.32$$

-439-

9. (Continued)

(b) $D = Mdt$

$ = \$6,000 \times 0.09 \times \dfrac{61}{360}$

$D = \$91.50$

 $p = M - D$
$ = \$6,000.00 - \$91.50$
$p = \$5,908.50$

(c) $D = Mdt$
$ = \$6,500 \times 0.12 \times 0.25$
$D = \$195$

 $p = M - D$
$ = \$6,500 - \$195$
$p = \$6,305$

(d) $D = Mdt$
$ = \$9,000 \times 0.10 \times 0.50$
$D = \$450$

 $p = M - D$
$ = \$9,000 - \$450$
$p = \$8,550$

10.

	Maturity Value	Discount Rate	Date	Due Date	Time	Proceeds
(a)	$7,500	8%	2/19	6/19	4 mos.	$7,300
(b)	2,000	6	11/15	12/15	1 mo.	1,990
(c)	5,600	9	8/1	11/29	120 days	5,432
(d)	4,200	10	9/5	11/4	60 days	4,130

(a) $D = Mdt$

$ = \$7,500 \times 0.08 \times \dfrac{1}{3}$

$D = \$200$

 $p = M - D$
$ = \$7,500 - \$200$
$p = \$7,300$

(b) $D = Mdt$

$ = \$2,000 \times 0.06 \times \dfrac{1}{12}$

$D = \$10$

 $p = M - D$
$ = \$2,000 - \$10$
$p = \$1,990$

(c) $D = Mdt$

$ = \$5,600 \times 0.09 \times \dfrac{1}{3}$

$D = \$168$

 $p = M - D$
$ = \$5,600 - \$168$
$p = \$5,432$

(d) $D = Mdt$

$ = \$4,200 \times 0.10 \times \dfrac{1}{6}$

$D = \$70$

 $p = M - D$
$ = \$4,200 - \$70$
$p = \$4,130$

11. M = $10,000

    d = 11%

    $t = \dfrac{90}{360} = 0.25$

    D = Mdt

      = $10,000 × 0.11 × 0.25

    D = $275

    p = M − D

      = $10,000 − $275

    p = $9,725

12. M = $4,000

    d = 9%

    $t = \dfrac{60}{360} = \dfrac{1}{6}$

    p = ?

    D = Mdt

      $= \$4,000 × 0.09 × \dfrac{1}{6}$

    D = $60

    p = M − D

      = $4,000 − $60

    p = $3,940

13. D = $156

    M = $7,800

    d = 8%

    t = ?

    D = Mdt

    $156 = $7,800 × 0.08 × t

    156 = 624t

    $\dfrac{1}{4} = t$

    $\dfrac{1}{4}$ of 12 mos. = 3 mos. or

    90 days

14. D = $70

    M = $3,500

    d = 12%

    t = ?

    D = Mdt

    $70 = $3,500 × 0.12 × t

    70 = 420t

    $\dfrac{1}{6} = t$

    $\dfrac{1}{6}$ × 12 mos. = 2 mos. or

    $\dfrac{1}{6}$ × 360 days = 60 days

15. D = $9,400 - $8,554 = $846   D = Mdt

    M = $9,400 $846 = $9,400 × d × 0.75

    d = ?   846 = 7,050d

    $t = \frac{270}{360} = \frac{3}{4} = 0.75$ 12% = d

16. D = $15,000 - $14,550 = $450   D = Mdt

    M = $15,000 $450 = $15,000 × d × $\frac{1}{3}$

    d = ?   450 = 5,000d

    $t = \frac{120}{360} = \frac{1}{3}$ 9% = d

17. April   4 = 94 day
    January   4 = - 4 day
                  90 days

    M = $6,000   D = Mdt   p = M - D
                      = $6,000 × 0.13 × 0.25   = $6,000 - $195
    D = ?   D = $195   p = $5,805

    d = 13%

    $t = \frac{90}{360} = 0.25$

    p = ?

18. June   20 = 171 day
    February 20 = - 51 day
                   90 days

    M = $9,000   D = Mdt   p = M - D
                                                = $9,000 - $240
    D = ?   = $9,000 × 0.08 × $\frac{1}{3}$ p = $8,760

    d = 8%   D = $240

    $t = \frac{120}{360} = \frac{1}{3}$

    p = ?

19.　M = \$3,000

　　d/r = 9%

　　t = $\frac{6}{12}$ = 0.50

Simple interest note:
$$M = P(1 + rt)$$

　　\$3,000 = $P(1 + .09 \cdot 0.50)$

　　3,000 = $P(1 + 0.045)$

　　3,000 = $P(1.045)$

　\$2,870.81 = P (present value)

Simple discount note:
$$p = M(1 - dt)$$

　= \$3,000$(1 - .09 \cdot 0.5)$

　=　3,000$(1 - 0.045)$

　=　3,000(0.9555)

p = \$2,865

20.　M = \$6,000

　　d/r = 12%

　　t = $\frac{4}{12}$ = $\frac{1}{3}$

Simple interest note:
$$M = P(1 + rt)$$

　\$6,000 = $P\left(1 + 0.12 \cdot \frac{1}{3}\right)$

　　6,000 = $P(1.04)$

　\$5,769.23 = P (present value)

Simple discount note:
$$p = M(1 - dt)$$

　= \$6,000$\left(1 - 0.12 \cdot \frac{1}{3}\right)$

　=　6,000(0.96)

p = \$5,760

21. M = \$54,750

　　d = ?

　　t = $\frac{60}{365}$

　　D = \$54,750 - \$53,940 = \$810

　　p = \$53,940

　　　　　　D = Mdt

　\$810 = \$54,750 × d × $\frac{60}{365}$

　　810 = 9,000d

　　9% = d

22. M = $40,150

    d = ?

    $t = \dfrac{30}{365} = \dfrac{6}{73}$

    D = $40,150 - $39,886 = $264

    p = $39,886

                             D = Mdt

                 $\$264 = \$40,150 \times d \times \dfrac{6}{73}$

                   264 = 3,300d

                    8% = d

23. M = $10,000

    d = 10%

    $t = \dfrac{26 \times 7}{360} = \dfrac{182}{360} = \dfrac{91}{180}$

    D = ?

    p = ?

    (b) $10,000

    (a) $p = M(1 - dt)$

           $= \$10,000\left(1 - 0.10 \cdot \dfrac{91}{180}\right)$

           $= 10,000(1 - 0.0505555)$

           $= 10,000(0.9494445)$

      $p = \$9,494.44$

    (c) D = M - p

          = $10,000.00 - $9,494.44

        D = $505.56

24. M = $20,000

    d = 9%

    $t = \dfrac{13 \times 7}{360} = \dfrac{91}{360} = \dfrac{91}{360}$

    D = ?

    p = ?

    (b) $20,000

    (a) $p = M(1 - dt)$

           $= \$20,000\left(1 - 0.09 \cdot \dfrac{91}{360}\right)$

           $= 20,000(1 - 0.02275)$

           $= 20,000(0.97725)$

      $p = \$19,545$

    (c) D = M - p

          = $20,000 - $19,545

        D = $455

Section 2, page 424

1.

	Proceeds	Discount Rate	Date	Due Date	Time	Maturity Value
(a)	$6,860	12%	10/18	12/17	60 days	$7,000
(b)	1,925	9	6/1	10/29	150 days	2,000
(c)	8,721	18	7/9	9/9	2 mos.	9,000
(d)	4,275	15	2/25	6/25	4 mos.	4,500

(a) October 18 = 291 day
$$ + 60 \text{ days}$$
Due date = 351 day = December 17

$$p = M(1 - dt)$$

$$\$6,860 = M\left(1 - 0.12 \cdot \frac{1}{6}\right)$$

$$6,860 = M(1 - 0.02)$$

$$6,860 = M(0.98)$$

$$\$7,000 = M$$

(b) June 1 = 152 day
$$ +150 \text{ days}$$
Due date = 302 day = October 29

$$p = M(1 - dt)$$

$$\$1,925 = M\left(1 - 0.09 \cdot \frac{5}{12}\right)$$

$$1,925 = M(1 - 0.0375)$$

$$1,925 = M(0.9625)$$

$$\$2,000 = M$$

(c) September 9 = 252 day
July 9 = −190 day
$$ 62 \text{ days}$$

1. (c) (Continued)

$$p = M(1 - dt)$$

$$\$8,721 = M\left(1 - 0.18 \cdot \frac{31}{180}\right)$$

$$8,721 = M(1 - 0.031)$$

$$8,721 = M(0.969)$$

$$\$9,000 = M$$

(d) June   25 =   176 day
     February 25 = $\underline{- 56 \text{ day}}$
                    120 days

$$p = M(1 - dt)$$

$$\$4,275 = M\left(1 - 0.15 \cdot \frac{1}{3}\right)$$

$$4,275 = M(1 - 0.05)$$

$$4,275 = M(0.95)$$

$$\$4,500 = M$$

2.

	Proceeds	Discount Rate	Date	Due Date	Time	Maturity Value
(a)	$17,595	9%	8/14	11/12	90 days	$18,000
(b)	14,700	12	9/7	11/6	60 days	15,000
(c)	5,220	10	2/5	6/5	4 mos.	5,400
(d)	19,750	15	6/25	7/25	1 mo.	20,000

(a) August 14 =   226 day
                $\underline{+ 90 \text{ days}}$
     Due date =   316 day = November 12

$$p = M(1 - dt)$$
$$\$17,595 = M(1 - 0.09 \cdot 0.25)$$
$$17,595 = M(1 - 0.0225)$$
$$17,595 = M(0.9775)$$
$$\$18,000 = M$$

(b) September 7 =   250 day
                 $\underline{+ 60 \text{ days}}$
     Due date   =   310 day = November 6

2. (b) (Continued)

$$p = M(1 - dt)$$

$$\$14,700 = M\left(1 - 0.12 \cdot \frac{1}{6}\right)$$

$$14,700 = M(1 - 0.02)$$

$$14,700 = M(0.98)$$

$$\$15,000 = M$$

(c) June   5 =   156 day
     February 5 = - 36 day
                    120 days

$$p = M(1 - dt)$$

$$\$5,220 = M\left(1 - 0.10 \cdot \frac{1}{3}\right)$$

$$5,220 = M(1 - 0.033333)$$

$$5,220 = M(0.966667)$$

$$\$5,400 = M$$

(d) July 25 =   206 day
     June 25 = -176 day
                   30 days

$$p = M(1 - dt)$$

$$\$19,750 = M\left(1 - 0.15 \cdot \frac{1}{12}\right)$$

$$19,750 = M(1 - 0.0125)$$

$$19,750 = M(0.9875)$$

$$\$20,000 = M$$

3.

		Original Note			Rediscounted Note			
	Maturity	Rate	Time	Proceeds	Rate	Time	Proceeds	Net Interest Earned
(a)	$7,600	13%	270 da	$6,859	14%	90 da	$7,334.00	$475.00
(b)	8,500	9	120 da	8,245	10	30 da	8,429.17	184.17
(c)	6,400	14	90 da	6,176	12	60 da	6,272.00	96.00

3. (Continued)

(a) Original Note:
$$D = \$7,600 \times 0.13 \times 0.75$$
$$D = \$741$$

$$p = \$7,600 - \$741$$
$$p = \$6,859$$

Rediscounted Note:
$$D = \$7,600 \times 0.14 \times 0.25$$
$$D = \$266$$

$$p = \$7,600 - \$266$$
$$p = \$7,334$$

Net interest earned = $7,334 - $6,859 = $475

(b) Original Note:
$$D = \$8,500 \times 0.09 \times \frac{1}{3}$$

$$D = \$255$$

$$p = \$8,500 - \$255$$
$$p = \$8,245$$

Rediscounted Note:
$$D = \$8,500 \times 0.10 \times \frac{1}{12}$$

$$D = \$70.83$$

$$p = \$8,500.00 - \$70.83$$
$$p = \$8,429.17$$

Net interest earned = $8,429.17 - $8,245.00 = $184.17

(c) Original Note:
$$D = \$6,400 \times 0.14 \times 0.25$$

$$D = \$224$$

$$p = \$6,400 - \$224$$
$$p = \$6,176$$

Rediscounted Note:
$$D = \$6,400 \times 0.12 \times \frac{1}{6}$$

$$D = \$128$$

$$p = \$6,400 - \$128$$
$$p = \$6,272$$

Net interest earned = $6,272 - $6,176 = $96

4.

		Original Note			Rediscounted Note			
	Maturity	Rate	Time	Proceeds	Rate	Time	Proceeds	Net Interest Earned
(a)	$10,000	7.5%	120 da	$ 9,750	6.5%	45 da	$ 9,918.75	$168.75
(b)	12,000	9	150 da	11,550	8	60 da	11,840.00	290.00
(c)	9,000	10	300 da	8,250	12	120 da	8,640.00	390.00

(a) Original Note:
$$D = \$10,000 \times 0.075 \times \frac{1}{3}$$

$$D = \$250$$

Rediscounted Note:
$$D = \$10,000 \times 0.065 \times \frac{1}{8}$$

$$D = \$81.25$$

4. (a) (Continued)

p = \$10,000 - \$250   p = \$10,000.00 - \$81.25
p = \$9,750   p = \$9,918.75

Net interest earned = \$9,918.75 - \$9,750.00 = \$168.75

(b) <u>Original Note:</u>   <u>Rediscounted Note:</u>

$D = \$12,000 \times 0.09 \times \frac{5}{12}$ $D = \$12,000 \times 0.08 \times \frac{1}{6}$

D = \$450   D = \$160

p = \$12,000 - \$450   p = \$12,000 - \$160
p = \$11,550   p = \$11,840

Net interest earned = \$11,840 - \$11,550 = \$290

(c) <u>Original Note:</u>   <u>Rediscounted Note:</u>

$D = \$9,000 \times 0.10 \times \frac{5}{6}$ $D = \$9,000 \times 0.12 \times \frac{1}{3}$

D = \$750   D = \$360

p = \$9,000 - \$750   p = \$9,000 - \$360
p = \$8,250   p = \$8,640

Net interest earned = \$8,640 - \$8,250 = \$390

5. (a) <u>Simple Interest Note:</u>   <u>Discounted Note:</u>
P = \$1,600   M = \$1,660

r = 15%   d = 12%

$t = \frac{90}{360} = 0.25$ $t = \frac{30}{360} = \frac{1}{12}$

I = Prt   D = Mdt

= \$1,600 × 0.15 × 0.25 $= \$1,660 \times 0.12 \times \frac{1}{12}$

I = \$60   D = \$16.60

M = P + I   p = M - D
= \$1,600 + \$60   = \$1,660.00 - \$16.60
M = \$1,660   p = \$1,643.40

5. (a) (Continued)

Net interest earned = $1,643.40 - $1,600.00 = $43.40

(b) <u>Simple Interest Note:</u>   <u>Discounted Note:</u>
P = $8,000   M = $8,400

r = 12%   d = 10%

$$t = \frac{150}{360} = \frac{5}{12} \qquad\qquad t = \frac{45}{360} = \frac{1}{8}$$

I = Prt   D = Mdt

$$\quad = \$8,000 \times 0.12 \times \frac{5}{12} \qquad\quad = \$8,400 \times 0.10 \times \frac{1}{8}$$

I = $400   D = $105

M = P + I   p = M − D
  = $8,000 + $400   = $8,400 − $105
M = $8,400   p = $8,295

Net interest earned = $8,295 − $8,000 = $295

6. (a) <u>Simple Interest Note:</u>   <u>Discounted Note:</u>
P = $4,000   M = $4,180

r = 9%   d = 8%

$$t = \frac{180}{360} = 0.5 \qquad\qquad t = \frac{45}{360} = \frac{1}{8}$$

I = Prt   D = Mdt

$$\quad = \$4,000 \times 0.09 \times 0.5 \qquad\quad = \$4,180 \times 0.08 \times \frac{1}{8}$$

I = $180   D = $41.80

M = P + I   p = M − D
  = $4,000 + $180   = $4,180.00 − $41.80
M = $4,180   p = $4,138.20

Net interest earned = $4,138.20 − $4,000.00 = $138.20

6. (Continued)

(b) Simple Interest Note:
P = $1,500

r = 6%

$t = \dfrac{60}{360} = \dfrac{1}{6}$

I = Prt

$= \$1,500 \times 0.06 \times \dfrac{1}{6}$

I = $15

M = P + I
= $1,500 + $15
M = $1,515

Discounted Note:
M = $1,515

d = 7.5%

$t = \dfrac{20}{360} = \dfrac{1}{18}$

D = Mdt

$= \$1,515 \times 0.075 \times \dfrac{1}{18}$

D = $6.31

p = M − D
= $1,515.00 − $6.31
p = $1,508.69

Net interest earned = $1,508.69 − $1,500.00 = $8.69

7. May   10 = 130 day
   January 10 = − 10 day
                120 days

p = $3,800

d = 15%

$t = \dfrac{120}{360} = \dfrac{1}{3}$

M = ?

$p = M(1 - dt)$

$\$3,800 = M\left(1 - 0.15 \cdot \dfrac{1}{3}\right)$

$3,800 = M(1 - 0.05)$

$3,800 = M(0.95)$

$\$4,000 = M$

8. December 16 = 350 day
   November 16 = −320 day
                  30 days

8. (Continued)

p = $15,840

d = 12%

$t = \dfrac{30}{360} = \dfrac{1}{12}$

M = ?

$$p = M(1 - dt)$$

$$\$15,800 = M\left(1 - 0.12 \cdot \dfrac{1}{12}\right)$$

$$15,800 = M(1 - 0.01)$$

$$15,800 = M(0.99)$$

$$\$16,000 = M$$

9. July   20 = 201 day
    February 20 = - 51 day
                  150 days

p = $8,470

d = 9%

$t = \dfrac{150}{360} = \dfrac{5}{12}$

M = ?

$$p = M(1 - dt)$$

$$\$8,470 = M\left(1 - 0.09 \cdot \dfrac{5}{12}\right)$$

$$8,470 = M(1 - 0.0375)$$

$$8,470 = M(0.9625)$$

$$\$8,800 = M$$

10. May   15 = 135 day
    March 15 = + 74 day
                61 days

p = $6,381.18

d = 9%

$t = \dfrac{61}{360}$

M = ?

$$p = M(1 - dt)$$

$$\$6,381.18 = M\left(1 - 0.09 \cdot \dfrac{61}{360}\right)$$

$$6,381.18 = M(1 - 0.01525)$$

$$6,381.18 = M(0.98475)$$

$$\$6,480 = M$$

11. June 3   = 154 day
               + 90 days
    Due date = 244 day = September 1

11. (Continued)

(a) M = $20,000   D = Mdt   p = M - D

d = 16%   = $20,000 × 0.16 × 0.25   = $20,000 - $800

$t = \frac{90}{360} = 0.25$ D = $800   p = $19,200

September 1 = 244 day
                 - 30 days
Due date   = 214 day = August 2

(b) M = $20,000   D = Mdt   p = M - D

d = 15% $= \$20,000 \times 0.15 \times \frac{1}{12}$ = $20,000 - $250

$t = \frac{30}{360} = \frac{1}{12}$ D = $250   p = $19,750

(c) Cullman National made $19,750 - $19,200 = $550

(d) $800 - $550 = $250 (or $20,000 - $19,750 = $250)

12. August 16 = 228 day
              +120 days
Due date = 348 day = December 14

(a) M = $60,000   D = Mdt   p = M - D
                                            = $60,000 - $2,000

d = 10% $= \$60,000 \times 0.10 \times \frac{1}{3}$ p = $58,000

$t = \frac{120}{360} = \frac{1}{3}$ D = $2,000

December 14 = 348 day
November 14 = -318 day
                 30 days

(b) M = $60,000   D = Mdt   p = M - D
                                            = $60,000 - $450

d = 9% $= \$60,000 \times 0.09 \times \frac{1}{12}$ p = $59,550

$t = \frac{30}{360} = \frac{1}{12}$ D = $450

(c) Tri State Bank made $59,550 - $58,000 = $1,550

12. (Continued)

(d) Tri State Bank could have made $450 more

13. (a) March 16 =   75 day
                    +120 days
    Due date =   195 day = July 14

    P = $9,000   I = Prt   M = P + I
                                                  = $9,000 + $420
    r = 14%   = $9,000 × 0.14 × $\frac{1}{3}$ M = $9,420

    t = $\frac{120}{360}$ = $\frac{1}{3}$ I = $420

    July 14 = 195 day
    May   15 = -135 day
               60 days

    M = $9,420   D = Mdt   p = M - D
                                                  = $9,420 - $188.40
    d = 12%   = $9,420 × 0.12 × $\frac{1}{6}$ p = $9,231.60

    t = $\frac{60}{360}$ = $\frac{1}{6}$ D = $188.40

(b) $9,231.60 - $9,000.00 = $231.60

(c) $420.00 - $231.60 = $188.40 (or $9,420.00 - $9,231.60 = $188.40)

14. (a) September 1 =   244 day
                     + 90 days
    Due date   =   334 day = November 30

    P = $18,000   I = Prt
                                     = $18,000 × 0.07 × 0.25
    r = 7%   I = $315

    t = $\frac{90}{360}$ = 0.25

    M = P + I
      = $18,000 + $315
    M = $18,315

14. (a) (Continued)

    November 30 = 334 day
    November 10 = $\underline{-314}$ day
     20 days

$M = \$18,315$ $\qquad\qquad$ $D = Mdt$

$d = 9\%$ $\qquad\qquad\qquad\qquad$ $= \$18,315 \times 0.09 \times \dfrac{1}{18}$

$t = \dfrac{20}{360} = \dfrac{1}{18}$ $\qquad\qquad\quad$ $D = \$91.58$

$p = M - D$
$ = \$18,315.00 - \$91.58$
$p = \$18,223.42$

(b) $\$18,223.42 - \$18,000.00 = \$223.42$

(d) $\$18,315.00 - \$18,223.42 = \$91.58$

15. (a) June 25 $\quad=$ $\quad$ 176 day
     $\underline{+120}$ days
    Due date $=$ $\quad$ 296 day $=$ October 23

$M = \$6,300$ $\quad$ $D_1 = Mdt$ $\qquad\qquad$ $p_1 = M - D$
 $\qquad\qquad\qquad\qquad$ $ = \$6,300 - \$210$
$d = 10\%$ $\qquad$ $= \$6,300 \times 0.10 \times \dfrac{1}{3}$ $\quad$ $p_1 = \$6,090$

$t = \dfrac{120}{360} = \dfrac{1}{3}$ $\quad$ $D_1 = \$210$

(b) October 23 $=$ $\quad$ 296 day
    July $\quad$ 25 $=$ $\underline{-206}$ day
     90 days

$M = \$6,300$ $\quad$ $D_2 = Mdt$ $\qquad\qquad$ $p_2 = M - D$
 $= \$6,300 \times 0.09 \times 0.25$ $\quad$ $ = \$6,300 - \$141.75$
$d = 9\%$ $\qquad$ $D_2 = \$141.75$ $\qquad\qquad$ $p_2 = \$6,158.25$

$t = \dfrac{90}{360} = 0.25$

(c) Radford earned $\$6,158.25 - \$6,090.00 = \$68.25$

(d) Radford lost $\$210.00 - \$68.25 = \$141.75$

16. (a) February 24 =   55 day
                     +300 days
    Due date   = 355 day = December 21

    M = $24,000   D_1 = Mdt

    d = 9%   = $24,000 × 0.09 × $\frac{5}{6}$

    $t = \frac{300}{360} = \frac{5}{6}$ D_1 = $1,800

    p_1 = M − D
       = $24,000 − $1,800
    p_1 = $22,200

(b) December 21 = 355 day
    September 22 = −265 day
                    90 days

    M = $24,000 D_2 = Mdt
                                  = $24,000 × 0.08 × 0.25
    d = 8% D_2 = $480

    $t = \frac{90}{360} = 0.25$

    p_2 = M − D
       = $24,000 − $480
    p_2 = $23,520

(c) $23,520 − $22,200 = $1,320

(d) D_2 = $480

17. (a) May 13   = 133 day   P = $4,200
                  + 90 days
    Due date = 223 day = Aug. 11   r = 12%

                                     $t = \frac{90}{360} = 0.25$

    I = Prt   M = P + I
      = $4,200 × 0.12 × 0.25   = $4,200 + $126
    I = $126   M = $4,326

17. (a) (Continued)

Aug. 11 = 223 day $M = \$4,326$

June 22 = -173 day $d = 11\%$

         50 days $t = \dfrac{50}{365} = \dfrac{10}{73}$

$D = Mdt$

$\quad = \$4,326 \times 0.11 \times \dfrac{10}{73}$

$D = \$65.19$

$p = M - D$

$\quad = \$4,326.00 - \$65.19$

$p = \$4,260.81$

(b) $\$4,260.81 - \$4,200.00 = \$60.81$

(c) $\$4,326.00 - \$4,260.81 = \$65.19$

18. (a) April 6 =   96 day $P = \$30,000$

           +150 days $r = 10\%$

Due date = 223 day = Sept. 3 $t = \dfrac{150}{360} = \dfrac{5}{12}$

$I = Prt$

$\quad = \$30,000 \times 0.10 \times \dfrac{5}{12}$

$I = \$1,250$

$M = P + I$

$\quad = \$30,000 + \$1,250$

$M = \$31,250$

September 3 = 246 day $M = \$31,250$

July   20 = -201 day $d = 8.5\%$

          45 days $t = \dfrac{45}{365} = \dfrac{9}{73}$

$D = Mdt$

$\quad = \$31,250 \times 0.085 \times \dfrac{9}{73}$

$D = \$327.48$

$p = M - D$

$\quad = \$31,250.00 - \$327.48$

$p = \$30,922.52$

18. (Continued)

(b) $30,922.52 - $30,000.00 = $922.52

(c) D = $327.48

Section 3, page 428

Amount of Invoice	Sales Terms	Amount Needed (Proceeds)	Time of Note	Discount Rate	Face Value of Note	Amount Saved
1. (a) $6,404.64	3/10,N/30	$6,212.50	20 da	9%	$6,243.72	$160.92
(b) 7,614.80	2/15,N/30	7,462.50	15 da	12	7,500.00	114.80
(c) 4,242.86	2/15,N/30	4,158.00	45 da	8	4,200.00	42.86

(a)
$$\% \text{ Pd} \times L = N$$
$$0.97(\$6,404.64) =$$
$$\$6,212.50 = N$$

$$p = M(1 - dt)$$
$$\$6,212.50 = M\left(1 - 0.09 \cdot \frac{1}{18}\right)$$
$$6,212.50 = M(1 - 0.005)$$
$$6,212.50 = M(0.995)$$
$$\$6,243.72 = M$$

$6,404.64 Amount of invoice
-6,243.72 Face value of note
$ 160.92 Savings

(b)
$$\% \text{ Pd} \times L = N$$
$$0.98(\$7,614.80) =$$
$$\$7,462.50 = N$$

$$p = M(1 - dt)$$
$$\$7,462.50 = M\left(1 - 0.12 \cdot \frac{1}{24}\right)$$
$$7,462.50 = M(1 - 0.005)$$
$$7,462.50 = M(0.995)$$
$$\$7,500 = M$$

$7,614.80 Amount of invoice
-7,500.00 Face value of note
$ 114.80 Savings

1. (Continued)

(c)
$$0.98(\$4,242.86) = $$
$$\$4,158 = N$$

$$p = M(1 - dt)$$

$$\$4,158 = M\left(1 - 0.08 \cdot \frac{1}{8}\right)$$

$$4,158 = M(1 - 0.01)$$

$$4,158 = M(0.99)$$

$$\$4,200 = M$$

$\$4,242.86$ Amount of invoice
$\underline{-4,200.00}$ Face value of note
$\$\quad 42.86$ Savings

	Amount of Invoice	Sales Terms	Amount Needed (Proceeds)	Time of Note	Discount Rate	Face Value of Note	Amount Saved
2. (a)	$ 5,051.02	2/10,N/30	$4,950.00	20 da	18%	$ 5,000	$ 51.02
(b)	8,206.19	3/15,N/30	7,960.00	15 da	12	8,000	206.19
(c)	10,193.30	3/15,N/60	9,887.50	45 da	9	10,000	193.30

(a)
$$0.98(\$5,051.02) = $$
$$\$4,950 = N$$

$$p = M(1 - dt)$$

$$\$4,950 = M\left(1 - 0.18 \cdot \frac{1}{18}\right)$$

$$4,950 = M(1 - 0.01)$$

$$4,950 = M(0.99)$$

$$\$5,000 = M$$

$\$5,051.02$ Amount of invoice
$\underline{-5,000.00}$ Face value of note
$\$\quad 51.02$ Savings

(b)
$$0.97(\$8,206.19) = $$
$$\$7,960 = N$$

$$p = M(1 - dt)$$

$$\$7,960 = M\left(1 - 0.12 \cdot \frac{1}{24}\right)$$

$$7,960 = M(1 - 0.005)$$

$$7,960 = M(0.995)$$

$$\$8,000 = M$$

2. (b) (Continued)

$8,206.19 Amount of invoice
-8,000.00 Face value of note
$ 206.19 Savings

(c)   % Pd × L = N $p = M(1 - dt)$
0.97($10,193.30) =
$9,887.50 = N $\$9,887.50 = M\left(1 - 0.09 \cdot \dfrac{1}{8}\right)$

$$9,887.50 = M(1 - 0.01125)$$

$$9,887.50 = M(0.98875)$$

$$\$10,000 = M$$

$10,193.30 Amount of invoice
-10,000.00 Face value of note
$ 193.30 Savings

3. (a)   % Pd × L = N $p = M(1 - dt)$
0.97($5,613.40) =
$5,445 = N $\$5,445 = M\left(1 - 0.18 \cdot \dfrac{1}{18}\right)$

$$5,445 = M(1 - 0.01)$$

$$5,445 = M(0.99)$$

$$\$5,500 = M$$

(b) $5,613.40 Amount of invoice
-5,500.00 Face value of note
$ 113.40 Savings

4. (a)   % Pd × L = N $p = M(1 - dt)$
0.97($16,432.99) =
$15,940 = N $\$15,940 = M\left(1 - 0.09 \cdot \dfrac{1}{24}\right)$

$$15,940 = M(1 - 0.00375)$$

$$15,940 = M(0.99625)$$

$$\$16,000 = M$$

(b) $16,432.99 Amount of invoice
-16,000.00 Face value of note
$ 432.99 Savings

5. (a)
$$\% \text{ Pd} \times L = N$$
$$0.97(\$3,073.45) =$$
$$\$2,981.25 = N$$

$$p = M(1 - dt)$$
$$\$2,981.25 = M\left(1 - 0.15 \cdot \frac{1}{24}\right)$$
$$2,981.25 = M(1 - 0.00625)$$
$$2,981.25 = M(0.99375)$$
$$\$3,000 = M$$

(b) $3,073.45 Amount of invoice
 <u>-3,000.00</u> Face value of note
 $ 73.45 Savings

6. (a)
$$\% \text{ Pd} \times L = N$$
$$0.98(\$20,153.06) =$$
$$\$19,750 = N$$

$$p = M(1 - dt)$$
$$\$19,750 = M\left(1 - 0.09 \cdot \frac{5}{36}\right)$$
$$19,750 = M(1 - 0.0125)$$
$$19,750 = M(0.9875)$$
$$\$20,000 = M$$

(b) $20,153.06 Amount of invoice
 <u>-20,000.00</u> Face value of note
 $ 153.06 Savings

7. (a)
$$\% \text{ Pd} \times L = N$$
$$0.96(\$9,259.11) =$$
$$\$8,888.75 = N$$

$8,888.75 Net cost of mdse.
<u>+   21.25</u> Freight
$8,910.00 Proceeds

$$p = M(1 - dt)$$
$$\$8,910 = M\left(1 - 0.09 \cdot \frac{1}{9}\right)$$
$$8,910 = M(1 - 0.01)$$
$$8,910 = M(0.99)$$
$$\$9,000 = M$$

(b) $9,259.11 Merchandise
 <u>+   21.25</u> Freight
 $9,280.36 Amt. of invoice
 <u>-9,000.00</u> Face value of note
 $ 280.36 Savings

8. (a)   % Pd × L = N
          0.98($4,020.41) =
                         $3,940 = N

$$p = M(1 - dt)$$

$$\$3,980 = M\left(1 - 0.06 \cdot \frac{1}{12}\right)$$

$$3,980 = M(1 - 0.005)$$

$$3,980 = M(0.995)$$

$$\$4,000 = M$$

$3,940 Net cost of mdse.
+   40 Freight
$3,980 Proceeds

(b) $4,020.41 Merchandise
+   40.00 Freight
$4,060.41 Amt. of invoice
-4,000.00 Face value of note
$ 60.41 Savings

9. (a)   % Pd × L = N
          0.98($2,715) =
                         $2,660.70 = N

$$p = M(1 - dt)$$

$$\$2,679 = M\left(1 - 0.14 \cdot \frac{1}{18}\right)$$

$$2,679 = M(1 - 0.007778)$$

$$2,679 = M(0.992222)$$

$$\$2,700 = M$$

$2,660.70 Net cost of mdse.
+   18.30 Freight
$2,679.00 Proceeds

(b) $2,715.00 Merchandise
+   18.30 Freight
$2,733.30 Amt. of invoice
-2,700.00 Face value of note
$ 33.30 Savings

10. (a)   % Pd × L = N
          0.96($5,093.75) =
                         $4,890 = N

$$p = M(1 - dt)$$

$$\$4,950 = M\left(1 - 0.12 \cdot \frac{1}{12}\right)$$

$$4,950 = M(1 - 0.01)$$

$$4,950 = M(0.99)$$

$$\$5,000 = M$$

$4,890 Net cost of mdse.
+   60 Freight
$4,950 Proceeds

(b) $5,093.75 Merchandise
+   60.00 Freight
$5,153.75 Amt. of invoice
-5,000.00 Face value of note
$ 153.75 Savings

Section 4, page 431

1. $P = \$5,000$

    $r = 11\%$

    $t = \dfrac{45}{360} = \dfrac{1}{8}$

    $I = Prt$

    $ = \$5,000 \times 0.11 \times \dfrac{1}{8}$

    $I = \$68.75$

    $M = P + I$
    $ = \$5,000.00 + \$68.75$
    $M = \$5,068.75$

2. $P = \$4,500$

    $r = 8.5\%$

    $t = \dfrac{120}{360} = \dfrac{1}{3}$

    $I = Prt$

    $ = \$4,500 \times 0.085 \times \dfrac{1}{3}$

    $I = \$127.50$

    $M = P + I$
    $ = \$4,500.00 + \$127.50$
    $M = \$4,627.50$

3. $M = \$3,960$

    $d = 10\%$

    $t = \dfrac{40}{360} = \dfrac{1}{9}$

    $D = Mdt$

    $ = \$3,960 \times 0.10 \times \dfrac{1}{9}$

    $D = \$44$

    $p = M - D$
    $ = \$3,960 - \$44$
    $p = \$3,916$

4. $M = \$9,000$

    $d = 11\%$

    $t = \dfrac{270}{360} = 0.75$

    $D = Mdt$

    $ = \$9,000 \times 0.11 \times 0.75$

    $D = \$742.50$

    $p = M - D$
    $ = \$9,000.00 - \$742.50$
    $p = \$8,257.50$

5. (a) <u>Interest Note:</u>
    $P = \$1,600$

    $r = 15\%$

    $t = \dfrac{120}{360} = \dfrac{1}{3}$

<u>Discount Note:</u>
$M = \$1,600$

$d = 15\%$

$t = \dfrac{120}{360} = \dfrac{1}{3}$

5. (a) (Continued)

Interest Note:	Discount Note:
$I = Prt$	$D = Mdt$
$= \$1,600 \times 0.15 \times \dfrac{1}{3}$	$= \$1,600 \times 0.15 \times \dfrac{1}{3}$
$I = \$80$	$D = \$80$

(b) Amount received: Interest note = $1,600
Discount note = $1,600 - $80 = $1,520

(c) Maturity value: Interest note = $1,600 + $80 = $1,680
Discount note = $1,600

6. (a)

Interest Note:	Discount Note:
$P = \$10,800$	$M = \$10,800$
$r = 7\%$	$d = 7\%$
$t = \dfrac{90}{360} = 0.25$	$t = \dfrac{90}{360} = 0.25$
$I = Prt$	$D = Mdt$
$= \$10,800 \times 0.07 \times 0.25$	$= \$10,800 \times 0.07 \times 0.25$
$I = \$189$	$D = \$189$

(b) Amount received: Interest note = $10,800
Discount note = $10,800 - $189 = $10,611

(c) Maturity value: Interest note = $10,800 + $189 = $10,989
Discount note = $10,800

7. (a) p = $2,352

d = 12%

$t = \dfrac{60}{360} = \dfrac{1}{6}$

M = ?

$$M = \frac{p}{1 - dt}$$

$$= \frac{\$2,352}{1 - 0.12 \cdot \dfrac{1}{6}}$$

$$= \frac{2,352}{1 - 0.02}$$

$$= \frac{2,352}{0.98}$$

$$M = \$2,400$$

7. (Continued)

(b) $2,400 = Maturity value = face value

8. (a) p = $11,910

d = 9%

$t = \dfrac{30}{360} = \dfrac{1}{12}$

M = ?

$M = \dfrac{p}{1 - dt}$

$= \dfrac{\$11,910}{1 - 0.09 \cdot \dfrac{1}{12}}$

$= \dfrac{11,910}{1 - 0.0075}$

$= \dfrac{11,910}{0.9925}$

$M = \$12,000$

(b) $12,000 = Maturity value = face value

9. (a) M = $4,190

r = 9.5%

$t = \dfrac{180}{360} = 0.50$

P = ?

$M = P(1 + rt)$

$\$4,190 = P(1 + 0.095 \cdot 0.50)$

$4,190 = P(1 + 0.0475)$

$4,190 = P(1.0475)$

$\$4,000 = P$

(b) The maker received the face value (principal) = $4,000.

10. (a) M = $15,375

r = 10%

$t = \dfrac{90}{360} = 0.25$

P = ?

$M = P(1 + rt)$

$\$15,375 = P(1 + 0.10 \cdot 0.25)$

$15,375 = P(1 + 1.025)$

$\$15,000 = P$

(b) I = M - P
= $15,375 - $15,000
I = $375

11. M = $7,000

d = 10%

$t = \dfrac{90}{360} = 0.25$

r = ?

D = Mdt

= $7,000 × 0.10 × 0.25

D = $175

p = M − D

= $7,000 − $175

p = $6,825

I = Prt

$175 = $6,825 · r · 0.25

175 = 1,706.25r

10.25% = r (nearest 1/4%)

12. M = $18,000

d = 12.5%

$t = \dfrac{120}{360} = \dfrac{1}{3}$

r = ?

D = Mdt

$= \$18,000 × 0.125 × \dfrac{1}{3}$

D = $750

p = M − D

= $18,000 − $750

p = $17,250

I = Prt

$\$750 = \$17,250 · r · \dfrac{1}{3}$

750 = 5,750r

0.1304 = r

13% = r (nearest 1/4%)

13. Present value of a
Simple Interest Note:
M = $8,400

r = 15%

$t = \dfrac{120}{360} = \dfrac{1}{3}$

P = ?

Proceeds of a
Bank Discount Note:
M = $8,400

d = 15%

$t = \dfrac{120}{360} = \dfrac{1}{3}$

p = ?

13. (Continued)

Present value of a
Simple Interest Note:
$$M = P(1 + rt)$$

$$\$8,400 = P\left(1 + 0.15 \cdot \frac{1}{3}\right)$$

$$8,400 = P(1 + .05)$$

$$8,400 = P(1.05)$$

$$\$8,000 = P$$

Proceeds of a
Bank Discount Note:
$$p = M(1 - dt)$$

$$= \$8,400\left(1 - 0.15 \cdot \frac{1}{3}\right)$$

$$= 8,400(1 - 0.05)$$

$$= 8,400(0.95)$$

$$p = \$7,980$$

14. Present value of a
Simple Interest Note:
M = $9,600

r = 9%

$$t = \frac{30}{360} = \frac{1}{12}$$

P = ?

Proceeds of a
Bank Discount Note:
M = $9,600

d = 9%

$$t = \frac{30}{360} = \frac{1}{12}$$

p = ?

$$M = P(1 + rt)$$

$$\$9,600 = P\left(1 + 0.09 \cdot \frac{1}{12}\right)$$

$$9,600 = P(1.0075)$$

$$\$9,528.54 = P$$

$$p = M(1 - dt)$$

$$= \$9,600\left(1 - 0.09 \cdot \frac{1}{12}\right)$$

$$= 9,600(0.9925)$$

$$p = \$9,528$$

15. December 22 = 356 day
August   22 = -234 day
              122 days

P = $1,080

r = 10%

$$t = \frac{122}{360} = \frac{61}{180}$$

I = Prt

$$= \$1,080 \times 0.10 \times \frac{61}{180}$$

I = $36.60

M = P + I
  = $1,080.00 + $36.60
M = $1,116.60

15. (Continued)

M = $1,116.60

r = 9%

$$t = \frac{122}{360} = \frac{61}{180}$$

$$M = P(1 + rt)$$

$$\$1{,}116.60 = P\left(1 + 0.09 \cdot \frac{61}{180}\right)$$

$$1{,}116.60 = P(1 + 0.0305)$$

$$1{,}116.60 = P(1.0305)$$

$$\$1{,}083.55 = P \text{ (present value)}$$

16. April 12 = 102 day
    January 12 = − 12 day
                    90 days

P = $11,000

r = 12%

$$t = \frac{90}{360} = 0.25$$

M = ?

$$M = P(1 + rt)$$

$$= \$11{,}000(1 + 0.12 \cdot 0.25)$$

$$= 11{,}000(1.03)$$

$$M = \$11{,}330$$

M = $11,330

r = 11%

$$t = \frac{90}{360} = 0.25$$

P = ?

$$M = P(1 + rt)$$

$$\$11{,}330 = P(1 + 0.11 \cdot 0.25)$$

$$11{,}330 = P(1.0275)$$

$$\$11{,}026.76 = P \text{ (present value)}$$

17. July 5 = 186 day
    February 5 = − 36 day
                    150 days

P = $5,200

r = 12%

$$t = \frac{150}{360} = \frac{5}{12}$$

17. (Continued)

$I = Prt$

$\quad = \$5,200 \times 0.12 \times \dfrac{5}{12}$

$I = \$260$

$M = P + I$
$\quad = \$5,200 + \$260$
$M = \$5,460$

$M = \$5,460$

$r = 10\%$

$t = \dfrac{90}{360} = 0.25$

$M = P(1 + rt)$

$\$5,460 = P(1 + 0.10 \cdot 0.25)$

$5,460 = P(1 + 0.025)$

$5,460 = P(1.025)$

$\$5,326.83 = P \text{ (present value)}$

18. November 1 = 305 day
    September 1 = -244 day
    _____
                61 days

$P = \$40,000$

$r = 9\%$

$t = \dfrac{61}{360}$

$M = ?$

$I = Prt$

$\quad = \$40,000 \times 0.09 \times \dfrac{61}{360}$

$I = \$610$

$M = P + I$
$\quad = \$40,000 + \$610$
$M = \$40,610$

$M = \$40,610$

$R = 10.5\%$

$t = \dfrac{30}{360} = \dfrac{1}{12}$

$M = P(1 + rt)$

$\$40,610 = P\left(1 + 0.105 \cdot \dfrac{1}{12}\right)$

$40,610 = P(1.00875)$

$\$40,257.74 = P \text{ (present value)}$

19. (a) July   8 = 189 day
        January 8 = - 8 day
        _____
                 181 days

$P = \$8,000$

$r = 18\%$

$t = \dfrac{181}{360}$

19. (a) (Continued)

$I = Prt$

$\quad = \$8,000 \times 0.18 \times \dfrac{181}{360}$

$I = \$724$

$M = P + I$
$\quad = \$8,000 + \$724$
$M = \$8,724$

July 8 = 189 day
April 9 = - 99 day
          90 days

$M = \$8,724$

$d = 15\%$

$t = \dfrac{90}{360} = 0.25$

$p = M(1 - dt)$

$\quad = \$8,724(1 - 0.15 \cdot 0.25)$

$\quad = 8,724(1 - 0.0375)$

$\quad = 8,724(0.9625)$

$p = \$8,396.85$

(b) Cook Construction Co. made $8,396.85 - $8,000.00 = $396.85.

(c) The bank earned the discount $8,724.00 - $8,396.85 = $327.15.

20. (a) December 9 = 343 day
       October 9 = -282 day
                    61 days

$P = \$5,000$

$r = 9\%$

$t = \dfrac{61}{360}$

$I = Prt$

$\quad = \$5,000 \times 0.09 \times \dfrac{61}{360}$

$I = \$76.25$

$M = P + I$
$\quad = \$5,000.00 + \$76.25$
$M = \$5,076.25$

December 9 = 343 day
November 9 = -313 day
             30 days

$p = M(1 - dt)$

$\quad = \$5,076.25\left(1 - 0.08 \cdot \dfrac{1}{12}\right)$

$\quad = 5,076.25(1 - 0.006667)$

$\quad = 5,076.25(0.993333)$

$p = \$5,042.41$

20. (Continued)

(b) $I = \$5,042.41 - \$5,000.00 = \$42.41$

(c) $D = \$5,076.25 - \$5,042.41 = \$33.84$

21. (a) December 15 =   349 day
        August   15 = -227 day
                          122 days

$M = \$6,000$

$d = 9\%$

$t = \dfrac{122}{360} = \dfrac{61}{180}$

$p_1 = M(1 - dt)$

$ = \$6,000\left(1 - 0.09 \cdot \dfrac{61}{180}\right)$

$ = 6,000(1 - 0.0305)$

$ = 6,000(0.9695)$

$p_1 = \$5,817$

(b) December 15 =   349 day
     October   16 = -289 day
                       60 days

$M = \$6,000$

$d = 8.5\%$

$t = \dfrac{60}{360} = \dfrac{1}{6}$

$p_2 = M(1 - dt)$

$ = \$6,000\left(1 - 0.085 \cdot \dfrac{1}{6}\right)$

$ = 6,000(1 - 0.014167)$

$ = 6,000(0.985833)$

$p_2 = \$5,915$

(c) American Bank earned $\$5,915 - \$5,817 = \$98$

(d) The second bank earned $\$6,000 - \$5,915 = \$85$

22. (a) September 18 =   261 day
         June   18 = -169 day
                           92 days

22. (a) (Continued)

$M = \$10,000$

$d = 12\%$

$t = \dfrac{92}{360} = \dfrac{23}{90}$

$p = ?$

$p_1 = M(1 - dt)$

$\quad = \$10,000\left(1 - 0.12 \cdot \dfrac{23}{90}\right)$

$\quad = 10,000(1 - 0.030667)$

$\quad = 10,000(0.969333)$

$p_1 = \$9,693.33$

(b)
```
September  18 =   261 day
July       20 =  -201 day
                  60 days
```

$M = \$10,000$

$d = 11\%$

$t = \dfrac{60}{360} = \dfrac{1}{6}$

$p = ?$

$p_2 = M(1 - dt)$

$\quad = \$10,000\left(1 - 0.11 \cdot \dfrac{1}{6}\right)$

$\quad = 10,000(1 - 0.0183333)$

$\quad = 10,000(0.9816667)$

$p_2 = \$9,816.67$

(c) Marbury Bank earned $\$9,816.67 - \$9,693.33 = \$123.34$

(d) Marbury Bank lost $\$10,000.00 - 9,816.67 = \$183.33$

CHAPTER XVII

MULTIPLE PAYMENT PLANS

This chapter is closely related to the simple interest chapter. It includes both payments made at irregular intervals (the United States rule) and payments made at specified regular intervals (the installment plan). Also presented are two methods for determining unearned interest on installment plan payments (the actuarial method and the rule of 78s).

1.   United States Rule:

This topic actually has two applications. The most obvious is for irregular prepayments on a simple interest note which is not yet due. However, both simple interest notes and bank discount notes state that, when the note is past due, interest will be charged (often at an increased rate) on the face value of the note. Hence, the procedure described here will apply to both types of notes once they are past maturity.

The United Sates rule is presented in the text in a manner which emphasizes that the partial payment must first be applied toward the interest due since the previous payment. However, since it would be a rare instance when a partial payment is not sufficient to pay the accrued interest, all payments in the student problems are large enough to more than cover this interest. Thus, having made it clear to the student that the payment must at least equal the interest due at the time of the partial payment, you might wish to teach the United States rule by the following alternative method:

Example 1 (alternate):
An alternative method is the PIM method as shown below:

A $1,500 note dated April 1 drew interest at 10% for 90 days. Partial payments were $700 on May 1 and $300 on May 16.

P_1 April 1		$1,500.00
I_1 on $1,500 \times 10\% \times \dfrac{30}{360}$		+ 12.50
M_1 May 1		$1,512.50
1st payment, May 1		− 700.00
P_2 May 1		$ 812.50
$I_2 = \$812.50 \times 10\% \times \dfrac{15}{360}$		+ 3.39
M_2 May 16		$ 815.89
2nd payment, May 16		− 300.00
P_3 May 16		$ 515.89
$I_3 = \$515.89 \times 10\% \times \dfrac{45}{360}$		− 6.45
M_3 June 30		$ 522.34

The calculations shown in example 1 in the text could also be set up in tabular form similar to example 1 of topic 2, installment plans.

2.   Installment Plans -- Open End:

Prior to passage of the Federal Truth in Lending Law, most people who made purchases on the installment plan knew only the amount of their monthly payment; they seldom knew how much extra was charged to finance the purchase and had no idea whatsoever what interest rate they were paying. If an interest rate were quoted to them, it was usually the misleading simple interest rate rather than the effective rate applicable to multiple payments.

Although the Truth in Lending Law has accomplished a great deal in informing consumers, some misunderstanding still exists. (In particular, many people do not understand what a 21% effective rate means, for example, and may think that the finance charge represents 21% of the original outstanding balance.) Hence a careful study of installment plan calculations is still an important topic for business students, despite the required Truth in Lending disclosures. Of special importance are the problems which involve both simple and effective rate (for comparison) and the verifications of effective rates.

Example 1 illustrates an installment plan with a monthly interest rate applied to the outstanding balance, such as is used by many retail stores offering revolving charge accounts. Although such accounts may seldom be paid off entirely in actual practice, for the sake of illustration, these accounts will be paid in full for the text problems. This procedure is usually easy for the student to grasp and will not require lengthy explanation.

Interest computed by the average daily balance method is illustrated in example 2. Conceptually, students can readily comprehend that interest is paid on the preceding balance until a payment is received and then paid on the adjusted balance during the remainder of the month. Actually doing the calculations, however, especially with additional purchases also occurring, tends to generate many errors. This example could be omitted entirely for a basic class or only used for class discussion.

When discussing methods of computing interest on revolving charge accounts, it would be of interest to know which methods are used by various local retailers. This information would be available from their credit application forms or from the contract that arrives with the charge card (which many people save since it contains their account number). The instructor and/or students might collect some of these forms prior to the related class session.

3.   Installment Plan -- Set Payments:

The examples in this section pertain to the standard installment purchase or loan, which requires a specified number of equal payments. Example 1 and example 2 show the computation of the regular installment payment. The only difficulty which sometimes arises here is that some students try to compute the finance charge on the cash price, rather than on the outstanding balance remaining after the down payment. Example 2 also includes determination of the annual percentage rate. Examples 3 and 4 continue the study of the annual percentage rate and also cover the important verifications of these rates.

Some texts include a formula that computes the _effective_ interest rate equivalent to a given simple interest rate applied in an installment plan. The Annual Percentage Rate Table for Monthly Payment Plans (Truth in Lending annual percentage rates) is preferable because it finds the _actuarial_ rate applicable to standard amortization payments of a uniform amount each month (composed of increasing principal and diminishing interest). Formulas for effective interest apply when the principal is divided into equal parts, and the unequal total payments include the uniform principal plus the interest due on the outstanding principal. The rates found by the two methods, however, are almost the same. Thus, you may wish your better students to compare the rates obtained by both methods.

Typical for computing effective interest rates is the formula:

$$e = \frac{2nr}{n + 1}$$

where e = effective interest rate
      n = number of payments
      r = annual simple (nominal) interest rate

Using example 3 for comparison (a $480 loan at 9% simple interest for 6 months):

$$e = \frac{2nr}{n + 1} = \frac{2(6)(9)}{6 + 1} = 15.43$$

This compares with 15.25% by the actuarial method in the text. The rate can be verified similarly to example 3, by making monthly payments of $480/6 = $80 principal plus whatever interest is due.

4.   Installment Plan Prepayments:

The interest saved by paying off an installment plan early becomes a more important topic when interest rates are high. The actuarial method shown in example 1 is more closely correlated to the Truth in Lending rates computed previously. However, the calculations for students are rather tedious -- particularly if calculators are not available. The traditional rule of 78s is, in fact, still used by a significant number of lending institutions. This, together with the fact that the student problems contain more compatible numbers, makes the rule of 78s the preferable method from a teaching standpoint (example 2).

Example 3 is included simply to confirm the calculations of example 1 for the student. No assignment problems of this type are included.

If time is short, this entire topic may be omitted. The actuarial method (examples 1 and 3) may be omitted in any case.

Although this chapter is in many respects more related to simple interest than to compound interest, Chapters XV - XVII contain more material than the typical student can effectively study for one test and more material than the instructor can effectively cover on an hour exam. Thus, the authors prefer to include this chapter on the test with Chapters XVIII - XX, since they contain less material and their problems can also be computed faster.

CHAPTER 17 - MULTIPLE PAYMENT PLANS
PROBLEM SOLUTIONS

Section 1, page 439

1. (a)

$P = \$6,000$

$r = 12\%$

$t_1 = \dfrac{20}{360} = \dfrac{1}{18}$

$I_1 = Prt$

$= \$6,000 \times 0.12 \times \dfrac{1}{18}$

$I_1 = \$40$

$t_2 = \dfrac{60}{360} = \dfrac{1}{6}$

$I_2 = Prt$

$= \$4,000 \times 0.12 \times \dfrac{1}{6}$

$I_2 = \$80$

$t_3 = \dfrac{70}{360}$

$I_3 = Prt$

$= \$2,580 \times 0.12 \times \dfrac{7}{36}$

$I_3 = \$60.20$

Original principal		$6,000.00
1st partial payment	$2,040	
Less: int. (20 days)	− 40	
Payment to principal		−2,000.00
Adjusted principal		$4,000.00
2nd partial payment	$1,500	
Less: int. (60 days)	− 80	
Payment to principal		−1,420.00
Adjusted principal		$2,580
Interest due (70 days)		+ 60.20
Balance due		$2,640.20

1. (Continued)

   (b)

P = \$3,600	Original principal			\$3,600.00

$$r = 15\%$$

$$t_1 = \frac{20}{360} = \frac{1}{18}$$

1st partial payment	\$2,030	
Less: int. (20 days)	− 30	

$I_1 = Prt$

$= \$3,600 \times 0.15 \times \dfrac{1}{18}$	Payment to principal	−2,000.00
	Adjusted principal	\$1,600.00

$I_1 = \$30$

2nd partial payment	\$1,030
Less: int. (45 days)	− 30

$$t_2 = \frac{45}{360} = \frac{1}{8}$$

Payment to principal	−1,000.00
Adjusted principal	\$ 600.00

$I_2 = Prt$

$= \$1,600 \times 0.15 \times \dfrac{1}{8}$	Interest due (25 days)	6.25

$I_2 = \$30$

Balance due \$ 606.25

$$t_3 = \frac{25}{360} = \frac{5}{72}$$

$I_3 = Prt$

$= \$600 \times 0.15 \times \dfrac{5}{72}$

$I_3 = \$6.25$

1. (Continued)

(c)

$P = \$8,000$ Original principal $8,000

$r = 10\%$

$t_1 = \dfrac{90}{360} = \dfrac{1}{4}$ 1st partial payment $2,200

Less: int. (90 days) $-\ \ \ 200$

$I_1 = Prt$ Payment to principal $-2,000$

$= \$8,000 \times 0.10 \times \dfrac{1}{4}$ Adjusted principal $6,000

$I_1 = \$200$ 2nd partial payment $2,875

Less: int. (45 days) $-\ \ \ 75$

$t_2 = \dfrac{45}{360} = \dfrac{1}{8}$ Payment to principal $-2,800$

Adjusted principal $3,200

$I_2 = Prt$ Interest due (135 days) $+\ \ 120$

$= \$6,000 \times 0.10 \times \dfrac{1}{8}$ Balance due $3,320

$I_2 = \$75$

$t_3 = \dfrac{135}{360} = \dfrac{3}{8}$

$I_3 = Prt$

$= \$3,200 \times 0.10 \times \dfrac{3}{8}$

$I_3 = \$120$

2. (a)

$P = \$9,000$

$r = 10\%$

$t_1 = \dfrac{90}{360}$

$I_1 = Prt$

$= \$9,000 \times 0.10 \times \dfrac{90}{360}$

$I_1 = \$225$

$t_2 = \dfrac{45}{360}$

$I_2 = Prt$

$= \$8,000 \times 0.10 \times \dfrac{45}{360}$

$I_2 = \$100$

$t_3 = \dfrac{45}{360}$

$I_3 = Prt$

$= \$6,100 \times 0.10 \times \dfrac{45}{360}$

$I_3 = \$76.25$

Original principal		$9,000.00
1st partial payment	$1,225	
Less: int. (90 days)	- 225	
Payment to principal		-1,000.00
Adjusted principal		$8,000.00
2nd partial payment	$2,000	
Less: int. (45 days)	- 100	
Payment to principal		-1,900.00
Adjusted principal		$6,100.00
Interest due (45 days)		+ 76.25
Balance due		$6,176.25

2. (Continued)

(b)

$P = \$7,200$	Original principal $7,200.00
$r = 8\%$	
$t_1 = \dfrac{30}{360}$	1st partial payment $3,288
	Less: int. (30 days) $- \underline{\quad 48}$
$I_1 = Prt$	Payment to principal $\underline{-3,240.00}$
$\quad = \$7,200 \times 0.08 \times \dfrac{30}{360}$	Adjusted principal $3,960.00
$I_1 = \$48$	2nd partial payment $2,000
	Less: int. (75 days) $- \underline{\quad 66}$
$t_2 = \dfrac{75}{360}$	Payment to principal $\underline{-1,934.00}$
	Adjusted principal $2,026.00
$I_2 = Prt$	Interest due $+ \underline{\quad 6.75}$
$\quad = \$3,960 \times 0.08 \times \dfrac{75}{360}$	Balance due $2,032.75
$I_2 = \$66$	

$$t_3 = \frac{15}{360}$$

$I_3 = Prt$

$\quad = \$2,026 \times 0.08 \times \dfrac{15}{360}$

$I_3 = \$6.75$

2. (Continued)

(c)

$P = \$5,000$

$r = 9\%$

$t_1 = \dfrac{120}{360}$

Original principal		$5,000.00
1st partial payment	$3,150	
Less: int. (120 days)	− 150	
Payment to principal		−3,000.00
Adjusted principal		$2,000.00
2nd partial payment	$ 950	
Less: int. (60 days)	− 30	
Payment to principal		− 920.00
Adjusted principal		$1,080.00
Interest due		+ 16.20
Balance due		$1,096.20

$I_1 = Prt$

$\quad = \$5,000 \times 0.09 \times \dfrac{120}{360}$

$I_1 = \$150$

$t_2 = \dfrac{60}{360}$

$I_2 = Prt$

$\quad = \$2,000 \times 0.09 \times \dfrac{60}{360}$

$I_2 = \$30$

$t_3 = \dfrac{60}{360}$

$I_3 = Prt$

$\quad = \$1,080 \times 0.09 \times \dfrac{60}{360}$

$I_3 = \$16.20$

3.

$$P = \$10,000$$

$$r = 12\%$$

$$t_1 = \frac{60}{360} = \frac{1}{6}$$

$$I_1 = Prt$$

$$= \$10,000 \times 0.12 \times \frac{1}{6}$$

$$I_1 = \$200$$

$$t_2 = \frac{90}{360} = \frac{1}{4}$$

$$I_2 = Prt$$

$$= \$8,000 \times 0.12 \times \frac{1}{4}$$

$$I_2 = \$240$$

$$t_3 = \frac{30}{360} \times \frac{1}{12}$$

$$I_3 = Prt$$

$$= \$5,000 \times 0.12 \times \frac{1}{12}$$

$$I_3 = \$50$$

Original principal, 4/5		$10,000
1st partial payment, 6/4	$2,200	
Less: int. (60 days)	- 200	
Payment to principal		- 2,000
Adjusted balance		$ 8,000
2nd partial payment, 9/2	$3,240	
Less: int. (90 days)	- 240	
Payment to principal		- 3,000
Adjusted principal		$ 5,000
Interest due (30 days)		+ 50
Balance due, 10/2		$ 5,050

4.

$P = \$10,000$

$r = 9\%$

$t_1 = \dfrac{60}{360}$

$I_1 = Prt$

$= \$10,000 \times 0.09 \times \dfrac{60}{360}$

$I_1 = \$150$

$t_2 = \dfrac{60}{360}$

$I_2 = Prt$

$= \$8,000 \times 0.09 \times \dfrac{60}{360}$

$I_2 = \$120$

$t_3 = \dfrac{60}{360}$

$I_3 = Prt$

$= \$4,120 \times 0.09 \times \dfrac{60}{360}$

$I_3 = \$61.80$

Original principal, 4/14		$10,000.00
1st partial payment	$2,150	
Less: int. (60 days)	– 150	
Payment to principal		– 2,000.00
Adjusted principal		$ 8,000.00
2nd partial payment	$4,000	
Less: int. (60 days)	– 120	
Payment to principal		– 3,880.00
Adjusted principal		$ 4,120.00
Interest due		+ 61.80
Balance due, 12/10		$ 4,181.80

5.

$P = \$12,000$

$r = 18\%$

$t_1 = \dfrac{20}{360} = \dfrac{1}{18}$

$I_1 = Prt$

$\quad = \$12,000 \times 0.18 \times \dfrac{1}{18}$

$I_1 = \$120$

$t_2 = \dfrac{45}{360} = \dfrac{1}{8}$

$I_2 = Prt$

$\quad = \$10,000 \times 0.18 \times \dfrac{1}{8}$

$I_2 = \$225$

$t_3 = \dfrac{25}{360} = \dfrac{5}{72}$

$I_3 = Prt$

$\quad = \$5,000 \times 0.18 \times \dfrac{5}{72}$

$I_3 = \$62.50$

Original principal, 6/10		$12,000.00
1st partial pmt., 6/30	$2,120	
Less: int. (20 days)	− 120	
Payment to principal		− 2,000.00
Adjusted principal		$10,000.00
2nd partial pmt., 8/14	$5,225	
Less: int. (45 days)	− 225	
Payment to principal		− 5,000.00
Adjusted principal		$ 5,000.00
Interest due (25 days)		+ 62.50
Balance due, 9/8		$ 5,062.50

6.

$P = \$12,000$ Original principal, 6/15 $12,000.00

$r = 10\%$

$t_1 = \dfrac{30}{360}$ 1st partial payment $2,100

           Less: int. (30 days)   − 100

$I_1 = Prt$ Payment to principal   − 2,000.00

$= \$12,000 \times 0.10 \times \dfrac{30}{360}$ Adjusted principal $10,000.00

$I_1 = \$100$ 2nd partial payment $5,000

           Less: int. (90 days)   − 250

$t_2 = \dfrac{90}{360}$ Payment to principal   − 4,750.00

           Adjusted principal $ 5,250.00

$I_2 = Prt$ Interest due   + 43.75

$= \$10,000 \times 0.10 \times \dfrac{90}{360}$ Balance due, 11/12 $ 5,293.75

$I_2 = \$250$

$t_3 = \dfrac{30}{360}$

$I_3 = Prt$

$= \$5,250 \times 0.10 \times \dfrac{30}{360}$

$I_3 = \$43.75$

Section 2, page 444

1. (a)

Pmt. No.	Balance Due	Interest ($1\frac{1}{4}$%)	Monthly Payment	Payment Toward Bal. Due	Adjusted Balance Due
1	$175.00	$2.19	$ 25.00	$ 22.81	$152.19
2	152.19	1.90	25.00	23.10	129.09
3	129.09	1.61	25.00	23.39	105.70
4	105.70	1.32	25.00	23.68	82.02
5	82.02	1.03	25.00	23.97	58.05
6	58.05	0.73	25.00	24.27	33.78
7	33.78	0.42	25.00	24.58	9.20
8	9.20	0.12	9.32	9.20	0.00
	Totals	$9.32	$184.32	$175.00	

The interest is $9.32.

(b)

Pmt. No.	Balance Due	Interest (1%)	Monthly Payment	Payment Toward Bal. Due	Adjusted Balance Due
1	$500.00	$ 5.00	$ 50.00	$ 45.00	$455.00
2	455.00	4.55	50.00	45.45	409.55
3	409.55	4.10	50.00	45.90	363.65
4	363.65	3.64	50.00	46.36	317.29
5	317.29	3.17	50.00	46.83	270.46
6	270.46	2.70	50.00	47.30	223.16
7	223.16	2.23	50.00	47.77	175.39
8	175.39	1.75	50.00	48.25	127.14
9	127.14	1.27	50.00	48.73	78.41
10	78.41	0.78	50.00	49.22	29.19
11	29.19	0.29	29.48	29.19	0.00
	Totals	$29.48	$529.48	$500.00	

The interest is $29.48.

2. (a)

Pmt. No.	Balance Due	Interest $(1\frac{1}{2}\%)$	Monthly Payment	Payment Toward Bal. Due	Adjusted Balance Due
1	$400.00	$ 6.00	$ 50.00	$ 44.00	$356.00
2	356.00	5.34	50.00	44.66	311.34
3	311.34	4.67	50.00	45.33	266.01
4	266.01	3.99	50.00	46.01	220.00
5	220.00	3.30	50.00	46.70	173.30
6	173.30	2.60	50.00	47.40	125.90
7	125.90	1.89	50.00	48.11	77.79
8	77.79	1.17	50.00	48.83	28.96
9	28.96	0.43	29.39	28.96	0.00
	Totals	$29.39	$429.39	$400.00	

The interest is $29.39.

(b)

Pmt. No.	Balance Due	Interest (1%)	Monthly Payment	Payment Toward Bal. Due	Adjusted Balance Due
1	$500.00	$ 5.00	$ 75.00	$ 70.00	$430.00
2	430.00	4.30	75.00	70.70	359.30
3	359.30	3.59	75.00	71.41	287.89
4	287.89	2.88	75.00	72.12	215.77
5	215.77	2.16	75.00	72.84	142.93
6	142.93	1.43	75.00	73.57	69.36
7	69.36	0.69	70.05	69.36	0.00
	Totals	$20.05	$520.05	$500.00	

The interest is $20.05.

3.

Mo.	Date	Prev. Balance	Payment	Adj. Bal.	Avg. Bal.	2% Int.	Purchases	Current Balance
1	18	$300.00	$ 50	$250.00				$250.00
	20						$20	270.00
	30				$280.00[1]	$ 5.60		275.60
2	15	275.60	75	200.60				200.60
	19						25	225.60
	25						10	235.60
	30				238.10[2]	4.76		240.36
3	12	240.36	45	195.36				195.36
	28						30	225.36
	30		____		213.36[3]	4.27	____	229.63
		Totals	$170			$14.63	$85	

3. (Continued)

(1) $\dfrac{(\$300 \times 18) + (\$250 \times 12)}{30} = \$280.00$

(2) $\dfrac{(\$275.60 \times 15) + (\$200.60 \times 15)}{30} = \$238.10$

(3) $\dfrac{(\$240.36 \times 12) + (\$195.36 \times 18)}{30} = \$213.36$

```
Check:
$300.00  Beginning balance
+ 85.00  Purchases
+ 14.63  Interest
$399.63
-170.00  Payments
$229.63  Ending balance
```

4.

Mo.	Date	Prev. Balance	Pmt.	Adj. Bal.	Avg. Bal.	2% Int.	Purch.	Current Balance
1	12	$1,500.00	$ 40	$1,460.00				$1,460.00
	16						$ 50	1,510.00
	30				$1,476.00	$29.52		1,539.52
2	15	1,539.52	150	1,389.52				1,389.52
	20						25	1,414.52
	25						10	1,424.52
	30				1,464.52	29.29		1,453.81
3	5	1,453.81	400	1,053.81				1,053.81
	12						60	1,113.81
	20	1,053.81	200	853.81				913.81
	30				1,053.81	21.08		934.89
		Totals	$790			$79.89	$145	

(1) $\dfrac{(\$1,500 \times 12) + (\$1,460 \times 18)}{30} = \$1,476$

(2) $\dfrac{(\$1,539.52 \times 15) + (\$1,389.52 \times 15)}{30} = \$1,464.52$

(3) $\dfrac{(\$1,453.81 \times 5) + (\$1,053.81 \times 15) + (\$853.81 \times 10)}{30} = \$1,053.81$

4. (Continued)

Check:
$1,500.00 Beginning balance
-   790.00 Payments
+   79.89 Interest
+   145.00 Purchases
$ 934.89 Ending balance

5.

Pmt. No.	Balance Due	Interest (1%)	Monthly Payment	Payment Toward Bal. Due	Adjusted Balance Due
1	$300.00	$ 3.00	$ 50.00	$ 47.00	$253.00
2	253.00	2.53	50.00	47.47	205.53
3	205.53	2.06	50.00	47.94	157.59
4	157.59	1.58	50.00	48.42	109.17
5	109.17	1.09	50.00	48.91	60.26
6	60.26	0.60	50.00	49.40	10.86
7	10.86	0.11	10.97	10.86	0.00
	Totals	$10.97	$310.97	$300.00	

The interest will total $10.97

6.

Pmt. No.	Balance Due	Interest ($1\frac{1}{4}$%)	Monthly Payment	Payment Toward Bal. Due	Adjusted Balance Due
1	$400.00	$ 5.00	$ 60.00	$ 55.00	$345.00
2	345.00	4.31	60.00	55.69	289.31
3	289.31	3.62	60.00	56.38	232.93
4	232.93	2.91	60.00	57.09	175.84
5	175.84	2.20	60.00	57.80	118.04
6	118.04	1.48	60.00	58.52	59.52
7	59.52	0.74	60.26	59.52	0.00
	Totals	$20.26	$420.26	$400.00	

The interest will total $20.26

7.

Mo.	Date	Prev. Balance	Payment	Adj. Bal.	Avg. Bal.	1% Int.	Purchases	Current Balance
1	15	$ 85.00	$10	$ 75.00				$ 75.00
	20						$ 30	105.00
	30				$ 80.00[1]	$0.80		105.80
2	18	105.80	20	85.80				85.80
	25						45	130.80
	30				97.80[2]	0.98		131.78
3	12	131.78	20	111.78				111.78
	21						25	136.78
	30				119.78[3]	1.20		137.98
		Totals	$50			$2.98	$100	

$$(1) \quad \frac{(\$85 \times 15) + (\$75 \times 15)}{30} = \$80.00$$

$$(2) \quad \frac{(\$105.80 \times 18) + (\$85.80 \times 12)}{30} = \$97.80$$

$$(3) \quad \frac{(\$131.78 \times 12) + (\$111.78 \times 18)}{30} = \$119.78$$

Check:
$ 85.00 Beginning balance   (a) Total payments = $ 50.00
+100.00 Purchases   (b) Total interest = $ 2.98
+ 2.98 Interest   (c) Ending balance = $137.98
$187.98
- 50.00 Payments
$137.98 Ending balance

8.

Mo.	Date	Prev. Balance	Pmt.	Adj. Bal.	Avg. Bal.	1% Int.	Purch.	Current Balance
1	10	$ 60.00	$15	$ 45.00				$ 45.00
	15						$ 20	65.00
	30				$ 50.00[1]	$0.50		65.50
2	5	65.50	15	50.50				50.50
	10						80	130.50
	30				53.00[2]	0.53		131.03
3	13						25	156.03
	20	131.03	20	111.03				136.03
	30				124.36[3]	1.24		137.27
		Totals	$50			$2.27	$125	

8. (Continued)

(1) $\dfrac{(\$60 \times 10) + (\$45 \times 20)}{30} = \$50.00$

(2) $\dfrac{(\$65.50 \times 5) + (\$50.50 \times 25)}{30} = \$53$

(3) $\dfrac{(\$131.03 \times 20) + (\$111.03 \times 10)}{30} = \$124.36$

```
Check:
$ 60.00 Beginning balance
- 50.00 Payments
+  2.27 Interest
+125.00 Purchases
$137.27 Ending balance
```

Section 3, page 455

1. (a)
Cash price	$500
Down payment	− 50
Outstanding balance	$450
Finance charge	+ 20
Total of payments	$470

$\dfrac{\$470}{10} = \$47/\text{month}$

(b)
Cash price	$960
Down payment (25%)	−240
Outstanding balance	$720
Finance charge	+ 30
Total of payments	$750

$\dfrac{\$750}{12} = \$62.50/\text{week}$

(c)
Cash price	$645
Down payment (1/3)	−215
Outstanding balance	$430
Finance charge	+ 86
Total of payments	$516

(= $430 × 0.10 × 2)

$\dfrac{\$516}{24} = \$21.50/\text{month}$

2. (a)
Cash price	$1,000
Down payment	− 50
Outstanding balance	$ 950
Finance charge	+ 25
Total of payments	$ 975

(b)
Cash price	$1,500
Down payment (10%)	− 150
Outstanding balance	$1,350
Finance charge	+ 50
Total of payments	$1,400

2. (a) (Continued)

$$\frac{\$975}{5} = \$195/month$$

(b) (Continued)

$$\frac{\$1,400}{20} = \$70/week$$

(c)
Cash price	$1,100
Down payment (1/4)	− 275
Outstanding balance	$ 825
Finance charge	+ 66
Total of payments	$ 891

(= $825 × 0.08 × 1)

$$\frac{\$891}{12} = \$74.25/month$$

3. (a) $\dfrac{\text{Finance charge}}{\text{Amount financed}} \times 100 = \dfrac{\$20}{\$120} \times 100 = \$16.67$

$16.67 finance charge per $100 financed over 9 months = 38.5% actuarial rate

(b) $\dfrac{\text{Finance charge}}{\text{Amount financed}} \times 100 = \dfrac{\$30}{\$300} \times 100 = \$10$

$10 finance charge per $100 financed over 12 months = 18% actuarial rate

(c) Simple interest rate × time = 14% × 3 = 42
$42 interest per $100 financed over 36 months = 24.5% actuarial rate

(d) Simple interest rate × time = $12\% \times \dfrac{5}{12} = 5$

$5 interest per $100 financed over 5 months = 19.75% actuarial rate

4. (a) $\dfrac{\text{Finance charge}}{\text{Amount financed}} \times 100 = \dfrac{\$60}{\$900} \times 100 = \$6.67$

$6.67 finance charge per $100 financed over 10 months = 14.25% APR

(b) $\dfrac{\text{Finance charge}}{\text{Amount financed}} \times 100 = \dfrac{\$90}{\$1,200} \times 100 = \$7.50$

$7.50 finance charge per $100 financed over 12 months = 13.5% APR

4. (Continued)

   (c) Simple interest rate × time = 10% × 2 = 20
       $20 finance charge per $100 financed over 24 months =
       18.25% APR

   (d) Simple interest rate × time = 9% × $\frac{1}{2}$ = 4.5

       $4.50 finance charge per $100 financed over 6 months =
       15.25% APR

5.

Month	Prt	=	I	Payment to Principal
1	$800.00 × 0.17 × $\frac{1}{12}$	=	$11.33	$128.67
2	671.33 × 0.17 × $\frac{1}{12}$	=	9.51	130.49
3	540.84 × 0.17 × $\frac{1}{12}$	=	7.66	132.34
4	408.50 × 0.17 × $\frac{1}{12}$	=	5.79	134.21
5	274.29 × 0.17 × $\frac{1}{12}$	=	3.89	136.11
6	138.18 × 0.17 × $\frac{1}{12}$	=	1.96	138.04
			$40.14	$799.86

($0.14 difference in total interest and total payment to
principal is due to rounding interest and usage of an
effective interest rate correct only to the nearest 1/4%.)

6.

Month	Prt	=	I	Payment to Principal
1	$400.00 \times 0.3925 \times \dfrac{1}{12}$	=	$13.08	$ 74.92
2	$325.08 \times 0.3925 \times \dfrac{1}{12}$	=	10.63	77.37
3	$247.71 \times 0.3925 \times \dfrac{1}{12}$	=	8.10	79.90
4	$167.81 \times 0.3925 \times \dfrac{1}{12}$	=	5.49	82.51
5	$85.30 \times 0.3925 \times \dfrac{1}{12}$	=	2.79	$ 85.21
			$40.09	$399.91

($0.09 difference in total interest and total payments to principal is due to rounding interest and usage of an effective interest rate correct only to the nearest 1/4%.)

7.
Cash price	$336
Down payment (1/3)	−112
Outstanding balance	$224
Finance charge	+ 40
Total of payments	$264

$$\frac{\$264}{12} = \$22/month$$

8.
Cash price	$1,400
Down payment (1/4)	− 350
Outstanding balance	$1,050
Finance charge	+ 60
Total of payments	$1,110

$$\frac{\$1,110}{24} = \$46.25/month$$

9.
Cash price	$2,500
Down payment (30%)	− 750
Outstanding balance	$1,750
Finance charge	+ 50
Total of payments	$1,800

$$\frac{\$1,800}{18} = \$100/month$$

10.
Cash price	$1,600
Down payment (20%)	− 320
Outstanding balance	$1,280
Finance charge	+ 70
Total of payments	$1,350

$$\frac{\$1,350}{18} = \$75/month$$

11. (a)
List price	$520
Down payment (25%)	−130
Outstanding balance	$390
Finance charge	+ 39
Total owed	$429

$\left(= \$390 \times 0.12 \times \dfrac{10}{12} \right)$

The finance charge = $39

11. (Continued)

(b) $\dfrac{\$429}{10} = \$42.90/month$

(c)
Total payments	$429		$520 List price
Down payment	+130	or	+ 39 Finance charge
Total cost	$559		$559 Total cost

(d) Simple interest rate × time = 12% × $\dfrac{10}{12}$ = 10 or

$\dfrac{\text{Finance charge}}{\text{Amount financed}}$ × 100 = $\dfrac{\$39}{\$390}$ × 100 = 10

$10 finance charge per $100 financed over 10 months = 21.25% actuarial rate

12. (a)
Cash price	$1,000	
Down payment (10%)	− 100	
Outstanding balance	$ 900	
Finance charge	+ 243	(= $900 × 0.09 × 3)
Total of payments	$1,143	

The finance charge = $243

(b) $\dfrac{\$1,143}{36} = \$31.75/month$

(c)
Total payments	$1,143		$1,000 Cash price
Down payment	+ 100	or	+ 243 Finance charge
Total cost	$1,243		$1,243 Total cost

(d) $\dfrac{\text{Finance charge}}{\text{Amount financed}}$ × 100 = $\dfrac{\$243}{\$900}$ × 100 = 27

$27 finance charge per $100 financed over 36 months = 16.25% APR

13. (a) $125 × 24 payments = $3,000 Total payments
$\qquad\qquad\qquad\qquad\qquad$ −2,600 Amount borrowed
$\qquad\qquad\qquad\qquad\qquad$ $ 400 Finance charge

(b) $\dfrac{\text{Finance charge}}{\text{Amount financed}}$ × 100 = $\dfrac{\$400}{\$2,600}$ × 100 = 15.38

$15.38 per $100 financed over 24 months = 14.25% APR

14. (a) $70 × 18 payments = $1,260 Total payments
                                    -1,150 Loan
                              $ 110 Finance charge

   (b) $\dfrac{\text{Finance charge}}{\text{Amount financed}} \times 100 = \dfrac{\$110}{\$1,150} \times 100 = 9.57$

      $9.57 finance charge per $100 financed over 18 months = 11.75% APR

15. (a) $35 × 18 payments = $630 Total payments
                                    -580 List price
                              $ 50 Finance charge

   (b) $\dfrac{\text{Finance charge}}{\text{Amount financed}} \times 100 = \dfrac{\$50}{\$580} \times 100 = 8.62$

      $8.62 per $100 financed over 18 months = 10.5% APR

16. (a) $57 × 36 payments = $2,052 Total payments
                                    -1,600 Loan
                              $ 452 Finance charge

   (b) $\dfrac{\text{Finance charge}}{\text{Amount financed}} \times 100 = \dfrac{\$452}{\$1,600} \times 100 = 28.25$

      $28.25 finance charge per $100 financed over 36 months = 17% APR

17. (a) $56 × 24 payments = $1,344 Total payments
                                   + 200 Down payment
                              $1,544 Total cost when
                                          purchased on credit

   (b) $1,544 Total cost   (c) $1,400 Cash price
      -1,400 Cash price   - 200 Down payment
      $ 144 Finance charge $1,200 Amount financed

     $\dfrac{\$144}{\$1,200} \times 100 = 12$ $12 per $100 financed
                                  over 24 months = 11.25% APR

18. (a) $95 × 12 payments = $1,140 Total payments
                                   + 100 Down payment
                              $1,240 Total cost

18. (Continued)

    (b) $1,240 Total cost
       -1,100 Cash price
       $ 140 Finance charge

    (c) $\dfrac{\text{Finance charge}}{\text{Amount financed}} \times 100 = \dfrac{\$140}{\$1,000} \times 100 = 14$

       $14 finance charge per $100 financed over 12 months = 25% APR

19. (a) $35 × 36 payments = $1,260 Total payments
                        + 250 Down payment
                       $1,510 Total cost on the
                                installment plan

    (b) $1,510 Total cost   (c) $1,300 Cash price
       -1,300 Cash price   - 250 Down payment
       $ 210 Finance charge $1,050 Amount financed

       $\dfrac{\$210}{\$1,050} \times 100 = 20$ $20 per $100 financed
                                over 36 months = 12.25% APR

20. (a) $140 × 15 payments = $2,100 Total payments
                        + 200 Down payment
                       $2,300 Total cost

    (b) $2,300 Total cost
       -2,000 Cash price
       $ 300 Finance charge

    (c) $\dfrac{\text{Finance charge}}{\text{Amount financed}} \times 100 = \dfrac{\$300}{\$2,000} \times 100 = 15$

       $15 finance charge per $100 financed over 15 months = 21.5% APR

21. <u>14% simple interest</u>

    (a) <u>12 monthly installments</u>
       Rate × time = 14 × 1 = 14
       $14 per $100 financed over 12 months = 25% annual rate

21. (Continued)

    (b) <u>18 monthly installments</u>

        Rate × time = $14 \times \dfrac{18}{12} = 21$

        $21 per $100 financed over 18 months = 25% annual rate

    (c) <u>9 monthly installments</u>

        Rate × time = $14 \times \dfrac{9}{12} = 10.5$

        $10.50 per $100 financed over 9 months = 24.5% annual rate

22. (a) Simple interest rate × time = 9% × 1 = 9
        $9 finance charge per $100 financed over 12 months = 16.25% APR

    (b) Simple interest rate × time = 9% × 2 = 18
        $18 finance charge per $100 financed over 24 months = 16.5% APR

    (c) Simple interest rate × time = $9\% \times \dfrac{10}{12} = 7.5$

        $7.50 finance charge per $100 financed over 10 months = 16% APR

23. (a) $I = Prt$ (b) $M = P + I$

        $= \$2,400 \times 0.09 \times \dfrac{1}{2}$ $= \$2,400 + \$108$

                          $M = \$2,508$

        $I = \$108$ $\dfrac{\$2,508}{6} = \$418/month$

    (c) Simple interest × time = $9\% \times \dfrac{1}{2} = 4.5$

        $4.50 per $100 financed over 6 months = 15.25% actuarial rate

23. (Continued)

(d)

Month	Prt	=	I	Payment to Principal
1	$2,400.00 \times 0.1525 \times \dfrac{1}{12}$	=	\$ 30.50	\$ 387.50
2	$2,012.50 \times 0.1525 \times \dfrac{1}{12}$	=	25.58	392.42
3	$1,620.08 \times 0.1525 \times \dfrac{1}{12}$	=	20.59	397.41
4	$1,222.67 \times 0.1525 \times \dfrac{1}{12}$	=	15.54	402.46
5	$820.21 \times 0.1525 \times \dfrac{1}{12}$	=	10.42	407.58
6	$412.63 \times 0.1525 \times \dfrac{1}{12}$	=	5.24	412.76
	Totals	=	$107.87	$2,400.13

($0.13 difference in totals is due to rounding and use of the actuarial rate correct only to nearest 1/4%.)

24. (a) $I = Prt$

$\qquad = \$800 \times 0.10 \times \dfrac{3}{12}$

$\quad I = \$20$

(b) $\dfrac{\$820}{3} = \$273.33/\text{month}$

(c) Simple interest rate × time $= 10\% \times \dfrac{3}{12} = 2.5$

$2.50 finance charge per $100 financed over 3 months = 15% APR

24. (Continued)

(d)

Month	Prt	=	I	Payment to Principal
1	$800.00 × 0.15 × $\frac{1}{12}$	=	$10.00	$263.33
2	536.67 × 0.15 × $\frac{1}{12}$	=	6.71	266.62
3	270.05 × 0.15 × $\frac{1}{12}$	=	3.38	269.95
		Totals	$20.09	$799.90

($0.09 difference in totals is due to rounding and the use of the actuarial tables correct only to 1/4%.)

25. (a) I = Prt

$$= \$2,200 \times 0.12 \times \frac{5}{12}$$

I = $110

(b) $\frac{\$2,310}{5}$ = $462/month

(c) Simple interest rate × time = 12% × $\frac{5}{12}$ = 5

$5 finance charge per $100 financed over 5 months = 19.75% APR

(d)

Month	Prt	=	I	Payment to Principal
1	$2,200.00 × 0.1975 × $\frac{1}{12}$	=	$ 36.21	$ 425.79
2	1,774.21 × 0.1975 × $\frac{1}{12}$	=	29.20	432.80
3	1,341.41 × 0.1975 × $\frac{1}{12}$	=	22.08	439.92
4	901.49 × 0.1975 × $\frac{1}{12}$	=	14.84	447.16
5	454.33 × 0.1975 × $\frac{1}{12}$	=	7.48	454.52
		Totals =	$109.81	$2,200.19

($0.19 difference in totals is due to rounding and use of actuarial tables correct only to the nearest 1/4%.)

26. (a) $I = Prt$

$\quad\quad = \$800 \times 0.09 \times \dfrac{6}{12}$

$\quad I = \$36$

(b) $\dfrac{\$836}{6} = \$139.33/\text{month}$

(c) Simple interest rate × time $= 9\% \times \dfrac{1}{6} = 4.5$

$4.50 finance charge per $100 financed over 6 months = 15.25% APR

(d)

Month	Prt	=	I	Payment to Principal
1	$800.00 × 0.1525 × $\dfrac{1}{12}$	=	$10.17	$129.16
2	670.84 × 0.1525 × $\dfrac{1}{12}$	=	8.53	130.80
3	540.04 × 0.1525 × $\dfrac{1}{12}$	=	6.86	132.47
4	407.57 × 0.1525 × $\dfrac{1}{12}$	=	5.18	134.15
5	273.42 × 0.1525 × $\dfrac{1}{12}$	=	3.47	135.86
6	137.56 × 0.1525 × $\dfrac{1}{12}$	=	1.75	137.58
	Totals	=	$35.96	$800.02

(Differences in totals are due to rounding and the use of the actuarial tables correct only to nearest 1/4%.)

Section 4, page 462

1. (a) Value for 6 payments at 18.25% = 5.39

$$\dfrac{n \times \text{Pmt} \times \text{Value}}{100 + \text{Value}} = \dfrac{6 \times \$110 \times 5.39}{100 + 5.39}$$

$$= \dfrac{3,557.40}{105.39}$$

$$= \$33.75 \quad \text{Interest saved}$$

1. (a) (Continued)

$660.00 Total of 6 remaining payments of $110 each
- 33.75 Interest saved
$626.25 Balance due

(b) Value for 5 payments at 26.75% = 6.79

$$\frac{n \times Pmt \times Value}{100 + Value} = \frac{5 \times \$237.50 \times 6.79}{100 + 6.79}$$

$$= \frac{8,063.125}{106.79}$$

$$= \$75.50 \quad \text{Interest saved}$$

$1,187.50 Total 5 remaining payments of $237.50 each
-      75.50 Interest saved
$1,112.00 Balance due

2. (a) Value for 4 payments at 16% = 3.36

$$\frac{n \times Pmt \times Value}{100 + Value} = \frac{4 \times \$860 \times 3.36}{100 + 3.36}$$

$$= \frac{11,558.40}{103.36}$$

$$= \$111.83 \quad \text{Interest saved}$$

$3,440.00 Total of 4 remaining payments of $860 each
-   111.83 Interest saved
$3,328.17 Balance due

(b) Value for 5 payments at 21.5% = 5.44

$$\frac{n \times Pmt \times Value}{100 + Value} = \frac{5 \times \$46.67 \times 5.44}{100 + 5.44}$$

$$= \frac{1,269.424}{105.44}$$

$$= \$12.04 \quad \text{Interest saved}$$

$233.35 Total of 5 remaining payments of $46.67 each
- 12.04 Interest saved
$221.31 Balance due

3. (a) <u>Rule of 78s</u>: 6 months early out of 24:

Numerator:

$$\frac{6(6+1)}{2} = \frac{42}{2} = 21$$

Denominator:

$$\frac{24(24+1)}{2} = \frac{600}{2} = 300$$

$$\frac{21}{300} \times \$440 = \$30.80 \text{ Interest saved}$$

$660.00 Total of 6 remaining payments of $110 each
- 30.80 Interest saved
$629.20 Balance due

(b) <u>Rule of 78s</u>: 5 months early out of 15:

Numerator:

$$\frac{5(5+1)}{2} = \frac{30}{2} = 15$$

Denominator:

$$\frac{15(16)}{2} = \frac{240}{2} = 120$$

$$\frac{15}{120} \times \$562.50 = \$70.31 \text{ Interest saved}$$

$1,187.50 Total of 5 remaining payments of $237.50 each
-    70.31 Interest saved
$1,117.19 Balance due

4. (a) <u>Rule of 78s</u>: 4 months early out of 10:

Numerator:

$$\frac{4(4+1)}{2} = \frac{20}{2} = 10$$

Denominator:

$$\frac{10(10+1)}{2} = \frac{110}{2} = 55$$

$$\frac{10}{55} \times \$600 = \$109.09 \text{ Interest saved}$$

$3,440.00 Total of 4 remaining payments of $860 each
-   109.09 Interest saved
$3,330.91 Balance due

(b) <u>Rule of 78s</u>: 5 months early out of 12:

Numerator:

$$\frac{5(5+1)}{2} = \frac{30}{2} = 15$$

Denominator:

$$\frac{12(12+1)}{2} = \frac{156}{2} = 78$$

4. (b) (Continued)

$$\frac{15}{78} \times \$60 = \$11.54 \text{ Interest saved}$$

$233.35 Total of 5 remaining payments of $46.67 each
- 11.54 Interest saved
$221.81 Balance due

5. (a) I = Prt

$$= \$2,800 \times 0.10 \times \frac{24}{12}$$

I = $560

(b) M = P + I
     = $2,800 + $560
   M = $3,360

$$\frac{\$3,360}{24} = \$140/\text{month}$$

(c) $$\frac{\$560}{\$2,800} \times 100 = 20$$

$20.00 per $100 financed over 24 months = 18.25%

(d) $$\frac{n \times Pmt \times Value}{100 + Value} = \frac{14 \times \$140 \times 11.78}{100 + 11.78}$$

$$= \frac{23,088.80}{111.78}$$

$$= \$206.56 \text{ Interest saved}$$

(e) $1,960.00 Total of 14 remaining payments of $140 each
- 206.56 Interest saved
$1,753.44 Balance due

6. (a) I = Prt

$$= \$3,300 \times 0.08 \times 1$$

I = $264

(b) M = P + I
     = $3,300 + $264
   M = $3,564

$$\frac{\$3,564}{12} = \$297/\text{month}$$

(c) Simple interest rate × time = 8% × 1 = 8
$8 finance charge per $100 financed over 12 months = 14.5%
APR

6. (Continued)

(d) $\dfrac{n \times Pmt \times Value}{100 + Value} = \dfrac{4 \times \$297 \times 3.04}{100 + 3.04}$

$= \dfrac{3,611.52}{103.04}$

$= \$35.05$ Interest saved

(e) $\$1,188.00$ Total of 4 remaining payments of $297 each
$-\quad 35.05$ Interest saved
$\$1,152.95$ Balance due

7. (a) I = Prt

$= \$7,500 \times 0.11 \times \dfrac{15}{12}$

$I = \$1,031.25$

(b) M = P + I
$= \$7,500.00 + \$1,031.25$
$M = \$8,531.25$

$\dfrac{\$8,531.25}{15} = \$568.75/\text{month}$

(c) $\dfrac{\$1,031.25}{\$7,500} \times 100 = 13.75$

$13.75 per $100 financed over 15 months = 19.75%

(d) $\dfrac{n \times Pmt \times Value}{100 + Value} = \dfrac{6 \times \$568.75 \times 5.84}{100 + 5.84}$

$= \dfrac{19,929}{105.84}$

$= \$188.29$ Interest saved

(e) $\$3,412.50$ Total of remaining 6 payments of $568.75 each
$-\quad 188.29$ Interest saved
$\$3,224.21$ Balance due

8. (a) I = Prt

$= \$3,000 \times 0.08 \times \dfrac{10}{12}$

$I = \$200$

(b) M = P + I
$= \$3,000 + \$200$
$M = \$3,200$

$\dfrac{\$3,200}{10} = \$320/\text{month}$

8. (Continued)

(c) Simple interest rate × time = 8% × $\frac{10}{12}$ = 6.67

$6.67 finance charge per $100 financed over 10 months =
14.25% APR

(d) $\frac{n \times Pmt \times Value}{100 + Value} = \frac{4 \times \$320 \times 2.99}{100 + 2.99}$

$= \frac{3,827.20}{102.99}$

= $37.16 Interest saved

(e) $1,280.00 Total of remaining 4 payments of $320 each
   -    37.16 Interest saved
   $1,242.84 Balance due

9. (a) I = Prt

    = $3,600 × 0.14 × $\frac{9}{12}$

    I = $378

(b) M = P + I
    = $3,600 + $378
   M = $3,978

$\frac{\$3,978}{9}$ = $442/month

(c) <u>Rule of 78s</u>: 5 months early out of 9:

Numerator:

$\frac{5(5+1)}{2} = \frac{30}{2}$ = 15

Denominator:

$\frac{9(9+1)}{2} = \frac{90}{2}$ = 45

$\frac{15}{45}$ × $378 = $126 Interest saved

(d) $2,210 Total of 5 remaining payments of $442 each
   -    126 Interest saved
   $2,084 Balance due

10. (a) I = Prt
    = $5,000 × 0.10 × 1
    I = $500

(b) M = P + I
    = $5,000 + $500
   M = $5,500

$\frac{\$5,500}{12}$ = $458.33/month

10. (Continued)

   (c) <u>Rule of 78s</u>:   4 months early out of 12:

     Numerator: Denominator:

$$\frac{4(4+1)}{2} = \frac{20}{2} = 10 \qquad\qquad \frac{12(12+1)}{2} = \frac{156}{2} = 78$$

$$\frac{10}{78} \times \$500 = \$64.10 \text{ Interest saved}$$

   (d) $1,833.32 Total of 4 remaining payments of $458.33 each
      -     64.10 Interest saved
     $1,769.22 Balance due

11. (a) $I = Prt$ (b) $M = P + I$
                                  $= \$1,200 + \$180$

$$= \$1,200 \times 0.12 \times \frac{15}{12} \qquad M = \$1,380$$

$$I = \$180 \qquad\qquad\qquad \frac{\$1,380}{15} = \$92/\text{month}$$

   (c) <u>Rule of 78s</u>:   9 months early out of 15:

     Numerator: Denominator:

$$\frac{9(9+1)}{2} = \frac{90}{2} = 45 \qquad\qquad \frac{15(15+1)}{2} = \frac{240}{2} = 120$$

$$\frac{45}{120} \times \$180 = \$67.50 \text{ Interest saved}$$

   (d) $828.00 Total of remaining 9 payments of $92 each
      - 67.50 Interest saved
     $760.50 Balance due

12. (a) $I = Prt$ (b) $M = P + I$
        $= \$1,200 \times 0.08 \times 2$ $= \$1,200 + \$192$
       $I = \$192$ $M = \$1,392$

$$\frac{\$1,392}{24} = \$58/\text{month}$$

12. (Continued)

(c) <u>Rule of 78s</u>: 10 months early out of 24:

Numerator: Denominator:

$$\frac{10(10+1)}{2} = \frac{110}{2} = 55 \qquad\qquad \frac{24(24+1)}{2} = \frac{600}{2} = 300$$

$$\frac{55}{300} \times \$192 = \$35.20 \text{ Interest saved}$$

(d) $580.00 Total of remaining 10 payments of $58 each
   - 35.20 Interest saved
   $544.80 Balance due

CHAPTER XVIII

COMPOUND INTEREST

Despite the deceptive terminology, compound interest is much simpler for the student than is "simple" interest. This is due to the fact that computation in this chapter (and in the remaining chapters) usually involves only one multiplication using a value from a table; so, provided the student uses the right table, the "problem" presents no difficulty at all. Only the basic amount and present value problems are included, as these are sufficient to meet business math objectives.

1.   Compound Interest (by Computation):

Although manual computation of compound interest is rather tedious, the student needs to compute a few problems in this manner in order to develop an understanding of what compound interest really is. Example 1 shows the difference between simple interest and compound interest for a period of three years, but presented from a simple interest standpoint. The terminology used in the computation of compound interest is then introduced, and examples 2 and 3 demonstrate the computation of the number of conversion periods and the rate per period at compound interest. Finally, example 4 shows the manual computation of compound interest as such. The student problems require the manual computation of compound interest for only a limited number of periods, but a sufficient number to illustrate the procedure involved.

2.   Compound Amount (using Tables):

This section introduces the compound amount formula, $M = P(1 + i)^n$. Example 1 demonstrates the application of this formula without use of the table, in order to illustrate how the tabular entries were derived. The example is then reworked using the compound amount table; example 2 presents a similar example. When the student first begins using the compound amount formula, the parentheses $(1 + i)^n$ usually give some students the impression that "1" must be added to the tabular value; emphasize that this must not be done. It will probably be necessary to review from Chapter 1 the section regarding the number of tabular decimal places which must be used to ensure accuracy to the nearest cent. As you work examples for the class, ask them how many digits must be used before you write the tabular value.

The problems computed manually in section 1 were for such short periods of time that the student could not fully appreciate the advantage of compound interest. You can bring out the difference by comparing the $1,032.89 compound interest of example 2 with the corresponding simple interest: $2,000 invested at 7% for 6 years = $840 simple interest.

Example 3 is a two-part problem where the principal changes. Diagrams are extremely helpful here, and the students should be encouraged to use them.

Problems in the simple interest chapter emphasized that interest doubled, tripled, halved, etc., whenever the corresponding change occurred in principal, rate, or time. Problems 9 through 14 of this topic emphasize that only principal has a direct effect on compound interest.

The information below shows how the compound amount formula $M = P(1 + i)^n$ is derived. This will be of interest to your better students who have a good algebra background. The accumulation factor $(1 + i)^n$ is fundamental to all the formulas of Chapters XVIII through XX.

i =   rate per period n = number of periods

I_1 $= Pi$ M_1 $= P + I_1$

                                              $= P + Pi$

                                         M_1 $= P(1 + i)$

I_2 $= [P(1 + i)]i$ M_2 $= P(1 + i) + P(1 + i)i$

                                               $= P[(1 + i) + (1 + i)i]$

                                               $= P[(1 + i)(1 + i)]$

                                         M_2 $= P(1 + i)^2$

.   .
.   .
.   .

I_{n-1} $= P(1 + i)^{n-2}i$ M_{n-1} $= P(1 + i)^{n-2} + P(1 + i)^{n-2}i$

                                               $= P[(1 + i)^{n-2}(1 + i)]$

                                         M_{n-1} $= P(1 + i)^{n-1}$

I_n $= P(1 + i)^{n-1}i$ M_n $= P(1 + i)^{n-1} + P(1 + i)^{n-1}i$

                                               $= P[(1 + i)^{n-1}(1 + i)]$

                                         M_n $= P(1 + i)^n$

3.   **Interest Compounded Daily**:

This topic reflects the current business practice of most institutions offering interest compounded daily. Daily compounding, of course, slightly increases the amount of interest earned; and some institutions may also pay from 1/4 to 1/2% higher interest than others. [Actually, deposits may have to remain invested until the end of the quarter in order to earn interest; that is, funds may be required to be on deposit for three months in order to earn interest to date of withdrawal. The student problems meet these requirements, although this is not brought out in the text.]

You might wish to omit example 4 from basic courses. Student problems 3 and 4 point out the advantage of interest compounded daily over interest compounded quarterly; all other problems illustrate various deposit/withdrawal transactions during a quarter.

4.   **Present Value (at Compound Interest)**:

The concept of present value learned during the study of simple interest also applies to compound interest; thus, this topic does not present the problem that present value did earlier. As was done for simple interest, the present value formula is presented as an adaptation of the amount formula. The introductory material describes how the present value formula, $P = M(1 + i)^{-n}$, is derived; and example 1 demonstrates that a present value problem could be solved using either the "amount at compound interest" table or the "present value at compound interest" table. (However, students will not be required to solve any present value problems using the compound amount table.) As before, the similarity of the compound amount and present value formulas will present difficulties in the students' memorization. Emphasize that they should memorize carefully, and stress that the minus sign must be included in the present value formula.

Example 2 is an application of present value at compound interest. Example 3 is a two-part problem where present value differs from the principal; as indicated above, this problem will be practically "routine" for the students, having mastered the basic procedure as part of the study of simple interest.

CHAPTER 18 - COMPOUND INTEREST
PROBLEM SOLUTIONS

Section 1, page 470

1. (a) 6 years × 1 period per year = 6 periods

$$\frac{4.5\%}{1 \text{ period per year}} = 4.5\% \text{ per period}$$

(b) 2 years × 12 periods per year = 24 periods

$$\frac{9\%}{12 \text{ periods per year}} = 0.75\% \text{ per period}$$

(c) 5 years × 2 periods per year = 10 periods

$$\frac{7.5\%}{2 \text{ periods per year}} = 3.75\% \text{ per period}$$

(d) 8 years × 4 periods per year = 32 periods

$$\frac{6\%}{4 \text{ periods per year}} = 1.5\% \text{ per period}$$

(e) 9 years × 2 periods a year = 18 periods

$$\frac{5\%}{2 \text{ periods per year}} = 2.5\% \text{ per period}$$

2. (a) 8 years × 1 period per year = 8 periods

$$\frac{5.8\%}{1 \text{ period per year}} = 5.8\% \text{ per period}$$

(b) 4 years × 12 periods per year = 48 periods

$$\frac{3\%}{12 \text{ periods per year}} = 0.25\% \text{ per period}$$

(c) 6 years × 2 periods per year = 12 periods

$$\frac{8\%}{2 \text{ periods per year}} = 4\% \text{ per period}$$

2. (Continued)

(d) 4 years × 4 periods per year = 16 periods

$$\frac{8.5\%}{4 \text{ periods per year}} = 2.125\% \text{ per period}$$

(e) 3 years × 2 periods per year = 6 periods

$$\frac{5.6\%}{2 \text{ periods per year}} = 2.8\% \text{ per period}$$

3. (a) 4 years × 1 period per year = 4 periods

$$\frac{7\%}{1 \text{ period per year}} = 7\% \text{ per period}$$

Period 1	Principal	$4,000.00	
	Interest	280.00	(7% of $4,000)
Period 2	Principal	$4,280.00	
	Interest	299.60	(7% of $4,280)
Period 3	Principal	$4,579.60	
	Interest	320.57	(7% of $4,579.60)
Period 4	Principal	$4,900.17	
	Interest	343.01	(7% of $4,900.17)
Compound amount		$5,243.18	

Compound amount $5,243.18
Original principal -4,000.00
Compound interest $1,243.18

(b) 4 years × 2 periods per year = 8 periods

$$\frac{7\%}{2 \text{ periods per year}} = 3.5\% \text{ per period}$$

Period 1	Principal	$4,000.00	
	Interest	140.00	(3.5% of $4,000)
Period 2	Principal	$4,140.00	
	Interest	144.90	(3.5% of $4,140)
Period 3	Principal	$4,284.90	
	Interest	149.97	(3.5% of $4,284.90)
Period 4	Principal	$4,434.87	
	Interest	155.22	(3.5% of $4,434.87)
Period 5	Principal	$4,590.09	
	Interest	160.65	(3.5% of $4,590.09)
Period 6	Principal	$4,750.74	
	Interest	166.28	(3.5% of $4,750.74)

3. (b) (Continued)

```
Period 7      Principal    $4,917.02
              Interest        172.10  (3.5% of $4,917.02)
Period 8      Principal    $5,089.12
              Interest        178.12  (3.5% of $5,089.12)
         Compound amount   $5,267.24
```

```
Compound amount     $5,267.24
Original principal  -4,000.00
Compound interest   $1,267.24
```

4. (a) 3 years × 1 period per year = 3 periods

$$\frac{5\%}{1 \text{ period per year}} = 5\% \text{ per period}$$

```
Period 1      Principal    $2,500.00
              Interest        125.00  (5% of $2,500)
Period 2      Principal    $2,625.00
              Interest        131.25  (5% of $2,625)
Period 3      Principal    $2,756.25
              Interest        137.81  (5% of $2,756.25)
         Compound amount   $2,894.06
```

```
Compound amount     $2,894.06
Original principal  -2,500.00
Compound interest   $  394.06
```

(b) 3 years × 2 periods per year = 6 periods

$$\frac{5\%}{2 \text{ periods per year}} = 2.5\% \text{ per period}$$

```
Period 1      Principal    $2,500.00
              Interest         62.50  (2.5% of $2,500)
Period 2      Principal    $2,562.50
              Interest         64.06  (2.5% of $2,562.50)
Period 3      Principal    $2,626.56
              Interest         65.66  (2.5% of $2,626.56)
Period 4      Principal    $2,692.22
              Interest         67.31  (2.5% of $2,692.22)
Period 5      Principal    $2,759.53
              Interest         68.99  (2.5% of $2,759.53)
Period 6      Principal    $2,828.52
              Interest         70.71  (2.5% of $2,828.52)
         Compound amount   $2,899.23
```

4. (b) (Continued)

    Compound amount $2,899.23
    Original principal   <u>-2,500.00</u>
    Compound interest $ 399.23

5. (a) 1 year × 2 periods a year = 2 periods

$$\frac{5\%}{2 \text{ periods per year}} = 2.5\% \text{ per period}$$

    Period 1   Principal $3,000.00
                Interest   <u>75.00</u> (2.5% of $3,000)
    Period 2   Principal $3,075.00
                Interest   <u>76.88</u> (2.5% of $3,075)
         Compound amount $3,151.88

    Compound amount $3,151.88
    Original principal   <u>-3,000.00</u>
    Compound interest $ 151.88

   (b) 1 year × 4 periods a year = 4 periods

$$\frac{5\%}{4 \text{ periods per year}} = 1.25\% \text{ per period}$$

    Period 1   Principal $3,000.00
                Interest   <u>37.50</u> (1.25% of $3,000)
    Period 2   Principal $3,037.50
                Interest   <u>37.97</u> (1.25% of $3,037.50)
    Period 3   Principal $3,075.47
                Interest   <u>38.44</u> (1.25% of $3,075.47)
    Period 4   Principal $3,113.91
                Interest   <u>38.92</u> (1.25% of $3,113.91)
         Compound amount $3,152.83

    Compound amount $3,152.83
    Original principal   <u>-3,000.00</u>
    Compound interest $ 152.83

6. (a) 1 year × 2 periods per year = 2 periods

$$\frac{8\%}{2 \text{ periods per year}} = 4\% \text{ per period}$$

6. (a) (Continued)

```
Period 1    Principal    $6,000.00
            Interest        240.00  (4% of $6,000)
Period 2    Principal    $6,240.00
            Interest        249.60  (4% of $6,240)
       Compound amount   $6,489.60
```

```
Compound amount      $6,489.60
Original principal   -6,000.00
Compound interest    $  489.60
```

(b) 1 year × 4 periods per year = 4 periods

$$\frac{8\%}{4 \text{ periods per year}} = 2\% \text{ per period}$$

```
Period 1    Principal    $6,000.00
            Interest        120.00  (2% of $6,000)
Period 2    Principal    $6,120.00
            Interest        122.40  (2% of $6,120)
Period 3    Principal    $6,242.40
            Interest        124.85  (2% of $6,242.40)
Period 4    Principal    $6,367.25
            Interest        127.35  (2% of $6,367.25)
       Compound amount   $6,494.60
```

```
Compound amount      $6,494.60
Original principal   -6,000.00
Compound interest    $  494.60
```

7. (a) $\frac{9}{12} = \frac{3}{4}$ year × 4 periods a year = 3 periods

$$\frac{6\%}{4 \text{ periods a year}} = 1.5\% \text{ per period}$$

```
Period 1    Principal    $7,000.00
            Interest        105.00  (1.5% of $7,000)
Period 2    Principal    $7,105.00
            Interest        106.58  (1.5% of $7,105)
Period 3    Principal    $7,211.58
            Interest        108.17  (1.5% of $7,211.58)
       Compound amount   $7,319.75
```

```
Compound amount      $7,319.75
Original principal   -7,000.00
Compound interest    $  319.75
```

7. (Continued)

(b) $\dfrac{3}{4}$ year × 12 periods a year = 9 periods

$$\dfrac{6\%}{12\text{ periods a year}} = 0.5\%\text{ per period}$$

Period 1	Principal	$7,000.00	
	Interest	35.00	(0.5% of $7,000)
Period 2	Principal	$7,035.00	
	Interest	35.18	(0.5% of $7,035)
Period 3	Principal	$7,070.18	
	Interest	35.35	(0.5% of $7,070.18)
Period 4	Principal	$7,105.53	
	Interest	35.53	(0.5% of $7,105.53)
Period 5	Principal	$7,141.06	
	Interest	35.71	(0.5% of $7,141.06)
Period 6	Principal	$7,176.77	
	Interest	35.88	(0.5% of $7,176.77)
Period 7	Principal	$7,212.65	
	Interest	36.06	(0.5% of $7,212.65)
Period 8	Principal	$7,248.71	
	Interest	36.24	(0.5% of $7,248.71)
Period 9	Principal	$7,284.95	
	Interest	36.42	(0.5% of $7,284.95)
	Compound amount	$7,321.37	

Compound amount $7,321.37
Original principal -7,000.00
Compound interest $ 321.37

8. (a) $\dfrac{1}{2}$ year × 4 periods per year = 2 periods

$$\dfrac{4.5\%}{4\text{ periods per year}} = 1.125\%\text{ per period}$$

Period 1	Principal	$4,500.00	
	Interest	50.63	(1.125% of $4,500)
Period 2	Principal	$4,550.63	
	Interest	51.19	(1.125% of $4,550.63)
	Compound amount	$4,601.82	

Compound amount $4,601.82
Original principal -4,500.00
Compound interest $ 101.82

8. (Continued)

(b) $\frac{1}{2}$ year × 12 periods per year = 6 periods

$$\frac{4.5\%}{12 \text{ periods per year}} = 0.375\% \text{ per period}$$

Period 1	Principal	$4,500.00	
	Interest	16.88	(0.375% of $4,500)
Period 2	Principal	$4,516.88	
	Interest	16.94	(0.375% of $4,516.88)
Period 3	Principal	$4,533.82	
	Interest	17.00	(0.375% of $4,533.82)
Period 4	Principal	$4,550.82	
	Interest	17.07	(0.375% of $4,550.82)
Period 5	Principal	$4,567.89	
	Interest	17.13	(0.375% of $4,567.89)
Period 6	Principal	$4,585.02	
	Interest	17.19	(0.375% of $4,585.02)
Compound amount		$4,602.21	

Original Amount $4,602.21
Original principal   -4,500.00
Compound interest $ 102.21

9. More interest is earned when interest is compounded more often.

10. How often interest is compounded.

Section 2, page 477

1. (a) P = $4,000 $M = P(1 + i)^n$
        i = 7% $= \$4,000(1 + 7\%)^4$
        n = 4 $= 4,000(1.3107960)$
                                       M = $5,243.18

    I = M - P
      = $5,243.18 - $4,000.00
    I = $1,243.18

1. (Continued)

   (b) P = $4,000 $M = P(1 + i)^n$
       i = 3.5% $= \$4,000(1 + 3.5\%)^8$
       n = 8 $=\ 4,000(1.3168090)$
                                  $M = \$5,267.24$

       I = M − P
         = $5,267.24 − $4,000.00
       I = $1,267.24

2. (a) P = $2,500 $M = P(1 + i)^n$
       i = 5% $= \$2,500(1 + 5\%)^3$
       n = 3 $=\ 2,500(1.1576)$
                                  $M = \$2,894.06$

       I = M − P
         = $2,894.06 − $2,500.00
       I = $394.06

   (b) P = $2,500 $M = P(1 + i)^n$
       i = 2.5% $= \$2,500(1 + 2.5\%)^6$
       n = 6 $=\ 2,500(1.1597)$
                                  $M = \$2,899.23$

       I = M − P
         = $2,899.23 − $2,500.00
       I = $399.23

3. (a) P = $3,000 $M = P(1 + i)^n$
       i = 2.5% $= \$3,000(1 + 2.5\%)^2$
       n = 2 $=\ 3,000(1.050625)$
                                  $M = \$3,151.88$

       I = M − P
         = $3,151.88 − $3,000.00
       I = $151.88

   (b) P = $3,000 $M = P(1 + i)^n$
       i = 1.25% $= \$3,000(1 + 1.25\%)^4$
       n = 4 $=\ 3,000(1.050945)$
                                  $M = \$3,152.84$

       I = M − P
         = $3,152.84 − $3,000.00
       I = $152.84

4. (a) P = $6,000   M = P(1 + i)^n
       i = 4%   = $6,000(1 + 4%)^2
       n = 2   =   6,000(1.0816)
                                       M = $6,489.60

       I = M - P
         = $6,489.60 - $6,000.00
       I = $489.60

   (b) P = $6,000   M = P(1 + i)^n
       i = 2%   = $6,000(1 + 2%)^4
       n = 4   =   6,000(1.0824)
                                       M = $6,494.59

       I = M - P
         = $6,494.59 - $6,000.00
       I = $494.59

5. (a) P = $7,000   M = P(1 + i)^n
       i = 1.5%   = $7,000(1 + 1.5%)^3
       n = 3   =   7,000(1.045678)
                                       M = $7,319.75

       I = M - P
         = $7,319.75 - $7,000.00
       I = $319.75

   (b) P = $7,000   M = P(1 + i)^n
       i = 0.5%   = $7,000(1 + 0.5%)^9
       n = 9   =   7,000(1.045911)
                                       M = $7,321.37

       I = M - P
         = $7,321.37 - $7,000.00
       I = $321.37

6. (a) P = $4,500   M = P(1 + i)^n
       i = 1.125%   = $4,500(1 + 1.125%)^2
       n = 2   =   4,500(1.0226)
                                       M = $4,601.82

       I = M - P
         = $4,601.82 - $4,500.00
       I = $101.82

6. (Continued)

(b) $P = \$4,500$

$i = 0.375\%$

$n = 6$

$M = P(1 + i)^n$

$= \$4,500(1 + 0.375)^6$

$= 4,500(1.0227)$

$M = \$4,602.20$

$I = M - P$

$= \$4,602.20 - \$4,500.00$

$I = \$102.20$

7. (a) $P = \$500$

$i = \dfrac{5}{12}\%$

$n = 36$

$M = P(1 + i)^n$

$= \$500\left(1 + \dfrac{5}{12}\%\right)^{36}$

$= 500(1.161472)$

$M = \$580.74$

$I = M - P$

$= \$580.74 - \$500.00$

$I = \$80.74$

(b) $P = \$1,700$

$i = 1.5\%$

$n = 20$

$M = P(1 + i)^n$

$= \$1,700(1 + 1.5\%)^{20}$

$= 1,700(1.346855)$

$M = \$2,289.65$

$I = M - P$

$= \$2,289.65 - \$1,700.00$

$I = \$589.65$

(c) $P = \$3,200$

$i = 3.5\%$

$n = 12$

$M = P(1 + i)^n$

$= \$3,200(1 + 3.5\%)^{12}$

$= 3,200(1.511069)$

$M = \$4,835.42$

$I = M - P$

$= \$4,835.42 - \$3,200.00$

$I = \$1,635.42$

(d) $P = \$4,500$

$i = \dfrac{2}{3}\%$

$n = 48$

$M = P(1 + i)^n$

$= \$4,500\left(1 + \dfrac{2}{3}\%\right)^{48}$

$= 4,500(1.375666)$

$M = \$6,190.50$

7. (d) (Continued)

$$I = M - P$$
$$= \$6,190.50 - \$4,500.00$$
$$I = \$1,690.50$$

(e) P = $8,100
i = 2.25%
n = 28

$$M = P(1 + i)^n$$
$$= \$8,100(1 + 2.25\%)^{28}$$
$$= 8,100(1.8645450)$$
$$M = \$15,102.81$$

$$I = M - P$$
$$= \$15,102.81 - \$8,100.00$$
$$I = \$7,002.81$$

8. (a) P = $1,400
i = 0.5%
n = 60

$$M = P(1 + i)^n$$
$$= \$1,400(1 + 0.5\%)^{60}$$
$$= 1,400(1.348850)$$
$$M = \$1,888.39$$

$$I = M - P$$
$$= \$1,888.39 - \$1,400.00$$
$$I = \$488.39$$

(b) P = $2,500
i = 1.25%
n = 16

$$M = P(1 + i)^n$$
$$= \$2,500(1 + 1.25\%)^{16}$$
$$= 2,500(1.219890)$$
$$M = \$3,049.73$$

$$I = M - P$$
$$= \$3,049.73 - \$2,500.00$$
$$I = \$549.73$$

(c) P = $5,200
i = 2%
n = 6

$$M = P(1 + i)^n$$
$$= \$5,200(1 + 2\%)^{6}$$
$$= 5,200(1.126162)$$
$$M = \$5,856.04$$

$$I = M - P$$
$$= \$5,856.04 - \$5,200.00$$
$$I = \$656.04$$

8. (Continued)

(d) P = \$9,000

$i = \dfrac{7}{12}\%$

n = 72

$M = P(1 + i)^n$

$= \$9,000\left(1 + \dfrac{7}{12}\%\right)^{72}$

$= \ 9{,}000(1.520106)$

M = \$13,680.95

I = M − P
  = \$13,680.95 − \$9,000.00
I = \$4,680.95

(e) P = \$800
i = 2%
n = 8

$M = P(1 + i)^n$
$= \$800(1 + 2\%)^8$
$= \ 800(1.171659)$
M = \$937.33

I = M − P
  = \$937.33 − \$800.00
I = \$137.33

9. (a) P = \$500

$i = \dfrac{5}{12}\%$

n = 36

$M = P(1 + i)^n$

$= \$500\left(1 + \dfrac{5}{12}\%\right)^{36}$

$= \ 500(1.161472)$

M = \$580.74

I = M − P
  = \$580.74 − \$500.00
I = \$80.74

(b) P = \$1,000

$i = \dfrac{5}{12}\%$

n = 36

$M = P(1 + i)^n$

$= \$1,000\left(1 + \dfrac{5}{12}\%\right)^{36}$

$= \ 1{,}000(1.161472)$

M = \$1,161.47

I = M − P
  = \$1,161.47 − \$1,000.00
I = \$161.47

9. (Continued)

(c) $P = \$2,000$

$i = \dfrac{5}{12}\%$

$n = 36$

$M = P(1 + i)^n$

$ = \$2,000\left(1 + \dfrac{5}{12}\%\right)^{36}$

$ = 2,000(1.161472)$

$M = \$2,322.94$

$I = M - P$
$ = \$2,322.94 - \$2,000.00$
$I = \$322.94$

(d) Doubling the principal doubles the interest when interest rate and time are the same.

10. (a) $P = \$800$

$i = \dfrac{7}{12}\%$

$n = 48$

$M = P(1 + i)^n$

$ = \$800\left(1 + \dfrac{7}{12}\%\right)^{48}$

$ = 800(1.322054)$

$M = \$1,057.64$

$I = M - P$
$ = \$1,057.64 - \$800.00$
$I = \$257.64$

(b) $P = \$1,600$

$i = \dfrac{7}{12}\%$

$n = 48$

$M = P(1 + i)^n$

$ = \$1,600\left(1 + \dfrac{7}{12}\%\right)^{48}$

$ = 1,600(1.322054)$

$M = \$2,115.29$

$I = M - P$
$ = \$2,115.29 - \$1,600.00$
$I = \$515.29$

(c) $P = \$3,200$

$i = \dfrac{7}{12}\%$

$n = 48$

$M = P(1 + i)^n$

$ = \$3,200\left(1 + \dfrac{7}{12}\%\right)^{48}$

$ = 3,200(1.322054)$

$M = \$4,230.57$

10. (c) (Continued)

$$I = M - P$$
$$= \$4,230.57 - \$3,200.00$$
$$I = \$1,030.57$$

(d) Doubling the principal doubles the interest when interest rate and time are constants.

11. (a) $P = \$1,000$ $M = P(1 + i)^n$
    $i = 1\%$ $= \$1,000(1 + 1\%)^8$
    $n = 8$ $= 1,000(1.082857)$
                    $M = \$1,082.86$

$$I = M - P$$
$$= \$1,082.86 - \$1,000.00$$
$$I = \$82.86$$

(b) $P = \$1,000$ $M = P(1 + i)^n$
    $i = 2\%$ $= \$1,000(1 + 2\%)^8$
    $n = 8$ $= 1,000(1.171659)$
                    $M = \$1,171.66$

$$I = M - P$$
$$= \$1,171.66 - \$1,000.00$$
$$I = \$171.66$$

(c) $P = \$1,000$ $M = P(1 + i)^n$
    $i = 4\%$ $= \$1,000(1 + 4\%)^8$
    $n = 8$ $= 1,000(1.368569)$
                    $M = \$1,368.57$

$$I = M - P$$
$$= \$1,368.57 - \$1,000.00$$
$$I = \$368.57$$

(d) No

12. (a) $P = \$1,000$ $M = P(1 + i)^n$
    $i = 0.75\%$ $= \$1,000(1 + 0.75\%)^{20}$
    $n = 20$ $= 1,000(1.161184)$
                    $M = \$1,161.18$

$$I = M - P$$
$$= \$1,161.18 - \$1,000.00$$
$$I = \$161.18$$

12. (Continued)

(b) P = \$1,000
  i = 1.5%
  n = 20

$M = P(1 + i)^n$
 $= \$1,000(1 + 1.5\%)^{20}$
 $= 1,000(1.346855)$
$M = \$1,346.86$

I = M - P
 = \$1,346.86 - \$1,000.00
I = \$346.86

(c) P = \$1,000
  i = 3%
  n = 20

$M = P(1 + i)^n$
 $= \$1,000(1 + 3\%)^{20}$
 $= 1,000(1.806111)$
$M = \$1,806.11$

I = M - P
 = \$1,806.11 - \$1,000.00
I = \$806.11

(d) No

13. (a) P = \$1,000
   i = 3%
   n = 4

$M = P(1 + i)^n$
 $= \$1,000(1 + 3\%)^4$
 $= 1,000(1.125509)$
$M = \$1,125.51$

I = M - P
 = \$1,125.51 - \$1,000.00
I = \$125.51

(b) P = \$1,000
  i = 3%
  n = 8

$M = P(1 + i)^n$
 $= \$1,000(1 + 3\%)^8$
 $= 1,000(1.266770)$
$M = \$1,266.77$

I = M - P
 = \$1,266.77 - \$1,000.00
I = \$266.77

(c) P = \$1,000
  i = 3%
  n = 16

$M = P(1 + i)^n$
 $= \$1,000(1 + 3\%)^{16}$
 $= 1,000(1.604706)$
$M = \$1,604.71$

I = M - P
 = \$1,604.71 - \$1,000.00
I = \$604.71

13. (Continued)

    (d) No

14. (a) P = $1,000$ $M = P(1 + i)^n$
         i = 2.5% $= \$1,000(1 + 2.5\%)^6$
         n = 6 $= 1,000(1.159693)$
                                    $M = \$1,159.69$

         I = M - P
           = $1,159.69 - $1,000.00
         I = $159.69

    (b) P = $1,000$ $M = P(1 + i)^n$
         i = 2.5% $= \$1,000(1 + 2.5\%)^{12}$
         n = 12 $= 1,000(1.344889)$
                                    $M = \$1,344.89$

         I = M - P
           = $1,344.89 - $1,000.00
         I = $344.89

    (c) P = $1,000$ $M = P(1 + i)^n$
         i = 2.5% $= \$1,000(1 + 2.5\%)^{24}$
         n = 24 $= 1,000(1.808726)$
                                    $M = \$1,808.73$

         I = M - P
           = $1,808.73 - $1,000.00
         I = $808.76

    (d) No

15. $P_1 = \$1,000$ $P_2 = \$1,200$

    (a) $P_1 = \$1,000$ $M_1 = P_1(1 + i)^n$
         i = 1% $= \$1,000(1 + 1\%)^2$
         n = 2 $= 1,000(1.0201)$
                                 $M_1 = \$1,020.10$

    (b) $1,200.00 - $1,020.10 = $179.90

    (c) $P_2 = \$1,200$ $M_2 = P_2(1 + i)^n$
         i = 1% $= \$1,200(1 + 1\%)^4$
         n = 4 $= 1,200(1.040604)$
                                 $M_2 = \$1,248.72$

15. (Continued)

    (d) $1,248.72 Maturity$_2$ I_1 = $20.10
       -1,179.90 Total deposits (or) I_2 = +48.72
      $ 68.82 $68.82

16. P_1 = $2,200 P_2 = $2,400

    (a) P_1 = $2,200 M_1 = $P_1(1 + i)^n$
       i = 1.5%   = $2,200(1 + 1.5\%)^2$
       n = 2   = 2,200(1.030225)
                        M_1 = $2,266.50

    (b) $2,400.00 - $2,266.50 = $133.50

    (c) P_2 = $2,400 M_2 = $P_2(1 + i)^n$
       i = 1.5%   = $2,400(1 + 1.5\%)^4$
       n = 4   = 2,400(1.061364)
                        M_2 = $2,547.27

    (d) $2,547.27 Maturity$_2$ I_1 = $ 66.50
       -2,333.50 Total deposits (or) I_2 = +147.27
      $ 213.77 $213.77

17. P_1 = $1,000 P_2 = $1,400

    (a) P_1 = $1,000 M_1 = $P_1(1 + i)^n$
       i = $\frac{5}{12}$%   = $1,000\left(1 + \frac{5}{12}\%\right)^3$
       n = 3   = 1,000(1.012552)
                   M_2 = $1,012.55

    (b) $1,400.00 - $1,012.55 = $387.45

    (c) P_2 = $1,400 M_2 = $P_2(1 + i)^n$
       i = 1.5%   = $1,400(1 + 1.5\%)^4$
       n = 4   = 1,400(1.061364)
                  M_2 = $1,485.91

    (d) Interest, CD#1 $12.55 $1,485.91 Maturity$_2$
       Interest, CD#2 +85.91 (or) -1,387.45 Total deposits
       Total interest $98.46 $ 98.46 Total interest

18. P_1 = \$2,000 P_2 = \$2,100

  (a) P_1 = \$2,000 $M_1 = P_1(1 + i)^n$
       i = 3.5%   = \$2,000$(1 + 3.5\%)^1$
       n = 1   = 2,000(1.035)
                                       M_1 = \$2,070

  (b) \$2,100 - \$2,070 = \$30

  (c) P_2 = \$2,100 $M_2 = P_2(1 + i)^n$
       i = 1.75%   = \$2,100$(1 + 1.75\%)^4$
       n = 4   = 2,100(1.071859)
                                       M_2 = \$2,250.90

  (d) \$2,250.90 Maturity$_2$ I_1 = \$ 70.00
       -2,030.00 Total deposits (or) I_2 = +150.90
       \$ 220.90   \$220.90

19. P_1 = \$1,000 P_2 = \$1,400

  (a) P_1 = \$1,000 $M_1 = P_1(1 + i)^n$

       i = $\dfrac{5}{12}$%   = \$1,000$\left(1 + \dfrac{5}{12}\%\right)^6$

       n = 6   = 1,000(1.025262)

                                       M_1 = \$1,025.26

  (b) \$1,400.00 - \$1,025.26 = \$374.74

  (c) P_2 = \$1,400 $M_2 = P_2(1 + i)^n$
       i = 1.75%   = \$1,400$(1 + 1.75\%)^8$
       n = 8   = 1,400(1.148882)
                                       M_2 = \$1,608.43

  (d) Interest, CD#1 \$ 25.26   \$1,608.43 Maturity$_2$
       Interest, CD#2 +208.43   (or) -1,374.74 Total deposits
       Total interest \$233.69   \$ 233.69 Total interest

20. P_1 = \$600 P_2 = \$700

  (a) P_1 = \$600 $M_1 = P_1(1 + i)^n$
       i = 1%   = \$600$(1 + 1\%)^2$
       n = 2   = 600(1.0201)
                                       M_1 = \$612.06

  (b) \$700.00 - \$612.06 = \$87.94

20. (Continued)

    (c) $P_2 = \$700$ $M_2 = P_2(1 + i)^n$
          $i = 2.5\%$ $= \$700(1 + 2.5\%)^4$
          $n = 4$ $= 700(1.103813)$
                                     $M_2 = \$772.67$

    (d) $\$772.67$ Maturity$_2$ $I_1 = \$12.06$
       $\underline{-687.94}$ Total deposits (or) $I_2 = \underline{+72.67}$
       $\$\ 84.73$ $\$84.73$

Section 3, page 484

1. (a) $P = \$1,000$

      $I = P \times$ Dep. tab. $M = P + I$
         $= \$1,000(0.0072759)$ $= \$1,000.00 + \$7.28$
      $I = \$7.28$ $M = \$1,007.28$

    (b) $P = \$800$

      $I = P \times$ Dep. tab. $M = P + I$
         $= \$800(0.01068)$ $= \$800.00 + \$8.54$
      $I = \$8.54$ $M = \$808.54$

    (c) $P = \$4,000$

      $I = P \times$ Dep. tab. $M = P + I$
         $= \$4,000(0.001877)$ $= \$4,000.00 + \$7.51$
      $I = \$7.51$ $M = \$4,007.51$

    (d) $P = \$600$

      $I = P \times$ Dep. tab. $M = P + I$
         $= \$600(0.01043)$ $= \$600.00 + \$6.26$
      $I = \$6.26$ $M = \$606.26$

2. (a) $P = \$1,000$

      $I = P \times$ Dep. tab. $M = P + I$
         $= \$1,000(0.0070241)$ $= \$1,000.00 + \$7.02$
      $I = \$7.02$ $M = \$1,007.02$

2. (Continued)

(b) P = $350

I = P × Dep. tab.   M = P + I
  = $350(0.0101758)   = $350.00 + $3.56
I = $3.56   M = $353.56

(c) P = $2,300

I = P × Dep. tab.   M = P + I
  = $2,300(0.0020019)   = $2,300.00 + $4.60
I = $4.60   M = $2,304.60

(d) P = $700

I = P × Dep. tab.   M = P + I
  = $700(0.0090401)   = $700.00 + $6.33
I = $6.33   M = $706.33

3. (a-1) P = $7,500   (a-2) P = $7,500

I = P × Dep. tab.   I = P × Dep. tab.
  = $7,500(0.011313)   = $7,500(0.01125)
I = $84.85   I = $84.38

(b-1) P = $4,500   (b-2) P = $4,500

I = P × Dep. tab.   I = P × Dep. tab.
  = $4,500(0.0113128)   = $4,500(0.01125)
I = $50.91   I = $50.63

4. (a-1) P = $5,000   (a-2) P = $5,000

I = P × Dep. tab.   I = P × Dep. tab.
  = $5,000(0.0113128)   = $5,000(0.01125)
I = $56.56   I = $56.25

(b-1) P = $600   (b-2) P = $600

I = P × Dep. tab.   I = P × Dep. Tab.
  = $600(0.0113128)   = $600(0.01125)
I = $6.79   I = $6.75

5. (a) I = P × Dep. tab.

				Balance
I_1 = $700(0.0113128)	=	$ 7.92		$ 700.00
I_2 = $500(0.0086618)	=	4.33		500.00
I_3 = $300(0.0057662)	=	1.73		300.00
I_4 = $400(0.0032551)	=	1.30		400.00
Total interest		$15.28		15.28
				$1,915.28

(b) I = P × Dep. tab.

				Balance
I_1 = $600(0.0113128)	=	$ 6.79		$ 600.00
I_2 = $200(0.0076537)	=	1.53		200.00
I_3 = $400(0.0060177)	=	2.41		400.00
I_4 = $300(0.0027536)	=	0.83		300.00
Total interest		$11.56		11.56
				$1,511.56

6. (a) I = P × Dep. tab.

				Balance
I_1 = $1,000(0.0111864)	=	$11.19		$1,000.00
I_2 = $ 200(0.0081576)	=	1.63		200.00
I_3 = $ 500(0.0072759)	=	3.64		500.00
I_4 = $ 400(0.0003751)	=	0.15		400.00
Total interest		$16.61		16.61
				$2,116.61

(b) I = P × Dep. tab.

				Balance
I_1 = $1,500(0.0113128)	=	$16.97		$1,500.00
I_2 = $ 900(0.0075277)	=	6.77		900.00
I_3 = $1,000(0.0051378)	=	5.14		1,000.00
I_4 = $ 600(0.0035059)	=	2.10		600.00
Total interest		$30.98		30.98
				$4,030.98

7. (a) P = $10,000 - $1,000 = $9,000

	Interest	Balance
I_1 = P × Dep. tab.		$10,000.00
= $9,000(0.0113128)	$101.82	- 1,000.00
I_1 = $101.82	4.26	+ 106.08
	$106.08	$ 9,106.08
I_2 = W × W/D tab.		
= $1,000(0.004259)		
I_2 = $4.26		

7. (Continued)

(b) P = $5,500 - $100 - $400 = $5,000

	Interest	Balance
I_1 = P × Dep. tab.	$56.56	$5,500.00
= $5,000(0.0113128)	0.50	- 100.00
I_1 = $56.56	3.06	- 400.00
	$60.12	+ 60.12
I_2 = W × W/D tab.		$5,060.12
= $100(0.00501)		
I_2 = $0.50		

I_3 = W × W/D tab.
   = $400(0.00765)
I_3 = $3.06

8. (a) P = $6,800 - $800 = $6,000

	Interest	Balance
I_1 = P × Dep. tab.	$64.84	$6,800.00
= $6,000(0.0108073)	6.53	- 800.00
I_1 = $64.84	$71.37	+ 71.37
		$6,071.37
I_2 = W × W/D tab.		
= $800(0.0081576)		
I_2 = $6.53		

(b) P = $2,400 - $200 - $500 = $1,700

	Interest	Balance
I_1 = P × Dep. tab.	$17.30	$2,400.00
= $1,700(0.0101758)	0.95	- 200.00
I_1 = $17.30	5.02	- 500.00
	$23.27	+ 23.27
I_2 = W × W/D tab.		$1,723.27
= $200(0.004761)		
I_2 = $0.95		

I_3 = W × W/D tab.
   = $500(0.0100495)
I_3 = $5.02

9. (a) P_1 = $5,600 - $1,000 = $4,600
       P_2 = $500

9. (a) (Continued)

$I_1 = P_1 \times$ Dep. tab.

	Interest	Balance
$= \$4,600(0.0113128)$	$\$52.04$	$\$5,600.00$
$I_1 = \$52.04$	3.83	$-1,000.00$
	$\underline{5.14}$	$+\ \ 500.00$
$I_2 = P_2 \times$ Dep. tab.	$\$61.01$	$+\ \ \ \underline{61.01}$
$= \$500(0.00765)$		$\$5,161.01$
$I_2 = \$3.83$		

$I_3 = W \times$ W/D tab.
  $= \$1,000(0.005138)$
$I_3 = \$5.14$

(b) $P_1 = \$4,900 - \$600 - \$400 = \$3,900$
   $P_2 = \$800$
   $P_3 = \$1,000$

$I_1 = P_1 \times$ Dep. tab.

	Interest	Balance
$= \$3,900(0.0113128)$	$\$44.12$	$\$4,900.00$
$I_1 = \$44.12$	5.62	$-\ \ 600.00$
	2.38	$-\ \ 400.00$
$I_2 = P_2 \times$ Dep. tab.	1.13	$+\ \ 800.00$
$= \$800(0.00702)$	$\underline{4.02}$	$+1,000.00$
$I_2 = \$5.62$	$\$57.27$	$+\ \ \ \underline{57.27}$
		$\$5,757.27$

$I_3 = P_3 \times$ Dep. tab.
  $= \$1,000(0.002378)$
$I_3 = \$2.38$

$I_4 = W \times$ W/D tab.
  $= \$600(.00188)$
$I_4 = \$1.13$

$I_5 = W \times$ W/D tab.
  $= \$400(.01005)$
$I_5 = \$4.02$

(c) $P_1 = \$5,100 - \$200 - \$900 = \$4,000$
   $P_2 = \$400$
   $P_3 = \$100$

9. (c) (Continued)

	Interest	Balance
$I_1 = P_1 \times$ Dep. tab.	$45.25	$5,100.00
$\quad = \$4,000(0.0113128)$	4.17	$-$ 200.00
$I_1 = \$45.25$	0.65	$-$ 900.00
	0.68	$+$ 400.00
$I_2 = P_2 \times$ Dep. tab.	9.04	$+$ 100.00
$\quad = \$400(0.0104284)$	$59.79	$+$ 59.79
$I_2 = \$4.17$		$4,559.79

$I_3 = P_3 \times$ Dep. tab.
$\quad = \$100(0.0065208)$
$I_3 = \$0.49$

$I_4 = W \times$ W/D tab.
$\quad = \$200(0.0033805)$
$I_4 = \$0.68$

$I_5 = W \times$ W/D tab.
$\quad = \$900(0.0100495)$
$I_5 = \$9.04$

10. (a) $P_1 = \$7,000 - \$600 = \$6,400$
$\quad\quad P_2 = \$300$

	Interest	Balance
$I_1 = P_1 \times$ Dep. tab.	$72.40	$7,000.00
$\quad = \$6,400(0.0113128)$	0.98	$-$ 600.00
$I_1 = \$72.40$	3.23	$+$ 300.00
	$76.61	$+$ 76.61
$I_2 = P_2 \times$ Dep. tab.		$6,776.61
$\quad = \$300(0.0032551)$		
$I_2 = \$0.98$		

$I_3 = W \times$ W/D tab.
$\quad = \$600(0.0053891)$
$I_3 = \$3.23$

(b) $P_1 = \$3,600 - \$600 - \$200 = \$2,800$
$\quad P_2 = \$1,000$
$\quad P_3 = \$1,000$

10. (b) (Continued)

	Interest	Balance
$I_1 = P_1 \times$ Dep. tab.	$31.68	$3,600.00
$= \$2,800(0.0113128)$	7.53	− 600.00
$I_1 = \$31.68$	3.76	− 200.00
$I_2 = P_2 \times$ Dep. tab.	0.45	+1,000.00
$= \$1,000(0.0075277)$	1.98	+1,000.00
$I_2 = \$7.53$	$45.40	+ 45.40
		$4,845.40

$I_3 = P_3 \times$ Dep. tab.
$\quad = \$1,000(0.0037568)$
$I_3 = \$3.76$

$I_4 = W \times$ W/D tab.
$\quad = \$600(0.0007502)$
$I_4 = \$0.45$

$I_5 = W \times$ W/D tab.
$\quad = \$200(0.0099233)$
$I_5 = \$1.98$

(c) $P_1 = \$6,000 - \$1,000 - \$600 = \$4,400$
$\quad P_2 = \$800$
$\quad P_3 = \$500$

	Interest	Balance
$I_1 = P_1 \times$ Dep. tab.	$49.78	$6,000.00
$= \$4,400(0.0113128)$	4.71	−1,000.00
$I_1 = \$49.78$	1.75	− 600.00
$I_2 = P_2 \times$ Dep. tab.	2.50	+ 800.00
$= \$800(0.0058919)$	6.79	+ 500.00
$I_2 = \$4.71$	$65.53	+ 65.53
		$5,765.53

$I_3 = P_3 \times$ Dep. tab.
$\quad = \$500(0.0035059)$
$I_3 = \$1.75$

$I_4 = W \times$ W/D tab.
$\quad = \$1,000(0.0025030)$
$I_4 = \$2.50$

$I_5 = W \times$ W/D tab.
$\quad = \$600(0.0113128)$
$I_5 = \$6.79$

Section 4, page 489

1. (a) M = \$3,200

       i = 2%

       n = 4

$P = M(1 + i)^{-n}$

$= \$3,200(1 + 2\%)^{-4}$

$= \ 3,200(0.9238454)$

$P = \$2,956.31$

$I = M - P$

$= \$3,200.00 - \$2,956.31$

$I = \$243.69$

  (b) M = \$2,500

       i = 1.25%

       n = 20

$P = M(1 + i)^{-n}$

$= \$2,500(1 + 1.25\%)^{-20}$

$= \ 2,500(0.780009)$

$P = \$1,950.02$

$I = M - P$

$= \$2,500.00 - \$1,950.02$

$I = \$549.98$

  (c) M = \$6,800

       $i = \dfrac{7}{12}\%$

       n = 48

$P = M(1 + i)^{-n}$

$= \$6,800\left(1 + \dfrac{7}{12}\%\right)^{-48}$

$= \ 6,800(0.756399)$

$P = \$5,143.51$

$I = M - P$

$= \$6,800.00 - \$5,143.51$

$I = \$1,656.49$

  (d) M = \$1,800

       i = 2.5%

       n = 2

$P = M(1 + i)^{-n}$

$= \$1,800(1 + 2.5\%)^{-2}$

$= \ 1,800(0.951814)$

$P = \$1,713.27$

$I = M - P$

$= \$1,800.00 - \$1,713.27$

$I = \$86.73$

  (e) M = \$4,400

       i = 1.5%

       n = 12

$P = M(1 + i)^{-n}$

$= \$4,400(1 + 1.5\%)^{-12}$

$= \ 4,400(0.836387)$

$P = \$3,680.10$

$I = M - P$

$= \$4,400.00 - \$3,680.10$

$I = \$719.90$

2. (a) M = $1,400 $P = M(1 + i)^{-n}$
        i = 1.25% $= \$1,400(1 + 1.25\%)^{-20}$
        n = 20 $= 1,400(0.7800085)$
                                           P = $1,092.01

        I = M - P
          = $1,400.00 - $1,092.01
        I = $307.99

    (b) M = $40,000 $P = M(1 + i)^{-n}$
        i = 4% $= \$40,000(1 + 4\%)^{-6}$
        n = 6 $= 40,000(0.7903145)$
                                           P = $31,612.58

        I = M - P
          = $40,000.00 - $31,612.58
        I = $8,387.42

    (c) M = $5,200 $P = M(1 + i)^{-n}$
        i = 0.5% $= \$5,200(1 + 0.5\%)^{-72}$
        n = 72 $= 5,200(0.698302)$
                                           P = $3,631.17

        I = M - P
          = $5,200.00 - $3,631.17
        I = $1,568.83

    (d) M = $10,000 $P = M(1 + i)^{-n}$
        i = 1.75% $= \$10,000(1 + 1.75\%)^{-8}$
        n = 8 $= 10,000(0.8704116)$
                                           P = $8,704.12

        I = M - P
          = $10,000.00 - $8,704.12
        I = $1,295.88

    (e) M = $8,700 $P = M(1 + i)^{-n}$
        $i = \dfrac{5}{12}\%$ $= \$8,700\left(1 - \dfrac{5}{12}\%\right)^{-48}$
        n = 48 $= 8,700(0.819071)$
                                           P = $7,125.92

        I = M - P
          = $8,700.00 - $7,125.92
        I = $1,574.08

Business Mathematics: A Collegiate Approach

3. (a) M = $5,000

i = 0.5%

n = 12

$P = M(1 + i)^{-n}$

$= \$5,000(1 + 0.5\%)^{-12}$

$= 5,000(0.941905)$

P = $4,709.53

(b) I = M − P

= $5,000.00 − $4,709.53

I = $290.47

4. (a) M = $25,000

i = 2%

n = 8

$P = M(1 + i)^{-n}$

$= \$25,000(1 + 2\%)^{-8}$

$= 25,000(0.8534904)$

P = $21,337.26

(b) I = M − P

= $25,000.00 − $21,337.26

I = $3,662.74

5. (a) M = $75,000

i = 2%

n = 8

$P = M(1 + i)^{-n}$

$= \$75,000(1 + 2\%)^{-8}$

$= 75,000(0.8534904)$

P = $64,011.78

(b) I = M − P

= $75,000.00 − $64,011.78

I = $10,988.22

6. (a) M = $30,000

$i = \dfrac{7}{12}\%$

n = 24

$P = M(1 + i)^{-n}$

$= \$30,000\left(1 + \dfrac{7}{12}\%\right)^{-24}$

$= 30,000(0.8697119)$

P = $26,091.36

(b) I = M − P

= $30,000.00 − $26,091.36

I = $3,908.64

7. (a) M = $100,000

i = 4.5%

n = 12

$P = M(1 + i)^{-n}$

$= \$100,000(1 + 4.5\%)^{-12}$

$= 100,000(0.5896639)$

P = $58,966.39

7. (Continued)

(b) I = M - P
= $100,000.00 - $58,966.39
I = $41,033.61

8. (a) M = $200,000 $P = M(1 + i)^n$
i = 2.25% $= \$200,000(1 + 2.25\%)^{-20}$
n = 20 $= 200,000(.64081647)$
                       $P = \$128,163.28$

(b) I = M - P
= $200,000.00 - $128,163.28
I = $71,836.72

9. (a) P = $7,000 $M = P(1 + i)^n$
i = 1.5% $= \$7,000(1 + 1.5\%)^{16}$
n = 16 $= 7,000(1.268986)$
                       $M = \$8,882.90$

(b) M = $8,882.90 $P = M(1 + i)^{-n}$

$i = \dfrac{5}{12}\%$ $= \$8,882.90\left(1 + \dfrac{5}{12}\%\right)^{-48}$

n = 48 $= 8,882.90(0.819071)$

                       $P = \$7,275.73$

10. (a) P = $9,000 $M = P(1 + i)^n$
i = 1.25% $= \$9,000(1 + 1.25\%)^{20}$
n = 20 $= 9,000(1.282037)$
                       $M = \$11,538.33$

(b) M = $11,538.33 $P = M(1 + i)^{-n}$
i = 3% $= \$11,538.33(1 + 3\%)^{-10}$
n = 10 $= 11,538.33(0.7440939)$
                       $P = \$8,585.60$

11. (a) P = $6,000   I = Prt   M = P + I
r = 11% $= \$6,000 \times 0.11 \times 2$ $= \$6,000 + \$1,320$
t = 2 yrs.   I = $1,320   M = $7,320

11. (Continued)

(b) M – $7,320 $P = M(1 + i)^{-n}$

$i = \dfrac{7}{12}\%$ $= \$7,320\left(1 + \dfrac{7}{12}\%\right)^{-24}$

n = 24 $= 7,320(0.869712)$

P = $6,366.29

12. (a) P = $10,000   I = Prt   M = P + I

r = 9% $= \$10,000 \times 0.09 \times 3$ $= \$10,000 + \$2,700$

t = 3 yrs.   I = $2,700   M = $12,700

(b) M = $12,700 $P = M(1 + i)^{-n}$

$i = \dfrac{7}{12}\%$ $= \$12,700\left(1 + \dfrac{7}{12}\%\right)^{-36}$

n = 36 $= 12,700(0.8110790)$

P = $10,300.70

13. (a) P = $5,000   I = Prt   M = P + I

r = 9% $= \$5,000 \times 0.09 \times 1$ $= \$5,000 + \$450$

t = 1 yr.   I = $450   M = $5,450

(b) M = $5,450 $P = M(1 + i)^{-n}$

i = 0.5% $= \$5,450(1 + 0.5\%)^{-12}$

n = 12 $= 5,450(0.941905)$

P = $5,133.38

14. (a) P = $1,000   I = Prt   M = P + I

r = 6% $= \$1,000 \times 0.06 \times 1$ $= \$1,000 + \$60$

t = 1 yr.   I = $60   M = $1,060

(b) M = $1,060 $P = M(1 + i)^{-n}$

i = 1.25% $= \$1,060(1 + 1.25\%)^{-4}$

n = 4 $= 1,060(0.951524)$

P = $1,008.62

CHAPTER XIX

ANNUITIES

Annuities (and sinking funds and amortization, as well) can be covered in business math at only the most elementary level. However, the course would be incomplete if students did not at least learn what an annuity is and something about its applications.

As indicated previously, computation in all compound-interest-related problems is extremely easy for the students -- provided they know what type of problems they are dealing with; but herein lies the problem. If the instructions say, "Find the amount at compound interest" or "Find the present value of an annuity," then the problem will be trivial for the students. But written problems where the type of problem is not so obviously defined will pose a greater obstacle. Hence, a good deal of class discussion will be needed to thoroughly acquaint the students with the different types of problems and the distinctions among them.

Strict mathematical formulas* for annuity problems would be meaningless to most students and are not essential to the solutions. Therefore, the formulas are replaced by abbreviated procedures, such as: M = Pmt. × Amt. ann. tab.$_{n]i}$. In addition to defining a meaningful solution for the problem, these procedures help guarantee a correct solution: if students have learned the procedure correctly, they know exactly which table to use for the calculation. However, if you feel these procedures are too informal, you may require the students to use the alternate procedures indicated in the footnotes, such as: M = Pm$_{n]i}$. These alternate procedures are standard and widely used in math of finance textbooks.

Point out to the students that for all compound-interest-related problems (including annuities, sinking funds, and amortization) they would always use the table with the same title as

---

*The amount of an annuity formula is $M = P\left(\dfrac{(1 + i)^n - 1}{i}\right)$; the present value formula is $A = P\left(\dfrac{1 - (1 + i)^{-n}}{i}\right)$, where M denotes amount, A represents present value, P is the periodic payments (or rent), i = interest rate per period, and n = number of periods.

the aspect being calculated. Thus, compound amount is found using the "amount at compound interest" table; present value of an annuity is found using the "present value of annuity" table, and so on. This will aid the students in learning the procedures correctly and help ensure that the correct table is used for each problem. Caution the students to be extremely careful, however, as it is easy to stray into the wrong table even when one knows which table is correct.

1.   Amount of an Annuity:

Simply defining "annuity" may not be sufficient to make students realize the basic difference between annuities and ordinary compound interest. Stress that, "whereas basic compound interest problems involved a single deposit made at the beginning of the problem and left invested for the whole time period, annuities involve a series of equal deposits made at regular intervals during the time period."

Example 1 presents the calculation for amount of an annuity. As a comparison, it would be helpful to demonstrate a compound amount problem where the same total principal ($2,400) was deposited at 8% compounded quarterly for 6 years. There is a difference of $818.06 between the compound amount ($3,860.25) and the maturity value of the annuity ($3,042.19). Of course, this large difference results because the entire $2,400 was on deposit for the complete 6 years in the compound amount problem. In the annuity problem, however, only the first payment of $100 earned interest for basically the entire time;* the remaining annuity payments earned interest for shorter portions of the 6 years. [*Recall that the first payment of an "ordinary" annuity is not made until the end of the first period.]

2.   Present Value of an Annuity:

This topic can be covered at the same time as amount of an annuity since, by this time, students will feel quite comfortable working with present value.

"Present value" denotes a slightly different concept when related to annuities, since it represents a beginning balance from which the annuity will be regularly withdrawn. Emphasize to the class that an annuity problem can be identified as pertaining to present value when the account contains its largest amount at the beginning of the time period. Also stress that, although funds are being withdrawn from the account at regular intervals, the account continues to earn interest as long as any balance remains; thus, altogether the annuity pays considerably more than the original balance.

Example 1 introduces the basic computation of present value of an annuity. Observe that in both Section 1 and Section 2, each example 1 uses Pmt. = $100; n = 24; and I = 2% -- the Section 1 example building up an account (by <u>making</u> the $100 annuity payment) and the Section 2 example depleting an account (by <u>receiving</u> the $100 payment). The total interest is $642.19 in Section 1 and is $508.61 in Section 2. The interest differs since, in the first case, each $100 payment is entirely principal, and interest is earned in addition. In the second case, each $100 includes some interest, and the payments exhaust both principal and interest. (That is, the interest is greater in the first case because the principal there is greater.)

Example 2 is a two-part problem combining annuities and compound interest. The example shows what deposit (present value at compound interest) would have to be made now in order to finance a given annuity at retirement (present value of an annuity).

CHAPTER 19 - ANNUITIES
PROBLEM SOLUTIONS

Section 1, page 496

1. (a) Pmt. = $500

   i = 1.5%

   n = 28

$M = \text{Pmt.} \times \text{Amt. ann. tab.}_{n|i}$

$= \$500 \times \text{Amt. ann. tab.}_{28|1.5\%}$

$= 500(34.481479)$

$M = \$17,240.74$

Total deposits = $500 × 28 payments = $14,000
Total interest = $17,240.74 - $14,000.00 = $3,240.74

   (b) Pmt. = $800

   i = 1.75%

   n = 12

$M = \text{Pmt.} \times \text{Amt. ann. tab.}_{n|i}$

$= \$800 \times \text{Amt. ann. tab.}_{12|1.75\%}$

$= 800(13.225104)$

$M = \$10,580.08$

Total deposits = $800 × 12 payments = $9,600
Total interest = $10,580.08 - $9,600.00 = $980.08

1. (Continued)

(c) Pmt. = $300

M = Pmt. × Amt. ann. tab.$_{n|i}$

i = 4%

= $300 × Amt. ann. tab.$_{16|4\%}$

n = 16

= 300(21.82453)

M = $6,547.36

Total deposits = $300 × 16 payments = $4,800
Total interest = $6,547.36 - $4,800.00 = $1,747.36

(d) Pmt. = $1,500

M = Pmt. × Amt. ann. tab.$_{n|i}$

i = 1.25%

= $1,500 × Amt. ann. tab.$_{24|1.25\%}$

n = 24

= 1,500(27.788084)

M = $41,682.13

Total deposits = $1,500 × 24 payments = $36,000
Total interest = $41,682.13 - $36,000.00 = $5,682.13

(e) Pmt. = $1,100

M = Pmt. × Amt. ann. tab.$_{n|i}$

i = 0.5%

= $1,100 × Amt. ann. tab.$_{36|0.5\%}$

n = 36

= 1,100(39.336105)

M = $43,269.72

Total deposits = $1,100 × 36 payments = $39,600
Total interest = $43,269.72 - $39,600.00 = $3,669.72

2. (a) Pmt. = $1,500

M = Pmt. × Amt. ann. tab.$_{n|i}$

i = 3.5%

= $1,500 × Amt. ann. tab.$_{8|3.5\%}$

n = 8

= 1,500(9.051687)

M = $13,577.53

Total deposits = $1,500 × 8 payments = $12,000
Total interest = $13,577.53 - $12,000.00 = $1,577.53

(b) Pmt. = $2,000

M = Pmt. × Amt. ann. tab.$_{n|i}$

i = 1.5%

= $2,000 × Amt. ann. tab.$_{20|1.5\%}$

n = 20

= 2,000(23.123667)

M = $46,247.33

Total deposits = $2,000 × 20 payments = $40,000
Total interest = $46,247.33 - $40,000.00 = $6,247.33

2. (Continued)

(c) Pmt. = $600

$$i = \frac{5}{12}\%$$

n = 48

$$M = Pmt. \times Amt.\ ann.\ tab._{\overline{n}|i}$$
$$= \$600 \times Amt.\ ann.\ tab._{\overline{48}|\frac{5}{12}\%}$$
$$= 600(53.014885)$$
$$M = \$31,808.93$$

Total deposits = $600 × 48 payments = $28,800
Total interest = $31,808.93 - $28,800.00 = $3,008.93

(d) Pmt. = $1,800

i = 2%

n = 32

$$M = Pmt. \times Amt.\ ann.\ tab._{\overline{n}|i}$$
$$= \$1,800 \times Amt.\ ann.\ tab._{\overline{32}|2\%}$$
$$= 1,800(44.227030)$$
$$M = \$79,608.65$$

Total deposits = $1,800 × 32 payments = $57,600
Total interest = $79,608.65 - $57,600.00 = $22,008.65

(e) Pmt. = $50

i = 0.75%

n = 48

$$M = Pmt. \times Amt.\ ann.\ tab._{\overline{n}|i}$$
$$= \$50 \times Amt.\ ann.\ tab._{\overline{48}|0.75\%}$$
$$= 50(57.52071)$$
$$M = \$2,876.04$$

Total deposits = $50 × 48 payments = $2,400
Total interest = $2,876.04 - $2,400.00 = $476.04

3. Pmt. = $500

i = 1.75%

n = 8

(a) $$M = Pmt. \times Amt.\ ann.\ tab._{\overline{n}|i}$$
$$= \$500 \times Amt.\ ann.\ tab._{\overline{8}|1.75\%}$$
$$= 500(8.507530)$$
$$M = \$4,253.77$$

(b) Total deposits = $500 × 8 = $4,000

(c) Total interest = $4,253.77 - $4,000.00 = $253.77

4. Pmt. = $300

i = 1%

n = 16

(a) $$M = Pmt. \times Amt.\ ann.\ tab._{\overline{n}|i}$$
$$= \$300 \times Amt.\ ann.\ tab._{\overline{16}|1\%}$$
$$= 300(17.257864)$$
$$M = \$5,177.36$$

4. (Continued)

(b) Total deposits = $300 × 16 = $4,800

(c) Total interest = $5,177.36 - $4,800.00 = $1,377.36

5. Pmt. = $500

    i = 0.5%

    n = 60

(a) M = Pmt. × Amt. ann. tab.$_{n|i}$

    = $500 × Amt. ann. tab.$_{60|0.5\%}$

    = 500(69.770031)

    M = $34,885.02

(b) Total deposits = $500 × 60 = $30,000

(c) Total interest = $34,885.02 - $30,000.00 = $4,885.02

6. Pmt. = $1,000

    i = 3.5%

    n = 16

(a) M = Pmt. × Amt. ann. tab.$_{n|i}$

    = $1,000 × Amt. ann. tab.$_{16|3.5\%}$

    = 1,000(20.971030)

    M = $20,971.03

(b) Total deposits = $1,000 × 16 = $16,000

(c) Total interest = $20,971.03 - $16,000.00 = $4,971.03

7. (a) Total investment = $6,000 × 5 payments = $30,000

(b) Pmt. = $6,000

    i = 8%

    n = 5

M = Pmt. × Amt. ann. tab.$_{n|i}$

    = $6,000 × Amt. ann. tab.$_{5|8\%}$

    = 6,000(5.8666010)

M = $35,199.61

(c) Total interest = $35,199.61 - $30,000.00 = $5,199.61

8. (a) Total investment = $5,000 × 10 payments = $50,000

(b) Pmt. = $5,000

    i = 6%

    n = 10

M = Pmt. × Amt. ann. tab.$_{n|i}$

    = $5,000 × Amt. ann. tab.$_{10|6\%}$

    = 5,000(13.180795)

M = $65,903.98

8. (Continued)

   (c) Total interest = \$65,903.98 - \$50,000.00 = \$15,903.98

9. (a) Total investment = \$8,000 × 20 = \$160,000

   (b) Pmt. = \$8,000 $M = \text{Pmt.} \times \text{Amt. ann. tab.}_{\overline{n}|i}$

        i = 1.5% $= \$8,000 \times \text{Amt. ann. tab.}_{\overline{20}|1.5\%}$

        n = 20   = 8,000(23.123667)

                    M = \$184,989.33

   (c) Total interest = \$184,989.33 - \$160,000.00 = \$24,989.33

10. (a) Total investment = \$800 × 24 payments = \$19,200

   (b) Pmt. = \$800 $M = \text{Pmt.} \times \text{Amt. ann. tab.}_{\overline{n}|i}$

        $i = \dfrac{5}{12}\%$ $= \$800 \times \text{Amt. ann. tab.}_{\overline{24}|\frac{5}{12}\%}$

        n = 24   = 800(25.185921)

                    M = \$20,148.74

   (c) Total interest = \$20,148.74 - \$19,200.00 = \$948.74

Section 2, page 501

1. (a) (1) Pmt. = \$1,000 $P.V. = \text{Pmt.} \times \text{P.V. ann. tab.}_{\overline{n}|i}$

          i = 7.5% $= \$1,000 \times \text{P.V. ann. tab.}_{\overline{16}|7.5\%}$

          n = 16   = 1,000(9.141507)

                    P.V. = \$9,141.51

   (2) \$1,000 × 16 = \$16,000

   (3) \$16,000.00 - \$9,141.51 = \$6,858.49

   (b) (1) Pmt. = \$1,500 $P.V. = \text{Pmt.} \times \text{P.V. ann. tab.}_{\overline{n}|i}$

          i = 0.75% $= \$1,500 \times \text{P.V. ann. tab.}_{\overline{36}|0.75\%}$

          n = 36   = 1,500(31.446805)

                    P.V. = \$47,170.21

1. (b) (Continued)

      (2) $\$1,500 \times 36 = \$54,000$

      (3) $\$54,000.00 - \$47,170.21 = \$6,829.79$

  (c) (1) Pmt. = $\$3,000$ P.V. = Pmt. × P.V. ann. tab.$_{\overline{n}|i}$

           i = 2%   = $\$3,000$ × P.V. ann. tab.$_{\overline{40}|2\%}$

           n = 40   = $3,000(27.355479)$

                      P.V. = $\$82,066.44$

      (2) $\$3,000 \times 40 = \$120,000$

      (3) $\$120,000.00 - \$82,066.44 = \$37,933.56$

  (d) (1) Pmt. = $\$1,700$ P.V. = Pmt. × P.V. ann. tab.$_{\overline{n}|i}$

           i = 3%   = $\$1,700$ × P.V. ann. tab.$_{\overline{24}|3\%}$

           n = 24   = $1,700(16.935542)$

                      P.V. = $\$28,790.42$

      (2) $\$1,700 \times 24 = \$40,800$

      (3) $\$40,800.00 - \$28,790.42 = \$12,009.58$

  (e) (1) Pmt. = $\$2,600$ P.V. = Pmt. × P.V. ann. tab.$_{\overline{n}|i}$

           i = 3%   = $\$2,600$ × P.V. ann. tab.$_{\overline{10}|3\%}$

           n = 10   = $2,600(8.530203)$

                      P.V. = $\$22,178.53$

      (2) $\$2,600 \times 10 = \$26,000$

      (3) $\$26,000.00 - \$22,178.53 = \$3,821.47$

2. (a) (1) Pmt. = $\$1,000$ P.V. = Pmt. × P.V. ann. tab.$_{\overline{n}|i}$

           i = 4%   = $\$1,000$ × P.V. ann. tab.$_{\overline{30}|4\%}$

           n = 30   = $1,000(17.292033)$

                      P.V. = $\$17,292.03$

      (2) $\$1,000 \times 30 = \$30,000$

      (3) $\$30,000.00 - \$17,292.03 = \$12,707.97$

2. (Continued)

(b) (1) Pmt. = \$1,600   P.V. = Pmt. × P.V. ann. tab.$_{n|i}$

$i = \dfrac{5}{6}\%$ = \$1,600 × P.V. ann. tab.$_{36|\frac{5}{6}\%}$

n = 36   = 1,600(30.991236)

P.V. = \$49,585.98

(2) \$1,600 × 36 = \$57,600

(3) \$57,600.00 - \$49,585.98 = \$8,014.02

(c) (1) Pmt. = \$2,400   P.V. = Pmt. × P.V. ann. tab.$_{n|i}$

i = 2.25%   = \$2,400 × P.V. ann. tab.$_{32|2.25\%}$

n = 32   = 2,400(22.637674)

P.V. = \$54,330.42

(2) \$2,400 × 32 = \$76,800

(3) \$76,800.00 - \$54,330.42 = \$22,469.58

(d) (1) Pmt. = \$3,500   P.V. = Pmt. × P.V. ann. tab.$_{n|i}$

i = 1.75%   = \$3,500 × P.V. ann. tab.$_{8|1.75\%}$

n = 28   = 3,500(7.405053)

P.V. = \$25,917.69

(2) \$3,500 × 8 = \$28,000

(3) \$28,000.00 - \$25,917.69 = \$2,082.31

(e) (1) Pmt. = \$1,200   P.V. = Pmt. × P.V. ann. tab.$_{n|i}$

i = 2.5%   = \$1,200 × P.V. ann. tab.$_{12|2.5\%}$

n = 12   = 1,200(10.257765)

P.V. = \$12,309.32

(2) \$1,200 × 12 = \$14,400

(3) \$14,400.00 - \$12,309.32 = \$2,090.68

3. (a) (1) Pmt. = $6,000   M = Pmt. × Amt. ann. tab.$_{n|i}$
           i = 2%   = $6,000 × Amt. ann. tab.$_{32|2\%}$
           n = 32   = 6,000(44.227030)
                            M = $265,362.18

      Total payments = $6,000 × 32 = $192,000
      Interest = $265,362.18 - $192,000.00 = $73,362.18

      (2) P.V. = Pmt. × P.V. ann. tab.$_{n|i}$
              = $6,000 × P.V. ann. tab.$_{32|2\%}$
              = 6,000(23.468335)
          P.V. = $140,810.01

      Interest = $192,000.00 - $140,810.01 = $51,189.99

   (b) (1) Pmt. = $300   M = Pmt. × Amt. ann. tab.$_{n|i}$
           i = 3.5%   = $300 × Amt. ann. tab.$_{24|3.5\%}$
           n = 24   = 300(36.66653)
                            M = $10,999.96

      Total payments = $300 × 24 = $7,200
      Interest = $10,999.96 - $7,200.00 = $3,799.96

      (2) P.V. = Pmt. × P.V. ann. tab.$_{n|i}$
              = $300 × P.V. ann. tab.$_{24|3.5\%}$
              = 300(16.05837)
          P.V. = $4,817.51

      Interest = $7,200.00 - $4,817.51 = $2,382.49

   (c) (1) Pmt. = $4,900   M = Pmt. × Amt. ann. tab.$_{n|i}$
           i = 0.5%   = $4,900 × Amt. ann. tab.$_{48|0.5\%}$
           n = 48   = 4,900(54.097832)
                            M = $265,079.37

      Total payments = $4,900 × 48 = $235,200
      Interest = $265,079.37 - $235,200.00 = $29,879.37

3. (c) (Continued)

(2) P.V. = Pmt. × P.V. ann. tab.$_{\overline{n}|i}$

= \$4,900 × P.V. ann. tab.$_{\overline{48}|0.5\%}$

= 4,900(42.580318)

P.V. = \$208,643.55

Interest = \$235,200.00 - \$208,643.55 = \$26,556.45

4. (a) (1) Pmt. = \$5,000   M = Pmt. × Amt. ann. tab.$_{\overline{n}|i}$

    i = 2.5%   = \$5,000 × Amt. ann. tab.$_{\overline{28}|2.5\%}$

    n = 28   = 5,000(39.859801)

                    M = \$199,299

Total payments = \$5,000 × 28 = \$140,000
Interest = \$199,299 - \$140,000 = \$59,299

(2) P.V. = Pmt. × P.V. ann. tab.$_{\overline{n}|i}$

= \$5,000 × P.V. ann. tab.$_{\overline{28}|2.5\%}$

= 5,000(19.964889)

P.V. = \$99,824.45

Interest = \$140,000.00 - \$99,824.45 = \$40,175.55

(b) (1) Pmt. = \$8,000   M = Pmt. × Amt. ann. tab.$_{\overline{n}|i}$

    i = 4.5%   = \$8,000 × Amt. ann. tab.$_{\overline{20}|4.5\%}$

    n = 20   = 8,000(31.371423)

                    M = \$250,971.38

Total payments = \$8,000 × 20 = \$160,000
Interest = \$250,971.38 - \$160,000.00 = \$90,971.38

(2) P.V. = Pmt. × P.V. ann. tab.$_{\overline{n}|i}$

= \$8,000 × P.V. ann. tab.$_{\overline{20}|4.5\%}$

= 8,000(13.007936)

P.V. = \$104,063.48

Interest = \$160,000.00 - \$104,063.48 = \$55,936.52

4. (Continued)

(c) (1) Pmt. = \$900 $M = \text{Pmt.} \times \text{Amt. ann. tab.}_{\overline{n}|i}$

$$i = \frac{7}{12}\%$$

$$= \$900 \times \text{Amt. ann. tab.}_{\overline{60}|\frac{7}{12}\%}$$

$$n = 60$$

$$= 900(71.592902)$$

$$M = \$64,433.61$$

Total payments = \$900 × 60 = \$54,000
Interest = \$64,433.61 − \$54,000.00 = \$10,433.61

(2) $\text{P.V.} = \text{Pmt.} \times \text{P.V. ann. tab.}_{\overline{n}|i}$

$$= \$900 \times \text{P.V. ann. tab.}_{\overline{60}|\frac{7}{12}\%}$$

$$= 900(50.501994)$$

$$\text{P.V.} = \$45,451.79$$

Interest = \$54,000.00 − \$45,451.79 = \$8,548.21

5. Pmt. = \$450   (a) $\text{P.V.} = \text{Pmt.} \times \text{P.V. ann. tab.}_{\overline{n}|i}$

$$i = 1.5\%$$

$$= \$450 \times \text{P.V. ann. tab.}_{\overline{12}|1.5\%}$$

$$n = 12$$

$$= 450(10.90751)$$

$$\text{P.V.} = \$4,908.38$$

(b) \$450 × 12 = \$5,400

(c) \$5,400.00 − \$4,908.38 = \$491.62

6. Pmt. = \$250   (a) $\text{P.V.} = \text{Pmt.} \times \text{P.V. ann. tab.}_{\overline{n}|i}$

$$i = \frac{5}{12}\%$$

$$= \$250 \times \text{P.V. ann. tab.}_{\overline{12}|\frac{5}{12}\%}$$

$$n = 12$$

$$= 250(11.681222)$$

$$\text{P.V.} = \$2,920.31$$

(b) \$250 × 12 = \$3,000

(c) \$3,000.00 − \$2,920.31 = \$79.69

7. Pmt. = $600   (a) P.V. = Pmt. × P.V. ann. tab.$_{n|i}$

    i = 1.25%   = $600 × P.V. ann. tab.$_{8|1.25\%}$

    n = 8   = 600(7.568124)

                          P.V. = $4,540.87

   (b) $600 × 8 = $4,800

   (c) $4,800.00 - $4,540.87 = $259.13

8. Pmt. = $150   (a) P.V. = Pmt.× P.V. ann. tab.$_{n|i}$

    i = $\frac{5}{12}$%   = $150 × P.V. ann. tab.$_{60|\frac{5}{12}\%}$

    n = 60   = 150(52.990706)

                          P.V. = $7,948.61

   (b) $150 × 60 = $9,000

   (c) $9,000.00 - $7,948.61 = $1,051.39

9. Pmt. = $700   (a) P.V. = Pmt. × P.V. ann. tab.$_{n|i}$

    i = 4%   = $700 × P.V. ann. tab.$_{8|4\%}$

    n = 8   = 700(6.73274)

                        = $4,712.92

                  P.V. = $4,700 (to nearest hundred)

   (b) M = $4,700   P = $M(1 + i)^{-n}$

      i = 4%   = $4,700(1 + 4\%)^{-20}$

      n = 20   = 4,700(0.45638)

                     = $2,145.02

                P = $2,100 (to nearest hundred)

   (c) $700 × 8 = $5,600

      $5,600 - $2,100 = $3,500

10. (a) Pmt. = $2,500   P.V. = Pmt. × P.V. ann. tab.$_{n|i}$

       i = 1.75%   = $2,500 × P.V. ann. tab.$_{24|1.75\%}$

       n = 24   = 2,500(19.460686)

                     = $48,651.72

                P.V. = $48,700 (to nearest hundred)

10. (Continued)

(b) M = $48,700 $P = M(1 + i)^{-n}$
    i = 1.75% $= \$48,700(1 + 1.75\%)^{-40}$
    n = 40 $= 48,700(0.499601)$
                           $= \$24,330.57$
                           P = $24,300 (to nearest hundred)

(c) $2,500 × 24 = $60,000
    $60,000 - $24,300 = $35,700

11. (a) Pmt. = $350   P.V. = Pmt. × P.V. ann. tab.$_{n\rceil i}$
        i = 0.5% $= \$350 ×$ P.V. ann. tab.$_{48\rceil 0.5\%}$
        n = 48 $= 350(42.58032)$
                           P.V. = $14,903.11 or $14,900

(b) M = $14,900 $P = M(1 + i)^{-n}$
    i = 0.5% $= \$14,900(1 + 0.5\%)^{-72}$
    n = 72 $= 14,900(0.6983024)$
                          P = $10,404.71 or $10,400

(c) $350 × 48 = $16,800
    $16,800 - $10,400 = $6,400

12. (a) Pmt. = $10,000   P.V. = Pmt. × P.V. ann. tab.$_{n\rceil i}$
        i = 3% $= \$10,000 ×$ P.V. ann. tab.$_{6\rceil 3\%}$
        n = 6 $= 10,000(5.417191)$
                               $= \$54,171.91$
                           P.V. = $54,200 (to nearest hundred)

(b) M = $54,200 $P = M(1 + i)^{-n}$
    i = 3% $= \$54,200(1 + 3\%)^{-4}$
    n = 4 $= 54,200(0.888487)$
                          $= \$48,156$
                          P = $48,200 (to nearest hundred)

(c) $10,000 × 6 = $60,000
    $60,000 - $48,200 = $11,800

13. (a) $3,000 × 72 = $216,000 + $25,000 down payment = $241,000
        total cost

13. (Continued)

(b) Pmt. = \$3,000   P.V. = Pmt. × P.V. ann. tab.$_{n|i}$

    $i = \dfrac{5}{6}\%$ = \$3,000 × P.V. ann. tab.$_{72|\frac{5}{6}\%}$

    $n = 72$ = 3,000(53.978665)

                     P.V. = \$161,935.99

Equivalent cash price: \$161,935.99
                        + 25,000.00 down payment
                        \$186,935.99

14. (a) \$6,000 × 60 = \$360,000 + \$50,000 down payment = \$410,000 total cost

(b) Pmt. = \$6,000   P.V. = Pmt. × P.V. ann. tab.$_{n|i}$

    $i = \dfrac{7}{12}\%$ = \$6,000 × P.V. ann. tab.$_{60|\frac{7}{12}\%}$

    $n = 60$ = 6,000(50.501994)

                     P.V. = \$303,011.96

Equivalent cash price: \$303,011.96
                        + 50,000.00 down payment
                        \$353,011.96

15. (a) \$2,000 × 12 = \$24,000 + \$5,000 down payment = \$29,000 total cost

(b) Pmt. = \$2,000   P.V. = Pmt. × P.V. ann. tab.$_{n|i}$

    $i = 2.25\%$ = \$2,000 × P.V. ann. tab.$_{12|2.25\%}$

    $n = 12$ = 2,000(10.414779)

                    P.V. = \$20,829.56

Equivalent cash price: \$20,829.56
                        + 5,000.00 down payment
                        \$25,829.56

16. (a) \$5,000 × 8 = \$40,000 + \$8,000 down payment = \$48,000 total cost

16. (Continued)

(b) Pmt. = \$5,000

$\quad$ i = 2%

$\quad$ n = 8

P.V. = Pmt. $\times$ P.V. ann. tab.$_{\overline{n}|i}$

$\quad$ = \$5,000 $\times$ P.V. ann. tab.$_{\overline{8}|2\%}$

$\quad$ = 5,000(7.325481)

P.V. = \$36,627.41

Equivalent cash price: $\quad$ \$36,627.41

$\qquad\qquad\qquad\qquad$ + 8,000.00 down payment

$\qquad\qquad\qquad\qquad$ \$44,627.41

CHAPTER XX

SINKING FUNDS AND AMORTIZATION

The topics of sinking funds and amortization are basically the inverse of the annuities studied previously; whereas the annuity problems gave the periodic payments and asked for the amount or the present value, these problems give the amount or the present value and ask for the periodic payment.

1.   Sinking Funds and Bonds:

This topic is explained as a variation of amount of an annuity; the students are asked to find the periodic payment (to a sinking fund) which will produce the required maturity value. The introduction explains that a sinking fund payment can be computed using the amount of an annuity table; however, students will not be required to solve any problem in this manner. Example 1 is a practical example of a sinking fund and uses the sinking fund table only.

Example 2 contains a sinking fund schedule which verifies that a given periodic payment produces the required maturity value. The authors recommend that this example be at least discussed in all classes, so that the students can see how the fund grows; however, it may not be necessary to have students in basic classes prepare sinking fund schedules themselves.

Bonds are included here, since their redemption is the purpose of many corporate sinking funds. The selling price of bonds (at a premium, par, or discount) is the topic of example 3. Example 4 determines the current yield to the buyer, which first requires that the bond interest be computed. Emphasize to the class that any corporation or governmental body that issues bonds must pay the periodic bond interest in addition to making the payments to any sinking fund created to provide the redemption value of the bonds.

2.   Amortization:

This topic begins with an illustration to show why, for long-term loans, financial institutions require periodic payments including interest at an effective interest rate. This leads directly into a definition of amortization. In your class discussion, emphasize strongly that the borrower never pays compound interest; the lender earns effective compound interest only by lending the borrower's interest to another person, thereby earning "interest on interest" indirectly. The manner in which the individual borrower pays interest can be correlated to the verification of effective rates of interest, studied as part of the installment plan section of Chapter XVII.

The concept of the payment to a sinking fund as a variation of amount of an annuity is easy for students to accept. The idea of amortization as a variation of present value of an annuity is somewhat more difficult to comprehend, however. This is probably because the basic applications of present value of an annuity involves receiving an annuity, whereas amortization involves making a payment. Amortization can best be explained as a variation of present value because the maximum amount of debt exists at the beginning of the time period.

Example 1 presents a typical amortization situation, using the amortization procedure and table. An amortization schedule is later completed (example 3) to show that the payment found in example 1 will actually amortize the loan correctly. As in the case of sinking fund schedules, the authors would discuss the amortization schedule in all classes, but would not assign these schedules to basic classes.

Real estate mortgages are the most familiar type of amortization payment, and a discussion of alternative financing methods would be of interest to your students. The text contains a table that enables students to compute the monthly payment on mortgages covering a fairly wide range of interest rates.

Several class examples should be presented to demonstrate not only the substantial variation in monthly payments at different rates (and to a less extend for different time periods) but especially the tremendous differences in the total amounts paid during the life of the mortgage. Bring out the amount of interest included and its ratio to the loan principal, since most people (consumers as well as students) think only in terms of the "monthly payment" and have no conception of the magnitude of the overall values involved. Also emphasize the large difference in total amounts paid between, say, a 25 vs. 30 year loan at the same rate.

Figure 20-2 shows the amortization schedule for a $50,000 loan at 9% with monthly payments for 10 years. This schedule can provide the basis for an excellent class discussion. Point out the high amount of interest which the earlier payments include. Notice the last two payments are slightly different from the other 118 payments. The total interest of $26,005.58 on a $50,000 loan seems outrageous to students. However, you can comfort them somewhat by showing them what the simple interest on a $50,000 loan would be -- $45,000. There is an error of 12¢ over the 120-payment period due to rounding the interest each period. This is normal for a computerized amortization schedule.

The text also contains a table illustrating the difference in amounts of interest between effective and simple rates on a $25,000 loan at 12% for 10, 20, or 30 years.

The text examples of (1) why the borrower cannot afford simple interest but (2) the lender does not profit by simple interest, yet (3) the lender earns compound interest although (4) the borrower does not pay compound interest will probably merge into one vague, indistinct maze in the students' minds. Hence, the authors would never require that students be able to reproduce them. Such examples do serve a useful purpose, however, in that they reassure the class that things are as they should be and that the procedures actually used work to the advantage of all concerned.

3.   Review:

As in the case of simple interest and bank discount, a review of compound-interest-related problems is needed to provide practice for the students in distinguishing among the various types of problems. The topic contains a summary table of the various problems, some identifying characteristics of each, and the corresponding formula or procedure. The review contains only the basic problems of finding amount, present value, and periodic payment; interest compounded daily and variations of the basic problems are not included.

CHAPTER 20 - SINKING FUNDS AND AMORTIZATION
PROBLEM SOLUTIONS

Section 1, page 511

1. (a) (1) M = $30,000   Pmt. = M × s.f. tab.$_{n|i}$

          i = 1.75%   = $30,000 × s.f. tab.$_{20|1.75\%}$

          n = 20   =   30,000(0.0421912)

                              Pmt. = $1,265.74

     (2) Total payments = $1,265.74 × 20 = $25,314.80

     (3) Total interest = $30,000.00 - $25,314.80 = $4,685.20

1. (Continued)

(b) (1) M = $50,000   Pmt. = M × s.f. tab.$_{n|i}$

      i = 4%   = $50,000 × s.f. tab.$_{12|4\%}$

      n = 12   = 50,000(0.0665522)

                     Pmt. = $3,327.61

   (2) Total payments = $3,327.61 × 12 = $39,931.32

   (3) Total interest = $50,000.00 - $39,931.32 = $10,068.68

(c) (1) M = $75,000   Pmt. = M × s.f. tab.$_{n|i}$

      i = 0.5%   = $75,000 × s.f. tab.$_{84|0.5\%}$

      n = 84   = 75,000(0.009609)

                     Pmt. = $720.68

   (2) Total payments = $720.68 × 84 = $60,537.12

   (3) Total interest = $75,000.00 - $60,537.12 = $14,462.88

(d) (1) M = $100,000   Pmt. = M × s.f. tab.$_{n|i}$

      i = 1.25%   = $100,000 × s.f. tab.$_{11|1.25\%}$

      n = 16   = 100,000(0.05684672)*

                     Pmt. = $5,684.67

                     *Mental math used since most
                      calculators will not take 8
                      decimal places.

   (2) Total payments = $5,684.67 × 16 = $90,954.72

   (3) Total interest = $100,000.00 - $90,954.72 = $9,045.28

(e) (1) M = $200,000   Pmt. = M × s.f. tab.$_{n|i}$

      i = 0.75%   = $200,000 × s.f. tab.$_{36|0.75\%}$

      n = 36   = 200,000(0.0242997)

                     Pmt. = $4,859.94

   (2) Total payments = $4,859.94 × 36 = $174,957.84

1. (e) (Continued)

    (3) Total interest = $200,000.00 - $174,957.84
                               = $25,042.16

2. (a) (1) M = $80,000   Pmt. = M × s.f. tab.$_{\overline{n}|i}$

           i = 2%   = $80,000 × s.f. tab.$_{\overline{40}|2\%}$

           n = 40   =   80,000(0.0165557)

                       Pmt. = $1,324.46

    (2) Total payments = $1,324.46 × 40 = $52,978.40

    (3) Total interest = $80,000.00 - $52,978.40 = $27,021.60

  (b) (1) M = $500,000   Pmt. = M × s.f. tab.$_{\overline{n}|i}$

           i = 4.5%   = $500,000 × s.f. tab.$_{\overline{16}|4.5\%}$

           n = 16   =   500,000(0.04401537)

                       Pmt. = $22,007.65

    (2) Total payments = $22,007.65 × 16 = $352,122.40

    (3) Total interest = $500,000.00 - $352,122.40
                              = $147,877.60

  (c) (1) M = $275,000   Pmt. = M × s.f. tab.$_{\overline{n}|i}$

           i = $\frac{5}{6}$%   = $275,000 × s.f. tab.$_{\overline{60}|\frac{5}{6}\%}$

           n = 60   =   275,000(0.0129137)

                       Pmt. = $3,551.27

    (2) Total payments = $3,551.27 × 60 = $213,076.20

    (3) Total interest = $275,000.00 - $213,076.20
                              = $ 61,923.80

  (d) (1) M = $60,000   Pmt. = M × s.f. tab.$_{\overline{n}|i}$

           i = 1.75%   = $60,000 × s.f. tab.$_{\overline{48}|1.75\%}$

           n = 48   =   60,000(0.013466)

                       Pmt. = $807.96

2. (d) (Continued)

    (2) Total payments = $807.96 × 48 = $38,782.08

    (3) Total interest = $60,000.00 - $38,782.08 = $21,217.92

  (e) (1) M = $140,000   Pmt. = M × s.f. tab.$_{n|i}$

        i = 1%   = $140,000 × s.f. tab.$_{24|1\%}$

        n = 24   = 140,000(0.0370735)

                   Pmt. = $5,190.29

    (2) Total payments = $5,190.29 × 24 = $124,566.96

    (3) Total interest = $140,000.00 - $124,566.96
                       = $ 15,433.04

3.

	Price Quote	Selling Price	Premium or Discount	Interest Rate	Annual Interest	Current Yield
(a)	101	$1,010.00	$ 10P	$6\frac{1}{4}\%$	$ 62.50	6.19%
(b)	88	880.00	120D	$5\frac{1}{8}$	51.25	5.82
(c)	100	1,000.00	Par	$9\frac{3}{4}$	97.50	9.75
(d)	$95\frac{1}{2}$	955.00	45D	$8\frac{1}{2}$	85.00	8.90
(e)	$106\frac{1}{4}$	1,062.50	62.50P	10	100.00	9.41

(a) 101% × $1,000 = $1,010
$1,010 - $1,000 = $10P
0.0625 × $1,000 = $62.50

(b) 88% × $1,000 = $880
$1,000 - $800 = $120D
0.05125 × $1,000 = $51.25

$$\text{Cur. yield} = \frac{\text{Interest}}{\text{Price}}$$

$$= \frac{\$62.50}{\$1,010}$$

c.y. = 6.19%

$$\text{Cur. yield} = \frac{\text{Interest}}{\text{Price}}$$

$$= \frac{\$51.25}{\$880}$$

c.y. = 5.82%

(c) 100% × $1,000 = $1,000 (Par)
0.0975 × $1,000 = $97.50

(d) 95.5% × $1,000 = $955
$1,000 - $955 = $45D
0.085 × $1,000 = $85

3. (c) (Continued)

$$\text{Cur. yield} = \frac{\text{Interest}}{\text{Price}}$$

$$= \frac{\$97.50}{\$1,000}$$

c.y. = 9.75%

(d) (Continued)

$$\text{Cur. yield} = \frac{\text{Interest}}{\text{Price}}$$

$$= \frac{\$85}{\$955}$$

c.y. = 8.9%

(e)   106.25% × $1,000 = $1,062.50
$1,062.50 - $1,000 = $62.50P
    0.10 × $1,000 = $100

$$\text{Cur. yield} = \frac{\text{Interest}}{\text{Price}}$$

$$= \frac{\$100}{\$1,062.50}$$

c.y. = 9.41%

4.

	Price Quote	Selling Price	Premium or Discount	Interest Rate	Annual Interest	Current Yield
(a)	106	$1,060.00	$ 60P	$5\frac{1}{2}$%	$55.00	5.19%
(b)	94	940.00	60D	5	50.00	5.32
(c)	100	1,000.00	Par	$7\frac{3}{4}$	77.50	7.75
(d)	$85\frac{1}{2}$	855.00	145D	$6\frac{1}{4}$	62.50	7.31
(e)	$104\frac{1}{4}$	1,042.50	42.50P	8	80.00	7.67

(a)   106% × $1,000 = $1,060
$1,060 - $1,000 = $60P
0.055 × $1,000 = $55

$$\text{Cur. yield} = \frac{\text{Interest}}{\text{Price}}$$

$$= \frac{\$55}{\$1,060}$$

c.y. = 5.19%

(b)   94% × $1,000 = $940
$1,000 - $940 = $60D
0.05 × $1,000 = $50

$$\text{Cur. yield} = \frac{\text{Interest}}{\text{Price}}$$

$$= \frac{\$50}{\$940}$$

c.y. = 5.32%

4. (Continued)

(c)   100% × $1,000 = $1,000 (Par)   (d)   85.5% × $1,000 = $855
       0.0775 × $1,000 = $77.50 $1,000 - $855 = $145D
                                             0.0625 × $1,000 = $62.50

$$\text{Cur. yield} = \frac{\text{Interest}}{\text{Price}} \qquad\qquad \text{Cur. yield} = \frac{\text{Interest}}{\text{Price}}$$

$$= \frac{\$77.50}{\$1,000} \qquad\qquad\qquad = \frac{\$62.50}{\$855}$$

c.y. = 7.75%   c.y. = 7.31%

(e)   104.25% × $1,000 = $1,042.50
       $1,042.50 - $1,000 = $42.50P
          0.08 × $1,000 = $80.00

$$\text{Cur. yield} = \frac{\text{Interest}}{\text{Price}}$$

$$= \frac{\$80}{\$1,042.50}$$

c.y. = 7.67%

5. (a) M = $75,000   Pmt. = M × s.f. tab.$_{\overline{n}|i}$

   i = 2.25%   = $75,000 × s.f. tab.$_{\overline{16}|2.25\%}$

   n = 16   = 75,000(0.0526166)

                        Pmt. = $3,946.25

   (b) $3,946.25 × 16 = $63,140

   (c) $75,000 - $63,140 = $11,860

6. (a) M = $250,000   Pmt. = M × s.f. tab.$_{\overline{n}|i}$

   i = 1.75%   = $250,000 × s.f. tab.$_{\overline{8}|1.75\%}$

   n = 8   = 250,000(0.11754293)

                        Pmt. = $29,385.73

   (b) $29,385.73 × 8 = $235,085.84

   (c) $250,000.00 - $235,085.84 = $14,914.16

7. (a) M = $25,000   Pmt. = M × s.f. tab.$_{n|i}$
      i = 3.5%   = $25,000 × s.f. tab.$_{4|3.5\%}$
      n = 4   = 25,000(0.2372511)
                        Pmt. = $5,931.28

   (b) $5,931.28 × 4 = $23,725.12

   (c) $25,000.00 - $23,725.12 = $1,274.88

8. (a) M = $1,000,000   Pmt. = M × s.f. tab.$_{n|i}$
      i = 3%   = $1,000,000 × s.f. tab.$_{10|3\%}$
      n = 10   = 1,000,000(0.08723051)*
                        Pmt. = $87,230.51

      *Mental math was used since most
       calculators will not show 8 decimal
       places.

   (b) $87,230.51 × 10 = $872,305.10

   (c) $1,000,000 - $872,305.10 = $127,694.90

9. (a) M = $1,000,000   Pmt. = M × s.f. tab.$_{n|i}$
      i = 0.75%   = $1,000,000 × s.f. tab.$_{96|0.75\%}$
      n = 96   = 1,000,000(0.007150203)*
                        Pmt. = $7,150.20

      *Mental math was used since most
       calculators will not show 9 decimal
       places.

   (b) $7,150.20 × 96 = $686,419.20

   (c) $1,000,000.00 - $686,419.20 = $313,580.80

Business Mathematics: A Collegiate Approach

10. (a) M = $1,000,000   Pmt. = M × s.f. tab.$_{\overline{n}|i}$

    $i = \frac{2}{3}\%$ $= \$1,000,000 \times \text{s.f. tab.}_{84|\frac{2}{3}\%}$

    n = 84 $= 1,000,000(0.00891955)$

                            Pmt. = $8,919.55

    (b) $8,919.55 × 84 = $749,242.20

    (c) $1,000,000.00 - $749,242.20 = $250,757.80

11. (a) 104% of $1,000 = $1,040

    (b) $1,040 - $1,000 = $40 premium per bond

    (c) $1,040 × 500 bonds = $520,000

    (d) 8.25% × $1,000 = $82.50 interest per year per bond

    (e) Current yield $= \frac{\text{Annual interest}}{\text{Current price}} = \frac{\$82.50}{\$1,040} = 7.93\%$

    (f) $82.50 × 500 bonds = $41,250

12. (a) 96% of $1,000 = $960

    (b) $1,000 - $960 = $40 premium

    (c) $960 × 5,000 bonds = $4,800,000

    (d) 10.25% × $1,000 = $102.50 interest per year per bond

    (e) Current yield $= \frac{\text{Annual interest}}{\text{Current price}} = \frac{\$102.50}{\$960} = 10.68\%$

    (f) $102.50 × 5,000 bonds = $512,500

13. (a) M = $8,000   Pmt. = M × s.f. tab.$_{\overline{n}|i}$

    i = 2% $= \$8,000 \times \text{s.f. tab.}_{8|2\%}$

    n = 8 $= 8,000(0.116510)$

                            Pmt. = $932.08

13. (a) (Continued)

Payment	Pd. Interest (i = 2%)	Periodic Payment	Total Increase	Balance End of Period
1	0	$ 932.08	$ 932.08	$ 932.08*
2	$ 18.64	932.08	950.72	1,882.80
3	37.66	932.08	969.74	2,852.54
4	57.05	932.08	989.13	3,841.67
5	76.83	932.08	1,008.91	4,850.58
6	97.01	932.08	1,029.09	5,879.67
7	117.59	932.08	1,049.67	6,929.34
8	138.59	932.08	1,070.67	8,000.01
	$543.37	$7,456.64		

*If the Excel spreadsheet is used, there may be differences of a few cents in the answers. The software stores and saves the numbers with full precision even though the student rounded to the nearest cent.

(b) M = $20,000   Pmt. $= M \times$ s.f. tab.$_{n|i}$

   i = 6% $= \$20{,}000 \times$ s.f. tab.$_{5|6\%}$

   n = 5 $= 20{,}000(0.177396)$

                 Pmt. = $3,547.92

Payment	Pd. Interest (i = 6%)	Periodic Payment	Total Increase	Balance End of Period
1	0	$ 3,547.92	$3,547.92	$ 3,547.92*
2	$ 212.88	3,547.92	3,760.80	7,308.72
3	438.52	3,547.92	3,986.44	11,295.16
4	677.71	3,547.92	4,225.63	15,520.79
5	931.25	3,547.92	4,479.17	19,999.96
	$2,260.36	$17,739.60		

*See note at the end of Problem 13a.

14. (a) M = $10,000   Pmt. $= M \times$ s.f. tab.$_{n|i}$

    i = 2.5% $= \$10{,}000 \times$ s.f. tab.$_{4|2.5\%}$

    n = 4 $= 10{,}000(0.2408179)$

                 Pmt. = $2,408.18

14. (a) (Continued)

Payment	Pd. Interest (i = 2.5%)	Periodic Payment	Total Increase	Balance End of Period
1	0	$2,408.18	$2,408.18	$ 2,408.18*
2	$ 60.20	2,408.18	2,468.38	4,876.56
3	121.91	2,408.18	2,530.09	7,406.65
4	185.17	2,408.18	2,593.35	10,000.00
	$367.28	$9,632.72		

*See note at the end of Problems 13a.

(b) M = $60,000   Pmt. = M × s.f. tab.$_{n|i}$

   i = 7%   = $60,000 × s.f. tab.$_{6|7\%}$

   n = 6   = 60,000(0.1397958)

Pmt. = $8,387.75

Payment	Pd. Interest (i = 7%)	Periodic Payment	Total Increase	Balance End of Period
1	0	$ 8,387.75	$ 8,387.75	$ 8,387.75*
2	$ 578.14	8,387.75	8,974.89	17,362.64
3	1,215.38	8,387.75	9,603.13	26,965.77
4	1,887.60	8,387.75	10,275.35	37,241.12
5	2,606.88	8,387.75	10,994.63	48,235.75
6	3,376.50	8,387.75	11,764.25	60,000.00
	$9,673.50	$50,326.50		

*See note at the end of Problem 13a.

Section 2, page 522

1. (a) (1) P.V. = $300,000   Pmt. = P.V. × Amtz. tab.$_{n|i}$

      i = 4%   = $300,000 × Amtz. tab.$_{30|4\%}$

      n = 30   = 300,000(0.0578301)

Pmt. = $17,349.03

   (2) $17,349.03 × 30 = $520,470.90

   (3) $520,470.90 - $300,000.00 = $220,470.90

1. (Continued)

(b) (1) P.V. = \$150,000   Pmt. = P.V. × Amtz. tab.$_{n|i}$

    i = 2.25%   = \$150,000 × Amtz. tab.$_{40|2.25\%}$

    n = 40   =   150,000(0.0381774)

                            Pmt. = \$5,726.61

   (2) \$5,726.61 × 40 = \$229,064.40

   (3) \$229,064.40 - \$150,000.00 = \$79,064.40

(c) (1) P.V. = \$80,000   Pmt. = P.V. × Amtz. tab.$_{n|i}$

    i = $\frac{7}{12}$%   = \$80,000 × Amtz. tab.$_{60|\frac{7}{12}\%}$

    n = 60   =   80,000(0.0198012)

                            Pmt. = \$1,584.10

   (2) \$1,584.10 × 60 = \$95,046

   (3) \$95,046 - \$80,000 = \$15,046

(d) (1) P.V. = \$500,000   Pmt. = P.V. × Amtz. tab.$_{n|i}$

    i = 5%   = \$500,000 × Amtz. tab.$_{14|5\%}$

    n = 14   =   500,000(1.01023970)

                            Pmt. = \$50,511.95

   (2) \$50,511.95 × 14 = \$707,167.30

   (3) \$707,167.30 - \$500,000.00 = \$207,167.30

(e) (1) P.V. = \$20,000   Pmt. = P.V. × Amtz. tab.$_{n|i}$

    i = 0.75%   = \$20,000 × Amtz. tab.$_{96|0.75\%}$

    n = 96   =   20,000(0.0146502)

                            Pmt. = \$293

   (2) \$293 × 96 = \$28,128

   (3) \$28,128 - \$20,000 = \$8,128

2. (a) (1) P.V. = \$60,000   Pmt. = P.V. × Amtz. tab.$_{n|i}$

   i = 6%   = \$60,000 × Amtz. tab.$_{10|6\%}$

   n = 10   =   60,000(0.1172305)

   Pmt. = \$7,033.83

   (2) \$7,033.83 × 10 = \$70,338.30

   (3) \$70,338.30 - \$60,000.00 = \$10,338.30

(b) (1) P.V. = \$900,000   Pmt. = P.V. × Amtz. tab.$_{n|i}$

   i = 1.25%   = \$900,000 × Amtz. tab.$_{48|1.25\%}$

   n = 48   =   900,000(0.02783075)

   Pmt. = \$25,047.63

   (2) \$25,047.63 × 48 = \$1,202,286.20

   (3) \$1,202,286.20 - \$900,000.00 = \$302,286.20

(c) (1) P.V. = \$280,000   Pmt. = P.V. × Amtz. tab.$_{n|i}$

   i = $\frac{2}{3}$%   = \$280,000 × Amtz. tab.$_{84|\frac{2}{3}\%}$

   n = 84   =   280,000(0.0155862)

   Pmt. = \$4,364.14

   (2) \$4,364.14 × 84 = \$366,587.76

   (3) \$366,587.76 - \$280,000.00 = \$86,587.76

(d) (1) P.V. = \$550,000   Pmt. = P.V. × Amtz. tab.$_{n|i}$

   i = 4.5%   = \$550,000 × Amtz. tab.$_{16|4.5\%}$

   n = 16   =   550,000(0.08901537)

   Pmt. = \$48,958.42

   (2) \$48,958.42 × 16 = \$783,334.72

   (3) \$783,334.72 - \$550,000.00 = \$233,334.72

2. (Continued)

(e) (1) P.V. = \$90,000   Pmt. = P.V. × Amtz. tab.$_{n|i}$

$i = \dfrac{5}{12}\%$ $= \$90,000 \times$ Amtz. tab.$_{36|\frac{5}{12}\%}$

n = 36   = 90,000(0.0299709)

Pmt. = \$2,697.38

(2) \$2,697.38 × 36 = \$97,105.68

(3) \$97,105.68 - \$90,000.00 = \$7,105.68

3. (a) $ 7.34 per \$1,000 @ 8%
×   200
$ 1,468 Monthly payment
×   360 Mos. in 30 yrs.
\$528,480 Total payments
-200,000 Principal
\$328,480 Total interest

(b) $ 8.84 per \$1,000 @ 8.75%
×   300
$ 2,652 Monthly payment
×   240 Mos. in 20 yrs.
\$636,480 Total payments
-300,000 Principal
\$336,480 Total interest

(c) $ 8.57 per \$1,000 @ 9.25%
×   60
$ 514.20 Monthly payment
×   300 Mos. in 25 yrs.
\$154,260 Total payments
- 60,000 Principal
$ 94,260 Total interest

(d) $ 9.00 per \$1,000 @ 9%
×   90
$ 810 Monthly payment
×   240 Mos. in 20 yrs.
\$194,400 Total payments
- 90,000 Principal
\$104,400 Total interest

4. (a) $ 7.87 per \$1,000 @ 8.75%
×   120
$ 944.40 Monthly payment
×   360 Mos. in 30 yrs.
\$339,984 Total payments
-120,000 Principal
\$219,984 Total interest

(b) $ 8.68 per \$1,000 @ 8.5%
×   75
$ 651.00 Monthly payment
×   240 Mos. in 20 yrs.
\$156,240 Total payments
- 75,000 Principal
$ 81,240 Total interest

(c) $ 8.40 per 1,000 @ 9%
×   360
$ 3,024 Monthly payment
×   300 Mos. in 25 yrs.
\$907,200 Total payments
-360,000 Principal
\$547,200 Total interest

(d) $ 8.60 per \$1,000 @ 9.75%
×   500
$ 4,300 Monthly payment
×   360 Mos. in 30 yrs.
\$1,548,000 Total payments
- 500,000 Principal
\$1,048,000 Total interest

5. (a) P.V. = $30,000 Pmt. = P.V. × Amtz. tab.$_{n|i}$

    i = 0.75% = $30,000 × Amtz. tab.$_{36|0.75\%}$

    n = 36 = 30,000(0.031800)

    Pmt. = $954

    (b) Total payments = $954 × 36 = $34,344
    Total interest = $34,344 - $30,000 = $4,344

6. (a) P.V. = $150,000 Pmt. = P.V. × Amtz. tab.$_{n|i}$

    $i = \frac{2}{3}\%$ = $150,000 × Amtz. tab.$_{48|\frac{2}{3}\%}$

    n = 48 = 150,000(0.0244129)

    Pmt. = $3,661.94

    (b) Total payments = $3,661.94 × 48 = $175,773.12
    Total interest = $175,773.12 - $150,000.00 = $25,773.12

7. (a) P.V. = $60,000 Pmt. = P.V. × Amtz. tab.$_{n|i}$

    i = 2% = $60,000 × Amtz. tab.$_{28|2\%}$

    n = 28 = 60,000(0.0469897)

    Pmt. = $2,819.38

    (b) Total payments = $2,819.38 × 28 = $78,942.64
    Total interest = $78,942.64 - $60,000.00 = $18,942.64

8. (a) P.V. = $1,000,000 Pmt. = P.V. × Amtz. tab.$_{n|i}$

    i = 1.75% = $1,000,000 × Amtz. tab.$_{20|1.75\%}$

    n = 20 = 1,000,000(0.059691225)*

    Pmt. = $59,691.23

    *Mental math was used since most
    calculators will not show 9 decimal
    places.

    (b) Total payments = $59,691.23 × 20 = $1,193,824.60
    Total interest = $1,193,824.60 - $1,000,000.00
    = $193,824.60

9. (a) P.V. = \$145,000 - \$25,000 = \$120,000

$$i = 2\%$$
$$n = 20$$

Pmt. = P.V. × Amtz. tab.$_{n|i}$

= \$120,000 × Amtz. tab.$_{20|2\%}$

= 120,000(0.0611567)

Pmt. = \$7,338.80

(b) \$7,338.80 × 20 = \$146,776
\$146,776 - \$120,000 = \$26,776

(c) \$146,776 + \$25,000 = \$171,776

10. (a) P.V. = \$108,000 - \$8,000 = \$100,000

$$i = 2.25\%$$
$$n = 40$$

Pmt. = P.V. × Amtz. tab.$_{n|i}$

= \$100,000 × Amtz. tab.$_{40|2.25\%}$

= 100,000(0.03817738)

Pmt. = \$3,817.74

(b) \$3,817.74 × 40 = \$152,709.60
\$152,709.60 - \$100,000.00 = \$52,709.60

(c) \$152,709.60 + \$8,000.00 = \$160,709.60

11. (a) P.V. = \$175,000 - \$25,000 = \$150,000

$$i = \frac{7}{12}\%$$
$$n = 60$$

Pmt. = P.V. × Amtz. tab.$_{n|i}$

= \$150,000 × Amtz. tab.$_{60|\frac{7}{12}\%}$

= 150,000(0.01980120)

Pmt. = \$2,970.18

11. (Continued)

   (b) $2,970.18 × 60 = $178,210.80
       $178,210.80 - $150,000.00 = $28,210.80

   (c) $178,210.80 + $25,000.00 = $203,210.80

12. (a) P.V. = $650,000 - $20,000 = $630,000

       $i = \dfrac{2}{3}\%$

       $n = 24$

       Pmt. = P.V. × Amtz. tab.$_{n|i}$

            = $630,000 × Amtz. tab.$_{24|\frac{2}{3}\%}$

            = $630,000(0.04522729)$

       Pmt. = $28,493.14

   (b) Total payments = $28,493.14 × 24 = $683,835.36
       Total interest = $683,835.36 - $630,000.00 = $53,835.36

   (c) $683,835.36 + $20,000.00 = $703,835.36

13. P.V. = $245,000 - $15,000 = $230,000

       $i = 9\dfrac{1}{2}\%$

   (a) 20 Years, $9\dfrac{1}{2}\%$:   25 Years, $9\dfrac{1}{2}\%$:

       $ 9.33 Per $1,000 $ 8.74 Per $1,000
       ×   230   ×   230
       $2,145.90 Monthly pmt. $2,010.20 Monthly pmt.

   (b) $2,145.90 $2,010.20
       ×   240 Months   ×   300 Months
       $ 515,016 Total pmts. $ 603,060 Total pmts.

   (c) $515,016 $603,060
       + 15,000 Down pmt.   + 15,000 Down pmt.
       $530,016 Total cost $618,060 Total cost

   (d) $618,060 - $530,016 = $88,044

14. (a)

25 Years, 8.75%	30 Years, 8.75%
$ 8.23 Per $1,000	$ 7.87 Per $1,000
× 375	× 375
$3,086.25 Monthly pmt.	$2,951.25 Monthly pmt.

(b)

$3,086.25	$ 2,951.25
× 300 Months	× 360 Months
$ 925,875 Total pmts.	$1,062,450 Total pmts.

(c)

$925,875	$1,062,450
+ 40,000 Down pmt.	+ 40,000 Down pmt.
$965,875 Total cost	$1,102,450 Total cost

(d) $1,202,450 − $965,875 = $136,575

15. (a) P.V. = $5,000   Pmt. = P.V. × Amtz. tab.$_{n|i}$

     i = 7%   = $5,000 × Amtz. tab.$_{5|7\%}$

     n = 5   = 5,000(0.2438907)

                                          Pmt. = $1,219.45

Payment	Principal Owed	Interest (i = 7%)	Pmt. to Principal ($1,219.45 − I)
1	$5,000.00	$ 350.00	$ 869.45*
2	4,130.55	289.14	930.31
3	3,200.24	224.02	995.43
4	2,204.81	154.34	1,065.11
5	1,139.70	79.78	1,139.67
	Totals	$1,097.28	$4,999.97

*See note at the end of Problem 13a, Section 1

(b) P.V. = $6,000   Pmt. = P.V. × Amtz. tab.$_{n|i}$

     i = 4%   = $6,000 × Amtz. tab.$_{6|4\%}$

     n = 6   = 6,000(0.1907619)

                                          Pmt. = $1,144.57

15. (b) (Continued)

Payment	Principal Owed	Interest (i = 4%)	Pmt. to Principal ($1,144.57 - I)
1	$6,000.00	$240.00	$ 904.57*
2	5,095.43	203.82	940.75
3	4,154.68	166.19	978.38
4	3,176.30	127.05	1,017.52
5	2,158.78	86.35	1,058.22
6	1,100.56	44.02	1,100.55
	Totals	$867.43	$5,999.99

*See note at the end of Problem 13a, Section 1

16. (a) P.V. = $10,000

$$\text{Pmt.} = \text{P.V.} \times \text{Amtz. tab.}_{\overline{n}|i}$$

i = 1.5%

$$= \$10,000 \times \text{Amtz. tab.}_{\overline{8}|1.5\%}$$

n = 8

$$= 10,000(1.3358402)$$

$$\text{Pmt.} = \$1,335.84$$

Payment	Principal Owed	Interest (i = 1.5%)	Pmt. to Principal ($1,335.84 - I)
1	$10,000.00	$ 150.00	$ 1,185.84*
2	8,814.16	132.21	1,203.63
3	7,610.53	114.16	1,221.68
4	6,388.85	95.83	1,240.01
5	5,148.84	77.23	1,258.61
6	3,890.24	58.35	1,277.49
7	2,612.75	39.19	1,296.65
8	1,316.10	19.74	1,316.10
	Totals	$ 686.72	$10,000.00

*See note at the end of Problem 13a, Section 1

(b) P.V. = $12,000

$$\text{Pmt.} = \text{P.V.} \times \text{Amtz. tab.}_{\overline{n}|i}$$

i = 8%

$$= \$12,000 \times \text{Amtz. tab.}_{\overline{12}|8\%}$$

n = 12

$$= 12,000(0.9458572)$$

$$\text{Pmt.} = \$11,350.29$$

16. (b) (Continued)

Payment	Principal Owed	Interest (i = 8%)	Pmt. to Principal ($11,350.29 - I)
1	$12,000.00	$ 80.00	$ 963.86*
2	11,036.14	73.58	970.28
3	10,065.86	67.11	976.75
4	9,089.11	60.60	983.26
5	8,105.85	54.04	989.82
6	7,116.03	47.44	996.42
7	6,119.61	40.80	1,003.06
8	5,116.55	34.11	1,009.75
9	4,106.80	27.38	1,016.48
10	3,090.32	20.60	1,023.26
11	2,067.07	13.78	1,030.08
12	1,036.99	6.91	$ 1,036.95
	Totals	$526.36	$11,999.96

*See note at the end of Problem 13a, Section 1

Section 3, page 528

1. (a) P = $5,000 $\quad$ M = $P(1 + i)^n$
   i = 2.25% $\qquad\qquad$ = $5,000(1 + 2.25\%)^{28}$
   n = 28 $\qquad\qquad\quad$ =   5,000(1.8645450)
   $\qquad\qquad\qquad\qquad$ M = $9,322.73

   (b) I = $9,322.73 - $5,000.00 = $4,322.73

2. (a) P = $20,000 $\qquad\quad$ M = $P(1 + i)^n$

   $i = \dfrac{5}{6}\%$ $\qquad\qquad\quad$ $= \$20,000\left(1 + \dfrac{5}{6}\%\right)^{48}$

   n = 48 $\qquad\qquad\qquad$ =   20,000(1.4893541)

   $\qquad\qquad\qquad\qquad$ M = $29,787.08

   (b) I = $29,787.08 - $20,000.00 = $ 9,787.08

3. (a) M = $30,000 $\qquad\quad$ P = $M(1 + i)^{-n}$
   i = 4% $\qquad\qquad\qquad$ = $30,000(1 + 4\%)^{-16}$
   n = 16 $\qquad\qquad\qquad$ =   30,000(0.53390818)
   $\qquad\qquad\qquad\qquad$ P = $16,017.24

   (b) $30,000.00 - $16,017.24 = $13,982.76

4. (a) $M = \$6,000$

$\quad i = \dfrac{5}{12}\%$

$\quad n = 36$

$P = M(1 + i)^{-n}$

$\quad = \$6,000\left(1 + \dfrac{5}{12}\%\right)^{-36}$

$\quad = 6,000(0.8609762)$

$P = \$5,165.86$

(b) $\$6,000.00 - \$5,165.86 = \$834.14$

5. (a) $M = \$200,000$

$\quad i = 2\%$

$\quad n = 32$

$\text{Pmt.} = M \times \text{s.f. tab.}_{n|i}$

$\quad = \$200,000 \times \text{s.f. tab.}_{32|2\%}$

$\quad = 200,000(0.0226106)$

$\text{Pmt.} = \$4,522.12$

(b) $\$4,522.12 \times 32 = \$144,707.84$

(c) $\$200,000.00 - \$144,707.84 = \$55,292.16$

6. (a) $M = \$175,000$

$\quad i = \dfrac{7}{12}\%$

$\quad n = 60$

$\text{Pmt.} = M \times \text{s.f. tab.}_{n|i}$

$\quad = \$175,000 \times \text{s.f. tab.}_{60|\frac{7}{12}\%}$

$\quad = 175,000(0.0139679)$

$\text{Pmt.} = \$2,444.38$

(b) $\$2,444.38 \times 60 = \$146,662.80$

(c) $\$175,000.00 - \$146,662.80 = \$28,337.20$

7. (a) $P = \$25,000$

$\quad i = 3\%$

$\quad n = 8$

$\text{Pmt.} = \text{P.V.} \times \text{Amtz. tab.}_{n|i}$

$\quad = \$25,000 \times \text{Amtz. tab.}_{8|3\%}$

$\quad = 25,000(0.1424564)$

$\text{Pmt.} = \$3,561.41$

(b) $\$3,561.41 \times 8 = \$28,491.28$

(c) $\$28,491.28 - \$25,000.00 = \$3,491.28$

8. (a) P = \$350,000 Pmt. = P.V. × Amtz. tab.$_{n|i}$

   i = 2%   = \$350,000 × Amtz. tab.$_{24|2\%}$

   n = 24   = 350,000(0.05287110)

             Pmt. = \$18,504.89

 (b) \$18,504.89 × 24 = \$444,117.36

 (c) \$444,117.36 - \$350,000.00 = \$94,117.36

9. (a) Pmt. = \$100,000 M = Pmt. × Amt. ann. tab.$_{n|i}$

   i = 1.25%   = \$100,000 × Amt. ann. tab.$_{20|1.25\%}$

   n = 20   = 100,000(22.56297854)*

            M = \$2,256,297.85

      *Mental math was used since most
      calculators will not show 8
      decimal places.

 (b) \$100,000 × 20 = \$2,000,000

 (c) \$2,256,297.85 - \$2,000,000.00 = \$256,297.85

10. (a) Pmt. = \$10,000 M = Pmt. × Amt. ann. tab.$_{n|i}$

   i = $\frac{7}{12}$%   = \$10,000 × Amt. ann. tab.$_{36|\frac{7}{12}\%}$

   n = 36   = 10,000(39.3901007)*

           M = \$399,301.01

      *Mental math was used since most
      calculators will not show more
      than 9 numbers.

 (b) \$10,000 × 36 = \$360,000

 (c) \$399,301.01 - \$360,000.00 = \$39,301.01

11. (a) Pmt. = $600

    i = 0.5%

    n = 48

$$P.V. = Pmt. \times P.V. \text{ ann. tab.}_{\overline{n}|i}$$
$$= \$600 \times P.V. \text{ ann. tab.}_{\overline{48}|0.5\%}$$
$$= 600(42.58032)$$
$$P.V. = \$25,548.19$$

(b) Total payments = $600 × 48 = $28,800
    Total interest = $28,800.00 − $25,548.19 = $3,251.81

12. (a) Pmt. = $2,000

    i = 1.75%

    n = 8

$$P.V. = Pmt. \times P.V. \text{ ann. tab.}_{\overline{n}|i}$$
$$= \$2,000 \times P.V. \text{ ann. tab.}_{\overline{8}|1.75\%}$$
$$= 2,000(7.4050530)$$
$$P.V. = \$14,810.11$$

(b) Total payments = $2,000 × 8 = $16,000
    Total interest = $16,000.00 − $14,810.11 = $1,189.89

13. (a) M = $15,000
    i = 0.5%
    n = 48

$$P = M(1 + i)^{-n}$$
$$= \$15,000(1 + 0.5\%)^{-48}$$
$$= 15,000(0.7870984)$$
$$P = \$11,806.48$$

(b) $15,000 − $11,806.48 = $3,193.52

14. (a) M = $40,000

    $i = \dfrac{7}{12}\%$

    n = 36

$$P = M(1 + i)^{-n}$$
$$= \$40,000\left(1 + \frac{7}{12}\%\right)^{-48}$$
$$= 40,000(0.81107896)$$
$$P = \$32,443.16$$

(b) $40,000.00 − $32,443.16 = $7,556.84

15. (a) Pmt. = $7,000

    i = 1.75%

    n = 16

$$M = Pmt. \times Amt. \text{ ann tab.}_{\overline{n}|i}$$
$$= \$7,000 \times Amt. \text{ ann. tab.}_{\overline{16}|1.75\%}$$
$$= 7,000(18.281677)$$
$$M = \$127,971.73$$

15. (Continued)

    (b) $7,000 × 16 = $112,000
        $127,971.73 - $112,000.00 = $15,971.73

16. (a) Pmt. = $10,000 $M = \text{Pmt.} \times \text{Amt. ann tab.}_{\overline{n}|i}$

        i = 2% $= \$10,000 \times \text{Amt. ann. tab.}_{\overline{20}|2\%}$

        n = 20 $= 10,000(24.2973698)*$

                            M = $242,973.70

                            *Mental math was used since most
                            calculators will not show 7
                            decimal places.

    (b) Total payments = $10,000 × 20 = $200,000
        Total interest = $242,973.70 - $200,000.00 = $42,973.70

17. (a) P.V. = $50,000 $\text{Pmt.} = \text{P.V.} \times \text{Amtz. tab.}_{\overline{n}|i}$

        i = 5% $= \$50,000 \times \text{Amtz. tab.}_{\overline{6}|5\%}$

        n = 6 $= 50,000(0.1970175)$

                        Pmt. = $9,850.88

    (b) Total payments = $9,850.88 × 6 = $59,105.28
        Total interest = $59,105.28 - $50,000.00 = $9,105.28

18. (a) P.V. = $12,000 $\text{Pmt.} = \text{P.V.} \times \text{Amtz. tab.}_{\overline{n}|i}$

        i = 4.5% $= \$12,000 \times \text{Amtz. tab.}_{\overline{10}|4.5\%}$

        n = 10 $= 12,000(0.12639788)$

                        Pmt. = $1,516.55

    (b) Total payments. = $1,516.55 × 10 = $15,165.50
        Total interest = $15,165.50 - $12,000.00 = $3,165.50

19. (a) Pmt. = $400 $\text{P.V.} = \text{Pmt.} \times \text{P.V. ann. tab.}_{\overline{n}|i}$

        i = 0.5% $= \$400 \times \text{P.V. ann. tab.}_{\overline{24}|0.5\%}$

        n = 24 $= 400(22.56287)$

                        P.V. = $9,025.15

19. (Continued)

    (b) $400 × 24 = $9,600

    (c) $9,600.00 - $9,025.15 = $574.85

20. (a) Pmt. = $300   P.V. = Pmt. × P.V. ann. tab.$_{n|i}$

        $i = \dfrac{5}{12}$%   = $300 × P.V. ann. tab.$_{48|\frac{5}{12}\%}$

        n = 48   = 300(43.422956)

                            P.V. = $13,026.89

    (b) $300 × 48 = $14,400

    (c) $14,400.00 - $13,026.89 = $1,373.11

21. (a) M = $800,000   Pmt. = M × s.f. tab.$_{n|i}$

        i = 4.5%   = $800,000 × s.f. tab.$_{20|4.5\%}$

        n = 20   = 800,000(0.0318761)

                     Pmt. = $25,500.88

    (b) $25,500.88 × 20 = $510,017.60

    (c) $800,000.00 - $510,017.60 = $289,982.40

22. (a) M = $20,000   Pmt. = M × s.f. tab.$_{n|i}$

        $i = \dfrac{7}{12}$%   = $20,000 × s.f. tab.$_{24|\frac{7}{12}\%}$

        n = 24   = 20,000(0.038939)

                     Pmt. = $778.78

    (b) $778.78 × 24 = $18,690.72

    (c) $20,000.00 - $18,690.72 = $1,309.28

23. (a) P = $1,000 $M = P(1 + i)^n$

        i = 1.25% $= \$1,000(1 + 1.25\%)^{12}$

        n = 12   = 1,000(1.160755)

                   M = $1,160.76

23. (Continued)

    (b) $1,160.76 - $1,000.00 = $160.76

24. (a) $P = \$4,500$ $M = P(1 + i)^n$

           $i = 1.5\%$ $= \$4,500(1 + 1.5\%)^{16}$

           $n = 16$ $= 4,500(1.268986)$

                                   $M = \$5,710.44$

    (b) $5,710.44 - $4,500.00 = $1,210.44

TRANSPARENCY MASTERS FOR
BUSINESS MATHEMATICS, A COLLEGIATE APPROACH, 8e

TRANSPARENCY MASTERS, continued

EXPONENT AND BASE

Example 4

(a) $x^2 \xleftarrow{\text{exponent}} = x \cdot x \xleftarrow{\text{base}}$

(b) $5^3 \xleftarrow{\text{exponent}} = 5 \cdot 5 \cdot 5 = 125$
$ \xleftarrow{\text{base}}$

(c) $2^4 = 2 \cdot 2 \cdot 2 \cdot 2$
$ = 16$

(d) $(1.02)^3 = (1.02)(1.02)(1.02)$
$ = 1.061208$

589

Roueche & Graves
Business Mathematics: A
Collegiate Approach, 8/e

PARENTHESES WITH COEFFICIENTS

Example 8

<table>
<tr><td align="center"><u>RIGHT</u></td><td align="center"><u>WRONG</u></td></tr>
</table>

$$P(1 + rt) = \$600\left(1 + \frac{5}{100} \cdot \frac{1}{3}\right) \qquad P(1 + rt) = \$600\left(1 + \frac{5}{100} \cdot \frac{1}{3}\right)$$

$$= 600\left(1 + \frac{5}{300}\right) \qquad\qquad = \$600\left(1 + \frac{5}{300}\right)$$

$$= 600\left(\frac{300}{300} + \frac{5}{300}\right) \qquad\qquad = \overset{2}{\cancel{600}}\left(1 + \frac{5}{\cancel{300}}\right)$$

$$= \overset{2}{\cancel{600}}\left(\frac{305}{\cancel{300}}\right) \qquad\qquad = 2(6)$$

$$= \$610 \qquad\qquad\qquad = \$12$$

Example 9

(a) $\quad P(\overset{\frown}{1 + rt}) = P \cdot 1 \quad + \quad P \cdot rt = P + Prt$

(b) $\quad M(\overset{\frown}{1 - dt}) = M \cdot 1 \quad - \quad M \cdot dt = M - Mdt$

(c) $\quad M(1 - dt)$ with $M = \$400$ and $d = \frac{6}{100}$ becomes

$$M(1 - dt) = \$400\left(\overset{\frown}{1 - \frac{6}{100}t}\right)$$

$$= 400 \cdot 1 \quad - \quad \overset{4}{\cancel{400}} \cdot \frac{6}{\cancel{100}}t$$

$$= 400 - 24t$$

Roueche & Graves
*Business Mathematics: A
Collegiate Approach*, 8/e

EQUATIONS WITH %

Example 1

(a)   16% of 45 is what number?

$$0.16 \times 45 = n$$
$$7.2 = n$$

(b)   What percent of 30 is 6?

$$r \times 30 = 6$$
$$30r = 6$$
$$\frac{30r}{30} = \frac{6}{30}$$
$$r = \frac{1}{5}$$
$$r = 20\%$$

(c) $66\frac{2}{3}\%$ of what number is 12?

Because $66\frac{2}{3}\%$ is exactly $\frac{2}{3}$, we will use $\frac{2}{3}$:

$$\frac{2}{3} \times n = 12$$
$$\frac{2n}{3} = 12$$
$$\frac{3}{2} \times \frac{2n}{3} = 12 \times \frac{3}{2}$$
$$n = 18$$

Roueche & Graves
Business Mathematics: A
Collegiate Approach, 8/e

WORD PROBLEMS WITH %

Example 1

A direct-mail campaign by a magazine produced \$16,000 in renewals and new subscriptions. If renewals totaled \$10,000, what percent of the subscriptions were renewals?

$$\underline{\text{What percent}} \quad \underline{\text{of}} \quad \underline{\text{subscriptions}} \quad \underline{\text{were}} \quad \underline{\text{renewals?}}$$

$$\underline{\quad\quad}\% \quad \times \quad \$16{,}000 \quad = \quad \$10{,}000$$

$$16{,}000r \quad = \quad 10{,}000$$

$$\frac{16{,}000r}{16{,}000} \quad = \quad \frac{10{,}000}{16{,}000}$$

$$r \quad = \quad 0.625$$

$$r \quad = \quad 62.5\%$$

Example 2

Thirty-five percent of a payment made to a partnership land purchase was tax deductible. If a partner receives a notice that he qualifies for a \$700 tax deduction, how much was his total payment?

$$\underline{35\%} \quad \underline{\text{of}} \quad \underline{\text{payment}} \quad \underline{\text{was}} \quad \underline{\text{tax deduction}}$$

$$35\% \quad \times \quad p \quad = \quad \$700$$

$$0.35p \quad = \quad 700$$

$$\frac{0.35p}{0.35} \quad = \quad \frac{700.00}{0.35}$$

$$p \quad = \quad \$2{,}000$$

Roueche & Graves
Business Mathematics: A Collegiate Approach, 8/e

WORD PROBLEMS

Example 3 A quarterback completed 40% of his attempted passes in a professional football game. If he attempted 65 passes, how many did he complete?

40%	of	attempted passes	were	completed passes
0.4	×	65	=	c
		0.4(65)	=	c
		26	=	c

Example 4 Last year's sales were $45,000; sales for this year totaled $48,600. What was the percent of increase in sales?

Original = $45,000   ____.% of Original = Change?

Change = $48,600 − $45,000   ____ % of $45,000 = $3,600

= $3,600 $45,000r = 3,600

$$\frac{45,000r}{45,000} = \frac{3,600}{45,000}$$

$$r = 0.08$$

$$r = 8\%$$

Roueche & Graves
*Business Mathematics: A
Collegiate Approach, 8/e*

593

Percent Equivalents of Common Fractions

The following percents (many with fractional remainders) will be given in many problems so that students without calculators can conveniently use the exact fractional equivalents. (Students using calculators may also use the fractional equivalents by entering the numerators and denominators separately.)

$\frac{1}{2} = 50\%$

$\frac{1}{3} = 33\frac{1}{3}\%$ $\qquad$ $\frac{2}{3} = 66\frac{2}{3}\%$

$\frac{1}{4} = 25\%$ $\qquad$ $\frac{3}{4} = 75\%$

$\frac{1}{5} = 20\%$ $\qquad$ $\frac{2}{5} = 40\%$ $\qquad$ $\frac{3}{5} = 60\%$ $\qquad$ $\frac{4}{5} = 80\%$

$\frac{1}{6} = 16\frac{2}{3}\%$ $\qquad$ $\frac{5}{6} = 83\frac{1}{3}\%$

$\frac{1}{7} = 14\frac{2}{7}\%$ $\qquad$ $\frac{2}{7} = 28\frac{4}{7}\%$ $\qquad$ $\frac{3}{7} = 42\frac{6}{7}\%$

$\frac{1}{8} = 12\frac{1}{2}\%$ $\qquad$ $\frac{3}{8} = 37\frac{1}{2}\%$ $\qquad$ $\frac{5}{8} = 62\frac{1}{2}\%$ $\qquad$ $\frac{7}{8} = 87\frac{1}{2}\%$

$\frac{1}{9} = 11\frac{1}{9}\%$ $\qquad$ $\frac{2}{9} = 22\frac{2}{9}\%$ $\qquad$ $\frac{4}{9} = 44\frac{4}{9}\%$ $\qquad$ $\frac{5}{9} = 55\frac{5}{9}\%$

$\frac{1}{10} = 10\%$ $\qquad$ $\frac{3}{10} = 30\%$ $\qquad$ $\frac{7}{10} = 70\%$ $\qquad$ $\frac{9}{10} = 90\%$

$\frac{1}{12} = 8\frac{1}{3}\%$

Roueche & Graves
*Business Mathematics: A
Collegiate Approach, 8/e*

WEIGHTED AVERAGE

The same model of microwave oven is available from several appliance stores. Prices and number of ovens sold are shown below. What is (a) the average price per store, and (b) the average price per oven sold?

Store	Number Sold	Price
1	40	$450
2	60	400
3	120	350
4	80	375

(a) Average price per store = $\dfrac{\text{Sum of prices at all stores}}{\text{Total number of stores}}$

$$\frac{\$450 + \$400 + \$350 + \$375}{4} = \frac{\$1,575}{4}$$

$$= \$393.75 \quad \text{(average price per store)}$$

(b) Average price per oven = $\dfrac{\text{Sum of prices of all ovens}}{\text{Total number of ovens}}$

For this average, the various prices must be weighted according to the number of ovens sold at each price.

Number		Price		
40	×	$450	=	$ 18,000
60	×	400	=	24,000
120	×	350	=	42,000
+ 80	×	375	=	30,000
300				$114,000

$$\frac{\$114,000}{300} = \$380 \quad \text{(average price per oven)}$$

Roueche & Graves
*Business Mathematics: A
Collegiate Approach*, 8/e

595

AVERAGE INVESTMENT PER MONTH

David Cohen invested $5,000 in a business on January 1. On May 1, he withdrew $200; on July 1, he reinvested $1,000; and on August 1, he invested another $1,400. What was his average investment during the year?

$$\text{Average investment} = \frac{\text{Sum of investments of all months}}{\text{Total number of months}}$$

Date	Change	Amount of Investment		Months Invested		
January 1		$5,000	×	4	=	$20,000
May 1	− $200	4,800	×	2	=	9,600
July 1	+ 1,000	5,800	×	1	=	5,800
August 1	+ 1,400	7,200	×	5	=	36,000
				12		$71,400

$$\frac{\$71,400}{12} = \$5,950 \qquad \text{(average investment)}$$

Roueche & Graves
Business Mathematics: A
Collegiate Approach, 8/e

STANDARD DEVIATION

Assume that the mean size of women's dresses is size 12, with a standard deviation of 4, as shown below. Use the percent categories of the normal curve to answer each question.

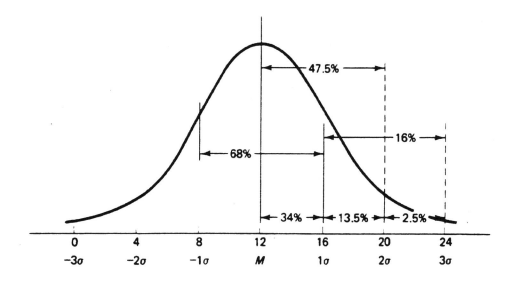

(a) What percent of the women are size 12 or larger?   50%

(b) What percent of the women are size 16 or larger?   16%

(c) What percent are 24 or smaller?   100%

(d) What percent are smaller than size 4?   2.5%

(e) What percent are smaller than size 4 *or* larger than size 20?   2.5% + 2.5% = 5.0%

(f) If a dress company plans to manufacture 5,000 dresses, how many of those should be in sizes 8 through 16?   68% × 5,000 = 3,400

Roueche & Graves
Business Mathematics: A
Collegiate Approach, 8/e

SPREADSHEET

KOENIG BUILDING DISTRIBUTORS, INC					
	20X1	20X2	20X3	20X4	20X5
Net sales	$ 180,000	$ 210,000	$ 160,000	$ 220,000	$ 237,000
Cost of goods sold	105,000	110,000	80,000	112,000	95,000
Net profit	25,000	32,000	8,000	10,000	42,000

598

Roueche & Graves
*Business Mathematics: A
Collegiate Approach, 8/e*

Sales Analysis,
Koenig Building Distributors, Inc.
20X1-20X5

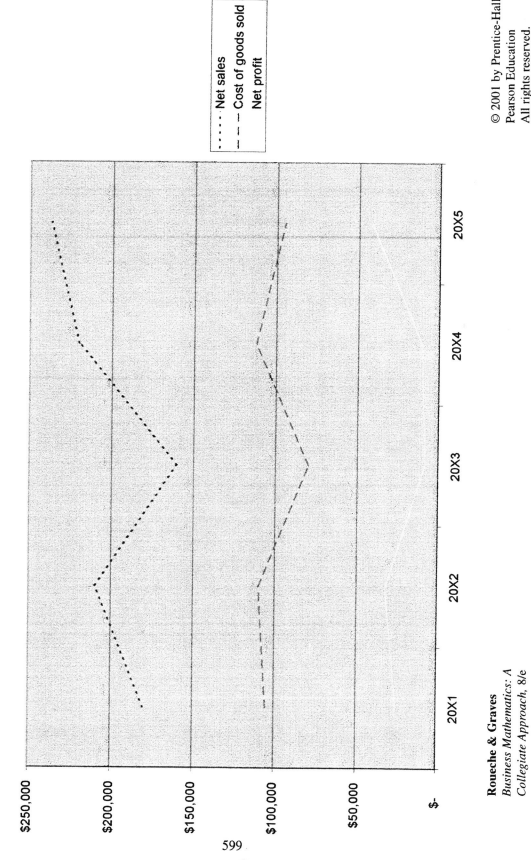

- · · · · · Net sales
- — — Cost of goods sold
- ———— Net profit

Roueche & Graves
*Business Mathematics: A
Collegiate Approach, 8/e*

PROPERTY TAX RATE FORMULA

$$\text{Rate} = \frac{\text{Total tax needed}}{\text{Total assessed valuation}}$$

Example 1

Markly County has an annual budget of $4,800,000. If the taxable property in the county is assessed as $300,000,000, what will be the tax rate for next year? Express this rate (a) as a percent, (b) as an amount per $100, (c) as an amount per $1,000, and (d) in mills.

$$\text{Rate} = \frac{\text{Total tax needed}}{\text{Total assessed value}}$$

$$= \frac{\$4,800,000}{\$300,000,000}$$

$$\text{Rate} = 0.016$$

(a) The property tax rate is 1.6% of the assessed value of property.

(b) When the rate is expressed per $100, the decimal point is marked off after the hundredths place. Thus, the rate is $1.60 per C (or per $100).

(c) The rate per $1,000 is found by marking off the decimal point after the thousandths place. Hence, the rate is $16.00 per M (or per $1,000).

(d) The rate in mills is found the same way as in part (c), but the $ sign is not used (16 mills).

Roueche & Graves
Business Mathematics: A
Collegiate Approach, 8/e

600

TABLE 6-1. Annual Fire Insurance Premiums per $100 of Face Value

TERRITORY	STRUCTURE CLASS				CONTENTS CLASS			
	A	B	C	D	A	B	C	D
1	$0.45	$0.56	$0.66	$0.75	$0.51	$0.79	$0.79	$0.98
2	0.58	0.64	0.78	0.80	0.68	0.86	0.91	1.03
3	0.63	0.72	0.85	0.93	0.71	0.89	0.95	1.12

TABLE 6-2. Short-Term Rates Including Cancellations by the Insured

Months of Coverage	Percent of Annual Premium Charged	Months of Coverage	Percent of Annual Premium Charged
1	20%	7	75%
2	30	8	80
3	40	9	85
4	50	10	90
5	60	11	95
6	70	12	100

Roueche & Graves
Business Mathematics: A
llegiate Approach, 8/e

TABLE 6-3. Driver Classifications

Multiples of Base Annual Automobile Insurance Premiums

			Pleasure; Less Than 3 Miles to Work Each Way	Drives to Work, 3 to 9 Miles Each Way	Drives to Work, 10 Miles or More Each Way	Used in Business
No young operators	Only operator is female, age 30–64		0.90	1.00	1.30	1.40
	One or more operators age 65 or over		1.00	1.10	1.40	1.50
	All others		1.00	1.10	1.40	1.50
Young females	Age 16	DT[a]	1.40	1.50	1.80	1.90
		No DT	1.55	1.65	1.95	2.05
	Age 20	DT	1.05	1.15	1.45	1.55
		No DT	1.10	1.20	1.50	1.60
Young males (married)	Age 16	DT	1.60	1.70	2.00	2.10
		No DT	1.80	1.90	2.20	2.30
	Age 20	DT	1.45	1.55	1.85	1.95
		No DT	1.50	1.60	1.90	2.00
	Age 21		1.40	1.50	1.80	1.90
	Age 24		1.10	1.20	1.50	1.60
Young unmarried males (not principal operator)	Age 16	DT	2.05	2.15	2.45	2.55
		No DT	2.30	2.40	2.70	2.80
	Age 20	DT	1.60	1.70	2.00	2.10
		No DT	1.70	1.80	2.10	2.20
	Age 21		1.55	1.65	1.95	2.05
	Age 24		1.10	1.20	1.50	1.60
Young unmarried males (owner or principal operator)	Age 16	DT	2.70	2.80	3.10	3.20
		No DT	3.30	3.40	3.70	3.80
	Age 20	DT	2.55	2.65	2.95	3.05
		No DT	2.70	2.80	3.10	3.20
	Age 21		2.50	2.60	2.90	3.00
	Age 24		1.90	2.00	2.30	2.40
	Age 26		1.50	1.60	1.90	2.00
	Age 29		1.10	1.20	1.50	1.60

[a] "DT" indicates completion of a certified driver training course.

Roueche & Graves
Business Mathematics: A Collegiate Approach, 8/e

TABLE 6-4. Automobile Liability and Medical Payment Insurance

Base Annual Premiums

	BODILY INJURY				PROPERTY DAMAGE		
Coverage	Territory 1	Territory 2	Territory 3	Coverage	Territory 1	Territory 2	Territory 3
15/30	$ 81	$ 91	$112	$ 5,000	$83	$ 95	$100
25/25	83	94	115	10,000	85	97	103
25/50	86	97	120	25,000	86	99	104
50/50	88	101	125	50,000	87	101	107
50/100	90	103	129	100,000	90	103	108
100/100	91	104	131				
100/200	94	108	136		MEDICAL PAYMENT		
100/300	95	110	139	$ 1,000	$62	$63	$64
200/300	98	112	141	2,500	65	66	67
300/300	100	115	144	5,000	67	68	69
				10,000	70	72	74

TABLE 6-5. Comprehensive and Collision Insurance

Base Annual Premiums

Model Class	Age Group	TERRITORY 1			TERRITORY 2			TERRITORY 3		
		Comprehensive	$250-Deductible Collision	$500-Deductible Collision	Comprehensive	$250-Deductible Collision	$500-Deductible Collision	Comprehensive	$250-Deductible Collision	$500-Deductible Collision
(1)	1	$55	$ 82	$ 76	$59	$ 92	$ 80	$73	$100	$ 91
A-G	2,3	52	77	73	56	86	76	58	94	85
	4	49	71	67	51	79	70	54	85	78
(3)	1	63	111	101	69	128	108	75	141	127
J-K	2,3	59	103	95	64	118	101	68	131	118
	4	54	93	86	57	106	91	61	116	105
(4)	1	68	123	112	76	143	120	83	169	142
L-M	2,3	64	125	104	70	133	112	75	138	132
	4	57	102	94	62	117	100	66	129	117
(5)	1	77	140	126	86	164	136	95	183	162
N-O	2,3	70	130	117	77	151	126	85	168	150
	4	62	115	105	68	133	112	73	147	132

Roueche & Graves
Business Mathematics: A Collegiate Approach, 8/e

TABLE 6-7. Annual Life Insurance Premiums
Per $1,000 of Face Value for Male Applicants[a]

Age Issued (Years)	Term 10-Year	Whole Life	Variable Universal	Limited Payment 20-Year
18	$ 6.81	$14.77	$18.36	$24.69
20	6.88	15.46	19.81	25.59
22	6.95	16.12	20.28	26.53
24	7.05	16.82	21.33	27.53
25	7.10	17.22	22.17	28.06
26	7.18	17.67	23.43	28.63
28	7.35	18.64	24.79	29.84
30	7.59	19.73	26.05	31.12
35	8.68	23.99	30.87	35.80
40	10.64	28.26	35.55	40.34
45	14.52	33.79	41.24	46.01
50	22.18	40.77	48.11	53.24
55	32.93	51.38	57.62	64.77
60	—	59.32	—	70.86

[a] Because of women's longer life expectancy, premiums for women approximately equal those of men who are 5 years younger.

Roueche & Graves
Business Mathematics: A Collegiate Approach, 8/e

TABLE 6-8. Nonforfeiture Options* on Typical Life Insurance Policies

Issued at Age 25

| Years in Force | WHOLE LIFE | | | | 20-PAYMENT LIFE | | | | VARIABLE UNIVERSAL |
| | Cash Value | Paid-Up Insurance | EXT. TERM | | Cash Value | Paid-Up Insurance | EXT. TERM | | Cash Value |
			Years	Days			Years	Days	
3	$ 9	$ 19	1	190	$ 32	$ 94	10	84	$ 44
5	31	87	9	200	74	218	19	184	95
10	93	248	18	91	187	507	28	186	321
15	162	387	20	300	319	768	32	164	595
20	251	535	22	137	470	1,000	Life		1,030
40	576	827	—	—	701	—	—	—	2,979

* The "cash value" and "paid-up insurance" nonforfeiture values are per $1,000 of life insurance coverage. The time period for "extended term insurance" applies as shown to all policies, regardless of face value. The cash value for variable universal life represents a reasonable estimate of the increase in value rather than a guaranteed amount.

TABLE 6-9. Settlement Options

Monthly Installments per $1,000 of Face Value

| OPTIONS 1 AND 2: FIXED AMOUNT OR FIXED NUMBER OF YEARS | | OPTIONS 3 AND 4: INCOME FOR LIFE | | | | |
| Years | Amount | Age When Annuity Begins | | Life Annuity | Life with 10 Years Certain | Life with 20 Years Certain |
		Male	Female			
10	$9.60	40	45	$4.60	$4.56	$4.44
12	8.52	45	50	5.16	5.07	4.80
14	7.71	50	55	5.30	5.28	5.00
15	6.89	55	60	6.13	6.00	5.46
16	6.43	60	65	6.56	6.31	5.65
18	6.08	65	70	7.22	6.70	5.78
20	5.66					

Roueche & Graves
Business Mathematics: A Collegiate Approach, 8/e

© 2001 by Prentice-Hall, Inc.
Pearson Education
All rights reserved.

PARTS OF CHECK; ENDORSEMENTS

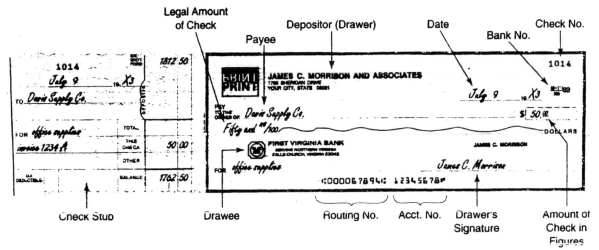

Courtesy of First Virginia Bank

FIGURE 7-1   Parts of Check

BLANK

RESTRICTIVE

SPECIAL

Endorsements

Roueche & Graves
*Business Mathematics: A
Collegiate Approach, 8/e*

BANK STATEMENT

FIRST VIRGINIA BANK
Member FDIC

S1 3

110

STATEMENT CLOSING DATE
06-30-99
ACCOUNT NUMBER
8888-8888

FOR INFORMATION ABOUT
YOUR ACCOUNT, PLEASE CALL
THIS NUMBER:
703-241-3240

22

117

XYZ INDUSTRIES
1234 MAIN STREET
ARLINGTON, VA 22222

PAGE 1

ACCOUNT SUMMARY

ACCOUNT TYPE	PREVIOUS BALANCE	ADDITIONS TO ACCOUNT	SUBTRACTIONS FROM ACCOUNT	NEW BALANCE
CHECKING	11,768.55	7,540.32	10,061.59	9,247.28

.... CHECKING ACCOUNT   8888-8888 ....

DATE	AMOUNT	DESCRIPTION OF ACTIVITY		BALANCE
05-28		PREVIOUS BALANCE		11,768.55
06-01	1,964.83+	DEPOSIT	RF 01849669	13,733.38
06-01	301.14-	CHECK 4622	RF 01849649	13,432.24
06-01	1,336.46 -	CHECK 4620	RF 01787456	12,095.78
06-04	341.10-	CHECK 4628	RF 02425733	11,754.68
06-04	157.50-	CHECK 4624	RF 01432690	11,597.18
06-07	406.42-	CHECK 4625	RF 02683978	11,190.76
06-08	2,085.45+	DEPOSIT	RF 02881943	13,276.21
06-08	306.39-	CHECK 4629	RF 02881940	12,969.82
06-08	38.00-	CHECK 4626	RF 02767954	12,931.82
06-09	105.49-	CHECK 4627	RF 01114317	12,826.33
06-11	341.10-	CHECK 4634	RF 02289624	12,485.23
06-14	2,003.16+	DEPOSIT	RF 02704733	14,488.39
06-14	529.00-	CHECK 4635	RF 02655504	13,959.39
06-14	300.16-	CHECK 4633	RF 02704717	13,659.23
06-17	350.00-	CHECK 4637	RF 02034602	13,309.23
06-17	56.00-	CHECK 4630	RF 02041553	13,253.23
06-17	8.65-	CHECK 4631	RF 01983543	13,244.58
06-18	341.10-	CHECK 4640	RF 01228826	12,903.48
06-18	4,000.00-	CHECK 4636	RF 02190347	8,903.48
06-21	216.86-	CHECK 4638	RF 01327057	8,686.62
06-21	209.00-	CHECK 4632	RF 01344566	8,477.62
06-22	1,486.88+	DEPOSIT	RF 02655535	9,964.50
06-22	297.75-	CHECK 4641	RF 02655524	9,666.75
06-23	28.54-	CHECK 4639	RF 02824054	9,638.21
06-25	341.10-	CHECK 4643	RF 02272566	9,297.11
06-25	49.83-	CHECK 4642	RF 02295577	9,247.28

AVERAGE BALANCE   11,134.93

*************************************   SUMMARY OF ACTIVITY   *************************************

	PREVIOUS BALANCE		11,768.55
4	DEPOSITS AND CREDITS	7,540.32	
22	CHECKS AND DEBITS	10,061.59	
0	SERVICE CHARGES	.00	
22	ENCLOSURES		
	ENDING BALANCE		9,247.28

****

VISIT OUR WEBSITE AT WWW.FIRSTVIRGINIA.COM

NOTICE: SEE REVERSE FOR IMPORTANT INFORMATION

Roueche & Graves
Business Mathematics: A
Collegiate Approach, 8/e

607

STRAIGHT COMMISSION

Edith Reilly receives an 8% commission on her net sales. Find her commission if her gross (original) sales were $5,680 and sales returns and allowances were $180.

Gross sales $5,680 $\% \times S = C$

Less: sales returns
and allowances $-\ \underline{180}$ $8\% \times \$5,500 = C$

Net sales $\overline{\$5,500}$ $\$440 = C$

608

Roueche & Graves
Business Mathematics: A
Collegiate Approach, 8/e

OVERTIME EXCESS METHOD

A worker who earns $5 per hour works 46 hours. Compare these earnings (a) by standard overtime and (b) by overtime excess.

(a) 40 hours @ $5.00 = $200.00   Straight-time wages
    6 hours @ $7.50 =   45.00   Overtime wages
    46 hours   = $245.00   Total gross wages

(b) One-half the regular rate is $\frac{1}{2}$ of $5.00 = $2.50 per hour for the excess hours over 40.

    46 hours @ $5.00 = $230.00   Regular-rate wages
    6 hours @ $2.50 =   15.00   Overtime excess
    46 hours   = $245.00   Total gross wages

Roueche & Graves
Business Mathematics: A Collegiate Approach, 8/e

Form W-4

Department of the Treasury
Internal Revenue Service

Employee's Withholding Allowance Certificate

▶ For Privacy Act and Paperwork Reduction Act Notice, see page 2.

OMB No. 1545-0010

1999

1 Type or print your first name and middle initial

Sarah B.

Last name

Bingham

2 Your social security number

987 | 65 | 4321

Home address (number and street or rural route)

4120 Frosty Court

City or town, state, and ZIP code

Birmingham, AL 35209

3 ☑ Single ☐ Married ☐ Married, but withhold at higher Single rate.
Note: *If married, but legally separated, or spouse is a nonresident alien, check the Single box.*

4 If your last name differs from that on your social security card, check
here. **You** must call 1-800-772-1213 for a new card . . . . ▶ ☐

5 Total number of allowances you are claiming (from line H above or from the worksheets on page 2 if they apply) . | **5** | **1**

6 Additional amount, if any, you want withheld from each paycheck . . . . | **6** | $

7 I claim exemption from withholding for 1999, and I certify that I meet **BOTH** of the following conditions for exemption:
- Last year I had a right to a refund of **ALL** Federal income tax withheld because I had **NO** tax liability **AND**
- This year I expect a refund of **ALL** Federal income tax withheld because I expect to have **NO** tax liability.

If you meet both conditions, write "EXEMPT" here . . . . ▶ | **7**

Under penalties of perjury, I certify that I am entitled to the number of withholding allowances claimed on this certificate, or I am entitled to claim exempt status.

Employee's signature
(Form is not valid
unless you sign it) ▶ Sarah B. Bingham

Date ▶ August 1, 2000

8 Employer's name and address (Employer: Complete 8 and 10 only if sending to the IRS)

**MacArthur Electronics, Inc.; 2001 Second Avenue, South
Birmingham, AL 35200**

9 Office code
(optional)

10 Employer identification number

11 | 222222

Cat. No. 10220Q

610

Roueche & Graves
*Business Mathematics: A
Collegiate Approach,* 8/e

FORM 941

2	Total wages and tips, plus other compensation	**2** 47,800
3	Total income tax withheld from wages, tips, and sick pay	**3** 6,200
4	Adjustment of withheld income tax for preceding quarters of calendar year . .	**4**
5	Adjusted total of income tax withheld (line 3 as adjusted by line 4—see instructions) . . .	**5** 6,200
6	Taxable social security wages . . **6a** 46,700 × 12.4% (.124) =	**6b** 5,791
	Taxable social security tips . . **6c** × 12.4% (.124) =	**6d**
7	Taxable Medicare wages and tips . **7a** 47,800 × 2.9% (.029) =	**7b** 1,386
8	Total social security and Medicare taxes (add lines 6b, 6d, and 7b). Check here if wages are not subject to social security and/or Medicare tax. ▲ ☐	**8** 7,177
9	Adjustment of social security and Medicare taxes (see instructions for required explanation) Sick Pay $ _____ ± Fractions of Cents $ _____ ± Other $ _____ =	**9**
10	Adjusted total of social security and Medicare taxes (line 8 as adjusted by line 9—see instructions)	**10** 7,177
11	**Total taxes** (add lines 5 and 10)	**11** 13,377
12	Advance earned income credit (EIC) payments made to employees	**12**
13	Net taxes (subtract line 12 from line 11). **If $1,000 or more, this must equal line 17, column (d) below (or line D of Schedule B (Form 941))**	**13** 13,377
14	Total deposits for quarter, including overpayment applied from a prior quarter	**14** 13,377
15	**Balance due** (subtract line 14 from line 13). See instructions	**15** 0

611

Roueche & Graves
Business Mathematics: A
Collegiate Approach, 8/e

WEEKLY PAYROLL PERIOD — SINGLE PERSONS

Wages: $0 — $599.99

(For Wages Paid in 1999)

If the wages are—		And the number of withholding allowances claimed is—										
At least	But less than	0	1	2	3	4	5	6	7	8	9	10
		The amount of income tax to be withheld is—										
$0	$55	0	0	0	0	0	0	0	0	0	0	0
55	60	1	0	0	0	0	0	0	0	0	0	0
60	65	2	0	0	0	0	0	0	0	0	0	0
65	70	2	0	0	0	0	0	0	0	0	0	0
70	75	3	0	0	0	0	0	0	0	0	0	0
75	80	4	0	0	0	0	0	0	0	0	0	0
80	85	5	0	0	0	0	0	0	0	0	0	0
85	90	5	0	0	0	0	0	0	0	0	0	0
90	95	6	0	0	0	0	0	0	0	0	0	0
95	100	7	0	0	0	0	0	0	0	0	0	0
100	105	8	0	0	0	0	0	0	0	0	0	0
105	110	8	1	0	0	0	0	0	0	0	0	0
110	115	9	1	0	0	0	0	0	0	0	0	0
115	120	10	2	0	0	0	0	0	0	0	0	0
120	125	11	3	0	0	0	0	0	0	0	0	0
125	130	11	4	0	0	0	0	0	0	0	0	0
130	135	12	4	0	0	0	0	0	0	0	0	0
135	140	13	5	0	0	0	0	0	0	0	0	0
140	145	14	6	0	0	0	0	0	0	0	0	0
145	150	14	7	0	0	0	0	0	0	0	0	0
150	155	15	7	0	0	0	0	0	0	0	0	0
155	160	16	8	0	0	0	0	0	0	0	0	0
160	165	17	9	1	0	0	0	0	0	0	0	0
165	170	17	10	2	0	0	0	0	0	0	0	0
170	175	18	10	2	0	0	0	0	0	0	0	0
175	180	19	11	3	0	0	0	0	0	0	0	0
180	185	20	12	4	0	0	0	0	0	0	0	0
185	190	20	13	5	0	0	0	0	0	0	0	0
190	195	21	13	5	0	0	0	0	0	0	0	0
195	200	22	14	6	0	0	0	0	0	0	0	0
200	210	23	15	7	0	0	0	0	0	0	0	0
210	220	25	17	9	1	0	0	0	0	0	0	0
220	230	26	18	10	2	0	0	0	0	0	0	0
230	240	28	20	12	4	0	0	0	0	0	0	0
240	250	29	21	13	5	0	0	0	0	0	0	0
250	260	31	23	15	7	0	0	0	0	0	0	0
260	270	32	24	16	8	0	0	0	0	0	0	0
270	280	34	26	18	10	2	0	0	0	0	0	0
280	290	35	27	19	11	3	0	0	0	0	0	0
290	300	37	29	21	13	5	0	0	0	0	0	0
300	310	38	30	22	14	6	0	0	0	0	0	0
310	320	40	32	24	16	8	0	0	0	0	0	0
320	330	41	33	25	17	9	1	0	0	0	0	0
330	340	43	35	27	19	11	3	0	0	0	0	0
340	350	44	36	28	20	12	4	0	0	0	0	0
350	360	46	38	30	22	14	6	0	0	0	0	0
360	370	47	39	31	23	15	7	0	0	0	0	0
370	380	49	41	33	25	17	9	1	0	0	0	0
380	390	50	42	34	26	18	10	3	0	0	0	0
390	400	52	44	36	28	20	12	4	0	0	0	0
400	410	53	45	37	29	21	13	6	0	0	0	0
410	420	55	47	39	31	23	15	7	0	0	0	0
420	430	56	48	40	32	24	16	9	1	0	0	0
430	440	58	50	42	34	26	18	10	2	0	0	0
440	450	59	51	43	35	27	19	12	4	0	0	0
450	460	61	53	45	37	29	21	13	5	0	0	0
460	470	62	54	46	38	30	22	15	7	0	0	0
470	480	64	56	48	40	32	24	16	8	0	0	0
480	490	65	57	49	41	33	25	18	10	2	0	0
490	500	67	59	51	43	35	27	19	11	3	0	0
500	510	68	60	52	44	36	28	21	13	5	0	0
510	520	70	62	54	46	38	30	22	14	6	0	0
520	530	71	63	55	47	39	31	24	16	8	0	0
530	540	74	65	57	49	41	33	25	17	9	1	0
540	550	77	66	58	50	42	34	27	19	11	3	0
550	560	80	68	60	52	44	36	28	20	12	4	0
560	570	82	69	61	53	45	37	30	22	14	6	0
570	580	85	71	63	55	47	39	31	23	15	7	0
580	590	88	73	64	56	48	40	33	25	17	9	1
590	600	91	76	66	58	50	42	34	26	18	10	2

Roueche & Graves
Business Mathematics: A Collegiate Approach, 8/e

612

WEEKLY PAYROLL PERIOD — MARRIED PERSONS

Wages: $0 — $739.99

(For Wages Paid in 1999)

If the wages are–		And the number of withholding allowances claimed is—										
At least	But less than	0	1	2	3	4	5	6	7	8	9	10
		The amount of income tax to be withheld is—										
$0	$125	0	0	0	0	0	0	0	0	0	0	0
125	130	1	0	0	0	0	0	0	0	0	0	0
130	135	1	0	0	0	0	0	0	0	0	0	0
135	140	2	0	0	0	0	0	0	0	0	0	0
140	145	3	0	0	0	0	0	0	0	0	0	0
145	150	4	0	0	0	0	0	0	0	0	0	0
150	155	4	0	0	0	0	0	0	0	0	0	0
155	160	5	0	0	0	0	0	0	0	0	0	0
160	165	6	0	0	0	0	0	0	0	0	0	0
165	170	7	0	0	0	0	0	0	0	0	0	0
170	175	7	0	0	0	0	0	0	0	0	0	0
175	180	8	0	0	0	0	0	0	0	0	0	0
180	185	9	1	0	0	0	0	0	0	0	0	0
185	190	10	2	0	0	0	0	0	0	0	0	0
190	195	10	2	0	0	0	0	0	0	0	0	0
195	200	11	3	0	0	0	0	0	0	0	0	0
200	210	12	4	0	0	0	0	0	0	0	0	0
210	220	14	6	0	0	0	0	0	0	0	0	0
220	230	15	7	0	0	0	0	0	0	0	0	0
230	240	17	9	1	0	0	0	0	0	0	0	0
240	250	18	10	2	0	0	0	0	0	0	0	0
250	260	20	12	4	0	0	0	0	0	0	0	0
260	270	21	13	5	0	0	0	0	0	0	0	0
270	280	23	15	7	0	0	0	0	0	0	0	0
280	290	24	16	8	0	0	0	0	0	0	0	0
290	300	26	18	10	2	0	0	0	0	0	0	0
300	310	27	19	11	3	0	0	0	0	0	0	0
310	320	29	21	13	5	0	0	0	0	0	0	0
320	330	30	22	14	6	0	0	0	0	0	0	0
330	340	32	24	16	8	0	0	0	0	0	0	0
340	350	33	25	17	9	1	0	0	0	0	0	0
350	360	35	27	19	11	3	0	0	0	0	0	0
360	370	36	28	20	12	4	0	0	0	0	0	0
370	380	38	30	22	14	6	0	0	0	0	0	0
380	390	39	31	23	15	7	0	0	0	0	0	0
390	400	41	33	25	17	9	1	0	0	0	0	0
400	410	42	34	26	18	10	2	0	0	0	0	0
410	420	44	36	28	20	12	4	0	0	0	0	0
420	430	45	37	29	21	13	5	0	0	0	0	0
430	440	47	39	31	23	15	7	0	0	0	0	0
440	450	48	40	32	24	16	8	1	0	0	0	0
450	460	50	42	34	26	18	10	2	0	0	0	0
460	470	51	43	35	27	19	11	4	0	0	0	0
470	480	53	45	37	29	21	13	5	0	0	0	0
480	490	54	46	38	30	22	14	7	0	0	0	0
490	500	56	48	40	32	24	16	8	0	0	0	0
500	510	57	49	41	33	25	17	10	2	0	0	0
510	520	59	51	43	35	27	19	11	3	0	0	0
520	530	60	52	44	36	28	20	13	5	0	0	0
530	540	62	54	46	38	30	22	14	6	0	0	0
540	550	63	55	47	39	31	23	16	8	0	0	0
550	560	65	57	49	41	33	25	17	9	1	0	0
560	570	66	58	50	42	34	26	19	11	3	0	0
570	580	68	60	52	44	36	28	20	12	4	0	0
580	590	69	61	53	45	37	29	22	14	6	0	0
590	600	71	63	55	47	39	31	23	15	7	0	0
600	610	72	64	56	48	40	32	25	17	9	1	0
610	620	74	66	58	50	42	34	26	18	10	2	0
620	630	75	67	59	51	43	35	28	20	12	4	0
630	640	77	69	61	53	45	37	29	21	13	5	0
640	650	78	70	62	54	46	38	31	23	15	7	0
650	660	80	72	64	56	48	40	32	24	16	8	0
660	670	81	73	65	57	49	41	34	26	18	10	2
670	680	83	75	67	59	51	43	35	27	19	11	3
680	690	84	76	68	60	52	44	37	29	21	13	5
690	700	86	78	70	62	54	46	38	30	22	14	6
700	710	87	79	71	63	55	47	40	32	24	16	8
710	720	89	81	73	65	57	49	41	33	25	17	9
720	730	90	82	74	66	58	50	43	35	27	19	11
730	740	92	84	76	68	60	52	44	36	28	20	12

Roueche & Graves
Business Mathematics: A
Collegiate Approach, 8/e

STRAIGHT-LINE METHOD

Example 3

A machine that manufactures keys is purchased for $5,100. It is expected to last for 5 years and have a trade-in value of $900. Prepare a depreciation schedule by the straight-line method.

First, the depreciable value must be computed and divided by the years of use to determine each year's depreciation charge:

Original cost	$5,100
Trade-in value	− 900
Depreciable value	$4,200

$$\frac{\text{Depreciable value}}{\text{Years}} = \frac{\$4,200}{5}$$

$$= \$840 \quad \text{Annual depreciation}$$

Depreciation Schedule
Straight-Line Method

Year	Book Value (End of Year)	Annual Depreciation	Accumulated Depreciation
0	$5,100	—	—
1	4,260	$840	$ 840
2	3,420	840	1,680
3	2,580	840	2,520
4	1,740	840	3,360
5	900	840	4,200

Residual value   Depreciable value

Roueche & Graves
*Business Mathematics: A
Collegiate Approach,* 8/e

DECLINING-BALANCE METHOD

(a) A new vending machine that cost $4,800 has an expected residual value of $600 and a life of 5 years. Prepare a depreciation schedule by the declining-balance method.

Because the machine will be used for 5 years, it can be depreciated at a rate of

$$2 \times \frac{1}{5} = \frac{2}{5} = 40\% \text{ annually}$$

Each succeeding book value will be multiplied by 40% (or 0.4) to find the next annual depreciation. The following depreciation schedule shows dollar amounts rounded to whole dollars.

Depreciation Schedule
Declining-Balance Method

Year	Book Value (End of Year)	Annual Depreciation	Accumulated Depreciation
0	$4,800	—	—
1	2,880	$1,920	$1,920
2	1,728	1,152	3,072
3	1,037	691	3,763
4	622	415	4,178
5	600	22[a]	4,200

[a] This is an adjusted final depreciation value, not a declining-balance calculation.

(c) Cost = $4,800
Residual value = 0
Life = 5 years

Year	Book Value (End of Year)	Annual Depreciation	Accumulated Depreciation
0	$4,800	—	—
1	2,880	$1,920	$1,920
2	1,728	1,152	3,072
3	1.037	691	3,763
4	622	415	4,178
5	—	622	4,800

MACRS FACTORS

TABLE 9-2 MACRS COST RECOVERY FACTORS

For Property Placed into Service in 1987 and Thereafter

RECOVERY YEAR(S)	3-YR. CLASS	5-YR. CLASS	7-YR. CLASS	10-YR. CLASS
1	0.333333	0.200000	0.142857	0.100000
2	0.444444	0.320000	0.244898	0.180000
3	0.148148	0.192000	0.174927	0.144000
4	0.074074	0.115200	0.124948	0.115200
5	—	0.115200	0.089249	0.092160
6	—	0.057600	0.089249	0.073728
7	—	—	0.089249	0.065536
8	—	—	0.044624	0.065536
9	—	—	—	0.065536
10	—	—	—	0.065536
11	—	—	—	0.032768

RECOVERY YEARS	15-YR. CLASS	20-YR. CLASS	27.5-YR. CLASS	31.5-YR. CLASS	39-YR. CLASS
1	0.050000	0.037500	0.034848	0.030423	0.024573
2	0.095000	0.072188	0.036364	0.031746	0.025641
3	0.085500	0.066773	0.036364	0.031746	0.025641
4	0.076950	0.061765	0.036364	0.031746	0.025641
5	0.069255	0.057133	0.036364	0.031746	0.025641
6	0.062330	0.052848	0.036364	0.031746	0.025641
7	0.059049	0.048884	0.036364	0.031746	0.025641
8	0.059049	0.045218	0.036364	0.031746	0.025641
9–15	0.059049	0.044615	0.036364	0.031746	0.025641
16	0.029525	0.044615	0.036364	0.031746	0.025641
17–20	—	0.044615	0.036364	0.031746	0.026541
21	—	0.022308	0.036364	0.031746	0.025641
22–27	—	—	0.036364	0.031746	0.025641
28	—	—	0.019697	0.031746	0.025641
29–31	—	—	—	0.031746	0.025641
32	—	—	—	0.017196	0.025641
33–39	—	—	—	—	0.025641
40	—	—	—	—	0.001068

INCOME STATEMENT
DEMO 1

Smithfield Supply Co. Income Statement For Year Ending December 31, 20X2				
Income from sales:				
Sales	$ 850,000		106.3%	
Sales discounts	50,000		6.3%	
Net sales		$ 800,000		100.0%
Cost of goods sold:				
Inventory, January 1	$ 45,000			
Net purchases	255,000			
Goods avail. for sale	$ 300,000			
Inventory Dec. 31	60,000			
Cost of goods sold		$ 240,000		30.0%
Gross profit		$ 560,000		70.0%
Operating expenses:				
Salaries	$ 219,000		27.4%	
Rent	100,000		12.5%	
Depreciation	52,000		6.5%	
Insurance	26,000		3.3%	
Advertising	15,000		1.9%	
Office supplies	11,000		1.4%	
Miscellaneous	10,000		1.3%	
Total expenses		433,000		54.1%
Net inc. from operations		$ 127,000		15.9%
Income taxes		32,000		4.0%
Net inc. after taxes		$ 95,000		11.9%

BALANCE SHEET
DEMO 2

<table>
<tr><td colspan="6">**Stella's World of Beauty**
Balance Sheet, June 30, 20X3</td></tr>
<tr><td>*Assets*</td><td></td><td></td><td></td><td></td><td></td></tr>
<tr><td>Current assets:</td><td></td><td></td><td></td><td></td><td></td></tr>
<tr><td>Cash</td><td></td><td>$ 5,800</td><td></td><td>1.8%</td><td></td></tr>
<tr><td>Accounts receivable</td><td></td><td>11,200</td><td></td><td>3.5%</td><td></td></tr>
<tr><td>Supplies</td><td></td><td>500</td><td></td><td>0.2%</td><td></td></tr>
<tr><td>Inventory</td><td></td><td>19,000</td><td></td><td>5.9%</td><td></td></tr>
<tr><td>Total current assets</td><td></td><td></td><td>$ 36,500</td><td></td><td>11.4%</td></tr>
<tr><td>Plant assets:</td><td></td><td></td><td></td><td></td><td></td></tr>
<tr><td>Equipment</td><td>$ 44,000</td><td></td><td></td><td></td><td></td></tr>
<tr><td>Less: Accum. Depreciation</td><td>9,000</td><td></td><td></td><td></td><td></td></tr>
<tr><td>Net equipment</td><td></td><td>$ 35,000</td><td></td><td>10.9%</td><td></td></tr>
<tr><td>Building</td><td>$ 400,000</td><td></td><td></td><td></td><td></td></tr>
<tr><td>Less: Depreciation</td><td>350,000</td><td></td><td></td><td></td><td></td></tr>
<tr><td>Net building</td><td></td><td>50,000</td><td></td><td>15.6%</td><td></td></tr>
<tr><td>Land</td><td></td><td>200,000</td><td></td><td>62.2%</td><td></td></tr>
<tr><td>Total plant assets</td><td></td><td></td><td>285,000</td><td></td><td>88.6%</td></tr>
<tr><td>Total assets</td><td></td><td></td><td>$ 321,500</td><td></td><td>100.0%</td></tr>
<tr><td></td><td></td><td></td><td></td><td></td><td></td></tr>
<tr><td>*Liabilities and Equity*</td><td></td><td></td><td></td><td></td><td></td></tr>
<tr><td>Current liabilities:</td><td></td><td></td><td></td><td></td><td></td></tr>
<tr><td>Accounts payable</td><td></td><td>$ 10,000</td><td></td><td>3.1%</td><td></td></tr>
<tr><td>Notes payable</td><td></td><td>8,000</td><td></td><td>2.5%</td><td></td></tr>
<tr><td>Total current liabilities</td><td></td><td></td><td>$ 18,000</td><td></td><td>5.6%</td></tr>
<tr><td>Long-term liabilities:</td><td></td><td></td><td></td><td></td><td></td></tr>
<tr><td>Mortgage note payable</td><td></td><td></td><td>84,000</td><td></td><td>26.1%</td></tr>
<tr><td>Total liabilities</td><td></td><td></td><td>$ 102,000</td><td></td><td>31.7%</td></tr>
<tr><td>Stockholders' equity:</td><td></td><td></td><td></td><td></td><td></td></tr>
<tr><td>Common stock</td><td></td><td>$ 119,000</td><td></td><td>37.0%</td><td></td></tr>
<tr><td>Retained earnings</td><td></td><td>100,500</td><td></td><td>31.3%</td><td></td></tr>
<tr><td>Total equity</td><td></td><td></td><td>219,500</td><td></td><td>68.3%</td></tr>
<tr><td>Total liabilities and equity</td><td></td><td></td><td>$ 321,500</td><td></td><td>100.0%</td></tr>
</table>

Roueche & Graves
Business Mathematics: A
Collegiate Approach, 8/e

COMPARATIVE INCOME STATEMENT
DEMO 3

Murphy's Golf Co.
Comparative Income Statement
For Years Ending Dec. 31, 20X2 and 20X1

	20X2	20X1	Increase or (Decrease) Amount	Increase or (Decrease) Percent	Percent of Net Sales 20X2	Percent of Net Sales 20X1
Income:						
Net sales	$ 166,000	$ 170,000	4,000	2.4%	100.0%	100.0%
Cost of goods sold:						
Inventory, Jan. 1	$ 53,000	$ 39,000	(14,000)	-35.9%	31.9%	22.9%
Purchases	91,000	94,000	3,000	3.2%	54.8%	55.3%
Goods avail. for sale	$ 144,000	$ 133,000	(11,000)	-8.3%	86.7%	78.2%
Inventory, Dec. 31	60,000	53,000	(7,000)	-13.2%	36.1%	31.2%
Cost of goods sold	84,000	80,000	(4,000)	-5.0%	50.6%	47.1%
Gross profit	$ 82,000	$ 90,000	8,000	8.9%	49.4%	52.9%
Expenses:						
Salaries	$ 56,000	$ 60,000	4,000	6.7%	33.7%	35.3%
Advertising	-	1,400	1,400	100.0%	0.0%	0.8%
Utilities	3,000	2,800	(200)	-7.1%	1.8%	1.6%
Depreciation	8,000	8,000			4.8%	4.7%
Property taxes	5,000	5,200	200	3.8%	3.0%	3.1%
Total expenses	72,000	77,400	5,400	7.0%	43.4%	45.5%
Net profit	$ 10,000	$ 12,600	2,600	20.6%	6.0%	7.4%

Roueche & Graves
Business Mathematics:: A Collegiate Approach, 8/e

COMPARATIVE BALANCE SHEET
DEMO 4

Campbell Supply Co.
Comparative Balance Sheet
December 31, 20X2 and 20X1

	20X2	20X1	Increase or (Decrease) Amount	Increase or (Decrease) Percent	Percent of Total Assets 20X2	Percent of Total Assets 20X1
Assets						
Current assets:						
Cash	$ 7,000	$ 8,000	$ 1,000	12.5%	0.9%	1.1%
Marketable securities	1,500	2,000	500	25.0%	0.2%	0.3%
Accounts receivable	83,500	85,000	1,500	1.8%	11.1%	11.3%
Inventory	60,000	45,000	(15,000)	-33.3%	8.0%	6.0%
Total current assets	$ 152,000	$ 140,000	$(12,000)	-8.6%	20.2%	18.7%
Total plant assets	600,000	610,000	10,000	1.6%	79.8%	81.3%
Total assets	$ 752,000	$ 750,000	$ (2,000)	-0.3%	100.0%	100.0%
Liabilities and Equity						
Current liabilities	$ 37,500	$ 40,000	$ 2,500	6.3%	5.0%	5.3%
Long-term liabilities	197,000	210,000	13,000	6.2%	26.2%	28.0%
Total liabilities	$ 234,500	$ 250,000	$ 15,500	6.2%	31.2%	33.3%
Stockholders' equity:						
Preferred stock	$ 75,000	$ 75,000	$ -	0.0%	10.0%	10.0%
Common stock	330,000	325,000	(5,000)	-1.5%	43.9%	43.3%
Retained earnings	112,500	100,000	(12,500)	-12.5%	15.0%	13.3%
Total equity	$ 517,500	$ 500,000	$(17,500)	-3.5%	68.8%	66.7%
Total liabilities and equity	$ 752,000	$ 750,000	$ (2,000)	-0.3%	100.0%	100.0%

620

Roueche & Graves
*Business Mathematics: A
Collegiate Approach, 8/e*

INVENTORY TURNOVER

Example 2   The bookstore in Example 1 had net sales during the year of $56,800. What was the stock turnover for the year at retail?

$$\text{Inventory turnover} = \frac{\text{Net sales}}{\text{Average inventory (at retail)}}$$

$$= \frac{\$56,000}{\$16,000}$$

$$= 3.55 \text{ times} \quad (\text{at retail})$$

Example 3   The income statement of the store above shows that its $43,200 "cost of goods sold" is 75% of net sales. Find the bookstore's inventory turnover at cost.

The average inventory at retail (sales) value was $16,000. In general, the store's goods cost 75% of sales value. Thus, the average inventory cost is computed as follows:

$$\text{Cost} = 75\% \text{ of sales}$$

$$C = 0.75 \times \$16,000$$

$$C = \$12,000$$

The average inventory at cost was $12,000. Thus, inventory turnover at cost is

$$\text{Inventory turnover} = \frac{\text{Cost of goods}}{\text{Average inventory (at cost)}}$$

$$= \frac{\$43,200}{\$12,000}$$

$$= 3.6 \text{ times} \quad (\text{at cost})$$

Roueche & Graves
*Business Mathematics: A
Collegiate Approach*, 8/e

INVENTORY VALUATION METHODS

Example 1   Assume that a new valve came on the market this year and that the following purchases were made during the year: 15 at $5, 9 at $6, and 12 at $8. Twenty valves were sold (leaving 16 in inventory) for a total net sales of $300. Evaluate the ending inventory by the following methods: (a) weighted average, (b) FIFO, and (c) LIFO. (d) Compare the effect of each inventory method on the income statement.

(a)   Weighted Average Method

$$
\begin{array}{ll}
15 @ \$5 = & \$\ 75 \\
9 @ \$6 = & 54 \\
+12 @ \$8 = +\ \underline{96} \\
\hline
36 \text{ items} & \$225 \qquad \text{Total cost} \\
\text{purchased}
\end{array}
$$

$$\frac{\$225}{36} = \$6.25 \qquad \text{Average cost}$$

16 items @ $6.25 = $100   Inventory value at cost by weighted average method

(b)   FIFO Method

The 16 items remaining are assumed to be the last 12 plus 4 from the previous order:

$$
\begin{array}{ll}
12 @ \$8 = & \$96 \\
+\ 4 @ \$6 = +\ \underline{24} \\
\hline
16 & \$120 \qquad \text{Inventory value} \\
& \qquad\quad \text{at cost by FIFO}
\end{array}
$$

(c)   LIFO Method

The 16 items remaining are assumed to be the first 15 plus 1 from the second order:

$$
\begin{array}{ll}
15 @ \$5 = & \$75 \\
+\ 1 @ \$6 = +\ \underline{6} \\
\hline
16 & \$81 \qquad \text{Inventory value} \\
& \qquad\ \text{at cost by LIFO}
\end{array}
$$

(d)   Income Statements

	WEIGHTED AVERAGE		FIFO		LIFO	
Net sales		$300		$300		$300
Cost of goods sold:						
Beginning inventory	$0		$ 0		$ 0	
Purchases	+ 225		+ 225		+ 225	
Goods available	$225		$225		$225	
Ending inventory	− 100		− 120		− 81	
Cost of goods		− 125		− 105		− 144
Gross profit		$175		$195		$156
Gross profit as a % of net sales		58.3%		65%		52%

Roueche & Graves
Business Mathematics: A
Collegiate Approach, 8/e

STOCK DIVIDENDS

Artcraft Sales, Inc., has 1,000 shares of 5%, $100 par-value preferred stock outstanding and 10,000 shares of common stock. The board declared a $50,000 dividend. What dividends will be paid on (a) the preferred stock, and (b) the common stock?

(a) Dividends on preferred stock are always computed first, as follows:

$$\text{Total preferred dividend} = \underbrace{\% \times \text{Par value}} \times \begin{pmatrix} \text{Number of} \\ \text{preferred shares} \end{pmatrix}$$

$$= \begin{pmatrix} \text{Dividend} \\ \text{per share} \end{pmatrix} \times \begin{pmatrix} \text{Number of} \\ \text{preferred shares} \end{pmatrix}$$

$5\% \times \$100 \text{ par value} = \$5$	Dividend on each share of preferred stock
$\$5 \text{ per share} \times 1,000 \text{ shares} = \$5,000$	Required to pay dividends on all preferred stock

(b)

$50,000	Total dividend
− 5,000	Dividend on all preferred stock
$45,000	Dividend allotted to common stock

$$\frac{\text{Total common stock dividend}}{\text{Number of common shares}} = \frac{\$45,000}{10,000} = \$4.50 \qquad \text{Dividend per share of common stock}$$

Hence, the preferred stockholders receive their full dividend of $5 per share, and a dividend of $4.50 per share will be paid to common stockholders.

Roueche & Graves
Business Mathematics: A
Collegiate Approach, 8/e

© 2001 by Prentice-Hall, Inc.
Pearson Education
All rights reserved.

PARTNERSHIP DISTRIBUTIONS

Original investment

Partners A and B opened a business with a $10,000 investment from A and an $8,000 investment by B. Partner B later invested another $6,000. Their partnership agreement stipulated that profits or losses would be divided according to the ratio of their original investments. What portion of a $7,200 profit would each partner receive?

$$\$10,000 + \$8,000 = \$18,000 \qquad \text{Total original investment}$$

$$A \quad \text{had} \quad \frac{\$10,000}{\$18,000} \quad \text{or} \quad \frac{5}{9} \text{ of the original investment}$$

$$B \quad \text{had} \quad \frac{\$8,000}{\$18,000} \quad \text{or} \quad \frac{4}{9} \text{ of the original investment}$$

Thus, A will receive $\frac{5}{9}$ of the profit and B receives the other $\frac{4}{9}$:

$$A: \quad \tfrac{5}{9}(\$7,200) = \$4,000$$
$$B: \quad \tfrac{4}{9}(\$7,200) = \underline{3,200}$$
$$\text{Total profit} = \$7,200$$

A's share is $4,000 and B has earned $3,200.

Investment at beginning of the year

A variation of the foregoing "original-investment" distribution is to divide profits according to each partner's investment at the beginning of the year. Suppose that partners A and B (above) use this method during their second year of operations. Partner A still has $10,000 invested, while B's investment is now $8,000 + $6,000 = $14,000, giving a total investment by both partners of $24,000.

Therefore, following the second year of operations,

$$A \text{ would receive } \frac{\$10,000}{\$24,000} \quad \text{or} \quad \frac{5}{12} \text{ of the profit}$$

$$B \text{ would receive } \frac{\$14,000}{\$24,000} \quad \text{or} \quad \frac{7}{12} \text{ of the profit}$$

Roueche & Graves
*Business Mathematics: A
Collegiate Approach, 8/e*

PARTNERSHIP DISTRIBUTIONS

Average investment per month

When partners C and D began operations on January 1, C had $4,000 invested, which did not change during the year. D had $5,800 invested on January 1; on May 1, he withdrew $200; and on August 1, he reinvested $800. If profits are to be shared according to each partner's average investment per month, how much of a $12,500 profit should each receive?

Partner C's average investment is $4,000, since his investment did not change during the year. D's average investment is computed as follows:

Date	Change	Amount of Investment		Months Invested		
January 1	—	$5,800	×	4	=	$23,200
May 1	−$200	5,600	×	3	=	16,800
August 1	+$800	6,400	×	+ 5	=	+ 32,000
				12		$72,000

$$\frac{\$72,000}{12} = \$6,000 \qquad \text{Average investment per month}$$

$$
\begin{array}{ll}
\$\ 4,000 & \text{C's average investment} \\
+\ \ \ 6,000 & \text{D's average investment} \\
\hline
\$10,000 & \text{Total of average investments}
\end{array}
$$

Thus, C receives $\dfrac{\$4,000}{\$10,000}$ or $\dfrac{2}{5}$ of the profit. D's investment earns $\dfrac{\$6,000}{\$10,000}$ or $\dfrac{3}{5}$ of the profit.

$$
\begin{array}{lll}
\text{C:} & \tfrac{2}{5}(\$12,500) = & \$\ 5,000 \\
\text{D:} & \tfrac{3}{5}(\$12,500) = & \underline{\ 7,500} \\
& \text{Total profit} = & \$12,500
\end{array}
$$

C earns $5,000 of the total profit, and D receives $7,500.

Roueche & Graves
Business Mathematics: A Collegiate Approach, 8/e

EARNINGS PER SHARE

EXAMPLE 5

THE POWERS CO. HAD A NET INCOME OF $1,000,000 LAST YEAR. THE BOARD OF DIRECTORS DECLARED A CASH DIVIDEND OF ONLY $600,000, RETAINING THE REMAINDER FOR FUTURE PLANT EXPANSION. THERE WERE 50,000 SHARES OF COMMON STOCK AND 75,000 SHARES OF 8%, $50 PAR-VALUE PREFERRED STOCK OUTSTANDING. (A) WHAT WAS THE DIVIDEND PER SHARE? (B) WHAT WAS THE EARNINGS PER SHARE ON COMMON STOCK?

(A)   8% x $50   = $4 DIVIDEND ON EACH
                                        PREFERRED SHARE

       $4 x 75,000 SHARES = $300,000 TOTAL PREFERRED
                                            DIVIDEND

         $600,000 TOTAL DIVIDEND
       - 300,000 TOTAL PREFERRED DIVIDEND
         $300,000 ALLOCATION FOR COMMON DIVIDEND

          $300,000   = $6 DIVIDEND ON EACH COMMON
           50,000   SHARE

(B)   NET INCOME - PREFERRED DIVIDEND = EARNINGS PER SHARE
       COMMON SHARES OUTSTANDING

       $1,000,000 - $300,000   = $14
              50,000

Roueche & Graves
*Business Mathematics: A
Collegiate Approach, 8/e*

INVOICE

EAST STREET HARDWARE SUPPLY	Invoice
P. O. Box 239	#2414
Richmond, VA 23222	

TO: Handy Hardware Co.
1241 Post Drive
Alexandria, VA 22301

DATE: Sept. 9, 19xx

TERMS: Net 30

Your Order	Received	Shipped	Freight
#534	11/6/xx	11/8/xx	F.O.B.Richmond

Quantity	Cat. #	Description	List	Extension
5	S301	Lounge Chair	$18.50	$ 92.50
6	S302	Folding Chair	12.75	76.50
10	D20	Aluminum Grill	9.50	95.00
		SubTotal		$264.00
		Less 20% discount		52.80
		Net		$211.20
		Freight		37.80
		Total Due		$249.00

Figure 12-1 Invoice from Wholesale Supplier

Roueche & Graves
*Business Mathematics: A
Collegiate Approach*, 8/e

627

FINDING LIST PRICE OR DISCOUNT %

Example 5

Following trade discounts of 20% and 15%, a furnace cost a dealer $374.
(a) What is the list price? (b) What is the net cost rate factor? (c) What single discount percent is equivalent to discounts of 20% and 15%?

(a)
$$\% \text{ Pd} \times L = N$$

$$(0.8)(0.85)L = 374$$

$$0.68L = 374$$

$$\frac{0.68L}{0.68} = \frac{374}{0.68}$$

$$L = \$550$$

(b) Net cost rate factor = 0.68.

(c) The single discount equal to discounts of 20% and 15% is

$$100\% - 68\% = 32\%$$

Example 6

The suggested retail price of a television set is $400. If the net cost is $320, what single discount rate was offered?

$\% \text{ Pd} \times L = N$ The price changed by $400 − $320 = $80:

$$x \cdot 400 = 320 \quad \text{or} \quad \_\_ \% \text{ of Original} = \text{Change?}$$

$$\frac{400x}{400} = \frac{320}{400} \qquad\qquad x \cdot 400 = 80$$

$$x = \frac{4}{5} \qquad\qquad \frac{400x}{400} = \frac{80}{400}$$

$$x = 80\% \qquad\qquad x = \frac{1}{5}$$

But $x = \%$ Pd. Thus, a $x = 20\%$ discount

20% discount was given.

Roueche & Graves
Business Mathematics: A
Collegiate Approach, 8/e

MARKUP BASED ON COST

A merchant has found that his expenses plus the net profit he wishes to make usually run $33\frac{1}{3}\%$ of the cost of his goods. For what price should he sell a dress that cost him $36?

(a) We know that the markup equals $33\frac{1}{3}\%$ or $\frac{1}{3}$ of the cost. Since $\frac{1}{3}$ of $36 = $12, then

$$C + M = S$$

$$\$36 + \$12 = S$$

$$\$48 = S$$

(b) This same problem can be computed in another way. Since markup equals $\frac{1}{3}$ of the cost $(M = \frac{1}{3}C)$, by substitution

$$C + M = S$$

$$C + \frac{1}{3}C = S$$

$$\frac{4}{3}C = S$$

But since cost equals $36,

$$\frac{4}{3}(\$36) = S$$

$$\$48 = S$$

MARKUP AT SALE PRICE

Example 1   Using a markup of 30% on sales, price an item that costs $42.

As before, we start with the equation $C + M = S$. We know that the markup equals 30% of sales, or $M = 0.3S$. Thus, we substitute $0.3S$ for M in the formula $C + M = S$.

$$C + M = S$$

$$C + 0.3S = S$$

$$C + 0.3S - 0.3S = S - 0.3S$$

$$C = 0.7\,S$$

$$\$42 = 0.7S$$

$$\frac{1}{0.7}(\$42) = 0.7S\left(\frac{1}{0.7}\right)$$

$$\$60 = S$$

Roueche & Graves
*Business Mathematics: A
Collegiate Approach,* 8/e

630

MARKUP ON PERISHABLES

Example 1   A grocer bought 100 pounds of bananas at 45¢ per pound. Experience indicates that 10% of these will spoil. At what price per pound must the bananas be priced in order to obtain a margin of 50% on cost?

The bananas cost 100 pounds × 45¢, or $45. Since the markup will be 50% on cost ($M = 0.5C$), then

$$C + M = S$$

$$C + 0.5C = S$$

$$1.5C = S$$

$$1.5(\$45) = S$$

$$\$67.50 = S$$

At least $67.50 must be made from the sale of the bananas.

The grocer expects 10% or 10 pounds of bananas to spoil; thus, his needed $67.50 in sales must come from the sale of the other 90 pounds. Now, if p = price per pound of bananas, then

$$90p = \$67.50$$

$$p = \frac{\$67.50}{90}$$

$$p = 75¢ \text{ per pound}$$

631

Roueche & Graves
*Business Mathematics: A
Collegiate Approach, 8/e*

OPERATING AND ABSOLUTE LOSSES

Example 3

The regular marked price of a woman's suit was $144. The suit cost $120, and related selling expenses were $18. The suit was later marked down by 25% during a clearance sale. (a) What was the operating loss? (b) What was the absolute loss? (c) What was the percent of gross loss (based on wholesale cost)?

The total handling cost $(C + \overline{OH})$ of the suit was $120 + $18 = $138. The actual net selling price (or sale price) of the suit was

$$\% \text{ Pd} \times L = \text{Net}$$
$$0.75(\$144) = \text{Net}$$
$$\$108 = \text{Net selling price } (S_2)$$

(a) Since the suit sold for less than its total handling cost,

Total handling cost	$138
Actual selling price	− 108
Operating loss	$ 30

(b) The absolute or gross loss is the difference between wholesale cost and the actual selling price:

Wholesale cost	$120
Actual selling price	− 108
Absolute (or gross) loss	$ 12

(c) Absolute loss is always computed as some percent of the wholesale cost, as follows:

What percent of wholesale cost was the absolute loss?

$$\_\_\%(\$120) = \$12$$
$$120x = 12$$
$$x = \frac{12}{120} \quad \text{or} \quad \frac{1}{10}$$
$$x = 10\% \text{ gross loss}$$

Roueche & Graves
*Business Mathematics: A
Collegiate Approach*, 8/e

SIMPLE INTEREST

Example 1   A loan of $900 is made at 16% for 5 months. Determine (a) the interest and (b) the maturity value of this loan.

(a) $P = \$900$ $I = Prt$

$r = 16\%$ or 0.16 $= 900 \times 0.16 \times \dfrac{5}{12}$

$t = 5$ months $= \dfrac{5}{12}$ year $I = \$60$

(b) $M = P + I$

$= \$900 + \$60$

$M = \$960$

Example 2   Rework Example 1, using the maturity value formula $M = P(1 + rt)$. As before, $P = \$900$, $r = 0.16$, and $t = \frac{5}{12}$ year.

(a) $M = P(1 + rt)$ (b) $P + I = M$

$= \$900\left(1 + 0.16 \times \dfrac{5}{12}\right)$ $I = M - P$

$= 900\left(1 + \dfrac{0.80}{12}\right)$ $= \$960 - \$900$

$= 900\left(\dfrac{1.80}{12}\right)$ $I = \$60$

$= 900(0.15)$

$M = \$960$

Roueche & Graves
Business Mathematics: A
Collegiate Approach, 8/e

SIMPLE INTEREST NOTE
WITH COLLATERAL

Consumer Note — Cardinal Bank   *Cardinal Bank*

William J. McDaniel   May 1, 20XX   Garden City
Borrower   Date   Originating Office

                                      4561-9121   B2-22314
Co-Borrower   Account No.   Note No.

3001 Dawes Avenue; Alexandria, VA 22311
Borrower's Address

Five thousand and no/100 dollars
Loan Amount

Dollars($ 5,000.00   )

In this Note, the words "you" and "your" mean the Borrower and any Co-Borrower. "We," "our," "us," and "the Bank" mean Cardinal Bank.

This note covers your loan with the Bank. When you sign it, each one of you is fully responsible for fulfilling all of the promises you make in this Note. By signing this Note, you acknowledge that you received a loan from us in the Loan Amount shown above and agree to pay to us at any of our offices, or at such place as the Bank may in writing designate, the Loan Amount shown above, plus or including interest, any other amounts due, upon the terms described below.

Terms of Note

☐ **Simple Interest Instalment Loan**
You will make a total of ____ monthly payments of principal and interest beginning on _____, 20__ and continuing on the same day of each succeeding month until this Note is paid in full. You will make _____ monthly payments of principal and interest equal to $_____ and then a final payment equal to the unpaid principal balance plus interest and any other amounts due.

☐ **Principal Plus Instalment Loan**
You will make a total of _____ monthly payments of principal and interest beginning on _____, 20__ and continuing on the same day of each succeeding month until this Note is paid in full. Each month for _____ months you will make a payment equal to $_____ in principal plus all interest accrued on the unpaid balance, and then a final payment equal to $_____ in principal plus all accrued interest any other amounts due.

☑ **Single Payment Loan** due on May 31, _____ 20xx (30 days from the date of this note). You will make one payment in full of principal plus interest from the date of this Note until this Note is paid in full plus any other amounts due.

☑ New obligation   ☐ Renewal — New disclosure required   ☐ Renewal — Same term and no new disclosure required

Interest

Interest on an Instalment Loan will accrue on a 30/360 day basis On all other loan types, interest will accrue daily on the basis of a 360-day year. Interest will accrue at the stated interest rate on the unpaid balance from the date of this Note until paid in full. Interest will continue to accrue after maturity, whether by acceleration or otherwise, at the stated interest rate until this Note has been paid full. Subject to the above, the interest rate applicable to this Note (the "Rate") is:

☑ 9.0 % per annum, fixed for the term of this Note.

Collateral

We will have a security interest in the property described below (the "Collateral"). The Collateral is described more fully in a

☐ Security Agreement dated_____   ☐ Assignment on Deposit dated_____

☐ Deed of Trust dated_____   ☐ Credit Line Deed of Trust dated_____

☑ Other Certificate of Deposit for $5,000 at Cardinal Bank dated March 1, 20XX
By signing below, you agree to all the terms of this Note and acknowledge receipt of a completed copy.

William J. McDaniel   _____
Borrower's Signature   (Seal)   Co-Borrower's Signature   (Seal)

Figure 15-2   *Note with Collateral*

PRESENT VALUE
(NOT ORIGINAL DAY)

Example 3 Find the (present) value on October 11 of a $720, 4-month note taken out on July 10 at 15%, if money is worth 12%.

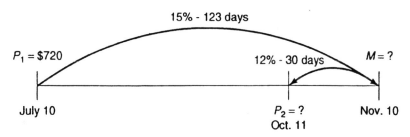

15% - 123 days

$P_1 = \$720$

12% - 30 days

$M = ?$

July 10

$P_2 = ?$
Oct. 11

Nov. 10

(a) $P_1 = \$720$ $I = Prt$ $M = P + I$

$r = 15\%$ $= \$720 \times 0.15 \times 123/360$ $= \$720 + \$36.90$

$t = \dfrac{123}{360}$ $I = \$36.90$ $M = \$756.90$

$M = ?$

(b) $M = \$756.90$ $P_2 = \dfrac{M}{1 + rt}$

$r = 12\%$

$t = \dfrac{30}{360}$ or $\dfrac{1}{12}$ $= \dfrac{\$756.90}{1 + 0.12 \times \dfrac{1}{12}}$

$P_2 = ?$

$= \dfrac{756.90}{1 + 0.01}$

$= \dfrac{756.90}{1.01}$

$P_2 = \$749.41$

Roueche & Graves
Business Mathematics: A
Collegiate Approach, 8/e

COMPARISION OF SIMPLE INTEREST
WITH SIMPLE DISCOUNT

Example 1   The face values of two notes are $1,500 each. The discount rate and the interest rate
are both 12%, and the time of each is 90 days.

Interest Note	*Discount Note*
$P = \$1,500$	$M = \$1,500$
$r = 12\%$	$d = 12\%$
$t = \dfrac{90}{360}$ or 0.25	$t = \dfrac{90}{360}$ or 0.25

$I = Prt$

$\quad = \$1,500 \times 0.12 \times 0.25$

$I = \$45$

$M = P + I$

$\quad = \$1,500 + \$45$

$M = \$1,545$

$D = Mdt$

$\quad = \$1,500 \times 0.12 \times 0.25$

$D = \$45$

$p = M - D$

$\quad = \$1,500 - \$45$

$p = \$1,455$

636

Roueche & Graves
Business Mathematics: A
Collegiate Approach, 8/e

REDISCOUNTING A NOTE

Example 2   City National Bank was the holder (payee) of a $1,200, 120-day note discounted at 12%. Thirty days before the note was due, City Bank rediscounted (or sold) the note to Capital Mortgage and Trust at 9%. (a) How much did City Bank receive for the note? (b) How much did City Bank actually make on the transaction?

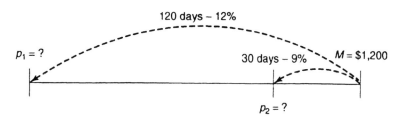

Original Note

$M = \$1,200$ $D = Mdt$

$d = 12\%$

$$= \$1,200 \times 0.12 \times \frac{1}{3}$$

$t = \dfrac{120}{360}$ or $\dfrac{1}{3}$ $= \$1,200 \times 0.04$

$p_1 = ?$ $D = \$48$

$$p = M - D$$

$$= \$1,200 - \$48$$

$$p_1 = \$1,152$$

Rediscounted Note

$M = \$1,200$ $p_2 = M(1 - dt)$

$d = 9\%$ $= \$1,200\left(1 - 0.09 \times \dfrac{1}{12}\right)$

$t = \dfrac{30}{360}$ or $\dfrac{1}{12}$ $= \$1,200(1 - 0.0075)$

$p_2 = ?$ $= \$1,200(0.9925)$

$$p_2 = \$1,191$$

(a)   The proceeds of the rediscounted note (p_2) were $1,191. That is, City Bank received $1,191 when it sold the note to Capital Mortgage and Trust.

(b)   City Bank made $1,191 − $1,152 = $39 on the transaction.

Roueche & Graves
Business Mathematics: A
Collegiate Approach, 8/e

US RULE

On April 1, Mary Carrington Interiors took out a 90-day note for $1,500 bearing interest at 10%. On May 1, Carrington paid $700 toward the obligation, and on May 16, she paid another $300. How much remains to be paid on the due date?

Original principal, 4/1		$1,500.00
First partial payment, 5/1	$700.00	
Less: Interest ($1,500, 10%, 30 days)	− 12.50	
Payment to principal		− 687.50
Adjusted principal		$ 812.50
Second partial payment, 5/16	$300.00	
Less: Interest ($812.50, 10%, 15 days)	− 3.39	
Payment to principal		− 296.61
Adjusted principal		$ 515.89
Interest due ($515.89, 10%, 45 days)		+ 6.45
Balance due, 6/30		$ 522.34

Roueche & Graves
*Business Mathematics: A
Collegiate Approach, 8/e*

INSTALLMENT PAYMENTS AND APR

Example 2   Gerald Wood bought a new color television that sold for $675 cash. He received a $35 trade-in allowance on his old set and also paid $40 cash. The store arranged a 2-year payment plan, including a finance charge computed at regular 8% simple interest. (a) What is Wood's monthly payment? (b) What will the total cost of the TV be? (c) How much extra will he pay for the convenience of installment buying? (d) What annual percentage rate must be disclosed under the Truth-in-Lending Law?

(a)   Wood's regular payment of $29 per month is computed as follows:

Cash price	$675	
Down payment	− 75	($35 trade-in + $40 cash)
Outstanding balance	$600	
Finance charge (I)	+ 96	$\left(\begin{array}{l} I = Prt \\ = \$600 \times 0.08 \times 2 \end{array}\right)$
Total of payments	$696	

$$\frac{\$696}{24} = \$29 \text{ per month}$$

(b)   The total cost of the TV will be $771:

Down payment: Trade-in	$ 35
Cash	40
Total of monthly payments	696
Total cost	$771

(c)   The $771 total cost includes an extra $96 interest (or finance or carrying) charge above the cash price.

(d) $\dfrac{\text{Finance charge}}{\text{Amount financed}} \times 100 = \dfrac{\$96}{\$600} \times 100 = 0.16 \times 100 = \$16$

ACTURIAL METHOD OF PREPAYMENT

Mason Jansen borrowed $600 at 13% simple interest, to be repaid in 12 monthly payments of $56.50. When making his eighth payment, Jansen also wishes to pay his remaining balance. (a) What annual (actuarial) percentage rate was charged on the loan? (b) How much interest will Jansen save, computed by the actuarial method? (c) How much is the remaining balance on that day?

(a) As presented in the preceding section, the value we look for in the table is the product of "rate × time":

$$13\% \times 1 \text{ year} = 13 \quad \text{Corresponding to a 23.25\%} $$
$$\text{annual percentage rate}$$

(b) Since 8 payments have been made, there are 4 payments remaining. Referencing the annual percentage rate table for 4 periods at 23.25%, we find a Value of 4.89. Thus, the unearned interest by the formula is

$$\frac{n \times Pmt \times \text{Value}}{100 + \text{Value}} = \frac{4 \times \$56.50 \times 4.89}{100 + 4.89}$$

$$= \frac{\$1,105.14}{104.89}$$

$$= \$10.54$$

Jansen will save $10.54 interest by the actuarial method.

(c) Since the remaining payments total 4 × $56.50 = $226, Jansen's remaining balance is as follows:

$226.00	Total of remaining payments
− 10.54	Interest saved
$215.46	Balance due

A payment of $215.46 will terminate Jansen's installment loan. (This is in addition to the regular $56.50 payment paid on that day.)

Roueche & Graves
Business Mathematics: A
Collegiate Approach, 8/e
640

RULE OF 78s

Refer to Mason Jansen's loan in Example 1, in which $600 was repaid in 12 monthly payments of $56.50. The loan is paid in full after the 8th installment payment.

Step 1 Determine the total amount of *interest* on the loan.

The installment payments for all 12 months total $12 \times \$56.50 = \$678$, which includes $78 interest:

$$\begin{array}{rl} \$678 & \text{Total payments} \\ -\ \underline{600} & \text{Principal} \\ \$\ 78 & \text{Total interest} \end{array}$$

Step 2 Determine the *numerator* for the remaining period by applying the formula from sum-of-the-years'-digits method, $\dfrac{n(n+1)}{2}$.

There are four payments remaining, so *n* is 4:

$$\frac{4(4+1)}{2} = \frac{20}{2} = 10$$

Step 3 Determine the *denominator* that is the sum-of-the-years'-digits for the entire loan period.

$$\frac{12(12+1)}{2} = \frac{156}{2} = 78$$

Step 4 Multiply the fraction $\dfrac{n}{d}$ times the total interest (step 1). The result is the amount of *interest saved*.

$$\frac{10}{78} \times \$78 = \$10 \text{ interest saved}$$

Step 5 Determine the total of the *remaining regular payments*.

Jansen has four remaining payments:

$$4 \times \$56.50 = \$226$$

Step 6 Subtract the amount of interest saved (step 4), from the total of the remaining installment payments (step 5), to determine the total *payment necessary to pay off the loan*.

$$\begin{array}{rl} \$226.00 & \text{Total of remaining payments} \\ -\ \underline{10.00} & \text{Interest saved} \\ \$216.00 & \text{Balance due} \end{array}$$

Jansen will owe $216 under the rule of 78s (as compared with $215.46 using the actuarial method).

Roueche & Graves
Business Mathematics: A Collegiate Approach, 8/e

Sum of Months' Digits

Number of Months	Sum: 1 through Largest Month
6	21
9	45
10	55
12	78
18	171
24	300
36	666

As a reminder, for convenience in finding the sum of a series of consecutive integers for months 1 through n, the following formula may be applied (as illustrated for the sum $8 + 7 + 6 + 5 + 4 + 3 + 2 + 1 = 36$):

$$\frac{n(n + 1)}{2} = \frac{8(9)}{2} = \frac{72}{2} = 36$$

642

Roueche & Graves
Business Mathematics: A Collegiate Approach, 8/e

PRESENT VALUE (AT COMPOUND INTEREST)

Example 2

Charles and Sue Baker would like to have $6,000 in 4 years for a down payment on a condominium. (a) What single deposit would have this maturity value if CDs earn 7% compounded quarterly? (b) How much of the final amount will be interest?

(a) $M = \$6,000$ $P = M(1 + i)^{-n}$ (b) $I = M - P$

$n = 16$

$$= \$6,000\left(1 + 1\frac{3}{4}\%\right)^{-16}$$

$i = 1\frac{3}{4}\%$

$$= 6,000(0.7576163)$$

$P = \ ?$

$$= 4,545.698$$

$$P = \$4,545.70$$

$$\begin{aligned} &= \quad \$6,000.00 \\ &- \ \underline{\ 4,545.70} \\ I &= \quad \$1,454.30 \end{aligned}$$

If the Bakers purchase a $4,545.70 CD now, it will earn interest of $1,454.30 during 4 years at 7% compounded quarterly and have a $6,000 maturity value.

Roueche & Graves
Business Mathematics: A
Collegiate Approach, 8/e

AMOUNT OF AN ANNUITY

(a) Determine the amount (maturity value) of an annuity if Leonard Feldman deposits $100 each quarter for 6 years into an account earning 8% compounded quarterly. (b) How much of this total will Feldman deposit himself? (c) How much of the final amount is interest?

(a) (Notice that deposits are made each quarter to coincide with the interest conversion date at the bank; we would not be able to compute the annuity if they were otherwise.)

$$\text{Pmt.} = \$100 \qquad M = \text{Pmt.} \times \text{Amt. ann. tab.}_{\overline{n}|i}$$

$$n = 24 \qquad \qquad = \$100 \times \text{Amt. ann. tab.}_{\overline{24}|2\%}$$

$$i = 2\% \qquad \qquad = 100(30.42186)$$

$$= 3{,}042.186$$

$$M = \$3{,}042.19$$

Feldman's account will contain $3,042.19 after 6 years.

(b) There will be 24 deposits of $100 each, totaling 24 × $100 or **$2,400.**

(c) The interest earned during this annuity period is

Amount of annuity	$3,042.19
Total deposits	− 2,400.00
Interest	$ 642.19

Roueche & Graves
Business Mathematics: A
Collegiate Approach, 8/e

PRESENT VALUE OF ANNUITY

EXAMPLE 1

Elaine Shaw wishes to receive a $100 annuity each quarter for 6 years while attending college and graduate school. Her account earns 8% compounded quarterly. (a) What must be the (present) value of Elaine's account when she starts to college? (b) How much will Elaine actually receive? (c) How much interest will these annuity payments include?

(a) $\text{Pmt.} = \$100$ $\text{P.V.} = \text{Pmt.} \times \text{P.V. ann. tab.}_{\overline{n}| i}$

$n = 24$ $= \$100 \times \text{P.V. ann. tab.}_{\overline{24}| 2\%}$

$i = 2\%$ $= 100(18.91393)$

$\text{P.V.} = \$1,891.39$

Elaine's account must contain $1,891.39 when she enters college.

(b) She will receive 24 annuity payments of $100 each, for a total of $2,400.

(c) The account will earn interest of

Total payments	$2,400.00
Present value	− 1,891.39
Interest	$ 508.61

Thus, from an account containing $1,891.39, Elaine may withdraw $100 each quarter until a total of $2,400 has been withdrawn. During this time, the declining fund will have earned $508.61 interest. After the final payment is received, the balance in her account will be exactly $0.

SINKING FUND
Example 1

Brandon County issued bonds totaling $1,000,000 in order to build an addition to the courthouse. The county commissioners set up a sinking fund at 9% compounded quarterly in order to redeem the 5-year bonds. (a) What quarterly rent must be deposited to the sinking fund? (b) How much of the maturity value will be deposits? (c) How much interest will the sinking fund earn?

(a) $M = \$1,000,000$

$n = 20$

$i = 2\frac{1}{4}\%$

Pmt. $= M \times$ S.F.tab.$_{\overline{n}|i}$

$= \$1,000,000 \times$ S.F.tab.$_{\overline{20}|2\frac{1}{4}\%}$

$= 1,000,000(0.04014207)$

Pmt. $= \$40,142.07$

A payment of $40,142.07 must be deposited into the sinking fund quarterly in order to have $1,000,000 at maturity.

(b) There will be 20 deposits of $40,142.07 each, making the total deposits 20 × $40,142.07, or $802,841.40.

(c) The interest earned is thus

Maturity value	$1,000,000.00
Total deposits	− 802,841.40
Interest	$ 197,158.60

SINKING FUND SCHEDULE
Example 2

Prepare a sinking fund schedule to show that semiannual payments of $949 for 2 years will amount to $4,000 when invested at 7% compounded semiannually.

The "interest" earned each period is found by multiplying the previous "balance at end of period" by the periodic interest rate i. (Example: $\$949 \times 3\frac{1}{2}\% = \$33.22$.)

Payment	Periodic Interest ($i = 3\frac{1}{2}\%$)	Periodic Payment	Total Increase	Balance at End of Period
1	$ 0	$ 949.00	$ 949.00	$ 949.00
2	33.22	949.00	982.22	1,931.22
3	67.59	949.00	1,016.59	2,947.81
4	103.17	949.00	1,052.17	3,999.98
Totals	$203.98	$3,796.00		

$3,999.98   Final balance

Roueche & Graves
Business Mathematics: A Collegiate Approach, 8/e

BONDS; CURRENT YIELD

Example 3

Three $1,000 bonds are quoted as shown, producing the indicated selling price and premium (or discount):

Quote	Face Value	Selling Price	Premium/Discount
104	$1000	$104\% \times \$1000 = 1040$	$40 premium
97	1000	$97\% \times 1000 = 970$	$30 discount
$108\frac{1}{2}$	1000	$108\frac{1}{2}\% \times 1000 = 1085$	$85 premium

Example 4

Two $1,000 bonds each pay 6 % simple interest annually. The quoted price of bond A was 98 and bond B was 114. Find the current annual yield on each:

Annual interest on each bond, by $I = Prt$, is

$$\$1000 \times \frac{6}{100} \times 1 = \$60$$

Bond A cost $980 and bond B was $1,140. Thus,

$$\text{Current yield} = \frac{\text{Annual interest}}{\text{Market or purchase price}}$$

$$\text{Bond A} = \frac{\$60}{\$980} = 6.12\% \text{ current yield}$$

$$\text{Bond B} = \frac{\$60}{\$1,140} = 5.26\% \text{ current yield}$$

Roueche & Graves
Business Mathematics: A
Collegiate Approach, 8/e

MORTGAGE PAYMENTS

The Townsends purchased a $98,000 home by making an $8,000 down payment and signing a 10% mortgage with monthly payments for 25 years. (a) Determine the Townsends' monthly payment. (b) What was the total of their payments, and how much of this was interest? (c) What was the total cost of their home?

(a) After their $8,000 down payment, the mortgage principal was $90,000. Their payment was thus

$$
\begin{array}{r}
\$ \ 9.09 \text{ per } \$1,000 \text{ at } 10\% \text{ for } 25 \text{ years} \\
\times \underline{\qquad 90} \\
\$818.10 \text{ monthly payment on } \$90,000 \text{ mortgage}
\end{array}
$$

(b) Twelve payments per year for 25 years equal 300 payments required to repay the mortgage. Their total payments and interest included would be

Monthly payment	$ 818.10
	× _____ 300
Total payments	$245,430
Principal	− _____90,000
Interest	$155,430

(c) Including their down payment, the Townsends' $98,000 home cost them

Total cost of loan	$245,430
Down payment	+ _____8,000
Total cost of home	$253,430

Roueche & Graves
*Business Mathematics: A
Collegiate Approach, 8/e*